Birth Control and the
Population Question in England,
1877–1930

BIRTH CONTROL
and the Population Question in England, 1877–1930

Richard Allen Soloway

The University of North Carolina Press
Chapel Hill London

© 1982 The University of North Carolina Press
All rights reserved
Manufactured in the United States of America

Library of Congress Cataloging in Publication Data

Soloway, R. A.
Birth control and the population question in England,
1877–1930

Bibliography: p.
Includes index.
1. Birth control—England—History—Public opinion—
Addresses, essays, lectures.   2. Public opinion—England—
History—Addresses, essays, lectures.   3. Family size—
England—History—Addresses, essays, lectures.
4. England—Population—History—Addresses, essays,
lectures.   I. Title.
✓ HQ766.5.G7S64   304.6′6   81-14791 ✓
ISBN 0-8078-1504-7   AACR2

For Maxine and Colin

Contents

Preface

This work owes much to the patience, kindness, and cooperation of numerous individuals and institutions. My colleague, Lamar Cecil, and former colleague, Joan Scott, read and reread the entire manuscript offering incisive criticism and consistently helpful recommendations for improvement. I trust they know how deeply grateful I am for their interest and much-needed assistance. Donald Mathews helped me clarify some difficult conceptual problems, and Gillian Cell's thoughtful counsel and assistance with some thorny issues is much appreciated. Rosalie Radcliffe not only typed the manuscript more times than she cares to remember, but she did so with tolerance, humor, and, on occasions, even interest. If she, like the others, failed to save me from my own mistakes it was not for want of trying.

I am also indebted to the staff of the British Library, particularly the librarians and archivists in the Division of Manuscripts and at the Newspaper Library in Colindale, as well as to the archivists at the Public Record Office, University College Library, the British Library of Political and Economic Science, the National Maritime Museum Library (Greenwich), and King's College Library, Cambridge. I must offer special thanks to S. E. Walters, general secretary of the Eugenics Society, whose help, while I was working in the society's library in London, was invaluable.

My research in this country was facilitated by the staffs of the Library of Congress, the Library of the American Philosophical Society, Widener Library, Harvard University, the Stirling Library, Yale University, the Perkins Library, Duke University, as well as those of the libraries of the University of Illinois, the University of Michigan, and of my own institution, the University of North Carolina. Finally, the project was generously supported by grants from the Research Council of the University of North Carolina and from the American Council of Learned Societies. I also acknowledge with appreciation the award from the University of North Carolina of a Kenan Research Professorship, which enabled me to conduct research in England.

Richard Allen Soloway
Chapel Hill
1 May 1981

Introduction

This book is a study of the often contentious debate surrounding the rapid decline in the birthrate and in family size that began in the late Victorian years and has more or less continued to the present day. It was, as people began to notice by the 1890s, a dramatic reversal of demographic trends that had persisted for more than a century. During the nineteenth century the country had been transformed from a comparatively uncrowded, largely rural nation of some nine million inhabitants to a populous, industrial, urbanized society of nearly thirty-seven million.

Until the 1880s, at least, this extraordinary increase was characterized by high annual birthrates averaging around thirty-four births per thousand of the population and reaching a recorded peak of 36.3 in 1876 before beginning to fall relentlessly. By 1901 fertility had dropped more than 24 percent and, by the outbreak of World War I in 1914, 33 percent. Despite minor fluctuations the descent continued until it finally leveled off at approximately 14.5 to 15 per 1,000 persons in the early 1930s. In the course of these fifty years the fertility of women between the presumably fecund ages of fifteen and forty-five declined by over 60 percent, and the average size of British families fell nearly two-thirds from what it had been in the mid-Victorian era.

These crude vital statistics lay at the heart of the "population question" as it came to be described in the early twentieth century. In contrast to the more famous population question raised by Malthus a century before, the modern query posed by his latter-day followers and critics was more complex. It involved the old Malthusian fear of unchecked population growth geometrically exceeding the arithmetical ability of a nation to provide adequate subsistence for its mushrooming numbers. But it also spawned a new realization, supported by impressive statistical evidence, that reduction of fertility was much more pronounced among the higher socioeconomic classes than among the populous lower classes, where reproduction remained disproportionately high.

The following chapters are, in effect, a series of self-contained, topical essays within a general, chronological structure. As such, they move back and forth within the time frame of the book, avoiding, I hope, repetition and confusion. They are primarily concerned with how the later Victorians, Edwardians, and their successors after World War I perceived, analyzed, and interpreted the profound demographic changes they observed within their own lifetimes. Though based upon a variety of contemporary and recent population statistics, this book is less a study in historical demography than it is an exploration of social thought and attitudes in generational transition. Consequently, the chapters also emphasize how people over the course of some sixty years explained and evaluated the statistical data that graphically illustrated the differing aspects of the population question. That question, as it evolved from the 1870s, eventually engaged prominent as well as peripheral figures of widely varying persuasions in government, politics, law, religion, education, journalism, literature, theater, science, medicine, and the armed forces. It intruded in one way or another into most contemporary issues—socialism, women's rights, imperialism, eugenics, the rise of labor—as men and women in ever-increasing numbers came to recognize that they were living through a revolution in reproductive behavior. They were at first interested in determining its causes and possible endurance; in time they became more concerned about its differential class characteristics and likely consequences for the future, and, depending upon their conclusions, advancing or reversing its direction.

If, as the first chapters argue, there was initially considerable confusion and disagreement about the reasons for the plummeting birthrate, by the early twentieth century, and certainly by World War I, it was widely acknowledged that the decided shift toward smaller families was not a result of later marriage, alterations in diet, or the diminished fecundity of an evolving, or, as the more pessimistic suggested, a decaying race. On the contrary, the decline was the effect of the rapid spread of family limitation, or birth control, as it was increasingly described after 1914, among various sectors of society.[1] Demographers have examined these population trends since the 1870s and their work is invaluable to students of modern British history.[2] But their quantitative analyses of census data and fertility surveys have not been concerned with how contemporaries comprehended and appraised the striking demographic developments reflected in the accumulating vital statistics.

In addition, historical works on the birth control movement such as Joseph Banks's pioneering study *Prosperity and Parenthood* (1954) and Joseph and Olive Banks's *Feminism and Family Planning in Victorian England* (1964), Peter Fryer's general survey, *The Birth Controllers* (1965), and, more recently, Rosanna Ledbetter's *History of the Malthusian League* (1976) and Angus McLaren's *Birth Control in Nineteenth-Century England* (1978) have noted, but not examined in depth, the rise of birth control in the wider context of declining fertility and the multiple ramifications it posed in the minds of the later Victorians and subsequent generations. Although this book obviously owes much to these studies and others, including the stimulating work of scholars of the American birth control movement, it has, in its emphasis upon the broader implications of the population question, attempted to take a very different approach to the topic and suggest some different interpretations.[3]

Moreover, in contrast to much of the historical literature on the population question, I am primarily concerned with developments in the twentieth rather than in the nineteenth century, which has attracted most of the scholarship dealing with birth control and the population debate. Audrey Leathard's *The Fight for Family Planning . . . 1921–1974* (1980) suggests that scholars are beginning to turn their attention to the historical aspects of demographic change since World War I. But Leathard, like Fryer and Ledbetter, devotes only a small section of her book to a descriptive survey of major developments in the critical interwar years, particularly the 1920s, when, as I have tried to show, the population question in general and the birth control issue in particular, reformulated by the experiences of the war, expanded in significant new directions.

Although references to birth control practices are evident in the text, this is not a history of contraception, but rather what overlapping generations of British men and women thought about the adoption of contraception and its likely consequences for their society, their empire, even their civilization. Until recently the striking fall in fertility evident not only in Britain, of course, but in many other parts of the world, has had little to do with scientific or technological developments. None of the late Victorian, Edwardian, or postwar analysts of the declining birthrate, whether they believed it a curse or a blessing, could point to any new contraceptive breakthrough to account for the demographic changes they traced to the 1870s. Indeed, despite the introduction of new appliances and devices, including the modern diaphragm and the latex rubber condom, the most prevalent restrictive practices, coitus interruptus, abstention, douching, or some type of occlusive pessary had been known for centuries.[4] Why married couples in unprecedented numbers began to employ them and other preventives as an important part of domestic culture was, for many of their contemporaries, as it is for historians today, an important question. The answers given by those who first pondered so sensitive and hidden an area of motivation and behavior reflected, I argue in the following chapters, their varying perceptions and responses to mounting internal economic, social, and political changes as well as new challenges from abroad. In addition, their analyses, like the behavior of those millions of couples who decided to raise smaller families, also reflected changing religious and moral values, new concepts of individual and public health, and evolving notions of marriage, gender roles, and sexuality.

Part I considers the growing awareness of demographic change in late Victorian and Edwardian England and describes the differing explanations and evaluations of the phenomenon. These were often influenced by Social Darwinism and anxieties about Britain's waning economic and political preeminence as the old century drew to a close and the new portended incalculable challenges for the future. It was also a period marked by the provocative activities of the Malthusian League, founded in 1877 as the first birth control organization in the world. Throughout most of its fifty-year life it remained a small, eccentric, rather disreputable society tenaciously pursuing its curious philosophical amalgamation of old-fashioned, laissez-faire political economy and radically new ideas of population control called Neo-Malthusianism. Nevertheless, before World War I, the league was singular in its efforts to advance the concept of rational, planned parenthood as the cornerstone of sound domestic strategy. By the opening of the twentieth century Neo-Malthusianism had become synonymous with "family limitation," "conception control," and other terms that preceded the advent of the expression "birth control." Many people sympathetic to population restriction who had no affiliation with the Malthusian League and often thoroughly disagreed with its philosophy and its campaign for smaller families were described as Neo-Malthusians. For purposes of clarification, however, in this work the term Neo-Malthusian, unless otherwise indicated, refers to supporters of the league, however tenuous their enthusiasm.

The institutional history of the Malthusian League has been written, and I have tried to avoid repeating it.[5] Instead I have attempted to discuss Neo-Malthusianism in the wider historical context of the population question and to consider it as one of several stages of the birth control movement, limited, like its successors, by ideological preconceptions and the changing values of the age. Those birth control advocates of the 1920s and 1930s, as well as more recent scholars, who viewed Neo-Malthusianism as a regressive, separate phase of the modern struggle for the acceptance of family planning, were, in my judgment, mistaken. The Neo-Malthusians were, in many ways, their own worst enemies, and by several standards a failure. But, in the final analysis, as they themselves always predicted, the success of their disturbing campaign was not marked by public acclaim, but by declining fertility.

This is not to argue that the activities of the Neo-Malthusians were responsible for the fall in the birthrate, as some of the league's zealous proponents and many of its critics before World War I believed. Because the league was the only organization advocating smaller families and because its appearance coincided with the drop in fertility statistics, it was an understandable, if overly simplistic conclusion. Neo-Malthusianism emerged as one of the numerous reform movements associated with deepening concerns in the late 1870s and 1880s about the "Condition of England." It was much more a result of changing reproductive habits than it was a cause, and although league propagandists undoubtedly provided many people with information and a rationale for raising smaller families, the rise of Neo-Malthusianism, as some perceptive analysts of the population question observed, coincided with a desire on the part of married couples to do so.

Although the Neo-Malthusians endured decades of abuse for trying to persuade their countrymen that overpopulation was the single most important cause of the economic distress and severe social problems plaguing the nation, their activities often stirred up greater anxieties about underpopulation and "race suicide." This latter dimension, closely associated with the differential characteristics of the declining birthrate, became a major consideration of the population question in the opening decade of the new century and was of particular concern to the newly founded eugenics movement in the prewar years. Unlike the Neo-Malthusians whose radical-secularist roots were highly suspect, the eugenists, mostly successful, well-educated middle-class scientists, physicians, academicians, churchmen, and other professionals, brought to the population question both social and scientific credibility. Eugenic assumptions and beliefs, I attempt to demonstrate, increasingly pervaded the debate over changing British fertility both before and after World War I. The demographic implications of a host of issues confronting the nation—democracy, urbanization, rural depopulation, emigration, alien immigration, female emancipation, socialism, the loss of religious and moral direction—were continually under discussion, and underlying much of the debate was a persistent fear of racial degeneration that threatened Great Britain's imperial destiny.

Part II of the book considers the impact of World War I on the population question and examines the rapid changes of the 1920s when the birth control cause was taken up by a new generation of individuals and organizations who expanded its dimensions, and, for the first time, propelled it into national politics. Despite serious efforts at modernization and reform, Neo-Malthusianism was quickly shunted aside as a curious, rather embarrassing legacy from the past, irrelevant to the future. Though the movement found a new, dynamic advocate in Marie Stopes, whose papers are a major source for several of the chapters that follow, her sensational writings and activities have overshadowed the equally important role played by others in the Workers Birth Control Group, the Society for the Provision of Birth Control Clinics, and, perhaps most important, the Women's Section of the Labour party.

Their collective efforts both influenced and reflected altered concepts of domestic propriety and individual sexuality, which, when merged with expanding concepts of social reform and public health, broke down many of the barriers confronted before the war in such influential areas of British life as the church, the medical profession, and local and national government. The turning point was reached in 1930, in the early months of the Great Depression, when, as the final chapters illustrate, the "walls of the citadel" crumbled. Birth control was reluctantly sanctioned by the established church, grudgingly declared to be safe and proper by the guardians of the medical profession, and, even more significantly, with Cabinet approval, accepted by the Ministry of Health to be a legitimate concern of local welfare authorities. At the same time the various birth control interests in the country came together to lay the organizational foundations of the modern Family Planning Association.

In the sexually freer climate of the 1920s birth control was more candidly linked to individual sexual enjoyment and emotional fulfillment, and observers of that period have contrasted its more positive, expansive attitude toward contraception with the negativism of population control prevailing before World War I. This contrast is, in my judgment, too simplistic. Although birth control was increasingly adopted by individuals for a complex variety of personal reasons associated with some degree of sexual liberation, as well as with economic considerations, better health, changing perceptions of women, marriage, the family, and the role and value of children, the birth control movement, I try to demonstrate, was still primarily concerned with reducing the fertility of the poorer classes. This was the goal of the early Neo-Malthusians in their "Crusade Against Poverty" and of the Eugenics Society's efforts to curb the proliferation of the unfit after the war. It motivated, for different reasons, the Workers Birth Control Group and the Women's Section of the Labour party to insist that their constituents have the same access to safe, reliable contraceptive information long enjoyed by the healthier, more prosperous middle classes. Even Marie Stopes, who claimed that her Society for Constructive Birth Control and Racial Progress was founded in 1921 in part to end the negative connotation of family limitation associated with Neo-Malthusianism, opened the first birth control clinic in Britain to serve the working poor. Like most others in the birth control movement, she directed much of her extraordinary energy toward checking the excessive fertility of working-class wives.

Consequently, the population question in Britain was tightly enmeshed in class attitudes, relations, and antagonisms. From the Neo-Malthusians of the 1870s to the birth control proponents and family planners of the 1920s and 1930s, it was commonly assumed that the rational control of fertility would devolve from the wealthier, better-educated middle classes to the skilled, semiskilled, and unskilled, ignorant working classes. The multiple benefits to be derived from birth control were seen as relative and proportionate to the character, needs, and aspirations of the differing classes—more subtle, complex, and individuated for men and women in the higher ranks, more basic, material, and direct for those in the lower. Initially, birth control was quietly accepted as an unspoken privilege of class until the Neo-Malthusians decided that it was a behavioral distinction the country could ill afford much longer. It was transformed gradually from a humane and useful gift to be taught the poor by their compassionate, far-sighted betters into a fundamental, natural right of all who wished to exercise it. Much like the struggle over abortion today in many countries, the transformation was passionately confused with changing religious and moral values and embroiled in class politics.

The campaign to provide the working poor with the desire and means for regulating their fertility was weakened by a tangle of motives, fears, and anxieties pulling in different directions. The birth control movement was part of a broader concern with improving the economic well-being and welfare of the lower classes by inculcating such solid virtues as prudence, foresight, and self-restraint. Most contraceptive methods required all three. The movement was also an extension of earlier efforts, evident in tighter controls over recreation and the drink trade, to civilize the laboring poor and curtail their animalistic and violent tendencies, as the Victorians described them. Birth control advocates, certain that the tensions resulting from squalor and overcrowding were responsible for drunkenness, crime, random violence, and vice, were always puzzled and frequently angered by the unwillingness of their contemporaries, many of whom admitted the connection, to support their campaign. Most thought prudish hypocrisy, or selfish vested interests, stood in the way of common sense. But much of the opposition, before World War I, was rooted not only in Victorian notions of propriety but also in a fear of unbridled sexuality and the further loss of social control if people, especially the poor, were free to indulge their carnal appetites without fear of the consequences.

At the same time there were sincere scientific and medical differences about the likely physiological and psychological effects of contraception that reinforced doubts and that were not effectively laid to rest until shortly before World War II. The revival of the population question and the rise of the birth control movement coincided with, and was in part stimulated by, the new threats Britain perceived to its economic and imperial position in the world. The curtailment of population in a country already geographically and demographically the inferior of aggressive new competitors such as Germany and the United States had military and imperial implications that many later Victorians and Edwardians found particularly alarming. The very notion that Great Britain could no longer sustain an expansive population at home or in its colonies abroad suggested a loss of strength and vigor that was not easy to accept.

As a result, despite the popular belief that birth control knowledge was transmitted by or "trickled down" from the higher classes to the lower, it is by no means clear that this was so. As the prolonged conflicts with churchmen, physicians, scientists, politicians, even feminists suggest, the adoption of birth control practices by different sectors of the working classes occurred despite the often formidable opposition of middle- and upper-class interests. Indeed, throughout the 1920s and 1930s, when it was increasingly evident that family size at nearly every level of society was diminishing, the birth control movement devoted much of its energy trying to persuade influential people in positions of authority that if they could not endorse the dissemination of contraceptive information to the poor, the least they could do was to stop trying to block it.

Resistance, however, was obvious in working-class circles as well, though for different reasons. Some socialists, especially the militant Marxists, were distinctly hostile to the birth control campaign from its inception, but it is questionable how representative they were of worker sentiment. Most socialists and trade unionists had surprisingly little to say about the issue until after World War I. Even then the divisions that surfaced within the Labour party had less to do with the advantages or disadvantages of birth control than with its relevance to the socialist cause and the political consequences of including it as a part of public health and social welfare programs.

As some contemporaries argued insightfully and as the reports of the first birth control clinics in the interwar years indicated, people probably learned much more about avoiding conception from friends, fellow workers, classmates, and, during the war, from servicemen, as well as from the millions of tracts and pamphlets published since the 1870s, than they ever did from the Malthusian League or its numerous successors. Like middle-class couples who began limiting their families earlier, increasing numbers of workers turned to birth control for a combination of individual and economic reasons. The desire of both men and women to avoid the physical and financial burdens of too many children coincided with a continually expanding network of contraceptive information and a rapidly changing social, political, cultural, and religious environment. It reinforced their inclinations, borne of new experiences and perceptions of the times, and made their restrictive behavior understandable, increasingly acceptable, and socially desirable. But the organizations and individuals who kept the population question before the public and who figure so prominently in this study did much to overcome the obstacles to change. They stimulated interest and created the climate of opinion in which family planning could emerge from the shadows of private lives to become a major public issue and, eventually, an important feature of modern society.

Abbreviations

BMJ	*British Medical Journal*
CBC	Society for Constructive Birth Control and Racial Progress (often referred to as Society for Constructive Birth Control)
NBCC	National Birth Control Council
NBRC	National Birth-Rate Commission
NCPM	National Council of Public Morals

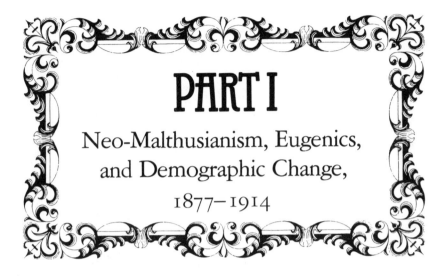

PART I

Neo-Malthusianism, Eugenics,
and Demographic Change,

1877–1914

CHAPTER 1

The Declining Birthrate

Although the English clergyman, Thomas Robert Malthus, was the most famous proponent of population restraint in the nineteenth century, his countrymen, however fascinated by his arguments, paid little attention to his recommendations. Despite Malthus's portentous calculations of the populace expanding geometrically while the means of its support increased only arithmetically, men and women throughout much of the century continued to marry and reproduce at an unprecedented rate.[1] They had already begun to do so a generation before Malthus revealed his demographic laws in 1798 and were unwilling or unable to dampen their procreative instinct significantly until the closing decades of Queen Victoria's long reign. By then the nearly nine million people enumerated in England and Wales in the first census of 1801 had increased almost fourfold. The average decennial rate of growth was 13.8 percent. It never fell below 11.6 percent during the century and soared as high as 18.06 from 1811 to 1821. Although the pace moderated somewhat in the middle decades of the century, it rose again sharply to nearly 14.4 percent in the 1870s before gradually tapering off in the last years of the Victorian era.[2]

The decline was not overly precipitous after the queen's death in 1901, and, during the nine-year reign of her son, Edward VII, the population of nearly thirty-three million grew by another 10.89 percent. Although this was a rate of increase somewhat below the decennial average obtained in the previous century, it was not compelling evidence that Great Britain was tottering on the edge of demographic catastrophe. Nevertheless, a great many people were uneasy with recent population trends. But in contrast to the issues raised during the first Malthusian debate, the population question, as it was posed in the late nineteenth and early twentieth century, focused much more on the causes and implications of precipitous decline rather than on unchecked growth. Furthermore, traditional demographic considerations were increasingly complicated by more elaborate statistical information about regional and socioeconomic class differentials in fertility. Under the pervasive impact of Social Darwinism and its ancillary new science of human heredity, eugenics, the problem of "race quality" became as important as that of "race quantity" as late Victorian and Edwardian Englishmen pondered the anticipated challenges to British civilization in the new century.

Basic to their deliberations and prognostications was a growing awareness that after more than a century of expansively high fertility the national birthrate had, since the mid-1870s, been steadily declining. For decades the crude rate had hovered around 34.3 births per thousand of the population. It reached a recorded peak of 36.3 in 1876, but by 1901 had fallen to 28.5, the lowest figure since vital statistics were first reported in 1838. The downward trend continued unabated and the decline of more than 21 percent at the turn of the century exceeded 33 percent in the months preceding the outbreak of World War I when fertility slid to around 24/1,000.[3] In spite of the diminishing birthrate the population since the 1870s continued to expand by more than 50 percent, from approximately twenty-four to thirty-seven million people, but this was often overlooked by analysts of the population question who riveted their attention on the accumulating evidence of decline.

Shortly after Edward VII ascended the throne the popular *Daily Mail* claimed that statesmen and publicists were no longer listening to the old Malthusian lamentations about the "devastating torrent of children" whose numbers assured the perpetuation of poverty. Instead of worrying about arresting the birthrate, the nation's leaders were trying to stop a decline that had "set in with ominous steadiness, and which is now beginning to menace the predominance of the race." Looking ahead to the challenges of the twentieth century the paper predicted that victory would belong "to the large unit; the full nursery spells national and race predominance."[4] J. A. Spender, editor of the Liberal *Westminster Gazette*, commented in 1907 on the revival of such arguments long after Malthus and his generation of political economists purportedly demolished that error and educated the nation to the dangers of overpopulation. Fertility had finally been checked, as the recent decline in the birthrate indicated, Spender wrote, but public opinion had again swung to the opposite pole. "What in 1830 and 1840 was regarded as the special aim of statesmanship is now regarded as a sign of decay." It was ironic that although the population had nearly quadrupled in the last century, "in these days we find most of the newspapers and all the preachers in a state of despair about the slightest check in the percentage of increase."[5]

Press and pulpit were only the more obvious oracles of gloom predicting, like the medical journal, the *Lancet*, "a national calamity seriously threatening the future welfare of our race."[6] In 1906 the Radical-Liberal journalist and M.P. for Tyneside, John Mackinnon Robertson, denounced these sentiments as "lugubrious humbug" while acknowledging the growing hold they had on the public mind. An old Malthusian and classical liberal economist, Robertson deplored the "deliberately insincere rhetoric about decay of national energy, the approaching extinction of the Anglo-Saxon, the fall in the vitality of the higher races, and all the rest of it," muddying discussions of the declining birthrate.[7] Although he welcomed the trend toward smaller families, Robertson recognized that many of his contemporaries were seriously disturbed by the racial, political, and economic implications of an apparent loss of vital procreative energy. They thrashed about in search of explanations and prognoses, fearful that a diminution of reproductive capacity was but another manifestation of the decline of Britain's imperial civilization.

It was eventually conceded that the decline in the birthrate, whether a menacing or salutary trend, was not a consequence of Darwinian evolution, cyclical dietary fluctuations, radical alterations in the age and frequency of marriage, or the sterilizing effects of industrialization and urbanization. On the contrary it was, as Robertson and countless others knew full well, a direct result of the rapid adoption of family limitation, or birth control, as it was later described. The increasingly sophisticated interpretation of governmental and private statistical inquiries in the decade and a half preceding the war gave decisive scientific credibility to that conclusion.

Although the crude, or uncorrected, fertility statistics provided in the quarterly and annual reports of the registrar-general as well as in the decennial censuses were widely quoted by the myriad analysts of the population question, the more astute stressed the importance of corrected fertility as a more precise measurement. By comparing the number of children born annually to married women of child-bearing age (fifteen to forty-five) it was, they reasoned, possible to demonstrate changes in fertility even more graphically. The registrar-general emphasized this point in his 1903 report, noting that corrected fertility, which had averaged 288 children per thousand women in this fecund category until the 1870s, had, after soaring to 304.1 in 1876, steadily fallen to 234.2 by the end of 1901. The *Lancet* analyzed the returns and calculated that more than 300,000 fewer children were being born to married couples each year than would have been the case if the corrected birthrate had remained the same as in the 1870s.[8]

Arthur Newsholme, medical officer of health for Brighton, and T. H. C. Stevenson, medical officer for the London County Council, played a major role in educating their contemporaries in the intricacies of corrected fertility. In a much-quoted paper, "The Decline of Human Fertility," presented to the Royal Statistical Society in 1905, they emphasized that, irrespective of changes in the overall composition of the British population, women of childbearing age were having less children with each passing year, whatever their marital status. Illegitimacy in the last quarter of the nineteenth century, they reported, had also dropped an astonishing 40 percent, indicating that some effective check to conception was clearly at work.[9] By 1914 corrected marital fertility was at 191.6/1,000, a decline of 37 percent since the prolific 1870s.[10]

Since nearly 80 percent of the population lived in and around cities by the end of the nineteenth century, it was often assumed that urbanization was in some way responsible for the declining birthrate. The number of towns with more than fifty thousand residents had doubled in the last thirty years of Queen Victoria's reign, and like observers of the urban scene from earlier times, many of her subjects complained of the sterilizing effects of crowded city life. It was frequently contended that no London family could survive more than three generations in the enervating atmosphere of the metropolis, and extensive rural migration to the great towns since the 1870s provoked much concern about the dilution of healthy British stock.

Although the birthrate declined in nearly all population centers, investigators quickly discovered that diminished fertility was by no means limited to townspeople. Newsholme wrote to the *Times* in 1906 that those who believed that the trend was an urban phenomenon were much mistaken. On the contrary, his studies revealed that since 1881 the fall in the rural birthrate actually exceeded the loss in the towns, compounding the recent depopulation of agricultural areas. No rural county since the 1870s had increased its birthrate, he reported; most had experienced a decline of around 20 percent compared with a drop of only 15 percent in urban districts.[11] Newsholme's general conclusion was confirmed the following year by Sidney Webb in his Fabian Society tract, *The Decline in the Birth-Rate.* Concentrating upon corrected fertility in such towns as Northampton, Halifax, Burnley, and Blackburn, he found that births had diminished by 32 percent between 1881 and 1901. Although the decline was not as sharp in the selected rural counties of Cornwall, Rutland, Sussex, Devonshire, and Westmoreland, it still ranged between 23 and 29 percent.[12]

The most ambitious of the unofficial investigations into regional fertility undertaken before World War I was Ethel Elderton's detailed study of the nine English counties north of the Humber. A research scholar in the Francis Galton Laboratory for National Eugenics at the University of London, Elderton supplemented vital statistics with questionnaires and interviews. Her *Report on the English Birth Rate,* which appeared in late 1914, clearly illustrated the striking decline in births apparent in every one of the diverse counties since the mid-1870s. Between 1851 and 1875, she reported, fertility rose in every county but one, although, with the exception of Northumberland and Durham, the increase was not particularly large. Since then, however, all nine counties showed a substantial loss, ranging in 1901 from 9.6 children per thousand in rural Westmoreland to 5.3 in coal-rich Durham. In recent years the decline had accelerated and actually doubled in the traditionally fecund mining counties of Durham and Northumberland. Elderton calculated that if the 1901–11 rate of decrease was extended back to 1876 the birthrate in nearly every area north of the Humber would be half the current figure.[13] The outbreak of the war prevented an extension of the investigation to other regions of the country, but by then it was clear that the overall pattern was similar throughout the nation. English families were on the average much smaller than they had been, and there was no indication that the trend, underway for at least three decades, was about to be reversed.

Lamentations about the demise of the large Victorian family and recurrent images of empty cradles became commonplace in the years before World War I. The royal family itself had once been a monument to the domestic fecundity of the age. If Queen Victoria was less than exhilarated by the experience of bearing nine children in eighteen years she at least understood her natural responsibilities. Nine children, while not uncommon, were nevertheless somewhat above the mid-Victorian average of approximately six, which prevailed until the 1880s. Although Edward VII, with his five offspring, and his heir, George V, with six, met the older norm, a great many of their subjects were markedly less prolific. Average family size dropped substantially to 3.4 children in Edward's reign and to under three by the outbreak of the war.[14]

The young statistician, Karl Pearson, Goldsmid Professor of Applied Mathematics and Mechanics at University College, London, had called attention to the trend in the mid-1890s. His growing interest in statistical probability, human heredity, and evolution had led him to plot a number of frequency curves extracted from fertility data contained in the reports of the registrar-general. They showed a distinct tendency toward a decrease in the number of families of five and six children, he reported, and a corresponding increase of those with two, three, and four offspring. The pattern was already well established in the 1890s, he noted, though it had not yet become a subject of national concern.[15] It did so rapidly in the next decade as professional and amateur statisticians alike ruminated in the popular press as well as in specialized journals upon the reduced incidence of childbirth recorded for each passing year. The registrar-general's quarterly and annual tabulations now became a subject of running commentary, frequently inspiring the most pessimistic visions of the future. They were often haunted by Britain's doubtful performance during the Boer War and the official and unofficial inquiries it provoked into the possibilities of advanced racial deterioration.[16] In the context of mounting worries about "national efficiency" preached by Darwinistically inspired imperialists, the extinction of the large family was to many another nail in the coffin of British hegemony.[17]

Although Balfour's Conservative government had rejected several appeals to appoint a royal commission to investigate the diminished birthrate, its Liberal successor was persuaded to sanction a national *Fertility of Marriage Census* in conjunction with the decennial census of 1911.[18] Its author, T. H. C. Stevenson, who had become superintendent of statistics in the General Register Office, was specifically concerned with trying to resolve the numerous controversies that surrounded the declining birthrate by gathering data on childbirth to an extent never before attempted. By surveying the fertility experience of married women at all levels of society since the mid-nineteenth century Stevenson anticipated that the true cause of the rapid move to smaller families would be conclusively revealed. The coming of the war delayed the publication of the tabulated statistics until 1917 and the report until 1923, but it was well known years before the volumes appeared that the returns proved emphatically that whatever domestic legacies the Victorians passed on to their successors large families were not among them. A second survey, less comprehensive, but based upon improved sampling techniques, was taken in 1946. When combined with the 1911 data this *Family Census* also makes it possible to trace the completed fertility experience of women who married in the two decades preceding World War I as well as in the years immediately following.[19]

Approximately 9 to 10 percent of Queen Victoria's contemporaries gave birth to as many children as their sovereign; yet fewer than 2 to 4 percent of their grandchildren equaled her accomplishment. In the most fertile decade on record, the 1870s, the number of marriages achieving nine or ten offspring (13.5 percent) exceeded those at the other end of the spectrum producing only one or two (12.5 percent). Within a generation, however, small families of one or two children had become far more prevalent, constituting the number born to nearly a third of all marriages celebrated in the years 1900–1909. By contrast families of nine and ten dropped off to less than 4 percent of the total. For couples marrying during World War I and in the following decade the difference was even greater. One or two children were the norm in 45 to 50 percent of these cases, while only 1.5 percent reported nine or ten. Moreover, since the 1870s the number of childless marriages doubled, rising from slightly more than 8 percent to 16 percent in the years after 1914.[20]

Most of these statistics, representing long-term generational fertility trends, were unavailable to Victorian and Edwardian analysts of the population question who had to rely on less comprehensive data. Although there was little dispute about the general pattern of decline, there was considerable disagreement about its cause. Having determined that families were becoming smaller it was logical for people to examine the institution of marriage itself to see if some dramatic change in the age and frequency of its celebration had occurred. Malthus, after all, had proclaimed that deferred marriage was the most rational and effective check on excessive population, although he assumed that only the better, more responsible classes would respond.[21]

Complaints were heard continually throughout the nineteenth century about the surplus of eligible young women of good birth being unable to find suitable husbands willing to assume the burdens of domestic life. Late Victorian and Edwardian critics of higher taxes, the cost of living, the expenses of educating children, diminishing economic opportunities, and other threats to the improvement and even maintenance of social status believed that among the middle classes at least marriage had become a casualty of changing times. As early as 1892, Arthur Lyttelton, master of Selwyn College, Cambridge, concluded that the recently discovered fall in the birthrate was the direct result of a decline in marriage. Like many of his contemporaries who shared this view Lyttelton was admittedly puzzled about why fertility was falling so much more rapidly than the marriage rate.[22]

Lyttelton was responding to a modest drop in the 1880s in the crude marriage rate, the number of people who married per thousand of the population. The rate had ranged from a high of 17.1 in the early 1850s and again in the 1870s to 14.7 in the next decade. It rose, however, in the 1890s to approximately 15.5, at which point it remained until World War I. At no time did the marriage rate vary markedly from the 16/1,000 average that had prevailed since statistics were first reported in 1838.[23] As in the case of the birthrate, the corrected figures for the incidence of nuptiality were more revealing. They showed a steady decline in the rate of marriages among eligible men and women over the age of fifteen and single or widowed. In the middle years of the century the rate hovered around 56/1,000 before it began to drop to 49.2 in the 1880s and then more gradually to around 47 in the decade preceding the war.[24] Even then, however, as the more astute observed, the loss was only half that of the birthrate. Moreover, the total percentage of the population married actually increased slightly to around 36.4 in 1911 compared with approximately 34, the figure that had prevailed throughout the second half of the nineteenth century.[25]

Of more immediate interest to those who surveyed the marriage variables was not the increase or decline in the number of marriages, but the age of brides and their potential childbearing years. Most perceived that the age of marriage was on the rise, and H. G. Wells, in one of his earlier prognostications on the future of mankind, was only one of many who singled it out as a major cause of diminished fertility in recent years.[26] Different people cited different figures as they dipped into the accumulating vital statistics to illustrate the upward trend. The prominent sexologist, Henry Havelock Ellis, suggested in 1912 that the rise had been fractional since the 1890s, increasing from an average of 28.4 to 28.8 for men and from 26.2 to 26.6 for women. More significant, from the standpoint of expected fertility, was the sharp diminution in the number of marriages of young people fifteen to twenty years of age. Quoting from a recent report of the registrar-general, Ellis noted that whereas in the years 1876–80 7.8 percent of newly married men and 21.7 percent of new brides fell into this youthful and highly fecund category, by 1909 the figures had dropped to 4.0 and 13.8 percent.[27]

Although these statistics, like those cited by other perceptive observers, were subject to correction and modification the general demographic picture they outlined was drawn more precisely by the 1911 *Fertility of Marriage Census* and its post-World War II successor. Concentrating upon the more critical average marriage age of women, analysts of the 1911 returns traced an incremental rise since the 1860s from 22.5 to 25.3.[28] The figures were admittedly imprecise and reflected corrected estimates for differing periods, but the enumerators believed them to be reasonably accurate. If Ellis made the common mistake of overestimating the age of marriage, he underestimated the shift away from younger nuptiality. The decline in the number of women marrying under the age of twenty dropped from approximately 20 percent in the 1870s to 7.6 percent in the five years preceding the 1911 census.[29]

A similar but less dramatic change occurred in the most popular marital age bracket, twenty to twenty-four, as the proportion of women marrying in that group fell from nearly 51 percent in the 1870s to 43 percent. The reduction in younger marriages was offset by a substantial rise in the matrimonial activity of older women. Whereas in the 1870s brides aged twenty-five to twenty-nine comprised only 20.6 percent of the total, by 1911 the proportion had reached 30 percent, after which it dropped only slightly before and during the war. Similarly women over thirty, who represented less than 9 percent of those marrying three decades earlier, constituted more than 19 percent of those taking their vows between 1906 and 1911. Furthermore, during the same period the overall proportion of women between the ages of fifteen and forty-four who were married declined from just under 45 percent to 40.9 percent, a trend that was not reversed until after World War I.[30]

In the absence of other variables it was logical to conclude that a shift to later matrimony and a reduction in the percentage of presumably fecund women who were married would significantly curtail exposure to pregnancy and result in the birth of fewer children. But, as the statistically more experienced pointed out, the gradual alterations in nuptial age had only raised the average age of marriage two to three years since the birthrate had started its precipitous descent. Whatever its impact upon fertility it was not enough to account for the size of families falling by half. Moreover, as the corrected data revealed, irrespective of the proportion of women of childbearing age who were not married, the measured loss in fertility was primarily within marriage. Ethel Elderton's analysis of nuptial patterns in the counties she surveyed north of the Humber convinced her that the increase in the marriage age of women since 1861 was not adequate to explain the extent and variation of diminished fertility she found in that diverse region of the county.[31]

Several years earlier, in 1906, G. Udny Yule, Newmarch Lecturer in Statistics at University College, London, had also ruled out the marriage-age variable that he knew carried a great deal of popular credence. A detailed study of birth and marriage statistics for the preceding half century, Yule told the Royal Statistical Society, revealed that "for some reason or other, the actual fecundity of married women has been falling with increasing rapidity during the past thirty years, and it is to this, and to no mere changes in the proportion of married women to the population, that the fall in the rate is due."[32]

Yule represented a school of thought that believed that the country was merely passing through one of the many natural infertility cycles common to all societies. He personally thought it was caused by changing economic and, consequently, nutritional factors, which could be closely correlated with rising prices over the past century. Elsewhere, in a 1912 address to the Congress of the Royal Sanitary Institute, the president of the Society of Medical Officers of Health, Sir Shirley Murphy, recalled comparable demographic fluctuations in the past and assumed that as nature had been the cause of rising birthrates, it was logical to assume that it was responsible for the current decline as well.[33] Similar arguments were presented the following year to a private National Birth-Rate Commission, established under the auspices of the prestigious National Council of Public Morals to discover the causes and possible consequences of the alarming decline in fertility. Dr. Archibald Chalmers, medical officer of health for Glasgow, cited parish statistics for that town dating from the seventeenth century to prove the existence of a natural ebb and flow of births. On the surface fertility seemed to fluctuate with economic opportunities affecting the rate and age of marriage, he reported, but after careful deliberation he concluded that "fluctuations in germinal activity" were of much greater importance.[34]

Several of the ecclesiastical and lay dignitaries who constituted the National Birth-Rate Commission wondered how it was possible to derive such physiological conclusions from musty old parish registers.[35] If Chalmers himself was unable to explain the mysteries of family reconstitution, his belief in cyclical reproductive capacity was quite common in authoritative circles. Dr. John Brownlee, statistician to the Medical Research Committee established under the 1911 National Insurance Act, testified that the nineteenth century had been an age of "advanced germinal activity" that had resulted not only in a larger population but in a greater proportion of men of genuine ability. As a result England had surged ahead of other countries to become the preeminent nation in the world. The recent fall in the birthrate was, according to Brownlee, only a periodic dip in reproductive energy that appeared with the regularity of such infectious diseases as scarlet fever. Under questioning by the commissioners he admitted that his was only a hypothesis based upon the assumption that in certain periods "racial energy" was stored up to be released later in energetic bursts of fecundity. Having passed through one of these dynamic eras, England was entering a period of germinal tranquillity, or "storage," which would in time give way to another explosion of reproductive vigor.[36]

Many of the ideas about cyclical or fluctuating fertility advanced in the years before World War I were stimulated by a revival of the nutritional population theories of the early Victorian radical and Malthusian critic, Thomas Doubleday. His *True Law of Population* (1842) advanced the formula that the fecundity of human beings and other species was inversely proportional to the availability of nutriment. Consequently, those less prosperous and ill-fed persons who struggled for existence were more prolific than those who were well-off and relatively content. In effect, Doubleday believed that the germinal characteristics of species were directly affected by the threat or lack of threat to their existence. As a result, when there was a surplus of nutriment, a "plethoric state" as he described it, the race was not in danger and the rapidity of multiplication was unnecessary. Conversely, in a "deplethoric state" fecundity was naturally aroused and fertility increased to keep the race from dying out. As long as the population put a strain upon food supplies, Doubleday concluded, organisms would actually increase until prosperity subdued their reproductive drives.[37]

If the *True Law of Population* failed to dislodge Malthus's *Essay on the Principle of Population* from its preeminent place in nineteenth-century demographic literature, it did survive an attack by John Stuart Mill and managed to find some respectability until Herbert Spencer, in the 1860s, unloaded a barrage of criticism upon its frail logical foundations.[38] Doubleday was rediscovered in the opening years of the twentieth century as Englishmen sifted through numerous answers to the population question. One of them, James W. Barclay, irritated by seemingly endless complaints about the declining birthrate, turned to Doubleday to set the record straight. Citing the *True Law of Population*, Barclay, in a 1906 article in the *Nineteenth Century*, insisted that the birthrate of a country was a "natural and impartial test of the social condition and progress of its people." As the struggle for existence had lessened in the later nineteenth century, fertility, in accordance with Doubleday's formula, had steadily diminished.

Nothing proved the point more clearly, Barclay argued, than the class differences in reproduction that so worried his contemporaries. They were well aware that fertility among the wealthier, better-educated classes was substantially lower than that of the laboring poor. Recent comparisons of London districts had shown, for example, that the birthrate in the most overcrowded, impoverished areas at 35.6/1,000 was nearly double that recorded for the most prosperous sections of the metropolis. All that it meant, Barclay maintained, was that the "harder the struggle for existence the higher the birth-rate, and the greater the well-being the fewer the births." This had always been so, he wrote, and, as Doubleday had shown, the difference was natural and beneficial. The poorer and less well-nourished classes were inevitably more prolific so that they could provide enough people of ability to climb the social ladder and fill the empty spaces left by their prosperous, well-fed, but less fecund betters.[39]

Assorted food faddists and vegetarians seized upon Barclay's writings to prove that the upper classes were eating themselves into extinction. Others found little comfort in the promise that the depleted ranks of the wealthy would in time be filled with recruits from the populous lower orders who were still vigorously reproducing themselves in accordance with Doubleday's law. Though the obscure Barclay soon faded from the scene, his explanations remained a subject of discussion until the war and even enjoyed a brief revival in the early 1920s. Serious critics such as Arthur Newsholme and T. H. C. Stevenson examined the arguments closely and found them statistically wanting. Newsholme, now medical officer to the Local Government Board, observed in 1911 that not only was there a considerable range of fertility among women of the same class within the country but that international dietary comparisons hardly helped Barclay's case. It was difficult to believe, he wrote, that the notoriously low birthrate of 21.6/1,000 recorded for the French was so much below that of other countries because of fabled Gallic cuisine. Nor were the English so satiated as to account for their birthrate of 28.4 as compared with 35.7 for the Prussians.[40]

Three years later Stevenson made a similar point in his testimony before the National Birth-Rate Commission. As a statistical consultant to that body he analyzed the great differences in fertility that prevailed within and between neighboring communities. Citing two towns in the same county, Hull and Bradford, he noted that in 1911 the birthrate in the first was 26.1 as against 17.9 in the other. Yet thirty years earlier the rates at 31.0 and 30.6 were virtually the same. Taking into account the various physiological and nutritional theories being advanced, Stevenson found it difficult "to conceive of a natural cyclical change reducing the fertility of Bradford by 41 percent while it only reduced that of Hull by 16 percent."[41]

Both Newsholme and Stevenson were disturbed by the popular assumption, frequently endorsed by scientific authorities, that the declining birthrate was indeed a consequence of some recent alteration in biological capacity. The absorption of Social Darwinism into popular culture left their contemporaries particularly vulnerable to physiological explanations that were easily reconciled with simplistic concepts of evolutionary change. Barclay's cyclical evocations of pre-Darwinian demography were disposed of fairly easily by rigorous critics. Far more respectable and enduring, however, were the biological answers to the plummeting birthrate derived from the evolutionist writings of Herbert Spencer.

In 1867, a decade before the birthrate began to fall, Spencer, in his imposing *Principles of Biology*, had analyzed and rejected Doubleday's nutritional hypothesis. Never one to pass up an opportunity to formulate a new law Spencer substituted one of his own. He thought that the evidence proved that prosperous, better-fed people were for the most part actually more fertile than those who were undernourished, but in refuting the nutritional dialectics of the *True Law of Population* Spencer endorsed the inevitability of diminished fertility in advanced societies. He explained it, however, not in cyclical terms, but as a natural, progressive characteristic of an evolutionary continuum of "individuation and genesis" in which increasingly complex organisms, as they became more heterogeneous, consumed greater energy and nutriment from available resources. This, according to Spencer, reduced the capacity of the environment to sustain a larger population so that heterogeneity, or individuation, occurred at the expense of fertility. The complexity and differentiation of more highly evolved individuals required a greater "expenditure of force; and this supposes consumption of digested and absorbed food, which might otherwise have gone to make new organisms, or the germs of them."[42]

Self-maintenance and the maintenance of the race were, by Spencer's reasoning, mutually antagonistic. The evolution of a species entailed the survival of more complicated, energetic individuals whose enlarged nutritional requirements increasingly impinged upon resources once adequate for the support of a less developed population.[43] In arguing that diminished powers of propagation were an inevitable consequence of evolutionary progress Spencer recognized that the conflict between individuation and genesis could result in the eventual elimination of the most advanced organisms, including man himself. To save the endangered species he tortuously formulated an additional law in which "each increment of evolution entails a decrement of reproduction which is not accurately proportionate, but somewhat less than proportionate. The gain in one direction is not wholly cancelled by a loss in the other direction, but only partially cancelled: leaving a margin of profit to the species." Genesis, in effect, decreased somewhat more slowly than individuation increased so that in the case of man at least a minimum of two children would suffice to maintain the race. Moreover, in accordance with the survival of the fittest, superior species were not only more vigorous and intelligent, but as a result of their longer existence they were more likely to leave sufficient offspring. As Spencer explained, although "the more evolved organism is the less fertile absolutely, it is the more fertile relatively."[44]

Although Spencer shared Darwin's belief that excessive fertility, overpopulation, and natural selection stimulated evolution, he thought the process was modified significantly by progressive individuation. In crowded, complex modern societies this was most clearly manifested in expanded emotional and intellectual activity rather than in physical competition. The enlarged, more convoluted brain of civilized man evolved at the expense of early sexual maturity, and the energy required to support it had to be drawn from nutritive reserves once used for reproduction.[45]

Spencer, a celibate bachelor engrossed in the presumably sterilizing task of constructing a monumental synthetic philosophy, was confident that cerebral progress would continue while fertility declined until some point in the future a physiological equilibrium would be reached among the most individuated sector of society. At that point fertility would no longer decline, indicating an end to the evolutionary development of the nervous system. Man would be in harmony with his environment and, though he would continue to differentiate and produce a heterogeneous assemblage of varying types, two or three children would serve to preserve his individuated paradise.[46]

Many of Spencer's contemporaries were intrigued. Some, like William Rathbone Greg, a Darwinian cotton manufacturer and later comptroller of the Stationary Office, thought the *Principles of Biology* would put an end to predictions of a "Malthusian crisis." It might have been possible in more primitive times, he wrote in 1872, but, by proving that cerebral development tended to lessen reproduction, Spencer had shown how the menace of overpopulation would be contained by progressive evolution. Like his brother-in-law Walter Bagehot, he hoped that the intellectual advances promised by Spencer would keep pace with the democratic forces released by the recent Reform Bill of 1867.[47]

Francis Galton, Darwin's cousin and a close friend of Spencer, was uninterested in the political implications of evolution when, in 1865, inspired by *The Origin of Species*, he launched his pioneering statistical inquiries into human heredity.[48] His genealogical analysis, *English Men of Science*, published ten years later, gave some quantitative support to Spencer's theories. Galton found that in most cases the families of the one hundred prominent contemporary scientists he studied were slightly smaller than those from which they came, although they had usually married earlier than did their parents. From this slender evidence he plotted a decline in fertility that he believed confirmed in part at least the Spencerian hypothesis. But, in contrast to his friend's prediction that even the most intellectual of the species would be likely to have two children, Galton discovered that one-third of his sample had none. Given what he believed to be their superior inheritable qualities Galton found the trend particularly disturbing.[49]

Although his hereditarian studies were to continue through the next decade and lay the foundation for the new science of eugenics, neither the scientific community nor the public showed much interest in the questions Galton raised about inheritance and selective breeding. Disappointed, he set aside that aspect of his extraordinarily rich and varied work until the differential patterns of fertility associated with the declining birthrate became an issue of national concern in the opening decade of the twentieth century.[50] By then Galton's earlier ideas had been taken up by a new generation of mathematical scientists led by Karl Pearson and the zoologist Walter F. R. Weldon who fashioned them in the 1890s into biometrics, the statistical study of biology. During the same period Spencer's philosophical constructs of individuation and genesis had, like his earlier theories about the survival of the fittest, become an integral part of popular evolutionary thought.[51] As people became conscious of the persistent fall in the birthrate many of them had little difficulty putting it into a biological, evolutionary context that seemed logical and scientifically credible.

Montague Crackanthorpe, a prominent London barrister and long-time student of demographic trends, commented in 1906 on the revival of Thomas Doubleday's anti-Malthusian explanations of population change. An old Malthusian and a vigorous proponent of eugenics, Crackanthorpe, who had changed his name from Cookson in 1888, was not persuaded by assurances that it was natural and racially beneficial for a population to be reinvigorated from the overly fecund lower orders. In resurrecting this dubious thesis James Barclay, in Crackanthorpe's opinion, had ignored the implications of Spencerian evolution, which proved that organisms actually multiplied in inverse ratio to the dignity and worth of individual life.[52] Malthus had perceived this phenomenon in his observations on poverty and excessive fertility, Caleb Saleeby, a young Edinburgh physician and ardent eugenics propagandist wrote elsewhere, but it was Spencer's masterly contribution to "philosophic biology" that put demography in the proper evolutionary context. Indeed, he believed that the *Principles of Biology* was the most important study of population since Malthus's famous essay.[53]

A number of Crackanthorpe and Saleeby's colleagues in the fledgling eugenics movement before World War I energetically endorsed the Spencerian dimension. Like most of the Edwardians who contemplated the population question they were disturbed by the prospect of a geometric proliferation of the poor, as Malthus had warned a century earlier. More recently, Saleeby pointed out, the imposing studies of Charles Booth in London and Seebohm Rowntree in York had confirmed what numerous social investigators had claimed since the 1880s: in spite of all the advances of the past hundred years the country was still unable to feed and house adequately its burgeoning population. Nearly 30 percent of the urban poor lived on the edge of starvation. In surveying the evidence, Saleeby looked to Spencer's formulation of individuation and retarded fertility as the principal hope for warding off a Malthusian disaster in the twentieth century.[54] Malthus, after all, never understood the laws of evolution and therefore failed to see that in the struggle for survival the highest types would tend to perpetuate themselves while diminishing in number. Whereas Malthus urged later marriages and fewer children to avoid famine, modern couples achieved the same end, not out of a fear of starvation but as a natural result of individuation.[55]

As Spencer had shown, the intensity and extent of individuation varied widely within a given species depending upon the stage of evolutionary progress. To Saleeby and other disciples of the *Principles of Biology*, this theory accounted for the wide disparities of fertility found at different levels of the social hierarchy. Certain classes were simply further along the evolutionary path, and their progress was reflected not only in the size of their families but in their expectations for their children. "*The very fact of progress,*" Saleeby emphasized in 1909, "*is the replacement of lower by higher life, the supersession of the quantitative by the qualitative criterion of survival value, the increasing dominance of mind over matter, the substitution of the intensive for the merely extensive cultivation of life.*"[56] Havelock Ellis, like

Saleeby, an early advocate of eugenic breeding, made a similar point in 1912 when he cautioned that "those who seek to restore the birth-rate of half a century ago are engaged on a task which would be criminal if it were not based on ignorance, and which is, in any case, fatuous. The whole course of zoological evolution reveals a constantly diminishing reproductive activity and a constantly increasing expenditure of care on the off-spring thus diminished in number."[57]

Ellis was an optimistic eugenist in an era of racial pessimism. A majority of his contemporaries who explained the declining birthrate in biological, evolutionary terms feared that before the blessings of individuation reached the less cerebral lower classes their numbers would overwhelm their more complex, highly differentiated countrymen and reverse the progressive course of race development. Well aware that concerns about the birthrate were entwined with broader worries about the possibility of race degeneration in an age of real and imagined challenges to Britain's economic, political, and imperial position in the world, Saleeby and Ellis recalled Spencer's assurance that although the more highly developed organism is the "less fertile absolutely," it is the "more fertile relatively."[58] At the same time, however, Saleeby was taking no chances. He energetically promoted a national eugenics program to encourage the marriage and procreation of the more individuated "fit" people in society who were readily identified by their professional, intellectual, economic, or social achievements.

Although pronounced eugenists were most vocal in offering biological explanations for the drop in the birthrate, their sentiments were shared by countless Social Darwinists who did not necessarily think in terms of heredity and selective breeding. At the 1904 meetings of the recently formed Sociological Society Dr. W. Leslie Mackenzie, medical inspector to the Local Government Board of Scotland, commented on the pervasive assumption that the recent decline in fertility was somehow linked with the advance of civilization. For one thing, he argued, the "universal fall in the birth-rate has been too rapid to justify *simpliciter* the conclusion that biological capacity has altered." Not only were there substantial variations within the United Kingdom and within similar classes, but declining fertility was as great if not greater in many of the colonies, in several European countries, and in some parts of the United States. To suggest that so profound a change on so wide a scale was attributable to some physiological modification occurring in the previous twenty-five or thirty years strained scientific credulity as well as common sense.[59]

Even Galton who, at the age of eighty-two, came out of retirement in 1904 to address the Sociological Society on his theory of eugenics, had become uncomfortable with several aspects of Spencer's argument. Noting its current popularity among critics of the population question, Galton intimated that the causes of diminished fertility were perhaps more numerous and obscure than once believed. His earlier statistical genealogical and biographical studies of eminent scientists, lawyers, and other successful men had at first persuaded him of the validity of Spencer's formula.[60] He now thought it very likely that types could be found, even among the intellectual giants of the race, who could sustain a high level of civilization without losing their enormously valuable powers of procreation.[61]

Galton did not deny that reproductive capacity was clearly associated with inherited biological qualities subject to the laws of evolution, but he had of late become much more aware of another, less deterministic variable—individual volition, or deliberate family limitation, as it was frequently described. He was probably persuaded of its importance by his protégé, Karl Pearson, who had in the mid-1890s become convinced that the conscious restriction of fertility better explained the recent shift toward smaller families than any biological reason he could isolate.[62] Over the next decade Pearson and the statisticians he trained in his biometric laboratory reinforced this preliminary view, concluding in 1909 that all of their correlative studies had failed "to find any character whatever *which organically is markedly associated with fertility*. Nature seems to have effectually hindered living forms undoing by reproductive selection her great achievements produced by natural selection." Referring specifically to Spencer's famous explanation of individuation and genesis, Pearson reported that no meaningful correlation could be found between intelligence and fecundity.[63]

It is evident from his correspondence with Pearson that Galton at first found it difficult to believe that so radical a change in the procreative habits of his countrymen was taking place. As a convinced Darwinist and the foremost student of human heredity in Victorian England, Galton invariably thought in evolutionary biological terms. Procreative energy, or its absence, was, to his eugenic way of thinking, as inheritable a characteristic as intelligence, scientific ability, musical talent, strength, courage, good disposition, humor, digestion, or, conversely, any number of negative features that blighted the personality, health, and racial value of the less desirable members of society. Nevertheless, the evidence compiled by Pearson and others seemed to prove that whatever inherited tendencies toward sterility or fecundity might exist, they were far less significant determinants of family size than was the willful prevention of conception. Galton's friend and neighbor, Crackanthorpe, described it as a new "D.E.," or "determining element" in marital fertility. For Malthus the "D.E." had been celibacy or deferred marriage, while for John Stuart Mill and others it took the form of education and "moral restraint." For the current generation it was contraception.[64]

Both those who applauded the trend as a laudable sign of social and economic maturity and others who denounced it as selfish, unnatural, and racially perilous frequently complained about popular theories of evolutionary determinism obscuring reality. The columns of specialized journals, as well as those of the monthlies and the daily press, reflected the widely differing responses to each new announcement of the further decline in fertility. Physicians were as divided as everyone else. When the cautious *British Medical Journal* periodically opened its prestigious pages to the subject it was inundated by letters and articles from doctors who ranged on all sides of the question. By 1906, however, after weighing the various arguments, the *BMJ* found itself in agreement with those members of the profession who rejected abstract biological hypotheses and instead concluded from their experience with patients that the principal reason for the falling birthrate was the widespread employment of restrictive practices on the part of married couples. Commenting in particular on the resurgence of Thomas Doubleday's cyclical-nutritional theories and Spencerian alternatives, the *BMJ* encouraged its readers to examine the recent statistical analyses of Newsholme and Stevenson, which proved that the association between low fertility and improved social conditions was casual not causal. The alarming drop in the birthrate, it concluded, was not due to any mysterious natural laws of inverse relationships but to the voluntary control of conception.[65]

Although spokesmen for the medical profession were for the most part exceedingly hostile to contraception, in admitting its causative role the *BMJ* reflected the growing awareness of a reality that was, no matter how unpalatable, becoming increasingly difficult to ignore. To accept it, however, was to acknowledge the explicit sexuality of the marriage relationship and to disprove the fiction that marital intercourse was primarily for reproduction. Victorian legacies died hard. If millions of English couples were, as their diminished fertility testified, using some form of contraception, they were very circumspect about it. Only the boldest of social radicals dared to flaunt sexual conventions and question sacrosanct concepts of respectable family life. Natural cyclical or evolutionary explanations of lower fertility, while sincerely believed by many, were also a convenient and flattering alternative to other less seemly reasons. They permitted the preservation of the old ideals of marital sex and accounted for the diminution in expected offspring by extolling the intellectual progress of modern civilization. Smaller families were in a way an outward sign of inner evolutionary grace. This mixture of prudery and scientific rationalization, both deeply entrenched Victorian values, tended to reinforce biological explanations of the falling birthrate even as the evidence mounted that the cause lay in changing domestic expectations, perceptions, and aspirations.

On the eve of World War I, Newsholme, Stevenson, Pearson, and others were still piling on statistics and publishing tables and graphs to disprove any physiological correlations with the continued slide in fertility. They also embellished their data with appeals to common sense. Citing a recent study tracing a decline of from 7.1 to 3.1 children born on the average to aristocratic families in the course of the nineteenth century, Newsholme ridiculed the idea that the "state of nutrition or the intellectual capacity of these parents had so increased to account for this."[66] Stevenson thought it equally foolish to explain the 1911 English birthrate of 24.3 being so much smaller than the 45.3 recorded for the Irish of Connaught as a sign of biological favor. Such extraordinarily high fertility was an aberration even in Ireland where the overall birthrate of 23.2, though up slightly since the turn of the century, was actually lower than in England. Few Englishmen, of course, would have entertained the notion that Paddy was a step up on the evolutionary ladder. Differences, whether between countries or within them, could only be explained as environmental and cultural phenomena that reflected the extent "artificial restraint" was being practiced by people in varying regions and communities.[67]

In spite of repeated invocations of statistical truth the spirit of Doubleday and Spencer was difficult to exorcise. Defenders of biological causation did not deny the significance of family limitation, but either thought it of secondary importance, or, as was more common, the most recent manifestation of Spencerian individuation. Descanting upon the latest nutritional cycle of "racial energy" Dr. Brownlee, in 1913, conceded that the spread of contraception was perhaps having some effect on the reduced birthrate. He was certain, however, that the adoption of "artificial methods" merely happened to coincide with a new cyclical phase.[68] Far more convincing were the arguments of Havelock Ellis who insisted that the rise of family restriction was not in conflict with evolutionary individuation. On the contrary, it was an obvious characteristic of complex cerebral differentiation, which resulted in the most advanced of the species rationally adjusting to their changing environment.[69]

Ellis had long advocated family limitation as a critical stage of evolutionary progress. Any species that could deliberately regulate its fertility in accordance with a rational evaluation of individual and community needs was obviously at a high stage of civilization. As a result Ellis was certain that birth control, while technically responsible for the steady decline in the birthrate, was also a phase of evolution as biologically natural as reproduction itself. He knew, however, how difficult it would be for the English to acknowledge that rationally controlled sexual fulfillment was not only normal and desirable, but an important manifestation of race elevation. For nearly two decades Ellis had been trying to persuade his inhibited, easily offended countrymen that their carnal desires were not simply a shameful legacy of a natural, if unfortunate, impulse for procreation. Much of his work had to be published in other countries where censorship of such matters was less rigorous.[70]

Nature has always pursued quantity, Ellis reasoned, especially among the lower forms of life. Through evolution she also seeks quality. The control of fertility, he explained, without violating the natural impulses of sexuality, made it possible to subordinate and check reproduction in order to evolve fewer, but higher and more complex beings. Consequently, although procreativity had slackened, the evolution of the species, in accordance with Spencer's *Principles of Biology*, had accelerated along ever more selective and varied lines. Ellis believed there had always been an inverse relationship between individuation and genesis, but it had been raised to a new level with the introduction of "rational, volitional control." Birth control, as he defined the practice, was in reality "an art directed precisely to the attainment of ends which Nature has been struggling after for millions of years." It made possible the natural identification of the human will with the "divinely appointed law of the world."[71]

Whether family limitation, wrapped in the mantle of Darwin, Spencer, and even the Creator, was welcomed as the latest stage of human evolution, or condemned as it was by the National Council of Public Morals as a dreadful sign of the "low and degrading views of the social instinct" that threaten not only our morals but "our very life as a nation," it was impossible by 1914 to deny its extraordinary impact.[72] Virtually every study that made a pretense of scientific objectivity, whatever its prognosis, made the same diagnosis. This was true of the two most famous inquiries undertaken before World War I, the 1911 *Fertility of Marriage Census* and that of the unofficial National Birth-Rate Commission.

The commission, established in 1913, was the first of a series of similar investigatory bodies set up under the auspices of the exceedingly respectable NCPM, the descendant of an earlier National Social Purity Crusade founded in 1901. The NCPM proved to be the most important of the numerous moral vigilance societies stirred up by the excesses perceived in the Edwardian era. It was particularly concerned with the collapse of domestic values, as its motto, taken from a 1911 speech of the new monarch, George V, indicated. "The Foundations of National Glory are set in the homes of the people," it proclaimed. "They will only remain unshaken while the family life of our race is strong, simple, and pure." Having apparently failed to find similar inspiration in either the words or behavior of the previous sovereign, the NCPM looked to the reign of his more temperate successor for the revivification of domestic morality. It launched its campaign in 1911 with a "manifesto" condemning the debasement of sexual mores in general and the plummeting birthrate in particular. The sixty-six worthies who endorsed the document included eight peers, three M.P.s, the heads of two Cambridge colleges, two medical editors, seven bishops, as well as leaders of most of the Nonconformist denominations. They were joined by General William Booth of the Salvation Army, and, for additional secular leavening, Beatrice Webb and James Ramsay MacDonald.[73]

Under the guidance of the Presbyterian minister, James Marchant, the NCPM published a number of "New Tracts for the Times" and other works critical of the diminishing birthrate and usually prophesying the destruction of domestic, national, and imperial institutions unless the slide toward moral and racial degeneration was halted. Although the NCPM was to a large extent an amalgam of conservative fears about changing religious, social, and moral values in the early twentieth century, it was willing to entertain opposing views as indicated by its curious publication in 1911 of Havelock Ellis's pro-birth control, eugenic treatise, *The Problem of Race Regeneration*. Similarly, its most important contribution, the National Birth-Rate Commission, opened its proceedings to a wide range of differing testimony.

The commission was established to resolve the often contradictory arguments and "endless explanations" surrounding the population question.[74] Efforts had been underway since the opening years of the century to persuade the government to appoint a royal commission to investigate the problem. Pointed questions about the physical quality of the race had been raised at the time of the Boer War both within parliament and without. The disproportionately large numbers of recruits from industrial towns who were unable to meet minimal physical requirements for military service fed earlier fears that urbanization was taking place at the expense of racial vigor. Talk of degeneration, already evident in the 1880s and 1890s, took on added significance in the context of the South African debacle and mounting complaints about plummeting fertility.[75] It was not placated by the conclusions of the Inter-Departmental Committee on Physical Deterioration (1904) that no conclusive evidence of progressive physiological deterioration could be found despite the obvious deprivation suffered by those who lived in overcrowded slums.[76] Though optimistic evolutionists insisted that the focus should be on progress, not decay, demands for a full-scale inquiry remained.

The 1911 *Fertility of Marriage Census* was one response; the National Birth-Rate Commission another. Under the cochairmanship of the Bishop of Ripon, William Boyd Carpenter, and the Dean of St. Paul's, William Ralph Inge, the commission undertook to explore all of the possible explanations for what it generally believed to be an alarming trend. Unlike the census enumerators who would be limited to gathering vital statistics, the commissioners would be free to scrutinize different causes, and, more important, to determine what the effects of the declining birthrate were on individual, family, and national life. The NCPM still believed that a royal commission was the appropriate agency for so momentous an inquiry, but Prime Minister Asquith, himself the father of seven children by two wives, declined the opportunity to appoint an official body to study the controversial subject.[77] He already had enough problems with disruptive suffragettes, militant labor unions, and a possible rebellion in Ireland, but he promised to follow the proceedings with interest.

Assisted by T. H. C. Stevenson and Arthur Newsholme the commissioners heard from numerous clergymen, physicians, medical officers, peers, and the representatives of various organizations interested in the population question. In addition they analyzed a large number of official and unofficial studies, including the still unpublished compilations of the 1911 *Fertility of Marriage Census*. Their sessions throughout 1913 and the early months of 1914 were regularly covered by the press, and, although the final report was delayed by the war until 1916, its conclusions were anticipated. To the surprise of very few who had followed the well-publicized proceedings, the commissioners discounted the diverse physiological, biological, and nutritional explanations paraded before them and announced that the precipitous fall in fertility over the preceding forty years had nothing to do with depleted fecundity. Rather it was the direct result of the "artificial limitation" of conception.[78]

Although the National Birth-Rate Commission, like the planners of the 1911 *Fertility of Marriage Census* and most other studies of declining fertility undertaken before the war, was ostensibly exploring the overall drop in the birthrate, it was invariably much more concerned about class differentials. If the revived interest in the population question had at first been aroused by awareness of a persistent fall in the number of children born, the focus soon shifted to the strikingly dissimilar pace at which the birthrate declined among different socioeconomic groups. For most people the population question was reduced to a simple and often alarming fact: the middle and upper classes were having fewer offspring with each passing year, while the laboring classes, especially the poorest, were continuing to reproduce themselves with reckless abandon. However one chose to explain or interpret the dwindling birthrate, its differential class characteristics, the reasons for them, and the momentous import they held for the future of the race were really at the core of the population debate.

CHAPTER 2
Fertility and Class

When, in the 1890s, Karl Pearson noted the trend toward smaller families in England, he tried to determine what sectors of the population were likely to produce the majority of future generations. On the basis of the current vital statistics and past censuses he projected that one-half of the next generation would be bred by no more than one-fifth or one-quarter of the present generation of married couples. As a result of recent changes in reproductive behavior, Pearson calculated, 60 percent of families had fewer than five children, while the minority of 40 percent, those with five or more, already accounted for nearly 70 percent of the national total. He predicted that this disparity would increase, since most of the later generations would in all probability come from large families of at least seven children whose parents made no attempt at limitation.[1]

Pearson, one of the creative pioneers of modern statistics, drew reproductive frequency curves that revealed that restraint was already being practiced by couples with four children or less. Since there was every reason to believe that restriction would continue and even increase among an expanding majority of them, the lack of control among a minority of overly fertile parents raised very serious questions about the future composition of the race. As a neo-Darwinist and a disciple of Francis Galton's elaborate quantitative theories of human heredity, Pearson warned that if half the next generation was indeed descended from the more prolific quarter of society, "any correlation between inheritable (physical or social) characteristics and fertility must thus sensibly influence the next generation."[2]

Not even the higher mortality traditionally associated with excessive fertility was sufficient any longer to alter radically the disproportionate role played by larger families in peopling the country. Natural selection was still at work, as the greater infant mortality suffered by the more populous classes revealed, but "it is not more evident than restraint, and

. . . appears to have at the present time no really significant influence on reproductive selection." Selective mortality, then, where still operative, was more than offset by selective marriage and fertility on the part of an ever-widening segment of the populace. For the foreseeable future, Pearson emphasized, "*in the case of civilised man natural selection . . . would appear to be quite secondary to reproductive selection as a factor of progressive evolution.*"[3] It might very well mean that in contrast to the "conditions which hold among lower types of life, or among races of uncivilised man, where the struggle for existence is more severe . . . survival of the most fertile, rather than the survival of the fittest, is very possibly now the keynote to evolution in civilised man."[4]

Pearson's formula and explanation was quoted often during the next decade by analysts of the declining birthrate concerned with its differential characteristics. Usually they had particular groups or classes in mind. The assumption that the lower orders were more prolific than their social betters had been postulated since antiquity, of course, and Social Darwinists like Spencer, Galton, and Pearson were only the most recent of a long line of learned observers of the phenomenon. Any excessive imbalance between reproduction and social rank, it had long been believed, was partially corrected by recruitment from below, but mainly by the greater mortality endured by the poor. Malthus had counted on it as one of the critical checks on overpopulation. Darwin, inspired by Malthus, assumed the prolificacy of lower organisms was essential to natural selection and the evolution of species. Images of swarming, struggling creatures governed by invariable competitive laws of nature, permitting only the fittest to survive, opened up an exciting new era of social speculation and demographic theorizing. The concept of natural selection, simplified and popularized, made a great deal of sense to successful Victorians raised on the improving virtues of individual struggle, competition, and manly self-reliance as the route to economic and social improvement. It also explained the association of higher fertility with lower organisms, or, when applied to societies, the poorer classes.

Herbert Spencer, in his influential *Principles of Biology*, had been careful not to draw invidious class distinctions in his formulation of the principles of individuation and genesis, though many Social Darwinists were not as discreet as they analyzed the condition of their country. A sympathetic though not an active Fabian socialist in the 1890s, Pearson was also cautious in avoiding specific class references as he worked out his demographic projections. He knew that a great many people instinctively associated high fertility with such antisocial traits as sloth, imprudence, short-sightedness, drunkenness, and chronic indigence. Though it was commonly assumed that these were regrettable characteristics of the laboring poor,

Pearson warned that the existing vital statistics were inadequate for an accurate comparison of birthrates or even marriage rates among different classes and occupational groups.[5]

Within a few years, when he became more stridently eugenist and clearer in his mind about the extent of differential fertility, Pearson did not hesitate to correlate "social value" and "civic worth" with the birthrates of various classes and vocations. In the 1890s, however, he was content to predict that the accumulated figures, though imperfect for social analysis, portended momentous change. It would not be long before statesmen, even more than statisticians, would have to concern themselves with the "relative degrees of fertility in the various classes of a community, and the correlation of various social or anti-social characteristics with fertility." Political economists from Malthus to Mill had preached the value of bringing no more children into the world than could be well provided for, and Spencer had suggested that nature was lending a hand in checking the problem. Still, Pearson cautioned, the "prudential restraint on marriage and parentage in the more educated members of the community, which we are apt to regard as a social virtue, may after all have its dark side," since the effects of natural selection are increasingly neutralized by the advance of modern civilization. Without making any specific class references, Pearson noted that not even the most democratic of political leaders had identified the "most fertile with the socially fittest."[6]

Pearson was being disingenuous. Like many academic social critics whose elitist inclinations drew them to the eugenics movement in the next decade, he believed England was rapidly being populated by the less capable sectors of society. His waning socialist sentiments and scientific training made him reluctant to speculate too far beyond his statistical evidence, as many social prophets were inclined to do. By 1903 he felt less restrained. Concluding the prestigious Huxley Lecture before the Anthropological Institute that year, Pearson complained of the absence of highly intelligent, able people in science, the arts, commerce, politics, the professions, and the skilled trades, and he could understand why many people were worried "that we are no match for Germans and Americans."

The only explanation he could offer for this loss of national efficiency was that "we are ceasing as a nation to breed intelligence as we did fifty to a hundred years ago. The mentally better stock in the nation is not reproducing itself at the same rate as it did of old, the less able, and the less energetic, are more fertile than the better stocks." Galton had made a similar observation nearly thirty years earlier, but, as Pearson knew, the declining birthrate put the question into different perspective. The outlook for the future of the race was not promising, Pearson reported. Contemplating the manifold challenges the empire faced in the new century, he gloomily predicted, "we stand . . . at the commencement of an epoch, which will be marked by a great dearth of ability." To confirm his impressions Pearson joined the chorus of critics demanding a thorough investigation of recent demographic trends. In particular he called for a census of the "effective size of families among the intellectual classes" as well as a study that would compare the fertility of the more intelligent workingman with that of the uneducated hand laborer. The results will show, he promised, that "grave changes have taken place in relative fertility during the last forty years."[7]

Eugenists, like Pearson, who believed that ability was primarily determined by heredity (or nature), were confident that a national survey of differential fertility would point up the racial dangers that lay ahead and would enhance the acceptance of eugenic proposals for race betterment. Similarly, social reformers who emphasized environmental causation (or nurture), believed that a comparative class analysis of birthrates and death rates would show obvious correlations with social and economic conditions that would strengthen their demands for improved welfare legislation. Although the desired census was not undertaken until 1911, the issue had become much too consequential to await the investigations of a government reluctant to become embroiled in so difficult a controversy. As a result, a number of unofficial inquiries were conducted, frequently building upon the studies of urban poverty made by Charles Booth and Seebohm Rowntree in the 1890s.

Their notable surveys of London and York called attention to the excessive fertility found in the most benighted areas. Rowntree discovered that approximately 22 percent of those living in "primary poverty" in York had five or more children and would not have been destitute if their families were smaller. Nearly one-quarter of the poor were from families of at least six, although, as he calculated, wages were so marginal that "every labourer who has as many as three children must pass through a time, probably lasting for about ten years, when he will be in a state of primary poverty; in other words, when he and his family will be underfed."[8]

Booth's *Life and Labour of the People of London* drew the familiar close correlations between poverty, overcrowding, and high fertility noted by social reformers throughout the nineteenth century. His comparative analysis of fifty London districts revealed birthrates ranging from 43.3/ 1,000 in the poorest areas to 13.5 in the wealthiest. On the average the birthrate in the "central districts," populated by the lower middle and skilled artisan classes, was approximately twice that of such professional and upper-middle-class boroughs as Hampstead and Kensington, and the difference was even greater in the more impoverished sectors of the East End. Booth, like many of his contemporaries, assumed that the differential was largely a consequence of the lower classes marrying earlier. Among the poorest in squalid, densely packed slums youthful nuptiality was compounded by an absence of self-restraint that Booth believed to be a normal cultural characteristic of such people.[9] He in effect assumed that unregulated procreation was a consequence of poverty rather than a cause, and, like Rowntree, saw it as a vicious circle.

In spite of the uncontrolled fertility observed in the eleven most wretched districts of the metropolis, where the birthrate hovered around 37/1,000, Booth reassured his readers that the rate of population increase in these areas was not appreciably larger than in the same number of more comfortable working- and lower-middle-class neighborhoods surveyed. Because death rates were so much higher among the poor their net growth was, at 14.1/1,000, virtually the same as that experienced in more fortunate districts. Less comforting, perhaps, was the revelation that in the eleven wealthiest parts of London, where the birthrate stood at 24.2, the overall rate of increase was only 9.5, or a net differential between rich and poor of nearly 31 percent. As Booth acknowledged, not even the very low death rates of these prosperous middle- and upper-middle-class areas, often half that of the poorest regions, could offset the much higher total fertility of those at the other end of the social spectrum.[10] Whereas Pearson forecast a geometric increase in the relative contribution of the most fertile group, especially as mortality rates were brought down, Booth found nothing quite so portentous in the differential statistics he cited. They merely indicated that, as always, there were more poor people than rich people, and their disproportionate numbers were a normal consequence of the social and economic realities he so industriously investigated.

Considerations of comparative fertility were but a small part of Booth's extraordinarily rich and varied description of the London poor in the closing years of Queen Victoria's long reign. They were, however, harbingers of more specialized inquiries into the differential birthrate in the metropolis, as well as other areas of the country, which began to multiply in the next decade. Booth's findings, along with those of Rowntree, Pearson, and the French demographer, Jacques Bertillon, were increasingly cited by Edwardian diagnosticians of the population question.

Bertillon, for example, in 1899 published a study of fertility among women aged fifteen to thirty living in Paris, Berlin, Vienna, and London, in which he showed a direct correlation between very high birthrates and dismal living conditions.[11] It was soon discovered by critics such as Montague Crackanthorpe who, in 1906, dwelt upon the tables for London showing that in "very poor quarters" the birthrate of women in the designated category stood at 147/1,000 compared with 107 in "comfortable" districts and only 87 in the "rich" areas. The disparity had widened of late,

Crackanthorpe believed. Citing the most recent metropolitan statistics he noted that the birthrate in such crowded East End boroughs and parishes as Bermondsey, Stepney, Shoreditch, Poplar, Bethnal Green, Whitechapel, Mile End, and St. George's-in-East averaged 35.6. By contrast the rate in fashionable Chelsea, Kensington, Hampstead and St. George's, Hanover Square, was, at 18.6, virtually half that inflated figure.[12]

Although Crackanthorpe arbitrarily lumped corrected and uncorrected rates together, the results were essentially the same. Differential fertility, he assumed, was inevitably deleterious in its long-range effects, and he was one of several people now who recalled Pearson's warning of nearly ten years earlier that the country was becoming populated by a prolific, less capable minority. No one could doubt any longer who they were and where they were multiplying.

Crackanthorpe's demographic musings reflected widespread misgivings about differential fertility evident by the middle years of the decade. Karl Pearson, annoyed by the indiscriminate bandying about of vital statistics by social critics, directed his students and colleagues in the Biometric and Galton Eugenics Laboratory into more comprehensive studies of differential fertility. As the proceedings of the Royal Statistical Society illustrate, medical authorities and others with mathematical inclinations also began looking into the problem more carefully. Similarly, the Fabian Society, sensitive to the class distinctions associated with the falling birthrate, in 1905 launched its own investigation under the direction of Sidney Webb. The most comprehensive of these precensus analyses, *On the Relation of Fertility in Man to Social Status*, was written by David Heron, one of Pearson's former students and a fellow in the recently established Eugenics Laboratory. Its appearance in 1906 as the first in a series pointedly entitled "Studies in National Deterioration" stirred up a good deal of worried comment.

Heron carefully analyzed the fertility in 1901 of a sample of married women in twenty-seven London districts representing a wide range of social, economic, occupational, and physical characteristics. The results confirmed what many of Heron's unhappy contemporaries already suspected. In such prosperous boroughs as Chelsea, Westminster, Kensington, and Hampstead, where there were a large proportion of professional men and sizable retinues of servants, married women had the fewest children. Poplar, Bethnal Green, St. Luke, Shoreditch, and other East End slums were by contrast swarming with the progeny of the poor. Housing density, health indexes, lunacy, and infant mortality provided additional comparative dimensions to Heron's innovative study, confirming a high correlation of unchecked fertility with overcrowding, disease, mental illness, and disproportionately high death rates.[13]

Only cancer, Heron found, was more prevalent in the better districts of the city where low fertility was the rule. Otherwise every test correlation proved that the "wives in the districts of least prosperity and culture have the largest families, and the morally and socially lowest classes in the community are those which are reproducing themselves with the greatest rapidity." When compared with the admittedly less complete birth and status indexes available for 1851, there was no escaping the conclusion that the intensity of the relationship between undesirable social conditions and reproduction had almost doubled in the preceding fifty years. Moreover, all of the evidence indicated that the primary reason was the adoption of restrictive practices by couples in the better sections of London rather than their later age of marriage.[14]

Though Heron was obviously disturbed by these observations he was reluctant to discuss the dangers they posed for the future composition of British society. Others who read his and similar findings were less restrained, and a number of commentators noted how Heron's study confirmed the earlier projections of his mentor, Karl Pearson. In referring to the excitement caused by Pearson and now Heron, G. Udny Yule recalled that his own examination of several London areas for the period 1871 to 1901 showed that although the fertility of married women had fallen by 19 percent, there had been virtually no decline in the poorest districts. Preliminary returns for some other parts of the country indicated that the contrast might not be as great, but, Yule told the Royal Statistical Society, it was no longer possible to deny that the "matter is one of the gravest social importance."[15]

Although Yule still thought that the differential had more to do with periodic nutritional factors than deliberate restraint, many others suspected that it was an index of physical degeneration starting at the top of the social scale. However one interpreted the evidence it seemed obvious that Pearson's prediction that one-quarter of the populace would produce at least half the next generation was coming true. If, like Sir James Crichton Browne, a prominent physician and psychologist, one also believed that mental and moral traits were no less hereditary than physical qualities, then the nation's "racial resistance" to deterioration was obviously imperiled by so great an imbalance. In imparting these portentous observations in his 1906 presidential address to the Sanitary Inspectors Association, Sir James was reflecting a common reaction to the literature of differential fertility.[16] He became a founding member of the Eugenics Education Society when it was established in 1907, but countless others who made no formal commitment to saving the race were nonetheless fearful of being swamped by the working poor.

It was an awareness of this growing class antagonism in discussions of the declining birthrate that prompted a subcommittee of the Fabian Society, under the chairmanship of Sidney Webb, to look into the question. Seven years earlier, in his study of *Industrial Democracy*, Webb had argued that the Malthusian dilemma had little to do with overpopulation. The realistic problem was the deliberate restriction of family size by the intelligent, prosperous, and thrifty sections of society.[17] Since then the situation had grown worse. In a preliminary report published in the fall of 1906, as well as in the completed Fabian tract, *The Decline in the Birth-Rate*, which appeared the next year, Webb called attention to the drop by five thousand in the number of children scheduled to start school in the London County region. Yet the population of the area had increased by 300,000 in the past ten years. Citing the recent studies of Newsholme, Stevenson, and Yule on corrected fertility, Webb was certain that his findings were characteristic of the entire country. Noting that the only exception to be found was in Catholic Ireland, he found it difficult to give credence to any explanation other than that of voluntary limitation.[18]

Webb was one of the first to emphasize that such restraint was not limited to the middle and upper classes, as many people complained, but was employed increasingly by skilled workers as well. He and his Fabian cohorts based their findings in part on the evidence compiled by David Heron and other statisticians. More importantly, however, they also examined the records of two friendly benefit societies, the Hearts of Oak and the Royal Standard, whose members were mainly skilled artisans, mechanics, and small shopkeepers of "good character" who earned at least twenty-four shillings a week. The Hearts of Oak Friendly Society, the largest in the country with 272,000 members, reported that lying-in claims, which had risen from 2,176 per 10,000 members to 2,472 in the years 1866 to 1880, had since declined to 1,165, a loss of 52 percent. Similarly, for the same period, the much smaller Royal Standard Benefit Society recorded a drop of approximately 56 percent in maternity claims by its 8,225 members. Webb calculated that had the number of beneficiaries in 1904 been proportionally the same as in 1880 seventy thousand babies would have been born since that year to the members rather than the thirty-two thousand reported.[19]

The statistics convinced Webb that at least among the more cautious, thrifty, and skilled sectors of the working and lower middle classes smaller families were more prevalent than in the nation at large because the rate of decline in the demand for lying-in benefits was substantially greater than the overall diminution in the national birthrate. If the Hearts of Oak and Royal Standard members had reproduced themselves at the national average since 1880 they would have had fifty-eight thousand children, nearly twice as many as the number actually born. "It looks," Webb surmised, "as if the birth-rate was falling most conspicuously, if not exclusively, not among the wealthy or the middle class as such, but among the sections of every class in which there is most prudence, foresight and self-control."[20]

Webb quickly added that the absence of similar evidence for semiskilled and unskilled workers did not necessarily mean, as many people charged, that they were breeding with reckless abandon in London and other great cities. Admittedly, all recent comparative examinations indicated the multiplication of the population from the poorest stock, but, Webb reminded readers, the most lamentable areas of London also contained the largest numbers of Catholic Irish and immigrant Jews who did not practice family limitation. "We cannot therefore infer . . . either that the birth rate of the poorest stratum of the English race in London is greater than that of the artisan or lower middle class." In areas uninfluenced by alien elements, mainly the "intermediate" boroughs described by Heron, restraint was distributed across class lines. Though aware of the concentration of Irish and Jews in the East End, Heron had failed to appreciate the distorted picture their high fertility gave of English workers, Webb charged. The same skewed results could probably be found in Liverpool, Salford, Manchester, Glasgow, Preston, or any large town populated by large numbers of Irish, he argued, although no evidence had yet been compiled for these cities.[21]

Like many socialists Webb was sensitive to the hostility toward the working classes implicit, and increasingly explicit, in discussions of the differential birthrate. He was deliberately trying to put the issue into perspective by assuring his anxious contemporaries that the social imbalance was not as great as it appeared on the surface, nor was its principal cause, voluntary limitation, a monopoly of the educated, professional, and prosperous middle classes. As Newsholme and Stevenson had shown, diminished fertility was also not uniquely urban; the decline was as great, if not greater, in rural counties populated by poorly paid agricultural laborers. Moroever, Webb asserted, it was not caused by healthy or unhealthy conditions, mental complexity, or cerebral retardation, physical advances, or racial deterioration. It was, instead, a characteristic exceptionally marked among people of all classes who were responsible and far-sighted and who were responding to changing times.[22]

Fabian efforts to democratize the declining birthrate received some support from social statisticians, such as Yule, who recognized that differential fertility was not as extreme when the higher classes were contrasted with more prosperous wage earners rather than with the poorest groups.[23] Most critics of Webb's *Decline in the Birth-Rate*, however, thought it only modified rather than altered the dangers they perceived in current demographic trends. If the better sort of people, irrespective of class, were alone limiting their families while the dregs of society remained beyond the bonds of self-control, it was obvious, as Pearson predicted, what sort of people were in the numerical ascendancy.

Another side of the Fabian investigation inadvertently supported this pessimistic interpretation. In addition to surveying lying-in benefits, Webb's committee sent out questionnaires on family limitation practices to 476 people. They ranged from skilled artisans to professional men and small property owners, half of whom lived in London and the remainder scattered throughout the country. To avoid the extremes of the socioeconomic scale laborers and wealthy investors whose income exceeded £1,000 were excluded. Of the 316 people who replied 242 admitted to restricting their families in contrast to 74 who claimed they took no particular precautions. The returns also revealed that the more recent the marriage the greater the likelihood of deliberate limitation. Indeed 107 of the 120 respondents married in the 1890s fell into this category, and their planned families, averaging 1.5 children, were only one-third the size of the general average prevailing in England and Wales twenty-five years earlier. Webb recognized that the sample represented a highly imperfect microcosm of the national scene, but nevertheless reasoned that from one-half to three-quarters of all married couples were consciously avoiding conception. The result was an estimated loss of approximately 200,000 potential children a year in all classes. It was this, not the imagined differentials in fertility, that had put Great Britain on the path to "race suicide," the Fabian study concluded.[24]

The Decline in the Birth-Rate was probably the most widely read of the precensus inquiries into differential fertility. Its popularity irritated professional statisticians like Pearson who condemned much of the methodology as haphazard and pronounced the conclusions doubtful. He attacked the inadequate selection process in the sample that had been surveyed. Not only were the recipients of the questions known to Webb and his committee, or personally recommended to them by other Fabians, but they included a disproportionate number of intellectuals, who were scarcely representative of the general population. Moreover, Webb's confident assumptions about lower-class restraint clashed with the evidence Pearson had accumulated in a still-incompleted study of 1,205 working-class marriages of at least fifteen years duration. Far from finding any substantial social leveling of fertility, his sample averaged 5.6 children per family, well above the national average and that reported in Webb's tract. Nevertheless, Pearson thought that the Fabian survey, in spite of its simplistic statistical techniques and dubious generalizations, helped call attention to the danger of excessive infertility among the intellectual classes, which was already leading to a dearth of ability at the higher levels of society.[25]

Pearson's criticism reflected his conviction that the question of differential reproduction had become much too important to be left to the imprecise conjecture of learned and not-so-learned social philosophers. The emergence of his Biometric Laboratory in the Department of Applied Mathematics, and the establishment of the journal *Biometrika*, in 1901, followed three years later by Francis Galton's handsome bequest of the Eugenics Laboratory, derived from the determination to place problems of social biology on a sound mathematical-scientific footing.[26] Since the mid-1860s, when Galton first attempted to quantify the transmission of inheritable characteristics, he and his comparatively few followers had traced with supposed geometric precision the diminishing contribution of physical, intellectual, and personality traits from one generation to another. Early on he had noted the rarity of those with outstanding ability, or "genius," in the general population, and as his principal follower, Pearson, often lamented, there was every indication that its frequency was diminishing. Mediocrity seemed triumphant, and there was nothing in the projected distribution of talent likely to emerge in the coming generation to indicate a reversal in the leveling trend.

As early as 1873 Galton had proposed a society to study the laws of ancestral inheritance. Its goal was the formulation of scientifically sound policies for improving the quality of the race by increasing the distribution of the hereditarily fit.[27] "Viriculture," as he first described his new science, gave way ten years later to "eugenics," a new "brief word" he coined from the Greek *eugenes*, meaning "well-born" or "good-in-stock." He meant it to take "cognizance of all influences that tend in however remote a degree to give the more suitable races or strains of blood a better chance of prevailing speedily over the less suitable than they otherwise would have."[28]

Eugenics made slow headway, barely penetrating the established scientific disciplines whose members were uninterested in individual human heredity and were often unable to comprehend the statistical formulas involved in plotting genetic probability.[29] Discouraged, Galton turned to other areas, but after setting the subject aside for more than a decade he again raised it in the 1901 Huxley Lecture before the Anthropological Institute.[30] His subject, "The Possible Improvement of the Human Breed," made little impression on the "thick-witted anthropologists," as Pearson described them, and three years later Galton turned to the less hidebound members of the newly founded Sociological Society. That eclectic group, its intellectual parameters still undefined, proved more receptive to his aim of bringing "as many influences as can be reasonably employed to cause the useful classes in the community to contribute *more* than their proportion to the next generation."[31]

Galton was encouraged to come out of retirement and preach eugenics to a new generation because of the obvious concerns about race deterioration and race suicide that became so pronounced in the opening years of the century. The plummeting birthrate and, more significantly, its alarming differential aspects convinced him that the age of eugenics had dawned and that the twentieth century would adopt his ideas as a new religion of racial salvation.[32] Pearson, whose career benefited considerably from Galton's generosity, was concerned about his elderly friend's renewed desire to popularize the eugenic faith. Biometric studies were time-consuming, often long-term projects based upon complex statistical correlations beyond the grasp of most scientists and virtually all educated laymen. The octogenarian Galton was eager for quick returns. He urged his young colleague to publish clear, less technical articles in the heavily statistical pages of *Biometrika* in hopes of attracting a wider audience. He approved of brilliant essays in the monthlies and obviously wanted to see eugenics accepted in his own day. To Pearson's regret Galton and many of his new followers "had not yet fully differentiated [eugenics] as a science from Eugenics as a creed of social action."[33] It would eventually become that—a "question of the market place, of morality, and of politics"—but not enough was known yet "to make the whole doctrine of descent, of inheritance, and selection of the fitter, part of our every day life, of our social customs and conduct."[34] The premature transition from one to the other, Pearson feared, would endanger the still fragile scientific credibility of both biometrics and eugenics.

Pearson remained aloof from the Eugenics Education Society, founded in 1907 to promote and popularize Galton's ideas. Though Galton became its honorary president Pearson distrusted many of the society's founders, whom he described as "high-strung, enthusiastic quacks" advocating schemes without reliable evidence. Teetotalism or votes for women might lend themselves to the propaganda of opinion-making groups, he complained, but eugenics was a science.[35] Dean Inge, who quickly joined the new organization, was exaggerating but was not far wrong when in 1909 he accused Pearson of arguing that the Eugenics Education Society should wait at least a half century before making any recommendations.[36] Inge, like most of the new members, found the differential birthrate so appalling that he could not conceive that the country had that much time left to save itself from racial oblivion.

Ironically, it was Pearson and his small coterie of biometricians who alerted the adherents of the new organization and others to the implications of differential fertility. Many of the founders of the Eugenics Education Society were also members of the Sociological Society, who had heard in Galton's 1904 address possible answers to the dilemma posed by Pearson's much-quoted projections about the demographic source of future generations. Pearson kept returning to his old formula, modifying it and refining it over the years by taking into account celibacy, marital sterility, and mortality. By 1909 he thought it possible that half the next generation might actually be recruited from no more than 12 percent of all individuals born. "It is of vital importance," he summarized, "to realise how relatively small an element of human society is responsible for the next generation."[37]

A few people were already at work attempting to determine who that small element was, and, equally important, who it was not. William Cecil Whetham, a distinguished physicist, agronomist, Fellow of Trinity College, Cambridge, and early stalwart of the Eugenics Education Society, suspected for some time that the aristocracy and the professional and intellectual classes were contributing insufficient progeny to assure the future of the empire. Disturbed by Webb's findings and Pearson's predictions, Whetham and his wife, Catherine, examined *Burke's Peerage*, *Who's Who*, and the Cambridge faculty to measure the "racial contributions" of important people whose titles and accomplishments brought them recognition. Their conclusions, published in 1909 in the *Family and the Nation* and in *Nineteenth Century*, confirmed a dangerously low level of reproduction among the abler classes.

According to the Whethams, a minimum of four children per family would sustain the population and compensate for celibacy, sterility, and early mortality. Yet their review of one hundred noble marriages contracted between 1830 and 1890 indicated that the average number of offspring had fallen from 7.1 in the 1840s to 3.1 at the end of the period, figures that demographers have shown to be considerably exaggerated. The turning point, the Whethams claimed, seemed to have come in the 1870s, when the average suddenly dropped to 4.3, and there was no reason to believe that the decline had ended. If not, they forecasted, the "extinction of these lines is clearly only a matter of a few generations." The effects of aristocratic infertility were already being felt in public life, the military, and the church, long the preserves of the scions of eminent families. Complaints about the lack of suitable men in these and other professions had become commonplace, the Whethams correctly noted, but "no younger sons are going into the Church and the Army for the simple reason that there are no younger sons to go."[38]

Recruitment from nontitled but still prominent political, professional, military, clerical, and academic families was not appreciably more promising. Samples extracted from *Who's Who* pointed to a similar decline in the number of their children, from an average of 5.2 before 1870 to 3.0 in more recent years. Among army officers the loss was even greater, falling from 4.9 to around 2.0. Only the Anglican clergy, whose capacity for the siring of unmarriageable daughters was legendary, had still not completely belied the popular image of Trollope's prolific Parson Quiverful. The more eminent of them, at least, continued to be fruitful and multiplied to the extent of an average of 4.2 children after 1870, compared with nearly five before the onset of that demographically fateful decade.[39]

Turning from the family histories of Victorian worthies to their Cambridge colleagues and acquaintances, the Whethams' tabulations added up to sixty-seven celibates, forty childless couples, and seventy families averaging 2.8 children. The number of adults outnumbered the young 287 to 199, and there was every reason to believe that academic marital fertility would decline further. Celibacy, which had been imposed upon the faculty until 1882, had, in the Whethams' opinion, proved disastrous to the reproduction of high intellectual ability and other desirable innate characteristics so desperately needed now by the nation. Since then, however, self-imposed restraints perpetuated and compounded the racial losses. "Actually and absolutely the next generation of these 'intellectuals' will be about thirty percent less than the previous one," the Whethams projected, and only about half of them would become parents in turn. Although no similar survey of fertility at Oxford was attempted, there was nothing to suggest that the faculty there "would show a better record of national responsibility than does Cambridge."[40]

The Whethams, along with a number of academics worried about declining race quality in an age of democratic leveling, flocked to the new Eugenics Education Society. Like the Whethams, the academics adorned the governing council of the consciously elitist organization and filled nearly 20 percent of the positions of leadership.[41] Although Whetham and his wife, themselves the parents of six children, came from wealthy manufacturing and ship-owning families, they were not particularly interested in the fertility of the commercial classes. Precise information about family size among most social and occupational groups was in any event rare before the 1911 *Fertility of Marriage Census*. The *Family and the Nation*, modeled on the geneological and biographical surveys Galton had made a generation earlier, was one of the few efforts made before the war to study specific classifications of people. Most conclusions about differential fertility in the Edwardian years were projected from the general socioeconomic composition of selected locales. Since many districts were very heterogeneous it was difficult, if not impossible, to isolate specific occupational categories for analysis. Webb's survey of middle-class intellectuals and skilled workers and the Whethams' biographical inquiries were inadequate attempts at greater precision in an era of contradictory demographic generalization.

Most discussions about differential fertility were replete with broad references to the middle class, the professional class, the "better classes," or the "fit," whose smaller families were contrasted with those of the poor, the lower classes, the unskilled, the working classes, or the "unfit." Dr. Alfred F. Tredgold, a London neurologist and authority on feeble-mindedness, was characteristically vague when in 1911 he commented on the proliferation of studies of the differential birthrate. They reminded him of his observation ten years earlier of forty-three "incompetent and parasitic" but frightfully fecund, unskilled working-class couples whose 7.4 children per family averaged twice the number born to ninety-one "thrifty and competent working-class families" with whom they were compared. There was no question in Tredgold's mind that his small sample was representative of the nation at large. It confirmed that the declining birthrate "is practically confined to the best elements; and that the worst elements, the insane, the feeble-minded, the diseased, the paupers, the thriftless, and in fact the whole parasitic class of the nation, are continuing to propagate with unabated and unrestricted vigour."[42] Tredgold's interspersing of qualitative evaluations and sweeping generalizations with broad social categories was typical of much of the debate over the population question.

Without denying that the demographic outlook was "gloomy," more temperate commentators such as Arthur Newsholme and T. H. C. Stevenson reminded their pessimistic contemporaries that inverse correlations between fertility and high social status were nothing new. Aristocracies had always been kept alive by engrafting from their social inferiors. The two medical statisticians recognized that the emergence of eugenics was in large measure a response to the British population's being replenished in greater proportion than in the past from the lower strata. Whether this meant, as many suspected, that the "less fit" were contributing a greater proportion than in previous eras was by no means certain. Special fitness was not a monopoly of class, Newsholme and Stevenson argued. They thought that after the experience of the past century few would any longer contend that the line of intellectual or physical endurance is horizontal and not oblique—that it is perhaps even perpendicular to social position.[43] Even if, as recent reports suggested, among the wage-earning classes only the careful and skilled were limiting their families, it had only been going on for at most two generations and might in time reach down to the very poor as well.[44] Stevenson's own *Fertility of Marriage Census* and Ethel Elderton's 1914 *Report on the English Birth-Rate* indicated that it had a long way to go.

Elderton's exploration of fertility patterns in the nine counties above the Humber went much further than earlier unofficial studies in its efforts to correlate the birthrate with specific groups. She supplemented census data with the distribution of questionnaires and even personal interviews in selected locales. Aware of the controversy and confusion generated by differing explanations of the falling birthrate, she was determined to be as precise as possible. At the same time, however, she assumed that most people, irrespective of causation, regarded the differential aspects of the decline as a serious menace to national efficiency. After an extensive analysis of economic, occupational, wage, and living conditions in each of the counties, she correlated the results with fertility statistics and, for purposes of comparison, equated them with returns from Yorkshire and Lancashire. In addition to the inescapable conclusion that the fall in the birthrate was a result of the deliberate limitation of the family, it was equally evident that the decline was much more prevalent "in the fitter elements of the population" who were better housed, better fed, better paid, and were in general healthier, more sober, and responsible.[45]

Elderton's report confirmed David Heron's findings in London and a preliminary study Elderton and a number of her colleagues in the Eugenics Laboratory had made in the industrial towns of Blackburn, Preston, and Salford. "The Correlation of Fertility with Social Value," as they described it, revealed that unemployed mothers living in dirty, overcrowded, low-rent, low-wage districts whose husbands were subject to irregular, unskilled employment and heavy drinking tended to have appreciably more children than mothers in the "better-class working portion of the population." It had become axiomatic that "in almost every case a bad social condition is associated with a large family," and the high selective death rates of the past had declined to the point that they no longer compensated for excessive imbalances. No objective person, Elderton believed, could deny any longer that "there is a really serious problem before the nation."[46]

As Elderton evaluated her data, scientific detachment gave way to polemic. Like all eugenists she readily associated social, economic, intellectual, physical, and behavioral characteristics with imprecise notions of hereditary fitness and "civic worth." But under the veneer of mathematical objectivity she articulated assumptions about the declining birthrate that were widely held by 1914. When she asserted that "no one who has even a feeble belief in the power of heredity can regard [differential fertility] . . . as anything but an unmixed evil," she was reiterating what many people who had never heard of biometrics or eugenics had been saying with increasing fervor since the early years of the century.[47] With their minds permeated by Darwinian explanations of the changes they perceived all around them, there was no escaping the "unassailable truth" that the "healthy, careful and thrifty are having smaller families than the unhealthy, careless and thriftless, and the selective deathrate . . . no longer weeds out the children of the less fit."[48]

Elderton recognized that since the time of Malthus most social investigators had concentrated upon the poor, who were usually burdened with far more children than they could adequately support. This lack of domestic foresight, as generations of Malthusian political economists explained, had severely restricted opportunities for individual self-improvement. When, however, that long-observed phenomenon was put into a Social Darwinian context and compared with the diminishing reproductivity of the nonlaboring classes, it took on entirely new significance. Elderton knew much more about the procreative habits of working classes than of their betters, and she pointedly complained about the difficulty of obtaining sufficient data for middle- and upper-class families. If specific details were lacking, the general picture was nevertheless clear.

Troubled, perhaps regretful, Elderton conceded that "it is impossible now, even if we would, to go back to the old days when nature worked unhindered, and a differential birth-rate would possibly be racially harmless since its effects would be corrected by a selective death-rate." The growing intervention of the state on behalf of the children of the poor was, in spite of its unforeseen effects, irreversible. Protective legislation, public health measures, compulsory education had all made an impact. Civilization was obviously at odds with natural selection, but "no community can allow its children to suffer more than can possibly be avoided from the carelessness and indifference of their parents, but by thus interfering with natural processes the community probably lays up racial trouble for the future." It was a Darwinian dilemma compounded by the inevitable interference of the modern welfare state. Though some extreme Darwinists denied it, Elderton recognized that "we must continue to help the helpless," but pleaded, "can nothing be done to increase the fertility of the racially fit?"[49]

The *Report of the English Birth-Rate* was set in type but not yet printed when hostilities broke out in 1914. Pearson, as director of the Eugenics Laboratory, considered delaying publication so as not to add to the nation's worries. In the end, however, he decided that "in such a time of stress men's minds are likely to be turned from the pursuit of pleasure and thus be more in the mood to consider what tends to our efficiency as a nation." Moreover, the war made the topic of urgent concern, because, to Pearson, the reconciliation of the laws of natural selection with the collectivist modifications of the environment contemplated by twentieth-century planners was the greatest problem the nation faced. No rational postwar reconstruction, he believed, was possible without taking it into account.[50]

T. H. C. Stevenson had no such option. As superintendent of statistics in the General Register Office, he was bound by governmental priorities and these forced him to postpone publication of his report on the 1911 *Fertility of Marriage Census* until after the war. Much of what the data revealed, however, was made available earlier, particularly to the National Birth-Rate Commission, and it went a long way toward clearing up the confusion that surrounded the population question. Of greater interest to contemporaries was that substantial portion of the census expressly devoted to the correlation of fertility with social status. For the first time comprehensive information was gathered on the middle and upper classes as well as on the much-studied working classes.

Eight occupational categories were established as indexes of social classification. Class I included the professions and the wealthiest economic interests in the country, whereas Class II represented similar people but with a lower level of skill, income, and status. These two categories represented the "upper and middle class," including the higher elements of landed society, and they were distinguished from the "working class," whose various components were reflected in Classes III through VIII. Skilled, semiskilled, and unskilled workers comprised the first three of these laboring classifications. The exceptionally low fertility of textile operatives and high fertility of miners and agricultural laborers led to their being placed in special designations, Classes VI through VIII.[51] As the census compilers were the first to admit, there was considerable imprecision and confusion in the pluralistic stratification of nearly three hundred occupations. It nevertheless represented a thoughtful evaluation of socioeconomic status in the Edwardian era.[52]

Citing from his preliminary analysis of the returns, Stevenson confirmed to the National Birth-Rate Commission in 1914 that, although the birthrate was falling in all categories, the decline was much greater among people in the higher social classifications. The responses of women over forty-five whose fertility was assumed to be complete and those whose marriages were of shorter duration and whose potential fertility was not yet completed showed the same trend. The longer a marriage lasted the greater were the procreative differences between people in the elevated status categories and those in the lower. Even the most recent marriages, celebrated in the five years preceding the 1911 census, indicated that the poor started their families earlier and would generally have more children during their married lives. Their social betters not only began having children a little later but ended much sooner.[53]

Shortly after the war, when he was preparing to publish his report as the second volume of the *Fertility of Marriage Census*, Stevenson asserted that the declining birthrate in Classes I, II, and III was "quite the most important fact established by the . . . tabulation." He described it as "new and formidable—how formidable is a question which must be left for the consideration of authorities on eugenics."[54] Indeed eugenist assumptions pervaded the report when it appeared in 1923 in spite of its author's efforts to avoid drawing qualitative social conclusions. It corroborated the persistent warnings of Pearson and others that the fecund lower-class minority in the country was producing somewhere between 30 and 50 percent of the next generation.[55] Was it any wonder when, as of 1911, the most fertile 10 percent of the married population whose wives were still of child-bearing age had twice as many children as the least fertile tenth? The latter, arrayed in Classes I and II, included doctors, teachers, clergymen, military officers, scientists, bankers, barristers, chemists, accountants, and various business officials. They managed to sire, on the average, only 1.8 offspring. In contrast the prolific coal miners and boilermakers were joined by general laborers, shipyard workers, dockers, riveters, pig iron workers, coal heavers, and scavengers to produce 3.7 children for the same standardized periods of marriage.[56]

Although the average family size was larger when marriages of completed fertility were compared, the differential was not appreciably different. Women in the least fertile tenth of the populace who were over forty-five in 1911 reported having 3.4 children, substantially fewer than the 6.1 recorded at the other end of the status scale. Noting that the largest families were usually fathered by unskilled manual workers, the report cautiously surmised that "broadly speaking, there seems to be an inverse relation between brain work and fertility, but this is, no doubt, open to more than one interpretation."[57]

Comparing the two extremes of the fertility spectrum obviously exaggerated the differences that existed in family size between the middle and working classes. But the statistics also revealed that semiskilled and unskilled workers had appreciably more children than the Class III men in the skilled trades whose fertility was not markedly greater than many members of the lesser middle class in Class II. Yet the differences between all groups in the middle of the nineteenth century had been quite modest, ranging from 7.6 and 7.4 births among the miners and agricultural laborers to a low of just under six among the upper and professional middle classes.[58] Stevenson believed that had an earlier fertility census been taken so that marriages in the first half of the century were included it might have "reached back to a time when the fertility of all classes was practically equal, or at least when any appreciable defect from the general average was small and limited to the upper and middle classes."[59]

Moreover, the report revealed that the moderate fertility differentials of the middle Victorian years were further reduced by the greater incidence of child mortality suffered by the lower orders. Miners, for example, the most prolific group in society, lost nearly three of the 7.6 children born to them so that their "effective" or net fertility of 4.6 actually fell below that of most other occupational groups, including the middle classes in Class II.

It was not significantly larger than the lowest net fertility of 4.3 surviving children enjoyed by the fortunate members of Class I. All families were vulnerable to high infant mortality, however, and even parents in the highest socioeconomic categories marrying in the 1850s and 1860s saw anywhere from 20 to 30 percent of their offspring die. In general there was a rough correlation between high fertility and high infant mortality, although the survival rate for the children of agricultural laborers (Class VIII), whose fertility was second only to the miners, was nearly that of the middle classes.[60] Whether from better diet, cleaner air, less crowding or a more developed understanding of nurturing the young, farm families managed to limit their losses to an average of two children and achieved the highest net fertility of any occupational group.

Census tabulators recognized that their surviving sample of marriage histories dating back to the mid-nineteenth century was comparatively small, but after correcting for this obvious limitation concluded that the findings were reasonably accurate. The general pattern of modest differential fertility remained essentially unchanged until the last quarter of the century. All classes showed a slight decrease in births in the twenty years after 1851, but in the subsequent two decades the gap between status groups began to widen noticeably. Fertility among middle- and upper-class couples in Classes I and II who married in the 1870s to the mid-1880s, the last years for which completed family information was available in 1911, dropped nearly 23 percent. This exceeded by a third the decline of 15 to 16 percent recorded for skilled and semiskilled workers in Classes III and IV. It was more than twice that experienced by the unskilled in Class V and was almost three times as great as the less than 8 percent reduction in miners' fertility.[61]

The sharp differential decline in the class birthrates was accompanied by a significant, but more evenly distributed diminution in child mortality. Couples in all classes who married in the 1870s and 1880s benefited from a 6 to 8 percent improvement in the survival rate of their offspring, compared with the cohorts of the previous two decades. This general trend toward lower child mortality continued the rest of the century and then accelerated in the decade before World War I. It seemed obvious to Stevenson, analyzing net fertility, that the widening class differences in family size were primarily a result of increasingly different birthrates rather than any radical alteration in children's death rates. Couples in Classes I and II who wed in the years 1851 to 1871 had on the average 4.6 surviving children compared with 5.1 for the miners and agricultural laborers at the other end of the scale. Effective family size among the 1881 to 1886 cohort fell to 3.7 in the two highest categories while remaining virtually unchanged in the most prolific ranks. Among the skilled and semiskilled workers in Classes III and IV the average declined from 4.7 to 4.3, slightly below the 4.5 recorded for the unskilled working class couples in Class V. Only textile workers, whose abnormally low fertility and high infant mortality had singled them out for special consideration as Class VI, approached the middle and upper classes in family size. Their average of almost 3.8 surviving children was actually below the 3.9 reported by couples in Class II and was only exceeded by the 3.45 of the professional and wealthier people who comprised the pinnacle of the rankings.[62]

Although the data was less conclusive for marriages celebrated after 1886 in which fertility was assumed to be incomplete, it was more comprehensive since it incorporated a much larger number of couples. If anything the differential patterns evident in the late Victorian years were accentuated in the Edwardian period even though the birthrates and child mortality rates continued to fall in every sector of society. The families of miners and agricultural workers marrying between 1896 and 1906 were, at the time of the census, nearly 50 percent larger than those of the middle and upper classes. Their reproductive energies notwithstanding, miners and farm workers were still only half as numerous as their middle-class contemporaries. Of much greater concern was the relatively high fertility of the workers listed in Classes III through V. Not only were there twice as many of them as in the two highest categories, but their families were on the average a third larger. The effective fertility of unskilled laborers, who frequently ranked near the bottom of the scales of "civic worth," was alone nearly 40 percent greater. Of all of the laboring occupations only the textile operatives continued to defy the correlation of higher fertility with lower status, reducing their families to an average of 1.9 children in the opening decade of the century, not much above the 1.8 recorded for middle-class marriages.[63]

Even before the 1911 *Fertility of Marriage Census* charted the unique demographic experience of textile workers, Webb, Elderton, and others noted the startling decline of the birthrate in the mill towns. They, like Stevenson later, attributed it to the exceptionally large number of women employed in the mills who were reluctant to give up their jobs, and, as Elderton suspected, benefited from a substantial reservoir of contraceptive information readily available from their more experienced fellow workers.[64] Social critics had for years observed a high correlation between female employment and excessive infant mortality in the textile districts, a fact that compounded the low fertility of the areas.

One of the variables that the census considered at length was the different ages at which people—especially women—in the social hierarchy married. They were well aware of the widely held belief that the later marriage age of the middle and upper classes, as well as their greater tendency not to marry at all, contributed substantially to their low reproductivity. Stevenson and Newsholme had challenged this assumption to some extent in 1905, and their doubts were confirmed by the data gathered in 1911. There was no question that marriage ages differed considerably between classes and the differential was becoming greater; nevertheless, the frequency of marriage was not a significant factor. Though middle- and upper-class men in Classes I and II delayed marrying, the proportion of them who eventually took brides was not markedly different from men in other occupational groups. By middle age, forty-five to fifty-five, when the vast majority of men in the country were married, the most married class, miners, was only 16 percent more married than the least married group, professional men. In many skilled and even unskilled occupations late marriages were the rule, not the exception, and the celibacy of agricultural laborers approached that of the professional classes. Perhaps the most important conclusion to be drawn, Stevenson wrote, "is that frequency of marriage differs comparatively little in the various classes, much less so than fertility when married."[65]

These findings made the marriage age of women a much more critical variable. Although the average for all classes had increased steadily since the mid-nineteenth century, from 22.5 to 25.3, the gradual rise contrasted with the abrupt differential alterations in the birthrate after the 1870s. Middle- and upper-class women continued to marry later, but in the opening decade of the twentieth century new brides in the highest categories, I and II, were on the average twenty-six years old, only two years older than women marrying unskilled workers in Class V, and miners and farm laborers in Classes VII and VIII. In the 1860s the difference had been one year. Still, a much greater proportion of working-class women married under the age of twenty, and failing that, by age twenty-five. Women in Classes I and II, by contrast, rarely wed before their twentieth birthday, but they usually did so between the age of twenty-five and thirty.[66]

Though a class differential in female marriage age was clearly evident in the middle of the nineteenth century, as it was in the early twentieth, all status groups had experienced a decided shift to later nuptiality. In the 1850s approximately 20 percent of women marrying in Classes I and II were not yet twenty, while nearly 57 percent were between the age of twenty and twenty-five. Only 9 percent of new brides in these higher status categories waited until their mid and late twenties to wed. During the Edwardian years the percentage of teenage brides in Class I and II fell to only 4.3 percent, while those marrying between the ages of twenty and twenty-five and twenty-five and thirty rose to slightly more than 36 percent in each bracket. Even more striking, however, was the extraordinary increase in the proportion of middle- and upper-class women taking husbands after they reached thirty. In the 1850s they had constituted a negligible 3 percent, but by 1911 they represented nearly 23 percent of the total.

In the half century preceding the *Fertility of Marriage Census* the nuptial age of working-class women had followed the same pattern although the changes were not as extreme in some age categories. Among skilled and semiskilled workers in Classes III, IV, and VI the number of brides under twenty fell from more than 22 percent in the 1850s and 1860s to less than 8 percent in the Edwardian era, a rate of decline approximating that of the middle classes. Similarly, over 45 percent of the marriage cohort in these three working-class categories took their vows between the ages of twenty and twenty-five, whereas a half century earlier the figure had been closer to 57 percent. During the same period the proportion delaying marriage until their mid and later twenties nearly doubled, from around 16 to 30 percent.

Early marriages in the new century were still common among miners (18 percent), unskilled manual workers (12.4 percent) and agricultural laborers (10.5 percent), but even these averages were half of what they had been forty and fifty years before. Virtually 50 percent of the women who married husbands in these occupational categories were twenty-five compared with 44 percent in the mid-Victorian years, and another 21 percent of them fell into the twenty-five to twenty-nine age bracket.[67] What it all added up to, Stevenson reported, was that although the age of marriage had increased for all groups in society, "there is scarcely an exception to the rule that the fertility of the marriages of any period is less than that of the preceding period, whatever the class and whatever the age at marriage concerned." Nevertheless, "the classes most fertile when married, age for age, also married earliest." But, he quickly added, it was also clear that women who married later and presumably lessened their opportunities for motherhood, also stopped having children long before their physiological capacity to do so was diminished.[68]

The explanation for this, Stevenson acknowledged, "will probably be found to leave much room for difference of opinion, but for the most part may be accounted for by the supposition that the fall for this social class is largely due to voluntary restraint." As all classes experienced varying degrees of decline that could not be explained physiologically, it was reasonable to assume that the movement to restrict natural fertility "must have percolated downwards throughout society from the upper to the lower strata."[69]

Even if the biological capacity of the populace was not a determining factor, the differential characteristics of family strategy were, Stevenson concluded, very serious indeed. He repeatedly singled out the professional

classes in Class I and constructed special tables to illustrate how their low
fertility contrasted with that of the still prolific semiskilled and unskilled
laborers, miners, and agricultural workers. Though the age of marriage
had increased for all categories, women at the most fertile end of the scale
still married much earlier than those marrying into the professional classes
at the other end. Not only were the wives of miners and unskilled laborers
likely to be more ignorant of the methods of self-restraint, but, as Stevenson complained, they would be at risk of pregnancy much longer. Mean-
while the fertility of the professional classes, the presumed intellectual
elite of the country, ran approximately 25 percent below the national
average whereas that of manual laborers and miners was 20 to 25 percent
above the norm.[70]

Summarizing these and other comparisons Stevenson stated what to
many of his contemporaries was painfully obvious: "Our population has
been recruited . . . under conditions fundamentally different from those
of the immediately preceding and probably of any previous period. No
appeal to English experience, accordingly, can indicate the probable effect
of the change that has taken place."[71] There was no denying, however, that
it had "much significance from the eugenic point of view." Like countless
others of his generation, Stevenson believed that "if the more successful
classes may be assumed to be in bulk better equipped than others with the
qualities adapted to command success, the failure of this stock to maintain
itself in proportion to the rest of the nation is evidently undesirable from
the national point of view." Since it appeared from the census returns that
"this failure is mainly if not altogether a new phenomenon," Stevenson
warned, "we cannot quiet any uneasiness as to the future which it may
excite by the assumption that in the past things have gone on fairly well
despite it."[72]

As the statistical evidence mounted biological generalizations about the
declining birthrate gave way to more precise descriptions and analyses of
differential fertility. In the process the population question quickly became
inseparable from the question of class. Many people continued to perceive
the issue as being one of total numbers and contemplated the possibilities
of "race suicide" in terms of the aggregate population needed to sustain an
industrial economy and worldwide empire. But the distribution of that
population across the social and economic spectrum was of even greater
concern to the profoundly class-conscious Edwardians and their late Victorian predecessors. Having determined, for better or for worse, that the
differential decline was primarily the result of a deliberate decision on the
part of married couples to restrict the size of their families, the question
still remained why and when they chose to do so.

CHAPTER 3
Neo-Malthusianism

Whether, as many witnesses before the National Birth-Rate Commission charged, smaller families were a regrettable consequence of selfishness, love of luxury, and irresponsibility, or, as others testified, an encouraging sign of individual, domestic, and social improvement, nearly all agreed that the decline in fertility since the 1870s was closely associated with two important developments in that decade. The first, the start of the Great Depression in agriculture and trade, convinced people that Britain's economic growth and predominance was coming to an end and compelled the more prudent classes to reassess the number of children they were prepared to support. The second, the sensational, if coincidental, trial of Charles Bradlaugh and Annie Besant in 1877 thrust the issue of birth control before the public and led directly to the establishment of the first birth control organization in the country, the Malthusian League.

Contemporaries recognized that the limitation of conception was also associated with changing religious and moral values, the altered position of women, and differing concepts of domestic management and child rearing. As the National Birth-Rate Commission concluded, however, most married couples who deliberately restricted fertility were attempting to preserve or improve their status and standard of living in an era of economic uncertainty, diminished opportunity, rising costs, declining profits, and soaring taxes.[1] Neo-Malthusianism, the restrictionist philosophy preached by the Malthusian League, reinforced this strategy and made people aware of how it might be successfully accomplished.

When Joseph and Olive Banks in their studies of family planning in later Victorian England emphasized these economic motives for the "flight from parenthood," they in effect reached the same conclusions as the first analysts of the declining birthrate.[2] More recent scholarship has questioned this interpretation by demonstrating that the beginning of the fall in the birthrate among the more prosperous urban middle classes preceded the depression of the last quarter of the century by at least a generation. Patricia Branca, among others, has argued persuasively that birth control was less a strategy of economic self-preservation encouraged by husbands, as the Bankses believed, than it was a progressive manifestation of modernization that transformed the role of married women. Their changing perception of health, sexuality, and domesticity resulted in more cooperative marriages in which the psychological, physiological, and economic advantages of spacing and limiting pregnancies were mutually acknowledged by both husband and wife.[3]

Late Victorian and Edwardian students of the declining birthrate recognized these multiple causes, but they generally believed them to be secondary to the economic determinants. Despite the modest diminution in the size of middle-class families in the prosperous 1850s and 1860s, the association of the much more dramatic decline in national fertility with the onset of depression in the 1870s and 1880s was a compelling correlation that contemporaries thought irrefutable. Even before the accumulated vital statistics began to confirm the persistent downward trend in the birthrate, the Liberal M.P. and writer for the *Times*, Leonard Courtney, predicted that as Britain's share of world markets declined and economic opportunities receded, people would be more cautious about bearing children if they wished to maintain a level of comfort for their families.[4]

By the opening of the new century marriage rate and birthrate were frequently scrutinized as barometers of national prosperity, and the depression of the 1870s was usually cited as the beginning of the drop in fertility. G. Yudny Yule, in isolating the cost of living as the single most important determinant "in the reproduction of the race" told his Royal Statistical Society colleagues in 1906 that in ten or fifteen years, when the economy readjusted, people would again have larger families.[5] Not everyone was persuaded of the cause and effect relationship between population growth and price indexes. Arthur Newsholme and T. H. C. Stevenson, for example, wondered why it was the rich, those least affected by fluctuations in the cost of living, who were the first to restrict their fertility. But even they concluded that a distorted desire to preserve and enhance the "standard of comfort" was the principal reason why the more prosperous classes had of late demonstrated "an almost pagan lack of communal responsibility."[6]

If, to some, the decline in the birthrate was a consequence of wanton self-indulgence on the part of people who could well afford a sizable family, to others, like Dean Inge, it was the selfless response of the "best men and women" to the growing burden of taxation to support the irresponsible, unemployable wastrels whose numbers proliferated, irrespective of the economy.[7] As another clergyman warned in 1913, until some relief was forthcoming the people who had to pay the mounting rates would continue to compensate by limiting the size of their families and neither condemnation nor pious platitudes would alter their behavior.[8] Such rhetoric was often accompanied by various tax reform proposals designed to induce the retrenching middle classes to marry earlier and have more children. The Eugenics Education Society in particular directed several appeals to the government before the war urging a more "race-conscious" taxation policy to reverse the dangerous demographic trends so recently identified.

To Havelock Ellis the popular economic arguments were overly simplistic; they failed to appreciate that the adoption of birth control was an advanced, complex response to evolutionary changes in a mature industrial society where forethought and restraint were important virtues. Whatever the state of the economy, Ellis believed, the era of high fertility was over and it was only a matter of time before the same rising expectations and changing qualitative values of the middle and higher classes would combine to moderate the procreative instincts of the working classes.[9] Indeed the Fabian Society's investigation of the declining birthrate in 1906 indicated that among skilled workers, at least, this was already the case. As Sidney Webb observed, many wage earners recognized that another child would have a deleterious effect upon their standard of living and would diminish opportunities for other members of the family. Given their lower level of expectation, Webb added, the sacrifices required by workers would be psychologically less depressing than they would be for the middle and professional classes.[10]

Similar perceptions of class response and motivation pervaded nearly all of the economic explanations of differential fertility. The economist J. A. Hobson was certain that the middle classes were more interested in comfort, personal freedom, and the education of their children. Moreover, the expansion of female interests outside of the home made modern women increasingly reluctant to accept the burdens and risks of a large family. Workers, by contrast, were more immediately affected by fluctuations in income, unemployment, low wages, rising food prices, inadequate housing, and the declining economic value of child labor. Though both classes were concerned with preserving the quality of life, workers were much less secure and genuinely feared a relapse into poverty. For nearly a century they had been admonished to emulate their prudent betters and look to the future. Now that the more successful workers were doing so, Hobson told the National Birth-Rate Commission, what they saw made them exceedingly anxious, and like their middle-class counterparts they had begun to limit their families.[11]

Eugenist statisticians, such as Karl Pearson and Ethel Elderton, were not satisfied with what they thought were highly subjective explanations of procreative behavior. Too often, Pearson warned, we erroneously assume that workers perceive the world as we do when in fact they are governed less by moral and intellectual considerations. Although children are of little economic worth to the higher classes, it is obvious that even in their diminished numbers they are a luxury whose care and nurturing satisfy more subtle and elevated emotions. The working classes, however, view their offspring primarily as material assets or liabilities rather than plea-surable indulgences, Pearson explained.[12] Several Eugenic Laboratory studies in industrial towns concluded that restrictive labor legislation and compulsory education had in the last decades of the nineteenth century led to as much as a 40 percent decline in the fertility of textile workers. The limitations on child labor, which coincided with economic depression, were met, Elderton reasoned, "not by a reduction in the standard of living, but by a reduction in the number of those among whom the earnings were to be spent."[13]

What most alarmed eugenists, however, was the discovery that as chil-dren did not repay the cost of nurture, only the skilled, responsible work-ers undertook to curtail their fertility, while the marginal, unskilled, fre-quently unemployed continued to reproduce an average of eight to ten genetically questionable offspring. The results were seen to confirm the eugenic belief that the rational control of fertility was a characteristic of the more highly evolved of the species whose greater self-respect and intelligence made them more adaptable to changing times.[14] It was equally plausible, others argued, to conclude that unregulated reproduction was a manifestation of despair and indifference on the part of people who had little chance of improving their condition and controlling their own lives.

Concentrating as they did on the correlation of the birthrate with eco-nomic change, contemporary analysts underestimated the extent to which older Victorian domestic ideals and values were breaking down even be-fore the fateful 1870s. The high fertility reflected in the registrar general's annual reports masked the growing reticence of the mid-Victorian middle-class wife to accept passively the risks and consequences of repeated child-bearing, while her husband seemed less inclined to insist on an overly large family. This tendency had become a decided trend by the 1880s as a newer generation, even less wedded to older domestic traditions and in-creasingly pressed by economic constraints, turned to a readily available solution implied, if not specifically recommended, by respectable political economists since the time of Malthus.

To those looking back to the critical 1870s it seemed obvious that the desire to have fewer children was given a dramatic boost by the much-publicized Bradlaugh-Besant trial in 1877. If historians have been inclined recently to discount the impact of that prosecution for publishing an obscene pamphlet and the aggressive proselytizing of the Malthusian League that followed, late Victorian and Edwardian investigators of the declining birthrate thought both were instrumental in accelerating the fall. In the 1890s when Karl Pearson and Sidney and Beatrice Webb began to notice the unrelieved drop in fertility, they connected it with the notorious prosecution nearly twenty years earlier.[15] Similarly, in the opening years of the new century they were joined by people as diverse as George Bernard Shaw, H. G. Wells, and Havelock Ellis in describing the trial and the publicity it unleashed as a breach in the walls of Victorian prudery and sexual repression. Couples, they claimed, were alerted to the revolutionary potential of the "artificial sterilisation of matrimony," and the bearing of children was rapidly transformed from an involuntary to a voluntary condition.[16]

The trial, Ethel Elderton explained in her *Report on the English Birth-Rate*, coincided with the economic doubts troubling the more responsible classes who, even during decades of prosperity, accepted the precept that people should not have more children than they could adequately support. Although the gravity of the issue was not appreciated at the time, Elderton saw in retrospect that the Bradlaugh-Besant prosecution "legitimised the teaching of practical methods for the limitation of the family, and within thirty years that teaching has revolutionised the sexual habits of the English people." Like most eugenists, and a great many other Edwardians, Elderton believed that the differential class response to the control of conception had proven racially disastrous. She spun a cloudy web of national and imperial deterioration and traced the first strands to what a generation earlier appeared to be a small matter—"the judgement as to whether a pamphlet was indecent or otherwise." It might in time prove to have been the "spark of a whole nation and may lead to a complete change in its position in the world."[17]

Neither Bradlaugh, president of the National Secular Society, nor his irrepressible colleague, Annie Besant, anticipated the decay of the race or the collapse of the Empire when they decided to defend the right to continue to publish Charles Knowlton's *Fruits of Philosophy*, a tract on family limitation available since the 1830s.[18] Radicals and freethinkers throughout most of the century had been distributing pamphlets and books about both Malthusian ideas concerning the relationship of poverty to overpopulation and the advantages and methods of contraception that could help people, especially the poor, limit their ruinous fertility. They recommended a wide variety of solutions including coitus interruptus, the "safe period," sponges, douches, spermicidal chemicals, condoms, and a number of occlusive pessaries for women. All the authors agreed that however perceptive Malthus was in his analysis of the problem of over-population his recommendations of celibacy, deferred marriage, or prolonged abstinence were unnatural, impractical, and harmful to both sexes.[19]

For nearly two decades before his confrontation with the authorities Bradlaugh had been advocating smaller families as the solution to poverty and a variety of other social ills.[20] Until provoked by obscenity charges leveled against Knowlton's old pamphlet, Bradlaugh and his allies were content to accept the "quiet infiltration" of birth control ideas and methods.[21] After 1877 the advocacy of family limitation became associated with an active movement. The trial, as the prosecutor and presiding judge feared, not only greatly stimulated sales of the once-obscure *Fruits of Philosophy*, but it provided the defendants a public forum for preaching the benefits of family limitation that, they noted, were already well understood by the more prosperous, better educated middle and upper classes.[22]

Social values and class stereotypes permeated the testimony at the trial as they did the birth control movement in subsequent decades. Much of the prosecutor's case reflected sexual anxieties about "dirty, filthy books" that decent husbands should at all costs keep from their wives.[23] But it also dwelt upon the dangers of unbridled sexual license among the poor. For decades the governing classes had been struggling to civilize what they perceived to be the animalistic instincts of their inferiors. As a result of education, regulation of the drink trade, sabbatarianism, less violent forms of recreation, and endless invocations of the indisputable advantages of prudence, moderation, and self-restraint, the lower orders by the 1870s seemed far less threatening than a generation earlier. Although Bradlaugh and Besant argued that the principles of Malthus combined with the practices described by Knowlton would reinforce this civilizing trend, the court was persuaded that the availability of the inexpensive pamphlet would have just the opposite effect. Indeed the prosecutor readily agreed with the defendants that the low cost of the condemned pamphlet was as much at issue as its contents.

Bradlaugh and Besant eventually escaped conviction on a legal technicality. A fellow freethinker, Edward Truelove, was, however, less fortunate. In a concurrent trial he was found guilty of publishing another obscene work on family limitation, Robert Dale Owen's *Moral Physiology*, and he was sentenced to four months' hard labor. As in the case of *Fruits of Philosophy*, sales of Owen's book soared, and the sixty-eight-year-old Truelove emerged from prison an ardent Neo-Malthusian martyr and revered monument to the initial battle for birth control in England.[24]

In tracing the origins of the declining birthrate back to 1877, Edwardians recognized that the legal confrontations had brought old Malthusian questions before the public in a provocatively new way. Even before the legal battles were resolved the Malthusian League was established to continue the fight when the trials were over. With the economy faltering and the "Condition of England," as well as the issue of family limitation, much on people's minds, the times seemed propitious for launching a campaign dedicated to ending the age-old curse of poverty.[25] Malthus had identified the cause, overpopulation, at the opening of the century; the new, or Neo-Malthusians, by promoting early marriage and normal sexual relations without the risk of pregnancy, offered the solution. It was a message, later observers explained, that millions of men and women were eager to receive.

From its inception the Malthusian League was dominated by its first president, Charles Robert Drysdale (1829–1907), his wife and successor, Alice Vickery (1844–1929), and, later their son, Charles Vickery Drysdale (1874–1961). The Drysdales, like nearly all of the first Neo-Malthusians, were freethinking, liberal utilitarians nurtured in the political economy of Adam Smith, Malthus, Jeremy Bentham, and James and John Stuart Mill. Initially the league was closely allied to the National Secular Society, sharing the same premises and many of the same members.[26] C. R. Drysdale, senior physician of the Metropolitan Free Hospital in London, and his wife, a former chemist and midwife who was then a medical student in Paris, were among the few expert witnesses willing to testify on behalf of Bradlaugh and Besant.[27]

The Malthusian League was not only a family avocation for the Drysdales, but it represented a "new faith" that its first president promised would transform the civilized world.[28] The continued promulgation of that faith for fifty years required periodic infusions of money that the Drysdales and other occasional benefactors generously provided. Since the membership of the league rarely rose above twelve hundred, income from dues and subscriptions usually failed to meet the organization's propaganda expenses.[29] Although recent scholarship has tended to depict the league as largely irrelevant to the rise of family planning, and its most recent historian has argued that the group's secularist origins and outmoded economic philosophy actually delayed the acceptance of birth control, the evidence is at best mixed.[30] Despite limited support the Malthusian League, by the time of its demise in 1927, had printed and distributed well over three million pieces of literature and delivered thousands of lectures advancing the multiple blessings of small families.[31] Moreover, in an age when periodicals appeared and disappeared with astonishing frequency it managed to sustain the publication of a monthly journal, the *Malthusian*, for nearly five decades.

Contemporaries, including Neo-Malthusians, were themselves divided about the league's impact upon changing fertility patterns, but until after World War I, at least, Neo-Malthusianism was, in the public's mind, synonymous with family limitation. Indeed a number of people sympathetic to birth control went to considerable lengths to disassociate themselves from the popular assumption that their restrictionist views implied that they were supporters of the Malthusian League. Others, however grudgingly, allied with the organization because, until 1921, there was no other dedicated to the promotion of smaller families among the distressed poor. The role of the league and of Neo-Malthusianism should not be exaggerated, but it should be understood in the wider context of the declining birthrate and the population questions it raised. In the later nineteenth and early twentieth centuries the Neo-Malthusians were most vocal in provoking these questions, and therefore their impact, like their propaganda, transcended their numbers. If, in contrast to what some of their more zealous supporters and many of their implacable enemies claimed, they were not responsible for the plummeting birthrate, they were the first to encourage it and help make it a national issue. As a result, it is perhaps premature to read them out of the history of the family planning movement.

The Neo-Malthusians repeatedly complained from the early 1880s on, when the decline in fertility was first noticed, that, although thousands of married couples were obviously following their advice, contemporary religious and moral prejudices precluded the league from receiving the acclaim it thought it deserved. George Standring, the organization's printer, counseled the membership, "we must never hope to stand bowing before a hurricane of popular applause."[32] On the contrary, the first Neo-Malthusians discovered that their efforts were more often ignored or condemned so that in the final analysis, as Standring predicted, they had to find their satisfaction in the vital statistics of each successive generation and in the certitude that their cause, if not their organization, would eventually prevail.

Curiously, although the Malthusian league emerged from a bold challenge to English law and Victorian values, its leadership until World War I was often admonished by sympathizers for being vague and timid in its reluctance to provide practical contraceptive advice. Shortly after its founding the league's governing council decided to concentrate upon promulgating the economic, social, ethical, and physiological rewards of parental prudence in accordance with the Malthusian law of population. By doing so the council hoped to avoid further prosecution as well as the highly prejudicial feelings that "obscure any discussion of physiology in this country."[33] But by emphasizing reasons for family limitation rather than means of contraception, the founders of the first birth control organization also hoped to demonstrate that their movement was within the respected tradition of British political economy. They thought of themselves as the legitimate heirs of early nineteenth-century philosophic radicalism and classical liberalism rather than the bastard offspring of hedonistic sexuality and free love, as their enemies often charged. Despite countless florid encomiums to early marriage and domestic happiness, the league, by its own admission, was never able to disassociate itself completely from the "popular idea" that it promoted a licentious "promiscuity, irresponsibility and irregularity" that threatened to destroy the family.[34]

Neo-Malthusian propagandists quickly discovered that the audience for philosophical commentaries on the laws of population and the virtues of self-control was much smaller than it was for contraceptive instruction. "You may preach for eternity upon the duty of moral restraint," one disgruntled correspondent complained in 1883, "and you will effect—just nothing! Spread the knowledge of the preventive checks to conception, and you will effect—everything!"[35] Cryptic allusions in the *Malthusian* to "Gallic inventiveness" and the "method of family prudence" described in Genesis 38:8–10 led to pleas for "plain and practical advice" from people who had no doubts about the economic advantages of small families but who wanted to know "in what way prudence might best be practiced."[36] C. R. Drysdale admitted to a certain imprecision in language, but he could see no alternative. Although some discussion of the physiological and psychological effects of preventive measures as well as advertisements for "Practical Malthusian Appliances" were eventually permitted in the *Malthusian*, league officials insisted that precise contraceptive information be obtained from books and pamphlets recommended, but not published, by their cautious organization.[37]

The most important of these were Annie Besant's *The Law of Population*, first published in 1877 as a modern alternative to Knowlton's *Fruits of Philosophy*, and Henry Arthur Allbutt's *The Wife's Handbook*, whose appearance in 1886 provoked prosecution by medical authorities and the expulsion of its author, a Leeds dermatologist, from the registers of the General Medical Council and other professional organizations. Both works were enormously successful. By 1891, when its restless author converted to theosophy, abandoned Neo-Malthusianism, and withdrew *The True Law of Population* from publication, 175,000 copies had been sold.[38] Despite the medical fraternity's condemnation of Allbutt as a disgraceful huckster and purveyor of salacious material, *The Wife's Handbook* sold over 250,000 copies by the end of the century and more than a half million before it disappeared in the interwar years.[39] Although the Malthusian League promoted both books as the most reliable guides to family limitation, neither were official league publications. Moreover, after Besant's defection to Eastern mysticism, the council refused to authorize an official alternative to replace her valuable tract and left it to individual members to write and publish its successor, *The Malthusian Handbook* (1893). In the face of mounting pressures to strike out in bold, new directions, the league entered the twentieth century committed to the promotion of small families but without "risking the prosecution that many bigots desired."[40]

Actually legal prosecution for the dissemination of birth control literature after 1877 was rare. Neo-Malthusians suffered petty harassment and moral condemnation, but neither Knowlton's pamphlet nor its successors were again challenged in court. Twice in the early 1890s and again shortly before World War I individual booksellers or itinerant missionaries were charged by local officials for selling or mailing offensive publications, but these few prosecutions were at worst haphazard and never constituted a trend.[41] Nevertheless, the Malthusian League cited the occasional case as evidence of the legal obscurity that surrounded its campaign and justified its reluctance to concentrate upon the clinical rather than the philosophical aspects of fertility control.

Such timidity appeared ludicrous to many of the league's own members in the decade before World War I. The birthrate had fallen by nearly one-third since 1877, "Malthusian appliances" were readily available in most major towns, and any number of publications were filled with contraceptive advice and advertisements. Yet the one organization in the country widely held to be responsible for these extraordinary developments remained reticent about telling people how to limit their families. Acknowledging that a new age of demographic enlightenment had dawned, the league's council finally conceded in 1913 that its society could no longer remain a "purely academic body," and it agreed to publish and distribute a "practical leaflet" on *Hygienic Methods of Family Limitation*.[42] To prevent it from falling into the hands of unmarried couples, applicants for the pamphlet were required to fill out duplicate declarations that they were married or about to be married and that they believed in the voluntary limitation of families. When he appeared before the NBRC, C. V. Drysdale refused to give the commissioners an examination copy until one of them signed the protective statement.[43]

These elaborate precautions after some thirty-five years of activity indicate the deep conservatism of Malthusian League tactics. When the organization's hierarchy finally conceded in 1913 that society might be prepared to tolerate more specific instruction, Drysdale promised that the "New Departure" would not divert the league from its principal task of persuading public opinion of the socioeconomic justifications for rational population control in accordance with the precepts of Neo-Malthusianism.[44] It was this, he insisted, much more than the fear of legal prosecution that had always determined the league's tactics. Neo-Malthusians were confident that once their philosophy reached the public, especially the poor, couples would quickly find ways to implement their desire for fewer children. The problem was, then, not one of contraceptive method, but of understanding the relationship of the eternal laws of population to the laws of supply and demand.

They professed to find them in the writings of Malthus, Ricardo, Bentham, Naussau Senior, and the other luminaries of political economy and utilitarianism. It was, however, John Stuart Mill's *Principles of Political Economy* even more than Malthus's *Essay on the Principles of Population* that provided continual inspiration to the first Neo-Malthusians. C. R. Drysdale thought it the "most important work on the science of this century," and for many years the front page of the *Malthusian* quoted Mill's admonition: "Little improvement can be expected in morality until the production of large families is regarded in the same light as drunkenness or any other physical excess."[45] Malthus had, of course, first demonstrated the connection between unrestrained population growth and the consequences of poverty, but he had consistently rejected "artificial and unnatural modes" of restraint, recommending instead celibacy, deferred marriage, or prolonged abstention from sexual intercourse as the only acceptable "prudential checks" on man's geometric propensity to reproduction.

Like earlier proponents of birth control who were persuaded that such solutions were unnatural and impractical, the new Malthusians consciously departed from the master in their aggressive advocacy of early marriage, normal conjugal relationships, and the use of contraceptive measures to avoid unwanted children.[46] This would "ensure sexual purity, domestic comfort, social happiness, and individual health," from which all classes would benefit, the Malthusian League predicted in 1879.[47] Annie Besant explained that Malthus, an Anglican parson, had reverted to ineffective biblical injunctions about sexual self-control that ran contrary to human needs and instincts. They caused much unnecessary suffering for the prudent middle classes but had little effect upon the unrestrained fertility of the laboring poor.

The problem had become more serious in recent years, the Neo-Malthusians believed, as war, famine, disease, and other positive checks on population growth receded while "the life-preserving attempts of science and of reason . . . and civilization" continued to advance. Even respected observers like Montague Cookson in the 1870s pointed to the need for some realistic alternative restraints to replace those long imposed on mankind by "nature and providence." Though Cookson was unwilling to have anything to do with the Malthusian League, whose unwanted endorsement caused him some embarrassment when he ran for parliament in 1879, his views and those of others persuaded league theoreticians that the country was ready to receive a new demographic gospel preaching humane and rational voluntary curbs on human fertility.[48] The alternative, league statisticians calculated, was the doubling of the English population every forty years, despite mounting evidence that the country was already unable to provide for millions of ill-fed, ill-housed, and underemployed wretches.

The "small family system," as C. R. Drysdale described it, would not only eliminate the endemic poverty and inevitable social misery accompanying overpopulation, but it would end such notorious "sexual diseases" as prostitution and celibacy. Both were a consequence of the reluctance of eligible young men to marry and face the expense of raising a family. The surplus women who turned to prostitution in order to survive were not only exploited by single men but also by husbands who, fearful of impregnating their wives, employed the harlot as a debased form of contraception.[49] Many of the first Neo-Malthusians, including Bradlaugh, Besant, and the Drysdales were active in Josephine Butler's prolonged campaign to repeal the Contagious Diseases Acts, but they were always critical of her failure to acknowledge the true cause of prostitution and join with them in advocating the obvious solution—early marriage and controlled parentage.[50]

Even more insidious to the Neo-Malthusians than prostitution was the "curse of celibacy." Not only had it long enjoyed an idealized place in Christian society, but as one of Malthus's original prudent checks it would take "the best minds of the age" to persuade people of its pernicious effects.[51] No end of social critics in the 1880s and 1890s agreed that prostitution was a disgraceful symptom of the moral corruption of urban, industrial England, but comparatively few of them likened the reluctance of men to marry to an equivalent sexual abuse. Yet it was well known in enlightened medical circles, at least, Neo-Malthusians argued, that physical and emotional repression were organically integrated and invariably resulted in a variety of aberrations ranging from "peevishness, restlessness, vague longings and mental instability" to insanity and death in men and chlorosis and hysteria in women.[52]

If Neo-Malthusians searched the lexicon of human maladies for the psychic and somatic horrors of sexual deprivation, they were the obverse of countless doctors, clergymen, and self-appointed authorities in Victorian England who were equally industrious in rooting out the physiological and mental grotesqueries awaiting the sexually indulgent. Moreover, the first generation of Neo-Malthusians were daring, often shocking pioneers in their candid association of sexual fulfillment with sound physical and mental health. Paradoxically, although they were consciously rebelling against what they believed to be the repressive, unnatural, and unhealthy sexual mores of the age, their confidence in home and family as repositories of saving grace was unabashedly Victorian. Nothing frustrated them more than their inability to persuade critics that their recommendations were not intrinsically hostile to marriage and sound domestic life.

The Neo-Malthusians were not content to counter such charges with ritual panegyrics to the family, but they were among the first to employ actuarial statistics to prove that early marriage was not only desirable and natural but much healthier. Citing studies of Scottish, French, and German mortality, the *Malthusian* noted that married men lived substantially longer than their unmarried counterparts and that in every age cohort the death rate of bachelors was significantly higher. Although the data for women was less complete, it clearly indicated that, even allowing for the risks of childbirth, wives held a decided advantage over spinsters.[53] When skeptics retorted that such comparisons were misleading because the unmarried were often less healthy and therefore less attractive to the opposite sex in the first place, the *Malthusian* noted that widowers in their thirties expired at a rate three times greater than that of husbands who still enjoyed their wives' companionship. Although the mortality differential moderated among older age groups, it was still apparent. It was obvious to the Neo-Malthusians that only the "exercise of all functions," including sex, was conducive to a long life, happiness, and health. Deferred marriage or celibacy, which was especially common among the middle classes, placed a dangerously large number of men and women between the ages of twenty and forty at risk.[54]

The evidence also suggested to Neo-Malthusian analysts that Social Darwinists like Spencer were wrong in believing that celibacy was a natural result of diminished sexuality associated with higher cerebral evolution. It was illogical to conclude that progressive individuation would occur at the expense of shortened lives among the more highly evolved sector of the population. Intellectual advances would not be reflected in diminished reproductive energy, Neo-Malthusians reasoned, but in the rational employment of scientific methods of contraception within the framework of early marriage and normal sexual relations. The families of more individuated couples would be limited to two or three children who would, like their enlightened parents, live healthier, longer lives free of vice, disease, and poverty.[55]

Without claiming that the French had necessarily evolved further than the British, Neo-Malthusians nevertheless encouraged their countrymen to emulate their Gallic neighbors whose birthrate (25.1/1,000) was the lowest in Europe in the closing years of the nineteenth century even though their marriage rate was the highest.[56] If many people, especially in France itself, regarded the low fertility statistics as a sign of degeneration since Napoleonic times, Neo-Malthusians continued well into the next century to admire the prudent, tight-fisted French peasant, whose small family reflected a sensible determination to maintain status and property.

Neo-Malthusians tried to construct their campaign for smaller families on the respectable foundations of orthodox Malthusianism. The time seemed especially felicitous. For decades optimistic critics had been able to point to unprecedented economic and technological progress as evidence of Great Britain's ability to support an expanding population. But economic depression, mounting competition, declining profit margins, and the persistence of distressing social problems in the great cities stimulated a resurgence of interest in Malthus reflecting in part a loss of confidence in the ability of the economy to sustain an ever-growing number of people. Shortly after starting publication in 1879 the *Malthusian* surmised that if Malthus were alive he would be more certain than ever of his demographic projections, but he would have to concede that his positive and moral checks on overpopulation were no longer effective. He would certainly advocate the rational "prudent checks" recommended by his modern disciples.[57]

Without denying that the momentous question of overpopulation was of great importance once again, many students of Malthusian political economy such as F. W. Farrar, the respected philologist and Dean of Canterbury, complained in 1888 that it had become associated with "dangerous or immoral" theories propounded by those who assumed Malthus's "pure and virtuous name" but rejected his teachings.[58] The author and journalist, Arnold White, despairing of the proliferation of the degenerate multitudes in the urban slums, accepted that the "interference with nature is the condition of civilization" but regretted that it was the Malthusian League that had taken upon itself the task of applying the maxim to the population question. Its links with "aggressive atheism" had made it difficult to separate the issue of family limitation from religious sensibilities, and it would perhaps be another generation before people would be able to do so.[59]

The eminent jurist and legal historian Sir Henry Maine and the master of Selwyn College, Cambridge, the Reverend Arthur Lyttelton, thought it unfortunate that people were reluctant to explore practical, viable solutions, although few would deny the theoretical importance of Malthusianism. Maine believed that the Malthusian factor was the "central seat in all Political Economy," but Lyttelton still doubted that the law of population was relevant to an expansive, modern, industrial society. Yet Lyttelton essentially agreed that it was no longer possible to discuss the "harsh facts about population" without considering the ways people might control their numbers and improve their lives. Whether the subject had been "spoiled by Mr. Bradlaugh and his colleagues," as White charged, Lyttelton thought that their arguments ought to at least have a fair hearing before they were rejected.[60]

Neo-Malthusians welcomed any recognition, however critical, as evidence of progress in overcoming the burden of "social prudery" and the displeasure of "Mrs. Grundy."[61] They continually complained of their inability to receive a fair hearing in the journals and newspapers, which printed a great deal about the relationship of overpopulation to urban poverty but rejected their letters and articles and generally avoided any mention of the Malthusian League's solution. When such people as Farrar, White, or Lyttelton acknowledged their existence in important periodicals in the 1880s and 1890s, the faithful seized upon it as evidence that their campaign was not going unnoticed in important circles.

Most of the league's encouragement, however, came not from popular recognition, but from the cumulative vital statistics emanating from the registrar-general and from the organization's chronic inability to keep up with the demand for speakers and propaganda literature. When, during and after the Boer War, the size and quality of the population rapidly became a serious national issue, the Neo-Malthusians were confident that their time had come. Not only was the plummeting birthrate causing widespread discussion, but, as the *Malthusian* boasted, the rates of illegitimacy and of poor relief applications were substantially less than when the league was founded. Despite dire warnings to the contrary, sexual promiscuity had not increased as a result of its teachings, and, as predicted, the decrease in family size had brought the population into closer balance with available resources. The decline in the proportion of people on relief since the 1870s, the *Malthusian* noted, actually exceeded the fall in the birthrate. In light of the statistics, C. R. Drysdale complained in 1903, it was "really afflicting to find our most prominent men in office contenting themselves with preaching emigration, colonisation, or trashy alterations of tariffs" in a vain effort to solve the problems of poverty.[62]

Besides the fall in the birthrate after 1877 nothing gave orthodox Neo-Malthusians more satisfaction than a parallel decline in the deathrate of nearly 34 percent by 1914. Malthusian League theoreticians were certain that fertility and mortality were invariably in direct correlation. Until reproduction was substantially curtailed so that the pressures on subsistence were reduced, little could be done about the high death rates, particularly among infants, which cut down the most populous classes in large numbers. They projected in 1880 that a birthrate of 20/1,000 and a death rate of 10/1,000 would be needed to end the age-old curse of poverty while maintaining a level of population growth in harmony with the nation's resources. The averages at that time stood closer to 34 and 22/1,000, although in some prosperous areas surveyed in London the ideal balance was close to being achieved. When, by 1912, the birthrates and death rates reached new lows of 23.9 and 13.3, the ten-point differential appeared within reach, but a small surge in mortality in 1913 and 1914 frustrated that expectation until after the war.[63]

Various critics challenged the Neo-Malthusian's simplistic birthrate, death rate equation, arguing that mortality had much more to do with the age distribution of the population than its size. Since high infant mortality traditionally had the greatest impact on the overall death rates, the Royal Statistical Society was told in 1915, the dramatic decline in the proportion of newborn children during the preceding forty years was bound to affect the mortality figures. At some point in the future, as the population grew older, a process accelerated by lower birthrates and recent improvement in longevity, the decline in the death rate would level off and, in all probability, eventually rise once more.[64]

Rigidly adhering to their conviction that all mortality projections were dependent upon the number of people relative to available subsistence, the most unreconstructed Neo-Malthusians refused even to concede that the significant decline in infant mortality experienced in the decade before World War I was closely associated with better pre- and postnatal care, improved sanitation and housing, healthier diet, hygienic education, and medical advances in the control of some childhood infectious diseases, as most Edwardians believed. Environmental progress, C. V. Drysdale told the NBRC in 1913, at best played a minor role in enhancing the survival rate of children. The 45 percent decrease in childhood mortality since the 1870s, most of it since 1900, was a direct consequence of fewer children being born in the first place; they could therefore enjoy a larger share of limited resources and parental care. In the final analysis, Drysdale assured the incredulous commissioners, social and medical advances had little impact upon the size and health of the population.[65]

Most other witnesses, several of them physicians, were as unpersuaded as the commission, and they urged even greater public health measures and more social services to reduce further the loss of much-needed children. If Neo-Malthusians thought it futile, the commissioners did not. They strongly recommended in their report that more be done to encourage the conception and survival of those who could one day go forward and people the vast empty spaces of the increasingly threatened British Empire.[66] The secretary of the NBRC, the Reverend James Marchant, who wrote the report, was more openly critical of Neo-Malthusian testimony in his own book, *Birth-Rate and Empire* (1917), in which he cited data from the 1911 census to disprove the existence of invariable demographic laws directly correlating mortality with fertility. Staggering war losses had only intensified Marchant's long-held fears about "race suicide," and like many of his contemporaries he thought it imperative that in these perilous times everything possible be done to set rocking again the "thousands of empty, silent cradles" that stood as mute testimony to Britain's abandonment of its great Empire.[67] The NBRC had determined even before the outbreak of the European conflict that the Empire was severely underpopulated and in need of a prolonged infusion of healthy Anglo-Saxon stock to ward off the hordes of Asians eager to fill the spaces left vacant by infertile whites.[68]

To the Neo-Malthusians this was merely the continuation of hysterical nonsense heard increasingly since the turn of the century. No amount of evidence demonstrating that the population was still increasing seemed to make much difference. The parallel decline in the birthrates and death rates meant that net fertility was not yet markedly altered, Neo-Malthusians explained, so that the population continued to grow by a thousand people a day, or nearly 11 percent a decade. The persistence of poverty and excessive mortality among the working classes nevertheless indicated that fertility was still too high and not yet in optimum harmony with vital resources.[69] Before World War I Neo-Malthusians never contemplated zero population growth or thought an absolute decrease in numbers possible or desirable. Instead, they envisioned a reasonable, if varying increment in population compatible with the means of supporting it in health and minimum comfort.

Their opponents never seemed to comprehend that the quality and energy of a people was far more indicative of strength than numbers, as the Japanese had demonstrated in their defeat of the more populous Russians and Chinese in the opening years of the century. Harrowing accounts of Asiatic fertility and fatalistic predictions about the decline of the West, Havelock Ellis, Drysdale, and others complained, were based upon the familiar blunder of mistaking birthrates for survival rates and equating population size with racial vitality. The majority of Asian countries, in fact, suffered from devastatingly high mortality and racially debilitating standards that for the foreseeable future left them vulnerable to even moderately efficient nations.[70]

For most Edwardians, however, the "Yellow Peril" was very distant; the more immediate danger lay closer to home. Nervous comparisons with Germany were far more common as the economic, political, military, and demographic rivalry between the two countries intensified. The Liberal M.P. Leo Chiozza Money, for example, noted in 1912 that the gap between the size of the German population and that of Great Britain had increased from ten to twenty million since 1880, and that the German rate of increase in the previous decade was, at 15.2 percent, the highest in Europe. Admittedly, the birthrate in Germany, as elsewhere, was also beginning to decline, but, as Money reminded the House of Commons, their most formidable challenger was still increasing by 900,000 people a year compared to only 111,519 in the United Kingdom.[71]

Proponents of family limitation were extremely sensitive to anxieties about the German menace and the melancholy predictions of war or economic decline it prompted. They encouraged their worried countrymen to examine the declining birthrate as a European-wide phenomenon, which would actually lessen dangerous competition for resources and markets and reduce the prospects of conflict.[72] Despite such assurances anguished complaints and alarming predictions of race suicide continued unabated. Neo-Malthusians were repeatedly accused of pandering to the most perverse and selfish instincts of the populace. Moreover, although they proclaimed their devotion to the principles of early nineteenth-century political economy, by recommending "hygienic means of prevention" to avoid unwanted children they advocated a strategy and concept of marriage that was utterly contrary to Malthus's own beliefs.

Though the more orthodox Neo-Malthusians, led by C. V. Drysdale, who assumed control of the league in 1907, refused to concede that their departure from the master's teaching was so fundamental that they could not justify using his name, a number of other Malthusian League supporters and sympathizers thought that their critics had a point. Havelock Ellis, for example, a friend of the Drysdales who endorsed their goals, if not their laissez-faire philosophy, conceded in 1912 that "Neo-Malthusianism" might be a convenient term to describe the voluntary limitation of family size, but it was not something Malthus himself would have condoned.[73] Even true believers like the old radical secularist and early Malthusian League stalwart, John Mackinnon Robertson, worried about the confusion caused by Malthus having given a "true diagnosis of the social malady and a hopelessly bad remedy."[74]

The problem, as Bessie Drysdale, C. V. Drysdale's wife, recognized, was that the terms "Malthusianism" and "Neo-Malthusianism" had become interchangeable synonyms in the public's mind for family limitation and had become increasingly detached from the philosopical presuppositions of the Malthusian League. Many people, like Ellis, who never joined the organization or shared its belief in individualism and classical economy, were Neo-Malthusians. Millions of other were silent Neo-Malthusians whose partial adherence to the league's goals was probably unknown to them and was only reflected in their connubial behavior. Since there was considerable confusion about terminology, widespread hostility and misunderstanding among the public, and serious doubts even among supporters, Bessie Drysdale suggested in 1912 that a new name might be found for the league's monthly journal, if not for the organization itself. A number of titles were proposed, but each was rejected by C. V. Drysdale, who was fearful that a change might dilute the league's commitment to promulgating the basic tenets of political economy and the law of population upon which they rested.[75] In the end, when none of the suggestions proved satisfactory, the name remained unchanged until the Drysdales were forced to step aside after the war.

Drysdale's resolve was bolstered by the courteous, if restrained, hearing he received from the National Birth-Rate Commission in 1913. That the much maligned Malthusian League had been asked to testify was in itself a major step forward, he believed, which suggested that it had become too important to be ignored by prestigious boards of inquiry. Although the commission's report denied that Britain was threatened by overpopulation and expressed alarm at the unrelenting fall in the birthrate, it concluded that the decline was a direct result of the spread of birth control practices that coincided with the rise of the Neo-Malthusian movement.[76] In spite of heated testimony to the contrary, the commissioners declined to condemn family limitation as selfish, immoral, and medically harmful, but they conceded the right of parents, whose motives were "pure," to regulate their families by restricting coitus to "safe periods."

Neo-Malthusians exulted that after four decades their campaign was "wholly and finally cleared from the stain of being immoral and injurious to public decency and welfare." They prematurely described the report as the "great and final victory of our cause."[77] The troubled bishops, clergymen, peers, peeresses, physicians, and other notables who comprised the commission scarcely considered their tepid acceptance of reality to be a confirmation of Neo-Malthusianism. On the contrary, most of them considered it a positive menace to the race, one that weakened Britain's ability to preserve its imperial civilization in the hostile twentieth century. By the time their report appeared in 1916 the nation was already staggering under the blows of a prolonged and devastating war of attrition that, if anything, intensified anxieties about the size and quality of the population.

Although some of the more single-minded zealots in the Malthusian League remained convinced that their movement had not only been completely exonerated but that it had been given due credit for causing the rapid fall in fertility since 1877, most of the members knew better. They recognized that the Bradlaugh-Besant trial and subsequent propaganda campaign coincided with more fundamental changes in British society that made a new generation more receptive to their message. As Neo-Malthusianism gradually became associated with family limitation in the public's mind, the league was certainly willing to take credit for the declining birthrate. But, in general, its supporters agreed with T. H. C. Stevenson, the *Fertility of Marriage Census*, the NBRC, and the statisticians in the Eugenics Laboratory that although the Neo-Malthusians "showed the possibility of separating marriage and parentage, . . . their views would not have been accepted so quickly had not the desire for children been much diminished owing to some social or economic cause."[78]

Contraception was, then, a means to an end that married couples increasingly desired to achieve. It not only provided a degree of economic security, but, as contemporary analysts recognized, it permitted people individual freedom, opportunity, and greater control over the quality of domestic life they desired. If, as critics charged, this was often distorted into the pursuit of selfish, material pleasure, even they acknowledged that the rapid adoption of restrictive measures was obviously a reflection of older values giving way to new, less noble, and less self-sacrificing aspirations.

None of the analyses of the declining birthrate before World War I identified any particular contraceptive as having a dramatic impact on fertility. In contrast to the birth control revolution, which has occurred since the 1960s, contraceptive technology played a minor role in the campaign of the late nineteenth and early twentieth centuries. The Malthusian League was not particularly interested in experimentation and development, and it was content to recommend books and pamphlets that described existing appliances and types of restrictive behavior. Most of the league's old guard went to their graves convinced that, because of its simplicity, reliability, and absence of cost, coitus interruptus was probably the only contraceptive strategy the great majority of people would ever adopt. Motivation was, therefore, always far more important than method to the Malthusian League. The debate over the population question focused upon the moral, physical, psychological, political, economic, and eugenic consequences of couples thwarting conception rather than the means they employed to accomplish their goals.

At the heart of Neo-Malthusianism was the certitude that family limitation was first and foremost the rational and responsible way for men and women of all classes to adjust to economic stringencies to preserve or improve their standard of living. Implicit issues of personal satisfaction and individual sexual fulfillment, though raised occasionally, remained secondary until the 1920s. The tactics of family retrenchment, as the founders of the Malthusian League insisted, were already well understood by many middle- and upper-class Victorians who were far too prudish or hypocritical to admit it but whose smaller families were testimony to their behavior. Once they understood the legitimate philosophical reasons for population control, Malthusian League theoreticians predicted, people in the more educated, enlightened ranks would feel less guilty and inhibited. The practice of family limitation would not only spread more widely throughout the middle classes but the informed would join in educating those who needed instruction the most—the ignorant, laboring poor who knew nothing of either theory or practice.

CHAPTER 4
Labor and Socialism

The revival of the population question in the last quarter of the nineteenth century was closely associated with the wider social and economic criticism of that period. In contrast to the majority of reform-minded diagnosticians of the "Condition of England" the Neo-Malthusians rejected the growing belief that inequity and poverty could be substantially alleviated by carefully planned, collectivist policies at the local and national level. Ardent defenders of laissez-faire individualism, they believed it was impossible to manipulate the economic and social environment in defiance of the laws of supply and demand. As long as fertility remained inordinately high, the Neo-Malthusians insisted, the labor market would be glutted, wages would remain at or below bare subsistence, and the proliferating surplus population would stay mired in poverty. Not even the unchallenged prosperity of the 1850s and 1860s had been able to overcome the inexorable forces of demographic determinism, and there was little reason to believe that Great Britain would ever enjoy such economic preeminence again. Faced with this reality, the Neo-Malthusians complained, the country was losing faith in individualism, and, regrettably, it was listening to the popular clamor of socialists, trade unionists, settlement house workers, conscience-stricken clergymen, crusading journalists, and legislative champions of futile social welfare schemes.

Like those extreme Social Darwinists who feared that the humane inclinations of modern civilization would impede evolutionary progress by interfering with natural selection, Neo-Malthusians decried state intervention as ineffectual and ultimately regressive. Over the years they not only denounced new plans for slum removal, working-class housing, health and accident insurance, old age pensions, the medical inspection and feeding of undernourished children as well as infant and maternal health programs, but also older policies encouraging the emigration of surplus population to the colonies. Neo-Malthusianism was, then, not only an affront to contemporary moral and religious sensibilities, but, equally important, it was profoundly at odds with, and increasingly isolated from, the prevailing trends of late Victorian and Edwardian social thought. As time passed and new people joined the birth control movement, the obdurate philosophical conservatism of the Malthusian League's leadership led to serious conflicts within the organization and alienated thousands of potential supporters who approved of its objectives but were appalled by its arcane economic and social doctrines.

The first Neo-Malthusians expected resistance from the working classes whose antipathy for the unpalatable truths of laissez-faire political economy was of long duration and well known. But they expected support from the middle classes, whose fathers and grandfathers had prospered in the age of economic liberalism and self-help, and who were already aware, to some extent, of the need to limit the size of their families to preserve their inheritance. During the Bradlaugh-Besant trial, the defendants, like most Victorians, assumed that elevating beliefs and virtues generally devolved from the more civilized sectors of society to the less civilized. Their Neo-Malthusian successors based their "Crusade Against Poverty" upon the supposition that as the middle classes adopted the strategy of family limitation they would, by example and endorsement of the league's propaganda efforts, enlighten the laboring poor.

If, as proved to be the case, the Neo-Malthusians found more resistance than they did support from the better-educated, more prosperous middle classes, their initial hopes were stimulated by those who, like the London barrister, Montague Cookson, called upon the higher classes to lead a Malthusian "revolution in public opinion." Though Cookson doubted that the "lowest strata of the English people" were mature and educated enough to undertake the "regulative control of the family" within marriage, and should therefore be encouraged to remain celibate longer than their betters, with proper guidance from above even the poorest classes could in time be taught the advantages of domestic self-restraint.[1] Such condescension, rooted in Victorian class perceptions, punctuated the birth control movement from its earliest days. Advocates of family limitation readily associated smaller families with reason, self-control, prudence, and responsibility—qualities usually ascribed to the middle classes but rarely noticed among the improvident poor. Conventional Malthusians, like Cookson, believed that the continued acquisition of moderating virtues had to precede the adoption of "regulative controls." By contrast, the new Malthusians thought that the poor were already eager for social and economic redemption, if shown the way.

During the Bradlaugh-Besant trial and throughout the history of the league's campaign, the frustrated complained of middle-class conspiracies to deny the laboring masses the means for ending their subservience.[2] Doctors were accused of profiting from the ill health of exhausted mothers and their weakened offspring; clergymen were charged with perpetuating the superstition upon which their authority rested; militarists and imperialists thought only of populating their ranks with surplus numbers; and capitalists recoiled at the prospect of having to pay higher wages to a smaller labor force.[3] These complaints were frequently accompanied by detailed examples of crimes, illness, drunkenness, and other costs of maintaining the hordes of "incompetents" who reproduced themselves generation after generation.

League spokesmen were sensitive to the accusation that they were contemptuous of the large families of the poor but did not denounce the large families reared by wealthier people. From the Malthusian standpoint the poor were the main problem; their numbers exceeded available resources, a difficulty not faced by the more prosperous classes whose fertility was, in any event, on the wane. If the poor were ever to enjoy a permanent improvement in their condition, they would have to bring their numbers into balance with the market demands for labor. As long as the working population exceeded the productive needs of the economy, C. R. Drysdale explained in 1880, their wages would remain marginal at best, and they would live out their abbreviated lives at the edge or below a line of impoverished degradation.[4] The cruelty of that truth had been understood by the first political economists who had tried to impart it to the less fortunate, the Neo-Malthusians contended, but their efforts had been thwarted by an unwarranted optimism about the endlessly expansive vitality of the British economy.[5] That miscalculation had come home to roost in the 1870s and 1880s, and the result was widespread industrial unemployment, rural distress and depopulation, and a resurgence of overseas emigration. Unless the critical relationship between population size and economic well-being was quickly acknowledged, Malthusian League economists predicted, even free trade, the cornerstone of British prosperity, might soon prove impossible in an increasingly competitive, protectionist world.[6]

Though heroic old Liberals like John Bright always denied that the law of population held any dangers for free trade, Neo-Malthusians, while swearing loyalty to the revered principle, insisted it was not immune to demographic forces. When, in the late 1890s and opening years of the new century, former Liberals like Joseph Chamberlain turned to a policy of preferential tariffs, league propagandists noted that the colonial secretary had earlier perceived the relationship of overpopulation to the nation's economic and social ills. If he failed to draw the obvious conclusion and mistakenly called for the further expansion of trade in a protectionist framework instead of urging a reduction of the country's surplus numbers, critics recalled their warnings about the vulnerability of free trade.[7]

The Neo-Malthusians were repeatedly frustrated in their efforts to persuade public figures who shared their assessment of the deleterious effects of overpopulation to embrace their controversial solution, or at least give it serious consideration. Eager to snare an ally, however unwitting, they mined parliamentary debates and the national and provincial press for nuggets of sympathy, and when, as in the case of the Lancashire M.P., Samuel Smith, they found someone who attributed depressed conditions to an excess of surplus labor and the loss of markets, they invited him to address the league. Usually they were ignored, but, as in Smith's case, they were sometimes sternly admonished for circulating "polluting works" that violated Holy Scripture or threatened the future of the race.[8] Many analysts obviously agreed that labor redundancy was a serious problem, but few were about to become embroiled with the notorious Malthusian League.

Not until shortly before World War I, when the population question was of much greater concern, were the Malthusian League's economic precepts given close attention. The National Birth-Rate Commission discussed the issue of surplus labor at length, and J. A. Hobson showed that real wages, despite league doctrine, had grown more rapidly than population from the 1850s through the 1870s, while in recent years, despite the adoption of family limitation by many workers, wages had made little improvement. Had many workers not turned to "anti-conceptive methods . . . as a half conscious defense," their position might be worse, Hobson conceded, and the league might yet prove to be right in the future when Britain will need a much smaller, mature, skilled labor force.[9]

To the league's dismay the NBRC concluded that a significant reduction in surplus workers would only attract cheap, foreign labor into the country while checking needed migration to the colonies.[10] For nearly a century the British assumed that in times of economic distress the redundant population would emigrate, reducing tensions at home and strengthening the Empire abroad. The second advantage had become increasingly more important in imperial calculations in the late nineteenth and early twentieth century as Britain pondered the problems of expanding and governing its enormous overseas holdings, and the NBRC, in spite of the testimony of skeptics like Hobson, reflected the prevalent belief that the preservation of the Empire required a steady infusion of white settlers.

The Malthusian League was established during one of the periodic surges of emigration spurred by depression, which heralded opportunities in new lands. Well over a million people left the British Isles in the 1880s; their departure, like that of the more than 7,500,000 who had preceded them, was, in the league's judgment, as cruel and mistaken a remedy as celibacy.[11] Emigration, C. R. Drysdale complained in 1881, had clearly proven to be a very faulty device as low wages, dwindling profits, mounting social unrest, and more than a million people on relief clearly indicated. Yet, with the return of hard times, it was again being endorsed by political leaders to keep the population of "this tight little island" peaceful and content. Would it not be far more sensible and humane, Drysdale asked, to reduce the pressures of overpopulation by reducing the size of families so as not to drive people from their native land?[12]

Emigration, to the Neo-Malthusians, was an insidious option that deflected able and ambitious people from limiting their families while the least capable sector of the population remained behind to reproduce themselves. It also left a legacy of spinsters whose chances for attracting a husband and experiencing the joys of a small family faded with the outbound ships on the horizon. Among the advantages of female suffrage, Alice Vickery Drysdale believed, would be the passage of legislation to facilitate early marriage and the subsequent end of misguided emigration policies.[13] In any event, Neo-Malthusians predicted as early as 1879, the issue would be resolved within a generation or two when the colonies and the United States tired of the apparently endless inundation of paupers from overcrowded Britain. Despite mounting complaints from colonial officials and anxious Americans about the low quality of immigrants reaching their shores, the exodus averaged 284,000 people a year in the first decade of the twentieth century and rose to nearly a half million when cut off by the outbreak of the war.[14]

Although Neo-Malthusians were frustrated that the declining birthrate had not yet reduced the impulse to leave, they noted with some satisfaction that the defenders of emigration were less inclined to advocate it as a solution to overpopulation and social unrest, but placed much more emphasis upon the need for surplus stock to strengthen and preserve the outposts of British power and civilization. "Responsibility" was cited as often as "safety valve" and "opportunity" in the prewar dialogues about the role of emigration in the twentieth century. The younger Drysdale, unlike his father, who never wavered in his dislike of colonization, was less adamant, but insisted that the preservation of the Empire required "more efficient," eugenically desirable colonizers who were the products of more selective procreation. But, he insisted, even qualitative emigration had nothing to do with population control; the solution to that problem and to Britain's social and economic difficulties was, as it had always been, dependent upon the reproductive behavior of the most numerous classes.[15]

If the folly of emigration was consistently obvious to the Neo-Malthusians, the issue of immigration was more complex. Most were strongly opposed to the influx of aliens, many of them Eastern European Jews, in the late nineteenth and early twentieth centuries. But they were also uncomfortable with the charge that restriction violated principles of free trade and Britain's long tradition as a haven for oppressed foreigners fleeing political and religious persecution. Having suffered considerable obloquy for their own unconventional, frequently outrageous views, secularists and Neo-Malthusians were hard-pressed to answer those who contended that the troublesome invasion of immigrants were but the latest casualties of autocracy and tyranny. Like earlier generations of Jews, Huguenots, and countless other victims of oppression, these immigrants sought sanctuary and protection for their lives and unorthodox ideas.[16] Occasionally Malthusian League members succumbed to nativist passions and fulminated against the "filthy scum and refuse" dumped on Britain's shores, and they sometimes endorsed the use of force to eject these "starving barbarians" who represented "not the survival of the fittest, but the unfittest." For the most part, however, the organization was content to endorse trade union efforts and Conservative legislation to place limits on the "alien infestation."[17]

Present-day immigrants, C. R. Drysdale rationalized, were not victims of oppression, but of overpopulation, the same force that drove millions of people from the United Kingdom. The solution was not to shift population from one overcrowded country to another, but to lower the birthrate in all countries so that everyone who came into the world could find a place at the "banquet of nature."[18] Despite considerable dissatisfaction with his analysis, the league's council was persuaded by Drysdale to put its not very decisive weight behind the Conservative government's controversial Aliens Act in 1905. The decision angered J. M. Robertson who, like many Liberals, strongly opposed the bill as a departure from the country's libertarian traditions. The immigrants, he argued, were no more responsible for poverty, crime, unemployment, disease, high rents, excessive fertility, and low wages than were the native-born, nor were they the incompetent "malodorous parasites" depicted in xenophobic tirades. Many were intelligent, highly skilled workers whose numbers were far smaller than the millions of people leaving the country, he told his old Malthusian League comrades, and he scolded them for endorsing thoughtless appeals to racial and political prejudices.[19]

Robertson's strictures touched a sensitive nerve, and, although the league welcomed the passage of the Aliens Act, it never criticized the Liberal government for its indifferent enforcement of the restrictive measure.[20] When C. V. Drysdale succeeded his father in 1907 he overcame his own eugenist anxieties about the "degenerate wretches" populating the East End and decided it was unwise to continue to pursue an issue so troublesome to the radical Neo-Malthusian conscience. Similarly, he recognized that there was even less support for another of his father's favorite schemes, the involvement of the state in the control of population size. One of the tangential attractions of the Aliens Act for the elder Drysdale was the possibility that it would establish a precedent for legislative restrictions upon the proliferation of undesirable sectors of the populace.

Since the founding of the league he and his wife had been trying to persuade their colleagues to sponsor a "Malthusian statute" based upon John Stuart Mill's maxim, in which the state should "guarantee ample employment to all who are born" in return for assurances that "no person shall be born without its consent." They were prepared to enforce the statute with fines and a denial of poor relief if couples exceeded their allotted number of children.[21] As with the reformed Poor Law of 1834, one advocate explained in response to criticism, the measure might at first appear harsh, but it was no less incompatible with individual freedom than was the infringement on the property and liberties of the prudent and conscientious resulting from the heavy burdens of supporting the thoughtless poor.[22] Few of Drysdale's colleagues were persuaded, and, despite the league president's repeated efforts to bring them around, George Standring correctly perceived in the mid-1880s that the "advocacy of State coercion is not generally approved by the Malthusian party."[23]

Buttressed by the widening fears of race deterioration and the dangers of differential fertility in the early years of the next century, as well as by the passage of the Aliens Act, Drysdale blew the dust off his copy of Mill's *Political Economy* in hopes that parliament, if not his own organization, was now prepared to listen. Shortly before his death he tried to persuade Robertson, elected to parliament in the Liberal sweep of 1905, to introduce a private member's bill penalizing parents with more than four offspring.[24] Even before taking his seat Robertson explained that there was absolutely no sentiment for such a move, even among the many members who shared the league's assessment of the relationship between overpopulation and poverty. It would be greeted with anger or hilarity in the Commons, he predicted, where it would fail to receive a single vote, including his own.[25] Robertson had long protested that such proposals smacked of state socialism in their violation of individual liberties, and he was certain they would be seen by most M.P.s in the same light. But in the final analysis, he assured his old friend, the measure was unnecessary. The birthrate was falling rapidly, even among the working classes, and the Neo-Malthusian cause transcended the league and was at last receiving a serious hearing.[26]

C. V. Drysdale realized that most of the league's supporters agreed with Robertson, and after his father's death there was no further discussion of legislative control. On the contrary the younger Drysdale was much more interested in thwarting additional legislation, which, in his judgment, merely obscured the true cause of the nation's difficulties by holding out collectivist solutions to individual problems. Neo-Malthusians had repeatedly warned that compulsory education, better housing, workmen's compensation, health and accident insurance, old age pensions, nutritious school meals, and the medical inspection of schoolchildren, however ameliorative, had little to do with the root cause of Britain's social and economic difficulties. They only raised false hopes, diverted the poor from the true solution to their problems, and sapped the resources of the middle classes. No legislation that failed to take into account the fertility of the laboring poor would ever succeed, Neo-Malthusians insisted, and the "Condition of England" would continue to deteriorate.[27] Nothing angered them more than the refusal of parliamentary committees and royal commissions in the 1880s and 1890s to hear testimony from league experts who had ready answers to the problems of housing, the sweated trades, or unemployment.[28]

According to Malthusian League dogma social problems were a consequence of economic problems that could best be solved in the free market where the laws of supply and demand and enlightened self-interest could function unrestrained. The freethinking, radical artisans, tradesmen, and shopkeepers who were the backbone of Victorian secularism and early Neo-Malthusianism were testaments to the basic truth "that hard work, sobriety, thrift and education are the only means by which an individual can attain to independence and comfort."[29] Many of them, like the Holyoakes, Bradlaugh, Standring, and Truelove were largely self-educated, self-made people who had overcome the disadvantages of low economic and social status to achieve at least a modest degree of success. The values they reflected were reinforced by middle-class secularists, like the Drysdales and Annie Besant, who saw in family limitation the revitalization of self-help.[30] It was not only the most effective cure for poverty, they insisted, but the least expensive. Most Neo-Malthusians initially agreed that social welfare programs were of little value, and they repeatedly likened the taxation required to finance them to robbery. There would come a day, Annie Besant promised before her conversion to socialism in the mid-1880s, when people would consider it "a sin against society when a large family comes upon the rates."[31]

Neo-Malthusians scarcely held a monopoly on such sentiments. They were standard fare in the late Victorian and Edwardian period as many people questioned the growing interference of the state in social problems and complained of the allegedly ruinous tax burden it placed upon them. The *Malthusian* had little difficulty culling out supportive statements from the parliamentary debates and periodicals of the day, but it rarely found any prominent person, however hostile to "state subsistence" for the "thoughtless and improvident" who was willing to advocate the obvious solution.

In spurning every important social reform proposal passed before World War I the Malthusian League rejected the arguments of those who acknowledged the destructive effects of too many children on the poor, but believed that excessive fertility was a consequence rather than a cause of poverty. Reformers often contended that thoughtless reproduction was a manifestation of despair on the part of people who saw no reason for restraining their natural impulses. If, as many analysts agreed, smaller families were a result of rising expectations and the desire to preserve or enhance a higher standard of living, it logically followed that the poor, properly assisted and given hope of improvement, would also be motivated to greater domestic prudence.[32]

With the exception of a brief flirtation in the 1880s with popular ideas of dividing land into small parcels as a way of stimulating self-reliance and forethought, orthodox Neo-Malthusians never wavered in their denial that changes in the social and economic environment could permanently better the condition of the poor. The decade was saturated with plans for the redistribution or nationalization of arable land as a way of halting rural depopulation while alleviating the severe problems of unemployment, overcrowding, and decay in the great cities. A number of Malthusian League stalwarts envisioned England as a nation of small landed proprietors, who, like the French, would out of self-interest restrict the size of their families to preserve their valuable holdings. When, after years of conflict over his atheism, Bradlaugh was finally permitted to take his seat in parliament in 1886, he promptly introduced legislation requiring the sale of all fertile land not being utilized.[33] Like many of the first Neo-Malthusians he had long believed that "what France has, we need. But we want it without revolution."[34]

By the end of the decade, however, the Malthusian League saw the error of its ways and rejected all panaceas promising to cure the ills of society by altering the environment rather than individual behavior. It was particularly disillusioned by the favorable reception given the American single-tax advocate Henry George's assurances that, if properly redistributed and taxed, the land in most countries could support a much larger population indefinitely.[35] Nevertheless, as reform proposals multiplied in the closing years of Queen Victoria's reign, and in the first decade of the new century, critics within the league questioned the wisdom of isolating Neo-Malthusianism from most other reform movements at a time when the declining birthrate indicated that, with modifications, it might attract a great many potential supporters.

C. R. Drysdale characterized advocates of this point of view as "Moderate Malthusians" who, unlike "Thorough Malthusians," doubted that reducing fertility could by itself eliminate poverty. Both agreed that the small family was "the *sine qua non* of happiness," but the moderates were more inclined to welcome legislation designed to improve the education and the working and living conditions of the poor. "Thorough Malthusians" believed all such measures were hopeless "without some well-devised scheme for checking the production of large families."[36] The elder Drysdale always believed that these were differences of emphasis that could be readily accommodated within the league. His son was much less conciliatory. He described himself as late as 1914 as an unreconstructed "laissez-faire Malthusian" implacably opposed to any further extension of social welfare.[37] Under his editorship the *Malthusian* reacted violently to the Liberal reforms after 1906, embellishing traditional arguments with vituperative, eugenic references to the racial dangers of differential fertility.

"Moderate Malthusians" attempted to steer the movement toward a tacit accommodation with Edwardian social reformers. J. M. Robertson pointed out that the regulation of fertility had always found greater acceptance in an improved environment, and he warned "thorough Malthusians" that it would be "extremely undesirable" for the doctrine of family limitation to be associated even indirectly in the public's mind with opposition to the reforms advocated by the triumphant new Liberal government. The "conjunction of Malthusian philosophy" with reactionary policies had always weakened the Neo-Malthusian cause, he recalled, but by rallying behind humane Liberal measures the league could shake off its unfortunate legacy and use the public debate as "a means of spreading the knowledge of the law of population."[38]

Instead, the league, at C. V. Drysdale's urging, not only condemned school meals and medical examinations for the poor, but old age pensions, improved workmen's compensation, better housing, and national health insurance while assuring the working classes that it alone had their best interests at heart. Robertson, who withdrew from league affairs as his political career advanced, was appalled by Drysdale's call for a tax revolt by those "who regulate their own families" against the "large and irresponsible mass of people, who imagine that the State has an inexhaustible coffer from which they can get maternity bonuses, free education and feeding of children, old age pensions, etc. merely by shouting loudly enough."[39] Too many of these people had the vote, but little sense of responsibility, he added in 1916, and until their birthrate demonstrated a dramatic change for the better, "the most truly democratic sociologist ought to have the gravest doubts as to the advisability of adult suffrage."[40]

In retrospect Robertson and the other "moderates" thought that the Malthusian League had missed its opportunity in 1906 to follow the Fabian Society model of cooperation with the Liberal party and the gradual permeation of its intellectual ranks. By siding with reactionary, propertied interests who wanted nothing to do with them or their campaign to help the laboring poor, the Neo-Malthusians cut themselves off from the mainstream of reform in the early twentieth century. They were spurned not only by the middle-class forerunners of the welfare state, who, however much they recognized the advantages of smaller families, rejected their single-minded archaic, individualistic resolution of the nation's problems, but also by the working classes as well who found far more palatable revelations in the gospels of socialist visionaries.

The first Neo-Malthusians knew that they would have to overcome an entrenched legacy of working-class antipathy toward Malthus. He and his philosophical heirs had long been denounced as enemies of the poor because their laissez-faire ideas epitomized the self-serving rationalizations of the propertied classes. The likelihood of persuading working people that their difficulties were a consequence of their own thoughtless fertility rather than the entrenched inequities of economic and political institutions was further complicated by the rapid emergence in the 1880s of socialism and a more aggressive trade unionism. Considering that one of the organization's first publications was the reprint of a secularist pamphlet extolling the virtues of self-help and condemning the futility of "socialism, red republicanism, and trades-unions," league speakers were surprised when they found working-class audiences, mostly skilled artisans, willing to hear them out.[41] It quickly became obvious, however, that what their listeners wanted were not lectures on the laws of political economy but practical contraceptive advice. When it was not forthcoming, the audiences, who did not have to be persuaded of the folly of overly large families, frequently became restive, and, when provoked by a minority of socialist agitators, antagonistic.[42]

Confrontations were at first described as minor skirmishes, but by 1883 league propagandists were complaining regularly of the "savage anti-Malthusian ravings" they endured at the hands of socialist zealots who insisted that the new Malthusians were no different from the old in their failure to recognize that poverty was not a result of individual ignorance but an inherent evil of capitalism.[43] More often than not the early Neo-Malthusians were baffled by the divergent strains of socialism they encountered. A number of them, like Edward Truelove, were former Owenites who were never comfortable with the harshness of Malthusian dogma and doubted its relevance to a cooperative community, but who nevertheless recognized that overpopulation among the lower orders seriously complicated the establishment of a "New Model Society." Socialism today, C. R. Drysdale complained in 1879, lacked even this minimal understanding of the law of population. It was, he believed, a foreign import, alien to the British way of life in its emphasis upon state intervention and "communistic legislation," which would invariably stimulate even greater fertility and undermine the effectiveness of any improvements.[44] Nevertheless, since Neo-Malthusianism and socialism were both dedicated to the elimination of poverty, Malthusian League officials tried for years to find some basis of cooperation.

It was a frustrating quest. Not only were the two movements philosophically at odds, but for most socialists family limitation was a minor, personal issue, which reflected rather than caused socioeconomic conditions. When Neo-Malthusians tried to make it central to all other reforms within a framework of suspect laissez-faire capitalism, they were denounced as reactionaries trying to divert the proletariat from the true cause of oppression. The size of worker families, even moderate socialists insisted, was a secondary question that would be solved by the equitable redistribution of wealth and the means of production following the triumph of their cause. In spite of growing demands to take the offensive against the "cheap abuse" and "vulgar ridicule" directed at them, Drysdale persuaded his colleagues that the size of the population and not the structure of society was at the heart of the problem. Therefore, the league's policy should be one of patient conciliation rather than confrontation.[45]

Though often angered by the vilification they met in socialist circles, the Neo-Malthusians found some satisfaction in the knowledge that they were not being ignored. Moreover, they recognized from the early 1880s on that most of the vitriol flowed from the militant, Marxist Social Democratic Federation whose credibility in the socialist fraternity was not overly impressive. In contrast to other socialist and labor groups the SDF took a special interest in combating Neo-Malthusianism as a reconstructed prop of corrupt, exploitative capitalism. Marx himself, while sharing the contempt for Malthus felt by most socialists, was not particularly interested in the population question. The problem of surplus labor exceeding the amount of "variable capital" committed to wages was, according to Marx, a corollary of capitalist control of the means of production that would disappear with the triumph of socialism.[46]

His troublesome disciples in the SDF made much more of this point than Marx ever did. For H. M. Hyndman, Herbert Burrows, J. L. Joynes, E. Belfort Bax, among others, Neo-Malthusianism, like trade unionism, temperance, or feminism, was a short-term palliative and dangerous diversion from the revolution that would alone lead to true social change. The revived population question since the Bradlaugh-Besant trial and the enticing promises of the Malthusian League were viewed by SDF militants as ploys to persuade workers that their degraded state was a consequence of individual rather than social inadequacies. Joynes, a former Eton house master turned Marxist, attended the league's annual meeting in 1883 and wrote a series of letters to the *Malthusian* arguing that irrespective of the size of worker families, their income, in accordance with Ricardo's "iron law of wages," would always be kept to a bare subsistence level by their employers.[47] The following year Bradlaugh was persuaded to defend the league's position in a heated, often acrimonious, public debate with Hyndman over the question, "Will socialism benefit the English people?"

Despite repeated Neo-Malthusian charges that the SDF obstructed their path into important working-class circles, both sides exaggerated the influence of the other. The SDF was never able to attract many people to its revolutionary ranks, and even at its peak it had fewer members than the twelve hundred or so who joined the Malthusian League. In both cases, however, the interest generated by their avowedly revolutionary, provocative campaigns greatly transcended their meager numbers.

Although Neo-Malthusian relations with socialism were at first domiated by conflicts with the SDF, the league gradually discovered that other groups, like the Fabian Society, were "less hotly antagonistic" toward family limitation.[48] It was one of the reasons why when Annie Besant lost her faith in the "older English Economists" in the mid-1880s and concluded that poverty was the "result of an evil system . . . inseparable from private ownership of the instruments of wealth production," she turned to the newly founded Fabians.[49] It was the least offensive route to socialism she could have taken. In contrast to the SDF the Fabian plan for social reconstruction acknowledged that overpopulation threatened the effectiveness of reforms, and its most important spokesmen saw no inherent antagonism between socialism and smaller families. Moreover, a number of other Neo-Malthusians, including George Standring and J. M. Robertson, had close Fabian connections, and they repeatedly held out the hope of an alliance to end the persistent antipathy the left felt for the "Law of Population of Malthus."[50] At the same time while admitting that past interpretations of Malthusianism justified the suspicions it aroused, they assured socialists that the "law of population is no more opposed to any moral or social reform than is the law of gravitation."[51]

Neo-Malthusian aspirations received a boost from Karl Pearson who discovered socialism while studying in Germany in the early 1880s. Upon his return to England he praised the Fabians as the least unscientific of the various socialist groups he encountered. Unlike the SDF, whose close-minded, anticapitalistic frenzy so addled their ability to evaluate evidence that they claimed that Britain was actually underpopulated, the Fabians were interested in dispassionate investigation and sound social planning. Whatever their antipathies toward old or new Malthusians, Pearson predicted in 1887, all truly scientific socialists would someday realize that "Socialism is the logical outcome of the law of Malthus."[52] Both the Neo-Malthusians and their rabid socialist opponents, however, shared the same mistaken belief that population problems would be resolved by individual couples adjusting their reproductive habits to economic realities.[53] In reality, Pearson explained, the control of the size and quality of the populace would only be possible in a planned socialist state where the demands of the "capitalistic plutocracy" for low-wage, surplus labor could be contained, the demographic requirements of society scientifically determined and, if necessary, enforced.[54]

Virtually all of Pearson's ideas were incorporated into the Fabian Society's schemes for social efficiency and reconstruction in the early twentieth century. By then he had become deeply engrossed in biometrics and eugenics, which only intensified his elitist and statist inclinations at the expense of socialist idealism. But he had long been distressed by the differential patterns of fertility, suggesting in the late 1880s that the stronger "animal instinct" of less skilled, highly fertile proletariat actually strengthened capitalism while weakening the quality of the race.[55] When asked to address the Malthusian League's annual meeting in 1894, Pearson made it clear that however much he admired the wisdom of Malthus, he wanted nothing to do with an organization whose failure to "distinguish between the fit and the unfit" in its promotion of smaller families had created "a grave national danger."[56] Sidney Webb soon thereafter expressed similar dismay at the failure of Malthusian prudence to reach the "degenerate hordes of a demoralized residuum" unfit for social life, and like Pearson, Shaw, and other Fabians, he concluded that only the intervention of the state offered any hope of directing qualitative reproduction.[57]

If C. R. Drysdale and his wife were not entirely averse to the idea that reproduction was too important to be left to individuals, most Neo-Malthusians considered government intervention to be an affront to personal liberty. But even the Drysdales recognized by the end of the century that, although the Fabians appeared to understand the law of population, they were no different from other socialists in their misguided belief that the redistribution of wealth in a collectivist state would in and of itself stimulate greater family prudence.[58] In 1907 the Fabian report, *The Decline in the Birth-Rate*, described the extent of restrictive practices among the professional, middle, and skilled working class, and it suggested that restrictive practices would rapidly spread to the unskilled poor in a socialist environment. In response Drysdale recalled that the great progress suddenly "discovered" by the Fabians had been made in an atmosphere of "unshackled freedom of competition . . . [and] well-advertised by the Malthusian League for the past thirty years" in spite of socialist opposition.[59]

That opposition was never as great as the Neo-Malthusians or later historians have assumed. Their perception was distorted by the league's clashes with the SDF, but most socialists either ignored the sensitive subject or agreed that family limitation was a valuable strategy for worker self-improvement. It was certainly tainted by its confusion with Malthusianism and the aridities of political economy, but as Annie Besant, George Standring, J. M. Robertson, and others discovered, Neo-Malthusians who encouraged birth control in the context of improved maternal health, better child care, a more secure domestic economy, social reform, and enhanced individual opportunity found considerable sympathy in socialist circles beyond the Fabian Society. The most popular of all socialist papers of the period, Robert Blatchford's *Clarion*, sometimes described the advantages enjoyed by the small working-class family, and one of its columnists occasionally printed extracts from Malthusian League publications, after an appropriate denunciation of the organization's economic philosophy. The *Clarion* was only one of many socialist voices that, in the aftermath of the Boer War, accused the "sweaters, landlords and Overmen" who decried the falling birthrate as a mark of race suicide of really being worried about the potential loss of surplus "wage slaves."[60]

Even deviationists within the SDF questioned the wisdom of attacking "Malthusian practices," which could end the proliferation of cheap, expendable workers whose exploitation was essential to the preservation of capitalism. Repeated inquiries to the organization's journal, *Justice*, suggested that some members were unpersuaded by explanations that the law of supply and demand did not apply when capitalists owned the means of production and could introduce machinery or foreign workers to offset labor shortages. British socialists were for the most part unconvinced that family limitation was futile.[61] Although it was not a solution to the great inequities suffered by the laboring classes those socialists willing to discuss the subject generally agreed that birth control was one of the few weapons individual workers had at their disposal to improve their well-being and weaken the oppressive hold of capitalists over their lives.

The inability of the SDF to see its value was, as Angus McLaren has recently shown, rooted in part in the strident antifeminism, even misogyny, of men such as Hyndman and Bax, who feared birth control would upset the woman's "natural sphere," alter sexual relations, threaten the family, and create divisive competition in the labor force that would threaten class solidarity.[62] Although Marx, as his daughter Eleanor reminded the SDF leadership, believed that true female emancipation could only occur when women were liberated from domestic drudgery, the columns of *Justice* relegated them to their traditional role as wives and mothers and were scathing in their ridicule of the feminist struggle for the vote. Bax, the most contemptuous of SDF critics, joined the Conservative-dominated Men's League for Opposing Women's Suffrage, convinced that women already possessed too much influence and too many rights.[63] In the idealized domestic paradise painted by such Victorian social moralists as Ruskin and Morris, and promised by SDF visionaries, birth control was repugnant and unnecessary.

Although the entrenched antifeminism of some of the SDF spokesmen accentuated their antipathy for Neo-Malthusianism, their views on the "Woman Question" were by no means universally shared by their comrades.[64] Furthermore, the Malthusian League, a firm supporter of women's rights, did not consider antifeminism an important factor in the hostility it encountered from the SDF. On the contrary, league analysts were always convinced that its rapid condemnation of family limitation was motivated not by principles but by tactics.[65] As early as 1883 league missionaries to the working men's clubs reported that the only consistent arguments they heard from the "violent" socialists "was that if families became small, it would make . . . [workers] less anxious, because less miserable, to consummate the Socialistic revolution."[66]

However reprehensible, it was a point of view that Neo-Malthusians readily understood. Like the most dedicated Marxists, they too believed that social improvements were useless palliatives that temporarily diverted the victimized poor from the true course to earthly salvation. Few socialists, however, were doctrinaire revolutionaries, as the Neo-Malthusians who associated with them knew. If socialists were unwilling to concede the centrality of family limitation to social and economic reconstruction, Standring argued in 1906, they, along with the Malthusians, were nevertheless really "two wings of the same army" assaulting the scourge of poverty. He agreed with Robertson that it was time for the league to abandon its rigid adherence to laissez-faire and, like the Fabians, become a research as well as a propaganda agency with a special interest in determining the optimum family size for which social reforms would be most effective.[67]

Though the league's first president had always been interested in cooperation, he doubted now that the ideological gap between individualism and collectivism could be bridged.[68] His son, C. V. Drysdale, at first willing to placate "moderate" Malthusians, proved after 1906 to be much more resistant and quickly shattered any hopes of conciliation. In the younger Drysdale's judgment, the huge majority enjoyed by the new, reform-minded Liberal government and the portentous appearance of twenty-nine Labour party representatives in parliament threatened to remove the last barriers to a flood of collectivist legislation. Conflict between the prudent, taxpaying middle classes and the newly elected architects of "state coercion" was inevitable, he predicted. There was no doubt in his mind that the wealthier classes, desperate for some means of checking the growth of the dependent poor, and the endless demands of socialist reformers would at last have to advocate publicly the principle of family limitation they adhered to privately. At that point, in Drysdale's scenario, the Malthusian League would step in and show the way to social reconciliation and peace.[69]

If the battles fought over the "People's Budget" of 1909 did not erupt into the class conflict anticipated by Drysdale and his more zealous followers, the turmoil within the socialist ranks before World War I was a welcome alternative. The *Malthusian* recorded, with delight, disputes between the SDF, the Fabians, and the Labour party, as well as the differences between trade unionists during the wave of strikes after 1911. With a characteristic misreading of the situation, the league's analysts concluded that the "stupid and ineffective" socialists were warring out of frustration and desperation since none of their schemes had succeeded in solving the nation's economic and social problems. The result was a loss of credibility with labor organizations and the eruption of self-defeating, if temporarily disruptive strikes.[70]

Although Neo-Malthusians savored the prospect of socialism disintegrating on a "rock of stubbornness," they were always much more ambivalent about trade unions. In a curious way the unions were viewed as allies whose growing militancy reflected the failures of social reform.[71] Workers were victims not only of their own fertility but of the "cowardly policy" of those in authority who had always encouraged them to increase and multiply. Nowhere was this more evident than in the overcrowded colliery districts in which the birthrate remained devastatingly high and where angry and redundant miners turned in desperation to futile, if understandable, collective action. The mine owners and their friends in government had no right to complain, the *Malthusian* charged in 1912, but they should atone for their past sins by supporting a "vigorous Neo-Malthusian [campaign] among the miners and other workers."[72]

Many of the radical secularists who founded the Malthusian League had supported the cooperative movement since the 1840s and cautiously welcomed trade unions as similar repositories of individual self-improvement through voluntary association.[73] If they were less comfortable with the aggressive new unions of the 1880s and 1890s, tainted as they were by socialism, the Neo-Malthusians nevertheless looked to them as logical copartners in educating the laboring poor. Annie Besant was active in organizing women matchworkers in the East End, and the *Malthusian* applauded the prolonged dock strike of 1889 as a way of focusing the nation's attention upon the problem of surplus labor.[74] Not everyone in the league's hierarchy, including its president and his wife, was tolerant of the "craze of strikes" in the 1890s because they often left the workers worse off and obscured the basic truth that the "only really useful strike is that against the appearance of a too numerous posterity."[75] But league missionaries repeatedly addressed local union meetings and reported considerable interest in their message, if not their philosophy.[76] When the prominent labor leader John Burns, who acknowledged the benefits of smaller families, joined the new Liberal government as president of the Local Government Board in 1906, C. R. Drysdale, in a moment of optimistic self-delusion, speculated about the possibility of a Malthusian party being built around the minister and the small nucleus of Labour members in parliament.[77]

In reality the trade unions and the labor movement generally ignored the population question until the 1920s. Even then, while individual workers were obviously free to do as they wished in their private lives, labor organizations were very reluctant to concede that a sharp reduction in their constituencies would somehow resolve the economic and social problems of the working classes. To C. V. Drysdale it was not unexpected. Unlike his father, a physician who had long cared for the working poor in central London, he was an electrical engineer, living in Hampstead, who rarely came in contact with them. He was openly critical of the "selfish" labor leaders who limited their own families but refused to endorse the practice for the rank and file, and he grew increasingly resentful of the ingratitude of the working classes in preferring socialism to Neo-Malthusianism.[78]

Not surprisingly, under C. V. Drysdale's direction, the league's tenuous relations with the expanding labor movement in the early twentieth century rapidly disintegrated. Although his mother, Alice Vickery, succeeded her husband as president in 1907, C. V. Drysdale assumed actual control of the organization and, along with his wife, of the *Malthusian*, in whose columns they emphasized that the preservation of laissez-faire capitalism was more important than the success, for the *wrong* reasons, of the league's campaign for family limitation. At a time when a widening circle of people were prepared to promote not only the economic, but the physical, psychological, even personal sexual benefits of birth control, Drysdale was determined to keep the purity of the faith. By resisting arguments that the Malthusian League should accommodate itself to the social, economic, political, and moral realities of the new century and welcome all advocates of small families, whatever their motives, Drysdale, at a critical juncture, locked the organization into an era that had already passed and whose lingering illusions were soon destroyed by World War I.

There were some signs shortly before the outbreak of that conflict that the moderates might prevail. The willingness of the league to concern itself more directly with the practical side of family limitation and to entertain a change of name and possibly of philosophy attracted a number of new, important recruits to the ranks, including H. G. Wells. These hesitant efforts to broaden the base of support for the movement and make it more attractive to social reformers and labor abruptly ended in 1915 when Drysdale, angered by mounting economic controls and a wave of strikes, slowdowns, and demands for higher wages unleashed a series of savage attacks upon the traitorous, socialist-run trade unions and the "cowardly and weak" politicians who posed a greater threat to the nation than the Kaiser.[79]

To the Drysdales the war was the ultimate confrontation between "Neo-Malthusian individualism" and the "crazy and rotten doctrine" of state socialism. The "better born and better reared" in Britain's free, competitive system were threatened as never before by the overpopulous "uneducated, underfed, discontented who cannot manage their own affairs and even elect competent officials." In article after article, they openly questioned whether the well-educated and well-to-do could continue to support such a democracy, and, in 1917, they warned that a victory over Hunnish autocracy had to be followed by the creation of a "true aristocracy of democracy" based upon individual competition and strict family limitation. It would weed out the incompetent and unsuccessful whose susceptibility to socialism threatened the battered nation with economic and military ruin.[80]

Although the Drysdales insisted that their sulfurous diatribes were their own personal views, not those of the Malthusian League, they were unable to mollify the numerous members who angrily protested that the couple's observations were recklessly divisive and totally at odds with the opinion of the rank and file. Many of them, including the wealthy investment consultant, Clifton Chance, who had reluctantly joined the league shortly before the war solely because no other group was willing to promote the "much-needed knowledge of birth-control methods in this country," found their position untenable.[81] Chance and others had never tied their commitment to family limitation to the fossilized economic doctrines of "individualism" preached by orthodox Neo-Malthusians. They had assumed, as a recent medical recruit explained, that, as long as everyone agreed that birth control is "an indispensable corollary of any scheme of social reform," all members were free to pursue their own "various Millennia." The Malthusian League, he naively thought, could, like the Anglican church, "comfortably accommodate any minor heresy."[82] To the league's puritans, he soon discovered, socialists were not minor heretics, but antichrist incarnate.

The most serious defection, however, was that of H. G. Wells. His interest in the possibility of combining eugenics and birth control to create a "voluntary nobility" of talent had attracted him to the league. He had been welcomed by Drysdale as an emissary from the "educated public" and persuaded to become a vice-president in 1915.[83] Though often critical himself of the antiscientific, small-minded attitudes of his fellow socialists, he was not prepared for the Drysdales' "preposterous attacks," and he condemned them as "childish, utterly silly . . . individualistic fads" that diverted the league from its proper task of "physiological enlightenment" and severely damaged the cause to which they were all committed.[84]

Drysdale's reply revealed how out of touch he was with the changing motivations and expectations of those moving into the birth control movement before and during the war. He confessed that he had never wanted the league to become involved in the"teaching of the actual methods of birth control," which was not even an objective until 1913. Our major goal, he reminded Wells and the "socialist Malthusians" who rallied behind him, has always been the promulgation of the law of population and its many ramifications, and he was determined to press on as one of a beleaguered minority.[85] But rather than have the league lose Wells's valuable support he and his wife resigned the editorship of the *Malthusian*.

It was a decision reinforced by medical advice. Drysdale was clearly exhausted. He was deeply involved in the Admiralty's antisubmarine warfare program while trying to keep the league intact, edit the *Malthusian*, and save the nation from the menace of state socialism. In turning the journal over to his more conciliatory, but reliably orthodox colleague, Dr. Binnie Dunlop, a wealthy, Glasgow-born physician who had joined the league in 1910 and later became treasurer, Drysdale guaranteed that little accommodation would be reached with those who were unprepared to concede the infallibility of the demographic wisdom enshrined in the tablets of nineteenth-century political economy. When Dunlop was called into military service in the fall of 1918, C. V. Drysdale resumed the editorship of the *Malthusian* and unrepentantly took off after "wicked" socialists once more.[86] Wells and his followers had already departed, and those who remained to turn the reluctant league in the direction of the future were advised by Drysdale to start their own organization.[87]

Though still alone in the field after forty years, the Malthusian League was further than ever from obtaining a popular following. The Drysdales were not surprised. Those who complained about the organization's philosophic liabilities and wanted to transform it into a comprehensive agency for social reform never understood the league's primary purpose, which was not birth control but the elimination of poverty and the simultaneous preservation of the capitalistic-competitive system. Ironically, C. V. Drysdale believed, the Marxists recognized this more clearly than many Neo-Malthusians. The SDF's hatred of the league from its inception was because of the Neo-Malthusians' fervent defense of the individualistic society Hyndman and his followers wanted to destroy. Implicit in Malthus's law of population was the danger of what C. R. Drysdale described as a "hunger-created revolution," which the socialists could exploit until fertility was brought under control.[88]

To his son the immediate danger in the twentieth century was not from violent revolution, but from the gradual triumph of state welfarism and socialist-controlled trade unions. The younger Drysdale's decision to divert the organization he inherited from its positive crusade against poverty to a negative bulwark against the most powerful trend of the age—collectivism—destroyed any chance, however slight, that the Malthusian League would lead the expanded drive for birth control and comprehensive family planning in the early twentieth century. It had not only failed to find much acclaim among the working classes most in need of its advice, but its success in enlisting middle- and upper-class support was at best marginal.

Nevertheless, millions of people were obviously practicing what the Neo-Malthusians preached and devouring the propaganda literature they distributed and the books they recommended. Though the decline in the birthrate charted so carefully by those concerned with the population question was alarming in its differential characteristics, it was evident by 1914 that birth control was even beginning to have a marked impact on working-class fertility. To what extent it was emulative is impossible to determine. Certainly the Neo-Malthusians had attempted to persuade the middle classes to teach their social inferiors, and they had insisted from the time of the Bradlaugh-Besant trial that they were merely trying to provide the same information to the poor that was readily available to the wealthier, better-educated classes. Moreover, much of the propaganda directed at the workers by birth control advocates, some of them socialists, emphasized that they were no less entitled to the benefits of regulating their fertility than the middle classes.

In all likelihood, however, working-class families probably began practicing birth control for many of the same personal and domestic reasons attributed to the middle classes. In many cases, far from heeding their betters, they were actually defying their advice. As the Neo-Malthusians correctly observed, the spread of family limitation occurred in spite of the professed sentiments and beliefs of influential sectors of the middle classes, such as clergymen and doctors who, theoretically at least, were important arbiters of moral and physical behavior.

CHAPTER 5

The Church and the Birthrate

The secularist founders of the Malthusian League braced themselves for a fierce assault from church and chapel. Their irreligion coupled with their campaign for smaller families was, they believed, certain to infuriate the many clergymen who had long admonished congregations to "increase and multiply, and replenish the earth." C. R. Drysdale recalled in 1879 that when the great Malthus, himself a parson, questioned the wisdom of this ancient injunction many of his fellow churchmen, like "clerical tyrants in the past," denounced him. Frustrated by the impotency of ecclesiastical law, they eventually compelled secular authorities to harass Malthus's disciples Charles Bradlaugh and Annie Besant.

Nevertheless, after centuries of insisting that the sole reason for marriage was the procreation of the race, countless slum clergymen, Drysdale wrote, were overwhelmed by the misery their demographic ignorance fostered. They could offer no better remedy to their impoverished parishioners than unnatural celibacy or impractical, joyless abstinence.[1] Malthus had recognized the enormity of the problem even if his own religious presuppositions prevented him from offering an effective solution. The new Malthusians, unburdened by hoary scriptural injunctions and inspired by scientific revelations, in part saw their fight for early marriage and the rational control of fertility as another, perhaps the ultimate, attack on the crumbling citadel of priestly obscurantism.

Much to their surprise the Neo-Malthusians found themselves hotly embroiled with socialists rather than clergymen. The anticipated confrontation with organized religion was slow to develop. Although an occasional divine condemned the disgusting and immoral recommendations of Bradlaugh and Besant, clerical reaction to their famous trial was uncommonly restrained. Besant claimed that several clergymen serving slum parishes expressed sympathy for her struggle, although only two of them, the Reverend Edward Horsley and the outspoken Anglo-Catholic, Christian socialist Stewart Headlam, agreed to testify. She did not, however, consider the clergy particularly hostile at that point.[2] Though Headlam's provocative support probably contributed to his ouster from his Bethnal Green parish in 1878, it is difficult to determine how aware churchmen were of the Knowlton controversy. Religious journals ignored the proceedings, and the sermons, charges, memoirs, and biographies of Victorian ecclesiastics do not mention them.

Clerical silence during the trial and in the early years of the Malthusian League's history puzzled its members. They scanned the popular and religious press, examined accounts of meetings and clerical assemblies, read sermons and episcopal charges in search of some evidence that their activities were making an impact on so important a segment of public opinion. Whether out of ignorance, indifference, or, as was more likely, respectable discretion, neither the Anglican nor the Nonconformist clergy acknowledged the league's existence.[3] Neo-Malthusians persuaded themselves that their message was so threatening to the control of the faithful in a "priest-ridden land" like England that a conspiracy of silence had been imposed on press and pulpit. The explanation was less sinister. Most clergymen, like most Victorians, believed family limitation was an extremely sensitive, personal issue the public discussion of which bordered on the obscene. Despite the Neo-Malthusians' beliefs, few clergymen perceived the problem as either relevant or threatening to their ministry, and in the absence of any ecclesiastical direction thought it a subject best ignored.

The first important breach in the clerical wall of silence occurred in 1885 when the Honorable Arthur Lyttelton delivered a paper, "Marriage and Neo-Malthusianism," to the Junior Clergy Society of London. A High Church, Liberal clergyman and nephew of Mrs. Gladstone, Lyttelton thought it time his brethren overcame their natural repugnance for the topic and examined Neo-Malthusian claims. He confessed that after much personal reflection on the problem of poverty he had come to appreciate the Malthusian League's concerns about overpopulation and its claims for the advantages of early marriage. He could not, however, endorse the use of "physical checks" to avoid unwanted children, convinced that it reflected a "low, animal view of marriage," which permitted sexual gratification without responsibility. The only acceptable compromise for Christian couples, Lyttelton concluded, was the cessation of all sexual relations once the optimum number of children for a family's resources was reached.[4]

League officials were quick to point out that Malthus had made the same futile recommendation nearly a century earlier, but they were nevertheless delighted that a prominent churchman had at last spoken out. If his solution was ill-conceived, Lyttelton was still the scion of a distinguished family and the head of an important Cambridge college. His voice would assuredly be heard in clerical circles where any acknowledgment of the existence of Neo-Malthusianism was welcomed by the league as a major advance.

In the months following the London meeting the *Malthusian* began reporting accounts of other clerical groups discussing Neo-Malthusianism. Most were critical, but at least one "well-known London divine" astonished a league member by informing him that scores of clergymen were recommending Malthusian methods to their poorest parishioners.[5] Younger clergy, Drysdale announced at the league's annual meeting in 1888, were more willing to admit the obvious connection between large families and the impoverishment of their charges.[6] Few were ready to prescribe the Neo-Malthusian remedy, but an occasional parson, like H. R. Haweiss, was less reticent, and, as a result, incurred the wrath of his brethren and bishop.

Haweiss had participated in the Junior Clergy Society meeting of 1885 and was disturbed by the narrow interpretation of Christian marriage enunciated by evangelical fundamentalists who dominated the group. Like Stewart Headlam, who had challenged their rigid views, Haweiss welcomed Lyttelton's assessment of the population question, but he suggested that Neo-Malthusian answers were perhaps more acceptable to the rational Christian than either the master of Selwyn or the biblical literalists believed. In the aftermath of the meeting Haweiss recalled that nearly everyone admitted that overpopulation made the life of the poor a purgatory, but they would offer nothing more comforting than the "old blessing of 'increase and multiply.'" Though once "suitable for a sparsely peopled land," he complained, it "has become the great curse of our crowded centres. . . . You may say children are from God; I reply, so is the cholera."[7]

Neo-Malthusians liked to believe that Haweiss's views represented the unspoken opinion of compassionate clergy in all denominations. They were, however, hard pressed to find supportive evidence and made much of an isolated reference to the "conjugal prudence" of the French mentioned by a rural Anglican curate and an oblique allusion to "science" made by a Unitarian minister discussing separating early parentage from early marriage.[8] A few Unitarians populated the ranks of the Malthusian League in the nineteenth century, but aside from Headlam only one Anglican clergyman, Arthur E. Whatham of St. George's-in-the-East, London, seems to have openly endorsed Neo-Malthusian methods.

As a member of the Church of England Purity Society and former cosecretary of the Liverpool Society for the Suppression of Immorality, Whatham believed his moral credentials were in order when in 1887 he published a reply to Lyttelton's paper. He rejected the contention that contraception was unlawful for Christians and reflected a "low view of marriage," noting that it was not forbidden in the New Testament. Unlike animals fated to suffer the consequences of their natural impulses man was blessed with rational intellect. That he should not use it to plan for his domestic well-being was preposterous and relegated the poor in particular to suffer the consequences of ignorance. God would not have wished it so, he argued, and has nowhere condemned artificial limitation as inimical to the Christian ideal of marriage. Indeed, if the recommendations in Annie Besant's *Law of Population* were widely adopted, the institution of marriage, far from being debased, would be elevated to new heights.[9]

The most shocking part of Whatham's pamphlet, however, was his likening of sexual intercourse to any other "pleasant and lawful . . . sensuous desire" that contributed to health and human happiness. It was absurd for "anti-preventionists" to suggest that sex was always, or even usually, undertaken "between the most respectable and virtuous of married couples" with the idea of having children.[10]

C. R. Drysdale sent Whatham a letter of appreciation and reprinted most of his pamphlet in the *Malthusian*.[11] Whatham's bishop, Frederick Temple, also sent him a letter; it forbade distribution of the tract to any but medical men. When this proved ineffectual he ordered Whatham in 1889 to withdraw it entirely. The contumacious author instead departed for Canada leaving behind his unhappy diocesan and the notorious pamphlet, which subsequently went through at least ten editions before World War I. Neo-Malthusians referred to it time and again as a turning point in their struggle against religious obscurantism. In 1891, after reviewing developments since Lyttelton's address to the Junior Clergy Society, the Malthusian League Council announced that "ere long, clerical prejudices against [our] . . . doctrines would die out."[12]

Considering that the league had been able to identify at best no more than ten to twelve obvious sympathizers out of a ministerial population exceeding thirty thousand a more cautious assessment might have been in order. But in their enthusiasm Neo-Malthusians tended to greet every clergyman's concern about overpopulation as a veiled endorsement of their proposals. Socially conscious ministers were, like other analysts of the "Condition of England" in the 1880s and 1890s, well aware of a revived Malthusian dimension to the nation's serious economic problems. Most clerical demographers, however, recommended emigration rather than contraception. Yet, when clergymen with small incomes and large families were advised in 1885 by the Archbishop of York to call upon their congregations for supplementary assistance, the *Malthusian* commented on how quickly church dignitaries forgot about emigration when pondering the "genteel paupers" inhabiting overcrowded parsonages.[13] The few prelates who ventured to discuss the relationship of overpopulation to poverty invariably denounced the improvident marriages and absence of self-control on the part of the poor whose only recourse was celibacy, continence, or the colonies.

No bishop took any notice of Neo-Malthusianism until the next century. Other clergy were less reticent, however, and in 1888 a speaker at the Manchester church congress condemned the "awful heresy" of population restraint by artificial means, which seemed to be spreading rapidly through the country.[14] The following year the Church of England's Moral Reform Union published Francis W. Newman's polemic, *The Corruption Now Called Neo-Malthusianism*. Newman, the religiously erratic brother of the celebrated cardinal, had long been an enemy of the old Malthusianism, and he denounced the "foul doctrine" that of late had assumed its name. To counter the "odious monstrosity," Newman cited medical testimony, including that of the first woman physician, Elizabeth Blackwell, as well as Holy Scripture, to sustain his charge that contraception not only violated God's commandments but polluted marriage and was physically dangerous.[15]

The divine injunction in Genesis, "Be fruitful and multiply. Replenish the earth and subdue it," was for scriptural anti-Malthusians reinforced by the fateful sin of Onan. Although Neo-Malthusians argued repeatedly that Onan was destroyed for violating the Mosaic code obliging a man to marry his brother's widow and sire children rather than for the technical offense of spilling his seed upon the ground, their religious opponents insisted that the Lord's reprisal was a condemnation not only of masturbation but of coitus interruptus and any other unnatural method of thwarting God's procreant command.[16] Even that was open to interpretation, league theologians countered, for the order was first given when there were only two people on earth, and again, after the flood, when there were but eight. Propagation of the species in such extreme circumstances was obviously necessary, but by the time of Christ the world was sufficiently populated to call forth a new commandment—"that ye love one another. We realize but imperfectly what love is, but we know that love worketh no evil."[17] The irony of freethinking Neo-Malthusians debating scriptural demography with biblical fundamentalists was not lost on those league skeptics who reasoned that if people were so foolish as to be governed by ancient tales, New Testament myths were clearly more relevant to an overcrowded world than those of the Old Testament.

Most of the Malthusian League's theological disputations were with Anglicans rather than Nonconformists. Representatives of the free churches on the National Birth-Rate Commission explained that in the absence of clear interpretation and special revelation their ministers preferred to leave the vexatious question to the individual conscience. People who could not resolve the issue for themselves were encouraged to discuss it with their local minister, but they could expect no denominational guidance.[18] Consequently, the Nonconformist press rarely alluded to the subject. It was briefly raised in an anonymous but sympathetic article in the *Christian World* in 1893 prompted by a series of letters detailing the problems of poor women with too many children. Though the author argued that intelligent, sensible Christians no longer believed that voluntary limitation was an affront to Providence, his observations prompted no response.[19]

Arthur Lyttelton's brother, Edward, the headmaster of Haileybury School and later of Eton, complained in 1898 of the lack of clerical discussion of Neo-Malthusianism. Reviewing an anti-Malthusian tract, he noted that after a brief flurry of activity a few years earlier churchmen had once again become reluctant to discuss even the moral consequences of the "general increase in artificial preventives." Unlike his older brother, Edward believed that when the health of a wife was in danger, or a family was threatened by indigence, "preventive checks" were probably justified. Under no circumstances were they to be used for mere "self-indulgence," of course, but unless spiritual authorities were prepared to offer clearer guidance to the faithful the line between morally acceptable prudence and immoral fleshly gratification would become hopelessly blurred.[20]

Lyttelton, like his brother a decade earlier, wanted to provoke church leaders to consider the question of family limitation while there was still time. It was an issue that obviously involved the interpretation of Scripture, Christian morality, and the sanctity of marriage—subjects upon which the church should be prepared to speak with a clear voice. What finally propelled the ecclesiastical hierarchy to take up the distasteful problem was the shock of the Boer War and the multiple concerns it generated about the size and vitality of the British race. In this the church, as usual, followed public opinion rather than led it.

One of the first church dignitaries to speak out, William Boyd Carpenter, the Bishop of Ripon (1884–1911), was as distressed by the differential characteristics of the declining birthrate as he was by the gloomy accounts of physical deterioration he surveyed. In 1904 he condemned as an "indulgence in unsubdued lust" those "fashionable marriages" in which parenthood is shirked. People who could afford to rear large families refused to do so, he charged, "and it is left to the tramp, to the hooligan, and the lounger to maintain the population. This is not the way to rear up a great Imperial race," he warned, and he expressed fears that if the trend continued it would thwart God's plan for the exemplary dominance of British civilization throughout the world.[21]

The bishop, like the late queen, whose chaplain and favorite he had been, could not himself be accused of frustrating this divine scheme, having fathered eleven children in two marriages. An outspoken Liberal

imperialist and vigorous episcopal advocate of the cult of national efficiency, Boyd Carpenter was impressed by the dynamic growth of Germany
and enjoyed the friendship of its impulsive Kaiser. Britain, he told the
House of Lords in 1905, by contrast appeared to be in a position of
relative decline as its "strength and populous vigour" at home and in the
colonies headed toward stagnation.[22]

Two years before, Boyd Carpenter had supported the Earl of Meath and
others when they pressed the government to create a royal commission to
investigate the plummeting birthrate and the possible deterioration of the
race. The bishop thought that most analysts agreed that had fertility continued at the same level as twenty years earlier, at least a million more
children would have been born, most of them to the more energetic
classes. An investigation by a prominent commission would, he explained,
alert public opinion to the danger and determine whether the declining
birthrate was primarily the result of deliberate prevention or a dangerous
loss of "racial vigour."[23]

Although the findings of the Inter-Departmental Committee on Physical Deterioration (1904) satisfied those who disputed pessimistic diagnoses
of incipient decay and sufficed to quiet politicians who were for the most
part content to steer clear of the emotional issue, it did little to silence
aroused churchmen. The scattered discussions of Neo-Malthusianism,
which had taken place in religious circles in the 1880s and 1890s, reflected
little awareness of vital statistics. By the opening years of the new century,
however, the reality of the falling birthrate gave an urgency to the arguments of those clergymen who bemoaned the declining morals of the age
and predicted the disintegration of the sacred values of family life. They
began to speak out at all levels reinforced by the quarterly and annual
reports of the registrar-general. The *Malthusian* boasted in 1904 that its
campaign had not only dropped the nation's fertility to a new low, but had
at last succeeded in flushing church leaders into the open.[24]

One of the most distinguished to bolt, Arthur Foley Winnington-Ingram,
the evangelical Bishop of London (1901–39), caused a sensation during his
1905 diocesan visitation by angrily denouncing the falling birthrate and
condemning those responsible for practicing the "deliberate prevention of
conception." In his *Charge* he confessed to being embarrassed at having to
raise "one of those delicate subjects on which it is impossible to speak in
great detail." His being a bachelor perhaps contributed to his reluctance,
but having introduced the subject he pursued it with unexpected fervor.
Citing comparative statistics at home and abroad, the prelate insisted that
it was no longer possible for church authorities to ignore the evidence of
the nation's folly accumulated since artificial prevention "was first encouraged and taught in England some thirty-five years ago." It had "spread like

a blight over the middle class population of the land" and created a national malaise affecting all sectors of the populace.[25]

Winnington-Ingram recognized that the country was going through restless, changing times and admitted that he did not like the values of the new age. They discounted the responsibilities of married life and the "glory of motherhood," substituting a "deplorable selfishness which thinks first of creature comforts or social pleasures." Family limitation was, for him, the logical outcome of the corrosive influence of the "miserable gospel of comfort which is the curse of the present day." Unwilling to concede that it might also reflect a greater sense of domestic responsibility and an enhanced concern for the health and welfare of mothers and their existing children, he summarily condemned all who employed restrictive measures and summoned the forces of the church "to stem this gigantic evil."[26]

The Bishop of London's observations were widely reported in the national and provincial press and his published *Charge* was the subject of much commentary. Many praised his courage and echoed his views. One of his clergy, who had feared that "Malthus reigns instead of Christ," had criticized his superiors for remaining so circumspect while "England's homes are withering under a Malthusian blight." He now welcomed the prelate's visit as an answer to his prayers.[27] Dr. John Taylor, president of the British Gynaecological Society, whose criticisms of contraception the bishop had cited at length, returned the compliment by endorsing his "stern and solemn call" to end the "allied sins of cowardly but comfortable living." The outlook was not promising, Taylor confessed, though he was sure that Winnington-Ingram's strong admonition would give pause for serious thought.[28]

What to some was an ominous sign of domestic decadence was to others irrefutable evidence of an elevated sense of familial responsibility conforming to altered social and economic conditions. In making this point, numerous critics accused the Bishop of London of casting unfair aspersions on his prudent countrymen. The debunking of ecclesiastical demography was gleefully reported by the *Malthusian*, which reveled in the publicity the bishop's visitation *Charge* brought the Neo-Malthusian movement. Winnington-Ingram not only acknowledged the impact of the Bradlaugh-Besant trial and the activities of the league in lowering the birthrate, but he recklessly accused millions of men and women of being self-indulgent materialists whose luxuriant appetites were not only immoral but unpatriotic. It was ironic, one of the bishop's critics remarked, that the most prominent church dignitary to condemn the voluntary limitation of families was "a gentlemen who enjoys celibacy on an income of £10,000 a year."[29] Unlike that other early episcopal enemy of restriction, the progenetive Bishop of Ripon, the ascetic, unmarried Winnington-Ingram was an obvious target for jokes by Neo-Malthusians and other birth controllers who battled his unreconstructed opinions until his retirement in 1939.

In 1905, however, Winnington-Ingram's provocative comments reflected a wider concern about the relevancy of spiritual values and religious attachments in an era of science and materialism. Complaints about the ineffectiveness of organized religion, the difficulties of clerical recruitment, and the diminishing influence of the ministry were commonplace among the Anglican faithful in the closing years of Queen Victoria's reign. Surveys of church attendance in London indicated that the allegiance of middle-class and skilled-artisan congregations, long the backbone of most denominations, was waning.[30] In spite of the church's teachings about marriage and the family every study of differential fertility indicated that the declining birthrate was most pronounced among those whom the established church thought most loyal to its moral guidance. Fear of the weakening hold of religion on the less fertile younger generation contributed directly to the revitalization of a number of "purity societies" in the Edwardian period, such as the National Council of Public Morals, determined to restore the moral and spiritual structure of British family life.

For critics such as Boyd Carpenter, Winnington-Ingram, or their medical champion, Dr. Taylor, birth control was an insidious corruption of the "sanctity and honour of English family life"; its success threatened to sweep away the old order, and with it, a great imperial Christian civilization. Taylor, in a flight of medieval fancy, inflated the Bishop of London's visitation to the first step in "a new quest of the Holy Grail. . . . We shall not lack our Percevals and Galahads, nor Sir Percevale's sister, nor good Sir Bors," he promised. But unless the search was pressed, "the cultured family of knightly sons and queen-like daughters" will have vanished "and given place to the *menage* of one." At that point, Taylor lamented, "the sacred fellowship of the Table Round will once again be broken."[31]

The bishops of the Anglican communion who assembled for the Lambeth Conference in 1908 were perhaps less heroically Arthurian than the doctor had in mind, but their conclusions were everything he wished for. Prodded by the Bishop of London and his supporters the episcopacy collectively examined "with alarm, the growing practice of the artificial restriction of the family." In calling upon "all Christian people to discountenance the use of all artificial means of restriction as demoralising to character and hostile of national welfare," the conference endorsed the recommendations of a prelatical committee under the chairmanship of George F. Browne, the Bishop of Bristol (1897–1914).[32] The bishops also agreed that the Christian ideal of marriage and the purity of home life was already partially subverted, and they overwhelmingly affirmed the committee's view "that the deliberate tampering with nascent life is repugnant to Christian morality."[33]

In formulating their resolution Bishop Browne and his colleagues made substantial use of fertility statistics and considered the various explanations then current for the declining birthrate in Great Britain and the colonies. They also studied the worrisome diminution of "old English-speaking stocks" in the United States whose reproduction lagged far behind that of the "foreign stocks." There was no longer any question that the "loss of the sense of responsibility to God for the fruits of marriage" had opened the way for the "deliberate avoidance or prevention of child-bearing." The committee described it as "preventive abortion" and claimed that, as the "old reserve of modesty" disappeared, doctors were constantly consulted "by those who desire to avoid the burden of a family."[34]

Medical testimony was introduced to prove that "serious local ailments" were as likely to result from preventive practices as moral decay. The verdict of nature, "many eminent physiologists" agreed, appeared to endorse the moral instinct. Several of the ill effects noted by medical observers resembled those resulting from "self abuse." These included nervous enfeeblement and impaired mental and moral vigor, and the question was raised whether recent increases in insanity might be attributable to "these habits of restriction." The bishops conceded that there were cases in which a "natural wish to spare the wife from suffering" seemed to compel the prevention of conception, but they suspected that in the long run it entailed "far more suffering than can arise from allowing Nature to take her course."[35] Even then, however, the Lambeth Conference was unwilling to sanction any other forms of restriction than prolonged absention or the safe period. These alone, the prelates were assured by doctors, conformed to nature and physiology. More important, they appeared to conform to Scripture.

The ecclesiastical dignitaries also considered the standard economic arguments for smaller families and discussed whether the rearing of fewer children reflected, as birth control advocates claimed, a higher quality of parental love and responsibility for those already born. They concluded that, although children in a large family might be deprived of greater emotional support and material resources and opportunities, the benefits to be derived from self-denial, personal exertion, and responsibility were far more important in establishing a "wholesome discipline of life." But the bishops doubted that economic considerations were paramount in couples' minds, as many students of the population question believed. On the contrary, the data indicated that restrictive practices were far more prevalent "among the well-to-do than among the poor." Social ambition appeared to be a much stronger motive than "foresight under the stress of poverty." With some insight episcopal analysts argued that it arose from the "wish to escape burdens which might lessen social prestige or limit the opportunities of pleasure." Even Neo-Malthusians conceded that this was an important motivation, although they denied the conference's conclusion that it was also a "symptom of the spirit which shirks responsibility and repudiates self-denial, and which results in the weakening of character."[36]

Throughout their deliberations the bishops dwelt upon a strength of character as the "best asset of nations" and cited many indications of its growing "enfeeblement." The prelates obviously believed it had once been a special quality of the middle and upper classes, and when they discussed its decline in conjunction with the differential birthrate they readily drew obvious eugenic conclusions. Citing judicial statistics on divorce, which only the richer classes could afford, Bishop Browne's committee reported that between 1896 and 1906 40 percent were granted to childless couples, while an additional 40 percent had no more than one or two children.[37] The threat to the institution of marriage and the loss to the race of potential well-bred offspring was, in the committee's judgment, deplorable and eugenically dangerous.

Qualitative racial considerations permeated the Lambeth resolutions regarding the declining birthrate and dominated the conference's closing thoughts on the subject. They contemplated the "danger of deterioration whenever the race is recruited from the inferior and not from the superior stocks." It led the bishops to conclude that "there is the world danger that the great English-speaking peoples, diminished in number and weakened in moral force, would commit the crowning infamy of race-suicide, and so fail to fulfill that high destiny to which in the Providence of God they have been manifestly called."[38]

Although the Lambeth Conference resolutions lacked any formal synodical authority, their supporters hoped the pronouncements on marriage and the family would resolve the confusion about artificial limitation that had grown within the Anglican communion in recent years. They were quickly disappointed. The bishops' instructions further polarized public opinion as the conference's deliberations and conclusions were heatedly discussed in newspapers and journals for several months, and, in some cases, years. The *Malthusian* was ecstatic. Although the resolutions proved to be as unenlightened as expected, their summary condemnation of the demographic realities of the past thirty years had raised the population question to a new level of public consciousness. Furthermore, in specifically denouncing the "Malthusian Society" and demanding legislation to end the promotion and sale of "so-called Neo-Malthusian appliances," the church hierarchy, according to Malthusian League analysts, had inadvertently acknowledged the great success of their campaign.[39]

Clerical responses to the Lambeth Conference resolutions indicated greater division within the church's ranks than even the league anticipated. Although many ministers welcomed an authoritative reaffirmation of their own views, a smaller number were disturbed by the bishops' unrealistic response to those most in need of the church's help, the poor and their too numerous offspring. While the conference was still in session a few clergy appealed to the delegates not to take refuge in the past, but to recognize that many of their less exalted brethren welcomed the falling birthrate as a last opportunity for their impoverished parishioners to break free of chronic indigence. Some confessed that their hostile attitude toward family limitation had been changed by their searing experiences in slum parishes. In disagreeing with their diocesans they argued that religion, like civilization itself, was evolving. A "progressive revelation," it inspired the modern Christian with the certainty that it was wrong to bring into the world a "sickly, miserable and diseased child" who, if he survives, will grow up in desperate poverty.[40]

The Reverend James Peile, Archdeacon and Canon of Coventry, wondered if the church was wise in making sweeping pronouncements on a question "on which the best opinion, both moral and scientific, is still strongly divided." As a member of the new Eugenics Education Society, Peile was no less concerned than his ecclesiastical superiors about the dangers of "character enfeeblement" and "race suicide" to be found in the differential birthrate. Nevertheless, he was persuaded that the complex issue of restricting fertility was a "matter for the doctor and not for the parson." Nonconformists, in wisely eschewing any overall direction to the faithful on the thorny subject, were, in the opinion of Peile and many other Anglicans, sparing themselves prolonged and fruitless controversy.[41]

The Lambeth Conference resolutions, as critics predicted, made no difference as the birthrate of Anglicans and Nonconformists alike continued to decline. Observers noted that Catholics and Jews alone seemed unaffected by the downward trend. Testifying before the National Birth-Rate Commission in 1914, Nonconformist spokesmen explained that none of the free churches had taken a stand on family limitation, nor had their council ever discussed the subject. There had been no pressure from denominational ministries to do so, and it seemed clear to the general secretary of the Wesleyan Methodist Union for Social Services that most clergy wished to avoid becoming embroiled in so intimate and complex an area of individual human behavior.[42] Owing to the independence of most Nonconformists, free church authorities doubted that many congregations would in any event submit to the judgment of their ministers on such a personal matter. This did not mean, however, the NBRC feebly concluded, that if actually confronted with the problem, the great majority of Non-

conformists would not also "unhesitatingly condemn the use of all mechanical or chemical means of prevention, and would strongly insist on the
voluntary moral control of all natural functions."[43]

Regardless of such assurances there was no denying that Protestants of
all persuasions were increasingly curtailing the size of their families by one
method or another. Moreover, Neo-Malthusians reminded their adversaries, the clergy were themselves in the vanguard of the restrictionists.
Citing an 1874 actuarial survey of the professional and upper classes, C. V.
Drysdale noted that clergymen had an average of 5.2 children, which was
close to the national norm. More recently, however, as the 1911 census
revealed, that figure had dropped to 2.3, considerably below the declining
national average of 2.8. When marriages of completed fertility were analyzed, the gap proved to be even wider with clerical families numbering
2.8 offspring compared with nearly 3.7 for the entire population. Younger
marriages did not promise to be more fruitful, as minister's wives of child-
bearing age continued to have 1.9 children rather than the 2.3 reported for
the nation as a whole.

Clerical fertility was actually even lower than family size indicated. Men
of the cloth not only fathered fewer children in the first place, but more of
their well-cared-for offspring survived. Over 20 percent of children born
to the general population as of 1911 died in infancy compared with 13
percent in ministers' families. As infant mortality declined to around 17
percent in marriages of incomplete fertility, it fell to nearly 9 percent for
the clergy. Among Anglican ministers the figure was only 6.8 percent, the
lowest rate of infant mortality suffered by any occupational group studied in
the *Fertility of Marriage Census*. Critics of the Lambeth Conference resolutions never tired of reminding parsons and their diocesans that they denied
their impoverished charges the selective blessings they reserved for themselves and thus condemned poor parents to the loss of nearly a quarter of
their young. Perhaps, Drysdale mockingly suggested, the celibate Bishop
of London and his clergy had discovered since the Knowlton trial that although "the wages of sin is death, . . . the wages of birth control is healthier
and longer life."[44]

The hypocrisy of the Anglican clergy was a continual theme in Neo-
Malthusian propaganda. It assumed that the small families inhabiting the
parsonages of the land were a result of artificial contraception. Most clergymen, however, probably limited fertility by exercising prolonged and frustrating abstinence, and, less often, coitus interruptus. Fragmented evidence
from the 1920s suggests that this was the case.[45] Churchmen were more
concerned about motivation than method and preached the commendable
virtues of self-denial. Although "preventives" were readily associated with
unbridled sexuality and self-indulgence, prudent restraint on the part of

married couples was not necessarily equated with the deliberate thwarting of conception. Moreover, although a few clergy were prepared to conjure up the sin of Onan, most seemed as confused as the general public as to whether coitus interruptus was actually a form of contraception since it involved no chemicals or "Malthusian appliances."

Indeed, inadequate surveys and reports of birth control clinics during the interwar years indicate that a great many people, including men of the cloth, still did not equate withdrawal with the douches, sponges, condoms, spermicidal suppositories, and rubber devices that "immoral purveyors of lustful gratification" recommended to control fertility. The evidence, meager though it is, certainly suggests that the appliances played little role in the domestic strategies of clerical families. For most Neo-Malthusians before the war the distinctions were irrelevant. Although there were always dissenters, the Malthusian League hierarchy recommended coitus interruptus as the most effective form of contraception. Because of its simplicity and the absence of cost, it was especially suitable for the poor; but league spokesmen correctly assumed that it was widely practiced by people in all classes. Consequently, whatever subtle distinctions clergymen might make in justifying their own behavior, Neo-Malthusians derided them as self-serving hypocrites.

No one ranked higher in this clerical demonology than the increasingly outspoken Bishop of London. Emboldened by the Lambeth Conference and angered by the continual slide in the birthrate, he escalated his assault on the "miserable gospel of comfort," as he described family limitation, and in 1911 he condemned it as a "sin."[46] His elevation of birth control to a higher transgression provoked a renewed surge of protests from clergy and laity alike, causing the surprised prelate to claim that he had been misunderstood and that his denunciation applied only to the use of artificial devices, not methods of self-control.[47]

A few of Winnington-Ingram's colleagues, including Cosmo Gordon Lang, the Archbishop of York (1909–29), rallied to his defense. They reaffirmed the church's conviction that marriage was solely for procreation and any deviation was a violation of a divine mandate. Lang admitted that while the church had been sleeping the enemy had been "sowing his tares, . . . checking the harvest of human life." Now awakened, he promised, the church would continue to speak out.[48] Most of its leaders were, however, apparently uncertain as to what to say, and they remained discreetly silent. Those who hesitantly took up the challenge, like Edgar C. S. Gibson, the Bishop of Gloucester (1905–23), vacillated when pressed by his clergy for some realistic guidance in persuading their dwindling congregations of the dangers birth control posed for the race as well as their immortal souls. The prelate could only recommend a rereading of the Lambeth Conference resolutions.[49]

Although many churchmen were obviously skeptical of such advice, only one dignitary, W. R. Inge, the Dean of St. Paul's, openly questioned his ecclesiastical superiors. At a meeting of the Sociological Society in 1912 Inge denied that the parents of small families were selfish, as some bishops charged. On the contrary, he said, the clergy should be inculcating among the poor the virtues of self-control and qualitative family planning evident in the reduced fertility of the higher classes. To a rabid eugenist like Inge, the "great menace to our civilisation was not so much the stationary birth-rate of the upper classes as the great increase among the poor and ill-fed population of our great towns."[50] His defections from the Lambeth guidelines became more pronounced as his eugenic pessimism increased. On the eve of the Great War he was dismayed that his own church seemed to be inadvertently allying itself with greedy militarists and competitive, throat-cutting capitalists who looked upon men "as food for powder" or as "an unlimited quantity of cheap labour" without any thought for the racial well-being of their decaying nation.[51]

The "gloomy dean's" continual complaints about the mediocre cast of contemporary society reflected deeply ingrained, elitist sentiments revolted by the proliferation of "wastrels" and "incompetents." Without specifically recommending that the lower classes employ contraceptives to reduce their unwanted numbers, Inge strongly believed that the clergy ought not to discourage the poor from emulating their responsible betters. He paid less attention to the individual physical and economic benefits the poor would derive from curtailing their fertility than he did to the genetic advantages a reduction in their progeny could bring to the race.

On the basis of their experience in fetid slums and impoverished rural parishes a small but increasingly vocal body of clergymen began to question whether their bishops knew what they were talking about when they rambled on about the curse of selfish materialism and the myriad blessings of the large family. In a series of letters to the *Evening Standard* in 1912, a Surrey parson, J. P. Bacon-Phillips, complained that the concept of selfishness had become hopelessly confused by some prelates in the recent discussions of the declining birthrate. Who were the truly selfish, he asked? Those condemned couples who prudently evaluated their prospects and resources and limited their families accordingly; or those who, as some would wish, "bring a large number of children into the world without the wherewithal to provide for them?"[52]

Most clerical arguments were an admixture of compassion and eugenics. When W. J. Somerville, the outspoken Rector of St. George's, Southwark, derided episcopal admonitions and urged his poor parishioners to copy the restrictive practices of the middle classes, he was hoping to improve their lives while restoring a qualitative balance in class reproduction. His warning that a "nation which constantly renews itself from below . . . and which breeds from its most undesirable elements is well on the way to reaping a disastrous harvest," was so pleasing to the *Malthusian* that it quoted it in February, 1914, as its "Saying of the Month."[53]

It is doubtful that either Somerville or his virulently anti-Malthusian diocesan, H. M. Burge, appreciated the honor, but Drysdale was equally willing to acknowledge scathing denunciations of the league and its activities. When a partisan of the Bishop of London excoriated the organization as a "horror . . . which has advocated and promoted with appalling success child restriction by genetic fraud [and] family suicide leading to racial decay," Drysdale gleefully reported it as further evidence of the league's effectiveness.[54] He suspected that the intensity of such opposition masked a fear of extensive, if silent support for birth control within ministerial ranks. When in 1913 Binnie Dunlop offered to send a copy of Drysdale's book, *The Small Family System*, to any clergyman who requested it, he quickly received two hundred and fifty applications.[55] The *Malthusian* even thought it possible the next year that a "Church Malthusian League" might be established in the near future.[56]

This delusion was reinforced by the serious consideration the heavily clerical NBRC gave to Drysdale's testimony. More encouraging, however, was the commission's acknowledgment that wide differences of opinion prevailed among the clergy because of the absence of any recognized authoritative teaching on the subject of family limitation. Furthermore, ministerial objections to the practice had grown decidedly weaker since the beginning of the century, the commissioners concluded.[57] Although the Free Church Council was for the first time considering a report on the family and the home, its inquiry was interrupted by the war. Even then, however, its spokesmen told the commission, there was no intention of trying to impose an orthodox interpretation on the sturdily independent Nonconformist clergy or their congregations.[58]

The fundamental problem, the Methodist representative, W. F. Lofthouse, explained, was that a great many free churchmen, himself included, did not believe that the Old Testament definitely decreed that the purpose of marriage was the unrestricted production of children. Whatever personal objections they had to "preventive checks" had nothing to do with biblical condemnation, but rather with a lack of "filial trust in God" that their use implied. With the exception of the "safe period," Lofthouse reasoned, all methods of contraception challenged God's desire and the state's need for numerous children growing up in good homes. As the enjoyment of sexual intercourse was God-given, so were the consequences. Preventives allowed the "random indulgence of impulses" without any sense that they might be part of a higher plan.[59]

Although pressed hard by some of the established church commissioners to take the next logical step and condemn artificial methods of contraception, Lofthouse refused even to denounce the use of condoms since no clear scriptural rule prescribed such a conclusion. It was a dilemma, he admitted, but he was certain that the churches would lose what little opportunity they had for moral guidance on the subject if they categorically denounced the use of preventives. Dubious biblical exhortations and angry charges of selfishness would continue to have little effect, given the complexity and diversity of motives for rearing fewer children. Lofthouse, with typical class prejudice, suggested that an appeal to the higher sense of social responsibility possessed by the well-to-do might persuade them to diminish their amusements more and their families less. Those below them, whose altruistic senses were perhaps less refined, might be better encouraged by maternity endowments, improved housing, and expanded educational opportunities. Even people at the bottom of the ladder, who "can find little relaxation and amusement save in drink and sexual pleasure" will be less inclined to reckless indulgence as their standard of life improves.[60] Lofthouse essentially argued that the state could do as much, if not more, than the churches to halt the precipitous drop in the nation's fertility.

The Anglican bishops on the commission were particularly interested in Lofthouse's testimony. Two of them, Winnington-Ingram and the commission's chairman, Boyd Carpenter, had been instrumental in the preparation in 1913 of a private episcopal memorandum, "The Misuse of Marriage," which was to be circulated to clergy and laity seeking clarification of the church's position. Although the memorandum essentially reaffirmed the 1908 resolutions, it was more explicit in its toleration of the safe period as a method of controlling fertility. Restricting intercourse to the supposedly infertile days of a woman's monthly cycle, in the bishops' judgment, met the Christian criteria of "reasonable and conscientious self-restraint." Moreover, it constituted self-denial rather than self-indulgence, and self-denial was at the core of the memorandum. The faithful were warned that if, for economic or physiological reasons, they wished to avoid bringing more children into the world, they had to expect to endure long periods of continence throughout much of their married life.[61]

Determining the safe period was, the bishops knew, subject to medical dispute, and was, therefore, a notoriously unreliable method of contraception. But it had the dubious merit of requiring a "courageous readiness to trust God." If, as frequently happened, it proved ineffective, Christian couples were obligated to accept the consequences. God, after all, preferred large families, the memorandum asserted, and under no circumstances were the odds to be tilted against Providence by the use of any artificial devices or coitus interruptus. Wives in particular were warned of the mental and physical infirmities as well as the spiritual desolation they could suffer if they employed such repugnant methods. When, however, an insensitive husband insisted, his wife should submit, comforted by her good conscience and the surety that she at least "would still be welcomed at the Lord's table."[62]

With the exception of Bishop Burge of Southwark, who refused even to concede the acceptability of the safe period, the bench agreed that its harsh memorandum represented the position of the established church. Burge, the former headmaster of Winchester School and the father of two, adamantly insisted that conception was the only reason for intercourse. Any relaxation of this standard degraded the marital union, he told the unconvinced commissioners, and, as soon as the age of childbearing was over, all sexual relations between husband and wife must cease.[63]

Nonconformist and Anglican commissioners alike were incredulous, but in spite of repeated prodding Burge refused to moderate his austere views. It is doubtful that it mattered; the memorandum, "The Misuse of Marriage," was clearly so at odds with connubial behavior that it proved no more satisfactory for the faithful than did the Lambeth Conference resolutions the document was designed to clarify. The NBRC in its final report, acknowledged the wide differences of opinion in the religious community and frankly doubted that congregations were as uncertain as their ministers about the moral acceptability of contraception. Even within the established church, despite episcopal directives to the contrary, there were many "high-minded laymen and women . . . who openly justify the use of preventives, and this attitude has become far more common during the last few years."[64]

When the commission's report appeared in 1916, its editor, James Marchant, regretted the differing opinions and lack of influence the clergy had on the population question. The Catholic church, he observed, stood alone in its ability to guide the reproductive behavior of its followers, something that ought to give pause to a Protestant imperial race. If the higher classes continued to restrict their numbers while the Catholics, most of them of Irish working-class origin, proliferated at the current level, the religious as well as the racial structure of the nation could in time be permanently altered. Marchant prayed that the war would stimulate a great religious revival that would cause people to reflect on the dangers to the faith from the continued spread of birth control.[65]

Marchant touched upon a sensitive area of the population question that was rarely mentioned until shortly before the war. Bishop Boyd Carpenter in 1912 had forecast an increase in the proportion of heathens in the world if the birthrate of European Christians continued to drop, but it aroused little comment.[66] Comparative demographic studies frequently contrasted the fertility of Ireland or other Catholic countries to illustrate the importance of cultural factors in population trends, but the specter of barren Protestants being overrun by multitudes of pullulating papists was not raised very often. A 1914 article in the learned Anglican *Hibbert Journal* suggested that more attention should be paid to religious correlations by analysts of the declining birthrate. Its author, Meyrick Booth, described the high fertility recorded for such towns as Liverpool, Salford, Manchester, Glasgow, and the East End of London where large numbers of Jews and, more importantly, Irish Catholics, resided. In contrast to what many believed, he argued, it was not poverty that stimulated the hordes of children in these crowded areas, but religion and race. A substantial fertility differential was equally obvious among the upper classes. The Whethams had noted in their study, *The Family and the Nation*, that the size of Catholic landed families between 1871 and 1890 was on the average 6.6 compared with only 3.7 for Protestants of the same class. Since then, Booth was certain, the gap had widened. If Protestants were unaware or indifferent to these trends, Catholics were not. The most recent *Catholic Year Book*, Booth quoted, expressed pleasure that the birthrate of communicants in the Roman dioceses of England and Wales averaged 38.6/ 1,000 compared with only 24 for the country as a whole.[67]

The cause, Booth recognized, was the adoption by Protestants of "Malthusian customs" and a diminished religiosity among the middle- and well-to-do artisan classes. As a result the British were threatened by Irish, Jews, and other poorer "foreign stocks." Clergyman did not have to look far for the explanation of the decline of the Protestant churches in the country: "let them rather look to the empty cradles in the homes of their own congregations." There was no comfort to be found in evolutionist assertions that diminished fertility was a natural consequence of higher Protestant civilization. On the contrary, Booth thought it more likely a sign of ethical and religious degeneration that caused Protestants to embrace Neo-Malthusianism "in *practice* if not in theory" when it first appeared in the 1870s. Catholicism held firm, he lamented, while Protestantism has seen the "cream of its human material . . . suffering gradual extinction."[68]

The NBRC considered the correlation between religion and fertility, but it came to no conclusion. The Chief Rabbi of Great Britain acknowledged that Jewish fertility was proportionally higher in many English, Russian, and North American cities, but he noted that in other places, such as Bavaria and Breslau, it was much lower. Although most Jews believed preventives to be unclean and demoralizing and welcomed large families, there were obviously complex "racial and cultural differences" modifying attitudes in different parts of the world. In general, however, every Jew was expected to marry and have a substantial number of children, the rabbi explained, unless physically or mentally unfit.[69]

Catholic witnesses attributed their success in maintaining high fertility to the Roman church's strong guidance on domestic matters. Monsignor W. F. Brown, Vicar-General of the Diocese of Southwark and Pronotary Apostolic told the NBRC that his church had never wavered in its contention that the primary purpose of marriage was procreation. No "anticonceptual precautions or appliances of any sort" were permissible, and "onanism" or coitus interruptus, which Brown believed to be the most common method of restriction, was specifically condemned as a grave sin. He frankly admitted that the confessional gave the Catholic church a decided advantage in educating the faithful, and the denial of the sacraments to tormented souls was a potent weapon of enforcement.[70]

Much had been said about the Neo-Malthusians, Brown added, but he thought their influence was greatly exaggerated. People have always known how to avoid too many children, and they responded accordingly when the economic burdens became too great in the last quarter of the century, he believed. Only the faith of Catholics and the discipline of their church prevented their taking the same expedient route as the Protestants. The emergence of Neo-Malthusianism perhaps facilitated the process, but Brown was unconvinced that the Malthusian League had been very instrumental in persuading or teaching people what to do.[71]

Brown's implied criticism of Protestant religiosity and ecclesiastical discipline was particularly painful to those Anglican bishops who had prayed that the Lambeth resolutions would restore their credibility and authority in the area of connubial relations. Obviously they had not. The Bishop of London and his defenders had praised the Catholic church for refusing to waver in its condemnation of contraception as a sin, and he thought it incumbent upon the Church of England not to be content "with a lower standard." They envied the "power of religious faith and practice" in Catholic communities to stem the "tide of luxurious selfishness and social suicide."[72] Monsignor Brown assured his Anglican colleagues that his church did not really differ from them on the issue; it simply had a more effective means of implementing its rules. Like the Church of England, the Catholic church accepted the "safe period" since it did not interfere with conception and conformed to the desirable qualities of moderation and self-restraint that all Christians were admonished to inculcate.[73]

Although Neo-Malthusians seized upon this concession as evidence of inconsistency and equivocation they paid little attention to Catholic opposition before World War I. The Catholic church was acknowledged to be an implacable foe of family limitation, but compared to other religious groups its influence on public opinion seemed minimal. Convinced that economic realities and comparisons with the living conditions of their more enlightened neighbors would eventually propel Catholics into the restrictionist ranks, Neo-Malthusians were content to wait. Similarly, Catholic authorities largely ignored the Neo-Malthusian campaign. The continued high birthrate of the faithful probably assuaged any concerns Catholics might have had about the loss of fertility among other denominations. Shortly after the outbreak of the war, however, the *Malthusian* correctly predicted that the Catholic church would not be able to insulate itself from compelling demographic realities much longer. Unless the Catholic hierarchy came to grips with the issue fairly soon it would be confronted with a "pretty little internal quarrel."[74] Indeed when the expanded birth control movement of the 1920s began to impinge upon Catholic neighborhoods, the inherent antagonisms erupted for the first time into open conflict.

If, however, Catholics still appeared united in 1914, the Neo-Malthusians were certain that their other religious opponents were in a state of disarray, unable to mount an effective counteroffensive against the rapid spread of the "small family system." Religious barriers were crumbling everywhere, according to the *Malthusian*, and they could never be rebuilt. Catholicism was fast becoming the last holdout, but the power of its celibate leadership could only delay, not prevent, the inevitable outcome.[75]

As the postwar decade was to prove, the *Malthusian* was somewhat premature in its optimistic assessment. It was, however, more realistic about the difficulties the cause of birth control still faced in another vital quarter—the medical profession. Even more than the socialists and the Anglican hierarchy, the leaders of the medical fraternity were perceived by Neo-Malthusians before the war and birth control advocates after it, as their most formidable adversaries. Physicians not only shared many of the moral concerns of churchmen and the environmental assumptions of social reformers, but they were able to provide opponents of family limitation with physiological arguments about the effects of contraception that were not effectively refuted until the 1920s.

CHAPTER 6
Medicine and Malthusianism

The first Neo-Malthusians expected to be condemned by the clergy; they did not, however, anticipate prolonged resistance from the medical profession. Charles Knowlton and George Drysdale, whose writings formed the scientific core of the Malthusian League's propaganda, were both physicians. Charles R. Drysdale, the organization's first president, Johannes Swaagman, its treasurer, and Henry Allbutt, a member of the council, were all members of the medical fraternity. Although neither Charles Bradlaugh nor Annie Besant were trained in the caducean arts they were optimistic that doctors, out of a professional and compassionate interest in healing the afflictions of the poor, would logically be attracted to the Neo-Malthusian cause.

Little in the past history of the medical field warranted such confidence. Only a decade earlier, in 1868, when Viscount Amberley, at a meeting of the Dialectical Society, had agreed with Charles Drysdale about the benefits of family limitation and encouraged doctors to provide needed guidance, he was fiercely denounced by the medical press and his political opponents.[1] Medical spokesmen angrily denied that contraception was a medical problem worthy of their consideration. The artificial control of fertility was a form of self-help or folk medicine traditionally associated with quacks, midwives, and purveyors of rubber goods whose practices were beyond the interest of the medical profession.

Most conservative, middle-class Victorian doctors were content with this arrangement. Their practices were in any event oriented toward the treatment of disease rather than its prevention. If contraception was a medical problem requiring their skills, it was so only after the use of artificial methods or devices caused a pathological condition. The remedy seemed obvious, and physicians in the nineteenth century did not hesitate to prescribe it along with a strong dose of moral righteousness.

Despite the assertions of Bradlaugh and Besant in 1877 that Knowlton's contraceptive recommendations were reliable and safe and that respectable medical texts were far more explicit than anything in the condemned pamphlet, the medical press remained silent. It was perhaps unwilling to add to the extensive publicity given their sensational trial. More probable, medical authorities thought it a subject best ignored as there was little disposition within the profession to become embroiled in an inappropriate and rather salacious controversy. Their reticence was soon abandoned, however, when in August 1878, an eminent gynecologist, Charles Henry Felix Routh, flogged the newly established Malthusian League and urged his medical colleagues to join in driving "this many-headed monster from the realm."[2] It was the first salvo of a battle that was to last through the 1920s.

In a scalding address to the Obstetrical Section of the British Medical Association, Routh, senior physician to the Samaritan Hospital for Women and Children, reminded his colleagues of their obligations not only to the sick, but to healthy, trusting, virtuous women. Doctors could not remain silent when "our happy homes" were endangered by the promotion of "habits of immorality, which are so vile in their character, so dishonourable in their development, so degrading in their practice."[3]

Routh, like his son, Amand, a generation later, was one of the most antagonistic medical foes Neo-Malthusians faced. He was the articulate embodiment of the accumulated assumptions, prejudices, science, and pseudo-science that often characterized nineteenth-century medical knowledge about sexual physiology. "Conjugal onanism," as he described all forms of contraception, was not only a "great moral crime" equivalent to "trafficking with the devil," but it was the cause of a plethora of physiological and psychological horrors. Wives faced the prospect of contracting everything from metritis, leucorrhoea, menorrhagia, haematocele, hysteraligia, and hyperaesthesia of the genital organs to galloping cancer, ovarian dropsy, ovaritis, sterility, nymphomania, and a pronounced tendency to suicide. Male perpetrators of "sexual frauds" were warned to prepare for a life of nervous prostration, mental decay, loss of memory, intense cardiac palpitations, and, like their disintegrating mates, a mania for self-destruction.[4] Whereas neither sex had much to look forward to if they indulged in so toxic a perversity as family limitation, women, it was obvious, were susceptible to a far greater range of retributive maladies. As she was the guardian of chastity outside of marriage and the defender of the higher virtues within, it was, by Victorian standards, reasonable that a woman's afflictions should be commensurate with the seriousness of her failures.

If the new Malthusians succeeded with their "abominable" campaign, Routh warned, not only would the individual consequences be terrible, but the population as a whole would soon start to diminish and the vigorous English race would follow the infertile French down the road to decadence. The recent collapse of the demoralized Second Empire in 1870 and the savage Paris Commune that followed graphically demonstrated the effects of decades of sexual self-indulgence and "unholy debauches" that left France vulnerable to attack by the "sturdy [Prussian] sons of the North."[5]

This confusing of religious, moral, social, and political prejudices with doubtful physiology plagued medical discussions of family limitation well into the twentieth century. Although it embodied the deeply conservative and conventional values of the medical profession, it also reflected a prevalent ignorance of the sexual organic process that encumbered Victorian physicians and their medical successors until the interwar years. Those who presumably knew most about the subject, obstetricians and gynecologists, were among the most resistant to the countervailing evidence presented over the years by birth control advocates. As no scientific studies of contraception were undertaken in Great Britain until the 1920s, and the results were not formally introduced into the medical school curriculum until the 1930s, doctors who questioned the horrific prognoses of specialists like Routh were dependent upon their own personal observations and experience. Many felt that their background was inadequate, even after World War I, to challenge the testimony of the leaders of their profession.

In the absence of adequate scientific data at home, British physicians on both sides of the question frequently turned to continental authorities to support their opinions. Routh, for example, cited "several French writers" who confirmed his assessment. Drysdale countered with the testimony of two respected Parisian physicians who denied that contraception caused cancer, hysteria, or "any other disease worth mentioning."[6] The imprecision of the debate and the lack of evidence often resulted in arguments about morality rather than medicine. Though the subjects of chastity, fidelity, and Christian responsibility repeatedly intruded into medical denunciations of Neo-Malthusianism, most doctors in the late Victorian period shared the conviction that most contraceptive methods were physiologically harmful.

In 1880 the Malthusian League established a medical branch, which it hoped would become a repository of scientific information related to sexual physiology and would in time win the confidence of the medical profession.[7] C. R. Drysdale assumed the presidency of the group whose members included physicians from Holland, Spain, France, Greece, Italy, and India, but very few from Great Britain. Their meetings were scheduled to coincide with international medical congresses, but at home the branch remained a paper organization nurtured along by Drysdale for propaganda purposes until the end of the century. When he finally abandoned the project, he conceded that it had failed to find a following in British medical circles, which had proven far more difficult to penetrate than he had imagined.

Within a few months of the end of the Bradlaugh-Besant proceedings Drysdale introduced the question of higher fertility and excessive mortality to a section of the British Medical Association meetings. In subsequent years he read papers in Amsterdam, Turin, Copenhagen, Berlin, and Washington, D.C., as well as in various cities in the United Kingdom. On occasions he was joined by Swaagman or Allbutt, but he usually carried the Neo-Malthusian message alone, sustained by the small fraternity of physicians from other countries who shared his views. None of Drysdale's presentations dealt with the physiology of contraception. They invariably explored the relationship of overpopulation to poverty, disease, infant mortality, or shortened life expectancy—appropriate subjects of obvious concern to conscientious doctors.

Most physicians believed these problems could be alleviated by improved diet, sanitation, better housing, and more medical care; they were not overly sympathetic to Drysdale's repeated argument that these recommendations, like charity, only dealt with symptoms rather than causes. Those doctors who agreed usually denied Drysdale's explanation, however, and insisted that excessive fertility was not a cause of poverty and ill-health, but was, like drunkenness, a symptom of the dissolute character of the lower orders.[8] Responding to one of Drysdale's papers in 1879, Routh described the English working classes as "more despicable" than those in any other country. They never paid their bills, habitually wasted their salaries on food and drink, and deprived their families of needed nourishment. The "accursed" trade unions were to Routh only second to public houses in luring improvident workers from their responsibilities. He reminded his medical colleagues that there were no "slothful strikes" among the upper classes, many of whom, like doctors, worked fifteen hours a day.[9] This tendency to assume that the proliferation of children among the poor was a consequence of low status, or a manifestation of a fundamental character defect that explained much of their reckless behavior, caused the Neo-Malthusians no end of controversy.

Drysdale found that comparatively few of his medical colleagues had any quarrel with his individualistic economic philosophy or with classical Malthusianism. Yet when it led him to advocate artificial checks on overpopulation, his suggestions were met with silence or fierce disagreement. By the mid-1880s the few Neo-Malthusian physicians complained that doctors were increasingly blaming a rise in "some of the severest and most obstinate forms of diseases peculiar to women" on the greater use of contraceptive practices. An angry Drysdale pointed out that obstetricians were particularly prone to such "childish dogmata" despite the obvious evidence that millions of healthy French peasants had for decades been limiting their families to two children without a noticeable increase in female maladies.[10] Moreover, as the *Malthusian* had reported earlier, the wives of French and Dutch physicians rarely bore more than two or three offspring, which was substantially below the 4.82 recorded for their English counterparts in 1874. Yet there was no proof that the spouses of continental doctors were suffering any more ill effects than their more fertile English sisters.[11]

Any lingering doubts about the official attitude of the medical profession were eliminated in 1887 when Allbutt's name was struck from the rolls of the General Medical Council, the Royal College of Physicians of Edinburgh, and the London Society of Apothecaries for publishing *The Wife's Handbook*. Their action was an unspoken, if confused, warning to the medical fraternity at large. Allbutt's approval of condoms, quinine solutions, and a number of pessaries was apparently less offensive to his prosecutors than the illustrations, advertisements, and suppliers addresses he included in the first edition.[12] These transgressions, which were quickly removed in subsequent editions, and its six-penny price, prompted the General Medical Council to condemn the "objectionable popular character of the book, its accessibility to unmarried women, and its tendency to demoralise the world."[13] That global potential was at the time rather minimal, for in spite of the council's claim that the work had been purchased extensively, a Leeds bookseller testified that he had only sold about thirty copies before the medical authorities struck.[14] As a result of the publicity stirred up by the case, much of it organized by the Malthusian League, *The Wife's Handbook*, like Knowlton's *Fruits of Philosophy*, quickly became a *succès de scandale*, passing through fifty editions and 500,000 copies by 1927.[15]

The Allbutt case was nevertheless a serious setback to Neo-Malthusian recruitment of medical allies. Not only was the name of one of the league's few physicians stricken from the professional registers, but the decision was upheld in the Court of Queen's Bench and the Court of Appeals. After a decade of trying to prove its respectability, the league was again closely linked to the prurient and salacious. How much the Allbutt prosecution affected its imperceptible inroads into medical circles is difficult to determine because commentary in the medical press was very sparse. Some physicians sympathetic to Neo-Malthusianism were probably intimidated, as league apologists rationalized, but there is no evidence to suggest that their numbers were very large.

After the Allbutt controversy, however, Drysdale found it increasingly difficult to present the Neo-Malthusian case at professional gatherings in Great Britain. In 1893 he arrived at the British Medical Association meetings in Newcastle only to discover that a paper he intended to read on high birthrates and premature mortality had been rejected by the council of that organization. His angry denunciations of "anti-Malthusian bigots" controlling his profession fell upon deaf ears, and, throughout the 1890s, medical lines if anything hardened.[16] The league's opponents drew more heavily than ever on the expert testimony of physicians, including such famous female doctors as Elizabeth Blackwell, to denounce the moral and physiological dangers of repudiated parentage.[17] Bertrand Russell recalled that his family physician had solemnly assured him in 1894 that "he knew the use of contraceptives to be almost invariably gravely injurious to health." It was hinted that contraceptives had made Russell's father, Viscount Amberley, epileptic, and, when his young heir announced his intention to marry but have no children, it produced "a thick atmosphere of sighs, tears, groans and morbid horror . . . in which it was scarcely possible to breathe."[18]

By 1901 the authoritative organ of the British Medical Association, the *British Medical Journal* confidently asserted that the "medical profession as a whole has set its face against such practices which are unnatural and degrading in their mental effect, and oft times injurious to both husband and wife in their physical results." It allowed that a small number of medical men held and taught other views, but their numbers were not significant. According to the journal's editor, the chief cause for the spread of the evil in recent years was the proliferation of cheap pamphlets and advertisements in weekly and other newspapers, "which under a very thin disguise offer facilities for procuring abortion or preventing conception."[19]

The confusion of contraception with abortion was a source of endless vexation for Neo-Malthusians. From its earliest days the Malthusian League struggled to keep the two separate in the public's mind, condemning abortion as illegal, dangerous, and unnecessary. It was particularly frustrating when physicians, who should have known better, contributed to the confusion by failing to make any distinction between abortifacients and contraceptives. Virtually any doctor who treated poor patients was familiar with the ravages of abortion in the late nineteenth century, but it was obvious that many of them were unclear about its relationship to contraception. During an 1879 meeting of the London Medical Society Drysdale had to explain that the high risk "operations" one of his colleagues described as a principal cause of maternal mortality were not the same as the prevention of conception. The perplexed physician was unable to see any difference since the goal, the deliberate thwarting of nature, was the same.[20]

A generation later Neo-Malthusians were still trying to keep the issue of abortion and birth control separate. C. V. Drysdale in 1913 complained of recent medical society resolutions urging the passage of legislation that would forbid the advertising and sale of all antenatal products whether for use before or after conception. The younger Drysdale, unlike his father, had little respect for the medical profession whose curative pretensions he found inflated and stubborn opposition unforgivable. Abortion is a consequence of the failure of prevention, he lectured them; one is criminal, the other is not. The failure of doctors to learn the difference after thirty-five years of Neo-Malthusian education suggested an obtuseness and perversity equaled only by the Anglican clergy.[21]

If the confusion of contraception and abortion remained so entrenched in an allegedly learned and scientific profession, it was not surprising to Neo-Malthusians that the National Council of Public Morals would be any less indiscriminate. They were outraged by an NCPM wartime film, "Where Are My Children?" in which abortion and birth control were condemned as the cause of the perilous falling birthrate. This first attempt to use the cinema as propaganda in the prolonged debate over the population question was embellished by an admonition from the 1908 Lambeth Conference resolutions warning of the sins of abortion and contraception. Malthusian League critics protested that the film "leads the ignorant poor, who flock to see it, to believe that rich women limit their families by the illegal and injurious abortion method," rather than, as was the case, by safe preventive methods. The perpetuation of such myths was, they charged, the result of years of medical and religious ignorance now combined in the unfortunate production.[22]

In its unwavering opposition to abortion, no matter how desperate a woman's plight, the Malthusian League promised that the termination of pregnancy would, like prostitution, become unnecessary and rare if the campaign for birth control succeeded. Consequently, despite some pressure from a few militant feminists during the war to countenance abortion, the league insisted that it would be folly to waste energy and resources championing an imperfect remedy, which would only seem to validate the malicious charges the organization had refuted for decades.[23]

Long-standing medical objections to Neo-Malthusianism took on an added dimension in the opening years of the new century as doctors became more aware of recent fertility trends. The British Medical Association raised the issue for the first time at its annual meetings in 1901 when Dr. J. W. Byer, president of the Obstetrics and Gynaecological Section, alluded briefly to the declining birthrate and recommended that maternal and infant care be intensified to keep further population losses to a minimum.[24] Thereafter the medical press began regularly to summarize and comment upon the registrar-general's periodic reports. Physicians attributed the loss in fertility to everything from a general atrophy of maternal capability to "hypernutrition," or overeating. Many of their colleagues shared the common belief that smaller families were a consequence of biological evolution or merely a cyclical variation in germinal activity. Still others, fearful of racial decadence and diminished destiny, complained of the sterilizing effects of urbanization compounded by the rapid diminution of healthy, reinvigorating rural stock. It took the debacle of the Boer War to reveal how deep the rot had already penetrated.[25]

A session of the 1910 British Medical Association meetings was specifically devoted to the social aspects of the falling birthrate. The doctors who attended thrashed about for acceptable diagnoses and possible cures. Prognoses were as varied as etiologies, but most of the participants were guarded in their assessment and uncertain about their prescriptions.[26] They recognized that the falling birthrate had less to do with some complex alteration in fecundity than it did with a European, even worldwide change in values. Dr. J. W. Taylor had cautiously noted in his 1904 presidential address to the British Gynaecological Association that fertility in continental countries and the settlement colonies was also on the decline. The main reason, as gynecologists knew, was the rapid adoption of preventive practices during the preceding thirty-five years. Despite the claims of optimists, as far as England was concerned, there was no evidence that the quality of life had improved, Taylor claimed. On the contrary, crime, lunacy, and alcoholism were on the rise, and as Karl Pearson had recently shown in his Huxley Lecture, education had failed to raise the qualitative level of the English race.[27]

Taylor was particularly upset by the enormous wastage of health-giving semen associated with artificial prevention. Sharing a popular medical belief that the male ejaculate was an important source of racial strength and vitality for women, Taylor was convinced that the wanton disregard of its beneficial properties had proven detrimental to both sexes. Men, of course, were plagued by the well-known enervating maladies long attributed to "self-abuse," but women perhaps suffered even more from being denied the salubrious absorption of male secretions. Moreover, their ovaries, which required the nine months of rest pregnancy alone provided, had been overstimulated with consequences still unknown. As an experienced gynecologist Taylor held that mothers of large families were invariably healthier than their less fertile counterparts and that all methods of prevention were harmful to some extent. The much-maligned French were again summoned forth to exhibit the stigmata of race degeneration associated with their restrictive habits. Taylor could not help but wonder if the recent orgy of anti-Semitism stimulated by the Dreyfus affair was somehow linked to the lower, animal instincts released by the prolonged use of contraceptive practices.[28]

In contrast to many of his contemporaries, Taylor was less troubled by patterns of differential fertility than he was by the decline of the birthrate. He recognized that it was most pronounced among the "well-to-do and middle classes," but the race suicide it portended threatened every level of society. All of the great gains in medicine and the extraordinary improvements in the human condition were in danger of being swept away "by the vicious and unnatural habits of the present generation." Reverting to a familiar anti-Malthusian argument, Taylor paraded a list of great men from Shakespeare and Lord Nelson to Wesley and the Duke of Wellington, who never would have been born if their parents had limited their family to only one or two children. How many men of similar contribution were first or second sons, he wondered, "in view of the present limitation of children and the noted absence of men of surpassing genius." It seemed obvious to Taylor, as one of the most vociferous medical enemies of birth control in the early Edwardian period, "that our mischievous meddling with great natural forces is very much like little children playing with edge tools or with fire."[29]

Much of the medical criticism of the declining birthrate in the prewar years cited Arthur Newsholme and T. H. C. Stevenson's findings that the smaller family was not a consequence of poverty, urban growth, or the tensions of modern life, but of increased education, declining religious authority, and the desire on the part of the more prudent classes to maintain a rising standard of comfort. People were, in other words, deliberately flaunting nature and putting the race in peril, however, innocent their motives. The *Lancet* made this point repeatedly, adding a pronounced eugenic dimension to its criticism of family limitation. It complained in 1907 that the curtailment of the once-large, middle-class family, the backbone of Victorian England, had seriously depleted the nation's reservoir of moral and intellectual talent. At the same time by repeatedly "stimulating a natural function into activity and . . . preventing its physiological purpose from being attained," the health and vitality of this valued, if diminishing, class, had been weakened, allowing "increased room for a growth of tares by which the harvest of a better humanity would be choked."[30]

Doctors, as their critics reminded them, were drawn primarily from the allegedly waning middle class, and they had fewer children than most other professions in that social category. At the time of Charles Ansell's actuarial formulations of 1874 the 4.82 children recorded for medical families was on the average less than the number attributed to clergymen, lawyers, landed aristocrats, merchants, bankers, or manufacturers. In subsequent years that figure steadily decreased though neither physicians nor their wives deteriorated into the pitiful, disease-wracked, mental degenerates depicted by their more excitable anti-Malthusian colleagues. C. V. Drysdale frequently referred to actuarial statistics as evidence of the kind of hypocrisy with which the Malthusian League had to contend. As with the Anglican clergy, the doctors' own connubial strategy mocked their professional advice. Drysdale was positive that the 1911 *Fertility of Marriage Census* would once and for all reveal how extensively family limitation had been adopted since the Knowlton trial by the very same groups who so bitterly condemned Neo-Malthusianism.[31]

He was correct. The census compilations showed that the marriages of medical practitioners were, like those of churchmen, among the least fertile, averaging slightly less than 2.1 children in contrast to 3.5 for the population at large and 2.5 for couples in the other professions. The gap had started to narrow in younger marriages of incomplete fertility, but doctors' wives in that category had still only given birth to 1.7 offspring compared with the national average of 2.8.[32] Despite the much-publicized pronouncements of leading medical authorities on the physical and mental consequences of prevention, a great many doctors obviously knew from their own experience that some methods of restriction were clearly harmless. Whether out of a sense of propriety, deference, uncertainty, or, as critics charged, class hypocrisy, they were reluctant to challenge the questionable diagnoses of their colleagues.

Even the staid *BMJ*, certainly no friend of birth control, recognized by 1910 that there was nevertheless considerable disagreement and confusion in doctors' minds about the causes and implications of the declining birthrate. These had surfaced at the annual meeting of that year, leading the journal to recommend that its members avoid attacks on the falling birthrate for medical reasons, in the absence of conclusive scientific proof. Such caution did not imply the countenancing of any contraceptive practices, the journal emphasized, but it thought that physicians would be on firmer professional ground if they concentrated upon lowering infant mortality, studying heredity, and providing better maternal and pediatric care to moderate the qualitative and quantitative losses to the population. This would sometimes require advising women on the spacing of pregnancies, it conceded, but to deny their patients such information doctors would leave them prey to quacks and Malthusian propagandists.[33]

Throughout much of the decade the *BMJ* had been extremely reticent in discussing the population question and had left the field to its more popular rival, the *Lancet*. But the questioning of traditional assumptions about birth control at the 1910 meeting and its failure to reaffirm the harmful medical effects of contraception provoked the journal's call for caution and restraint.[34] Neo-Malthusians interpreted such wariness as a turning point. The proliferation of medical dogma that flew in the face of observed experience and practice caused a substantial number of doctors at least to suspend judgment. It made little difference, of course, Drysdale added, since the latest fertility statistics clearly showed that the general public would make up its own mind with or without the blessing of its spiritual and medical advisers.[35]

Neo-Malthusians were further buoyed by the election in 1912 of the prominent Liverpool surgeon, Sir James Barr, to the presidency of the British Medical Association. Though scarcely a supporter of the Malthusian League, Barr was a vice-president of the Eugenics Education Society and a strong proponent of negative eugenics to stop the proliferation of the unfit. The encouragement of family limitation among the diseased, the incompetent, and the chronic poor was an obvious means of achieving this end, and Barr was not averse to including it among the methods of rational selection available to a civilized society. Like most eugenists, of course, he preferred to foster "race-betterment" in accordance with Galton's positive promotion of early marriage and extensive reproduction among the hereditarily more promising sectors of the populace. At the same time, however, Barr feared that the procreant habits of the laboring masses would, unless brought under control, continue to overwhelm the number of eugenically desirable children.[36]

At least two Malthusian League officials, C. V. Drysdale and Binnie Dunlop, joined the Eugenics Education Society in hopes of converting the membership to this point of view.[37] Few eugenists before the war, however, would contemplate any alliance with a movement that was still considered very unsavory in professional, middle-class circles. But they were also persuaded by Galton, Pearson, and the president of the society from 1911 to 1927, Major Leonard Darwin, that Neo-Malthusianism was actually a threat to eugenics because, as the differential birthrate revealed, it was the better-educated, responsible classes who limited their families, not their recklessly fertile inferiors. Drysdale suspected, with some justification, that a minority of Eugenics Education Society members, led by Caleb Saleeby and Darwin's predecessor, Montague Crackanthorpe, recognized the need for both negative and positive eugenic policies to achieve a racially beneficial balance in the population. Barr, he believed, was of a similar mind when, in his presidential address to the British Medical Association, he spoke of the need for deliberate and rational selection in procreation to improve the health and quality of the next generation.[38]

Physicians played a prominent role in the founding of the Eugenics Education Society in 1907 and before the war comprised one-quarter of its one hundred officers and council members.[39] Their articles were prominently featured in the *Eugenics Review*, and an increasing number of discussions of the population question in the medical press dwelt upon the racial implications of differential fertility. The British Medical Association meetings in 1913 introduced a new session devoted to "Medical Sociology" at which the subject of family limitation was raised in connection with a paper entitled "Eugenics from the Physicians' Standpoint." Binnie Dunlop was astonished when no one at that session protested the recommendation that doctors provide contraceptive advice as a means of preventing the continued proliferation of the unfit.[40]

Neo-Malthusian satisfaction was short-lived, however, for much to Drysdale's disgust he was unable to persuade the International Medical Congress held in London the same year to take up the issue. Some comfort was found in the report of the Hungarian delegation that a study of restrictive practices in its country found no evidence that they led to sexual disorders, sterility, or defective children. The silence of most medical authorities, however, convinced Drysdale that though doctors' attitudes were changing, they were still embarrassed and reluctant to admit their past mistakes. He confided that a prominent English physician nevertheless assured him that the Neo-Malthusian cause had been won and it was only a matter of time before it would receive active medical cooperation.[41]

While Drysdale chided doctors for their timidity and prodded them with reminders of their own low fertility, Dunlop, one of the few physicians in the Malthusian League, tried to understand their reticence. He told his colleagues at the 1913 British Medical Association meetings that, although many of his league associates were extremely critical of medical resistance to family limitation, he understood that doctors could not really run too far ahead of public opinion.[42] They had to be cautious in recommending procedures about which there was considerable medical dispute and which were long considered offensive to good taste. Less conciliatory birth control advocates insisted that the problem was not that doctors were ahead of public opinion but that they were behind it.

At the annual meeting of the Malthusian League that year it was decided to try once again to persuade physicians to take responsibility for the contraceptive needs of their patients instead of merely complaining about the quacks and chemists who did. For the first time the organization proposed that preventive advice should be provided not only by private physicians but by public health authorities as well—an objective that was to unify the diverse, often warring factions of the birth control movement in the 1920s. The medical profession in general, and hospital and public health personnel in particular, were urged to give "instruction in hygienic contraceptive methods to all married people who desire to limit their families, or who are in any way unfit for parenthood."[43]

This resolution and the accompanying decision to publish and distribute a practical pamphlet, *Hygienic Methods of Family Limitation*, under the league's official auspices were predicated upon the belief that the times had changed sufficiently to anticipate medical cooperation. Drysdale told the National Birth-Rate Commission a few months later that the pamphlet had induced several physicians to join the league while even more had written of their approval. The numbers were still paltry, he admitted, but then British doctors were a notoriously conservative lot when compared with their Dutch colleagues who had, with the government's blessings, openly supported a Malthusian League in that country for more than thirty years. More recently, Drysdale told the commissioners, the American Society of Medical Sociology had affiliated with the International Federation of Malthusian Leagues, an example he expected to be followed in time by British medical groups.[44]

He was fated to remain frustrated. No medical organization ever lent its support to the league. If resistance was clearly starting to crumble before the war, it was, as the NBRC learned, still deeply entrenched and formidable. Dr. Amand Routh, consulting obstetrician to Charing Cross Hospital, was as certain as his father had been a generation before that "prevention of maternity . . . invariably produces physical, mental, and . . . moral harm to those who resort to it." Some preventive methods were more dangerous than others, he assured the commissioners, but all injured the pelvic organs and enlarged the womb with the result that "later on, when parents are perhaps better off and want a child, they are not able to have one." Routh knew from his own flourishing practice that young couples, in contrast to their parents, now married with the intention of delaying childbirth or widely spacing their offspring, only to discover that they had destroyed their chances forever.[45]

Infertility was a complex, if common problem for doctors, who actually knew very little about it. In light of widespread medical suspicions about family limitation it is not surprising that an increasing number of obstetricians and gynecologists such as Routh would see a logical connection between early contraception and later sterility. Fertility statistics not only revealed the decline in family size but verified a substantial rise in the number of childless marriages. More people were clearly having fewer children, but more were also having none at all. That the one trend might be as deliberate as the other was incomprehensible to a society that assumed that all married couples would want at least one child. Indeed physicians' files were filled with accounts of unhappy patients seeking ways to have additional children, or even a first. Though there is no evidence that doctors made any effort to correlate restrictive practices and infertility, many of them, like Routh, assumed it as an obvious consequence of the changing sexual customs of the age.

Routh, one of the more eminent specialists in his profession, admitted under close questioning by Dean Inge that his views were not universally shared in other medical specialties. He was confident, however, that most of the authorities in his field agreed that, with the exception perhaps of the condom, all contraceptive devices were dangerous. Even the use of condoms, of course, deprived the wife of the "stimulating effect of the semen," whose powerful and nourishing qualities were not the least in doubt, even if the physiological process of absorption was not yet understood. Routh's testimony was an epitome of contemporary misconception carried over from the nineteenth century. Total abstinence was not particularly harmful, depending upon a person's "sexual instinct," but unless the "sexual cravings" of a pregnant woman were satisfied her child would be cursed with a "very strong sexual tendency." The only acceptable way to avoid pregnancy, he told the NBRC, was the safe period. Since, as he mistakenly believed, most women conceived immediately before or after menstruation, a little self-restraint at those times would not prove detrimental to health. Routh, however, was even uncomfortable with this concession and preferred total abstinence.[46]

If some of the doctors who appeared before the commission, or sat as members, were less certain than Routh of the physiological consequences of family limitation, nearly all of them agreed that it was, however deplorable, a conscious response to changing economic conditions and expectations. They shared a common concern about the decay of Christian values and its likely effects on the imperial race. One of the commissioners, Dr. Mary Scharlieb, a gynecologist at the London School of Medicine for Women, and later its president, prescribed a "bath of physiological righteousness" for the nation. A former midwife and the first woman medical graduate from the University of London, she endorsed Routh's testimony and castigated her countrymen for their selfish neglect of duty to the race.[47] Whether her own three children sufficed to exonerate her was unclear, but Dr. Scharlieb, like Routh, remained a powerful adversary of birth control well into the 1920s.

Though adamant in their opinions, both physicians realized even before the war that they were no longer as representative of their profession as they had once been. As another witness explained to the commission, a new generation of doctors, more sensitive to the problems of maternal health and the advantages of preventive medicine, were willing to terminate dangerous pregnancies and explain to their patients how to space the arrival of children. He personally believed that a year between pregnancies was probably sufficient for most women, but conceded that his younger colleagues frequently disagreed. Further study was obviously needed to reconcile the differences, he told the commission.[48]

Many of the commissioners were as confused as the testimony they elicited. Dr. Major Greenwood, a young epidemiologist and statistician at the Lister Institute, confessed during Routh's appearance that medical opinions were so much at variance that it was perhaps impossible to draw any valid conclusion. One of the main difficulties was that meaningful statistical evidence was unobtainable because doctors rarely kept adequate records about the sexual practices of their patients.[49] No efforts were made to do so until several years after World War I. In the absence of anything more substantial than the contradictory personal experiences and impressions of differing physicians, the NBRC would have been hard put to condemn the safety and reliability of all contraceptives.

Drysdale stressed this point during his appearance, insisting that there was so much prejudice and so little data within the medical community about the effects of limitation that it was impossible to speak of a medical position. At the same time he admitted that there was also no conclusive scientific evidence to prove that contraceptives were reliable and harmless. Drysdale was less disturbed by the absence of data than some of his more cautious supporters because it in no way disproved the social and economic arguments that gave rise to classical and Neo-Malthusianism in the first place.[50]

Drysdale's testimony accentuated a fundamental difference in philosophy between the medical profession and the Neo-Malthusians that repeatedly brought them into conflict. Doctors were essentially environmentalists who believed that the care they gave their patients, coupled with general improvements in sanitation, diet, and the administration of public health, had contributed substantially to the higher life expectancy and declining death rate recorded in recent decades. The physicians on the NBRC were not amused when Drysdale informed them that the collective efforts of their profession over the past forty years had made no significant impact on mortality. Only the decline in the birthrate, promoted in spite of medical objections, had brought down the death rate, he claimed, by greatly reducing infant and maternal deaths. No new medical skills nor hygienic advances could account for so dramatic a fall, Drysdale insisted.[51]

Neo-Malthusians had been making the same point since 1880 when Allbutt noted that twenty years of improving urban sanitation had scarcely altered the high death rates of the towns. As long as the fertility and the excessive infant mortality of the poor remained disproportionately high, any improvements in public health would be neutralized, he explained.[52] When a few years later the *Lancet*, commenting on a noticeable decline in the death rate, attributed it to the medically prescribed extension of drainage and sanitation, the *Malthusian* recalled that, although the public health movement dated from the 1840s, the frequency of mortality had changed little until the birthrate began to fall in the 1870s.[53] If fertility continued to decline, it predicted, mortality would do the same, irrespective of medical accomplishments, and for the next four decades the *Malthusian* claimed vindication with each quarterly or annual report from the registrar-general.

C. V. Drysdale had even less confidence in medical claims and environmental solutions than the first Neo-Malthusians. He was particularly vexed by doctors taking credit for the impressive decline in infant mortality experienced in the decade before the war. He told the incredulous commissioners that the fall in fertility was solely responsible for the improvement. Recent strides in public health and the control of childhood disease had no effect whatsoever, Drysdale asserted. "So rigidly do I conclude it," he added, "that I do not believe sanitation or medicine or any of these great advances have as yet . . . saved a life at all."[54]

Drysdale had on earlier occasions been slightly more conciliatory, acknowledging that doctors had perhaps helped to reduce infant mortality, but were only successful when their efforts were accompanied by family limitation. Unless the birthrate was restrained the "whole power of medical science" was utterly incapable of halting an increase in the death rate. He cited Toronto, Canada, as an example of a city whose birthrate, after falling for many years, had sharply increased in 1909, resulting in a surge of mortality that exceed the rate for the period 1880–85. To Drysdale these facts showed that the "whole medical profession is practically incompetent . . . to allay suffering and to prolong life . . . unless helped by family restriction."[55] Angered that physicians took credit for improvements that actually resulted from practices they had repeatedly denounced, Drysdale mockingly concluded that if doctors were able to perform the wonders they claimed, then they certainly could cure the multiple diseases allegedly contracted from the use of contraception.[56]

His analysis was not calculated to recommend Drysdale or his cause to the medical profession, but then Neo-Malthusians had been battling doctors for nearly forty years and, on several occasions, suspected them of being far worse than merely ineffective. Medical resistance to family limitation had since the 1880s raised questions about motives. C. R. Drysdale was one of several critics who noted that gynecologists and obstetricians, who obviously had a pecuniary interest in the proliferation of children, were the most rabid enemies of restriction.[57] During the Allbutt prosecution the General Medical Council was denounced repeatedly for trying to preserve a lucrative monopoly on the dissemination of healthful literature. It was sometimes suggested that medical ethics had become captive to the pursuit of wealth and social respectability so that many physicians who were known to have "sound private judgement on the matter" refused to speak out. Were they perhaps apprehensive, the *Malthusian* asked in

1892, that our success "will lessen the number of remunerative and disastrous *accouchements*, and accelerate the production of stronger children with native resistance to the infantile diseases that kill off the ill-begotten?"[58] These suspicions were reinforced by occasional articles in the medical press discussing the economic implications of the declining birthrate for doctors. Physicians' complaints about a possible decline in patients prompted one paper, *John Bull*, to ask in 1910, "Is There a Medical Conspiracy?" If, as doctors claimed, the fall in fertility threatened to reduce the need for their services, would it not seem to disprove their allegations that family limitation was harmful?[59]

Although it was not a prominent theme in Malthusian League propaganda, the question of medical ethics was always just below the surface ready to be asked during periods of frustrating conflict. Certainly some doctors were concerned about the effect a smaller population would have on their practices, but it was unlikely that many of them profited from delivering and caring for the children of the poor whose numbers the Neo-Malthusians hoped to reduce. On the contrary, that task was left primarily to midwives and the friends and relatives of the family. The diminished fertility of fee-paying, middle-class patients was logically of more direct concern, a distinction that Neo-Malthusian critics failed to develop. Despite some anxieties within the profession, there is no evidence that physicians suffered a dearth of patients. More often than not their worries about family limitation reflected genuine confusion and doubt about the propriety and effects of contraception rather than selfish cynicism, as angry Neo-Malthusians charged.

Obviously many doctors practiced contraception in their own marriages and quietly provided guidance for some of their patients while carefully avoiding any public controversy. Many others genuinely abhorred and feared birth control on moral and medical grounds, and, reinforced by the values of the age, did not hesitate to speak out. As their testimony before the NBRC clearly revealed, physicians were as bewildered as nonscientists about the reliability and safety of various preventive practices and "Malthusian appliances." It became apparent that doctors were dependent for their judgment upon their own professional and personal experience or beliefs and whatever other information they picked up haphazardly during their medical training or from other practitioners. Binnie Dunlop, who professed expertise on the subject, was astonished when it was discovered during the war that the majority of soldiers' wives who became pregnant did so within twenty-one days of the onset of their menstrual period. The findings seemed to disprove the long-held assumption that the "safe period" came in the middle of the monthly cycle and that maximum fecundity peaked just before menstruation in harmony with female passion. It had always seemed logical, he wrote to a friend, that, in accordance with natural selection, the "period of desire in women should be the likeliest time for conception," and as this occurred at the beginning of the cycle the risk of pregnancy should have been greatest at that time.[60]

Many doctors were even more puzzled than Dunlop, and they increasingly admitted before the war that their information was inadequate and unreliable. As a result they were reluctant to recommend contraceptive methods that might in time prove more harmful than helpful to their patients. Conflicting evidence, which, even in this current age of elaborate scientific testing, still surrounds the use of various contraceptives, remained a major stumbling block to the medical sanctioning of birth control until well after World War I. Neo-Malthusians grudgingly admitted the problem, but they insisted that the nation's experience since 1877 had sufficiently disproved most of the myths about artificial limitation to justify medical support for their cause. When it was not forthcoming, they suspected that other considerations were involved that had nothing to do with scientific reliability or the welfare of patients. This seemed especially evident in the support the Church of England received in its campaign against birth control from important medical authorities.

When in 1905 Bishop Winnington-Ingram of London delivered his first public indictment of the falling birthrate, he was praised by the *Lancet* for raising the delicate, if important issue and applauded for his vigorous denunciation of "filthy advertisements."[61] In both his 1905 and 1911 *Charge* the bishop emphasized that his condemnation was based upon spiritual and temporal considerations, citing the authoritative medical testimony of Dr. J. W. Taylor along with that of Scripture. Similarly, the Lambeth Conference resolutions of 1908 owed much to Taylor and other physicians who were extolled by the bishops for having "borne courageous testimony against the injurious practices spoken of."[62] An appendix to the resolutions cited British, French, and American medical authorities on the "sudden danger and chronic disease" inherent in artificial restriction. The conference report equated the symptoms with those attributed to "self-abuse" and warned of the psychological aberrations of sexual perversion revealed by Freud, Krafft-Ebing, Havelock Ellis, and others.[63]

The church-medical alliance was further cemented by the outspoken religious arguments against contraception that supplemented the professional judgment of many prominent physicians. Taylor and Routh, for example, contended that in violating nature and Holy Scripture restrictive practices injured the body and the soul. In his testimony before the NBRC Routh never doubted that God would provide for His progeny, however numerous, and insisted that the only form of limitation that conformed to both human physiology and the Bible was complete abstinence for a time by mutual consent.[64] Though Dr. Scharlieb, herself an ardent church-woman, endorsed these sentiments several of her fellow commissioners were by no means certain that they represented accurate theology or sound medicine.

A number of doctors and clergymen were troubled by the reciprocal endorsements that frequently accompanied criticism of family limitation before the war. Sir James Barr, in his presidential address to the British Medical Association in 1912, recognized that his eugenical support for rational selection would conflict with the church's preoccupation with an unrestricted birthrate. He thought, however, that a higher "racial morality" dictated that physicians take a special interest in the prevention of dysgenic breeding.[65] The *Malthusian* interpreted Barr's speech as an important break in the church-medical alliance, and it predicted that others would now be encouraged to speak out.[66] One of the first to do so was Charles Killick Millard, medical officer of health for Leicester, who bluntly challenged the selective use of medical opinion by the Lambeth Conference when doctors, despite their reticence, were far from agreement on the effects of contraception.

Millard, a devout churchman and the son of an Anglican vicar, wrote to the *Manchester Guardian* that he and many of his colleagues knew perfectly well that restrictive practices were regularly employed by the "ablest and most intelligent" sector of the population in all classes with no ill effects whatsoever. Although the Bishop of London regarded such prudence as immoral and deplored the "breach between the Church and the People, . . . it is scarcely to be expected that intelligent persons will feel drawn to a Church which denounces them as guilty of 'immorality' for doing what their own conscience and better judgement approve." To talk about morality without considering motivation was, in Millard's opinion, as theologically dubious as the sweeping pronouncements of some physicians against birth control were medically doubtful. Moreover, he thought it cruel for members of his profession to endorse clerical injunctions to the poor about self-control when they knew perfectly well that as a form of prevention it was ineffective and unreliable. Contrary to ecclesiastical and much medical logic, artificial means involved considerable self-control and the denial of immediate gratification, which was "one chief reason they [were] not resorted to by the more reckless, selfish, and depraved sections of the community."[67]

The outspoken Millard, whose fearless energy led him to take up flying at the age of sixty-three and motorcycling at eighty, rapidly emerged as one of the most vocal of a medical minority advocating birth control before the war. He joined the Malthusian League in 1914 and became a vice-president of the organization. Like many people who now entered the ranks he was not drawn to the league by its crusty economic and social philosophy but by its lone advocacy of practices he had believed for some time to be beneficial and inevitable. Millard was one of several physicians whose experience treating the poor persuaded them that it was imperative that the improvident lower classes learn what their more responsible and better-educated superiors already knew.

As another Leicester doctor, C. J. Bond, told a clerical audience in 1914, "we are confronted with this anomalous state of things, that the educated and thrifty portion of mankind is pursuing a line of conduct which the Church condemns; while the uneducated, the thriftless, and the feebler citizens are in this particular matter acting with the Church's approval." Bond, a successful surgeon, a respected Anglican layman, and a member of the Eugenics Education Society, warned a Ruri-Decanel Conference considering the bishops' recent memorandum, "The Misuse of Marriage," that the church faced a serious dilemma. In seeming to encourage the dangerous imbalances in class fertility that already threatened the future composition of the race, the Church raised serious questions about its judgment. Along with most critics of the bishops' position, Bond believed that the strong carnal appetites of the poor, reinforced by ignorance and overcrowding, precluded abstinence as a viable check on excessive reproduction. Although he ardently wished that the more successful classes would have more children and he condemned restriction for purely material reasons, he too believed that the church would do well to examine the purity of people's motives before issuing sweeping denunciations of their behavior. Ecclesiastical authorities might consider adding the words, "and in so far as human responsibility extends—'healthy'—before the word *children* in the passage in the Prayer Book which sets forth the reasons for which the state of matrimony was ordained."[68]

A few doctors willing to speak out on the eve of the war could see no reason for making any concessions to religious dignitaries whose pronouncements were medically wrong and socially unrealistic. Ecclesiastical worthies who fulminated against the "miserable gospel of comfort" and uttered threats of divine retribution in the form of "race suicide" were, according to the Preston physician James Rigby, howling at the winds of progress blowing over the land. Rigby, who practiced in a heavily Catholic working-class town, boldly announced in 1914 that the old-fashioned views of marriage, as well as the medical premises church authorities used to support their theological rationalizations, were hopelessly out of touch with the new century. He believed he was one of a growing number of people who welcomed the intellectual and technical progress that made it possible to have only as many children as could be maintained prudently in comfort and prosperity and who emphatically rejected a view of marriage that was so "sensual and lowdown" that it was limited "to the mere pro-creation of children and nothing else." Millions of couples already denied it by their actions, Rigby asserted, and his fellow physicians would not long allow their science to be distorted to preserve such reactionary and medically unsound values.[69]

Those doctors who challenged the hostile views inherited from the nineteenth century knew they were in a minority. But they all believed, with considerable justification, that they were far more representative than their numbers suggested. Many of their colleagues shared their opinions even though they were unwilling to speak out and defy decades of authoritative pronouncements. Most doctors simply went about their business quietly, some helping their patients with contraceptive problems, many more avoiding it. Medical opposition to family limitation was, then, never as complete as it seemed on the surface. Certainly some physicians were stubborn, opinionated, self-righteous hypocrites whose declarations on human sexuality and reproductive physiology appear in retrospect closer to quackery than science. Many more, however, were plagued by genuine doubts and confusion surrounding an area of medical experience in which little scientific research existed, which was traditionally secondary to their professional interests, and which was particularly susceptible to pervasive class concepts of social and individual morality and propriety. Their own changing domestic strategy, reflected in the diminishing fertility of their own marriages, must have left large numbers of doctors with serious doubts about the validity of the medical and moral claims of their outspoken anti-birth control colleagues.

The younger generation of physicians, whose fertility was lower than virtually any other group in society, were, as Millard frequently pointed out, less inclined to accept the old medical shibboleths. Though still very cautious, respectful, and respectable, these doctors would, as the moral climate permitted, begin to take a more assertive role in establishing a medical position on birth control that was more in conformity with experience and valid scientific evidence than it was with outmoded religious and moral precepts. During World War I Millard warned church leaders that when the conflict ended they would find little medical support in postwar Britain to sustain their limited, unrealistic ideal of modern family life. Unless they adapted quickly to the altered values of the age, he predicted, the church would find itself deserted not only by a new generation of doctors but by public opinion.[70] The church-medical alliance was reforged in the early 1920s, but it became, as Millard foresaw, a weakened amalgam of old Victorian moral and scientific values and prejudices rather than a durable barrier to the continued adoption of the "small family system."

CHAPTER 7
The Woman Question

Family planning played little part in early feminist campaigns. In the closing decades of the nineteenth century emancipationist goals emphasized educational and economic opportunities for women as well as the vote. Victorian advocates of women's rights thought largely in terms of single women and widows rather than wives and mothers, and few questioned that domestic management and raising of children were primal responsibilities of married women. There were of course individual feminists who boldly asserted that the control of her own fertility was essential to a wife's health, independence, and self-fulfillment, but it did not become a serious objective of the organized women's movement until well into the twentieth century. Though John Stuart Mill assumed that the "evil of overpopulation" would diminish as women achieved greater freedom, neither he nor most of his contemporaries linked the realization of feminist goals to smaller families.[1]

Antifeminists did not begin to associate female emancipation with restricted motherhood to any great extent until they became aware of the rapid decline in the birthrate in the later 1890s and opening years of the new century. Because it had not occurred to many opponents (or proponents) of feminism that women would deliberately spurn motherhood once married, the "flight from maternity" after the 1870s seems to have taken both camps by surprise.[2] Even then the quarrel with feminism was not about the issue of birth control. The issue was the threat that the women's movement posed to the traditional separation of natural gender spheres long held to be biologically and divinely determined. Emancipated women, it was feared, would not marry, or, if they did, would lack the capacity or desire to bear children. Others might neglect their offspring and husbands for a career outside the home. The unnatural aspirations of feminists smacked of sexual insubordination and threatened the highly idealized concepts of Victorian marriage and domesticity.

The Neo-Malthusians were, as a group, unique among feminists in tying the success of the women's struggle to the rearing of smaller families. It seemed obvious to the Drysdales, Bradlaugh, Annie Besant, and the other advocates of female emancipation who populated the ranks of the Malthusian League that there could be no solution to the Woman Question as long as wives were unable to control their fertility. They knew that virtually all feminists agreed in principle at least that motherhood should be voluntary, and they expected that the Malthusian League would be embraced as an ally by enlightened feminist organizations. Once again they were fated to be disappointed. The reluctance of the women's movement to consider birth control as a meaningful issue remained largely unaltered until after World War I. The efforts of Neo-Malthusians to expand feminist visions were mostly ignored or summarily rejected by the various suffrage groups who refused to respond to the league's repeated warning that millions of married women, a majority of them poor, would be effectively excluded from any benefits emancipation might bring the better-off members of their sex.

In 1877 Bradlaugh and Besant tried to recruit the feminist champions Millicent and Henry Fawcett for their defense, but Henry Fawcett denounced Knowlton's *Fruits of Philosophy*, refused to have anything to do with the case, and threatened to send his wife out of the country if any attempt was made to involve her in the distasteful proceedings.[3] No feminist publication mentioned the famous trial despite Annie Besant's strong defense of women's rights. In subsequent years Neo-Malthusians vainly surveyed the feminist press for some glimmer of recognition. They recognized that propriety and tactical considerations might impede respectable and cautious feminists from adopting the Malthusian league's entire program, but many of them had not hesitated to campaign against the sexual double standard implicit in the hated Contagious Diseases Acts.[4] Alice Vickery Drysdale had been involved in that fight and knew that many women had to overcome strong, prudish sensibilities and resistance from more reticent feminists to participate in the long campaign. She could not understand why Josephine Butler and other prominent defenders of women's rights were unable to see the much greater double standard that existed between rich and poor in the area of family limitation.

Feminists did not object to family limitation, but they considered it an inappropriate, divisive issue that could only weaken their struggle for the vote and for greater economic and educational opportunities. Many were, however, repelled by the use of artificial devices that were viewed as salacious, probably dangerous, and, perhaps more importantly, threatened to intensify the sexual subjugation of women already victimized by men's oppressive, carnal desires. If the threat of pregnancy were removed, husbands would presumably be more insatiable than ever, reducing marriage to a degraded state of legalized prostitution.[5] By contrast, prudent family restriction based upon continence and self-restraint not only conformed to popular morality but to feminist sensibilities as well.

To counter what it believed to be a commonplace, but wrong-headed perception, the *Malthusian* in its second issue promised feminists that the adoption of league proposals would actually give women greater control than ever in determining the size of their families—"the *sine qua non* of well being."[6] Year after year league spokesmen reiterated this argument, along with demands for immediate female enfranchisement. The adoption of Neo-Malthusian practices coupled with the vote would guarantee mothers of all classes the right to refuse to bring additional unwelcome children into an overcrowded world.[7] Moreover, many of the talented and independent spinsters active in the feminist cause would be more inclined to wed, Annie Besant promised, confident they could find self-fulfillment within marriage instead of sexual slavery, hordes of unwanted offspring, ill-health, and corrosive financial problems.[8]

Though several Neo-Malthusians doubted that it made much sense to demand enfranchisement or any other rights until women were equal participants in the control of population, most insisted that political and economic equality would provide wives the support they needed to resist the "will and wishes" of their husbands. As long as marital relations were governed by outmoded assumptions of female inferiority enshrined in repressive religious, economic, legal, and political institutions, it was essential to reform these barriers to progress. They had for centuries been perpetuated by inevitable cycles of high fertility that kept women in maternal bondage, the *Malthusian* explained, but at last it was possible to break this recurrent pattern.[9]

If many active feminists shared these sentiments, they rarely subscribed to them publicly and fled from any contact with the tainted Malthusian League. Individual voices were nevertheless raised occasionally in the 1880s and 1890s denouncing the "madness of large families" that jeopardized the health and happiness of overburdened mothers. A "Woman of the Day" suggested in the *Saturday Review* in 1895 that some women were less inclined to be a "mere breeding machine" and decried the "sorry waste of vitality" that others expended "in the meaningless production of children born into a country already over-populated." Prominent feminists such as Mrs. Mona Caird, Mrs. Wolstenholme Elmy, and Lady Florence Dixie assumed that smaller families would indeed result from greater sexual equality, and they thought it a good reason for women to battle for the vote.[10]

Such comments reinforced antifeminist accusations that the "New

Woman" was an unnatural enemy of marriage and maternity. But these charges were more in response to established social and demographic trends among the middle and upper classes than they were to any explicit feminist policies. The advocacy of smaller families remained an individual, secondary tributary to the mainstream of feminist demands. To what extent unspoken birth control considerations influenced emancipationist expectations and strategy is impossible to determine. Like feminism itself the deliberate control of fertility was probably more a result of greater female independence than a cause. Most contraceptive recommendations emphasized the wife's responsibilities and required that she play a conscious role in the determination of family size. With the exception of coitus interruptus, preferred for the poor by Neo-Malthusians, and the condom, much deplored by Annie Besant and other feminists as a license for male sexual indulgence, all other preventives were for use by women. Indeed, when critics began to rail against the selfishness of middle-class wives who limited their families, they were in large measure complaining about changing intermarital relations that reflected the gradual emergence of greater female independence, self-awareness, and expanded expectations. Although late Victorian feminism did not explicitly promote family planning, its quiet adoption by millions of couples nevertheless added an important if frequently inarticulated dimension to the Woman Question.

Neo-Malthusians predicted that once such feminist organizations as the National Society for Women's Suffrage, the federated National Union of Women's Suffrage Societies, and, later, the Women's Social and Political Union recognized the special needs of married women, they would be more inclined to acknowledge the importance of family limitation. Much of the Malthusian League's propaganda was devoted to persuading these and other groups that the emancipated wife was perhaps the most important of all emancipated women. Although some of its appeals were directed to wives alone, the league usually emphasized the need for mutual responsibility and cooperation between married couples. Such thoughtful arrangements, Neo-Malthusians suspected, were already common among the educated middle classes. Working-class women, however, were assumed to be at the mercy of their husbands' sexual appetites, which were often indulged with a reckless disregard for health and family welfare. It was these women, largely ignored by the middle-class suffrage societies, who the Malthusian League believed were most in need of liberation from the worst sort of oppression. Annie Besant was able to escape from her unhappy marriage to an Anglican clergyman by separation and divorce, but it was, as she knew, a solution few women even of her class could initiate or afford and one that was certainly of no use to the totally dependent wives of allegedly abusive workers.

Once the mutual advantages of rational parentage were accepted by both husband and wife, Neo-Malthusians expected that a new era of connubial and sexual maturity would replace the exploitative inequities of the past and end most domestic conflicts. This was one of the messages of George Noyes Miller's fictional dream of a feminist boycott, *The Strike of a Sex*, published by the Malthusian League in 1891. Inspired by the London dock strike of 1889, the women in Miller's imaginary town demanded a "Woman's Magna Charta," which guaranteed a woman the "perfect ownership of her own person" including the decision about the number of children she would bear.[11] After two weeks of conflict and separation, the lonely, frustrated men of the town succumbed, only to find that their equalized relationships were happier and more fulfilling than ever. Talented young women, in Miller's vision, now looked forward to marriage not as a burdensome necessity, but as an uplifting cooperative venture. The once-skeptical narrator awoke from his reverie passionately committed to female emancipation and Neo-Malthusianism. Despite Malthusian League hopes, *The Strike of a Sex* failed to electrify the feminist movement, and the women's journals ignored its short-lived appearance on the literary scene.

Those Neo-Malthusians who had ties with socialists also tried with little success to persuade them to consider the question of female labor and social and economic equality in terms of the working mother's plight. Although the antipathy of the Social Democratic Federation for feminism and Neo-Malthusianism was well known, more moderate socialists, particularly Fabians, were considered by Annie Besant, J. M. Robertson, and George Standring to understand the relationship between true female emancipation and fertility control. Yet in the nineteenth century Karl Pearson was rare in his acknowledgement of the Neo-Malthusian dimension of the problem, and he concluded that the moral legacies of the past were still so strong that the issue of family limitation, however relevant to modern feminism and socialism, would have to remain "outside the field of legitimate discussion" for the foreseeable future. He nevertheless was certain that society would one day have to face up to the Neo-Malthusian challenge since "no amount of hypocrisy will suffice to hide its existence."[12]

Feminism and socialism, Pearson wrote in 1887, are the "two most important movements of our era." Both were products of progressive economic and social evolution, he explained, and however reluctant people were to see it, the rational control of conception fell into the same category. Whether Neo-Malthusianism would advance the cause of feminism and socialism remained to be seen, but neither movement, he rightly observed, was yet willing to confront the implications of regulated maternity for the achievement of true equality.[13] If, as Pearson believed, women were as capable as men, it was unlikely that child-rearing would prove sufficiently satisfying to the best of their sex as more challenging alternatives became available. Moreover, he frankly doubted that a socialist state would merely accept children as a sufficient female contribution to the community unless they met a predetermined demographic need. Emancipated women, even mothers, in a socialist society would have to be free to provide "other forms of social labour" during their careers.[14]

Without being specific, Pearson assumed that some sort of "Neo-Malthusian practice" would eventually become commonplace in socialist marriages based upon mutual love, respect, and a shared desire to improve the living and working conditions of both sexes. Unchecked motherhood, even in a socialist environment, would perpetuate female dependency, he warned, which could jeopardize a woman's newfound freedom.[15] If Pearson's socialism faded during the next two decades, his support of female rights did not, even when many eugenists, including his friend and patron Francis Galton, were fearful that emancipation would take place at the expense of the "race-motherhood" they wanted so desperately to promote.

Many self-proclaimed champions of the feminist cause drew back when the "modern Woman's Movement" threatened to interfere "with this prime natural necessity of child-bearing." The writer Grant Allen, for example, thought it perfectly correct in 1889 for women to receive a better education, fairer property rights, and the vote as long as they were still able to provide the four to six children the nation needed to sustain reasonable growth. Like the Neo-Malthusians, whose arguments he acknowledged, Allen believed women should marry young, but for reasons of personal and community welfare they should not consider restricting the size of their families until after ten or twelve years. Having satisfied their "natural role" of wife and mother, women would then be free to enjoy the benefits of their newly won rights.[16]

Allen's "Plain Words on the Women's Question" were really addressed to middle-class women who were involved in the suffragist struggle and whose fertility was most in doubt. He did not consider the subject pertinent to the working classes. Galton, whom Allen quoted, had shown statistically that the ablest, most intelligent women, almost exclusively in the middle and upper classes, were reluctant to reproduce their own kind, while the "worst and lowest" sector of the populace showed no hesitation whatsoever.[17] As feminism became embroiled with the population question, it did so in terms of differential fertility and eugenics. It was widely feared that modern, educated, ambitious women of superior breeding would be either unwilling or physically unfit for motherhood. Consequently, even when suffragist sympathizers endorsed feminist aspirations, they frequently agreed with the antisuffragists that too many "feminine literati" and "unmarried school mistresses" were avoiding their primary biological and social obligations.[18]

There was considerable confusion in both camps as to whether the avoidance of these responsibilities was deliberate or an inevitable corollary of progressive evolution. Herbert Spencer had warned in the 1860s that increased mental exertion on the part of women in the more comfortable classes would lead to a "diminution of reproductive power" and a rise in "absolute sterility." He conjured up an enduring image of "flat-chested girls who survive their high-pressure education [but who] are incompetent to bear a well-developed infant and to supply it with the natural food for the natural period."[19] But a great many talented and learned women never even reached the stage of diminished reproduction because, it was commonly believed, their elevated expectations reduced the circle of men whom they found attractive, or their personal oddities frightened potential suitors away. Galton, for example, thought such women so "dogmatic and self-assertive" or so painfully "shy and peculiar" as to thwart eugenically desirable sexual selection.[20]

Neo-Malthusians countered that the low marriage and fertility rate of intelligent, educated females proved that the advancement of women was inextricably linked to the rational control of maternity. As family limitation became more acceptable, the best women and men, they promised, would be less reluctant to marry. Popular critics supported by numerous medical and scientific authorities were certain, however, that the prolonged expenditure of physical and emotional energy required to compete in the classroom or in the intellectual and economic marketplace would make most "advanced women" unfit for motherhood.[21] Physicians, who were grudgingly admitting women to their profession, warned of the dangers of sterility, prematurity, and an inability to nurse the "sickly offspring" who were likely to result from the strains of challenging a man's world. The ultimate test would come in the domestic arena, a Manchester professor of obstetrical medicine predicted in 1884, but he thought the outcome was already evident and the implications obvious. "To leave only the inferior women to perpetuate the species," he warned, "will do more to deteriorate the human race than all the individual victories at Girton will do to benefit it."[22]

To feminists such prognostications appeared to be self-serving justifications for keeping women dependent and confined to their traditional spheres. Nevertheless, the late Victorians and the Edwardians were clearly uneasy and confused about the impact of the Woman Question on the future of the race. Karl Pearson in 1885 complained that the issue was fast degenerating into a controversial jumble of emotional appeals, popular prejudices, and unproven, superficial assumptions about gender capacity and incapacity. He was as disturbed by the passionate invocation of John Stuart Mill and Mary Wollstonecraft by ardent feminists as he was by the allegedly scientific refutations of their opponents. It was time for a moratorium, he suggested, while a careful, scientific investigation tried to determine the probable outcome of the present revolution in sexual relations and social institutions. Nobody really knew much about the physical or mental capacity of women, or the likely effects of her emancipation on race reproduction. Until this was better understood, it was premature to talk about a woman's rights, "which are, after all, only a vague description of what may be the fittest position for her, the sphere of her maximum usefulness in the developed society of the future."[23]

Though frankly sympathetic to feminist aspirations, Pearson recognized that if race reproduction was left "to the coarser and less intellectual" women, it was possible that the "penalty to be paid for race predominance [would be] the subjection of women."[24] It was an unpalatable prospect, he confessed, but emancipation might only prove sensible for genuinely infertile, educated women, or those beyond child-bearing age. Whatever the outcome, Pearson could envision no justification for the continued disenfranchisement of women any more than intellectual or physical inferiority excluded men from the ballot. "There must be," he reasoned, "some other disqualification which deprives a George Eliot of the vote that is granted to the dullest yokel."[25]

If Pearson saw no reason for denying women the vote, his preliminary inquiries into differential fertility in the 1890s caused him to be more cautious about other areas of emancipation. Like Sidney Webb, Ethel Elderton, and others a decade later, Pearson was struck by the low fertility and higher incidence of miscarriage and infant mortality among working wives in the textile districts. He pondered the possibility that educated, middle-class women who attempted to pursue a career might face the same maternal difficulties suffered by their working-class sisters.[26]

These and other concerns about the likely effects of education and expanded opportunities for women prompted Eleanor Mildred Sidgwick in 1887 to undertake a unique inquiry into the relationship between female education and health, marriage, and fertility. Sidgwick, a sister of Arthur Balfour and principal of Newnham College, Cambridge, after 1892, analyzed 562 questionnaires returned by former students of that institution as well as Girton College and Lady Margaret and Somerville Halls at Oxford. The women provided detailed information not only on their own physical, marital, and maternal status, but also on that of 382 sisters and 68 first cousins who had not attended university.[27] Sixty-eight percent of the educated sample claimed to be in good or excellent health despite their college ordeal, compared with 59 percent of their sisters and cousins.[28]

Even more encouraging, nearly 75 percent of respondents who took honors described themselves as being as physically sound as they had been in their precollege days and reported no deleterious effects from their demanding regimen at school.[29]

Far less satisfying, however, was the low marriage rate of the college women. Only 10 percent of their number had yet married, compared to nearly 20 percent of their less educated relatives. Furthermore, the average length of marriage, 4.3 years, was only half that recorded for their sisters and cousins. Sidgwick recognized that the statistics seemed to confirm the opinions of those who claimed that advanced education for women was incompatible with matrimony, but she was quick to explain the difference as the obvious result of college girls being removed from the marriage market for an extended period of time. Many of them did not even matriculate until the age of twenty-two, and those who married did so on the average when they were nearly twenty-seven, almost a year and a half later than their less educated sisters and cousins. Although additional data gathered from the small number of college women in the sample who were over thirty suggested that eventually as many as a third of those who matriculated would marry, it seemed obvious to Sidgwick that whether they attended the university or not, only a minority of females in the educated classes ever married. It was not from want of physical attractiveness or desire, but from a lack of suitable men among the upper middle classes who tended to propose late, if at all. The problem existed long before the recent advent of women's colleges at Oxford and Cambridge, she contended, and had nothing to do with the inadequacies of learned young ladies.[30]

When college-educated women did marry, their reproductive ability was not markedly different from other women of their class. At the time of the survey the married respondents had on the average 1.53 children compared with 1.81 for their sisters and cousins. Because the college women started their families later and were slightly younger than their relatives, Sidgwick was not surprised. More intriguing, however, was the discovery that although total fertility was less among younger, educated wives, a substantially greater portion of them, 72.4 percent compared with only 63.2 percent of the other women, had at least one child.[31] These statistics, however limited, Sidgwick contended, more than disproved the claims of Grant Allen and the many like him who charged that educated women were "physically inefficient mothers" whose "reserve fund of strength" had been depleted in the quest for higher learning. Far from breaking down under the strains of maternity, Cambridge and Oxford girls who married were the healthy mothers of sound families quite up to the average of their class. They were, in fact, maternally more efficient. Fewer than 10 percent of their offspring failed to survive compared with a loss of 12.5 percent of infants born to their sisters and cousins. The only remotely negative effect of advanced education Sidgwick could find was a temporary decline in good health of about 5 percent while women were at the university. That, she concluded, was a normal result of overwork and irregular hours and was probably not restricted to female students.[32]

Feminists and Neo-Malthusians were reassured, though for different reasons. In proving that the low nuptiality and fertility of college-educated women was a characteristic of class rather than some academically induced affliction, the study strengthened the arguments of those who demanded even greater educational, professional, economic, and political opportunities for women unable or unwilling to devote their lives to motherhood. Though sympathetic, Sidgwick personally believed that a happy marriage was still the best career for any woman.[33] The Neo-Malthusians contended that rational family limitation could provide the best of both worlds, permitting young men to marry early while allowing talented, ambitious wives to blend a life of self-improvement and personal fulfillment with carefully planned motherhood. By ending the economic burdens of unchecked fertility on able men and the dangerous, stultifying effects of repeated, incapacitating confinements on intelligent women, the conflict between marriage and female emancipation could, the Neo-Malthusians insisted, be quickly resolved.

The conflict, however, became accentuated in the Edwardian era, stimulated by greater awareness of the plummeting birthrate, expanding eugenic concerns about the differential aspects of the decline, and the rapid, militant escalation of the suffrage campaign. Spencer's overly cerebral, "flat-chested girls" were considered by many to be at the heart of the problem. The sterilizing effects of higher education and competitive aspirations were particularly dangerous in a woman, Caleb Saleeby warned, because her body "is the temple of life to come—and *therefore* . . . the holy of the holies." Though more sympathetic to female emancipation than most of his eugenic colleagues, Saleeby warned in 1909 that it "cannot safely be carried to the point at which motherhood is compromised."[34] Much of the debate about the relationship of the Woman Question to the falling birthrate focused upon whether that critical juncture had been reached.

W. C. D. Whetham, the outspoken Cambridge University physicist and eugenist, thought the answer was obvious. He observed that the decline in fertility over the preceding thirty years closely paralleled the rise in feminism and, more specifically, female education. Only 22 percent of the three thousand women who had entered Cambridge had married, Whetham reported in 1909. Moreover, the greatest proportion of that minority had the good sense to withdraw before their final examinations, or declined to take honors. The young women who chose the most demanding field, mathematics, had the lowest marriage rate of all. Although there was no record of the number of children born to former students, Whetham knew that it was disconcertingly small.[35]

In the absence of comprehensive data, Whetham, like most worried analysts of recent demographic trends, extrapolated from small samples or regional investigations. He alluded to several studies contrasting the low birthrate in textile towns with the high fertility of mining districts where women had few opportunities for employment. Drawing the obvious lesson, Whetham described men as "income" to be spent freely by each generation. Women, however, constituted "life capital" to be spent sparingly and husbanded carefully for the future. Its reckless consumption by women determined to become teachers, nurses, factory inspectors, clerks, or something else incompatible with the rearing of sufficient progeny threatened to bankrupt the race. Nowhere was this more evident than in the low fertility or celibacy of the feminist leaders, Whetham complained, and he only wished more accurate figures were available to authenticate his observations.[36]

Variations on this familiar theme of feminist spinsterhood and sterility grew louder as the drive for suffrage legislation intensified before the war. The eugenic rendition was not original in its view of the ballot as symbolic of an orchestrated attack upon domestic life and traditional sex roles. Whetham, for example, had no doubt that women were as intellectually astute as men in making political decisions, but he feared that the exercise of that prerogative would, like advanced education and expanded occupational opportunities, divert the newly enfranchised from their natural roles and strengthen the already overweening "spinster influence" in the country. Because mothers would not have the leisure or energy to participate in public life on the same scale as the unmarried or childless, they would be more vulnerable to the latter's "mischievous authority." Whetham was one of many eugenists who urged that only mothers be given the vote.[37] Frederick D'Arcy, the Bishop of Down, Connor, and Dromore tried in 1914 to persuade his colleagues on the Eugenics Education Society Council to petition the government to restrict the ballot to wives who had at least four children.[38]

The society was in a quandary. Half its membership and a quarter of its officers were women. Forty percent of this number were unmarried and many of them were active in the moderate wing of the suffrage movement. All were middle and upper class, and although they supported the positive eugenic goal of encouraging greater fertility among the genetically promising—presumably people very much like themselves—few of this number were prepared to endorse permanent disenfranchisement as an inevitable corollary of greater procreation. Even without the vote, they knew, the women of their class were already among the least fertile and least married sector of the population. Despite substantial representation in the Eugenics Education Society, female eugenists rarely spoke out on the issue of women's rights. They were content to support Saleeby, D'Arcy, Whetham, and others who accepted enfranchisement as suitable for older women who had presumably fulfilled whatever maternal obligations they were destined to assume.

Saleeby went further than most of his eugenist colleagues, however, in reasoning that the same criteria should apply to women standing for parliament. He suspected that once the vote was granted, the suffrage forces would inevitably demand the right to sit in the Commons as well. In any event Saleeby believed that the sooner the women's political demands were met the better, because they diverted feminist energies from the much more important racial problems associated with widening differential class fertility.[39] He was comparatively rare among eugenists in his support of moderate female emancipation as a means of encouraging more enlightened and equitable marriages likely to produce genetically valuable, well-nurtured children. Similarly, before the war at least, he was one of a minority of Eugenics Education Society spokesmen who tended to agree with the Neo-Malthusian contention that any quantitative diminution of population resulting from emancipated women rationally planning their families would be substantially offset by qualitative advances.

Saleeby's views conflicted with those of Galton and others who complained that female emancipation would interfere with natural selection by reducing the attractiveness and availability of eugenically preferred women. Furthermore, unlike his protégé Karl Pearson, Galton had little regard for feminine talent. He opposed admitting females to the universities, lent his name in 1908 to the antisuffrage cause, and remained unpersuaded that intellectual, independent women would, as many feminists claimed, contract racially advantageous marriages based upon mutual attraction, respect, and compatibility.[40] Eugenic thinking was further confused by the insistence in 1908 of so eminent a naturalist as Alfred Russel Wallace who contended that instead of obstructing natural selection the extension of women's rights was an irreversible sign of progressive evolutionary individuation.[41] As early as 1890, after reading the American Edward Bellamy's family-centered, communitarian utopia *Looking Backward*, Wallace predicted that in a truly equitable, advanced society women would, like men, defer marrying while exercising their "higher faculties." Eventually, however, the laws of intellectual and physical attraction, unimpeded by shallow social and economic considerations, would draw together compatible men and women whose combined talents would be enhanced in their small, but eugenically efficient families.[42]

Neo-Malthusian eugenists making the same point claimed that contraception precluded the need for delaying such marriages until couples were in their late twenties or early thirties. C. V. Drysdale and Binnie Dunlop tried to convince the Eugenics Education Society that the rational control of parentage alone provided assurance that female emancipation was congenial with early, eugenic marriage.[43] Without explicitly acknowledging the Neo-Malthusian argument the society's president, Montague Crackanthorpe, basically agreed. For forty years Crackanthorpe had discreetly endorsed the advantages of prudent family limitation. As long as the procreative decisions of modern women were based upon qualitative considerations, he said in 1907, their diminished fertility would not by itself imperil the race but would, on the contrary, further the eugenics cause. In any event, Crackanthorpe reasoned, the clock could not be turned back. "Woman is now wide awake, her long slumber ended; to put her to sleep again is beyond human power." It was far wiser to welcome rather than resist her demands for a full share of responsibility in charting the future course of the race.[44]

Many of Crackanthorpe's eugenist colleagues grudgingly conceded that the inevitable advance of women's rights would probably entail a further decline in the fertility of middle- and upper-class women. Unlike Crackanthorpe, Saleeby, and Barr, most of the Eugenics Education Society membership was unwilling to endorse birth control as a form of negative eugenics useful in limiting the excessive reproduction of the less fit in society. Drysdale, his wife, and Dunlop had joined the society in 1909 in hopes of persuading it that "race-betterment" would never be possible until a powerful, voluntary check was imposed upon the inordinate fertility of the lower orders. Before the war most eugenics luminaries, led by Crackanthorpe's successor, Major Leonard Darwin, the fourth son of the great naturalist, concluded, with Galton and Pearson, that Neo-Malthusianism had proven racially disastrous in its adoption by the most successful classes while the remainder of the populace was as recklessly progenitive as ever.

Though some doubts were expressed in the society's council about the likelihood of success, most eugenists preferred to avoid any association with unsavory Neo-Malthusianism. Until the 1920s they were content to place their faith in the positive encouragement of increased reproduction among the fitter classes to offset the indiscriminate fertility of the less selective. In addition, they endorsed the confinement or the sterilization of the congenitally defective despite widespread uncertainty about the inheritance of various afflictions. But eugenists refused to heed Malthusian

League warnings that the impact of such measures would be slight compared to what could be accomplished by teaching the poor—supposedly the greatest repository of genetic incompetence—the rudiments of contraception.

Eugenic doubts about birth control were reinforced by the extensive scientific and medical testimony describing the consequences of deferred fertility and unnatural feminine competitive activity. Mrs. E. L. Somervell, president of the Anti-Suffrage Society and a eugenics sympathizer, buttressed her arguments with the reports of public health authorities citing the high incidence of childhood mortality, maternal deaths, disease, and moral decay in manufacturing districts with substantial female employment.[45] If middle-class women did not yet exhibit these tragic harbingers of physical incapacity, there was no lack of evidence about their psychological fragility. Modern females were indisputably more high strung and hysterical than their mothers and grandmothers, physicians reported, and this led to an alarming increase in obstetrical problems. Many of them could be readily traced to the confusion of sex roles stirred up by the feminist campaign.[46] Dr. Hope Grant claimed in the *British Medical Journal* in 1904 that the new woman was becoming masculine. She cycles, golfs, and plays hockey and other sports, which increased her muscles while diminishing her pelvis, he observed. He wondered if "her heart, which has hypertrophied already to the stimulus of gymnastics, [was] capable of further hypertrophy in response to the demands of puerperium." There was considerable doubt, however, that such women, like their highly educated, emancipated sisters, would be much interested in or able to attract men willing to test their reproductive and nurturing abilities.[47]

A number of Grant's medical colleagues doubted women were as fragile as was commonly believed and found from experience that exercise and athletic activity actually facilitated childbirth and postpartum recovery. As one Cheshire physician concluded, a paucity of adequate pelvises had little to do with the lower marriage and birthrates of active middle-class women. The explanation was more likely to be found in the insufficiency of clerks and professional men who could afford early marriage and a large family.[48] Nevertheless, six years later, at the 1910 British Medical Association meetings the respected gynecologist, Dr. J. W. Ballantyne, reported that one of his patients, "an enthusiastic hockey player," told him that young girls who participated in the sport were later unable to nurse their babies. He believed her and felt that such observations confirmed what specialists in his field already knew.[49]

As with birth control, hostile medical evaluations of female emancipation often reflected the diagnostician's gender perceptions and moral and social attitudes rather than rigorous clinical observation. The sexually rebellious, masculinizing tendencies of the women's movement particularly troubled doctors who diagnosed it as a symptom of a deep disturbance in the "emotional nature" of the modern female. It was manifest in "atrophied maternal instinct, loss of femininity and a lessened development of 'woman's ways.'"[50] Dr. R. Murray Leslie was typical in his conclusion that feminism had upset the critical balance of sexual selection. Its effect upon marriage and fertility was obvious, he added, but a close reading of the Lunacy Commission reports revealed other consequences reflected in the high rate of mental disturbance suffered by "intellectual women" in recent years.

A number of late Victorian pessimists had singled out reported increases in certifiable lunacy, especially among women, as irrefutable evidence of degeneration. Despite repeated claims by the Lunacy Commission that the statistics merely reflected better diagnoses of mental illness and expanded facilities to house the insane, the belief persisted into the Edwardian era that the stresses of modern life, coupled with a diminished capacity to cope, were driving more men and women out of their heads than ever before. Leslie was afraid that the "sex starvation" and sterility stimulated by the women's movement might well prove to be the major cause of increased female insanity. Though he did not question the intellectual ability of women to make important contributions in chosen spheres of professional or creative activity, he thought it time to adopt a new "Law of Consonance" requiring that a woman "only develop intellectually along lines that are consonant with the natural development of her capacity of race creativeness."[51] In practice, one distinguished chemist recommended in 1909, women with scientific talent should for the sake of the race marry and pass it on to their sons rather than pursue a career of their own.[52] If nothing else, Leslie added, such women should delay developing their cerebral endowments until after their childbearing years so as not to overtax their delicately balanced mental and physical resources.

It seemed to Leslie, Ballantyne, and their many colleagues in the medical profession that Neo-Malthusianism compounded the deleterious effects of female emancipation by providing married women the opportunity to pursue a variety of activities while postponing the fulfillment of their primary obligation. To them feminism and Neo-Malthusianism were complementary perversions of the modern age. The two had emerged together in the last quarter of the nineteenth century and jointly threatened the continued dominance of the British race in the twentieth. When fecund young women decided to have as few children as possible, the racial and demographic consequences of spinsterhood and sterility were multiplied many times over.

Even if the various suffrage organizations rejected any ties with the

Malthusian League, feminist leaders were suspected of secretly promoting Neo-Malthusianism. Dr. Francis Freemantle, the medical officer of health for Hertfordshire, believed the demand for the vote was a direct result of the "sexual indulgence" stimulated by the Bradlaugh-Besant trial of 1877. The moral and social ideals of women in the cultured, healthy, prosperous, and thrifty classes were rapidly eroded by the lure of artificial limitation. So-called advanced women were drawn from their "natural sphere," he claimed, and like those in decadent, ancient civilizations, they turned their attention to racially dangerous new diversions.[53] During the discussion of the social aspects of the falling birthrate at the 1910 British Medical Association meetings, Freemantle singled out for condemnation those girls' schools that boasted of strong, determined women equipped for the battle of life. "Their ideal," he complained, "seemed to be to beat man at his game, but the only result they attained was to get out of practice at their own game."[54]

Not all doctors passively acquiesced in the generalizations of their more eminent, outspoken colleagues. Some found the evidence for the harmful physiological and psychological effects of female emancipation unconvincing and were willing to say so. Whatever personal feelings physicians might have about the suffrage campaign and the acceptable parameters of a woman's role in society, they argued, they had no special insights that were any more valid than those of the general, educated public. A minority of female doctors were particularly irritated by the conservative pronouncements of various luminaries in their profession. Two gynecologists, Helen Hanson and Ethel Bentham, for example, thought it just as reasonable to argue that changing female values actually strengthened the integrity of family life while promoting the physical and mental health of previously intimidated, unhappy women. The educated women who did wed usually proved to be thoughtful, concerned mothers, aware of hereditarian factors, devoted to their children's future, and determined to employ rational family planning to maintain social status. Moreover, neither physician had ever seen any evidence that healthy muscular development or vigorous intellectual activity interfered with a woman's capacity for reproduction and motherhood. The falling birthrate, they insisted, was an economic rather than a biological response to the new age.[55]

A few cynical Neo-Malthusians shared the view of a number of feminists that medical opposition to women's suffrage was, as in the case of family limitation, motivated in part by a fear of pecuniary loss and control over their female patients. Emancipated women were less likely to provide greedy doctors with an endless supply of sickly children and compliant, exhausted mothers.[56] Although most proponents of women's rights, including Neo-Malthusians, recognized that their campaign appeared to threaten the dominant position of the male in society, they did not necessarily single out physicians as particularly sensitive to diminishing authority over dependent females. Medical men were no different from the rest of their sex in their traditional perceptions and evaluations of gender relationships however much they dressed their conclusions in the garb of clinical science. Nearly all men and most women needed to be educated to the mutual advantages of greater equality. The idea, implicit in Neo-Malthusianism and feminism, that women could function in society without the protection of men, violated deeply ingrained Victorian concepts of male and female capacity and responsibility. The more reasonable feminists and Neo-Malthusians appreciated the difficulties of cultural and psychological reassessment, even while they were impatient with the pace of change and suspicious of the reasons for delay.

The *Englishwoman*, for example, periodically acknowledged that the marriage and fertility statistics of educated, middle-class women had to give even the most ardent feminist pause for thought. Though it did not share the view that the figures, which many contemporaries found so distressing, were a frightening consequence of female education or other recent advances in women's rights, it could understand how men and women were predisposed to reach such a conclusion. Yet, the *Englishwoman* continued, closer analysis reveals that irrespective of new opportunities women of the better classes had for at least a generation or more been marrying less often and having fewer children than their social inferiors. In 1913 it recalled Eleanor Mildred Sidgwick's study from the 1880s and reconfirmed her conclusions about class and fertility in a less scientific survey. Although college-educated and professional women constituted only a small minority of the female population in such fashionable middle-class boroughs as Hampstead and Kensington, nearly 45 percent of the women in these areas between the ages of twenty-five and forty-five were unmarried, compared with only 17 or 18 percent in the working-class areas of Stepney, Shoreditch, and Poplar. Obviously, the *Englishwomen* reported, marital status was, as Sidgwick had determined a generation earlier, primarily a characteristic of class.[57]

Commenting on these and other figures, the Countess of Selborne concluded that since nearly half the men in the educated, professional middle classes were reluctant to marry until well established in their careers, girls might as well receive a good education and have the opportunity to lead a useful and satisfying life while waiting impatiently to be invited to the altar.[58] The 1911 census revealed that only 45.8 percent of professional men were married compared with a national average of 55.5 percent. Middle-class men in other occupations generally married later, but ultimately nearly as often as those in the working and agricultural classes.

Since it was assumed by census analysts that men married women of their own class and more females survived to adulthood than males, the proportion of spinsters in all classes, but especially in the professional, educated categories would be appreciably larger.[59] The eugenic implications of these differential patterns of nuptiality were a source of considerable anxiety to those who believed that the professional middle classes held the genetic key to the success of national efficiency.

If it was obvious that men and women in the educated categories married later and less often, the fertility of such women was still subject to much speculation because, as in the case of the *Fertility of Marriage Census*, it was usually extrapolated from male occupations. Confronted with this problem, the National Birth-Rate Commission invited two medical statisticians, Dr. Major Greenwood and Dr. Agnes Saville, to undertake a follow-up study of Sidgwick's unique survey of an earlier generation of college-educated women and their less-educated relatives. Of the 787 married women of similar age and background who responded to the new study, 481 were college graduates. They had on the average been married for 8.01 years and had given birth to 1.94 children, whereas the other women in the sample had been married 9.89 years and reported having 2.15 offspring. Furthermore, the mean age of marriage varied only by a year, with college women taking their vows at 27.8 compared with 26.8 for the remainder of the group. Correcting for differences of marriage age and duration Greenwood and Saville, like Sidgwick before them, concluded that "there is no physiological difference between the fertilities of the two classes."[60]

Unlike Sidgwick, however, the investigators for the first time daringly asked women about the reasons for their low fertility. Intrigued by the responses Sidney Webb had received from men in his Fabian Society study, *The Decline in the Birth Rate*, seven years earlier, Greenwood and Saville were emboldened to inquire about female contraceptive practices. Of the 541 who responded to this more intimate section of the questionnaire, 53 percent admitted to deliberate limitation while only 25.5 percent denied it. College women, who numbered 61 percent of the original sample, constituted nearly 72 percent of those willing to discuss contraception. Nearly 59 percent of them confessed to deliberate restriction compared with only 40 percent of noncollege women. More than a fifth of the replies were confusing or sufficiently imprecise to suggest that many women, college-educated or not, were uncertain as to what actually constituted deliberate limitation. Mechanical appliances, douches, and spermatocides were obvious contraceptives, but a sizable minority of the sample were unsure about how to categorize coitus interruptus, the safe period, or prolonged abstention from intercourse, though approximately half of the women who gave details about their practices employed these more "natural" methods.[61]

If the accumulated evidence effectively ruled out the possibility that the women's movement was somehow altering the biological makeup and reproductive capacity of the fair sex, it confirmed the claim that the more emancipated of their number were deliberately spurning their traditional domestic roles. Although Neo-Malthusians were not surprised by the findings of the NBRC, they obviously disagreed with its conclusion that small families were in some way a reflection of social and moral irresponsibility that could eventually imperil Britain's imperial civilization. They did, however, share the commission's concern about the lower marriage rate and delayed nuptiality of the better-educated, professional middle classes and had long argued that the antinuptial aspects of female emancipation need not be linked to the antinatal if only the Malthusian League's recommendations were adopted. When in 1904 Alice Vickery Drysdale, Lady Florence Dixie, and several other Neo-Malthusian feminists established a Woman's International Branch of the Malthusian League, they hoped to persuade the suffrage societies to endorse early marriage coupled with eugenic concepts of rational, selective motherhood.[62]

In contrast to popular opinion, the women argued, marriages of dependency actually interfered with natural eugenic selection by emphasizing one-sided superficial attractions and the quest for economic security. Neo-Darwinist eugenists should be particularly sensitive to this problem, Dr. Drysdale insisted, and encourage true sexual selection based upon racially sound criteria of mutual physical and intellectual attraction. Once this was achieved the compatibility of the women's movement with marriage and prudent race motherhood would quickly become obvious to feminists and antifeminists alike.[63] The task was of course complicated by the "ignorance and arrogance" of world leaders like Kaiser Wilhelm II and President Theodore Roosevelt in arbitrarily relegating women to *"Küche, Kinder, Kirche,"* or in denouncing the unmarried or mothers of limited families as race criminals deserving of "contemptuous abhorrence . . . by all healthy people." J. M. Robertson thought the American president's 1902 "prescription . . . will make a pleasing addition to the problem of the present relations of black and white" in that country.[64]

The league deplored the Kaiser's pronouncements on Teutonic domesticity and Roosevelt's anathemas against "race outlaws," but it welcomed the publicity and mixed reactions stirred up by such prominent sentiments. In 1905 it defiantly published its own *Programme of Women's Emancipation*, which added to the usual catalog of liberties the right of a married woman to retain her own name, and, if the eldest child, to inherit estates whether or not she had younger brothers.[65] In the final analysis, however, a woman's control over her own economic, intellectual, and political destiny depended upon her control over her own body. The state of contraceptive technology and understanding before World War I made it easier for women to regulate their fertility and coincided with the prevailing assumption that the wife, as the guardian of sexual purity and domestic morality, was far less passionate than her husband and thus able to control more effectively her subdued carnal impulses. Neo-Malthusian feminists maintained that the control of conception was not only a responsibility and a blessed convenience but an essential right as well.

Alice Vickery Drysdale thought this right was already understood by middle- and upper-class women in the early twentieth century whether or not they were active feminists. Those who were in the suffrage movement, the vanguard of feminist enlightenment, had a special responsibility to provide their less fortunate sisters not only equal political rights, but, more importantly, an appreciation of the liberties to be found in the aggressive regulation of their own fertility. Much to Dr. Drysdale's disgust the suffrage organizations, reflecting as they did the "mental cowardice of our middle-class ladies," continued to spurn Malthusian League overtures and refused any association with the ineffective Woman's International Branch.[66] Moderate feminists, such as Millicent Fawcett, president of the National Union of Women's Suffrage Societies, went further and explicitly denied that there was any logical connection between the suffrage campaign and the rise of family limitation. She noted in 1910 that the birthrate in New Zealand and Australia, where women were enfranchised, was actually slightly higher than in England, whereas in Canada, where women lacked the vote, fertility was substantially lower.[67]

Some of the more militant suffragettes associated with the Pankhursts in the Women's Social and Political Union were on occasion prepared to concede that the declining birthrate was related to the extension of female rights, even if the suffrage societies refused to acknowledge the connection. Teresa Billington-Grieg, for example, agreed that modern women were to some extent in revolt "against unwilling and too frequent motherhood" for economic reasons, but she thought that "in the main it is a personal rebellion due to the demand for liberty in the vital matters of life." Planned and willing motherhood was the "only fair way" for the new woman who recognized that "a few children well and willingly borne would be of greater value to the nation than a numerous and unwanted progeny."[68]

Another suffragette, Mary Knight, tired of the barbs and criticisms directed at the mothers of small families, was certain that the "maternal instinct," as French women had shown for decades, could be as satisfied with two or twenty children. Whether the needs of the Empire could be similarly satisfied in an era of mounting international rivalry was another question. Before answering Knight wanted to know what the country was prepared to guarantee "advanced women" and their valuable sons and daughters twenty years hence. What opportunities and rights would be available to them? What assurance will be given about the quality of life? When these questions were resolved, and able women were assured of a favorable political and economic climate, they would then perhaps give more thought to marrying and raising children. In the meantime, the "only people who do their duty to the State are the lower orders, the unthinking . . . so that the country had better hope that 'survival of the fittest' was still operative."[69]

Feminists were especially sensitive to charges that they were somehow disloyal and perverted from the female norm. In response, they insisted that low marriage rates and smaller families were not the result of some aberrant peculiarity of modern women, but the cumulative consequences of repressive laws, customs, and institutions. Mabel Atkinson allowed in 1910 that the first generation of feminists, hardened by the early battles, might have appeared to be indifferent or hostile to marriage and mother-hood, but their successors, endowed with a "new beauty and grace" born of greater independence, were certainly not that way. Many were already mothers, and countless others were prepared to become mothers as long as marriage did not mean a life of dull and dependent drugdery.[70] Emmeline Pethick Lawrence, the first treasurer of the Woman's Social and Political Union and editor of its journal, *Votes for Women*, forcefully denied the same year that the suffrage movement had ever disputed the supreme importance of motherhood. Its concerns were rather with the debased state in which women, many of them mothers, found themselves.[71]

Although feminist journals periodically described the woes of exhausted, exploited mothers of large families at the mercy of loutish, unfeeling, often diseased husbands, the Neo-Malthusian remedy, although occasionally implied, was rarely prescribed. Concerns about sexual propriety and a conscious reluctance to divert attention from the primary objective of the vote were central considerations. But there was also a strongly militant, antimale, antisexual orientation within the women's movement that alarmed contemporaries and that clearly affected its attitude toward birth control. The old feminist argument that birth control would only encour-age the sexual exploitation of women by their husbands was reinforced by some suffragette claims that men were actually unnecessary and were, in many cases, a positive menace to the health and well-being of the female sex.

Christabel Pankhurst, for example, bluntly proclaimed, in the most ex-treme phase of her career, that women would be better off without men.

A growing obsession with male vice and disease persuaded her that at least 75 percent of all men were contaminated by some venereal malady that caused sterility in their innocent wives, and, to a large extent, explained the falling birthrate that so alarmed contemporaries.[72] Marriage under such conditions was to be avoided. Intelligent women, Pankhurst observed, already recognized that under present laws and existing male standards, motherhood, no matter how great the desire, was not worth the price. If, however, an emancipated woman was able to find a suitable, uninfected mate, she alone should be able to decide how many children she would bear.[73] That was as close as most suffrage leaders came to discussing the question of birth control. Although comparatively few of their number shared Christabel Pankhurst's diagnosis of rampant masculine corruption, it was generally understood, if not explicitly spelled out, that the new woman would not only be more selective in choosing a husband but would have greater control over her own fertility than ever before.

Aware that it would be impolitic and divisive to intrude the issue of birth control directly into the suffrage campaign, Edith How-Martyn, honorary secretary of the Women's Social and Political Union, and her husband turned to the Malthusian League. They were rare catches indeed for that organization. But when they joined in 1910 it was not out of any sympathy with the league's individualistic economic philosophy, which, as members of the Independent Labour party, they frankly deplored. The How-Martyns, like several other social reformers, grudgingly allied with the league before the war simply because there was no other organization promoting family limitation, and it was clear that neither the suffrage groups nor the fledgling Labour party were about to take it up.[74]

Though the Malthusian League welcomed the occasional suffragette bold enough to join its suspect ranks, it lamented that its logical alliance with the women's movement failed as it had with socialism, eugenics, and the medical profession. For the time being it had to be content with the knowledge that individuals representing these various interests were quietly promoting family limitation, and a few of them were even willing to lend their names to the Neo-Malthusian cause. League propagandists continued to support votes for women as well as vetoes on unwanted pregnancies and were confident that it was only a matter of time before the two would be considered inseparable. C. V. Drysdale assured the NBRC in 1913 that despite their modesty most English women would soon realize after their enfranchisement, if not before, that "emancipation from excessive and undesired maternity" would alone make their new rights worth having. At that point the natural association between Neo-Malthusianism and the women's movement would be mutually acknowledged and welcomed.[75]

The sudden outbreak of World War I the following year brought the suffrage campaign to an abrupt halt. With characteristic single-mindedness Malthusian League zealots initially saw in the conflict a means of diverting women from maternity, particularly those in the working classes, who would, like their middle-class sisters, quickly come to appreciate the true freedom to be enjoyed once the bonds of excessive motherhood were broken. The shattering experience of the Great War compellingly revealed just how circumscribed Neo-Malthusian perceptions were not only about the Woman Question but about the twentieth century.

PART II
War, Reconstruction,
and Birth Control, 1914–1930

CHAPTER 8
Cradles or Coffins:
The Great War, 1914–1918

The National Birth-Rate Commission had nearly completed its work when the outbreak of World War I suddenly added a new dimension to its proceedings. As the casualty lists grew longer, the commissioners summoned additional witnesses and debated testimony with a quickening sense of urgency. In 1916 the commission's delayed report reflected the conviction that the devastating losses in combat and the disruption of family life had greatly compounded the dangers already associated with the prewar decline in fertility. In spite of a surge of marriages in late 1914 and 1915 the birthrate continued to plummet, and, on the basis of quarterly reports received as the NBRC's findings were being prepared in 1916, it was obvious that the year would close with the lowest fertility on record. Indeed, the birthrate slipped to 20.9 and two years later reached an unprecedented low of 17.7, bringing the overall wartime decline to 26 percent. Even more disturbing the ratio of children born to married women between the ages of fifteen and forty-five fell some 30 percent.[1]

Alarmed by these and other vital statistics a Conference on Marriage and Parenthood sponsored by various religious and lay organizations in 1918 urged the National Council of Public Morals to reactivate the NBRC. Unlike their predecessors who had been primarily interested in isolating the causes of diminished fertility and determining its implications, the new commissioners, under the presidency of Henry Russell Wakefield, the Bishop of Birmingham (1911–24), were governed by a wider mandate to explore virtually every facet of the quantitative and qualitative demographic aspects of "national and racial reconstruction."[2] Although the declining birthrate was now acknowledged to be only one of several critical elements of the population question, it remained central to the reconstituted commission. Even by the standard of the perilously low fertility ratio of 1914 it was estimated that some 543,087 children had not been born during the war who should have been.[3] With the loss of over 700,000 men of child-producing age, and more than 1,600,000 wounded and maimed weighing upon their deliberations, the commissioners were haunted by a morbid image of full coffins and empty cradles.

A number of members from the first commission were reappointed, but Dean Inge, one of the few sympathetic to birth control, was replaced as chairman by Dr. Caleb Saleeby. Inge admitted to Havelock Ellis that he had used his position "rather high-handedly . . . to induce the Birth-Rate Commision to abstain from misrepresenting the scientific evidence" and condemning family limitation as harmful. As a result he had been excluded from the new group whose members, he predicted, "are now preparing to eat their own published words." Their report, he expected, would be a "belated kick of the prewar mentality, with its timid and reactionary ethics, its reckless and thoughtless sentimentalism, its intellectual insincerity, too deep-seated to be called hypocrisy."[4]

In Saleeby the NCPM found a chairman who shared its perception of the menace posed by the declining birthrate. Although he had once been sympathetic to Neo-Malthusianism as a form of negative eugenics, the horrifying casualties of the war had convinced Saleeby that qualitative selection at the expense of quantity was a racial luxury Britain could ill afford in a world threatened by more populous, aggressive nations. Even before the war, Germany, with a population of seventy million, not only substantially outnumbered Britain but added twice as many people to its numbers each year. On the other side of the globe militant Japan, not yet an enemy, was, with fifty million people, larger than Britain and nearly as large as the "white population of our immense empire." When the low fertility of the mother country and its colonial settlements were added to the demographic costs of the war, Saleeby told the first NBRC, it was obvious that enemies of family limitation were correct in their assessment of the future of the Empire whatever the outcome of the European conflict.[5]

These concerns, coupled to calculations that the ranks of the surplus, unmarried women of childbearing age would be substantially enlarged by the war, prompted twenty-four of the twenty-seven commissioners to insist on an "Addition" to the 1916 report recommending measures to encourage early marriage, the birth of more children, and improvements in their chances of survival. Tax inducements, educational bonuses, better housing, expanded medical facilities, and improved prenatal and postnatal care to preserve as many of the newborn as possible would, the signers of the "Addition" anticipated, stimulate the demographic resurgence society required to survive. In their opinion the war had conclusively shown that the selfishness of the better classes in leading the flight from maternity was every bit as reprehensible and far more dangerous than the fabled recklessness of the poor.[6] Although no less saddened by the terrible losses on the battlefield and in the nursery, Inge, J. A. Hobson, and the psychologist James Crichton-Browne remained unconvinced that an enlarged birthrate and a greater population was either feasible or desirable and declined to sign the "Addition." None of them was reappointed to the new commission in 1918, and, as Inge foresaw, its report, published in 1920, was much more hostile to birth control than that of its predecessor.

Had the editor of the first report, the Reverend James Marchant, been free of the constraints imposed by the commission and Dean Inge, he would have censured the indulgent practitioners of birth control and proclaimed contraception a proven threat to individual health and sanity as well as to the nation. Unlike the commissioners who had been persuaded by the conflicting evidence to defer judgment on the physiological and psychological consequences of restrictive practices, Marchant in two of his own books, *Cradles and Coffins* (1916) and *Birth-Rate and Empire* (1917), claimed that contraception caused sterility and a host of other maladies. When added to the "life-destroying tragedies" of miscarriage and infant mortality, Marchant calculated that it had contributed to the loss of between 19,500,000 and 20,200,000 potential lives since the Knowlton trial of 1877. The war was the latest stage of this human wastage.[7]

Although the conflict was an incalculable disaster, Marchant prayed that it could revive the "claims of race or posterity" that had been undermined by materialism coupled to the momentous discovery of the control of propagation.[8] The "heroic energy" generated by the war might mark an end to the "general feeling of race-weariness" that Inge, among others, thought indicative of an evolutionary tendency of an older and tired power to withdraw from the struggle for existence and to sacrifice its future for the material, personal gratifications of the present. Declining trade, increased competition, internal conflicts, and self-doubt had certainly encouraged such beliefs before the war, Marchant conceded. But victory could mean renewal and a restoration of confidence. Automobiles might become less important than cradles once the "economic pressures and social ideas that have strangled the natural affections of motherhood and the home" were expunged from the national experience.[9]

Marchant recognized that Neo-Malthusianism ended any possibility of returning to the uncontrolled reproduction of earlier generations. But since 1914 the loss of "only sons" from good families and "great houses . . . where the pedigree has snapped" had taught a bitter lesson to people of all classes.[10] They had learned, as W. Hayes Fisher, president of the Local Government Board cautioned in 1918, that the "racial cradle" must be substantially larger than the "racial coffin" if a family or a civilization is to survive.[11] The comparison of extinct families with vanished empires was reinforced by the war experience. In each case, other people, perhaps of lesser quality and accomplishment, were prepared to fill the vacancies forfeited by those unable or unwilling to preserve their valuable legacies. Marchant recalled Francis Bacon's "Feast of the Family" in the New Atlantis honoring parents who produced thirty living descendants as creditors of the king. It might be instituted after the war, he suggested, "and our King might establish another Order of Merit for those who can show the largest number of healthy children."[12]

Far from piling up such procreant treasures, people in all walks of life seemed more determined than even during the war to restrict the size of their families. They did so despite repeated warnings from Marchant, Fisher, and countless others that France and Britain's waning fertility had whetted the expansionist appetites of the marauding Hun and his fecund allies in 1914. Had the French and British not fallen so far behind, Marchant contended, the Central Powers would have been much more reluctant to pursue their reckless course and would have been defeated much sooner.[13] Even then, a physician insisted, the war would eventually have been won by those who had children, not those who for a generation or more had evaded their racial responsibilities. Malthus had been turned on his head, and the country had paid a terrible price.[14] Despite innumerable warnings for at least two decades before the war, Britain entered the conflict with both a smaller and older population. Whatever the outcome, William Brend, a barrister and physician at Charing Cross Hospital, predicted that the vengeful Germans would continue to have a decisive numerical advantage for at least another generation even if population growth in both countries became static.[15]

The Malthusian League was profoundly disturbed by such wartime arguments and feared a demographic backlash that could threaten the progress of the past thirty-five years. It was not Malthus who had been turned on his head, its spokesmen countered, but his critics who contended that underpopulation had somehow caused the war. On the contrary, it was the overpopulation of the Central Powers that fueled their aggression. France, for example, had not been attacked by Germany because of Gallic infertility, but because of demographic pressures within the overcrowded Reich. The Malthusian League had been warning about such pressures not only in Germany but in Britain and elsewhere since 1879, encouraging the adoption of Neo-Malthusianism as the best safeguard against wars of external conquest as well as the only enduring cure for internal dissension.[16] In the aftermath of the Boer War and the Russo-Japanese War the elderly C. R. Drysdale recalled the league's many predictions that overpopulation would inevitably compel such countries as Russia, Japan, Germany, and

Britain to break the peace "in order to rob other nations" of their necessary resources.[17]

Neo-Malthusians were by no means alone in their populationist explanations of international tension. Edwardian political and military analysts gave considerable credence to demographic explanations of German restlessness and belligerency. The registrar-general frequently singled out German growth for particular comment, noting Britain's comparative disadvantages.[18] Such comparisons fed the periodic fears and at times almost fatalistic resignation to the inevitability of conflict. Montague Crackanthorpe, in 1906, thought the Germans were particularly dangerous because they were increasing by a million people a year and felt immured in a geographical prison, "the walls of which are spiked by the power of the Dual Alliance." Not surprisingly, Germany recklessly sought colonial outlets and fresh markets for "superfluous inhabitants." German growth had led to a national rivalry with England that could "one day develop into a hostile collision."[19] Neither enormous armament expenditures nor international conventions such as that planned for the Hague in 1907 could provide security, Crackanthorpe predicted. Only the control of population growth could reverse the ominous drift toward war inherent in the differential fertility of ambitious nations.[20]

By 1908 the *Malthusian* saw encouraging signs. The birthrate in Berlin had fallen from 36.5/1,000 to 24.3 since 1895, and there were indications that fertility was declining in other parts of the country. Germany still remained dangerous and unpredictable, however, as her economic progress had not kept pace with her population, and many militarists believed this discrepancy could only be corrected by expansion and conquest. Since all high-birthrate nations were suspect to Neo-Malthusian analysts, they found it perfectly understandable that Germany would ally with the overly fertile Austrians and encourage their adventures in the Balkans. Any country whose "social morality" condoned a birthrate of 36/1,000 and higher was not likely to be very scrupulous in honoring international agreements, the *Malthusian* proclaimed during the Bosnian crisis of 1908. Until treaties were based upon demographic and economic realities, it editorialized, they would prove of little value in preserving the peace.[21]

For many years before the war the Malthusian League advocated a pact between countries that "sensibly restrained their populations" to contain the aggression of "semi-civilised nations who have not learned how to restrain their population to their resources." It had welcomed the French entente in 1904 and hoped eight years later that its development into an alliance would be extended to include Scandinavia, Holland, Belgium, Switzerland, and the United States.[22] No mention was made of the irredeemably fecund Russians and the convention worked out with them in 1907. To Neo-Malthusian geopoliticians the world was divided into conflicting high and low fertility camps; only a formidable demonstration of unity by the latter was likely to halt the expansionist inclinations of the former. They were not alone in their assessment. Many of their contemporaries, like a writer in the Germanophobic *National Review* in 1912, envisioned a great conflict between the better-armed, overpopulated half of the world to extirpate the poorly armed and less populous. He was still uncertain as to which side Britain would be on.[23]

Although the pressures of overpopulation might have provoked conflicts in the earlier stages of national development, some optimistic Malthusians thought, like Havelock Ellis, that it was no longer a danger in modern times. Differing with Norman Angell's 1910 bestseller, *The Great Illusion*, Ellis asserted that only the wealthy and advanced nations could afford prolonged war on a grand scale, but those nations were the very ones whose birthrates were declining. England's ally, Russia, not Germany, where fertility was falling, was the one possible threat to peace. Even then, however, the high mortality of the backward Russians greatly reduced the dangerous effects of excessive reproduction. Moreover, the Russians had plenty of room to expand within their existing borders, and long before their empty spaces were filled, Ellis predicted, they will have joined other contentious peoples, like the Germans, in lowering their birthrate. Endorsing the conclusions of Stanford University's president, David Starr Jordan, and the Russian sociologist, Jacques Novikov, Ellis averred that declining fertility was, like the natural exhaustion of "the warlike spirit," a progressive, evolutionary attribute of civilized countries.[24]

C. V. Drysdale was not at all convinced that the German birthrate had fallen fast and far enough to defuse the population bomb that threatened to explode at any moment. Fertility in that aggressive country had dropped from 41/1,000 in 1876 to around 29/1,000, he wrote in early 1914, but it was by no means certain that Germany's expansionist momentum had slowed at the same rate.[25] The longer war could be avoided the more time there would be for German militaristic aspirations and the German birthrate to fall below a combustible level. When war erupted that summer, Drysdale sadly concluded that time had at last run out on the Malthusian clock. He calculated that it would have taken another ten years of declining fertility to lower the population pressure sufficiently to secure peace.

Having been ignored by the statesmen of Europe who sought security in futile alliances and spiraling expenditures for weapons, Drysdale was determined not to let them forget the true cause of the conflict. He bitterly recalled that family limitation had not even been mentioned at the Hague Conference seven years earlier despite Malthusian League efforts to have it placed on the agenda. As a result, the high-birthrate nations of central and eastern Europe that had been threatening the peace for decades could no longer contain their explosive tensions. The league's "Malthusian War Map" contrasted the excessive fertility of Austria (33.7), Hungary (35.7), Rumania (40.9), Bulgaria (42.2), Serbia (38.6), and Germany (31.7) during the years 1906 to 1910 with that of France (19.9), Belgium (21.3), and the United Kingdom (25.7). Russia, where the birthrate remained at an embarrassingly high 45.4, was the one exception to the Neo-Malthusian alliance system. Drysdale frankly wondered how long their unreliable, eastern ally would last.[26] The Russian Revolution three years later followed by the Soviet capitulation at Brest Litovsk confirmed his worst suspicions.

Virtually every aspect of the war was viewed demographically by Malthusian League zealots. Among the Kaiser's numerous sins, none was more offensive than his notorious hostility to birth control. The worst consequence of a German victory would be its retrogressive impact on the progress of family limitation. The moral fiber and tenacity of the various belligerents was determined by their fertility. Germany offered the "worst example of frigid and calculated violation of international morality on record." Belgium, by contrast, "with a birthrate not much higher than France, has given a heroic refusal to sell her honour . . . and has conducted a magnificent defense." Supposedly degenerate France has "shown herself calm and courageous in the face of wanton attack" and has fought the more numerous Hun to a standstill. Russia, with her huge numbers, was alone reeling before the assaults of her adversaries, demonstrating once again that the quality and efficiency of a population was more important than its size.[27] The less fertile nations have already gone on the offensive, a Neo-Malthusian strategist prematurely announced in 1915, and the epic battle "will settle the survival value of a low birth-rate in all its aspects."[28]

Another three years of relentless slaughter were required to resolve the issue, but few Neo-Malthusians wavered in their single-minded analysis of each advance or setback. By late 1917 J. M. Robertson was satisfied that the "nations with the longest-attained decline in the birth-rate . . . have held like iron on the Western Front. The Central Powers, relying on population have failed . . . after the first rush." Unfortunately, but not surprisingly, Russia, "with the largest population and the highest birth-rate of all, has shown the least power of continued effort, military, financial, moral, and administrative." The omens, Robertson concluded, are assuredly "not in favour of blind breeding."[29] Like Drysdale and others he believed the war had proven that irrespective of size a country would fight tenaciously to preserve a valued, prosperous way of life that was only possible when overpopulation was kept in check.

Advocates of these interpretations maintained them in the face of angry recriminations. As the casualty lists multiplied and the recruitment of sufficient replacements became more difficult, longtime proponents of smaller families were the targets of considerable abuse. Havelock Ellis, ordinarily the most restrained of men, scathingly attacked those "pseudo-patriots" in parliament, the press, and the churches who "tear their hair" and rage wildly about the smaller birthrate. In spite of the immediate tragedy, Ellis remained convinced that diminished fertility was a facet of progressive evolution that all of us "who abhor war cannot but pray . . . may be hastened." The dreary "apostles of race suicide" have never learned that a restricted birthrate, with its accompanying low death rate, was a result of the same valued qualities of reason, foresight, and self-restraint that marked a society's move to a higher step on the evolutionary ladder where it would no longer have primitive recourse to war to solve its problems.[30] Less optimistic defenders of family limitation were by no means certain that lower fertility was an effect of evolutionary enlighten-ment, recalling that man, as Thomas Huxley had said, was not a "fallen angel, but a risen ape."[31] The conscious struggle against natural fecundity was, therefore, Drysdale suggested, as much a cause of human progress as it was a consequence. Any relapse would result in socioeconomic regres-sion and a reversion to atavistic, aggressive tendencies in the species.

In light of the frightful war casualties Marchant could not comprehend how Ellis and Inge, "the most important champions of Malthusianism," could maintain that small families were a result of evolutionary progress rather than an "enfeebled sense of duty." He found their perverted, nega-tive eugenic notion that democracy could "become aristocracized by using the cradle for firewood" contemptible.[32] At the same time Marchant and many other wartime critics of Neo-Malthusianism knew that the clock could not be turned back. Birth control, Dr. Brend wrote in 1915, was here to stay. By the end of the war it would be practiced by couples in all sectors of society. Moreover, after the war women would continue in the labor force, and, as the experience of the textile districts revealed, they were unlikely to have many children. Every effort, therefore, had to be made "at the present crisis in our history" to discourage the view that Neo-Malthusianism was in any way beneficial to a country. The promotion and preservation of lives, not their prevention, was, Brend asserted, the most urgent task of reconstruction in the postwar world.[33]

Brend's demographic anxieties, like those of his contemporaries, were not only prodded by wartime manpower shortages but by the conviction that Germany, whose population would for many years exceed that of Great Britain, would, if defeated, certainly seek revenge. The rebuilding of human stock could not begin too soon. Much of the discussion, carried on as it was in middle- and upper-class circles, was tinged with eugenic, qualitative assumptions. It was widely believed during and after the war that the sons of the better-educated and more prosperous had flocked to the colors in disproportionately large numbers and thus bore the brunt of the casualties. Working-class enlistments in the first eighteen months of the war were greater than commonly perceived, but they were proportionally less numerous than the volunteers drawn from banking, finance, commerce, real estate, and the professions.[34] A great many of these early recruits were therefore presumed by eugenically conscious analysts to be from small, selective families whose higher racial qualities and lower fertility had been a source of worry throughout the prewar years.

Dr. Louis C. Parkes thought the racial outlook in 1915 looked very ominous. He reminded the Royal Sanitary Institute that excessive war losses among the least fertile and most capable sector of society—"the upper, the middle and the superior working classes"—had greatly reinforced the qualitative racial imbalance already created by the unrestricted breeding of the "least intelligent and most dependent elements of the population."[35] His views were reiterated by a number of speakers, including Dr. Phillip Boobbyer, the medical officer of health for Nottingham, who observed that the war, as nothing else, had shown the folly of small families. He grieved for the many parents "who mourned the death of an only child" and lamented that they had no other to comfort them and carry on the family. Their personal tragedy, multiplied thousands of times over, raised the frightening possibility that the scales of survival were weighted against the better classes.[36]

Eugenists continually complained that the war was being fought by the healthiest and most vigorous sector of the population while the less able and defective remained at home to propagate their weaknesses. Casualties were approximately two to three times greater among officers than among the common soldiers, and the roll of honor in every school and college bore witness to the talent that perished.[37] The loss of children, frequently only sons, in one notable family after another, was a constant reminder of the *Eugenics Review*'s somber prediction in the opening weeks of the conflict that the "eugenic and dysgenic effects of war are about to be put to the supreme test."[38]

Britain's initial reliance upon voluntary recruitment, eugenists protested, left her particularly vulnerable to the destruction of her bravest and fittest men. In contrast to countries with compulsory service, the *Eugenics Review* projected, Britain's "battle death-rate must strike unevenly and reduce the number of her males amongst the class from which it is most desirable that she should produce the stock of the future." The journal's strategists calculated that men who "are physically and mentally superior will volunteer" so that the "sample of those killed will not be the average of the race, but the best type of the race." The eugenists assumed metaphorically that the "cream of the race will be taken and the skimmed milk will be left."[39]

Until the adoption of conscription in 1916 there seemed to be no way to avert the disproportionate loss of the most "chivalrous, virile and courageous young men" who were, naturally, the first to take up arms. Their destruction, the Regius Professor of Natural History J. Arthur Thompson predicted, would lead not only to a "maternal depression" among women of their class, but would accentuate the overproduction of "under-average types" and inevitably lead to "some sort of race impoverishment."[40] Thompson, like the Cambridge University geneticist and eugenist, R. A. Fisher, and the Eugenics Education Society's president, Major Leonard Darwin, acknowledged that although conscription would moderate the racial imbalance in the casualty lists, it would by no means eliminate the problem of dysgenic reproduction. The medically unfit would still be rejected while the soundest stock continued to be exposed to death or maiming. Obviously inferior stock, or the "C3 population," as it came to be categorized by medical examiners, could not be sent to the front with the A1 troops without running an unacceptable risk of defeat. Still, Darwin decided, conscription was probably more desirable "because casualty lists would then more nearly represent a random sample of the population" even if the level of combat was less heroic.[41]

Such subtleties were lost on the military planners who, in their relentless quest for more troops to replace the staggering losses suffered in France and Belgium, gave little thought to the long-range hereditary implications of their enormously costly strategy. With its own ranks depleted by the demands of the war, the Eugenics Education Society nevertheless took upon itself the task of sensitizing the nation to the genetic implications of the great struggle while moderating the racially disastrous effects of differential wartime mortality. Darwin suggested that, if conscription proved necessary, older men should be called up first in order to preserve as many younger men as possible to rebuild the "nation's stock" after the war.[42]

"Race reconstruction" was not only imperilled by military policies at the front but by social and economic policies at home. Eugenics Education Society members were by no means alone in their concern that the disruptive economic impact of the war and the burdens of financing it would increase the reluctance of responsible people in the middle and higher classes to marry and raise large families. A deputation from the NCPM, led by the Bishop of Birmingham, appealed directly in 1916 to Walter Long at the Local Government Board for a reduction in taxes to encourage more people to wed and have children.[43] Sidney Webb, appearing in 1918 before the second NBRC claimed that as long as the tax burdens fell so heavily on the classes who should reproduce themselves, the community would continue to breed fastest "from its socially least desirable stocks."[44]

As early as 1915 R. A. Fisher began estimating the reproduction needed to recover a sufficient stock of able men over the age of eighteen if half the men in arms were killed. He calculated that if "those strains and types which have borne the brunt of the fighting" had five children to every four sired by the less fit civilian population, practically all of the wartime damage to the race could be repaired in three generations. It would of course be a "great eugenic achievement," he added, if the government made it economically possible for servicemen, particularly officers and noncomissioned officers, to marry young because it would probably accelerate the rate of race recovery. Special inducements, perhaps in the form of annual annuities, might be offered to those who have won military honors on the reasonable presumption that their courage and initiative was an inheritable quality that should be passed on to as many children as possible.[45] Every opportunity, Major Darwin added, must be provided returning soldiers to marry and settle down to raising a family "in order to promote the reappearance of their manly qualities in the coming generations."[46]

The Eugenics Education Society Council continually debated various promotional schemes to encourage troops, returning veterans, and even the wounded and maimed still capable of procreation to find a suitable wife as quickly as possible and start the regenerative process.[47] "If there is a patriotism in dying for our country," J. Arthur Thompson reasoned, "there is conceivable patriotism in marrying for her and in bearing children for her."[48] Not even the prospect of death on the battlefield was seen as a deterrent. The initial surge of marriages in the early months of the war was greeted with enthusiasm in eugenic circles, although Darwin hoped that officers and noncommissioned officers comprised the largest proportion of those rushing to the altars and registry offices. Quality, he cautioned, must not be lost in the eagerness for quantity.[49]

"Some of us," Caleb Saleeby told the NBRC, "are trying to persuade the men as far as possible to marry before they go," and he exhorted that eminent group to endorse legislation guaranteeing substantial allowances to the posthumous children of men killed in the war. Unlike a number of less perceptive eugenists, however, he doubted that either parliament or the public would tolerate the exclusion of offspring born to the fallen in the enlisted ranks. If the battlefield had become the principal agency of natural selection, it was imperative, Saleeby argued, to facilitate the birth of as many posthumous heirs as possible and let the future sort out their differing capabilities.[50]

The war not only stimulated demands for a reversal of the downward birthrate, but it also focused a great many disparate efforts on the lowering of infant mortality and improved maternal care. An immediate problem confronting military and public health authorities was the spread of venereal disease. It reached epidemic proportions in some sectors of the armed forces, threatening the health of the nation's defenders and their wives and children. When in 1916 Anglican churchmen attending convocation talked at length about the sanctity of the home and the "purity of life," they were reacting to the recent report of the Royal Commission on Venereal Disease. With approximately one serviceman in five infected with gonorrhea, syphilis, or some other venereal ailment, something had to be done to protect the diminished number of children born and their innocent mothers from such rampant promiscuous folly.[51] Consequently, although church assemblies and clerical authorities continued to condemn the sale of "preventives," there was no protest from religious quarters in 1917 when the distribution of condoms to the troops was officially sanctioned. Though ostensibly issued for prophylactic purposes, it was obvious that millions of men would use them as contraceptives. Whatever their dismay, the enemies of birth control thought the condoms a lesser evil under the circumstances than the continued contamination of mothers and their vulnerable, defective, short-lived offspring. At the same time, as Registrar-General Sir Bernard Mallet told the Institute of Public Health in 1918, no effort could be spared to preserve the infant survivors of the colossal European-wide scourge of race-suicide that had "filled the graves . . . [and] emptied the cradles" during the past four years.[52]

The medical profession was singled out as having special responsibilities, and its spokesmen, from the earliest days of the war, called for greater exertions on behalf of mothers and their children. The "war wastage" evident in first casualty lists was described in the medical press as the final blow after the low fertility of the preceding twenty or thirty years.[53] Various projections about the loss of potential lives from the continued spread of birth control, the disruption of family life, miscarriage, and infant mortality buttressed medical arguments. The hostility and anxiety that many doctors had felt about birth control in the prewar decade erupted in recriminations and accusations of selfish irresponsibility and racial cowardliness. As a result, one doctor anguished, we find our house "tenantless and . . . a prey to foes who have shown a wiser foresight and a truer appreciation of values than ourselves."[54] In light of existing and projected demographic realities, the *British Medical Journal* announced in 1915, it was imperative for the medical profession to do all that it could to reduce premature births and infant mortality so as to preserve as many children as possible for postwar reconstruction.[55]

Even then, a number of doctors speculated, it was doubtful whether their aging country would ever again have sufficient manpower to recover completely. Dr. E. J. Smith, a leading Bradford physician and a member of the new National Birth-Rate Commission, noted that middle-aged people already exceeded children by a ratio of three to two. The loss of so many fathers and potential fathers, plus the flood of women into new fields of service incompatible with motherhood, promised to exacerbate the age differences. Smith's solution, like that of so many others during the war, was the launching of a national campaign to protect the young by providing better housing, improved diet, clean milk, medical assistance, and any public health measures needed to aid mothers and their children.[56]

The availability of maternity and child services before the war was at best haphazard and dependent upon the varied initiatives of local authorities.[57] Mounting concern about the falling birthrate and the possibilities of physical deterioration stirred up by the Boer War had stimulated considerable interest in the care and welfare of children. It also contributed to the passage of Liberal legislation after 1906 establishing the systematic medical examination of elementary school students as well as providing them with adequate meals.[58] Earlier, in 1902, a Midwives Act established central registration, minimal standards, and medical supervision in an attempt to reduce maternal and infant mortality.[59] These efforts were supplemented by the work of voluntary groups organized in the aftermath of alarming medical reports on the rejection of military recruits and the poor health of school children.[60] Individuals of varying prominence joined with reform groups and the young Labour party in calling for government allowances, even pensions, for mothers while requiring parents to meet minimum standards for child care. H. G. Wells's autobiographical hero in his 1911 novel *The New Machiavelli* achieved his political notoriety by advocating a eugenically inspired scheme for the endowment of motherhood.[61]

Starting in 1908 a series of national conferences on infant mortality was held annually in London. Their reports, which reflected a deep sense of urgency about the need to offset the falling birthrate by a diminished infant death rate, were after 1910 often attached as supplements to those of the medical officer of health of the Local Government Board.[62] If there was considerable controversy about individual proposals to improve the care of mothers and their newborn, there was general agreement about the inadequacies of the registration of births and deaths of infants. Some local authorities, such as those in Huddersfield, required rapid notification by fathers, and, at the urging of medical officers of health, it was extended to the nation in 1907 and made compulsory in 1915. The new legislation not only provided more accurate statistics at a time when there was much

anxiety about the number of children born each year, but more importantly, it expedited the arrival of health visitors to assist new mothers and
their infants.[63]

The rapid expansion of these and other public health measures, coupled
to medical progress in the control of some childhood diseases, was reflected in the encouraging if erratic decline in infant mortality. By 1912 it
had fallen to an unprecedented 95 deaths per one thousand births, and,
although the rate rose again to 110 in 1915 it was well below earlier levels
and after that year never again exceeded 100. Though doctors were quick
to take much of the credit for the improvement and repeatedly dedicated
themselves to even greater achievements, the chances of a child surviving
during the war actually increased while the number of physicians available
to care for them decreased because of military needs. Neo-Malthusians,
who never believed doctors made much difference in any event, were
certain that the figures simply confirmed their old claim that death rates
were determined by birthrates. In all probability, however, the reduction
in infant mortality owed as much to the higher wages, improved diet, and
less crowded living conditions that many people on the home front enjoyed during the war as it did to any dramatic advance in medicine or
public health.

As "curtailing the waste of infant life" became a national concern throughout the war years, countless recommendations were proposed to assure
the good health of mothers and their diminished progeny. Benjamin
Broadbent, for example, called for the establishment of model maternal
communities where government, medicine, and philanthropy could demonstrate ways of "safeguarding all the new life that is given."[64] Women in
particular were urged to prod local authorities to recruit more health
visitors and establish infant and maternal welfare centers where mothers
and their children could be properly treated and nourished. Feminist organizations had supported the prewar demands for improved programs and
facilities, but they had played a decidedly secondary role in their establishment. Suffragists asserted that enfranchised women would be more effective advocates of maternal and child welfare than men, and they cited as
evidence the lower rates of infant mortality in Australia and New Zealand
where women had the vote.[65] The suffrage forces set aside their political
demands during the war, and they threw their weight behind the various
campaigns to advance the art of what was popularly known as "mother-
craft." They joined with others to badger local officials to end their "false
economies" and "parsimonious rate-saving tradition" while the war took its
daily toll of the "young manhood of the nation."[66] At the same time they
supported the National Birth-Rate Commission and other organizations
and individuals in asking the national government to assure that maternity

bonuses and financial assistance would be available to mothers of young children in the postwar years in order to encourage them to expand their families as soon as possible.[67]

Socialists and Labour party candidates had been advocating maternal subsidies for working-class mothers for nearly two decades, but the combined reality of the waning birthrate and massive wartime casualties made the idea appeal to people of widely differing political persuasions. Imperialists, worried about depopulation abroad, joined with anticolonialists calculating future demographic needs at home. Eugenists, who were scarcely enthusiastic about assisting the reproduction of the already too numerous poor, nevertheless endorsed maternity bonuses if they would also assist the hard-pressed wives of middle- and upper-class servicemen, mainly officers, to contribute a greater proportion of children than in the past to the task of race reconstruction. Shortly after the outbreak of the war the Eugenics Education Society in 1914 established its own Professional Classes War Relief Council to minimize the expected dysgenic effects of the conflict. J. Pierpont Morgan was prevailed upon to make his commodious house at Prince's Gate available for a maternity home for the wives of officers to assure the best of care for their genetically valuable offspring. Some 242 children of doctors, lawyers, university teachers, and other race heroes were born there over the next two years.[68]

The Eugenics Education Society was one of many groups responsible for the introduction of a National Baby Week in July, 1917. Modeled on a similar undertaking in the United States, the meetings, exhibits, and lectures on prenatal and postnatal care were designed to focus attention upon the need for healthy children to fill the stilled cradles of the land. Although the first Baby Week received comparatively little notice, its successor the following summer in Liverpool and London met with a great deal of favorable publicity and received the enthusiastic endorsement of prominent medical, clerical, social, and political figures.[69] In contrast, the impenitent leaders of the Malthusian League described Baby Week as an "atrocity." To them it was another stage in the battle they had been waging since the opening days of the war against eugenists and other "puritans" who, like the hated Kaiser himself, extolled the national and racial obligations of rearing a large family.[70]

Although the war sharply curtailed several of the league's activities, the organization pointedly declined the invitation of its opponents to emulate the suffragettes and halt its damaging campaign for the duration.[71] Instead the leadership determined that that clamor for a reversal in the declining birthrate necessitated greater vigilance than ever to preserve the gains achieved since 1877. The task was not easy. Membership, never very large, dropped off as the faithful were pressed into military service or war-related occupations. C. V. Drysdale's own engineering talents were co-opted by the Anti-Submarine Division of the Admiralty, and his wife Bessie and Binnie Dunlop had to carry most of the administrative and editorial burdens of the league and its publications.[72] Though requests for propaganda initially fell sharply, the war-induced interest in birth control soon reversed the trend. For the first time in years income exceeded expenditure, and the diminished staff had difficulty keeping up with demands for the league's practical leaflet, introduced shortly before the war.[73] The success was short-lived. The Drysdales' raging hostility to socialism and intemperate denunciations of reconstructionist welfare proposals alienated many of the tentative supporters who, like H. G. Wells and the How-Martyns, had grudgingly joined the league solely to advance the cause of birth control as a means of social improvement. Donations and subscriptions rapidly dwindled away leaving a balance of only £50 in the league's coffers and a severely depleted membership list when hostilities ground to a close.[74]

Perhaps the most painful blow the league had to bear, however, was not the defection from its ranks, but the accusation that its promotion of small families was not only immoral and irresponsible but disloyal. In a futile effort to curb the "charge that our movement was unpatriotic," the *Malthusian* announced in the summer of 1914 that a number of "distinguished foreign supporters" were to be dropped from the league's list of vice-presidents.[75] What outraged the league's accusers, however, was not its roster of officers, but its deplorable campaign for a moratorium on childbirth until the war was won. Within days of the outbreak of hostilities, Drysdale, alarmed by frantic cries for more children to compensate for anticipated losses, proclaimed the young a burden on the nation's limited resources. With the nation facing untold demands and its men a perilous future, it was foolish, he argued, to encourage women, many of whom will soon have no reliable means of support, to assume the obligation of raising children alone.[76]

Working people were reminded by Bessie Drysdale in a series of brief pamphlets that a rise in the birthrate would, by creating more surplus labor, only increase poverty and compound their difficulties after the war. Moreover, "war babies" were obviously of no use to the country during the conflict; they could only consume, not produce. Children in particular would suffer from harsh winters, fuel and food shortages, and the absence of their mothers recruited for war work. The high mortality suffered by the offspring of working mothers was well known, the pamphlets emphasized. Those children who survived would forever carry the scars of severe deprivation into an overcrowded postwar world where they would find

few opportunities to escape exploitation by greedy capitalists and dangerous, disgruntled socialists.[77]

Although Marchant and the enemies of family limitation grimly calculated the loss of potential new lives as a consequence of the war, Neo-
Malthusians projected the increase in new mouths to feed. Bessie Drysdale
estimated in 1915 that births would exceed battlefield deaths in that year
by twenty to one, and they would create a severe drain on the nation's
strapped resources.[78] The following year her casualty estimates doubled to
100,000, and, although somewhat chastened, she was still certain that the
replenishment ratio, if only ten to one, was more than sufficient for the
future.[79] Even then, Charles Killick Millard added, when many of the war
babies were ready to enter the labor market, they would find that their
jobs had been taken by modernized machinery and women. J. M. Robertson told the second NBRC that families of two to four would be more
than adequate in coming decades, but many of the more traditional Neo-
Malthusians thought that estimate too indulgent.[80]

Throughout the war Neo-Malthusians cited examples of severe food
shortages in various European countries, and they saw in them signs of the
great famines predicted by Malthus in his famous *Essay on the Principles of
Population*. A century of dazzling technological and scientific progress had
been unable to save the soil from exhaustion, the *Malthusian* gloated in
1917, so that even supposedly self-reliant Germany has discovered how
vulnerable it is to the consequences of excessive "baby production."[81] To
reinforce its contentious plan for a moratorium on children the *Malthusian*
extracted discussions of possible postwar famine from other publications
and gave them prominent play in its own columns.[82] It was particularly
taken with an article in the *Times* by Harold Cox, editor of the *Edinburgh
Review*, concluding that even if England ploughed up all of her sporting
grounds along with the rest of her arable land, there was no possibility of
the country feeding herself without a sharp decline in family size.[83] Cox, a
former Fabian and Liberal M.P., was a respected classical economist whose
concerns about overpopulation made him an important member of the
Neo-Malthusians in the 1920s. During the war, without explicitly endorsing the Malthusian League's moratorium, he questioned the wisdom of
promoting greater fertility when countries with smaller populations were
likely to have a real advantage in the competitive struggle for recovery that
would surely follow the end of hostilities.

Once it was apparent that the Malthusian League not only intended to
press on with its campaign, but actually viewed the war as an opportunity
to reduce the birthrate further, the reaction was swift and predictably
acrimonious. At a meeting in the Guildhall in October 1914, Sir James

Crichton Browne, no friend of unselective breeding, nevertheless called for an all-out effort to stop Drysdale and his followers from interfering with the "copious reinforcements of infant life . . . so vitally important to the economical future of the country." Certain as he was that Neo-Malthusian propaganda was largely "responsible for a marked diminution in the output of infants, and mostly of infants of those better stocks which it is most desirable to preserve," Sir James wondered "whether in wartime the Censor would not be better employed . . . if he interdicted Neo-Malthusian advertisements."[84]

Eugenic considerations were evident in much of the reaction to the Malthusian League's activities despite league assurances that it was primarily interested in curtailing the fertility of the populous working classes. With so many of the early casualties coming from small middle- and upper-class families, the worst fears of eugenists who had long been wary of birth control seemed vindicated. They were particularly horrified by the realization that more than 60 percent of the undergraduates from some universities were in the forces, in which capacity their superior progenitive qualities were at great risk of being buried on the western front. Even Caleb Saleeby, who at one time had supported the Neo-Malthusians in their attempt to advance birth control as the most effective means of checking the fertility of undesirable stocks, now had second thoughts. In retrospect he thought it might have encouraged German aggression, and he was deeply disturbed that the Malthusian League, led by the Drysdales, was urging yet a further cut in the birthrate.[85] The *New Statesman*, one of the few journals in Great Britain openly sympathetic to family limitation before the war, renounced its mistake in 1916 and openly joined the anti-Malthusian ranks. It cited dysgenic war losses, the differential birthrate, the increasing age of the population, and the need to preserve the Empire as its reasons for repudiating the Neo-Malthusian appeal.[86]

C. V. Drysdale entreated his opponents to recognize the deleterious racial consequences of what could happen if the older and unfit remained at home siring larger families while the genetically most valuable men were at the front. In addition, the ablest women in society were working as never before and were too anxious and fatigued to add to their responsibilities. A moratorium on childbirth would therefore not only benefit the war effort and facilitate postwar reconstruction, it would curtail further dysgenic imbalances in the differential birthrate.[87] In spite of such reasoning, Marchant was probably correct in his assessment that most English men and women were offended by the "unscrupulous efforts" of Drysdale, Dunlop, and their like "to urge parents to have no children during the war despite the irreparable losses of our young men."[88]

To counter the heated reaction to its antinatal policies the Malthusian

League produced "several military members" to certify that Britain was in no way endangered by the declining birthrate, nor was it unpatriotic to defer having children. Millions of the country's most loyal subjects had obviously come to the same conclusions as the rapid fall in marital fertility graphically illustrated. Moreover, there were no signs of degeneration or waning patriotic vitality among the people from small families who, it was commonly acknowledged, were making the greatest contribution to the war effort. The *Malthusian* repeatedly cited recruitment figures proving that men from more prosperous communities, where families were presumably smaller, comprised a disproportionately large percentage of the volunteers while the "large-familied proletariat" lagged behind.[89] Though critics were quick to point out that the first to go were also the first to be killed off, leaving few children to perpetuate their heroic qualities, the *Malthusian* chose to interpret the evidence differently.

It seemed obvious to Neo-Malthusians, at least, that any increase in the birthrate would not only compound the problems of postwar recovery but exacerbate the dysgenic tendencies of differential fertility. Since the prudent "better-off" classes, motivated as they were by economic realities and future uncertainties, were not about to take on the additional burdens of a too numerous progeny, it made no sense to encourage the less capable to breed more. Far from strengthening the country, their numbers would only necessitate higher taxes to pay for elaborate socialistic welfare programs that would in turn discourage the more successful classes from enlarging their own families.

Malthusian League theorists were especially frustrated by their inability to bring eugenists and feminists, whom they persisted in believing were natural allies, around to their way of thinking.[90] They hoped that the exigencies of the war would force them to see the light, and they were therefore infuriated when the Eugenics Education Society and the old suffrage organizations endorsed the "current popular Socialistic Dysgenics that culminated in BABY WEEK."[91] The Drysdales had resigned from the Eugenics Education Society in 1915 when it spurned the league's moratorium, but Dunlop had remained a member in hopes of influencing a change in policy. With the advent of Baby Week, however, he threatened to quit and joined in decrying baby bonuses, maternal allotments, milk funds, and all the other collectivist panaceas designed to lure women into the nursery. If the eugenists could not see the threat such schemes posed to selective reproduction, the feminist societies should certainly have rebelled at the prospect of condemning working-class women to continual poverty and exploitation.

Most puzzling to older Neo-Malthusians was the knowledge that many individual feminists now frankly agreed that birth control was absolutely essential to their economic and political independence. Among the most outspoken of these was Frances W. Stella Browne, a militant, working-class communist who, incongruous though it seemed, embraced the Malthusian League in spite of its infuriating, archaic economic philosophy and rabid antisocialism.[92] She believed birth control was a critical first step in freeing working-class women from capitalistic oppression, and the league, for better or for worse, was the only organization open to her. The Labour party, with its large Catholic constituency, was as yet unwilling to mention the subject, and the "incurably respectable tacticians of the old N.U.W.S.S. and W.S.P.U." remained adamant in maintaining their prewar position.[93] Consequently, Stella Browne decided to use the offices of the league, confident she could get her message across to laboring women without it being polluted by the laissez-faire, utilitarian nonsense usually spouted by the organization's orthodox propagandists. The league, in turn, gained a dynamic, articulate advocate of birth control who could carry at least part of its message to working-class audiences.

Despite their radically different visions of the future, Stella Browne and the league's hierarchy shared the conviction that solutions to the population question and the woman's question lay at the core of postwar reconstruction. The war had brought matters to a head and turned the feminist movement around. Women had been drawn into the labor market in unprecedented numbers, and they enjoyed new responsibilities and economic independence. They would be foolish to jeopardize these gains, they were warned, by responding to reactionary appeals to produce the "battalions of the future" thereby retying the bonds that had so recently enslaved them.[94]

The merger of Neo-Malthusianism with feminism and socialism was incorporated into the novelist Edwin Pugh's 1918 utopian fantasy, *The Great Unborn: A Dream of Tomorrow*. Disillusioned by the war and convinced that advocates of maternal and child assistance plans were more interested in an uninterrupted supply of cheap labor and canon fodder than in the welfare of women and their offspring, Pugh saw in the control of fertility a great weapon for social revolution. One of his characters ridiculed Baby Week as a middle-class exercise in self-congratulation in which wealthy suburban parents exhibited their one or two well-dressed, well-fed children while extolling the joys of motherhood to unhearing, impoverished working-class women and their hungry broods locked away out of sight in overcrowded, pestilential slums.[95]

When exposed to the horrors endured by the poor, Pugh's angry, enlightened hero excoriates the pious preachers of "race renewal," crying out, "Give us back our country and we will do our duty to our country, but so long as it remains your country—No More Babies!"[96] Socialist men and women in the novel at last rebel against their own reproductivity that had for so long left them vulnerable to the oppressive capitalists and militarists. "No More Babies!" joined "Votes for Women!" as the dual slogans of socialist reconstruction. Pinning his hopes for the workers' salvation on the "Great Unborn," a labor leader calculates that if they would sacrifice having children for ten, twenty, even thirty years if necessary, the demand for labor would become so critical and the workers so prosperous and powerful that they would easily overthrow the more numerous, but now surplus leisured classes.[97]

Stimulated by these fanciful projects, the narrator of the novel dreams of a peaceful world in which the "Apostles of the Great Unborn" preach the blessings of birth control to a working class in which women are fully emancipated. The "new women" in Pugh's infertile utopia lead the way in reducing fertility, but, in accordance with Neo-Malthusian canons, without repudiating marriage. They simply "hold back" and prevent conception until the ruling classes are brought to their knees. Three years after the war the birthrate is at 13.4; a decade later it is 3.0. Unable to exploit their shrinking labor force any longer, the capitalists lose their role in society, their industries are nationalized, and the exploiters quietly wither away. In the "one-class society" created by the "Triumph of the Great Unborn" family life soon revives, but, having learned the lessons of the past, no couple ever again has more than three or four children.[98]

Although most Neo-Malthusian readers doubted that their demographic utopia was compatible with socialism, they appreciated the imaginative reproductive calculus upon which it was based. Pugh's unsubtle novel, like Stella Browne's forceful proselytizing of working-class women, was nevertheless seen as a reflection of socialist and feminist recognition that, like it or not, meaningful social and political reform was inextricably bound up with the regulation of human fertility. When pressed, however, leaders of the women's movement still declined to go much beyond a cautious acknowledgment that much of the ill-health, unhappiness, and poverty endured by working-class mothers was the result of excessive childbearing. Similarly, although the Women's Cooperative Guild's *Maternity: Letters from Working Women* (1915), used by Pugh in his novel, recounted pathetic stories of too many children, too little food, overcrowded rooms, and dreadful cycles of miscarriage, disease, and infant mortality, its socialist editors were also unwilling to take the next logical step and advocate birth control.

Looking back, Eleanor Rathbone, an authority on maternal mortality, recalled in 1924 that "we feminists were very careful what we said, and in whose presence we spoke when treating of these matters."[99] Throughout the war years and immediately after, Havelock Ellis and Alice Vickery

Drysdale complained to their American friend, Margaret Sanger, about the difficulties of getting the so-called new woman to support birth control as part of her "right over herself." Dr. Drysdale, who preferred not to think about Stella Browne, excluded the Malthusian League's communist ally from her retrospective conclusion that, aside from Sanger and herself, Edith How-Martyn was the only woman during the war who understood, or had the courage to admit, that "Birth Control is the Pivot, the Cornerstone of reconstruction and . . . emancipation."[100]

The timid suffrage leaders had, in Dr. Drysdale's estimation, missed a great opportunity to advance their cause when they meekly settled for a limited franchise in 1918 that did little to free most of their sex. Instead of advancing the cause of birth control, she complained, the women's groups skirted the issue by supporting such "socialistic measures" as the Maternity and Child Welfare Act of 1918, which authorized the expenditure of funds by local authorities on health visitors, maternal and infant welfare centers, and "Schools for Mothers." Other legislation provided grants for the training and supervision of midwives. Some officials, like Hayes Fisher, thought the new bills would encourage a needed revival of births in the country, and Neo-Malthusians feared they would, but supporters of the legislation were primarily concerned with further reducing the risks of childbirth.[101]

The crowning folly of wartime legislation was, by Malthusian League standards, the creation of a National Ministry of Health in 1919 to administer the new acts and to take over the various public health responsibilities of other agencies, including the Local Government Board. Women's groups had joined the NCPM and other organizations in demanding a central organization at the ministerial level to control and coordinate the planning and distribution of health care. Many of these groups were particularly interested in the welfare of mothers and children, and they quoted in support of their case the frightful experiences of working-class mothers provided by the Women's Cooperative Guild. They were joined by physicians, scientists, and statisticians who emphasized that, although about 150 infant welfare centers had been established by local governments, most of the country lacked any facilities for expectant mothers or for children after they were born. It was generally agreed that only a national agency could begin to meet the desperate needs reflected in the unnecessarily high mortality statistics of the very young. The falling birthrate and soaring war losses kept the issue before the public as never before, and the decision to establish a Ministry of Health was greeted as official recognition that a "New Motherhood" would be required in the postwar world.[102]

In the course of the next decade the new agency found itself guiding a network of some two thousand local Maternal and Infant Welfare Centers and a principal target of a new, less inhibited generation of determined birth control activists. But for the fading generation of older Neo-Malthusians most of the wartime legislation, and certainly the Ministry of Health, were unnecessary and wrongly conceived. Perhaps some assistance should be given to widowed mothers, the Drysdales conceded, but only if the birthrate stayed below 20/1,000. But there was no justification for an elaborate and expensive new bureaucracy blind to the true causes of maternal ill health and excessive infant mortality. It was another nail in the coffin of the prudent middle classes already overburdened with taxes to support fruitless welfare programs that only encouraged the poor to perpetuate their misery.[103] When in 1921 the Ministry of Health budget exceeded £1,100,000 for maternity and child welfare, an angry Bessie Drysdale wondered how long the mothers and fathers of small families struggling to make ends meet would put up with the poor trying to solve their endless crises at public expense.[104]

If their formula for reconstruction was ignored by social planners, the Neo-Malthusians at least found satisfaction in the triumph of the "lowest birth-rate countries" over their high birthrate enemies. "Had it not been for the spread of birth control among the finer races, and among the better types in those races," Bessie Drysdale rejoiced at the end of the war, "democracy . . . would have gone down in the dust before Germany's false goals and awful military power." Quality had indeed mastered quantity, she boasted, adding rather lamely that, although it was a great shame that so many only sons were killed, the Malthusian League had never advocated single-child families, only small families.[105]

The future looked bright, as long as it was not clouded by a resurgence of unwanted births, C. V. Drysdale added. The new League of Nations, a "solid phalanx" of low birthrate victors, seemed destined to endure. Ultimately peace would be assured when the overpopulated Central Powers brought their fertility into line with their resources and could again associate with the "gentle nations" of Europe. Germany, in particular, should be restricted to a rate of demographic growth no larger than that of Great Britain, Malthusian League statesmen recommended to the peacemakers at Versailles. Moreover, their vanquished foe should not be permitted to increase its depleted population until all war debts were satisfied.[106] During the postwar conflicts about reparation payments the league repeatedly sided with the French, reminding unhearing government negotiators that if the Germans could afford more children they could afford to pay for the disasters their reckless fertility had so recently unleashed on their less populous neighbors.[107]

As was so often the case, however, the Malthusian League was fighting the last war rather than the current one. It barely emerged from World War I intact. Its insensitive campaign for a moratorium on children had managed to offend nearly everyone, including many of the league's members. Furthermore, the Drysdales' contumelious assault on socialism and humanitarian maternal and child welfare programs drove away all but the most determined new recruits who, however much they disagreed with the leadership, for the time being could see no other alternative. Eugenists and feminists so assiduously courted by Neo-Malthusian representatives before the war not only reaffirmed their distaste for the league's crusade, but invariably ended up on the opposite side of the important social welfare issues raised during the war.

Yet, once again, while the Neo-Malthusians were losing virtually every battle, they were, in one sense, winning the war in spite of themselves. If their nineteenth-century economic and social philosophy was more remote than ever from contemporary, collectivist reality, fertility had dropped beyond their most optimistic expectations. Whether, as the most obdurate of the old guard believed, the shrinking birthrate was in direct response to league propaganda, or, as the more realistic Neo-Malthusians appreciated, it was a consequence of profound changes in British society fortuitously coinciding with the league's campaign, both were certain that they had facilitated and accelerated its progress.

But even the most self-congratulatory of their number recognized by the end of the war that their "Crusade Against Poverty" had not yet succeeded in building the "New Jerusalem" so dear to the hearts of wartime planners. Rational family limitation remained primarily a strategy of the more prosperous, successful, and prudent classes who adopted it for a variety of personal motives that had nothing to do with the fear of general overpopulation or the avoidance of ruinous poverty. They had, in effect, adopted "Neo-Malthusian practices" with virtually no sense of Malthusian purpose. It was a source of continual disappointment to the league's dogmatic council. The council had insisted that the creation of a "land fit for heroes" was dependent upon the willingness of the demographically enlightened to share their practical knowledge with the ignorant poor. Chastened by the war, the poor were perhaps at last ready to receive from the league the enduring truths of Malthusianism and to do something for themselves to escape from chronic indigence. It was a strategy that proved irrelevant—even counter-productive—in a postwar society ready to promote and adopt family planning for numerous reasons that had little to do with Neo-Malthusianism.

CHAPTER 9

Neo-Malthusianism and the New Generation

Stimulated by demobilization and a shortlived economic boom, the birth-rate within two years of the end of the war rose to 25.5/1,000, a figure last approached in 1909. Several newspapers welcomed the surge of new children as a harbinger of a more populous future. Though apprehensive, Neo-Malthusians decided the increase was a euphoric but temporary phenomenon that would quickly fade as the realities of reconstruction became apparent.[1] By 1921 the peak was reached and two years later, C. V. Drysdale noted with satisfaction, fertility had receded to 22.4, the lowest peacetime level on record.[2] This trend continued throughout the 1920s, and, by the opening of the next decade, the birthrate hovered around 16/1,000, well below the Malthusian League's most optimistic dreams. Similarly the number of children born to women aged fifteen to forty-five, after rising to 101.7/1,000 in 1920, following a wartime low of 71.1, dropped steadily to 65.8 by the end of the decade.[3] League statisticians assumed that the death rate would continue to fall at about the same rate as fertility, permitting the population to increase at its prewar decennial figure of about 10 percent.[4] When the rate of growth slipped to only 6.2 percent in the 1920s, Neo-Malthusians were astonished and delighted by this unexpected bonus.[5]

The long-delayed publication in 1923 of the 1911 *Fertility of Marriage Census* confirmed that each succeeding generation of married couples since the 1870s was more determined than its predecessor to curtail family size. Even before the report's appearance a disheartened James Marchant thought it no longer possible to deny that most newlyweds started married life planning the number of children they would have.[6] Although observers in the 1920s were obviously unable to determine the completed fertility of couples marrying in the postwar years, it was clear to them that whereas the mean age of marriage, 24.7, and the marriage rate, 15.5/1,000, were virtually unchanged from Edwardian times, the size of families continued to shrink. Indeed, the *Family Census* of 1946 verified that women who took their vows in the years 1920 to 1929 gave birth on the average to 2.2 children compared with 2.8 for the 1910–19 cohort and 3.53 for marriages contracted in the first decade of the century.[7]

Until after World War II demographic analysts trying to plot class differentials were largely limited to studying the birthrate in various districts of the country where occupational and socioeconomic characteristics were generally definable. The Malthusian League was only one of several organizations watching such crowded working-class districts as Shoreditch and Poplar for indications of the democratization of family restriction. Although still well above the national average, the fertility in these populous areas fell to around 24/1,000 by 1925 and another 20 percent by the end of the decade.[8]

Wide reproductive variations between different occupational classifications remained, but, as the *Family Census* of 1946 established, they were no longer widening and in many instances were rapidly narrowing. For example, the overall decline in family size in the 1920s was virtually the same for manual and nonmanual occupations. Moreover, although the notoriously low fertility of the professional classes that had so distressed the eugenically minded author of the report on the 1911 *Fertility of Marriage Census* continued to fall by another 25 percent, the decline was increasingly shared and sometimes eclipsed by other sectors of the middle and working classes. Even miners marrying in the postwar years sired nearly one-third fewer children than prewar cohorts.[9] The numbers were still much too large, birth control advocates insisted, but family size was nevertheless fast diminishing as a class distinction.

Nearly everyone concerned with the population question believed that World War I had broken the remaining religious and moral restraints that had bound earlier generations to a different concept of domestic responsibility. Such gradualist terms as "erosion" and "diminution" now seemed tame and outdated to the National Council of Public Morals when it discussed the effects of changing values on family and sexual relationships. It was no longer possible to deter the faithful from birth control by describing it as "indelicate" or "debased," Marchant complained, nor was it conceivable, even in the face of enormous war losses, to imagine that people could ever again be induced to reproduce themselves at the old Victorian level.[10] A culture of restricted parenthood was already well established among the "better off" classes by 1914, and the leveling experience of the war assured its spread to other sections of society. Describing the rapid

progress of the idea of "birth regulation" as one of the "outstanding phenomena of the time," the novelist Arnold Bennett wrote in 1918 that the
war had made a mockery of efforts to deny the advantages of birth control
to the poor. Everyone knew, he added, that the "vast majority of its
instructed opponents practice in their private lives what they condemn for
others."[11]

Within three or four years birth control became an important public
issue. The clearest indication of this, George Bernard Shaw commented in
1923, was that its adversaries were "already . . . forced to talk more loudly
about it than its advocates" whose success was evident in the steady reduc-
tions in "national and in class birth rates."[12] Alarmist headlines in British
newspapers kept a tally on the nation's precipitate flight from maternity.
Each new report from the registrar-general set pessimistic calculators like
Sir Arthur Newsholme to work determining when the population would
cease growing entirely.[13] Others, like Sir William Beveridge, thought the
trend a "fortuitous result" of that "underground revolution" that had since
about 1880 launched an "epoch in human history as important as those
which witnessed the introduction of gunpowder or the printing press," and
they were already outlining social programs needed for an older, stationary
population.[14] However much they disagreed about the individual and national consequences of the continued decline in fertility, both proponents
and opponents of birth control agreed that it had become far more essential to domestic strategy than was believed possible before the war.

Even the Neo-Malthusians were surprised not only by the extent to
which family size diminished, but by the willingness of people in all walks
of life to discuss the issue with much greater candor than had been evident
only a few years earlier. Even though the traditionalists of the Malthusian
League boasted of having educated a new generation in the multiple advantages of rational parenthood, they justifiably felt themselves to be
prophets without honor in their own country. Neo-Malthusianism in the
1920s was abruptly shunted aside and overwhelmed by new populationist
interests and personalities whose broader concepts of sexuality and fertility control reflected more accurately the problems and values of the
present and the likely realities of the future. Accommodation to the collectivist trends in British society had never been easy for orthodox Neo-
Malthusians led by the Drysdales. The postwar years were no exception.
Internal conflicts erupted into bitter divisions while the league's desperate
efforts to remain in the vanguard of the burgeoning birth control movement proved pathetically ineffective. As the Drysdales were the first to
admit, there were too many alternatives after the war. A variety of new
organizations representing widening spheres of interest left little room in

the expanding constellation of birth control groups for their curious society with its quaint Victorian ideas about laissez-faire individualism and utilitarianism.

The years immediately following the war had nevertheless initially appeared very promising to the league. The birthrate, though briefly elevated, had not run amok and was on its way down. At the 1922 International Neo-Malthusian and Birth Control Conference in London the league played a prominent role and was optimistic about future successes.[15] Virtually everyone now agreed that the spectacular drop in fertility since the 1870s was a direct consequence of the spread of birth control rather than of some biological alteration in human fecundity. Even the registrar-general conceded that the nearly forgotten Bradlaugh-Besant trial of 1877 had been the turning point.[16]

Occasional voices still dissented and were heard with some sympathy. One of the most insistent in the early 1920s was that of Charles Edward Pell whose *Law of Births and Deaths* (1921) resurrected the recently buried nutritional cyclical theories of Thomas Doubleday and his Edwardian apostle J. W. Barclay. Like his predecessors Pell believed that population rose and fell in inverse correlation to prosperity and the availability of nutrition. Malthus was wrong in believing that man breeds up to his economic capacity, Pell explained, and his Neo-Malthusian followers were similarly incorrect in attributing the decline in the birthrate to their recommendations. Poverty, he believed, triggered higher fertility to preserve the race. The healthier, vigorous organisms that flourished in times of prosperity did not, by contrast, require as many offspring for perpetuation. Consequently, it was the growing prosperity of the nation that had reduced fecundity since the 1870s, Pell argued, not the adoption of artificial limitation.[17]

In effect Pell believed that the protein-rich diet enjoyed by the more prosperous classes acted as a natural contraceptive. That was why the very people who could best afford heirs and would logically desire a great many offspring had so few. Pell could not understand why this had escaped the notable men and women on the National Birth-Rate Commission who, in spite of their adamant opposition to the small family, had on the average sired or borne only 1.75 children. Indeed sixteen of the forty-one members Pell took the trouble to survey were childless. Similarly, among the twenty-eight officers of the Eugenics Education Society, dedicated though they were to self-replication, the average number of progeny was but 2.3. Moreover, a quarter of these race-conscious leaders had no children at all to endow with their superior genetic qualities.[18]

Pell was not being facetious. He thought it strained credulity to believe that all of these people were merely canting hypocrites. Infertility had nothing to do with feminism, education, Spencerian individuation, degeneration, race suicide, or birth control, he bravely informed the International Neo-Malthusian and Birth Control Conference, but it was the normal consequence of the most recent cycle of prosperity and high nutrition. If he was wrong, he admitted to the incredulous delegates, then the rise of birth control over the past forty years was the only reasonable explanation. But he thought that all of the evidence, when seen in historical perspective, pointed to causes "beyond the control of married couples."[19]

Though Pell had no personal objection to birth control and admired the courage of the Malthusian League, his ideas were welcomed by some environmentally oriented enemies of Neo-Malthusianism who had long contended that the reproductive habits of the lower classes would follow those of their more prosperous contemporaries as social and economic conditions improved. The socially and medically prominent physician, Lady Florence Barrett, praised Pell's book in her popular study, *Conception Control* (1922), without necessarily endorsing his dietary law. Like many of her allies who believed artificial contraception to be "unnatural and unclean" or "revolting," Lady Barrett was attracted by Pell's promise that extremes in differential fertility could in time be moderated.[20] Indeed Pell bluntly told the Neo-Malthusians that the way to get rid of the "slum types" was not by birth control but by bettering their home life.[21]

C. V. Drysdale responded with scorn and ridicule. He was angered by the favor Pell's book enjoyed in some circles and by an internal upheaval within the Malthusian League itself. *Births and Deaths*, with its detailed critique of Neo-Malthusian dogma, appeared at the same time the Drysdales were losing control of the organization and the cause they had for so long financed and championed. They felt challenged from within the ranks by a new generation of members and sensed that they were being bypassed by a more comprehensive and eclectic birth control movement. The danger had surfaced before the war when newer members had tried to expand the league's vision of family limitation and turn it away from its narrow association with irrelevant and antagonistic theories of political economy. The old guard reluctantly agreed to publish a practical pamphlet on contraception, considered changing the name of the *Malthusian*, and even seemed willing to embrace socialists and other environmental reformers whose interest in birth control was based upon very different premises.[22] When, during the war, the Drysdales' strained tolerance collapsed and they declared it "absolutely impossible for Socialists and Malthusians to join forces," they were to a large extent rebelling against the pressures that threatened to divert their crusade from its original purpose.[23]

Even then they knew they were fighting a rearguard action. The term "birth control" was already replacing "Neo-Malthusianism," and the "birth control movement," as it was increasingly described, had clearly moved beyond the prescribed philosophical perimeters laid out in the early years of the struggle. Many of its advocates were less interested in population control than they were in the many individual advantages and pleasures the regulation of fertility offered all married couples, irrespective of their social and economic status. Rather than see the true Neo-Malthusian faith absorbed and eventually erased by a more practical and comprehensive campaign for smaller families, the league hierarchy welcomed the immediate postwar efforts of George Standring and others to establish a separate "Birth Control Society." Unlike the league, it would encompass every philosophical point of view in its attempt to become a popular organization with a wide base of support. Neo-Malthusians would then be free to espouse their economic revelations while the league remained a haven for the "harassed tax-paying and employing classes, and all who wish to avert [socialist] revolution." Those who favored birth control for other reasons could go elsewhere.[24]

As Standring soon discovered the months after the war were not particularly auspicious for the inauguration of a new birth control society; his endeavor quickly collapsed in 1919 while the number of births soared. The Malthusian League remained, for better or for worse, the only alternative for another two years. When the investment consultant, C. F. Chance, and his wife, Janet, joined the league, though "opposed to much of [its] teaching called 'Individualism,'" they did so because there was no other "organization supplying the much-needed knowledge of birth control methods in this country."[25] It was, as Drysdale acknowledged, a grudging, expedient concession that even some trade unionists and socialists were willing to make, though most workers "showing a disposition to take up the advocacy of birth control . . . are deterred from doing so by the fear of being associated with Malthusian doctrines."[26]

Any hope that the Drysdales would be more conciliatory after the war was soon dashed. Militant labor demands, strikes, and additional social welfare programs merely fueled the fires ignited in 1917 and 1918. Instead of insisting on higher wages, the "Maffia" [sic] and other conspiratorial "banditti" among the striking coal miners in 1919 were told by the *Malthusian*'s editors to look to their own feckless proliferation of surplus workers and recognize that their "abominably selfish actions" are a consequence of their persistent defiance of economic law. By what right did labor claim a living wage, Bessie Drysdale asked the following year. No other class makes such "rapacious" demands and presents such a threat to democracy.[27]

Angry rejoinders poured in from league members and nonmembers alike who deplored the effect of such blatant class antagonism on efforts to broaden the base of support for birth control and promote it as the basis of social and economic reconstruction. Ameliorative pronouncements at the league's 1920 annual meeting only provoked the old leadership into repetitious digressions in defense of liberal economic orthodoxy.[28] When Drysdale succeeded his aging mother, Alice Vickery, as president of the badly divided organization the following February, he emphasized in his inaugural address the importance of employing "selective birth control" to weed out the unfit, whom he specifically defined as "everyone who is unable to support himself and his family in a state of free competition."[29] His decision to rejoin the Eugenics Education Society soon after was scarcely designed to endear him to his numerous working-class adversaries or to those newer Malthusian League members who challenged his confrontational policies and ideological rigidity.

One of the new recruits, Norman Haire, a young gynecologist recently arrived from Australia, spoke for those Neo-Malthusians who believed that the league should concentrate primarily upon the dissemination of practical birth control information to the laboring poor. In 1922 he revised and expanded the league's prewar pamphlet, *Hygienic Methods of Family Limitation*, qualifying or rejecting a number of its contraceptive recommendations, including coitus interruptus, in favor of more modern, reliable methods.[30] Although Drysdale was not enthusiastic about the revisions, he was persuaded by his wife and mother that a more aggressive program of birth control instruction could be introduced without threatening the league's ideological integrity.

The two women had even given some thought before the war to the opening of a clinic under the direction of a physician. C. R. Drysdale had encouraged Dr. Aletta Jacobs to open the first birth control clinic in Holland in 1882, and the Malthusian League had followed its success over the years with envious enthusiasm.[31] But as neither the British government nor the British trade unions were anywhere near as enlightened as their Dutch counterparts, the cautious league, worried about legal prosecution, was unwilling to duplicate the experiment. By 1913, however, it was possible to consider a similar facility in London. Two years later, when the visiting Margaret Sanger suggested establishing a clinic staffed by nurses instructed in contraceptive methods she had recently studied in Holland, Alice Vickery Drysdale and Bessie Drysdale were very interested. The Drysdales had befriended Sanger, found her lodgings next door to them in Hampstead, and introduced her to members of the English birth control fraternity when she fled the United States to avoid prosecution under the restrictive Comstock Law of 1873 prohibiting the dissemination of contraceptive information through the mails. Edith How-Martyn, one of the rare suffragettes willing to ally herself with Neo-

Malthusianism, promised to help and suggested that if Sanger ran a successful clinic in England, it might help her defense at home.[32]

Although the plans were not very far advanced when their new friend returned to New York to stand trial, the Drysdale women continued to discuss the scheme. Shortly after Sanger's Brooklyn clinic was defiantly opened and promptly closed by the police in 1917, Binnie Dunlop wrote to another of the league's recent recruits, Marie Stopes, that Dr. Vickery and her daughter-in-law were contemplating a similar facility, but they were worried that unscrupulous enemies would accuse them of promoting abortion.[33] Despite the Malthusian League's having carefully disassociated itself from Margaret Sanger's cautious allusion to abortion in her 1915 pamphlet, *Family Limitation*, its general endorsement of the tract nevertheless left the group vulnerable to accusation.[34] In the final analysis, however, the Malthusian League Council remained uncertain about the legality of such a venture, and given the hostility their campaign for a moratorium on children engendered during the war, the possibility of prosecution was one more burden they were unwilling to assume.

The question of opening a birth control clinic in London was revived by Sanger in 1920 during a return visit to England. She wrote to Marie Stopes, with whom she had also become friendly during her previous trip, that the idea had been broached by C. F. and Janet Chance while she was lecturing in Cambridge. They had already sent a check for £100 and promised another £1,000 when needed.[35] A paleobotanist by training, Stopes had, since the publication of her sensational books *Married Love* and *Wise Parenthood* two years earlier, quickly become the most visible figure in the British birth control movement, and she did not enjoy sharing her recent notoriety with her even more famous American acquaintance. Moreover, as she explained to Sanger, she and her wealthy husband of two years, Humphrey Verdon Roe, had "long been planning to found the first Birth Control Clinic in England as a memorial to our own marriage." The couple had in fact been introduced to each other by Binnie Dunlop in 1917 after a timid Manchester hospital had rejected Roe's generous offer to establish and endow a birth control clinic in that crowded manufacturing town.[36] Whether Stopes's warnings about the difficulties of finding suitable quarters and other vexing problems discouraged Sanger is unclear, but she decided against taking on the chore while trying to establish her own national birth control organization at home. Stopes was not the only person relieved. A number of Neo-Malthusians were afraid that Sanger, a socialist, was planning to launch her project under socialist auspices, and Dunlop complained about how little they had seen of the American who obviously preferred the company of her new left-wing allies to that of her old friends.[37] When Sanger left the country he wrote enthusiastically to

Marie Stopes, "hoping you will be first after all."[38] She was; in March of the following year she and her husband opened the first birth control clinic in the country in the north London district of Holloway.[39]

The Malthusian League, though slowed down by internal conflicts, was lumbering in the same direction. Many of the newer members, encouraged by Margaret Sanger, believed that the league should jettison some of its philosophical baggage in order to attract a wider audience for its message. A change in the name of the journal, they argued, would be a significant first step. The diversity of new objectives perceived for the old league can be seen in the recommendations that poured in: *Birth Control, Happy Families, The Population Journal, Matrimonial Economy, Motherhood, The Voice of Reason*, and, if all else failed, *Hope*.[40]

C. V. Drysdale viewed all such suggestions with great suspicion. They were in his judgment ill-conceived attempts to placate socialists eager to undermine the strongly individualistic foundations of the only birth control organization in Great Britain. When it was apparent that he could not prevail much longer, he vainly suggested dividing the *Malthusian*, and perhaps the league itself, into two sections. One, bearing a new title, would consider all aspects of the expanding birth control movement: contraception, child and maternal welfare, love, marriage, women's rights, sex education, eugenics, and anything else, including the establishment of clinics, that surfaced in the liberated atmosphere of the postwar era. The other section, still bearing the revered title, the *Malthusian*, would continue to promulgate population control in accordance with traditional Neo-Malthusian doctrine.[41]

These pathetic efforts to ward off accommodation with reality were suddenly undermined in October, 1921, by the public conversion to birth control of the distinguished churchman and the king's personal physician, Lord Dawson of Penn. Disturbed by the Lambeth Conference's reaffirmation the previous year of its prewar position on family limitation, Lord Dawson informed a shocked church congress in Birmingham that birth control was a beneficial practice that neither ecclesiastical nor medical condemnation could or should diminish. Its adoption, despite obscurantist objections by people who should know better, was, he insisted, not a result of selfishness and deteriorating morality, but a desirable response to a more elevated concept of love, marriage, and the family.[42]

Newspapers and journals throughout the country were inundated with articles and letters refuting or defending Lord Dawson's position. Birth control in a matter of weeks became a respectable subject for public discussion. Even Drysdale saw it would be folly not to take advantage of the larger readership since the provocative speech, and he sadly conceded that with its present title the *Malthusian* was unlikely to "be understood or

popular." Therefore, he announced, in accordance with his wife's suggestion, the journal would appear in the new year under the title, the *New
Generation*. Unlike the *Malthusian*, which had never been accepted for sale
by general trade, the *New Generation* was readily placed on the stalls of
news dealers where initially, at least, they reported a lively interest in its
contents.[43]

At the same time the league revived plans for opening a birth control
clinic. Margaret Sanger, who now recommended a network of such facilities, remained in touch with her Neo-Malthusian colleagues who assured
her that they were doing their best to persuade the reluctant Drysdale,
Binnie Dunlop, and others of its advantages. Bessie Drysdale proved to be
an important ally who was determined, a skeptical Dunlop wrote to Stopes
in July 1921, "to show that she could do what you and Mrs. Sanger have
done." He was still not convinced that the league should take so drastic a
step into the area of practical birth control, and he suspected that Mrs.
Drysdale's commitment to Neo-Malthusian orthodoxy was not all that it
should be.[44] Actually, even before the war, Bessie Drysdale had been
more flexible than her rigid husband; though she shared his abiding hatred
of collectivism and socialism, she seemed to understand better the need
for some accommodation with changing expectations if the Malthusian
League was to play any role in the future of population control. In the end
she persuaded him, along with a wealthy Cheshire physician, to provide
operating funds for a clinic for one year. It was located in a building
purchased for them by the Birmingham tea merchant, Sir John Sumner, in
Walworth, near the Elephant and Castle in south London.[45] The East
Street Welfare Centre for Pre-Maternity, Maternity and Child Welfare
opened its doors in November dedicated to preventing the very conditions described in its lengthy appellation.

The Malthusian League's association with the Walworth Women's Welfare Centre, as it was later called, was short-lived. It was dependent upon
the continued generosity of the Drysdales and a few other patrons who
were also burdened with trying to keep the fragmented league afloat. A
week after the clinic opened Bessie Drysdale complained to Margaret
Sanger that the old organization was at its "lowest ebb financially" and,
despite the selection of a new name for its journal, times were very hard.[46]
Expenses at the Walworth Centre proved greater than anticipated and
within three months the initial donations were exhausted and the league
was threatening to close the facility.[47] Like its parent organization the clinic
was also battered by internal conflicts, in particular those between its
abrasive medical director, Norman Haire, and the proprietary Bessie
Drysdale. League officials had agreed that it was imperative to have a
physician in charge of the clinic to avoid any risk of prosecution from

arbitrary local authorities, and Haire reluctantly agreed to take it on when it proved virtually impossible to find anyone else.[48]

His arrival on the scene solved one problem but created several more. The ebullient, aggressive Haire had no interest whatsoever in Neo-Malthusian theories, but he saw in the Walworth Centre an opportunity to promote safe and effective birth control practices among the poor. The simple, bare clinic facilities contrasted strikingly with his own opulent Harley Street consulting rooms, richly furnished with Chinese carpets, scarlet, black, and gold lacquer cabinets and elegant pieces of oriental porcelain. He was, Bertrand Russell's wife Dora remembered, shockingly frank about sex and birth control, describing "sex for the proletarian" as "fourpence and find your own railing."[49] But Haire was also very serious about his work and throughout the interwar years campaigned energetically against the ignorance and quackery touted in the name of birth control, including some methods and devices long favored by the Malthusian League itself.

Haire, who had studied at the successful Dutch birth control clinics, quarreled repeatedly with the less knowledgeable Mrs. Drysdale. She complained of his arrogant, domineering ways, and he confessed to a "personal lack of sympathy and incompatibility" with her and her methods.[50] When, at the end of its first year, the Walworth Centre was forced to close temporarily while the league sought new funds, Mrs. Drysdale vowed she would never again work with Haire if the clinic reopened.[51] When it did, early in 1923, it was no longer under the control of the league but had been taken over by a new, independent Society for the Provision of Birth Control Clinics.[52] Although C. V. Drysdale claimed that the separation was accomplished in part to keep "Dr. H. from dominating everything," the reasons were less personal and more practical.[53] Not only was the narrowly based league unable to support the facility, but even the Drysdales appreciated that an organization free from any ideological restrictions and focusing upon the single goal of providing safe contraceptive instruction to needy wives could draw upon resources closed to the tainted Neo-Malthusians. Moreover Haire stayed at the clinic for several months after it reopened, until, as Mrs. Drysdale gleefully reported, he was "chucked" and replaced by an advisory medical council of female physicians and a woman supervisor, Evelyn Fuller.[54]

Haire's departure was one of the Drysdales' few satisfactions in the early 1920s. The adoption of a new title for the *Malthusian* with its implication of more progressive policies was followed by an increase in new members, several of whom, like Sir James Barr, were impressive additions to the ranks. They brought with them, however, demands for additional changes, and, by the summer of 1922, the Malthusian League gave way to the New

Generation League in order, as Bessie Drysdale explained, "to bring in that very large body of popular and public opinion in favour of Birth Control on various terms and from various points of view."[55] It was a concession, Barr told Marie Stopes, that had been painfully extracted from the Drysdales.[56]

Adjustment was not easy, and although C. V. Drysdale was dissuaded from resigning as president of the league and as editor of its journal, it was clear that he lacked the temperament needed to direct the increasingly disparate membership. He and his wife had promised in the first issue of the *New Generation* "not to be committed to any sectarian or political doctrine." However, when it seemed possible that the Labour party might win the election in 1922, they reverted to form, describing Labourites as dupes of revolutionary socialists and communists who knew perfectly well that birth control, not the nationalization of the means of production, would alone help the working class. If the workers *"only knew what was best for themselves,"* Bessie Drysdale editorialized, there would be no objection to a Labour government, but so long as they remained mired in ignorance "we must regretfully endorse Mr. [Winston] Churchill's contention that Labour is not fit to govern."[57]

The reaction was immediate and predictable. Eden and Cedar Paul, prominent translators of Russian and German literature and communist advocates of family limitation, had, like many others, subscribed to the *New Generation* in hopes that it would indeed be an open forum "for rational birth control," as its subtitle proclaimed. Instead, they angrily complained, it proved to be the same old *Malthusian* preaching the individualistic irrelevancies of the eighteenth century. The Drysdales, like many of their old socialist adversaries, had never learned that birth control was not a question of Malthus versus Marx, the Pauls believed, but workers today recognized the error of past philosophical mistakes. In severing their brief affiliation with the *New Generation*, the Pauls noted the irony of its editors prattling on about "allaying revolutionary feeling" when the birth control doctrine they preached was itself so revolutionary.[58]

H. Jennie Baker, at the moderate end of the socialist spectrum, had also been persuaded to join the league by the nonpartisan promises of the *New Generation*, but quickly decamped. She had been recommending birth control to the working women she organized since the beginning of the century and hoped that the *New Generation*, purged of its antilabor prejudices, would facilitate her efforts. The Drysdales' remarks, however, again made it impossible for her "to pass on the paper to others as one would like to do by way of propaganda" and to continue "to be publicly associated" with its parent organization.[59]

As far as the Drysdales were concerned it was good riddance. Socialists would be better employed entreating the cowardly Labour party and its affiliated organizations to take up the cause of birth control. The *New Generation*, selling at six pence per copy, or seven shillings a year, was not written for workers in the first place, the unchastened Drysdales retorted, but for the successful, educated classes who would disseminate its teachings to those below them.[60] The first family of Neo-Malthusianism spiced their old recipes increasingly with eugenic warnings about the proliferation of the unfit and the need for the better classes to defend their "racial integrity" from the incursions of collectivist predators.[61]

Even the Drysdales' most loyal supporters realized that the situation was impossible. In January 1923, the couple again resigned from the editorship of the *New Generation* and their offices in the league, but efforts to persuade them to reconsider were perfunctory.[62] Bessie Drysdale was recovering from surgery, and, like her husband, felt that the campaign for birth control had moved beyond their psychological and physical capacity. They were distressed by the "wretched state of personal jealousies" stirred up by new personalities in the movement, and though "glad to be out of it," as they wrote Margaret Sanger, they were clearly bitter. At the same time, however, Drysdale recognized that he was "not an acceptable apostle to the working classes" whose conversion was now the principal aim of the expanding birth control forces. This had always been the goal of Neo-Malthusianism, of course, but it was based upon philosophical premises at odds "with most of the modern trend of thought." Nevertheless, Bessie Drysdale promised her American correspondent, "we shall stand for enlightened individualism, which is common sense, is nationally safe and gives us an opportunity to *real* socialization instead of the empty phrases which now stand for Socialism—a word accursed."[63]

Once the decision was made to resign and to "let others run the movement as they like," the Drysdales, with characteristic magnanimity, gave the New Generation League £500.[64] C. V. Drysdale was persuaded to remain as honorary president of the organization his family had led and financed for forty-five years, but the more important editorship of the journal was turned over to a fifty-six-year-old Scottish-born attorney, Robert Bird Kerr, who also assumed the secretaryship of the league. Kerr, who had migrated in 1893 to the United States and then to Canada, where he had practiced law before returning to England in 1922, had been a secularist and a Fabian socialist in his youth. He had become interested in birth control after reading a German edition of George Drysdale's *Elements of Social Science*, which he had discovered in a Munich bookstall in the early 1890s. He occasionally sent letters to the *Malthusian* from Canada urging the league to stress the individual benefits of family limitation rather than the broad, impersonal economic doctrines that meant little to those most in need of assistance.[65]

Kerr, who remained editor of the *New Generation* until his death in 1951, was hardly known to the Drysdales or to the other members of the league when he assumed responsibility for the troubled organization shortly after his arrival in London.[66] He might have been the only person willing to take on the thankless task, but it is also likely that his Fabian credentials and absence during the recent birth control battles sufficed to separate him from the Neo-Malthusian old guard. Many people thought it was too late. Earl Russell, Bertrand Russell's older brother and a partisan supporter of Marie Stopes's rival Society for Constructive Birth Control, was certain that the withdrawal of the Drysdales meant the end of the New Generation League.[67] C. V. Drysdale was scarcely more optimistic himself and doubted that Kerr's being "somewhat of a socialist" would be enough to attract adequate support from labor and other radical interests. Though publicly pledging his support for Kerr's plans, he privately felt that if that was how the battle was to be won, it was not much worth the winning.[68]

Despite such pessimism the membership of the league, which had started to rise with the introduction of the *New Generation*, continued to increase so that by 1925 it had nearly doubled to around 1,200, a figure not reached since the early years of the Neo-Malthusian campaign.[69] Far more important than the always insubstantial numbers was the prominence of many of the new recruits. The willingness of Sir James Barr, Sir William Arbuthnot Lane, Professor E. W. MacBride, Harold Cox, John Maynard Keynes, Lord and Lady Buckmaster, H. G. Wells, Arnold Bennett, and Eden Phillpotts to accept positions in the league and on its council did much to buoy up the faithful and enhance the league's attractiveness.

In courting new support Kerr emphasized that his commitment to Fabian pragmatism was stronger than his devotion to Neo-Malthusian individualism. The success of the birth control movement would ultimately be measured by the fertility statistics of the lower classes, he insisted, not the winning of abstruse philosophical debates. He knew that many individual labor leaders as well as party members were proponents and practitioners of family limitation even if the Labour party itself was wary of becoming embroiled in the divisive issue. In addition, the *Daily Herald* was more sympathetic to birth control than any other newspaper in the country.[70]

Under Kerr's editorship Frances W. Stella Browne rapidly emerged as the *New Generation*'s principal emissary to the working classes and the Labour party. She not only wrote most of the journal's articles and reviews concerning labor, but she was a dynamic and effective lecturer on behalf of the league. When her communist associates denounced her deviationist activities and refused to endorse her appeals for birth control, she quit their ranks. At her urging the league began concentrating most of its limited resources on working-class organizations, and in the summer of 1923 she led a mission to the Rhondda valley to preach birth control to the distressed miners. Timorous feminists and insensitive trade union and Labour party officials were as much targets of Browne's scathing criticism as were politicians, doctors, clergymen, and oppressive capitalists.

Orthodox Neo-Malthusians repeatedly complained about the leftward drift of the *New Generation* under Kerr's tutelage, and some suspected him of trying to turn it into a socialist journal.[71] He reminded his critics that the *New Generation* was an open forum on the population question and welcomed all views that furthered the cause of birth control. To those who found Stella Browne particularly horrifying, Kerr noted that she was really the first person in the league to make effective contact with the very workers whose procreant habits so distressed the membership. He found it difficult to chastise anyone who could collect nine hundred miners and their wives to listen to a lecture on birth control.[72]

After a brief respite the Drysdales once again began provoking labor with their familiar antisocialist tirades against the "can't works" and the "won't works," and the New Generation League could ill afford to repudiate those of its followers trying to cooperate with worker organizations.[73] If, as the Drysdales charged, socialists and communists were conspiring to maintain a high birthrate in order to foment revolution, why, Stella Browne asked, were many Labour party members and their leading newspaper endorsing the activities of the New Generation League and other birth control groups? It had become foolish since the war "to preach *birth control as a direct antithesis and alternative to Socialism*." The two, like it or not, had become allies in their pursuit of a prosperous and equitable future.[74]

As if to underline Stella Browne's argument, her former comrade, Eden Paul, returned to the fold in 1924 pleased by the balance of the *New Generation* and determined to erase from its cover a cherubic infant who, surrounded by fleecy clouds and a flowery ornamental circle, had adorned it since 1922. He had always deplored that "hideous, unwanted child" and thought it ludicrous "to have a baby on the cover *every* month, in a magazine devoted to the propaganda of birth control." A few months after Paul rejoined the league the incongruous infant disappeared without comment and was replaced by the old Malthusian League slogan, "*Non Quantitas. Sed Qualitas.*"[75]

Originally adopted in the early years of the century, the motto reflected a growing interest on the part of some Neo-Malthusians in the emerging field of eugenics. From the time of the Malthusian League's founding a number of members, including Annie Besant, insisted that the question of race quality could not be separated from that of race quantity. They were worried that the "wise and prudent" would respond to Neo-Malthusian propaganda, leaving the "selfish and foolish . . . more room to increase to the detriment of the race."[76] C. R. Drysdale and his wife, Alice Vickery, were, by contrast, never persuaded of the importance of qualitative considerations. In the discussion following Galton's 1904 address to the Sociological Society, they expressed serious reservations about class perceptions of inherited characteristics and the antidemocratic implications of eugenic evaluations. If qualitative breeding was possible it was so at all levels of society, the Drysdales argued, and only in this sense could the artificial control of the birthrate be considered a condition of eugenics.[77]

Their son, C. V. Drysdale, had no such reservations. He concluded that eugenists, in emphasizing positive selection rather than negative restriction, were making a serious error. He and his wife joined the Eugenics Education Society in 1909 to persuade the members that fertility among desirable families, which at best increased arithmetically, would never be sufficient in a democratic, welfarist society to offset the geometric proliferation of the racially inadequate.[78] Other Neo-Malthusians, however, balked at the younger Drysdale's assertion that they were "negative eugenists to the core."[79] J. M. Robertson was one of several members who doubted that the Malthusian League's radical, democratic tradition was compatible with unproven elitist theories, and he feared that any alliance with the Eugenics Education Society would only compound the league's difficulties in laboring circles. Havelock Ellis and Charles Killick Millard, by contrast, agreed with Drysdale that practical eugenics would not only benefit greatly from birth control but that the Neo-Malthusian movement stood to gain much-needed respectability and prestige by a eugenic endorsement. Millard was certain that eugenics, with its obvious appeal to the scientific, medical, and academic community, would have great influence in the future, but Ellis persisted in describing birth control and eugenics as inextricable manifestations of a higher stage of evolutionary development.[80]

Before the war a number of prominent eugenists, including Inge, Saleeby, and Montague Crackanthorpe, essentially agreed with Neo-Malthusianism, but none of them was prepared to embrace it. It still smacked of radical atheism, sleazy appliances, and a quasi-legal prurience that hardly recommended it to the respectable, often eminent, middle-class professional aspirants of a new aristocracy of talent and ability who populated the eugenic ranks. Moreover, most of them concurred with Galton, Pearson, and the great Charles Darwin himself that any "Malthusian check" would prove counterproductive because it would be adopted by the "prudent and self-denying" rather than the "impulsive and self-seeking."[81] Drysdale found such arguments particularly fatuous. As he knew, most eugenists were individualists who shared his distrust of social welfare and its disastrous effects upon natural selection. When the Eugenics Education Society declined to adopt his recommendations, he accused it of forgetting its Darwinian origins and joining with Christianity, sentimental socialism, and medical science in fostering hordes of "weakly and defective offspring."[82]

The Eugenics Education Society, even during the war, consciously avoided taking a formal position on the issue.[83] Major Leonard Darwin, who assumed the presidency of the society in 1911, knew that there was much more interest in birth control as a strategy of negative eugenics than he cared to admit, and he preferred to avoid a confrontation.[84] His own objections to any change in policy were, he admitted to Havelock Ellis in 1917, aided by the membership's apprehension that birth control was not yet a fit subject for decent people to discuss in public. That would soon change, Darwin predicted, and "possibly a bolder course might be better," but he thought it "politic with the audience I have to deal with" to avoid it as long as possible.[85]

Darwin acknowledged that birth control "was widely practiced" and "has come to stay." His opposition to it as eugenic policy went much deeper, however, than a reluctance to disturb the proprieties observed by the respectable ornaments of his organization. Darwin was convinced that the spread of family limitation since the last quarter of the nineteenth century had, as his father and subsequent eugenic apostles predicted, created a perilous imbalance in the differential birthrate. "I think probably where we differ most," he wrote Ellis in 1920, "is in my belief . . . that birth limitation will not be adopted voluntarily by the inferior types of the community to nearly the same extent as with the superior types."[86] Darwin was determined to keep the Eugenics Education Society wedded to its prewar policy of positive, selective reproduction. When complemented by the segregation or sterilization of congenital defectives, it seemed to be the most efficacious route to race betterment.

Like the Drysdales Darwin quickly discovered that he was unable to keep his organization within the narrow boundaries he had erected. Not only was birth control fast attracting a much wider and more respectable audience, but many eugenists now doubted that the numbers of the better classes, seriously depleted by years of low fertility compounded by disastrous war losses, could ever increase rapidly enough to counterbalance the reproduction of the less capable. Few students of the population question were unfamiliar with the countless contrasts made between the limited pool of healthy A1 recruits who were called to the colors and the far more numerous rejects who fell into the deplorable C3 category. In spite of its president's complaints, the Eugenics Education Society began a serious reevaluation of its previous policy. Binnie Dunlop, who, unlike the Drysdales, did not resign from the organization during the war, confidentially notified Marie Stopes early in 1920 that Millard and C. F. Chance were meeting privately with sympathetic members of the "Eugenics Society . . . [which] is still considering the question of taking up B. C."[87] When a short time later the *Eugenics Review* published a strong defense of the eugenic value of birth control, Dunlop was jubilant. He savored the thought that "Eugenic Society members who remember my brave persistence at meetings long before the war should be saying, 'Well, that terrible fellow Dr. B. D. was right after all.'"[88]

C. V. Drysdale felt similarly vindicated and, along with his wife, rejoined the organization in 1921 convinced that a balance of positive and negative eugenics was now possible to curtail quantity and advance race quality. In the lead article of the first issue of the *New Generation* he noted how quickly welfare benefits were overwhelmed during the current postwar slump by the surplus of unemployable, C3 people who were still encouraged to replicate themselves while the healthy, self-supporting A1 populace, burdened with the maintenance of the incapable, reduced the size of their own families still further. The future, he announced, requires a merging of the modified teachings of Darwin, Spencer, and Galton with those of Malthus in order to breed a "healthy, virile and competent" generation as a monument to the utilitarian pursuit of the greatest happiness for the greatest number.[89]

Drysdale's rekindled warmth for the eugenic cause came at a time when many eugenists themselves were becoming more cautious about the possibilities of biosocial engineering. Although the eugenic ideal of discriminate breeding remained, its more learned purveyors in the interwar years, many of them students of the new science of genetics, were better attuned to the complexities of human heredity. They recognized that many of the simplistic assumptions about nature and nurture held by Victorian and Edwardian eugenists and biometricians would not survive close empirical scrutiny. Moreover, the democratic forces unleashed by the war, coupled with the triumph of an allegedly deteriorating race, made it more difficult than ever to agree on what constituted "race fitness" or "civic worth." Would it not be wiser, they asked, to defer many qualitative judgments until much more was known about the mysteries of human inheritance? As research continued to seek answers, eugenists could concentrate on minimizing the proliferation of verifiable genetic defects by working for the institutionalization or sterilization of the congenitally afflicted, while encouraging the healthiest, most attractive, and most successful people to increase their fertility. In more muted tones eugenic scientists conceded that the spread of birth control information among the poorer, prolific classes would, in all probability, accelerate the process of race reconstruction.

Drysdale bridled at such caution. The minimal standards of racial fitness were obvious to him even if biologists and geneticists were unable to replicate them in the laboratory. Experience had long since proven that the only reliable criteria for eugenic selection was individual success, and the sons and daughters of those who achieved it in a competitive marketplace were the best candidates for the racial altar. Like middle-class eugenists in general Drysdale had no confidence in a hereditary aristocracy sheltered from the rigors of a natural selection now found primarily in the world of business and the professions. Workers at the other end of the social scale had been coddled by socialists, trade unions, and state welfare so that whatever individual talent they once possessed had been bred out of them. As a consequence, Drysdale proclaimed, the working classes were no longer capable of efficient production without continual capitalistic supervision.[90]

Drysdale was but one of a great many postwar critics who repeatedly tabulated the costs of collectivism in low productivity, high unemployment, militant trade unionism, rising taxes, and diminished trade. Not all of them, however, defined biological fitness in terms of economic viability and concluded, as did Drysdale, that anyone "who is unable to support himself and his family in a state of free competition" is as racially incompetent as people "afflicted with transmissible diseases or defects."[91] He found nothing humorous in the observation that in a welfare state those best adapted to living on the dole were obviously the fittest. It merely provoked him into describing England as a nation of Jukes and Kallikaks hiding behind such "catch phrases" as "Justice and Equality" while bowing reverently in "weak-kneed subservience to King Demos" and his legions of the unfit.[92]

The antidemocratic anxieties that underlay popular eugenics in the early twentieth century were rarely stated so explicitly. Eugenists were often accused of harboring such elitist sentiments, but the Eugenics Education Society always maintained that its objectives were not incompatible with a democratic society and would in fact strengthen it by the production of more efficient leaders. But in the 1920s Major Darwin and those within the society who shared his views were increasingly hard-pressed to keep the focus on positive selection when birth control appeared to offer so many more immediate eugenic returns if employed by the racially suspect. To Darwin's regret, a number of members, including several on the Eugenics Education Society's governing council, also joined the New Generation League, Marie Stopes's Society for Constructive Birth Control, or the Society for the Provision of Birth Control Clinics. The more outspoken of them, like Ernest W. MacBride, professor of Zoology at the Imperial

College of Science, were convinced that all realistic eugenic proposals "must come down to birth control in this country" if they were ever to succeed. Indeed MacBride, a vice-president of the Eugenics Education Society, predicted in 1924 that it would not be long before his organization would be fully integrated into the birth control movement.[93]

A compromise had been worked out a year or two earlier within the society's council, which acknowledged that although birth control was an acceptable way to reduce the fertility of the poor and racially unfit, it was not acceptable for couples of higher eugenic potential.[94] Despite Darwin's protests, the balance had clearly shifted toward a negative eugenic policy. The compromise opened the way for the Eugenics Education Society to associate itself with the expanding network of voluntary birth control clinics aimed at working-class women as well as with various groups favoring the establishment of similar facilities in government-supported welfare centers throughout the country. Cora Hodson, the society's secretary, notified Marie Stopes in 1923 that many members of the council and its honorary secretary, the distinguished geneticist R. A. Fisher, were "anxious to ascertain to how poor and incompetent a section of the community it may be hoped that Birth Control would penetrate if it were introduced into the Welfare Centres."[95] Soon after, the *Eugenics Review* began summarizing birth control developments, and its parent organization, with its large complement of scientists and physicians, became involved in monitoring the work of voluntary clinics to determine their eugenic potential.[96]

Major Darwin continued to insist that birth control had proven "simply disastrous to the race," but, as he complained to Henry Twitchin, the principal but anonymous benefactor of the Eugenics Education Society, the membership would only concede that it was a "potential danger."[97] Twitchin, a retired Australian sheep farmer whose doubts about his own hereditary fitness had prevented him from marrying, was not overly sympathetic. He thought the dangers of race deterioration were so great that we "should not be overscrupulous as to the means . . . of fighting it." In fact, he suggested, public authorities should consider imposing birth control upon those "who haven't the intelligence to know what is good for them[selves] or the country."[98] When Darwin, nearly eighty, retired in 1928 from the presidency of the society, urging "all men in the well-paid honourable employments" to have at least four children to keep up their class, he had become as anachronistic to the eugenics movement as C. V. Drysdale had to the birth control movement.[99]

Drysdale observed the growing accord between eugenics and birth control with genuine satisfaction.[100] His enthusiasm was not, however, shared by his editorial successor, R. B. Kerr, nor the many readers of the *New Generation* who resented Drysdale's elitist and contemptuous denunciations of the working classes. Kerr was frequently counseled to disassociate the journal from Drysdale's damaging assertions and affirm that the working men and women of Britain, whom eugenists want to sterilize, have always been the nation's true source of talent. They may not achieve the great financial success that, in the minds of some, singles them out as racially superior, one angry correspondent wrote in 1923, but neither do they end up as "middle-class fops and aristocratic wastrels."[101]

Though Kerr tried to placate adversaries with reminders that the *New Generation* welcomed differing points of view, he was worried that the "sterilizing fantasies" of some eugenic birth controllers would jeopardize the league's recent attempt to assuage laboring interests. Without denying the importance of heredity, he insisted that good stock was plentiful at all levels of society and cited America as an inspiring example of what great men of humble origins could achieve. Perhaps birth control would prove helpful in eliminating certain inherited disabilities such as deafness, insanity, or feeblemindedness, Kerr admitted, but he doubted it would ever have much of an effect on the hereditary capacity of the race, however much it contributed to the individual well-being of its practitioners.[102] Kerr's initial restraint gradually gave way to ridicule and finally contempt as Drysdale attempted to drag the New Generation League into the eugenics camp. The *Eugenics Review*, a target of repeated sniping, was even reprimanded for occasional misspellings with the observation that a "society which sets out to raise the intellectual level of mankind cannot afford to spell its literature badly." In 1928 Kerr described the publication, with its roster of scientists and academicians, as the "most highbrow paper in the country" and mockingly recommended that "while these great people are studying their humble neighbours, the latter are given a magnificent chance of returning the compliment."[103]

More pointedly, Kerr derided the notion that there was any probable correlation between wealth and hereditary superiority, suggesting that the City could disappear without the slightest effect upon the quality of the race. Indeed the notion that it was possible to breed desirable physical and mental characteristics in human beings was, in Kerr's judgment, only slightly more ludicrous than believing it was possible to reach any common consensus about what constituted fitness or unfitness. He had heard enough prattling about "social worth" and the importance of "good breeding." Like most other critics of eugenics he asked, good for what? "Can we suppose that there is one kind of gene which makes a man interested in business and another in bridge"; or a degenerate criminal in one country a heroic builder of empire in another? Kerr frankly thought that Freudian psychology, with its emphasis upon the role of early experience—the very opposite of eugenics—would in the long run explain far more about human behavior and how to alter it. As a result much of what passes as eugenic science today will have to be scrapped, he warned in 1929, and bluntly recommended that until that time eugenists use some common sense.[104]

The Eugenics Society, as it was renamed in 1926, was stung by these attacks. Professor MacBride, an enthusiastic promoter of a eugenics alliance with the birth control movement, complained about the *New Generation's* attacks on "eugenic snobbery" and ridiculed the suggestion that the "best people" might come from the working class.[105] Although Drysdale was sympathetic, believing as he did that "better eugenic selection . . . [was] more important now than greater restriction of the total birth rate," he no longer had much control over the journal.[106] In 1925, in a last-ditch effort to preserve the philosophical uniqueness of Neo-Malthusianism, he persuaded the officers of the New Generation League to revert to the old name, the Malthusian League. Since other groups and societies were now available for those who were primarily interested in the promotion of birth control for any variety of reasons, the Malthusian League, he concluded, was again free to advance its own "sound social philosophy" firmly rooted in the principles of Malthus and, increasingly, Darwin and Galton.[107] Since Drysdale continued to pay most of the organization's expenses, opposition to the change was minimal.

Unlike the league, however, the *New Generation*, with its wider audience, was relatively solvent.[108] It retained its more popular title and became even more independent after 1925. Though members of the league had been assured that the explicit return to Malthusian principles "would not mean any slackening of . . . practical propaganda," it was soon obvious that the Drysdales, Dunlop, and other unreconstructed remnants of the old guard were primarily interested in preserving the organization as a fortress of individualistic purity in a corrupt, collectivist age.[109] In returning to the old name and original ideas of the league, its defenders were also trying to defend traditional population theory from the incursions of modern demographic analysts like Kerr, Harold Cox, J. M. Keynes, and A. M. Carr Saunders. All were supporters of birth control as a means of population control, but whereas orthodox Neo-Malthusians always thought in terms of a natural increase regulated by available means of subsistence, new populationists discussed trends in terms of "optimum density," "zero population growth," "point of diminishing returns," and they actually contemplated the benefits of an absolute decrease in numbers. Although theories of static and even diminishing population were being formulated in the 1920s by economists and social planners troubled by urban congestion, environmental deterioration, and labor redundancy in such industries as mining, Drysdale continued to preach the virtues of competitive selection. It was one thing to reduce the rate of population growth to an optimum balance that would preserve the struggle for self-improvement while eliminating the worse excesses of poverty; it was quite another, however, to eliminate that primal, but necessary, motivation entirely. The result would not be an enhancement of the human condition, Drysdale warned, but regression.[110]

The Drysdales knew how obsolete their ideas seemed to contemporaries, and they had doubted for some time that their organization had much of a role to play in the modern birth control movement. Their revival of the Malthusian League in 1925 was a gesture to the past rather than a serious guide to the future. Nevertheless, if Neo-Malthusian economic philosophy seemed further than ever from popular acceptance, league stalwarts proclaimed as early as 1924 that the cause of family limitation had been won despite continued opposition "in R. Catholic and certain other Christian quarters."[111] Their optimism was reinforced by the Cambridge Union voting that year 479 to 236 in favor of a resolution proclaiming that the "wider application of Birth Control would constitute a major remedy of the social evils of today." In overcoming the formidable opposition of a team led by Lord William Cecil, the Bishop of Exeter, the victors, led by Lord Dawson of Penn, had, according to C. V. Drysdale, accomplished something of "immense significance." These "young intellectuals," he wrote to Margaret Sanger, "will be the leaders of thought in England in another decade or two."[112] Kerr, with characteristic good sense, reminded his exuberant colleagues that "to preach birth control in Cambridge is not the same as to practise it at Limehouse."[113] Still he was delighted when three years later, in 1927, the daring Cambridge students reaffirmed their earlier commitment. Oxford, it was noted, remained silent.[114]

Perhaps as a way of coping with their own irrelevancy to the expanding birth control movement the Drysdales and Dunlop talked as if the battle were over. Nearly all barriers to discussion had fallen since the war, they claimed, and in 1925 Drysdale predicted that the government was close to granting the "birth control philosophy and movement . . . official recognition and final victory." The struggle would probably then shift to the United States, he thought, where Margaret Sanger and other birth control crusaders continued to face harassment and prosecution. Great Britain, by contrast, was in a position to concentrate upon the selective, eugenic aspects of population control so that the triumph of quality over quantity could at last become a reality in the country that had inaugurated the dual philosophies that made it possible.[115]

Nearly everyone else in the birth control movement thought such pronouncements very premature. Edith How-Martyn and Kerr, for example, insisted that millions of poor women still had no idea of how to control conception safely and reliably.[116] What people needed, another critic suggested, were fewer proclamations of victory and more practical leaflets and clinics.[117] One person who did agree with Drysdale was his old enemy Sir Arthur Newsholme. He suggested to Binnie Dunlop in 1927 that the time had arrived "for the closing of the Malthusian League because your mission is fulfilled. Assuming things go on as now . . . twenty years hence the population will be stationary."[118]

Newsholme got his wish. In December, a few months after an elaborate fiftieth-anniversary jubilee dinner, Drysdale declared the work of the Malthusian League complete and disbanded its activities. Since the founding of the organization in 1877, he noted, the birthrate had fallen from 36/1,000 to under 18/1,000, and the once-alarming fertility differential between rich and poor was rapidly diminishing.[119] Annie Besant, who attended the festivities, admitted that she and Charles Bradlaugh had thought of birth control in the beginning as something for the "remote future"; they never suspected that it would come so soon.[120]

For his part Drysdale stubbornly reiterated that birth control has always been a "side issue for us," important only for the contribution it made to the achievement of Neo-Malthusian economic goals.[121] To Drysdale's chagrin, the "side issue" was invariably far more important to the public for whom family limitation was, until after World War I, synonymous with Neo-Malthusianism. Whatever success the Malthusian League had in attracting attention and support was a result of its interest in controlling fertility rather than its economic reasons for doing so. Although the league became the focal point of the birth control movement in spite of itself, its spokesmen never hesitated to take credit for the extraordinary decline in fertility that paralleled the organization's history, and they never tired of reminding the postwar generation of activists that the old league had broken the ground and paved the way for the future. It was a legacy that few of them chose to claim.

Although Drysdale withdrew the Malthusian League from the birth control ranks on a note of triumph, he was in fact saddened, depressed, and not a little bitter. He was burdened with a large financial deficit that probably contributed as much to the demise of the organization as did his inflated sense of accomplishment. He turned increasingly to the Eugenics Society where he had felt more comfortable in recent years. But, as his letters to Margaret Sanger reveal, it was difficult to adjust to the realization that after a half century of courageous sacrifice by his family, their work was swept aside with barely an acknowledgment. "The Birth Control people" are now totally in control, he sadly concluded in 1928, and "can afford to let the old people take their time to die off."[122] Three years later when

Edith How-Martyn proposed establishing an annual lecture and dinner honoring Malthus and the defunct league that bore his name, Kerr, who was still editing the *New Generation*, rejected the idea as unprogressive. Recalling the 1927 jubilee, he decided that one dinner honoring the dead was enough.[123]

CHAPTER 10
Marie Stopes and
Constructive Birth Control

When Margaret Sanger briefly contemplated extending her activities to England after World War I it was because she recognized that the Malthusian League's failure to widen its base of support had left the field open to others. Neo-Malthusians, she recalled, had never been able to escape their narrow concept of the population question, and she subsequently claimed that the term "birth control" was adopted in 1914 to separate her more comprehensive crusade from that of her English predecessors.[1] Although Sanger maintained a friendly alliance with the league throughout the 1920s and invited a pleased C. V. Drysdale to New York in 1925 to preside at the Sixth International Birth Control Conference, she viewed the old organization and its leaders as curious anachronisms from another era.[2] She admired the courage and devotion of the Drysdale family, but like many of her contemporaries, she was reluctant to acknowledge that the modern birth control movement owed much to the Malthusian League.

To the new generation of activists struggling in the interwar years to establish a network of birth control clinics and, more important, persuade politicians, bishops, scientists, medical authorities, trade union leaders, and the officers of women's organizations to join in pressuring a hesitant government to endorse their populationist demands, Neo-Malthusianism was a hindrance to be avoided rather than a historical legacy to be honored. The population question quickly became synonymous with birth control in the 1920s as it had been with Malthusianism and the declining birthrate in the late Victorian and Edwardian eras. One barrier after another, including, many would insist, the Malthusian League itself, gave way before the new movement and those whom a disgruntled C. V. Drysdale described as the "Birth Control People."

The most visible and dynamic of their number was Marie Stopes. No matter how much they resented her arrogant, overbearing, and quarrelsome ways, few of her numerous enemies would have disagreed with her sorely tried friends and supporters that the transition from Neo-Malthusianism to birth control was spearheaded by Stopes's sensational writings and provocative activities. When the Drysdales resigned their offices in the New Generation League in 1923 Bessie bitterly predicted that "Marie . . . will now sweep the board" and arouse enough publicity to carry the movement with her.[3] They had welcomed her interest and energy only a few years earlier, but they now found her "whimsical, catty, ill-bred and disagreeable," though unrivaled in her ability to keep the question before the public. "She *counts* everywhere in the Press," Mrs. Drysdale acknowledged, and "is in fact the only Birth Control name known."[4] Marie Stopes was the first to agree.

Unlike most early champions of birth control, including Margaret Sanger, Stopes emphasized the joys of romantic love and sexual fulfillment awaiting married couples freed from the threat of unwanted pregnancies. Neo-Malthusians had always alluded to these ancillary attractions and for years maintained that sexual relations for reasons other than procreation were normal, healthy, and necessary for happy marriages. It was, however, a secondary theme to Malthusian League propagandists who avoided topics that might be interpreted as salacious or criminally obscene by Victorian authorities. Personal sexual satisfaction seemed a minor benefit when compared to the momentous prospect of eliminating poverty. To orthodox Neo-Malthusians, steeped in nineteenth-century political economy rather than twentieth-century Freudian psychology, rational economic motivations for behavioral change seemed far more obvious than the subtle, shadowed, emotional mysteries of sexual passion.

When launching her own campaign for "constructive birth control" after the war, Stopes correctly perceived that people were ready to consider the subject in a much broader social and individual context. By emphasizing the right of married couples to sexual enjoyment, the right of women to happy motherhood, and the right of children to be desired and loved, Stopes, Edith How-Martyn recalled in 1930, offered a "new aspect of the birth control movement which proved more popular than the exposition of the doctrines of Malthus."[5] In contrast to the Neo-Malthusians, who for decades rigidly tied the amelioration of poverty to the decline of surplus labor, Stopes warmly envisioned improvement in a context of harmonious, love-filled, sexually satisfying marriages in which only wanted children were conceived and in which husband and wife found personal fulfillment.

Though she professed that her idealized marriages based upon sexual compatibility and family planning were available to all, her examples were drawn primarily from the middle and upper classes. It is doubtful that Stopes, any more than most Neo-Malthusians, really thought of the poor as individuals capable of sincere, romantic attachments and thoughtful, sexually mature relationships. Her pronounced eugenic sensibilities contributed to her difficulties in perceiving the fecund lower classes as genetically advanced enough to be motivated by other than thoughtless, animalistic instincts requiring immediate gratification. As a result, though much of her practical birth control work in the 1920s was directed at the same working-class mothers other birth control advocates were trying to reach, most of her writings appealed to a more elevated audience.

Married Love, the book that launched Marie Stopes's birth control career in 1918, scarcely discussed the subject.[6] It was a highly personal, eccentric work, inspired by her unconsummated five-year marriage to a Canadian botanist, Reginald Gates. Although she was a respected paleobotanist who had won her B.Sc. degree with double honors from the University of London, a Ph.D. from the University of Munich, and a D.Sc. from the University of London by the age of twenty-five, Stopes was still woefully ignorant about sex when she married six years later in 1911. Her parents, Henry and Charlotte Carmichael Stopes, had met at a meeting of the British Association for the Advancement of Science. He was a professional architect and well-traveled paleontologist and archaeologist, and she was a member of a well-established Edinburgh family, one of the first women students at its university and, later, a Shakespeare and Bacon scholar. Their precocious daughter learned much about paleontology and literature from her stimulating parents, but, like many women of her generation, little about the facts of life.[7] When it became apparent a year after her marriage that her generally satisfactory relationship with her husband nevertheless "lacked something," she began a systematic study of sex, spending long hours in the British Museum. Starting with the writings of Havelock Ellis, revelation followed revelation until four years later she was granted an annulment on the grounds of *virgo intacta*.

When she was introduced to Margaret Sanger in 1915, she invited Sanger to tea with the enticing announcement, "I am just finishing a book on the intimate marriage relation which will possibly electrify this country." During the visit she confided that the work in question was a consequence of her own sexual ignorance and the unhappiness it had brought her. She had resolved to make a scientific study of "the *realities* of sex" in order to spare other women the anguish she had endured.[8] Sanger was sympathetic, but she commented in her autobiography years later, when the two had become implacable enemies, that her troubled hostess knew nothing of birth control at the time and that she had enlightened Stopes on the subject. Stopes angrily scrawled in the margins of her copy of Sanger's autobiography, "full of errors . . . untrue."[9]

After nearly three years of study Stopes knew much more about sexual physiology and contraception than her American adversary had remembered. She was friendly with members of the Malthusian League and at that point had probably already joined the organization. The Drysdales and Binnie Dunlop were among the people to whom she submitted the manuscript of *Married Love* in 1917. Though troubled by her criticism of coitus interruptus, they were otherwise very supportive.[10] Since *Married Love* had already been rejected by two publishers, Dunlop offered to back it. He also knew a "rich young man (who wishes to start a Birth Control Clinic for poor women in Manchester) . . . who might well be glad to be the means of launching such a progressive work."[11] The gentleman in question, Humphrey Verdon Roe, son of a Manchester physician and brother of the famous aeronautical engineer, A. V. Roe, was a recent recruit to the Malthusian League. During a lunch arranged by Dunlop, Roe, then in the Royal Flying Corps, explained to Stopes how the timid board of a Manchester hospital had rejected his offer of £1,000 a year for five years and £12,000 at his death to establish a birth control facility. His companion had no hesitation in accepting his generosity and promptly negotiated a loan of £200 to support publication of her manuscript. She repaid it with an additional £100 interest within a month of the book's appearance, and as soon as the hotly pursued, though obviously fascinated, Roe was able to detach himself from an inconvenient engagement to another woman, the two were married.[12]

Married Love sold two thousand copies within two weeks of publication and went through seven editions the first year. By the outbreak of World War II sales exceeded a million copies, and the book was eventually translated into more than a dozen languages. Of Marie Stopes's many works only *Wise Parenthood*, published as a practical birth control supplement a few months after *Married Love*, approached the extraordinary success of her initial venture.[13] Though suggestive and tantalizingly oblique in parts, *Married Love* was, for the period, a very explicit, if cloyingly romantic examination of the emotional and physical aspects of marital sex its author had found lacking in her own first marriage. It emphasized that women were sexual creatures, capable of ardor, passion, and desire in harmony with their monthly cycles. Sexual physiology and the psychological importance of mutual understanding and respect were carefully explained. Ideal marriages were depicted as candid and sexually honest; women were allowed, even encouraged, to fulfill their sexual and individual potential. Although Stopes was an ardent feminist, she had not been notable in the suffragist cause. She went her own way doing what many emancipationists preached, and in *Married Love* she strongly implied that the new woman could achieve all of her goals and fulfill her biological obligations within the framework of enlightened matrimony. It was an argument that readily appealed to a new generation of women after the war and offered a compromise to sensitive, intelligent men worried about the reconciliation of feminist independence with the traditional maintenance of the family and the race.

Birth control was a means for achieving the physical freedom emancipated wives and their understanding husbands desired. The careful spacing of children, Stopes promised, would not only preserve a mother's health and produce sturdy offspring who were wanted and loved, but it would permit a sexually satisfying relationship free from the terrible anxieties of unexpected pregnancies. Not only did she proclaim that sexual delight was in and of itself a worthy goal in marriage, but she insisted that women need not be inhibited in the pursuit of such pleasure. If she dwelt at length upon the liberating advantages of birth control, the only practical contraceptive advice she offered was a brief reference to the use of vinegar and water or a quinine solution. Readers of *Married Love* learned much more about the unashamed delights of conception than they did about how to prevent it. They also learned about the mystical transmission of refined thought and sentiment to children still in the womb. Stopes was certain that if husbands read great literature, played beautiful music, and shared their highest thoughts with their pregnant wives, elevated taste and feeling would, through the mother's mind, be passed on to their fortunate progeny.

Contemporaries were shocked, amused, titillated, or deeply moved by her candid, sometimes ludicrous, but obviously sensitive account of natural sexual behavior and the torment caused by ignorance and repression. More liberated couples like Bertrand and Dora Russell "used to laugh at some of its passages, as for instance that a woman might allow her body to be seen by her husband 'in the clear water of her bath.'"[14] If they found *Married Love* absurdly sentimental in parts, and, later, its author insufferable, they acknowledged the importance of the work in breaking down taboos against sex and birth control. In at least one prominent men's club demand for the book was so great that members could read it for only an hour at a time; though they often started out giggling, it was reported, they soon became serious.[15] One excited correspondent wrote to the author, "you have done more to promote the happiness and welfare of humanity than all the priests, prophets, philosophers and social reformers in history." Stopes saw no reason to dispute such considered judgment, confessing to her new husband, "I have for a long time had the feeling I am a kind of priest and prophet mixed."[16]

Less inspiring perhaps was the flood of pathetic letters from men and women describing their own lamentable ignorance and anxiety about sex. The Stopes papers are filled with the guilt-ridden confessions of masturbators, the promiscuous, or the unsatisfied, as well as numerous accounts of the unhappiness caused by premature ejaculation or errant notions of sexual physiology. Many people, including George Bernard Shaw, wrote on behalf of "friends," "acquaintances," "parishioners," or, in the case of doctors, "patients" who sought relief from the myriad sexual afflictions torturing their lives.[17] One army chaplain, responsible for the sexual education of soldiers, confided that for years he had wanted to kiss his wife's breasts but feared that such unrestrained passion would harm the delicate protrusions. *Married Love*, he rejoiced, had freed him from his inhibitions.[18]

Stopes soon had to hire a secretary to keep up with the huge correspondence emanating from her astonishingly successful book.[19] Many of the letters contained inquiries about contraceptives and the legality of advocating or even practicing birth control. Indeed the possibility of prosecution had impeded the publication of *Married Love*, and the Drysdales and Binnie Dunlop anticipated legal difficulties after reading the manuscript.[20] Nevertheless, the Malthusian League helped to promote the book and delighted in its reception. When called to active duty at the end of the war, Dunlop reported that *Married Love* was making the rounds of the officer corps and that most who read it were deeply impressed. "Like Malthus," he wrote to its author, "you might well spend the remainder of a long and happy life bringing out new editions of your Essay with more and more data and evidence. *STOPES LAW. And it supplements the Laws of Malthus and George Drysdale.*"[21]

Wise Parenthood, which appeared late in 1918 as "A Sequel of *Married Love*," and *A Letter to Working Mothers* the following year, were practical, explicit guides to contraception and emphasized female control of fertility.[22] They were prompted by the avalanche of letters that followed the appearance of *Married Love*, requesting more precise information about the restrictive practices alluded to in the chapter entitled "Children." Roe suggested the title "Happy Families" or "Wise Parenthood" to his new bride as being more positive than "Birth Control."[23] Arnold Bennett was prevailed upon to write an introduction deploring the "ignorance and superstition" surrounding the subject, prompting some of Stopes's more conservative supporters, like the Reverend James Marchant, to question her judgment in soliciting the endorsement of "so-called advanced thinkers" for a "woman's book." As secretary to the National Council of Public Morals Marchant had tried to interest that respectable body in publishing *Married Love* in 1917, but he agreed with its board's decision that the "medical parts" were unacceptable in a popular work that might be purchased by young people.[24] Nevertheless, Marchant welcomed the book as far superior to the irresponsible publications of the Malthusian League, and he urged her to keep her work above the "low level" of that unfortunate organization.[25]

That was certainly one of Marie Stopes's goals. Like many recent recruits to the birth control movement she deplored the philosophical constraints and divisive policies promoted by the league's spokesmen. She disagreed with several of their contraceptive recommendations, including coitus interruptus, the condom, and douching, all of which she found to be either harmful, repugnant, or unreliable. During the war, when the league was urging a moratorium on children for the duration, and no more than two or three in the future, Stopes, already in her late thirties, was desperate for children, and saw nothing wrong with having four to six of them if they could be afforded and were spaced properly.[26] This, she told the readers of *Wise Parenthood*, could best be achieved by the use of a small occlusive vaginal rubber cap and a quinine pessary. Both, she believed, could be purchased from a chemist and could be self-fitted. If not, she naively promised, medical assistance was readily available.

Whereas the Malthusian League was primarily concerned with the economic consequences of overpopulation, Stopes was much more interested in the relationship of birth control to the enhancement of compatible sexuality and domestic happiness. It was of great importance to her that contraceptive methods in no way interfered with the natural joys of marital sex. Along with a number of learned medical authorities she believed that male "seminal secretions" were absorbed through the vaginal wall and were beneficial to a woman's health. Coitus interruptus and the condom not only left women dependent upon the self-control of their husbands, but denied them the advantages associated with the free mingling of bodily fluids during intercourse.[27] The vital, nutritional qualities of semen had long been upheld by sexual physiologists and gynecologists, and Stopes's tendency toward the mystical made her particularly susceptible to endowing the male ejaculate with special, undefined powers. She was less certain as to how men benefited from the commingling of bodily secretions, but she knew that true sexual fulfillment required maximum contact of the sex organs so that both partners could achieve the mutual orgasm they were entitled to experience.

This was heady stuff, far bolder than anything the Malthusian League had ever contemplated publishing. Some of it she extracted from the writings of Havelock Ellis and Edward Carpenter, but neither of them had been very helpful on birth control. When, however, she gave advice to working-class women, most of the erotic passages were deleted and the idyllic romance of sexual bliss gave way to less ethereal descriptions of the physical and economic hardships endured by the exhausted mothers of too many children.[28] *A Letter to Working Mothers* did not dally on the delights of married love savored by the liberated of higher station, but got right to the point. Conception was explained in simple terms and various popular, though unreliable, birth control methods were discussed and their inadequacies described. Abortion, which was, as Stopes knew, all too common among working-class women was singled out as dangerous, illegal, and unnecessary if wives would only purchase for two or three shillings and faithfully use the small rubber occlusive pessary she recommended. If that proved impractical, a sponge with soap powder or a soluble quinine pessary, "the wife's friend," could be inserted instead.[29]

Although *A Letter to Working Women* described the use of contraceptives, it was less precise in explaining how poor women were to obtain these precious items. Stopes suggested that her readers go to a chemist, district nurse, or medical officer of health, but recognizing that the women might be shy, intimidated, or sent away, she exhorted them to "be brave" and to persist until a nurse or doctor complied.[30] If all else failed, they were invited to write to her directly. Stopes was, like most advocates of birth control, unfamiliar with the operation of local public health facilities and the attitudes of the medical personnel who ran them. She soon learned that if she relied on the public health community, the country would soon be overrun with another generation of sickly, unwanted children. The only solution was to open a model clinic, as Humphrey Roe had proposed during the war, to demonstrate what could be accomplished at the local level at low cost. In time public authorities and perhaps even the new Ministry of Health would recognize the benefits of establishing similar facilities throughout the country.

The "Mothers' Clinic" that Roe and his wife opened in Holloway in 1921 was much less elaborate than Roe had originally hoped when he sketched out plans for a facility in Manchester in 1917.[31] It was not associated with a hospital, but it was located in a small, plainly furnished building where married women were examined by a staff of nurses directed by a midwife. If there were no obvious complications, patients were usually fitted with a rubber cap and shown how to use it in conjunction with quinine or some other spermicidal solution or suppository. Unusual cases were referred to a Harley Street gynecologist, Dr. Jane Lorimer Hawthorne, who agreed to serve as medical consultant. Though Roe was far more important to the conceptualization, planning, and operation of the first birth control clinic in Great Britain than has been recognized, he was from the start overshadowed by his more visible wife whose unrelenting drive for self-aggrandizement obscured the role played by her less assertive husband.

In contrast to the Malthusian League's Women's Welfare Centre, which was initially open only two afternoons a week when founded later in the year, Stopes could boast of *her* clinic being the "first in the world to be open all day and every day and devoted solely to a serious scientific consideration of the application of means of controlling conception."[32] Unlike her successors Stopes did not see any reason to require the attendance of a qualified gynecologist at all times. Trained nurses were, in her judgment, perfectly competent to fit contraceptive devices, and, as she correctly perceived, sufficient medical personnel were not available. This decision was to bring Stopes into continual conflict with the medical profession. It did not, however, prevent her attracting a number of prominent patrons, several of whom she shared with the New Generation League and the Society for the Provision of Birth Control Clinics, which took over its Walworth Centre and soon began opening other facilities.

Demonstrating a tenaciousness and boldness that continually marked her career, Stopes went after the prime minister himself. David Lloyd George, though sympathetic, declined any official support for a cause many voters still found disreputable. He suggested, however, that she might "change all that" by holding a "great public meeting . . . to make birth control respectable."[33] Stopes and her husband had already determined that the birth control movement needed to be disassociated from the negative connotations of the past, and they were contemplating a large rally to introduce a new campaign for "constructive birth control" that would emphasize all aspects of married life and the population question. This was the theme struck at the great Queen's Hall meeting held on 31 May 1921. Some two thousand people, many of them curious to see the sensational author of *Married Love*, assembled to hear the notorious lady and several other speakers explain the nation's qualitative and quantitative demographic needs. A number of the medical participants recounted the horrors experienced by the poor unable to control their fertility, and nearly all insisted that the same information readily available to women of the "better-to-do" classes should be accessible to the less fortunate. Some of the speeches were aggressively eugenic, decrying the disproportionate multiplication of wastrels and incompetents whose unregulated increase threatened the race and the Empire.[34]

Stopes, who was by her own reckoning, as well as others, the hit of the evening, offered veiled criticisms of the Malthusian League, regretting that the "words 'birth control' have become associated with a negative and repressive movement." Constructive birth control, by contrast, did not merely mean the "repression of lives which ought not to be started, but the bringing into the world of healthy, happy, *desired* babies." Indeed many of the inquiries she had received since 1918 concerned conception rather than its prevention, and she had tried to provide what information was available. The entire subject, however, was clouded by "unwholesome and tragic" ignorance and superstition. Constructive birth control was, by contrast, the "key to all racial progress . . . in which the race will be recruited only when love and knowledge combine for the conception." The result, Stopes promised, will be an "entirely new type of human creature, stepping into a future so beautiful, so full of the real joy of self-expression and understanding that we here today may look upon our grandchildren and think almost that the gods have descended to walk upon the earth."[35]

If these latter-day deities of constructive birth control have been slow to appear, it was not for want of their prophet's determined efforts to alter the course of evolution. Within three months of the Queen's Hall meeting Stopes and her husband formed the Society for Constructive Birth Control and Racial Progress as a more comprehensive alternative to the troubled Malthusian League. A few weeks later she was able to claim more members than the Malthusian League was able to enlist in forty years.[36] Although precise figures were not forthcoming, there is little question that the new society quickly eclipsed its predecessor, attracting directly and indirectly thousands of birth control supporters who could never overcome their aversion to the league's economic philosophy or their suspicion that it was a regressive, secularist, slightly prurient vestige of the past. Constructive birth control, by comparison, seemed modern and uncontaminated. Its deliberately broad mandate allowed people to find in it whatever they wished. As a result, eugenists, socialists, feminists, advocates of population control, proponents of greater sexual freedom, and even defenders of large but planned families found it to their liking.

For every new member countless others wrote to the CBC, as it was soon called, offering assistance and requesting literature for themselves or friends and neighbors. Many unsolicited letters contained harrowing personal accounts of the physical and economic consequences of bearing too many children, or, less commonly, the unhappiness of having too few. Frequently, correspondents were in some aspect of public health or social welfare, and, though reluctant to appear on the rolls of the new organization, wanted to endorse its efforts. Most were minor officials, nurses, medical officers, or midwives, but some were in positions of considerable influence. John Robertson, senior inspector for the Royal Society for the Prevention of Cruelty to Children in Scotland, for example, simply wrote to offer his help in Glasgow.[37] Similarly a representative of the National Council of the Young Men's Christian Association, which had never shown any interest in the subject, suddenly requested assistance for those of its working-class members who wanted to regulate the size of their families. Many YMCA members were opposed to his overture, the official admitted, but others were prepared to hear a CBC speaker.[38]

Not all unsolicited inquiries were welcomed. Nudists, advocates of free love, homosexuals, lesbians, and other champions of sexual liberation found no sympathy whatsoever for their respective causes and problems. Stopes always had a horror of being linked to anything salacious or obscene; her horror was only exceeded by her fear of being taken for a crank, or even worse, a quack. With numerous purveyors of "Malthusian appliances," potions, and abortifacients hovering on the fringes of the birth control movement, there was reason to be concerned. She was firmly convinced that the general acceptance of constructive family regulation was ultimately dependent upon freeing contraception from unsavory associations and winning the endorsement of respectable society. As a consequence Stopes was constantly on guard against the commercial use of her name or that of her organization, and she did not hesitate to hire private detectives to gather evidence against dubious rivals whose unscientific activities might prove embarrassing to her.[39]

She was as equally determined to grace her movement with distinguished patrons whose commendable reputations would redound to the credit of her society. Like the Neo-Malthusians before her, Stopes grasped at every intimation of estimable support, no matter how vague. But she was far more aggressive than her predecessors in the pursuit of the well known and well connected. Churchmen, doctors, lawyers, politicians, scientists, journalists, artists, writers, and of course the titled nobility were inundated with invitations to lend a portion of their reputation to her crusade. Though archbishops and prime ministers led the list of those who received her persistent attention, not even the royal family was spared occasional solicitation. Propriety, however, was as important as rank. When the scandalous personal life of Bertrand Russell's titled brother, Earl Russell, one of her first aristocratic converts, became an embarrassment in 1921, she quickly withdrew her offer to him of a vice-presidency in her fledgling organization.[40] He nevertheless remained a devoted and understanding supporter, and as soon as his marital affairs were settled he was elevated to the executive committee of the CBC.

Stopes's mulish refusal to accept an initial rejection of membership in her group usually wore her quarry down until the name was added to the growing list of supporters she was able to attract to the CBC cause in the 1920s. Even the reclusive Havelock Ellis, who long maintained a policy of not associating with any society, and had recently refused a vice-presidency in the "new Malthusian League," succumbed to her persistent flattery in late 1921, though privately she discounted his work and envied his reputation.[41] When soon after she began quarreling with the Neo-Malthusians and with Ellis's beloved friend, Margaret Sanger, he regretted his mistake in deviating from his earlier position and insisted that his name be removed from the rolls of the CBC.[42]

One of Stopes's most sought-after friends, George Bernard Shaw, managed to escape even a temporary alliance despite her decade-long campaign to ensnare him. The two met during the war when he consented to read some of her eugenically inspired dramatic offerings such as *The Race*, or *Ernest's Immortality*. He clearly admired her paleobotanical skills more than her dramaturgical talent, warning her that "until you take the stage more seriously than you take a coal mine you will never do anything with it."[43] Shaw viewed Stopes's birth control activities with good-humored if detached sympathy, delighting in her assault upon the conventional shibboleths of the day, but declining to be associated formally with her efforts. He parried her endless schemes to entice him to accept a vice-presidency with jokes, lectures, and suggestions that she stop bothering husbands and wives and "go off to some clime and have a good rest and book in the sunshine." He would not, however, even consent to preside at a dinner or meeting associated with the CBC.[44]

On a more serious note, Shaw explained to Stopes in 1928 that he had never been able to "find a satisfactory public position about B.C." An avowed positive eugenist, he had more confidence in the possibility of race improvement through selective marriage and reproduction than he did through family limitation. He knew, however, that his views, which had prevailed in eugenic circles before the war, were no longer as persuasive, and he urged Stopes to emphasize the racial rewards of selective, happy marriages as depicted in her first book, *Married Love*, rather than the negative advantages of contraception.[45]

Shaw touched a sensitive nerve. In stressing the "constructive" aspects of birth control Stopes and her husband had hoped to escape the negativism of the Malthusian League. Another of her books, *Radiant Motherhood* (1920), extolled the delights of conception, pregnancy, and the rearing of racially superior children in a eugenically conscious new world. But a number of her early supporters were primarily interested in weeding out the "ruck wastrels and throw-outs," as Charles Killick Millard described the offspring of "reckless breeding."[46] Like many who rallied to her movement, Sir James Barr, a patron of the new Mother's Clinic and a vice-president of the Society for Constructive Birth Control, wanted "to get rid of the C3 population," convinced as he was that "until we get a selective birth-rate, there can be no general elevation of the human race."[47] During one of her numerous libel suits, Stopes, in 1923, insisted that a reduction of the birthrate was not the purpose of her campaign; only "a reduction at the wrong end and an increase at the right end."[48]

In spite of her efforts to accentuate constructive parenthood, Stopes's writings and activities in the 1920s centered increasingly upon the prevention of conception among the lower classes. Between supervising her clinic, writing, editing, responding to thousands of letters, and speaking throughout the country and abroad, she had little time for "radiant" mothers. Though *Married Love* inspired a flood of imitative works platitudinously extolling the miracles of sexual compatibility, most remained very circumspect in their treatment of birth control practices. Stopes, by contrast, became bolder in her discussion of that aspect of marriage, and in 1923 published her most explicit statement on the subject, *Contraception (Birth Control): Its Theory, History, and Practice.* Similarly the *Birth Control News*, which she and her husband launched the previous year, placed much greater emphasis upon the limitation of families than it did upon the myriad pleasures of bountiful motherhood. Like the *New Generation*, which it hoped to displace, it regularly recounted the grim details of poverty, ill-health, abortion, infanticide, and occasional suicide traceable to unchecked fertility.

The *Birth Control News*, edited by Stopes, candidly described her as "impregnably honest, utterly fearless, incorruptible by the worldly lures which tend to weaken and deflect most reformers, yet sane, scientific and happy." In what might charitably be described as gratuitous self-deception the new journal offered the comforting assurance that "Dr. Stopes, hating all conflict, is fighting on behalf of others."[49] In fact she was compulsively belligerent and instinctively litigious, quarreling throughout her career with real and imagined enemies as well as with friends. Self-righteously intolerant, devious, manipulative, and not a little paranoid, she was able to work with few people and ultimately alienated many of those closest to her, including her husband and only son.[50] Consequently, the *Birth Control News* is as much a chronicle of Stopes's skewed perception of her unblemished virtues and her adversaries' duplicitous vices as it is of the birth control movement in the interwar years. As such it is a much less reliable source than the *Malthusian* or its more even-handed successor, the *New Generation*. But it is also a testament to Marie Stopes's extraordinary energy and success. If she was unable to recognize the achievements of others, while endlessly complaining that her own accomplishments were unappreciated, even her fiercest enemies, and they were legion, never denied her effectiveness as the principal advocate of birth control in Britain during the postwar decade. In her more euphoric moments Stopes extended the chronology back to the creation and widened her range of influence to encompass the globe.

Whereas the Malthusian League had for years been content with the gradual education of the public and only reluctantly turned to more aggressive proselytizing shortly before the war, Stopes enthusiastically exploited every opportunity to further her cause. She inundated the press with letters, articles, and announcements and raged bitterly when they were not printed or her exploits given the publicity she felt they deserved. The Neo-Malthusians grumbled when editors spurned their offerings; Marie Stopes threatened to sue.[51] The *Times* in particular drove her into a frenzy by not only closing its prestigious pages to her unsolicited contributions and advertisements, but by refusing to acknowledge her numerous academic degrees and referring to her as "Miss Stopes" or "Mrs. Stopes." She had insisted on retaining her own name at the time of marriage to underline her belief that it should be a partnership of equals, and she was always infuriated when her personal achievements were in any way diminished. Earl Russell, at her request, intervened on several occasions to ask the editor of the *Times* at least to show "Dr. Stopes" the courtesy of an accurate professional designation. At the same time he repeatedly reminded his irate friend that no law required editors to publish what they did not want, explaining once in exasperation, "You seem to think that newspapers are bound to behave nicely to people they do not like."[52]

In spite of her protests and threats Stopes actually received a great deal of press coverage throughout the 1920s, much of it fair, even supportive. When in 1923 she carried her campaign to the stage, writing and producing *Our Ostriches*, the first play to discuss birth control, reviewers were for the most part cautiously favorable. With the exception of the Catholic press, which was offended by the theme and by the villainous depiction of a devious priest, most critics described it as effective, if not very artful, propaganda. The International Neo-Malthusian and Birth Control Conference had in 1922 discussed the possibility of using the theater, but it was Stopes who made the first and only move in that direction.

Our Ostriches recounted in three acts the conversion of a young upper-class woman, Evadne, to the birth control movement after her visit to an overcrowded tenement filled with sickly, unwanted children and their unfit parents. Much of the play focused upon her efforts to persuade an insensitive, sometimes deceitful, birth control commission to endorse family limitation for the poor. The heroine was joined by an attractive, young medical officer of health whose efforts to help his fecund and impoverished charges had been thwarted by his cowardly superiors. Together the couple described the horrific scenes they had witnessed in the slums, but they failed to induce the commission, comprised of obtuse nobles, Darwinian professors, and ineffective clergy, all manipulated by the odious priest, even to interview a pathetic mother of twelve children, five of whom had died in infancy. One of the commissioners, Lady Highkno, wondered, "Where, if the poor are made free of the secrets of birth control, are we to get our servants from?"[53] Undeterred, Evadne broke her engagement to a bewildered aristocrat, and after pledges of mutual love she and her new ally vowed to continue their struggle for birth control.

If *Our Ostriches* confirmed George Bernard Shaw's doubts about his friend's dramatic gifts, the production, supported by infusions of the author's money, managed to run for twelve weeks at the Royal Court Theatre in London. The *New Generation*, though complimentary, correctly predicted that such costly ventures were not likely to be repeated.[54] Although Stopes dabbled with other plays and periodically contemplated revivals of *Our Ostriches*, she later turned her eclectic literary talents to the poetic arts where, in spite of the encouragement of such dimmed luminaries as Lord Alfred Douglas, she was not markedly more successful.

Like her heroine, Evadne, Marie Stopes often depicted herself as a lonely battler against the combined forces of social indifference, perverted science, economic exploitation, and religious obscurantism. All were dragged on the stage and held up to ridicule in her depiction of a committee that was obviously modeled on the National Birth-Rate Commission. Yet she had once been an enthusiastic supporter of the commission and its secretary, James Marchant. She had been satisfied with the group's first report in 1916 and warmed by Marchant's interest in *Married Love*. When, shortly after the book appeared, she was invited to sit on the new commission established in 1918, it was a sign of respectable approbation she greatly appreciated.[55] Though Binnie Dunlop and other Neo-Malthusians warned her to be careful and described the Presbyterian Marchant as a "Jesuit" who opposed birth control, Stopes defended him as an "earnest and inspired worker" for a stronger national home life and threatened to resign from the Malthusian League if it did not stop its criticism.[56]

Her confidence began to wane, however, when it became obvious that much of her testimony was not being recorded because, as she weakly explained, there are "far too many bishops to pacify" and Marchant has "to walk a tight rope."[57] Apprehension gave way to anger the following year when she realized the commission's report was being written without her assistance and that it was likely to prove very disappointing.[58] Her complaints to the former chairman, Dean Inge, were met with sympathy but not surprise. She asserted that the commission was reversing its neutral position on the safety and reliability of contraception by declaring all methods medically unsound. Certain that the "second commission was got together to undo the work of the first," Inge had known that the outcome was a foregone conclusion. All he could suggest was a "vigorous protest" against the new report.[59]

Our Ostriches was Marie Stopes's revenge. When in 1923 the NCPM established yet a third commission, this time to study the ethics of birth control, it declined her help. Her repeated attempts to get a hearing were fobbed off with the disingenuous explanation that the new investigation was concerned with moral issues rather than with science, the area of her expertise.[60] Even before the appearance of her play, however, Stopes had become too closely associated with birth control to find acceptance in NCPM circles. The new commission was even more critical of contraception than its predecessor. It warned of the "grave social perils" and the terrible illnesses associated with the use of "mechanical methods." Once the family was revitalized by the birth of at least four children, the commissioners declared, couples could, in good conscience, revert to the "safe period" or "continence" methods if there were sound medical reasons for avoiding additional offspring. Four of the seventeen commissioners refused to sanction even the "safe period." Although they agreed with the majority that a great birth control revolution was sweeping the country, the only ethical way they could see to stop it was by complete abstinence once the nursery was full.[61]

Stopes's conflicts with the NCPM were minor skirmishes compared to the war she launched against her former associates in the Malthusian League. Their early warnings to her about Marchant and the NBRC were met with suggestions that the old league had made little contribution to the birth control movement and had probably been an impediment to its success. She accused the Drysdales of jealousy, which seemed especially ungenerous in light of the welcome they had extended to her when she first entered the field. Dunlop assured her in 1919 that, far from being envious, they all "rejoiced" at her sudden success. Even if she was not particularly sympathetic to the Neo-Malthusian economic arguments for the control of parenthood, neither were Dr. Millard, Dean Inge, the Bishop of Birmingham, and many others like herself who were nevertheless making important contributions to the cause.[62]

For the next two years Dunlop tried desperately to patch over the deepening cracks in Stopes's relationship with the Malthusian League. Bessie Drysdale suspected that Stopes was merely using the organization for her own ends and would abandon it at the first opportune moment. When, on the eve of the Queen's Hall meeting in 1921, Stopes confessed to Dunlop that she and Roe had only kept up their membership in the league and refrained from criticizing it out of affection for him, he regretted that Mrs. Drysdale's assessment had hit the mark.[63]

Though she professed annoyance that the Malthusian League had been unwilling to underwrite her personal rally at the Queen's Hall, Stopes was obviously looking for an excuse to sever her connections with her old allies.[64] As her advocacy grew more confident and successful, supported as it was by the proceeds of her writings and her husband's considerable wealth, the league seemed more of a liability than an asset. Moreover, it was the Drysdales' organization, not hers. An emotionally religious, often mystical, visionary who had been raised "in the rigours of . . . stern Scottish old-fashioned Presbyterianism," Stopes suddenly remembered the Malthusian League's secularist origins.[65] A few days after her very successful Queen's Hall meeting she hesitatingly suggested to Dunlop that the atheism of Charles Bradlaugh and Annie Besant had irreversibly tainted the birth control movement and seriously hampered its progress. Exasperated, Dunlop recommended that she resign from the league—a suggestion that she and her husband promptly followed.[66]

Stopes's cautious criticism of the patron saints of Neo-Malthusianism was a mild portent of what was to come. Any semblance of cooperation between the old league and its newest antagonist was shattered five months later when Stopes, in her inaugural presidential address to the new Society for Constructive Birth Control, announced that the birth control movement owed nothing to Bradlaugh and Besant and the Neo-Malthusians. Her own research had revealed that efforts to advance family limitation had been around for years before the notorious, freethinking Bradlaugh and his hysterical ally "butted in" and diverted "untramelled physiological *control* in the interests of the race" to their own peculiar purposes. In foolishly deceiving themselves into thinking that "they were fighting for a great principle," Stopes charged, the two created difficulties for the dissemination of birth control that previously had not existed. Clergymen and law-abiding Christians, who were otherwise attracted to the ideals of family regulation, were offended and alienated by the charges of atheism and obscenity raised by the scandalous trial and the appearance of the Malthusian League. Her chronology somewhat confused, she implied that even the infamous Comstock Law, which made the United States the "most retrograde of the civilised countries," was somehow a consequence of the Bradlaugh-Besant trial, though it had actually been passed four years earlier.[67]

The purpose of Stopes's sudden attack quickly became obvious. Now that there was no longer only one organization in Great Britain promoting family limitation, it was possible for the birth control movement, through her new society, to renounce its unwanted legacy and attract to the cause alienated Christians and working people offended by the atheism and "intense anti-Socialism of the Malthusian League."[68] In a note added in 1923 to the third edition of her address, Stopes emphasized that Neo-Malthusianism was not the same as birth control, which is purely interested in health and is the "intimate physiological concern of each individual woman."[69]

Her unrelenting efforts to read the Neo-Malthusians out of the birth control movement continued that year in her book *Contraception* in which the medical profession was added to the important groups whose antipathy toward family limitation could be traced to the Malthusian League. If Bradlaugh's atheism had alarmed the clergy, the publication of Dr. Henry Allbutt's unfortunate *Wife's Handbook* in 1886, followed by his banishment from the medical society rolls the next year, frightened the doctors. Nothing the league had done since then had allayed medical suspicions that "Malthusianism is harmful."[70] The ultimate irony, she claimed, was that the decline in the birthrate since 1876 has occurred in spite of the Malthusian League. Its activities, like the Bradlaugh-Besant trial, may have given the issue unneeded prominence, but in reality they merely coincided with a downward trend following a "high water mark." While family size plummeted, she recalled, the league has remained "small and partial," unable after forty years to attract more than five hundred members.[71]

Although Stopes was often vindictive and unfair in her denunciations of Neo-Malthusianism, she was essentially correct in her conclusion that the league was a stumbling block to wider, more positive concepts of birth control. In adopting a new name and new policies the New Generation League conceded as much. Stopes was resolved, however, to avoid any connection between the CBC and the older group, whatever its title, though individual members were free to do as they wished. Many joined both organizations despite her efforts to persuade them to pledge allegiance to her society alone. The CBC was avowedly nonpartisan and assiduously avoided the political and ideological quicksand into which the Drysdales repeatedly led their organization. Stopes herself was politically conservative and was not demonstrably more sympathetic than her rivals to socialism or labor. But by contrast she was not openly hostile and was able to convince old socialists such as Robert Blatchford and the labor leader J. R. Clynes that she was sufficiently neutral for them to endorse her birth control campaign. She was at the same time cheered on by longtime enemies of the Malthusian League, including Marchant, who, after her scathing presidential address wrote, "I do sincerely hope that you succeed in burying the word 'Malthusian.' It has stuck in the throats of people until we are sick of the whole subject."[72]

When, the following year, the Malthusian League gave way to the New Generation League, the *Birth Control News* thought it an unnecessary tactic now that the CBC existed and predicted that it would prove to be but a frail rival to Dr. Stopes and her comprehensive organization.[73] In private Stopes was more apprehensive about the change. The Neo-Malthusians had managed to sponsor a very successful, much publicized international conference in July 1922 without her participation. She was annoyed by the prominence given to her American counterpart and increasingly more famous rival, Margaret Sanger, who, along with John Maynard Keynes, H. G. Wells, Harold Cox, and others led sections of the meetings. Stopes indignantly declined a last-minute invitation to attend and savored the thought that "after the precious 'Congress' the Malthusian League is busting up altogether and committing hari-kiri [*sic*]." At the same time she was obviously worried that what followed would be "an imitation CBC . . . cribbing almost our name as well as our policy."[74]

Actually the Neo-Malthusians were as pleased to be rid of Stopes as she was to be free of them. After her public disparagement of the Malthusian League and its revered founders, the *Malthusian* refused to publish paid announcements of the CBC or its clinic. The ostensible reason was the league's disapproval of some of the contraceptive methods prescribed in the clinic, but when Stopes angrily protested, C. V. Drysdale told her husband that it was best if the two birth control societies kept as far apart as possible.[75]

Even some of Stopes's friends thought her intemperate attacks on her Neo-Malthusian competitors went too far. Earl Russell, whose father, Viscount Amberley, had ruined his own political career in 1868 by an indiscreet advocacy of family limitation, told Stopes that she was completely wrong about Charles Bradlaugh. He was a man of principle and a strong advocate of free speech who, with Annie Besant, provoked the 1877 trial to defend that fundamental right. It was unfortunate that the issue of birth control became confused with atheism, but it in no way diminished what those brave defendants were trying to accomplish.[76]

J. M. Robertson, whose advocacy of Neo-Malthusianism had waned as his political career expanded, rallied to the defense of his old comrades, correcting Stopes's faulty history and suggesting that reviving the old specter of atheism did more harm than good to the birth control cause. In spite of the Malthusian League's secularist origins irreligion had never been a policy of the organization and played no role in its crusade for smaller families. Furthermore, Robertson added, that there were birth control advocates before Bradlaugh and Besant in no way diminished their accomplishment in bringing the issue before the public where it has remained ever since. Not even Stopes's "visions" and "religious frenzy" could alter the historical truth, and her efforts to do so only impeded the acceptance of birth control by the scientific community.[77]

Robertson was alluding to Stopes's embarrassing efforts two years earlier, in 1920, to persuade the bishops attending the Lambeth Conference that she had received a divine revelation "uniting physiology and the religion of man."[78] There had been shock but little outcry in Neo-Malthusian circles where it was decided that her spiritual peculiarities and increasing flirtation with the supernatural were her own concern. But when she proclaimed that birth control was a Christian movement perverted by the abhorrent atheists in the Malthusian League, it was too much for Robertson and the more forgiving Binnie Dunlop. Unable to restrain himself any longer, Dunlop denounced her "unjustifiable and hopeless effort to make B.C. appear to have been a Christian movement instead of leaving your own books to make it one." With rare ascerbity, the mild physician, who had tried to keep peace between the two camps, castigated his friend for being "hopelessly unscientific," "unbearably egotistical," and unable to work with anyone.[79] Only Dunlop's conciliatory nature permitted their curious friendship to survive, but it was marked by a new wariness.[80]

Stopes's battles with the Neo-Malthusians were intertwined with her conflicts with Margaret Sanger whose birth control campaign in the United States was faithfully reported in the *Malthusian* and, later, in the *New Generation*. Their initial friendship of 1915 was for several years sustained by letters of endearment and Stopes's circulation of a petition to President Wilson urging him to prevent New York authorities from prosecuting Sanger when she returned from European exile.[81] The American, for her part, enthusiastically endorsed *Married Love* and after considerable difficulty found a publisher willing to bring out an expurgated edition in the United States.

Ultimately, however, the two women proved incompatible. Both were driven by an inordinate sense of mission and self-righteousness that fed an uncompromising determination to succeed and dominate. Neither suffered other points of view with much civility or patience, and each found it positively painful to share authority or the limelight. Each was supported by a wealthy husband who had to subordinate himself and his fortune to his wife's ambitions. Though both women became committed eugenists in the course of their careers, Stopes distrusted Sanger's early socialist predilections, and the latter was offended by her British associate's mystical religiosity and Tory sympathies. By the time Sanger returned to England after the war Stopes was already uneasy about her popularity in British birth control circles and was not pleased by the attention lavished on the American by the Malthusian League. When, after months of looking for an adequate building for a birth control clinic, Stopes and her husband suddenly learned that their ambitious visitor was contemplating a similar facility in London, there was no hiding their disappointment and irritation.

What Sanger did not know at that time was that Stopes was being wooed by her principal rival in the United States, Mary Ware Dennett, president of the Voluntary Parenthood League. Dennett, who had recently broken with Sanger, initiated the relationship in 1919 by writing to Stopes of her admiration for *Married Love* and *Wise Parenthood*. Both, in her judgment, were superior to Sanger's famous pamphlet, *Family Limitation*, which she felt was "sadly lacking in the right atmosphere."[82] Dennett's subsequent letters were filled with complaints about her adversary's deviousness, arrogance, poor judgment, and bad taste. She offered to distribute Stopes's works in the United States and in 1921 discussed the possibility of opening several clinics in association with the newly established Society for Constructive Birth Control.[83] If Stopes was confused by the labyrinthine quarrels plaguing the American birth control movement, she was never reluctant to receive the scathing criticisms Dennett had of its most prominent leader.[84]

When Sanger learned in July that her British counterpart had agreed to come to New York, at her own expense, as the featured attraction of a Voluntary Parenthood League conference, she pleaded with Stopes not to attend, as "Mrs. D—— is outside the pale of honesty and decency."[85] Although she later professed innocent bewilderment, Stopes knew perfectly well that Mary Dennett's meeting was designed to eclipse the First National Birth Control Conference Sanger had scheduled for the following month in Chicago.[86] Unaware of the relationship that had developed between her enemy at home and her friend abroad, Sanger was puzzled and then enraged when Stopes not only ignored her frantic protests as mere hearsay, but forwarded the obviously private denunciations to their target.[87] Dennett in turn threatened a libel suit and indignantly, but vainly, demanded a retraction.[88] Sanger bitterly accused Stopes of betraying and splintering the birth control movement, and in spite of the latter's mellifluous invocation of the warm memories of 1915, refused to see her when she came to New York and never had anything to do with her again.[89]

The confrontation was probably inevitable. Neither woman was prepared to concede predominance in the birth control movement, and when they entangled themselves in each other's national concerns the explosion came quickly and the gap it created remained unbridged. The New Generation League allied itself with Sanger and endorsed her international and domestic activities to the exclusion of all her American rivals. Portions of her *Birth Control Review* were regularly featured in the *New Generation*. By contrast, Stopes's *Birth Control News* virtually ignored Sanger's activities and instead followed the declining fortunes of Mary Dennett and her embattled Voluntary Parenthood League.[90] On the other side of the Atlantic Sanger consigned Stopes and the CBC to comparative oblivion after 1921, leaving her American followers with the impression that, along with the Neo-Malthusians and a few other groups, she constituted the British birth control movement. Neither woman ever forgot or forgave. When, nearly thirty years later, Sanger proposed to carry her birth control campaign to the defeated Japanese after World War II, her old enemy gratuitously prevailed upon General Douglas MacArthur to quash what she described as a shoddy publicity stunt.[91]

Stopes, who was scarcely a neophyte in the scramble for publicity, resented the advantages Sanger enjoyed in flaunting the notorious Comstock Law in the 1920s, and she accused her of deliberately provoking prosecution to enhance "her personal popularity for other purposes."[92] Despite what some believed, Stopes insisted that in contrast to the United States there were no laws in Great Britain against the publication and dissemination of contraceptive information. The Neo-Malthusians were wrong in claiming that the unfortunate Bradlaugh-Besant trial had anything to do with the distribution of birth control literature; it was purely a prosecution for obscenity. So long as birth control advocates remained within the bounds of common decency, she argued, they have nothing to fear from the law.[93]

Her position seemed to be borne out in 1922 when the home secretary, Edward Shortt, was asked in the Commons if the government might follow France's recent example and make it illegal to publish or distribute birth control information and to sell or advertise contraceptives. No such legislation was contemplated, he replied; the local police would continue to deal with the problem if it seemed to contravene obscenity laws, but even then there was no surety that the courts would concur with their assessment.[94] This remained the standard reply of every government throughout the 1920s. Although parliament was not prepared to legislate in favor of birth control, it was not about to legislate against it.

If such rulings confirmed Stopes's point and made her exceedingly wary of any conflict involving questions of obscenity, the more vigorous defenders of freedom of expression, especially in the New Generation League, feared they left the birth control movement vulnerable to local harassment. Unlike Stopes, who cut a very fine path through the briars of controversy surrounding birth control in the postwar decade, the Neo-Malthusians continued to argue that the issue could not be separated from the large problem of censorship that Bradlaugh and Besant had challenged a generation earlier. The ban on some of Havelock Ellis's work was a continual target for the league, and when in 1928 Radclyffe Hall's shocking novel of lesbianism, *The Well of Loneliness*, was repressed, the *New Generation* quickly joined the battle against the ruling as it had in a number of cases involving censorship in the theater.[95]

Stopes, however, steered clear of such shoals, fearful they would threaten the fragile respectability she believed her campaign was at last bringing to the birth control movement. She complained repeatedly about extremists sullying the cause and warned her own people to be circumspect, proper, and on the alert for "distasteful" women who might be out to discredit the "whole movement, but especially the CBC."[96] Appeals for her help in defending booksellers and small publishers of birth control literature from local obscenity prosecutions were invariably refused, and she was furious when *Wise Parenthood* was briefly mentioned during a trial in Birmingham in 1921 in which the Malthusian League was, as usual, offering assistance. Though the defendent was found guilty of obscenity and blasphemy, Dunlop assured Stopes that neither her book nor the league was similarly condemned.[97]

The issue of legal harassment in the prosecution of the communist publishers Rose Witcop and her husband Guy Aldred in 1923 clearly showed how Stopes diverged from the rest of the birth control movement. In 1920 their Bakunin Press had introduced Margaret Sanger's popular pamphlet, *Family Limitation*, without difficulty, but three years later when they brought out a revised edition containing some added illustrations and a vague reference to abortion, it was seized by the police and Aldred was charged with publishing an obscene work. The New Generation League at once rallied support.[98] Dora Russell and John Maynard Keynes stood surety of £50 each, and the league hired a prominent attorney to defend the case. Upon learning of the prosecution Sanger immediately sent funds and offered to come over and testify if it would help. By the time she could make arrangements, however, the case was lost.[99] Aldred, who had once hewed to the old Social Democratic Federation line and strongly opposed birth control, was found innocent, but the pamphlet was judged to be obscene and the new edition was ordered burned. The authorities were apparently particularly offended by a diagram showing a finger placing a pessary in the correct position, fearing, as one of the defense attorneys explained, that "it might not be the finger of the woman concerned." But Dora Russell thought that the magistrates were even more troubled by the pamphlet's assertion that women could and should enjoy sexual intercourse.[100]

Stopes had perhaps been more successful than anyone else in persuading her contemporaries of the normality of such pleasure, yet she was conspicuous by her absence on the list of those willing to testify for the defense. Bertrand Russell, a member of the CBC, assumed that its president would contribute to Aldred's defense however much she was at odds with many people in the movement. But in this case, he wrote her, "all who stand for Birth Control should hang together, if only for fear of hanging separately."[101] His older brother, Earl Russell, gave her different advice and recommended that since the Sanger pamphlet seemed at one point to justify abortion the CBC should remain uninvolved. Stopes needed little persuading; in rejecting requests for help she explained that "as several of the recommendations are not in line with the attitude of our Medical Research Committee," neither she nor her organization could lend support.[102] Bertrand Russell, whom she privately described as a "very great thinker" who is "detested and distrusted" by responsible people, promptly resigned in disgust.[103]

Stopes could have pleaded the exigencies of preparing for her own pending libel action against a Catholic physician, Halliday Sutherland, who had accused her of experimenting on poor women visiting the Mother's Clinic. She considered it, but instead decided to state her objections to the way certain "enthusiasts" made their work vulnerable to prosecution. What was at issue, she argued, was not the legality of disseminating birth control information, but the way some people chose to go about it. Sanger, she delighted in explaining, should have tried to find a recognized, respectable publisher in order to avoid the questionable alterations and additions that had long plagued otherwise acceptable birth control works.[104] At the same time she resented sharing the attention of the press that her own case against Sutherland brought her. It was, as Mary Dennett complained, a great pity that Sanger's book had been prosecuted at that particular juncture. Not only did it detract from Marie's celebrated proceedings but it enabled Sanger to "revel in the publicity."[105]

In addition to sniping at her American nemesis, Stopes, in all probability, was also trying to avoid associating herself with the left-wing politics surrounding the defense of a communist publisher. But her position, whatever the complex of motives, was consistent with her earlier reluctance to become involved in obscenity cases and her analysis of what constituted legal and illegal birth control instruction. The entire controversy strengthened her resolve to avoid any more entangling alliances now that she had disassociated herself from Sanger and her old colleagues in the Malthusian League.

The Aldred prosecution proved to be the last. The appeal of the verdict was dismissed with costs in 1924 and plans for bringing out a new edition of Sanger's pamphlet, with a preface by H. G. Wells or by the respected suffragette, Emmeline Pethick Lawrence, were quietly dropped.[106] Later in the year a fourteenth edition of *Family Limitation* rolled off the Bakunin Press with Sanger's backing, but without the offending diagrams, and it was distributed without interference. Stopes appeared to be right, and although she eventually lost her own libel suit against Sutherland, the three-man appeal body of the House of Lords, which ruled against her in 1924, emphasized that its decision in no way questioned the legality of birth control or the dissemination of contraceptive advice.

By then Stopes's relations with most of the old and many of the new birth control people had deteriorated to a state of sullen resignation to the inevitability of continual conflict within the rapidly expanding movement. Although Stopes described the Drysdales' successor, Robert Kerr, as an "obstinate Scotchman," he was actually far more tolerant of her than were most of her adversaries. She showed little reciprocity. She was afraid that in seeking to widen its appeal the New Generation League under his leadership was making a "complete *volte face* and scrambling after us." His energetic encouragement of the Society for the Provision of Birth Control Clinics further indicated that the New Generation League had made a fundamental decision to commit itself to the practical problems of family limitation. But nothing upset Stopes more than Kerr's insistence that the growing interest in birth control among working-class women could be attributed to the heroic proselytizing efforts of people like Stella Browne rather than to her campaign.[107]

Kerr usually treated his vituperative detractor with restraint and good-humored patience. He recognized that despite her unpredictable combativeness and ludicrous sense of self-importance, Stopes was an influential and exceedingly effective propagandist. He reversed C. V. Drysdale's exclusionary policies and accepted advertisements for her books, her clinic, and the CBC. Most great movements, he reasoned, had more than one group providing places for those who disagreed about policies but who pursued the same beneficent end. More societies meant more workers, as far as he was concerned, and, in spite of the widening chasm between the CBC and the New Generation League, the birth control movement grew stronger not weaker.[108] At the same time Kerr could not resist reminding Stopes that her successful caravan rolled along a route paved and kept open by the Malthusian League for more than forty years. After all, he wrote elsewhere, she seemed to forget that no one had ever heard of her until 1918, and "by that time the essential work of the movement was already done." He was willing to give her the recognition she deserved since that date, but he recalled that when she opened the first clinic in 1921 the birthrate was already half what it had been in 1877, and no amount of rewriting history could alter that extraordinary fact.[109]

If Stopes was unnecessarily harsh in deprecating the accomplishments of her predecessors, she was not noticeably more generous to her contemporaries. Nevertheless, in spite of the wrangling, jealousy, and backbiting she sparked within the birth control movement, there was general agreement about the need to break the persistent opposition of the church and the medical profession while building a political constituency for policies of demographic restraint. Stopes was certainly in the forefront of the assault on the religious and medical establishment, where her provocative activities and daring confrontations stimulated public discussion throughout the decade. She was, despite her illusions, far less effective in the political arena where other groups and individuals proved far more adept at forcing reluctant governments to begin to face up to the birth control revolution they had preferred to ignore since its existence had first become obvious a generation earlier.

CHAPTER 11
Religion and Reconstruction

In his testimony before the second National Birth-Rate Commission in 1919 Dr. Charles Killick Millard bluntly told that heavily ecclesiastical body that it was time for church leaders to disavow the 1908 Lambeth Conference condemnation of birth control. The bishops, he complained, had confused it with abortion and selectively accepted the counsel of those doctors who believed contraception to be physically harmful. A majority of medical practitioners now knew this was not the case, Millard asserted, and the leaders of the national church should wake up to reality. The success of postwar reconstruction, in his judgment, depended on an end to the "population race." If the established church was to have any influence in shaping the future, its teachings had to become germane to the demographic realities of the new age.[1]

A few bishops, he knew, were cautiously sympathetic. At a meeting of the Lower House of Convocation at York the previous year, Francis Gurdon, the Bishop of Hull, had appealed for "moral restraint in the size of families" to facilitate recovery after the war and suggested that "if we are to have a League of Nations, the Church must reconsider her attitude of blessing large families and saying 'Be fruitful and multiply.'"[2] Although the *Malthusian* interpreted the prelate's remarks as irrefutable evidence of crumbling ecclesiastical resistance, Millard thought it was merely another of many signs that clergymen were uncomfortable with their church's prewar position. He knew that several of the commissioners were not pleased with his evaluation, but as a father of four he felt he could "view with complacency the diatribes of celibate ecclesiastics who think it their duty to denounce what they are pleased to refer to as 'race suicide.'"[3]

Like most of the birth control advocates in the 1920s who struggled to persuade the church to change its position, Millard recognized that comparatively few couples were about to accommodate their procreative behavior to the teachings of the Anglican communion. The birthrate obvi-

ously continued to decline precipitously in defiance of ecclesiastical admonitions, and fertility remained lowest among the very classes to whom
the church had the greatest appeal. If it was unable to command the
obedience of the faithful, the church was even less likely to have any
impact on the laboring masses who had long ignored its ministrations and
who were the principal targets of the birth control movement. Those who
pushed the church to modify its untenable resolutions had no illusions
then that it would have much of an effect on the reproductive strategy of
people at any level of society. Instead, they seemed to have been motivated by the enduring belief that the church's blessing would somehow
give their campaign a respectability they always felt was lacking. It could
also bring them allies, or at least reduce opposition, in the thousands of
parishes of the country and could help persuade local and national public
authorities to consider the economic, social, and eugenic advantages of
providing birth control information to the poor. But of equal importance
for many critics of the establishment, a number of whom, like Millard,
were devout churchmen, was the fear that by cleaving to their hopelessly
unrealistic response to the spread of family limitation, the ecclesiastical
hierarchy was destroying the church's remaining credibility and relevance
to the moral reconstruction of British domestic life.

At least one bishop on the NBRC—its chairman—concurred. In contrast to his predecessor in that industrial diocese, Charles Gore, Bishop
Henry Russell Wakefield of Birmingham had strong reservations about
the Lambeth resolutions. He thought that the economic gains for the poor
and the eugenic benefits for the nation to be derived from the adoption of
harmless birth control methods by the lower classes warranted reconsideration by his episcopal brethren. Millard told Marie Stopes in 1919 that
Wakefield had engineered a sympathetic debate on the subject at a recent
church congress in Leicester in which even the Archbishop of Canterbury
made no protest.[4]

Stopes had served with Wakefield in 1917 on a Cinema Commission of
Inquiry established by the ever vigilant National Council of Public Morals,
and she was familiar with his attitude. Whether the prelate, a widower with
four sons, was as entranced by the experience as she imagined, Stopes
claimed several years later that he was prepared to abdicate his episcopal
throne for her.[5] His passion clearly had limits, however, as he was one of
several church dignitaries who tactfully declined the opportunity to write a
preface for *Married Love* despite his professed admiration for the manuscript.[6] The following year he officiated at her marriage to Humphrey
Verdon Roe after persuading her with some difficulty that the word "obey"
in the ceremony did not mean "subjection" to or the "pampering" of a
husband, but only reverence and mutual respect.[7]

Though Wakefield proved to be a fair, even encouraging chairman to the birth control advocates who appeared before the NBRC, unlike Dean Inge he was not prepared to challenge the majority of his colleagues on that board. When he sided with them in expressing reservations about all scientific methods of birth control, Stopes was among the first to express her dismay and demanded any medical evidence he and his fellow commissioners possessed to support their unsound conclusions.[8] The bishop was obviously uncomfortable with the commission's retrograde conclusions, but he was under great pressure not to condone any further reduction in the birthrate. His differences with her, he lamely explained to Stopes, were over methods, not the principle of birth control.[9]

In supporting the report of the second NBRC Wakefield was also sensible of the pending Lambeth Conference called for the summer of 1920, and he was reluctant to challenge its earlier resolutions before the church had an opportunity to reconsider them. A number of rumors about the possibility of compromise made the rounds of the birth control camp as the opening of the conference approached. Malthusian League officials were greatly heartened, if surprised, when Randall Davidson, the Archbishop of Canterbury, agreed in February to discuss the issue in secret with Dr. Millard. "Very strictly *entre nous*," Dunlop informed Marie Stopes, "Dr. M. stayed last night at Lambeth Palace—strong ally in the A. of C. He came and told me this morning."[10] Whatever was said at the meeting, Millard at least thought it worthwhile to send a "Memorandum to the Archbishops and Bishops of the Anglican Communion" reviewing the "fresh light" shed on the birth control question since they had last assembled in 1908. Virtually all of the evidence disproved their warnings that contraception was physically dangerous and would encourage selfishness, promiscuity, and imprudence. Having endorsed the safe period in their 1913 memorandum, "Misuse of Marriage," the bishops had accepted the principle of birth control, he reasoned. It was time to take the next step and lift the ban on contraception that at present only perplexed rather than enlightened the true Christian.[11]

Millard's appeal was reinforced by Dean Inge who, on the eve of the Lambeth Conference, entreated his superiors to set aside their personal feelings, ignore the latest commission's dubious findings, and weigh the evidence with an open mind. It would prove indisputably that birth control constituted an irreversible revolution that had severed forever "any necessary connection between indulgence and procreation." Unless the leaders of the church faced up to this truth they would lose whatever chance still remained to "direct the birth control movement for the good of married life."[12]

Though Inge had persuaded the first commission to withhold judgment on the medical consequences of using contraceptive devices, he shared many of the doubts about their safety. He had cited these concerns and his respect for church authority when in 1918 he declined to endorse *Married Love*.[13] By 1920, however, the combination of "dysgenic war losses," the continued diminution of A1 families, and the proliferation of the C3 population had persuaded him that the "partial abstinence" he had earlier favored was, however safe and ethical, impractical and therefore racially dangerous. It required virtues of self-restraint beyond the capacity of the improvident lower classes. If, in the name of negative eugenics, Inge abandoned his reservations about contraceptives, he still consistently refused to lend his name to any birth control organization despite repeated appeals.[14]

Millard and Inge entreated the bishops on the temporal grounds of science, reason, and reality. Marie Stopes invoked higher powers. Shortly before the Lambeth Conference convened she was vouchsafed a divine message while walking alone in the "cool shades of the old yew woods" behind her home. Though a "trained and technical scientist," Dr. Stopes had suspected for some time that she was mystically attuned to the spirit of the universe. Consequently she was less surprised than most when the Creator singled her out as "His Prophet" to exhort His unsuspecting bishops to reverse their earlier stand on marriage and birth control. "I speak to you in the name of God," she told them in *A New Gospel*. "Paul spoke with Christ nineteen hundred years ago. I spoke with him yesterday," and he had enjoined her to preach of the "vivifying beauty of the love of mates." She extolled the "subtle internal secretions of the sacred organs of sex" released when men and women "are truly united . . . [in] biological oneness." With shocking, erotically romantic candor she rhapsodized on the divinity of two bodies pulsing together "to the highest climax" and remaining thereafter in a "long, brooding embrace without severance from each other by which and through which only can the vital interchange be perfect."[15] In orgasmic revelation Stopes discovered practical contraception, explaining to the newly awakened prelates that the holy commingling of bodily secretions was thwarted by celibacy, abstinence, coitus interruptus, and the condom. Devices such as rubber pessaries, which did not interfere with the divinely inspired mixing of coital fluids, were physically and spiritually sound.

The ultimate purpose of *A New Gospel* was to enlighten churches on new standards of connubial behavior that would make the marriage state more pleasing to God, who blesses sublime sexual love, if not to his misguided priests who continue to claim it is only for procreation. There were many reasons people should avoid conception, Stopes argued, but virtually none that precluded a satisfying sexual relationship. That is why

God through His scientific servant has now revealed how to have sex with "uncovered organs" while avoiding the curse of unwanted, racially dangerous births. "Harden not your hearts to the new revelation," she exhorted the bishops and implored them to extend their acceptance of the safe period to the more reliable contraceptives made available through science. Although she offered to deliver "God's latest Revelation" in person if summoned to the Lambeth Conference, the stony-hearted prelates declined to welcome the new prophet into their midst.[16] Much to the dismay of friend and foe alike in the birth control movement, Stopes instead published her extraordinary message.

Millard was only one of several confidants who tried desperately to dissuade her from sending *A New Gospel* to the bishops without first deleting many of the erotic passages that were bound to scandalize them.[17] He was aghast when it appeared in print. Binnie Dunlop was similarly horrified, and, like most Neo-Malthusians, feared for the scientific credibility of the birth control cause. Stopes protested that she had not intended to communicate with any of the bishops until suddenly overwhelmed by the awful responsibilities thrust upon her. Her correspondence, however, reveals that for three weeks prior to her extraordinary visitation she had tried unsuccessfully, directly and through intermediaries, to arrange a meeting with Archbishop Davidson.[18] As the opening of the conference drew near she grew more agitated, and her impatience and frustration perhaps made her particularly receptive to the voices intruding upon her solitary walk.

Archbishop Davidson responded to his receipt of *A New Gospel* by sending its author six White Cross League Canterbury leaflets on sex instruction for boys, which not only reaffirmed the church's conviction that sex was solely for procreation, but, less relevantly perhaps, detailed the satanic evils of "self abuse," which caused the young to grow up "feeble and flabby."[19] The leaflets were but a prelude to the conclusions of the great Anglican conference. Under the chairmanship of the Bishop of London, Winnington-Ingram, whose antipathy for birth control had, if anything, intensified since the war, the Committee on Problems of Marriage and Sexual Morality adamantly defended the 1908 resolutions. It refused to concede that birth control could ever be justified "on medical, financial and social grounds" and felt "called upon to utter an earnest warning against the use of any unnatural means by which conception is frustrated." Couples with too many children were instructed to abstain from sexual intercourse. Even the use of prophylactics to prevent venereal disease, though grudgingly acquiesced in during the war, was now unacceptable to the unyielding prelates.[20]

Ecclesiastical anxieties about domestic morality were intensified by continued warnings about race suicide implicit in the ever-falling birthrate. But they were also heightened by fears that additional feminist gains, building upon the vote, would come at the expense of maternity, and any encouragement of birth control would reinforce this dangerous trend. In the "Report on the Position of Women in the Church," another episcopal committee complained of the "sinister phenomenon" of increased celibacy and smaller families among the church's more devout "female communicants." Nothing should be done, it concluded, "which obscures or renders difficult woman's fulfillment of her characteristic function."[21]

The Malthusian League announced that the reactionary bishops had once again voted for poverty, war, and bolshevism.[22] Far less hostile voices were equally appalled. Dean Inge in the *Evening Standard* publicly decried the intransigence and futility of celibate bishops preaching total abstinence, while in his diary he wondered, "What am I doing in this galley?"[23] Other critics among the faithful appealed for more realistic guidance, and at least one church paper described the bishops' resolutions as one of the most unsatisfactory documents ever produced in the face of a crisis. A few prelates were personally embarrassed, including the Bishop of Wakefield, who suggested unconvincingly that the conference had been heavily influenced by the overseas bishops from sparsely populated lands.[24] There was, however, nothing in the resolutions that English bishops had not themselves advocated since the early years of the century.

For a spurned prophet Marie Stopes was surprisingly subdued. She knew from her extensive correspondence with clergymen that many Anglican ministers thoroughly disagreed with their ecclesiastical superiors. Some, like the Welsh Neo-Malthusian, Horace Corner, who helped her ready *A New Gospel* for publication, were openly defiant of the "hopeless" bishops.[25] Others, like Canon F. Hanes Dudden, master of Pembroke College, Oxford, were more circumspect, but still condemned the Lambeth Conference as "utterly deplorable" and the bishops as "utterly ignorant" or "hopelessly obstinate in trying to maintain an untenable position." Dudden, who had once been Winnington-Ingram's chaplain, had not expected much from a committee under the bishop's direction. He had not, however, anticipated that the entire conference would endorse so obdurate a report, and he felt no obligation to accept its conclusions or advise others to do so.[26] Nearly everyone agreed that, far from settling the troublesome issue of birth control for the faithful, the Lambeth Conference exacerbated it by trying to impose standards of behavior that were at variance with the beliefs and practices of possibly a majority of communicants and clergy.

Undeterred by the Lambeth resolutions Stopes, more certain than ever of her mission, offered a number of bishops, including Archbishop Davidson, an opportunity for repentance the following year by sending them tickets to her Queen's Hall rally. They all declined to attend, and a few months later lost another opportunity to embrace the "New Gospel" by refusing to lend their support to the new Society for Constructive Birth Control. Moreover, church publications rejected advertisements for her books and announcements of her clinic. Despite a great deal of sympathetic correspondence from men of the cloth, Horace Corner was the only Anglican clergyman willing to join the CBC when it was founded, and he was already a member of the Malthusian League.

His Neo-Malthusian colleagues, angered by the Lambeth resolutions, thought that people, especially the working poor, were even less inclined to pay any attention to the bishops than they were before the war. Stopes, however, was certain that the Archbishop of Canterbury was really a crypto "birth controller" whose public conversion would have an enormous impact on the success of her divinely ordained campaign. When he innocently suggested in 1922 that women with medical concerns about pregnancy consult a doctor, Stopes immediately wrote to thank him for his approval of her work and again urged him to lead the Anglican communion into the CBC camp. The agitated prelate quickly denied that any supportive construction for her ideas, most of which he found offensive, could be placed on his words.[27] She continued nevertheless to pursue and harass him throughout the remainder of the decade, motivated in part by the assurances of some of her supporters that Davidson and his wife were more realistic about the question than it was politic to admit.

Stopes had no such illusions about some other diocesans, particularly Arthur Headlam, the Bishop of Gloucester (1923–46), with whom she battled in the letter columns of the *Times* in 1925.[28] His adamant defense of the Lambeth Conference resolutions inspired his antagonist to some private doggerel:

> The patriot Bishop of Gloucester
> The British breed wishing to foucester
> To improve the home stock
> And increase his own flock
> Every nice girl he met he'd accouster.

After examining the bishop's domestic accomplishments in *Who's Who*, Humphrey Roe revised his wife's rhyme to read:

> The childless old Bishop of Gloucester
> A family wishing to foucester
> Was very much vexed
> To find himself undersexed
> When his fancy girl said—You Impoucester![29]

Despite continual denunciations of the hypocritical bishops and their timid clergy, birth control proponents were reassured by their own knowledge of ministers who readily provided contraceptive information to their parishioners. For every clergyman or clergyman's wife who wrote to Stopes for personal counseling, several others, including the Bishop of Wakefield, requested help for members of their congregations. An occasional inventive parson even sent along his own preventive recipe for her opinion, but far more common was the appeal of the harried minister who was simply at a loss as to what to tell anguished members of his flock.[30]

Slum parsons were particularly interested in obtaining advice for their populous charges and often embellished their letters with pathetic, even gruesome details of crowded family life in their impoverished districts. Others complained about the proliferation of the unfit and criminal classes and wondered what sort of birth control devices could be given to the ignorant, uncaring degenerates who threatened the race.[31] Nonconformists, especially Congregationalists and Methodists, were probably more active in the pursuit of reliable information than were their Anglican counterparts. In addition to seeking specific advice for individual worshipers several Nonconformist ministers arranged for Stopes or one of her CBC representatives to address the poor women of their congregations.[32] Even the Salvation Army expressed an interest in adding birth control to its arsenal and welcomed a speaker into its ranks.[33] Though the Anglican clergy in general were more cautious, a few of the more defiant boldly invited Stopes after the Lambeth Conference to visit their parishes and discuss the controversial resolutions.[34] Clerical correspondents were often more worried about the legal consequences of dispensing birth control information than they were about incurring the wrath of their diocesans. After writing for clarification or reassurance several joined the CBC, leading Horace Corner to predict that though most clergy "are humbugs in this matter," they would in time become important allies.[35]

Although the majority of ministers who wrote to Stopes praised her work, a few were abusive and accused her of demeaning love and marriage by reducing wives to the status of prostitutes. One enraged incumbent unleashed a ten-page salvo against old and new Malthusians when his son-in-law received twelve advertisements for contraceptives within a few days of the birth of his first child.[36] Stopes for the most part showed extraordinary patience in answering clerical inquiries and occasional denunciations sent to her over the years. Whether or not the bishops persisted in their arcane injunctions was of little consequence to her. She was sure that the quiet, underground clerical rebellion reflected in her letter files would soon sweep away the irrelevant Lambeth Conference resolutions and replace them with her own *New Gospel*.

To prove her contention that she, not the bishops, really spoke for Christ and the church on the controversial topic, Stopes, after the conference, audaciously sent out at random several hundred questionnaires to Anglican ministers asking about their marital status, number of children, and contraceptive practices. Although some indignantly returned the forms unanswered and many others explained that they were bachelors, nearly two hundred recipients or their wives actually responded to the specific questions. Approximately half claimed they used no artificial preventives whatsoever, but the rest confessed to employing coitus interruptus and condoms; an occasional respondent admitted to using occlusive pessaries or douching. Many of those who claimed to take no precautions admitted to employing the safe period or to abstaining from intercourse for long periods of time, but they were uncertain whether that constituted contraception. An occasional vitriolic respondent called Stopes a "whore" and regretted she was not a man so he could thrash her, but most replies were surprisingly courteous. Some people blessed her efforts even when declining to comply with her request.[37]

Although her sample of returns represented less than 1 percent of the more than 22,000 Anglican clergymen in Great Britain, Stopes was, with some justification, certain they accurately reflected the ambiguity, division, and hypocrisy within the established church. Moreover, as clerical fertility was among the lowest of any occupational group surveyed in 1911 and had further diminished since then, it seemed reasonable to conclude that birth control in ministerial families was even greater than the questionnaire indicated. There is no evidence that Stopes herself bothered to tabulate the data or to use it for some specific purpose. Unlike the Neo-Malthusians, her own religiosity made her reluctant to attack or humiliate the church, which she considered to be misguided but not unalterably perverse. She chose to use the returns not as a public weapon with which to flay the establishment, but as a private confirmation of the accuracy of her own perceptions.

When in the following year the king's personal physician, Lord Dawson of Penn, told the stunned Birmingham church congress that the "love envisioned by the Lambeth Conference [is] . . . an invertebrate joyless thing—not worth the having," Stopes, like nearly everyone else in the birth control movement, predicted that his comments would greatly weaken the church's professed opposition to the birth control cause.[38] Dawson, a cautious and deliberate man, had only spoken out when he had become convinced that the leaders of his church had so lost contact with "experience and reality" as to risk alienating an entire generation of young people who found their pronouncements on love, marriage, and birth control completely unacceptable. Sexual love, apart from parenthood, was to be prized and cherished for its own sake, he insisted, and to claim otherwise was to reduce marriage to an unnatural, passionless obligation. If the Roman Catholic church with its power and discipline was unable to erase birth control in France and Belgium, no Protestant church, he reasoned, was likely to be any more successful in England.[39]

Dawson could find nothing selfish, un-Christian, or antimaternal in people wanting to plan their families for honorable and cogent reasons. He would be the first to admit that some might misapply contraceptive knowledge, and he personally hoped that all couples would have at least three children to maintain the race. But the indiscriminate condemnation of birth control as "unnatural" and the advocacy of such unrealistic and possibly harmful alternatives as abstention was obviously no answer to the vast majority of decent, well-meaning people whose motives were above reproach. It was time for the church to leave the shadows of the past and abandon discredited arguments raised against the introduction of anesthetics and countless other scientific advances to alleviate human suffering. Issues, he concluded, must be faced in the light of modern knowledge and the needs of a new world.[40]

Lord Dawson's words were featured in virtually every major publication in the country and stimulated commentary and debate that ran on for months, and, in some cases, years. The *Malthusian* surveyed press opinion and was delighted to report that most of it was favorable. There were exceptions, but none quite as extreme as the *Sunday Express* decision that "Lord Dawson Must Go!" In donning the "grimy mantle of Malthus, the greasy robes of Bradlaugh and the frowsy garments of Mrs. Besant," the king's physician had raised the Neo-Malthusians from a "stealthy and furtive cult" to the high platform of a church congress where their "abominable gospel" has been given the imprimatur of medical science and social eminence.[41] The *Express* was clearly surprised by the volume of dissentient letters its comments generated, and subsequent efforts to moderate its language did little to mollify angry readers.

Combining impeccable religious and medical credentials, Lord Dawson's criticism was greeted by jubilant birth control proponents as unmistakable evidence of the crumbling of resistance within those formidable professional fortresses. One of the few discordant voices raised in the chorus of praise following the Birmingham address was that of Marie Stopes. She was on her way to Mary Ware Dennett's Voluntary Parenthood League rally in New York when she received the news, and she immediately wrote to her husband, "What a cad he was not to have mentioned my work. It would have made a huge difference."[42] Earlier in the year Dawson had declined to become a patron of Stopes's new clinic with the explanation that he could accomplish more at present by not too publicly identifying himself with "propganda on these sexual questions."[43] Once he came into the open, however, Dawson was fair game, and Stopes was only the most insistent of several birth control advocates who courted his endorsement throughout the decade. She reminded him on more than one occasion that she had paved the way for him by lifting the "subject out of the gutter"; the least he could do was to acknowledge her "pioneer work" and join the CBC.[44]

Disturbed by the uproar his opinions caused in religious and medical circles, Lord Dawson retreated from the public arena. With much forbearance he assured Stopes of his respect for her work, but he maintained that he still preferred to see birth control expand under medical direction.[45] Neither the Neo-Malthusians in 1922 nor Margaret Sanger in 1925 were any more successful in luring the famous physician to major birth control meetings. Sanger did arrange for him to come to the United States for a medical conference at the invitation of her ally, Dr. Raymond Pearl of the Johns Hopkins University, but she was unable to entice him even to send a message to the doctors attending the International Birth Control Conference in New York.[46] Furthermore, repeated efforts to persuade him to permit a reprinting of his 1921 address met with the reply, "I do not think it wise that I should appear before the public on this matter again, for the moment at any rate."[47]

The publicity given the birth control movement by the Lambeth Conference and the reactions it provoked was also sustained in part by the growing antagonism of the Catholic church. It was well known, of course, that the Roman hierarchy was implacably hostile to birth control, but before the war at least it had not proven especially aggressive in its condemnation. Monsignor Brown, the Catholic member of the first NBRC, was no more severe in his denunciations than were most of his Anglican colleagues. The fiery Jesuit, Father Bernard Vaughan, was one of the few Catholics who could be identified with anti-birth control propaganda before and during the war. His condemnation of Neo-Malthusianism in 1916 as a "national curse . . . poisoning the springs of our national life" was embellished with the usual warnings about luxuriant selfishness, demoralization, and race suicide. Along with clergymen of other denominations Father Vaughan grieved at the "massacre of innocents" at home as well as on the battlefields and, noting the correlation between empty church benches and empty cradles, predicted that "we shall have to make our cemeteries larger and our nurseries smaller."[48]

The Malthusian League believed that there was nothing exceptional or peculiarly Catholic about such familiar jeremiads. If Vaughan's coreligionists were less guilty of offenses against God and nature, they also only comprised about 5 percent of the population, Neo-Malthusians noted, and it was only a matter of time before economic realities and the example of their more prosperous, less fertile neighbors would bring the Catholic poor around. Although it was true that the power of superstitious, celibate priests over the ignorant faithful would retard the process somewhat, the low birthrates after the war in Catholic France, Belgium, Austria, Switzerland, and Bavaria indicated that the effectiveness of clerical displeasure was limited. Most Neo-Malthusians shared George Bernard Shaw's assessment that even the Irish would soon be as anticlerical and as enthusiastic for birth control as the French if only the English would leave them to their priests.[49]

C. V. Drysdale had often predicted that the Catholic church would be the last citadel of reaction to fall, and when, in the early 1920s, it became more vocal in its condemnation of birth control, he interpreted it as evidence of the movement's great success and an indication that the end of the battle was in sight. Earlier, when contraception was primarily practiced by the Protestant middle and skilled working classes and rarely threatened the poor Irish workers who comprised most of the Catholic congregations in Great Britain, the Roman church was not particularly alarmed. A number of people had suspected for years that the Catholic hierarchy secretly gloated over the differential fertility statistics, confident that its plentiful minions would eventually outnumber the increasingly barren Protestants. Father Vaughan confronted these insinuations and charges in 1916, sensibly pointing out that if the wily papists were really waiting until the sterility of the majority brought Britain back into the Catholic fold by demographic default, Protestants certainly knew how to avoid the fate. As much as he prayed to see the United Kingdom Catholic once again, Vaughan confessed, "I should be grieved and ashamed to feel that it had won in the race for population simply because Protestantism had too heavily handicapped itself by anti-conception practices."[50]

Some of Marie Stopes's earliest supporters in the CBC, especially in Glasgow, were persuaded that a Catholic plot had been hatched to overwhelm Protestants, and they recommended that the birth control forces combine to press for strict anti-Irish immigration laws before Britain went the way of the eastern United States.[51] Their religious concerns were often confused with eugenic fears about the excessive reproduction of people who were not only spiritually deficient but genetically retarded. Such anxieties were hardly allayed by Catholic Trust Society pamphlets praising the wonderful work of "our faithful Catholic mothers" while "wrong methods of birth control continue to prevail among the non-Catholics." The Society looked forward to the day when "their race will die out and the Catholic race will prevail and thus England will become again what it once was, a Catholic country."[52]

The Neo-Malthusians thought it all rhetorical nonsense. Catholics, they correctly surmised, were merely reacting to the intrusion of birth control into their own communities. The Roman hierarchy was already worried about the declining birthrate in Catholic countries, and its English representatives were fearful that its own congregations were becoming susceptible to the obvious advantages of smaller families. Catholic discipline would delay acceptance, but it would not prevent it. In the United States, Drysdale observed, Margaret Sanger reported in 1925 that Catholics were flocking to her clinic even as their priests launched frenzied assaults against birth control.[53] Robert Kerr added that Munich, though overwhelmingly Catholic, now had a lower birthrate than any town in Great Britain. It seemed clear to him that even if the country somehow became Catholic it would have little effect on the spread of birth control, which, as Neo-Malthusians had always maintained, had much more to do with economic considerations than it did with religious beliefs.[54] However militant the Catholics became in subsequent years, Neo-Malthusians insisted that the crucial point had been won in 1913 when Monsignor Brown had conceded that the safe period was acceptable for the faithful. In doing so he had broken with theological consistency dating back to St. Augustine and had set the Catholic church on the path toward birth control. It might fiercely resist other methods but, like the Church of England, it would in the end have to accept them, probably as a fait accompli.[55]

Marie Stopes was not so sanguine. Unlike Drysdale and other Neo-Malthusians who reacted to mounting Catholic hostility in the 1920s with the confident assurance that the clock could not be turned back, she viewed each obstacle as a formidable challenge to her destiny. Whereas they were content to let time and experience wear down their remaining foes, she was compelled to crush each one individually—the Malthusian League, Margaret Sanger, and now the Catholic church. Her initial relations with the Catholic community had been quite cordial. The first five editions of *Married Love* contained sympathetic comments by a Jesuit, Father Stanislaus St. John, but his approbation was soon withdrawn. Her explicit promotion of birth control in its sequel, *Wise Parenthood*, followed by what another Jesuit described as that "most profane compound of imaginary mysticism and pornography," *A New Gospel*, ended any illusions she had of leading the papists out of the middle ages.[56]

Aware, even pleased, that the Catholics now considered "Stopery," as they called it, a vile and satanic corruption to be exorcised as thoroughly as possible, she promised them a magnificent fight. Certain that Catholic spies would try to infiltrate her new clinic in 1921, she alerted her forces not to discuss their activities with anyone remotely suspected of being "an R.C.," because they were "up to no good."[57] Similar warnings about "perfidious R.C.s" sending devious agents to catch her up in some legal or moral violation flowed from her desk throughout the 1920s. In addition the *Birth Control News* was from its establishment in 1922 stridently anti-Catholic. Correspondents throughout the country reported on the anti-birth control machinations of priests, and the journal became a conduit for fears about Irish immigrants and their powerful clergy. By 1924 it was publishing lists of Catholic M.P.s so that the enemy within the political gates could readily be identified by the electorate.[58]

The Catholic press joined with local and national organizations in condemning birth control and calling upon Catholic physicians and politicians to ally with the clergy to demand an end to the advertising and sale of contraceptives. In 1922 the Westminster Catholic Federation succeeded in having the question raised in the House of Commons where it was made clear that the government had no inclination to pursue the matter.[59] Stopes was easily the most energetic and vituperative defender of the birth control cause, but it is difficult to separate her campaign against the Catholics from her insatiable need for confrontation and publicity. The *New Generation* could not understand why she responded so violently to what was at most a limited and temporary threat to the universal acceptance of family restriction. Several of her puzzled friends also cautioned her repeatedly about overreacting and tried to temper her pugnacious and litigious inclinations.

Stopes's correspondence with Mary Ware Dennett suggests that part of her intemperateness was motivated by envy. She was jealously aware of the publicity Sanger received from confrontations with Catholic officials and their police allies in New York and Boston. Though she professed to be disgusted with the "rows" provoked by the "Sanger crowd," she complained that in Britain "we face silence not attack."[60] By February 1922 she was looking for the "right case" to justify a "big *law suit* against Catholics" and was gathering affidavits testifying to her international reputation and prominence.[61] Stopes was primed for a major battle when the next month Dr. Halliday Sutherland, deputy commissioner for Tuberculosis Medical Services in England and Wales and a recent convert to Catholicism, referred in *Birth Control* to a "woman, who is a doctor of German philosophy (Munich)" who had recently opened a clinic "in the midst of a London slum . . . [to] make experiments" on poor women. He found it "truly amazing that this monstrous campaign . . . should be tolerated by the Home Secretary. Charles Bradlaugh was condemned to jail for a less serious crime."[62]

Stopes was at once furious and jubilant. The Lord had delivered her the "right case." Most of her friends as well as her attorneys were unconvinced, but they were unable to dissuade her from filing a libel suit against Sutherland. She was determined to break her Catholic antagonists once and for all.[63] Fortified by his prayers to the martyred St. Thomas More, a £400 contribution from the Cardinal-Archbishop of Westminster, and a fund established to pay all his costs, Sutherland delivered himself up as a compliant instrument of the faith.[64]

Most of the testimony during the trial centered upon the medical reliability rather than the theological acceptability of contraception. The presiding judge, Lord Chief Justice Hewart, was determined to prevent religious controversy in his court and warned counsel not to imply to the jury that there might be differences of opinion between Catholics and Protestants. Not even the plaintiff's damaging account of her message from God the previous year could divert the proceedings from their secular course for very long. The evidence was often perplexing, impressionistic, and contradictory, and when in the end the bewildered jury found that the words complained of were indeed defamatory yet true in substance and fact, but not "fair comment," everyone was confused. Although it awarded Stopes £100 in damages, Hewart, whose own prejudices and inept summary had compounded the problem, interpreted the jury's peculiar verdict as a vindication of Sutherland, denied the payment, and left Stopes with legal costs of several thousand pounds.[65]

Many people were outraged by the decision and the conduct of the Lord Chief Justice. Even members of the jury complained that their decision had been altered by the bench. The trial and Stopes's successful appeal later in the year stimulated enormous publicity for the birth control movement, much of it sympathetic. The Catholic press was unrestrained in its ringing denunciations of "Stopery" and the voluntary clinics it fostered. Stopes and her husband were inundated with poison-pen letters, some threatening her life. Newspapers were bombarded with derogatory letters about her work, and some succumbed to demands that all advertisements and references to her books and activities be stricken from their pages. The *Times*, whose receptivity to "Mrs. Stopes," as it called her throughout the trial, was at best erratic, again closed her out, and in 1924 it even refused to accept the announcement of the birth of her son.[66]

The harassment, which even extended to members of the Court of Appeals when it was considering the case, was exhausting and occasionally frightening. At the same time it fed Stopes's worst suspicions about the malevolence of the Catholic church. It also strengthened her monumental sense of mission and permitted her glimpses of a blessed martyrdom. She was certain that the pope himself was engineering the campaign against her, fearful that her success in Britain would soon be emulated in other parts of the world. Catholic invective only reinforced her belief that the Catholic church was an insidious force prepared to thwart her at all costs.

She knew that it encouraged and financed Sutherland's appeal to the House of Lords in 1924, and when a four-man body of judicial peers voted to overrule the Court of Appeals and uphold the original decision, the extent of papal power was suddenly clearer to her than ever before.[67]

The action had cost Sutherland and his supporters £10,000, and he won. The cost to Stopes and her husband was much greater, but the publicity and notoriety was everything she wished. Furthermore, in Sutherland's next book, *Birth Control Exposed*, he made no mention of Stopes's "experiments."[68] Their conflicts were by no means over, however, and they continued to assail each other into the next decade.[69] Stopes remained convinced that much of the press was intimidated by Catholics, and in 1927 she had to pay the editor of the *Morning Post* £200 and court expenses after she accused him of being controlled by a small clique of papists when he refused to publish her advertisements. Many papers, like the *Post*, pleaded that they were family-oriented, but others, especially in areas where Catholic readership was considerable, frankly admitted that they considered birth control to be a crime against God and nature.[70] Much of the press, though charged with being pawns of the Roman hierarchy, was not particularly unsympathetic to the birth control movement, but it was cautiously neutral.

Although few birth control activists in the 1920s doubted the intensity of Catholic opposition, most suspected that Stopes's antipathy for that faith was exaggerated by the publicity value she placed upon it. But it seems evident from her behavior and correspondence that she was also quite paranoid on the subject. At one point she was sure that local magistrates, who, in response to numerous complaints, demanded that she destroy her vicious chow "Wuffles," were Catholics trying to harass her. Not even the assurances of a detective she hired that the officials were all Protestants completely changed her view.[71] The Catholic church was of course the most visible organized opponent to birth control and as such was an obvious target not only for Stopes but for others. Though the Anglican hierarchy appeared to share the Catholic view, it was evident to birth control proponents that the Church of England was hopelessly compromised on the issue, with some of its most prominent members and countless of its clergy openly at odds with its bishops.

The free churches, by contrast, continued for the most part to avoid any official position although individual Nonconformists periodically expressed opinions about the controversy. The *New Generation* suggested that even if the free churches were more interested in fighting sin than in human suffering, birth control was practiced extensively by members of their congregations.[72] Indeed the fertility of Nonconformist ministerial families was, at approximately two children, only slightly larger than that recorded for their Anglican colleagues. The numerous Methodists, Congregational-ists, Presbyterians, and other free church adherents to the idea of construc-tive birth control did not complain of denominational conflicts, and Stopes, like the Neo-Malthusians, never had occasion to single them out for spe-cial condemnation.

The decision to leave birth control to the individual conscience had left Nonconformists without any clear moral theology to guide them, but it also prevented the tortured conflicts that plagued the Anglican faithful. This was strikingly evident at the 1924 Conference on Christian Politics, Economics, and Citizenship, which brought together socially concerned, progressive representatives from most of the denominations. The Angli-can conferees, in contrast to the Nonconformists, were highly agitated about the role of birth control in social reform and wrangled over the controversial Lambeth resolutions. While free churchmen stood aside, some Anglicans urged the conference to "face the facts" and endorse birth control clinics for the poor; others denounced contraception as "a dam-nable scandal . . . playing the very devil with the nation." Nothing was resolved.[73]

Similar differences began to appear in the episcopal ranks of the church. Though no bishop had dissented publicly from the Lambeth guidelines, a few were demonstrably uncomfortable with them. The former Bishop of Oxford, Charles Gore, testified in 1925 that he was often asked, even by his episcopal colleagues, "What is the use of the Christian Church fighting a losing battle against a practice which is sure to become prevalent?" If such resignation went unchallenged, he warned, human passion would be unchecked and we will be "exposed to tremendous perils . . . of race sui-cide, or the diminution of the best kind of stock which we should most desire to see propagated."[74] In the same year, however, Wakefield's suc-cessor at Birmingham, E. W. Barnes (1924–53), though equally worried about the eugenic implications of birth control, came to a totally different conclusion. A mathematician rather than a theologian, Barnes described the geometric capacity of human reproduction as a menace, not a blessing, and he assured the Royal Institute of Public Health that small families were fully in harmony with the Christian principles of self-renunciation. Birth control, the new prelate proclaimed, was an integral part of the new world created by public hygiene during the past one hundred years; it held out the best hope of curtailing the reckless fertility that threatened the better stocks and the community.[75]

Ecclesiastical resolve to defend the Lambeth Conference position was further shaken the following year when Archbishop Davidson, in a speech in the House of Lords, appeared to give his approbation to existing "birth control centers, which have been established for those who desire to use them and are supported by some exceedingly thoughtful people in this country."[76] The archbishop was actually speaking against a resolution introduced by the former Liberal lord chancellor, Lord Buckmaster, calling upon the government to permit medical officers of health to provide birth control information at local welfare centers. In opposing the motion Davidson not only claimed that voluntary clinics were sufficient to the task, but he mistakenly added that physicians were already free to prescribe birth control devices for women visiting public facilities. This was news to the various birth control groups who had been battling with the Ministry of Health for the past three years without success. The *Birth Control News* at once proclaimed that the Archbishop of Canterbury "does not oppose birth control clinics" and welcomed him as a great ally.[77] Stopes informed Davidson privately that he had been misled by the Ministry and that written instructions and an espionage system prevented birth control instruction from being offered in the welfare centers. When the archbishop realized his error but declined to correct his statement, Stopes publicly asked if he or the minister of health was a liar.[78]

Having once again been stung by an inadvertent confrontation with birth control and the determined Dr. Stopes, Davidson reverted to silence on the subject. To many, however, the archbishop's speech confirmed the belief in birth control circles that he, along with some others on the bench, had always been less adamant than the Lambeth resolutions suggested. Moreover, it seemed obvious by 1926 that church opposition was in sad disarray and that ecclesiastical discipline on the subject was negligible. Only one other bishop appeared with Davidson to vote against Lord Buckmaster's motion, which, to everyone's amazement, passed 57 to 44. The resolution was in no way binding on the government, but it clearly reflected the change in public opinion that had occurred since the war.

Dean Inge, commenting on the comparative equanimity with which the church received the surprising vote, thought it indicated that the "battle has really been won." In the waning years of the decade he was troubled by the possibility that the birth control movement had perhaps become too successful so that the "present birth-rate (15.3) is not sufficient to balance deaths."[79] Inge, who was always inclined to find cause for pessimism where others saw progress, now refused to take any further part in the movement and even refused to permit the reprinting of earlier articles he had written on the population question.[80]

Alarmed by the confusion, fragmentation, and lack of organized resistence among Christian opponents of birth control, Halliday Sutherland in 1926 established the League of National Life as an interdenominational alliance. As secretary, he was able to recruit a number of eminent people, including Lord Hugh Cecil, Edward Lyttelton, Charles Gore, Dr. Mary

Scharlieb, and the chief rabbi, Joseph Hirtz. A prominent gynecologist, Frederick J. McCann, agreed to serve as president. The league concentrated upon countering the "ethical sophistries . . . medical misstatements and statistical blunders of the contraceptionists." This also meant a detailing of the various physiological anomalies allegedly caused by contraceptives, including a new malady McCann described as "Malthusian uterus." In addition the group agitated for legislation to bring birth control organizations and retailers of contraceptives under the criminal law. In spite of Sutherland's ecumenical hopes of attracting birth control enemies from all areas of the religious spectrum, the League's membership, which never exceeded six hundred, was heavily dominated by Roman Catholics and Anglo-Catholics.[81] Consequently, it suffered from the suspicion that it was really a Catholic front organization with a thin veneer of interdenominationalism. Marie Stopes was of course certain of this, and she sent spies to monitor the league's meetings and infiltrate its ranks. On at least one occasion they were discovered and ejected.[82]

The League of National Life limped along between the wars carrying on the campaign in the pages of its journal, *National Life*. Its cause suffered an irreparable blow in 1930, however, when as Sutherland recalled, "we saw the white flag hoisted over Lambeth Palace."[83] He was referring to the outcome of the Lambeth Conference that year and its stunning reversal of its earlier resolutions on birth control. As the bishops of the Anglican communion prepared to meet once again, the polarization within clerical ranks over the issue was sharper than ever. It was now obvious that the defenders of the 1920 report clearly felt their position was in jeopardy. The old Bishop of London, Winnington-Ingram, and the Bishop of Lichfield, John Kempthorne, went out of their way to emphasize that their views had not changed. Edward Lyttelton persuaded the Norwich Diocesan Conference to petition the Lambeth conferees to reaffirm once and for all their unrepentant condemnation of all artificial means of thwarting conception.[84] Representatives of twenty-six religious organizations met in London in February to shore up the bulwarks against further birth control encroachments. Although they disagreed about details, they all joined in a resolution calling upon the Home Office to initiate legislation forbidding the advertising and public sale of contraceptives.[85]

Behind the scenes, however, concerted efforts were underway to work out a compromise that would at least partially accommodate the church to reality before its teachings on the regulation of fertility proved totally irrelevant. The new Archbishop of York (1929–42) and future Archbishop of Canterbury, William Temple, admitted in a "strictly confidential" letter to Stopes in November 1929, "I have long considered that the traditional attitude of the Church on this question is unwarrantable, and have (I think) done something to prepare the way for a modification." Secret discussions with some of his episcopal colleagues prompted him to predict a "more enlightened utterance from the Lambeth Conference than it gave us in 1920." Temple was by no means enthusiastic about the proliferation of birth control clinics during the preceding decade, but he thought that the conference might be persuaded to concede that physicians at least should be free to provide contraceptive information to married couples at family welfare clinics when medically appropriate.[86]

Although Stopes was not about to surrender the birth control movement to a medical monopoly, she knew a major concession when she saw it. She recognized that the church was inching closer to an endorsement of the position taken by all birth control organizations in recent years. As prelatical dignitaries maneuvered for compromise, many of the lesser clergy found themselves caught up in a conflict between authority and experience that left them puzzled, dissatisfied, and driven to follow their own inclinations. Several complained to Stopes that they prayed the confusion within the church would soon be resolved.[87]

She was once again determined to do her bit, but since the bishops had not been moved by her visionary exhortations in 1920, Stopes plied them with less ethereal evidence in 1930. She sent each of them a copy of her recent book, *Mother England*, a collection of letters written to her clinic in 1926 by working-class women who recounted the terrors of unwanted pregnancies, miscarriages, abortions, and death, which compelled them to find the means for controlling their fertility.[88] Their tragic plight was compounded by the indifference or ignorance of unfeeling doctors and contemptuous health visitors who neither sympathized with their desperation nor suggested the simple ways it might be avoided. Perhaps most shocking was Stopes's claim that the clinic had received more than twenty thousand requests for illegal abortions from frantic women who knew no other form of birth control.

Whether or not *Mother England* "touched their hearts" and persuaded the bishops to relent, as Stopes triumphantly claimed, they listened silently to an address by Dr. Helena Wright describing the advantages of birth control for the poor, and by a vote of 193 to 67 they adopted a new resolution on "marriage and sex."[89] It conceded that "in those cases where there is such a clearly felt moral obligation to limit or avoid parenthood, and where there is a morally sound reason for avoiding complete abstinence ... other methods may be used, provided that this is done in the light of ... Christian principles." In admitting the need for a fresh statement on the "noble and creative" subject of sex, and grudgingly sanctioning the use of contraceptives, the conference nevertheless reiterated that the primary purpose of married love remained procreation and the preferred form of limitation was abstention.[90]

By stressing motives rather than methods the bishops shifted the burden of responsibility to the individual conscience. If "selfishness, luxury, or mere convenience" were unacceptable reasons for restricting the size of the family, economic and medical considerations were now given ecclesiastical sanction. At the same time, however, the conference condemned that "propaganda which treats conception-control as a way of meeting those unsatisfactory social and economic conditions." It called for restrictions on advertisements and sales of appliances, but drew back from demanding laws that would actually outlaw contraceptives as many of the unconverted demanded.[91]

If to some the resolutions appeared equivocal and vague, they were hailed as a great triumph in birth control circles. Even Stopes was satisfied despite criticism that the bishops did not go far enough. She recognized that of greater importance than the specific statements on contraception was the conference's acknowledgment that opposition to birth control was rooted in tradition rather than in Scripture.[92] Nowhere was it mentioned in the New Testament nor had any ancient church council ever spoken on the subject. Even the Roman Catholics recognized that on some occasions restriction was acceptable.[93] These were of course the same arguments that the old Neo-Malthusians had been making for years.

Though the bishops waffled in their troubled efforts to find a satisfactory position, they were in the end forced to compromise with society as it was rather than as they wished it might be. As a result, their resolution read, "we cannot condemn the use of scientific methods to prevent conception, which are thoughtfully and conscientiously adopted." If the procreation of children was still the "primary end" of marital sex, it was evident that there were also "secondary ends" as well.[94] Though Marie Stopes assured all who would listen that *Mother England* and her influence with the church hierarchy had proven decisive in 1930, Cosmo Lang, who succeeded to the throne of Canterbury the previous year, had a simpler, more feasible explanation. He told the Lower House of Convocation after the conference that the bishops had acted "in the presence of a great and growing change, almost revolution, in the customs of married life throughout the whole world." With birthrates having already fallen by as much as 50 percent, the leaders of the church, whatever their personal feelings, could not act like ostriches and ignore their compelling responsibility to comment realistically on this momentous trend.[95]

Archbishop Lang's candid analysis was by implication hardly flattering to the leadership qualities of the Anglican hierarchy that had essentially caved in to the inevitable. Both Catholic and Protestant critics rushed to point this out. Cardinal Bourne, the Archbishop of Westminster, angrily denounced the bishops for having "abdicated any claim which they may have been thought to possess to be authorized exponents of Christian morality." In spite of the "destructive resolutions" approved by the Lambeth Conference, the Catholic church remained firm in its belief that birth control "is an unnatural vice" and was prepared to go it alone.[96] The new pope, Pius XI, confirmed Bourne's defiant stand when, in spite of the improbable offer of an alliance from Stopes, he issued on the last day of the year his encyclical on marriage, *Casti Conubii*, reaffirming the Catholic church's unwavering horror of the "grave sin" of contraception.[97]

Nearly fifty Anglican clergymen in the diocese of London alone signed protests against the Lambeth decisions.[98] Their sympathetic bishop, Winnington-Ingram, four years later was still lamenting the passing of the "old Victorian families," cursing the "filthy things" being sent to engaged couples, and contemplating the delights of dancing around a bonfire of condoms.[99] Less creative perhaps, the Bishop of Durham, Herbert Henson (1920–39), was content to warn of the grave risks to general morality involved in the continued spread of birth control, but he knew that many of his own clergy no longer shared his concern.[100] The irascible Dean Inge did not find it surprising considering the examples diocesans set for their ministers. Of the forty prelates in the country, he noted in 1934, one had five children, two others four, but the remaining thirty-seven managed to sire a mere twenty-eight offspring between them.[101] In the aftermath of the Lambeth Conference clergymen were much less circumspect about discussing birth control. Many now wrote to Stopes and the CBC for the first time requesting books and information for their parishioners, frequently adding that they shared the view of their Nonconformist brethren that family restriction, for whatever reason, was a decision of the individual conscience.[102]

Another generation passed before the bishops dropped their lingering reservations. The Lambeth Conference in 1958 decided that it was "clearly not true that all other duties and relationships in marriage must be subordinate to the procreative one." At the insistence of the overseas bishops whose more liberal social attitudes dominated the conference, the prelates now praised sexual intercourse as the "language of earthly love," which possessed qualities quite independent of any desire for children. "Family planning," as it was then described, was eulogized as a desirable strategy of "responsible parenthood" clearly in harmony with the human values implicit in the sexual union.[103] The reluctant ruling in 1930 that contraception was suitable only in cases of exceptional economic or medical need gave way to the liberating conclusion that, as long as the methods "are mutually acceptable to husband and wife in Christian conscience," birth control "is a right and important factor in Christian family life."[104] So complete was the church's abandonment of its prewar position that at least one manufacturer of condoms included with his product a short extract from the pertinent Lambeth resolution, suitably printed in gothic letters.[105]

For Marie Stopes, dying of cancer at the age of seventy-seven rather than at one hundred and twenty as she believed would happen, the conference, as several obituaries soon noted, was the long-delayed fulfillment of her curious prophecies.[106] But she, along with most of her contemporaries in the birth control movement, knew that the critical turning point had been reached in 1930 and that the church's qualified capitulation was only one aspect of the major breakthrough that occurred in that year. Though symbolically important, it was far less significant than the breaches made in the ranks of the medical profession and the Ministry of Health.

CHAPTER 12
Birth Control and the Medical Profession

In contrast to the Church of England the medical profession did not undergo a dramatic public conversion on the birth control question by the end of the decade. Instead it belatedly acquiesced to the inevitable out of an awareness that its hostility or indifference had proven irrelevant and because of the fear that unless doctors intervened quickly their authority in the area would be completely usurped by others. Charles Killick Millard was one of a few physicians before the war who tried in vain to warn his colleagues of this danger. He appealed to them not to endorse the retrogressive conclusion of the second National Birth-Rate Commission that all known methods of contraception were morally, racially, and medically dangerous, but instead to set their personal feelings aside and devote themselves to a dispassionate, scientific examination of the issue.

Millard knew many younger physicians who privately disputed the learned assertions of gynecological specialists that contraceptives were "genital frauds" the use of which resulted in a variety of condign punishments. Their own knowledge was, however, often very limited, and they were reluctant to challenge the eminent spokesmen of their profession whose entrenched moral sensibilities were as easily offended as their pride of expertise. The refusal of doctors to consider the establishment of an independent, scientific body to evaluate contradictory claims would, Millard feared, give the victory by default to medical moralists "who regarded the falling birthrate as a national calamity and the use of preventives as grossly immoral."[1]

To counter this possibility, Millard hurriedly sent out questionnaires in 1918 to more than one hundred physicians in four provincial towns asking them to recount the physiological effects they had observed in patients using contraceptives. Two-thirds of the seventy-four doctors who responded reported the devices to be effective and harmless, far superior to abstinence or the safe period, and they saw no evidence of their leading to estrangement between husbands and wives. The eleven practitioners who believed contraceptives to be injurious described their use as "unnatural," "disgusting," and "treason to the State," but only two of them actually had any medical experience with the appliances. Though they referred to the possibility of "septic irritation" and "severe protracted vaginitis," most of the sample reported no such difficulties. Several respondents commented on the widespread use of preventives "among the educated classes in both sexes" whose health was certainly above the average. They thought it "eminently desirable" for the medical profession to study the subject and provide "sound and authoritative advice as to the safest and least objectionable methods."[2]

Acknowledging that his sample was small, Millard nevertheless thought it fairly representative of what he had observed as a medical officer of health. It underlined his contention that, although the medical profession remained mired in futile moral condemnation, "birth control has clearly come to stay" and "whether we like it or not" it required the "most careful scientific consideration and study."[3] Millard hoped that his survey would convince the skeptical commission that the ignorance and prejudice paraded before it in the guise of professional expertise was not truly reflective of everyday medical experience. What, after all was to be made of the prominent gynecologist Amand Routh's learned assertion that labor unrest in recent years was the result of birth control reaching the working classes where its deleterious effects upon individual emotional and physical health were taking on collective characteristics? The Amalgamated Society of Engineers, which had been particularly militant of late, probably contained more practitioners of birth control than any other union, Routh estimated. "Don't you think," he asked the commission, "the unrest is simply due to the multiplication of congregations of individuals who are unsettled in their family life?"[4]

Much of the medical testimony was not appreciably more enlightening. Though the commission's report in 1920 was met with anger and dismay in birth control circles, the medical press was reserved and perfunctory in its comments. The contentious medical conclusions were largely ignored, and reviews in *Lancet*, the *British Medical Journal*, and elsewhere concentrated on the national and eugenic implications of the falling birthrate, which seemed to cause less division of opinion. Since its brief encounter with the controversial issue before the war the British Medical Association had excluded consideration of birth control from its meetings and, to a considerable extent, from the pages of the *BMJ*. When in 1921 that journal briefly opened its columns again to the subject, it quickly discovered that medical feelings were far more volatile than anticipated, and some disputatious physicians at least were no longer prepared to suffer in silence the sweeping moral pronouncements of the notable ornaments of their profession.

They were aroused by reports in the *BMJ* that Dame Mary Scharlieb, president of the London School of Medicine for Women, and Anne Louise McIlroy, director of the Obstetrical and Gynecological Unit of the Royal Free Hospital, had in separate meetings complained that birth control and the "sexual excesses" it encouraged were leading the nation down the path of effeminacy and degeneration. The seventy-six-year-old Dr. Scharlieb saw the barriers against rampant sexuality disintegrating in the "war against self-control" that had been unleashed by the unrestrained sexual appetites of men.[5] Her younger colleague, Dr. McIlroy, told the annual meeting of the Medico-Legal Society that women even used preventives on their wedding night, exposing themselves to a lifetime of illness and sterility and the Empire to further racial decay. The growth of birth control since the Bradlaugh-Besant trial, she warned, portended a calamity not seen since the collapse of Greece and Rome.[6]

Rhetoric of this sort was familiar enough by 1921, but McIlroy, in contrast to most earlier critics, thought it time for her profession to abandon its aloofness and bring the "use of contraceptives . . . now almost universal, under our advice and control."[7] The first Neo-Malthusians had urged doctors to take the lead in directing the spread of family limitation, and not a few of their successors found it ironic that only when it became obvious that medical approval or disapproval was of little consequence did physicians begin to agree. McIlroy reluctantly recommended that contraception, like therapeutic abortion, should only be permitted for medically certified reasons or for proven eugenic causes. The lively debate that followed her paper persuaded George Bernard Shaw that physicians would better serve their patients by not interfering in their private lives since they apparently knew little more about the subject than did priests.[8]

If the general tenor of the discussion supported the view that doctors should undertake a more realistic appraisal of their responsibilities, it also followed Lady Florence Barrett's admonition that the issue be left to medical women and their patients. Under no circumstances, she pleaded, should it become a subject for public discussion. The letters inspired by Scharlieb and McIlroy's comments quickly put an end to that hope. Many applauded their stand, although some thought the latter too conciliatory and urged the profession to agitate for prohibition, not control. One doctor called for the establishment of a national medical committee to determine who might use contraceptives, and he recommended that the devices be regulated along with such addictive drugs as morphine and cocaine.[9]

Critics hammered at the lack of scientific evidence to support condemnation. Their own experience with patients showed that birth control was safe and its practitioners generally less nervous, healthier, and happier than the parents of large families. No one knew this better than the educated middle classes, a Chester physician wrote, including the doctors who treated them. In spite of Scharlieb's prognosis, they did not appear to be a particularly lustful or effeminate lot as a consequence of their restrictionist habits.[10]

The testimony of birth control enthusiasts was often as emotional and as impressionistic as that of their opponents. The small family was usually endowed with robust good health, eugenic quality, mutual understanding, and idyllic happiness. Whatever the vision, doctors on both sides of the question recognized in the early 1920s that birth control could no longer be ignored or condemned by their profession and left to people who more often than not lacked medical credentials. Halliday Sutherland recommended a total moratorium on birth control until a scientific study of contraceptives could be completed, but even he recognized that his colleagues were increasingly worried about a weakening of their professional integrity and influence.[11] The rapid extension of birth control activity by nonmedical organizations threatened to exclude doctors from an area of responsibility and presumed expertise that a newer generation clearly thought belonged to them.

Any hope that the British Medical Association would take the lead in encouraging its members to approach birth control more clinically and integrate the latest teaching on the subject into their practices was soon dashed. Its governing authorities and the editors of the *BMJ*, disturbed by the intensity of feeling and discord surrounding the issue, instead chose to retreat as quickly as possible from the field of controversy.[12] Letters continued to arrive, but after the summer of 1921 the *BMJ* declined to reopen its columns to a free exchange of views for the remainder of the decade. This caution was abundantly evident in the journal's reaction to Lord Dawson's sensational speech before the church congress later that year. It regretted that the king's physician had not been precise in defending his position. Given the ramifications of the issue, the journal believed that birth control for the time being should remain a question of conscience for the individual doctor and his patient. Most practitioners would probably recommend some form of birth control for a patient whose life was endangered by further pregnancy, the *BMJ* hesitatingly conjectured, but as the profession is so badly divided only the "best and most innocuous method" is proper for consideration.[13]

If the *Lancet* was somewhat bolder than the rest of the medical press, it too deliberately avoided becoming a forum for discussion. Although the wife of its editor, Sir Squire Sprigg, helped establish the North Kensington Women's Welfare Centre birth control clinic in 1925, the *Lancet*, like the

BMJ, normally restricted its pages to official announcements of organizational activities and brief notices of parliamentary debates.[14] Both provided fair if restrained coverage of the Neo-Malthusian and Birth Control conferences in the 1920s and reported the findings of the several NBRCs established during the decade. The *Lancet* was more amenable to reviewing books dealing with birth control and more aggressive in its encouragement of the scientific investigation of contraception. Usually, however, its comments were in response to initiatives taken outside of formal medical organizations that carefully avoided involvement.

Most medical publications never broached the subject of birth control at all in the 1920s or, if they did, dropped it after a brief encounter. The *Journal of State Medicine*, for example, which first published Millard's survey of medical opinion in 1918, did not refer to the issue again until 1930, although many of its subscribers were under mounting pressure to prescribe contraceptives in public facilities. The *Proceedings of the Royal Society of Medicine* in 1921 alluded to birth control during a discussion of sterility by obstetricians and gynecologists, but it was not mentioned again in its massive volumes until the next decade.[15]

Striking in its exception was the appearance in July 1923 of an entire issue of the general physician's journal, the *Practitioner*, devoted to birth control. Although the editor acknowledged that the Bradlaugh-Besant trial had made it a subject of some consequence many years earlier, it had never been mentioned in the *Practitioner* before. But the rise of female emancipation and the impact of the war had ended the "intensive motherhood" of the Victorian era. Once forbidden in respectable circles, birth control, espoused by "women of unblemished virtue," had become a familiar topic in their clubs and even at "mixed tea tables."[16] Apparently the *Practitioner* decided it had become a fit subject for doctors as well. Unfortunately, the editor confessed, they knew little about it and were hardly in a position to provide much guidance through the maze of conflicting claims. Medical schools taught nothing of contraception, he reminded his readers, and though it would eventually be incorporated into the female program, he frankly doubted it would ever be permitted in the male curriculum. In the meantime most physicians, like the public at large, were dependent upon hearsay or literature "written by women with no medical qualification."[17] Convinced that the profession had to assert its leadership before birth control was entirely coopted by laymen, the *Practitioner* invited several recognized medical authorities of differing opinion to submit practical articles that would be useful and comprehensible to its audience.

Despite these good intentions the result was a familiar confusion of science, morality, religion, and popular prejudice. Barrett and McIlroy resented that public opinion had foisted the disagreeable issue on their profession, but they conceded that given the medical, moral, and eugenic impact of contraception doctors probably ought to learn something about it.[18] Some contributors rambled on about the warm family life enjoyed by the fecund poor. One of their more unreconstructed number denounced those who practiced birth control as "selfish cowards" who had probably graduated from such earlier perversions as masturbation.[19] If most of the authorities were more restrained, a majority of them still favored abstention as the ideal solution, though they acknowledged the futility of proposing it to modern couples. Enough had been learned about the unpredictability of the female cycle by the early 1920s to rule out the safe period, and withdrawal was unanimously rejected as psychologically punishing. Otherwise recommendations ran the gamut of preventive appliances. Barrett, for example, preferred quinine pessaries because they least interfered with the natural absorption of semen through the mucous membranes of the vaginal wall. McIlroy, who doubted the benefits of seminal fluid, recommended the condom as having the advantage of making men more responsible for their actions. Nearly everyone agreed that, whatever contraceptive was employed, its prolonged use would in all likelihood lead to sterility.

One of the exceptions, Eric Pritchard, medical director of the Infant's Hospital, Westminster, had once shared this view, and, as a member of the second NBRC, had rejected all contraceptives as harmful in 1920. Since then he had become convinced that this was not true of the "Dutch cap," or Mensinga diaphragm, which he now believed could be prescribed in good conscience by physicians for women who were determined to avoid further pregnancies. Pritchard's conversion, like that of other doctors, was facilitated by his recognition that since the war the spread of birth control among all classes had become so pervasive that unless his profession was prepared to exclude itself permanently from a new area of health care, physicians had best set their personal feelings aside and concentrate upon seeing that their patients were provided the safest contraceptives available.[20]

The medical fraternity, as Pritchard's comments suggest, was inching toward a new perception of birth control as an important part of the expanding field of preventive medicine. Major strides had been made in recent years toward the control of a number of contagious diseases. Immunology was a growing field that promised significant improvements in the area of public health, which taught that the avoidance of illness was as important as its treatment. In addition, the appeal of eugenics, still more comprehensible than genetics, convinced many doctors that, though pregnancy itself was not a pathological condition, its consequences on a number of levels most certainly could be, threatening not only the health and vitality of individual women but also society and the race. Norman Haire, the most knowledgeable of the physicians who wrote for the *Practitioner*, tried, on the basis of statistical data, to convince doctors that a safe and reliable contraceptive was available. A survey of 1,300 cases seen at the Walworth Clinic since 1921 confirmed that the Mensinga diaphragm had caused no problems and had only failed on four occasions in contrast to a 50-to-90 percent failure rate recorded for other devices.[21] The figures, which were at best preliminary and reflected short-term experience were, nevertheless, the only ones available in 1923.

Most of the women who came to the clinic, Haire reported, were mothers looking for a more reliable contraceptive rather than an introduction to birth control. Many had discovered that those doctors willing to help were often only marginally more knowledgeable than they were themselves. Haire was not surprised, considering that a substantial number of his colleagues still believed female orgasm was necessary for conception to take place, and they simply told their patients to control their climactic passion during coitus. Others remained so convinced of the benefit of mingling bodily secretions that they arbitrarily ruled out any appliances or spermatocides that might impede the absorption of semen. Haire pointed out that there was no scientific evidence that any such permeation actually took place. "Rosy cheeks" and serenity after intercourse probably had more to do with the flush of excitement and released tension than it did with the salubrious assimilation of the male ejaculate, he claimed. Though "one prominent nonmedical writer [Marie Stopes]" claimed she had proven the absorptive process when she was able to taste iodine within moments of having placed it in her vagina, Haire reminded her that iodine was a poison with very different characteristics from semen. Although he had already decided that Stopes was a bit of a humbug and something of a menace, Haire recognized that she, in contrast to most of the medical profession, was at least trying to learn something about sexual physiology. It was time, he pleaded, for reputable physicians to shift the debate from the individual and impressionistic to the collective and scientific, to rescue it "from the hands of quacks and charlatans and non-medical 'doctors' who write erotic treatises on birth control conveying misleading information in a highly stimulating form."[22]

The *Practitioner* agreed and challenged other medical journals to follow its lead and open their columns to a full and fearless discussion of the issue.[23] Having taken this courageous stand the editors avoided the subject for the remainder of the decade. Whether the *Practitioner*, like the *BMJ* two years earlier, was bombarded with rancorous correspondence that caused its publisher to have second thoughts is unclear, since nothing in subsequent issues even hinted that the extraordinary July number had ever been read.

The ambivalence of the medical press was not simply a result of the fundamental conservatism of the profession reasserting itself after momentary lapses of sober judgment. A great many doctors were obviously confused by conflicting testimony, and the journals had no authoritative information to give them. Millard found in another survey taken in 1922 that, although 56 to 65 doctors believed that the medical evidence would eventually support the safety and reliability of contraception, a substantial minority of their number thought that the declining birthrate among the prosperous classes was, as C. E. Pell recently argued, a result of nutritionally induced sterility rather than deliberate limitation.[24] What bothered Millard and the *Lancet* was the realization that the medical profession seemed uninterested in trying to resolve the contradictory assertions and explanations surrounding the subject of contraception and fertility. Its reticence was permitting Marie Stopes to become the recognized national authority and her clinic the principal center for birth control information and instruction in the country.[25]

Stopes, of course, enthusiastically agreed, and enjoyed reminding the prudish medical profession that she was merely filling a vacuum created by the ignorance and indifference of generations of doctors who had left the field open to Neo-Malthusians and an unregulated army of charlatans and quacks. Her conviction was strongly reinforced by her extensive correspondence with physicians who praised her work, offered suggestions, raised questions, and, more often, asked for specific advice.[26] Many frankly confessed that they knew little more than the embarrassed patients who came to them seeking help for everything from contraception to frigidity, sterility, and premature ejaculation. Though some doctors sensibly wondered if the commonplace premature ejaculation might be a consequence of extreme repression followed by uncontrollable anticipation, Stopes thought it was more likely caused by incipient gonorrhea.[27]

A substantial proportion of her correspondents turned to her after receiving conflicting counsel from fellow physicians, but many others confessed that they were reluctant to exhibit their ignorance by discussing questions of sex and birth control with their colleagues. Several writers clearly thought that Stopes was a member of the medical fraternity in spite of concerted efforts by her opponents to clarify her scientific credentials. Most, however, seemed to know that she had not been properly anointed, but they were so desperate for reliable information that they were prepared to accept it from any plausible source.

Many of Stopes's letters were from medical officers of health, like Richard Sandilands in Birmingham, who described the appalling ignorance of their working-class patients for whom "married love"consisted of drunken bouts of unchecked sexual passion. Although the abler artisans often knew about the sheath, he reported, their wives knew absolutely nothing. Most of his charges, however, were on the dole before and after they wed. They quickly learned about pregnancy, but they had a very difficult time learning about its prevention from the public health authorities upon whom they were dependent for medical advice. Progress was being made, Sandilands wrote, but his fellow physicians were still unpersuaded about the harmlessness and effectiveness of most contraceptive appliances.[28]

Whatever doctors knew about contraception was not learned in medical school. A number of Stopes's correspondents, including one of her former botany students studying at Charing Cross Hospital in 1921, complained about the absence of any birth control instruction in the curriculum. A number of women who had developed an interest in the subject as a result of their experiences in the hospital's outpatient clinic were bluntly told that most methods caused sterility and could not be recommended.[29] Intrigued by such reports Stopes in 1922 surveyed the twenty-three medical schools in Great Britain. Only one, the University of London's Royal Free Hospital, acknowledged that students in obstetrics and gynecology were introduced to contraception when and if it came up for discussion. Since the director of that department was Anne Louise McIlroy, it came as no surprise that she was no more receptive than officials in the other medical schools to Stopes's demand that a series of special lectures on birth control be added to their curricula.[30]

Students and physicians continued to protest to Stopes about the silence, indifference, or hostility they encountered when they tried to raise the subject, or, as in the case of C. P. Blacker, offered to teach contraception to the staff in gynecology and midwifery at Guy's Hospital in 1924. He was not optimistic that they would be willing to dispense preventives to needy mothers, nor was he sanguine "as to the possibility of inducing the very poor people of the Borough ever to overcome their native improvidence and irresponsibility to the extent of taking contraceptive precautions."[31] Blacker, who was beginning to emerge as an articulate medical advocate of birth control and negative eugenics, complained to Stopes about the irresponsibility of his profession. He was at the same time distressed that she was preempting the field of birth control with her "flowry and highly-coloured" books. They "inflame the imagination of both young and old," he charged, and are secretly read by boys and girls, while "flappers" and prostitutes regard them as "practical handbooks."[32] He soon discovered their author to be insensitive, uncooperative, and "ruthlessly uncompromising," and though he fought with her off and on for thirty years, he always admired Stopes's tenacity and vision. But he found it particularly galling that much of her influence and authority was initially built upon the timidity and confusion of his own profession.[33]

Nowhere was this more evident in the early 1920s than in the medical testimony elicited at Stopes's libel trial against Dr. Sutherland. Both sides paraded a number of experts before the court. If judge and jury were not sufficiently bewildered by the conflicting assessments they heard about the reliability of the plaintiff's clinical methods, they must have been startled by Sutherland's admission that he had not seen a gynecological patient in nearly twenty years. Dr. McIlroy grudgingly confessed under cross-examination that, although she was certain that rubber check pessaries were harmful, she knew of no specific case to substantiate her charge nor had she ever seen a patient who utilized the appliance.[34] Several medical journals reported the testimony without comment, but the *Lancet* found it embarrassing to the profession. Its editor, Robert Lyster, after listening to the doctors, concluded that birth control should be added to the medical curriculum where it could be studied scientifically, and a chapter on the subject should be included in every obstetrical manual.[35]

Stopes's major study, *Contraception* (1923), was offered to fill the gap in medical knowledge. Under some prodding from one of her associates, Dr. Maude Kerslake, the British Medical Association conceded in 1924 that it might be suitable reading for physicians were its author a member of the profession.[36] This impediment obviously failed to deter a large number of doctors who quickly added the book to their library and wrote Stopes about the possibility of purchasing quantities of the "pro race" rubber cap she recommended. As several medical authorities feared, her contemptuous boast, "I teach doctors," was proving all too true.[37] Not only were individual physicians turning to her for their education, but by the mid-1920s Stopes began to receive occasional invitations to address local branches of the British Medical Association, much to the displeasure of the central office. Though some branches, like Portsmouth, remained firm, others were less resolute and on several occasions withdrew invitations after local opposition became too vocal.[38] Areas with a substantial Catholic population were particularly difficult to penetrate, and as late as 1929 the Lancashire/Cheshire branch of the British Medical Association had to cancel an arranged address and discussion.[39]

The association found itself in a quandary. It wanted to gloss over the obvious differences doctors had about birth control while at the same time staking it out as a preserve of the medical profession in the future. Marie Stopes, to its official way of thinking, was an unqualified interloper whose claims were premature and whose scientific credentials and title were misleading and troublesome. Had she been willing, like midwives and nurses, to acknowledge the primacy of physicians and await their supervision, much of the association's resistance would probably have melted sooner. Stopes was of course certain that Catholic physicians had infiltrated the association's hierarchy and the editorial board of the *BMJ*, but as Sir James Barr and others found who tried to reason with the editors, her exclusion was based upon the considered decision to avoid controversy and to give no credibility to nonmedical authorities.[40]

The *New Generation* was irritated at the presumption of doctors, most of whom "know no more about birth control than a stevedore," denouncing it out of one side of their mouths while insisting out of the other that they alone should determine its use. After a half century of the "most gross and culpable negligence," the medical profession was not about to be given the monopoly it belatedly demanded.[41] Cooperation, however, was another matter; the Neo-Malthusians agreed that their Walworth Clinic, established in 1921, and the other facilities opened in subsequent years by the Society for the Provision of Birth Control Clinics, should be under medical direction and that all patients should be examined by a physician. The policy enjoyed the dual advantages of reducing the possibility of legal prosecution while blunting a good deal of medical criticism. However much doctors might deplore the falling birthrate and denounce the consequences of contraception, they were hard-pressed to challenge the professional competence of such eminent colleagues as Sir Humphrey Rolleston, physician-in-ordinary to George V and Regius Professor of Physic at Cambridge, who assumed the presidency of a new birth control clinic in that university town in 1925.

Although she employed professional consultants to prescribe for obvious physical abnormalities, Marie Stopes adamantly refused to share control of her clinic with physicians who were bound to know much less than she about the limitation of families. Defensive claims that a number of prominent doctors were officers in the Society for Constructive Birth Control failed to placate those who believed that a medical director should be in attendance at all times to supervise the nurses and midwives. Stopes, who was inclined to confrontation rather than conciliation, bristled at the prospect of sharing authority. Unlike Margaret Sanger, she never fully appreciated the importance of a medical endorsement to advance public and, eventually, governmental acceptance of birth control, and she was unwilling to cultivate the scientific community with the dexterity and shrewd patience of her American rival. The Neo-Malthusians, who endorsed Sanger's tactics, also saw little advantage in direct confrontation with an influential profession that was, like the church, struggling to accommodate itself to reality.

Stopes lacked their perspective. Her relations with the medical fraternity ranged openly from ambivalence to impatient, sometimes furious, contempt. Though individual doctors welcomed her accomplishments, she accepted their views on her terms or not at all. Much of her vituperation was aroused by the refusal of medical authorities to honor her scientific accomplishments and their inferences that her title of "doctor" was of lesser quality than their own. Another contributing factor was probably the traumatic stillbirth of her first child in 1919, which she always attributed to medical negligence rather than to a massive intrauterine infection revealed in an autopsy. Only when threatened with an action for slander did she finally stop accusing the attending physician of murder and begin deflecting her deep antipathy toward the profession as a whole.[42] That the profession had the poor judgment to question her vision rather than be guided by it guaranteed a stormy relationship over the next decade.

The tempest evolved rather than erupted. A number of physicians applauded her first works, and even avowed enemies of birth control, like Amand Routh, whom she subsequently employed as her personal physician, found considerable merit in *Married Love* and *Wise Parenthood*.[43] Several medical journals were also favorably impressed, and although they later noted the opening of the Mother's Clinic in early 1921 with a restrained wariness, there was no outright condemnation. When Humphrey Roe privately discussed the possibility of an endorsement with the editor of the *BMJ*, Dr. Scott Stevenson, he was assured confidentially that "our paper as a medical organ approves," but for the time being it seemed best to remain uninvolved.[44]

Despite Stevenson's reticence the *BMJ* was drawn into the open the following month when it published an anti-birth control letter from Mary Scharlieb in which she referred to "one well-known non-medical advocate of artificial prevention" who condones abortion at her clinic.[45] After a scathing reply from Stopes who emphasized that since she controlled the "*only* birth control clinic in Britain" Scharlieb was obviously referring to her, the physician agreed to an apology.[46] It was but a momentary retreat in Scharlieb's persistent war against contraception, and Stopes never tired of accusing the woman who had fought to open the field of medicine to her sex of abandoning her sisters when they stood to gain greater freedom than ever before.[47] If, during the subsequent debate over birth control that filled its letter columns, the *BMJ* declined to publish Stopes's increasingly rancorous observations, they found their way into print elsewhere. Halliday Sutherland first moved against Stopes in the fall of 1921 by sending to the *BMJ* excerpts of a letter she had sent to a number of local newspapers in which she accused "self-seeking" M.D.s of living off of women made ill by multiple pregnancies. Sutherland wanted his colleagues to know what the foremost proponent of birth control in the country thought of them.[48] Stopes made no effort to deny the statement, which was actually much milder than those expressed increasingly in her private correspondence.

Once aroused, as Sutherland soon discovered, his adversary was prepared to hound and harass her medical enemies at every opportunity. She waited years to revenge herself on Anne Louise McIlroy. Having learned from clinic patients in 1926 that McIlroy had relented and was quietly fitting women with contraceptive rubber caps in the outpatient clinic of the Royal Free Hospital, Stopes disguised herself as a poor, "work-grimed charwoman" and joined the crowd seeking assistance. "Three hours later," she reported triumphantly in the *Birth Control News*, "I left the hospital with a vaginal rubber cap, which had been advised and inserted in me by Professor McIlroy" after a "rude and perfunctory" examination.[49] Embarrassed hospital officials at first denied the story, but they soon reverted to denouncing the gloating Stopes's devious and time-consuming tactics.[50]

As Norman Haire knew very well Stopes's battles with doctors were by no means restricted to those who opposed birth control. When in the early years of the decade he questioned the harmlessness and reliability of an intrauterine device, the "gold pin" that she prescribed for some patients, and began to use the Mensinga diaphragm instead of her "pro-race" cap, Stopes became abusive and stopped referring people to him.[51] He realized that virtually all of her knowledge had been gleaned from the extensive reading she had done before World War I, and she showed little interest in the experiences and work of others. Though Stopes persuaded Haire to join the CBC in late 1921, he warned her that she must be prepared for occasional disagreements.[52] Within a month he was publicly questioning her judgment, complaining about the confusion of "Dr." and "M.D." in the public mind, and warning that, despite her distinction in some fields, "she has no practical knowledge of medical science whatever."[53]

Haire rubbed a raw nerve that was further inflamed during the Sutherland libel trial two years later. Although he still regarded her as a "medically deficient . . . useful propagandist—not much else," he agreed, at Binnie Dunlop's request, to help in the unlikely event that Stopes promised to treat him "courteously."[54] By then she had become convinced that there was something suspicious in Haire's Australian background, but after elaborate inquiries could find nothing more incriminating than that he was a Jew who had changed his name from Zions before emigrating to England.[55] Whether it was her pronounced anti-Semitism, or as was more likely, her inability to control Haire's testimony, she declined his qualified offer. He subsequently turned up as a reluctant defense witness who, however much he admired her objectives, questioned some of her contraceptive recommendations.[56]

Stopes was certain that only the jealousy of the medical profession and collusion within that self-serving fraternity could have prompted Haire to support, however unwillingly, a reactionary Catholic like Sutherland. Time and again friends and supporters appealed to her to temper her scathing language, reminding her that many doctors supported birth control, and it was neither wise nor fair to condemn an entire profession because of the behavior of individual members.[57] Perhaps, a Surrey doctor suggested, an occasional charitable interpretation of differences might prove beneficial. He reminded Stopes that, however improbable it seemed, she was not always right as her idiosyncratic denunciations of hypodermic injections indicated. When she ventured into areas that she knew nothing about, it only made her appear more eccentric and intensified medical distrust of her genuine accomplishments in the area of birth control.[58] Like many other well-intentioned rebukes, this one merely bounced off her impenetrable ego; she curtly replied that since doctors often differed in their diagnoses she would decide for herself.[59]

Support was not enough for Stopes; she wanted praise and adulation. It always galled her that doctors who wrote for advice and applauded her work in private were unwilling to acknowledge their debts in public. In the mid-1930s Haire wrote a conciliatory letter requesting that she stop vilifying him since they had enough opponents without making enemies of each other. Stopes angrily scrawled on the page that he had never publicly acclaimed "all the really big things" she had done.[60] Favored members of the profession who failed to acknowledge her triumphs were not treated much better. One of her supporters who had the temerity to defend birth control in the *Lancet* without alluding to her innovative leadership received an indignant rebuke. He tried without much success to explain that to mention her name in a medical publication was tantamount to waving a "red flag" in the face of many doctors whose conservatism, hypocrisy, and "queer mentality" he knew even better than she. Since most correspondence on the subject of birth control was returned by medical editors, he was fortunate to get his letter published at all.[61]

Whether placated or not Stopes knew the truth of this statement. If M.D.s met with countless refusals from their professional journals, it was nearly impossible for a "popular" rather than a "scientific" advocate of birth control like her to get correspondence printed. The *Lancet* remained the most accessible of the medical publications in the 1920s, willing to report noteworthy comments on birth control made by physicians at recognized meetings, and, on at least one occasion, permitting Stopes to reply to a critical speech made to the Manchester Medico-Chirurgical Society.[62] Though most of her other efforts to make a case in the pages of the *Lancet* were rejected, that journal did find merit in a proposal she made to the

General Medical Council in 1930 suggesting that the CBC refer corre-spondents needing birth control advice, but lacking a nearby clinic, to sympathetic local physicians on the council's rolls. After throwing up a number of patently thin obstacles, the council's registrar, rightly suspecting that Stopes was trying to associate her organization with his, made it clear that he wanted nothing whatsoever to do with her or with the CBC. Even the *Lancet*, which agreed to publish the correspondence, thought it was a sensible plan. It reminded the council that for years the profession had been demanding greater control over contraceptive practices yet it once again refused to seize the initiative even when aided by a longtime rival.[63]

A minority of physicians doubted that it mattered very much one way or the other. They remained persuaded that the decline in fertility was a consequence of some form of cyclical biological determinism triggered by population density and nutrition. Dr. F. A. E. Crew of the Animal Breed-ing Research Department of the University of Edinburgh knew more about reproduction than most of his medical colleagues, and he found it difficult to believe that deliberate limitation could account for the pro-longed drop in the birthrate. On the basis of his own studies he thought that G. Udny Yule and others were probably right in projecting that at some point in the near future, when the press upon living space and resources was sufficiently reduced, fecundity and fertility would revive. Birth control, like migration, he argued, alters only the proportion of groups in society not the size of the population. The same number of babies would be born even if contraception was unknown, except more of them would be in the suburbs rather than the slums.[64]

Critics who contrasted the excessively high fertility of desperately over-crowded countries like China and India with the very low birthrates of underpopulated nations such as Australia, New Zealand, and Canada found this to be a curious hypothesis. It was, however, one that appealed to medical eugenists like Florence Barrett who was convinced that diminished fecundity especially, but not exclusively, among the better classes was a more significant factor than the adoption of "unnatural practices" in ac-counting for recent demographic trends. Sterility, as most gynecologists knew, was a far more common complaint than fecundity and it was most evident among those women endowed with increased "mental and nervous energy."[65] Consequently, the modern woman does not need to take the risk of birth control, Barrett explained, since she is already demonstrably less fecund than her Victorian sisters who lived "sedative, confined, un-interesting lives."[66]

As a member of the Eugenics Education Society Council Barrett was particularly keyed to the dangers of differential fertility. She was therefore relieved to report that even with the poor, among whom "conception control" was much less common, families of ten or twelve had largely disappeared, suggesting that the Spencerian forces of individuation, combined with improved diet and better living conditions, were beginning to have a natural effect upon reproductive capacity. But even when multiple pregnancies occurred there was no evidence that they contributed to the premature aging and exhaustion of working-class mothers, as was frequently claimed. Since pregnancy was natural, not unnatural, she told the ethics committee of the National Council of Public Morals, the haggard state of overburdened mothers was a result of inherited weaknesses and nature's way of telling those frail women to avoid intercourse.[67]

Barrett represented a significant body of medical opinion that fought against the implication that multiple pregnancies were somehow a pathological aberration inimical to the well-being of women. To counter this dangerous assumption the assistant medical officer of health for Hull, Katherine Gamgee, reported in 1925 that a recent survey of "500 very poor families" revealed that the health of mothers of four or five offspring was better than that of women who had fewer children. Because the average interval between pregnancies among this "most improvident and fertile class" was over two years, Gamgee thought it disproved the contention that without restriction "babies would succeed one another so rapidly that the mother has not time to recover her strength." Her study indicated that the women "who has a child every four or five years is far more apt to suffer both mentally and physically than the woman who has one every two or three years."[68]

Gamgee's findings were endorsed by a roster of "prominent obstetricians" who shared her belief that birth control had little to do with good health but a great deal to do with self-indulgent women wanting *"an easy time"* as well as "a good time." Like many of her contemporaries, Gamgee was repelled by much more than birth control. She deplored the whole postwar moral climate. Abortion, birth control, and sexual license were all ingredients in the noxious brew of selfish corruption that threatened Britain with the same racial decadence long since obvious in France.[69] A number of her male allies would have added female emancipation as well, but most of the notable women doctors who lined up against birth control in the 1920s had been suffragists who had supported the women's movement. Before the war they had, like most feminists, avoided the birth control issue much to the disgust of Neo-Malthusians trying to find support in medical and women's circles. After the war, however, when increasing numbers of women, especially in the Labour party, began to contend that the ultimate achievement of feminist objectives and a woman's control of her own fertility were inseparable, female doctors both as physicians and emancipated leaders of their sex were forced to take a position.

In many instances they reverted to traditional feminist concerns about excessive male sexuality. Gamgee, for example, complained that the promoters of birth control seemed unaware that *"most of the suffering of our working-class women* arises from the unrestrained license and want of self-control of their husbands, especially after drinking bouts."[70] Barrett, in *Conception Control*, described the pitiful state of vulnerable women at the mercy of animalistic husbands who drunkenly fell upon them whenever lascivious passion dictated. Like Scharlieb, McIlroy, Gamgee, and others, she reasoned that, although birth control might reduce the number of children, it would not "diminish the excessive sexual demands made upon women" and might in fact increase them.[71] McIlroy warned that contraceptives meant greater slavery for her sex, since not even the threat of pregnancy would exist to curtail a husband's "uncontrolled desires."[72] All things being equal Barrett thought that for a working-class woman frequent childbearing was probably less harmful than the excessive demands of her husband, as she would at least have some respite during her many pregnancies.

Three years later, without noting the contradiction, Barrett informed the ethics committee of the NCPM that she had never met a woman who did not find contraceptives "repugnant," but most, nevertheless, were forced to use them by their husbands. This was particularly true for the "more primitive woman" whose "primitive instinct" tells her that "Nature should be left alone unless we are going to aid her."[73] Out of this jumble of middle- and upper-class assumptions about working-class behavior, men were damned if they did and damned if they did not. In gratifying their bestial lust without fear of the consequences they were uncaring, thoughtless brutes. If, however, husbands were prudent and encouraged birth control practices, they were "sordid and unnatural." In either case it was simply assumed that wives were passive victims rather than willing partners in perversity.

Feminist advocates of birth control continued to share many of these same opinions, but they concluded that only by providing for their own protection could women diminish the frightful consequences of unchecked male sexuality and truly gain equality and independence. They were angered that women M.D.s, of all people, did not as a group support them. Whether married or single, female physicians were looked up to as proud examples of what women could achieve, and they were continually reminded that they came from a class that had long since learned the benefits of smaller families. Although the CBC and the Society for the Provision of Birth Control Clinics were able to persuade a few women doctors to serve as consultants or supervise facilities, both organizations repeatedly complained about the lack of cooperation from female physicians. Stella Browne and Stopes fulminated about the "traitors" to their sex who, as debates in the Medical Women's Federation and occasional letters in the medical press indicated, did not necessarily share the views of Barrett, Scharlieb, or McIlroy, but were still unwilling to rally to the birth control cause and help their less fortunate sisters.

Physicians like Haire and Blacker who tried to analyze the differing opinions within their profession concluded that the conflicts had more to do with generational values and experience than with gender or scientific knowledge. Haire, for example, calculated in 1928 that the most vocal medical enemies of birth control in both sexes averaged sixty-two years of age and had little practical acquaintance with contraception. They had rarely, if ever, studied the subject or considered it as an area of professional treatment. M.D.s under the age of forty were, however, much more open-minded, personally familiar with various methods for limiting fertility, and more amenable to prescribing them, or at least withholding judgment until scientific studies were completed.[74]

Haire had in 1922 organized the first formal medical meetings in Britain to discuss birth control and in subsequent years kept a close check on the progress made within the profession. At that initial session nearly all of the 165 physicians from Europe and the United States echoed the need to treat birth control as a medical rather than a moral problem, and they complained about the inadequacies of the medical school curriculum and the absence of cumulative scientific data. They were alarmed that their role was being usurped by others whose ideas were sometimes "purely fanciful," and they urged the formation of medical societies to study contraception and make recommendations to the profession.[75]

Similar proposals made throughout the decade were occasionally endorsed by the *Lancet*, but research remained limited to a few individuals and the medical curriculum remained largely unchanged. Some data was accumulated in the voluntary clinics, and in 1925 Stopes reported, with considerable exaggeration, on her great success with the first five thousand women who visited her facility.[76] In addition, in the absence of any scientific testing agency, she and some of her married workers experimented on themselves with new contraceptives. The results were occasionally disgusting. She described one "sticky, slimy" chemical suppository sent her by an inventive physician seeking a CBC endorsement as "positively beastly . . . ; it took so many days to clear the thing out."[77]

By the mid-1920s the position of the medical profession was, like that of the church, becoming absurd. As demands for independent scientific evaluation mounted, the NCPM asked doctors for their views on the "ethics" of contraception. Lord Dawson, alluding to the birthrate, thought the inquiry academic, but most of the other physicians who appeared before its committee repeated the familiar litany of moral and physiological pitfalls associated with birth control.[78] Nearly all were now willing to concede, however, that if a woman had at least four children, or if her life was in danger, or even if the family was threatened by economic disaster, the risks associated with artificial restriction might be acceptable. But four members of the ethics committee, led by Dr. Letitia Fairfield, divisional medical officer of health for the London County Council, refused any such concession, with the pronouncement that the "use of contraceptives is a frustration of God's design in nature" and can never be justified.[79]

The thrust of the council's report in 1925 was that birth control required ethical, not medical, direction. However, because doctors had authoritative, responsible positions in society, they could help firm up moral guidelines.[80] This attempt to refurbish the prewar medical-religious alliance was continued the following year in James Marchant's compilation of *Medical Views on Birth Control.*[81] Despite an introductory appeal by a prominent physician, Sir Thomas Horder, for balance and discretion, most of the contributors, led by the implacable Scharlieb, reiterated their well-known opinions and discounted the need for statistics or other evidence.[82] When she claimed that all contraceptives caused sterility and none "has stood the test of practical use," Stopes wrote in the margin of her copy of *Medical Views,* "Liar! Oh you liar!" Dr. Arthur Giles's censure of all pessaries for "damming up the natural discharges from the uterus" was similarly embellished with "Idiot" and "Liar—what evidence?"[83]

Stopes was only slightly less offensive in print, but of greater importance was the reaction of the medical community. A number of reviewers in the medical press were embarrassed by the fears, prejudices, and unsupported opinions that paraded as science, and they worried about the impact of *Medical Views* on the profession's credibility.[84] To insist eight years after the war that abstinence was the only acceptable method of controlling family size was not likely to inspire confidence in medical judgment. In the face of so much disagreement it seemed prudent to many in the profession to do nothing. *Public Health,* which had avoided the birth control issue for several years, reasoned that the crudity of available preventives and the disputes about their use should convince medical officers of health that they should continue to maintain a "discreet silence, or at any rate . . . exercise a judicious reticence."[85] To the opponents of birth control who, like Fairfield, feared their position was eroding, this was welcome advice, and it made much more sense than "taking on the responsibility of intermeddling with the health of the country in a sphere where medical opinion is chaotic."[86]

In many ways the appearance of the NCPM *Ethics of Birth Control,* followed by its secretary's slanted collection of *Medical Views,* marked a turning point in the medical response to the birth control controversy. Despite efforts to leave the problem unresolved, several individuals and organizations were determined to exploit the anger and embarrassment caused by *Medical Views* within the younger, frequently reticent sectors of the medical community. Even Fairfield acknowledged that physicians of her persuasion were now on the defensive; their outspoken opposition to birth control had become counterproductive, and they were made to appear to be hopelessly reactionary or inhuman.[87]

The Eugenics Society, still undecided about the racial implications of birth control, was in 1926 the first organization to decide that it was time to undertake a serious medical study based on the accumulated experience of the few voluntary clinics that had been founded since 1921. Stopes, whose Mother's Clinic possessed the most complete records, refused to cooperate when the society asked Dr. Jane Hawthorne to represent the CBC on the investigation committee because she, not Stopes, possessed the requisite medical qualifications. After many apologies and lengthy negotiations, underscored by Stopes's less than charitable assessments of the intelligence and integrity of M.D.s, she finally relented and provided valuable data for the group.[88]

In contrast to *Medical Views of Birth Control* the report of the Eugenics Society Medical Committee of the Conference of Co-Operating Birth Control Clinics concluded that the rubber pessaries and suppositories prescribed by the various clinics were not only effective and harmless but that the health of the working-class women using them improved considerably. It was obvious, however, that even simpler contraceptives were needed because most women wishing to avoid conception did not have access to a clinic and were, in all probability, dependent on other women for most of their advice.[89] As eugenists the doctors on the committee were primarily interested in examining the viability of birth control as a negative strategy of race improvement. They were also trying to locate the "more defective types in the Community in which innate characteristics and modes of life would prevent the successful use of contraceptive measures" and might indicate the need for sterilization.[90] Despite its particular objectives, the committee was nevertheless the first medical group to analyze cumulative information about birth control practices and establish a continuing system of medical monitoring in cooperation with the clinics.

Norman Haire, who assisted the Eugenics Society Medical Committee, underlined its collective findings by publishing in 1928 a collection of individual articles by pro-birth control physicians and scientists pointedly entitled *Some More Medical Views on Birth Control*. The authors carefully eschewed moral judgment, and instead they dispassionately described the evidence available on the advantages and disadvantages of various contraceptives and methods. Even before Haire's obvious refutation of *Medical Views* appeared, the NCPM, stung by criticism of its recent publications, reconstituted its NBRC into a medical committee to reconsider what many of its own members feared was an unrealistic, perhaps ludicrous position. Under the chairmanship of a respected surgeon, Charles Gibbs, twelve M.D.s and a physiologist heard testimony from private practitioners, medical officers of health, biologists, statisticians, and the medical directors of several birth control clinics.[91] Even Stopes was invited this time, but she wrote the NCPM off as a nest of "medical reactionaries," refused to give evidence, and persuaded F. A. E. Crew not to appear.[92]

To nearly everyone's astonishment the medical committee concluded in 1927 that "no impediment should be placed in the way of those married couples who desire information as to contraceptives, when this is needed for medical reasons or because of excessive child-bearing or poverty." The evidence clearly revealed that contraception was not unhealthy, and in many cases it contributed substantially to the physical and psychological well-being of mothers with too many children. The committee members were particularly impressed by the four thousand cases Haire had followed over the years. They supported his findings that the Mensinga diaphragm, when used with lactic acid jelly, was safe and 95 percent reliable. Although some of the physicians on the committee were less enthusiastic than others, they all agreed that the spread of birth control was irreversible and that enough experience existed to justify a recommendation that hospitals, under careful medical supervision, become centers for instruction in family limitation.[93]

The willingness of the NCPM, of all groups, to underwrite and issue a report that ran so contrary to the position it had taken since the war revealed how much resistance to birth control had weakened. Though the cautious *BMJ* described the findings as an "interim report" worthy of study, the *Lancet*, *Public Health*, and other medical publications were more enthusiastic, and they encouraged their readers to give serious consideration to the establishment of medically supervised birth control clinics in the obstetrical and gynecological departments of hospitals.[94] Even the most vocal critics conceded they were now fighting a delaying campaign, and once-fervent medical preachers against the sin of contraception agreed to await new revelations based upon further scientific inquiry.

Sensing that the time was right Sir Humphrey Rolleston in 1927 joined with other physicians, scientists, and demographers to establish a permanent Medical Investigation Committee in conjunction with the North Kensington and Cambridge birth control clinics. Rolleston's appeal to the medical community for support was endorsed by the leading journals of the profession, and for the first time since 1912 the British Medical Association agreed to include in its 1928 annual meeting a session entitled "The Falling Birth-Rate."[95] Although most of the papers concentrated on the economic and biological determinants of smaller families, much of the discussion centered on birth control and the obligations of physicians toward patients who wanted to limit their fertility. Commenting on the debate, the *BMJ* concurred with those doctors who argued that it was not their responsibility to resolve the economic, social, religious, and moral considerations surrounding the use of contraceptives, but to concentrate upon the safety and reliability of the methods employed.[96]

They were increasingly dependent upon the reports of the voluntary clinics, or the Medical Investigation Committee, which assured doctors that most of the failures could be traced directly to human error and negligence rather than to a particular contraceptive.[97] Clinic authorities tended to exaggerate their successes as none of them had the facilities or personnel to conduct extensive follow-up studies on the working-class women who came only once or twice for assistance. As a result, although Haire and Stopes referred to as many as four, five, even ten thousand cases, a closer examination indicates that the number actually surveyed over a period of time was at best 10 percent of the clinic visitors.[98] By 1930 there were still only sixteen clinics and two private consultants in all of Great Britain. They had been visited by approximately 21,000 women since Stopes opened the first clinic in 1921, and many of her successors based their optimistic reports on no more than fifty of sixty cases whose progress could be followed.[99] They, like Stopes, generally assumed that if a woman did not return she was probably satisfied with her contraceptive prescription and was having no difficulty.

Rolleston and his colleagues at the Cambridge clinic were worried about the extravagant claims made by Stopes and others. Many contraceptives, they knew, were poorly manufactured and subject to failure, and people complained that they were cumbersome, inconvenient, and expensive. A careful survey of the first three hundred women who came to the Cambridge clinic between 1925 and 1927 turned up a failure rate not of 1 or 2 percent, as Stopes reported, but of closer to 50 percent. According to Lela Florence, who wrote the report in 1930, the principal reasons women abandoned the newer, more reliable appliances were ignorance, fear, disgust, fatigue, a lack of privacy, or some physical complication. Consequently coitus interruptus and, less often, the condom, soon replaced the rubber diaphragm and chemical suppository provided by the clinic, and many of the women became pregnant again.[100]

Most of the patients came to clinic from nearby rural villages, rather than from middle-class, academic Cambridge. A large proportion of them still felt that contraceptive appliances were unnatural and shameful, and they were haunted by fears that their neighbors would discover their secret. Many of them, Florence thought, were predisposed to failure. Because many of the women lived in "primitive conditions" and could or would not respond to letters, it was extremely difficult to conduct follow-up examinations or interviews. Though the problems were somewhat different in large cities like London, they could not, in Florence's judgment, account for the great disparities between the Cambridge experience and that reported by the "Mothers' Clinic." To assume, as Stopes did, that women who did not answer inquiries or return with complaints were satisfied and successfully controlling their fertility was, Florence argued, nonsense. Moreover, virtually all of the clinics had abandoned Stopes's "pro-race" cap in favor of the Mensinga diaphragm, which was much easier to fit and far more reliable.[101]

Stopes remained impervious to the experience of others and denounced the "amateur incompetents" who questioned her recommendations and claims of success. The Cambridge clinic was obviously as inept as all the rest, she decided, and reiterated that the failure rate at her clinic was certainly no greater than 2.5 percent. Indeed her own recent review of three hundred cases proved her methods to be virtually infallible.[102] What was evident from these squabbles over a small sample of patients was that the vast majority of people limiting their families were doing so without any assistance whatsoever from either clinics or doctors. Most women who learned about birth control probably did so from other women with whom they worked or, in the more prosperous classes, with whom they were educated.[103]

The voluntary clinics realized that nearly all of the women who came to them had already decided to limit their families and knew something about birth control, but were looking for more satisfactory methods. The birth control movement was no longer faced with persuading people of the multiple advantages of rational family planning, but with facilitating access to the best methods. In contrast to what many middle- and upper-class people believed, Florence reported, the working poor were not cursed with an excess of lust and a paucity of self-restraint. A great majority of the men whose desperate wives came to the Cambridge clinic were "extremely moderate and self-controlled." Wives were frequently encouraged to seek advice by their husbands who had tried to regulate fertility by spacing intercourse or practicing withdrawal, but found it debilitating and often unsuccessful. It was not then a surfeit of unchecked passion that condemned the poor to larger families, Florence insisted, but the unavailability of simple, reliable, inexpensive contraceptives that could be used without difficulty or shame.[104]

In summarizing the accomplishments of the birth control movement since the war, Haire made the same point in 1929. Our ability to reach those most in need of help, he wrote Stopes, has scarcely advanced at all. The ideal solution was the invention of an economical, trouble-free appliance that could be self-administered by the most ignorant of women. Though he perceived that it would be a high priority for the next generation of birth control advocates, he frankly doubted such a contraceptive would ever be developed.[105] In its absence Haire was persuaded that there were two effective alternatives to reduce significantly the fertility of the lowest classes. The first was to gain the support of the medical practitioners who treated them and the second was to persuade the minister of health to permit the more than two thousand local maternity and infant welfare centers in the country to form a national network of birth control clinics.

The cautious, piecemeal conversion of the reluctant medical profession was well on the way to accomplishment by the end of the decade even if, unlike the church, its changing attitude was not embodied in some dramatic declaration of principles. The doctors' grudging capitulation only awaited some definitive decision from the embattled Ministry of Health. That decision, enmeshed as it was in politics and in the expenditure of public funds to support highly personal and very controversial domestic behavior, proved more difficult to extract. Yet, as most leaders of the birth control movement during the interwar years recognized, it was their most important accomplishment, for it transformed their fragmented, voluntary efforts into a coordinated and critical campaign to alter basic government policy and decisively expand the nation's concept of public health.

CHAPTER 13
The Politics of Birth Control

When Marie Stopes and her husband opened the first birth control clinic in 1921 they thought of it as a unique model, a pilot project, rather than as the nucleus of a national network of similar facilities. They had no plans to open additional clinics and saw no justification for the Malthusian League and the Society for the Provision of Birth Control Clinics to establish their own accommodations.[1] Because it was unlikely that a few voluntary clinics would be able to reach more than a fraction of the poor women in need of instruction, Stopes believed it was more important to concentrate resources in a single clinic, her own, whose success might in time be emulated by government authorities. Part of Stopes's reasoning was self-serving, of course, but it also corresponded to the prevailing conclusion in birth control circles that the most promising way of reaching the lower classes was through the more than two thousand antenatal clinics and infant and maternal welfare centers distributed throughout the country. Though under the control of more than four hundred local authorities, they received financial grants from the new Ministry of Health, which was established in 1919. All that was needed to turn them into birth control clinics, Stopes perceived, was the "national will" to do so.[2] The climactic birth control battle of the interwar years was fought to persuade the reluctant Ministry of Health that such a national will existed.

A few Neo-Malthusians, including Alice Vickery Drysdale, had recognized the potential of the infant and maternal welfare centers during the war. She had persuaded her son that however much he opposed the establishment of a new welfare bureaucracy like that of the Ministry of Health it might eventually prove to be a valuable ally in the control of population.[3] There is no evidence that Lord Rhondda, Christopher Addison, and the other champions of the new Ministry remotely entertained such a possibility. Instead they concentrated on consolidating government departments concerned with public health and insurance and establishing guidelines for local authorities. The most effective weapon the minister of health possessed in dealing with boards and officials who rejected his directives was the withholding of supplementary grants. It was to prove very important when the young Ministry found itself drawn into the expanding controversy over birth control in the early 1920s.

A few local medical officers of health, such as Charles Killick Millard, had been trying for many years to interest their local boards in the public health implications of birth control. After the war, when it appeared that resistance might have softened, they found themselves confronting a new barrier—the possible curtailment of government funds. Binnie Dunlop discovered in 1921 that many welfare centers feared a loss of subsidies if the Ministry of Health learned that they were countenancing family limitation, but he was unable to discover any specific directive to substantiate the concern.[4] Stopes agreed that if the charge were true the birth control forces should challenge the Ministry, but her numerous inquiries failed to determine whether or not it had taken a position or ever even considered the matter. At least two medical officers of health recommended in their annual reports for that year that the Ministry consider national guidelines for birth control instruction in welfare facilities. The following July the mayor of Deptford, at his medical officer's request, agreed to hear arguments about opening the municipal public health centers for such purposes.[5] It was apparently the first time local authorities were prepared to consider the subject even if they were yet unwilling to authorize any change in policy.

Limited surveys at the time suggested that most medical officers of health were either divided over the place of birth control in their work or were noncommittal.[6] Ten municipalities were nevertheless sufficiently interested to send their medical directors to the Fifth International Neo-Malthusian and Birth Control Conference when it convened in London later in July and all of them supported the resolutions of the medical section. The *New Generation* was certain that the minister of health could not long resist the pressures caused by differential fertility and would have to sanction contraceptive instruction in every welfare center and hospital in the country.[7]

The reluctance of the Ministry to become involved in so contentious a matter only contributed to the confusion and rumors. When a deputation from the Catholic Women's League met with the minister of health, Sir Alfred Mond, in March 1922 to seek clarification and express their opposition to the use of public facilities for birth control, they found him sympathetic but disconcertingly vague.[8] Advocates of birth control were no more successful in extracting definitive answers because there were none. The new Ministry had never contemplated that it might be forced to contend with the issue and had not formulated a position. For the time being it was content to leave the problem to local officials.

Most local authorities assumed that the implementation of birth control counseling would probably place their government grants in jeopardy. Given the volatility of public opinion it was not only a reasonable conclusion, but convenient as well; comparatively few infant and maternal welfare centers seemed any more eager than the local authorities to take on the responsibilities and the controversies that were bound to follow. The Ministry's hand was finally forced, however, by the dismissal in December 1922 of Elizabeth Daniels, a nurse and health visitor in Edmonton, London, who, despite warnings from the medical officer, continued to provide birth control information to desperate women at the local maternity center. Her dismissal was met with an outcry from sympathizers, but, more significantly for the future, a deputation from the Unemployed Women's Committee in the district submitted a petition with five hundred names calling for Daniels's reinstatement.[9]

In rejecting the appeal, the Edmonton authorities indicated that they had not acted entirely independently. This was confirmed a few days later when a Ministry of Health official, Dr. Janet Campbell, proclaimed for the first time that it was not the function of a maternity center to give birth control instruction. Women in need of such assistance should be referred to a private physician or private hospital.[10] Critics immediately pointed out that few hospitals were able or willing to help, and, even if enough individual doctors were sympathetic, which was doubtful, the poor women who attended welfare clinics were hardly in a position to pay for private consultations. While the controversy swirled about her, Elizabeth Daniels slipped off to Holland to learn more about fitting birth control appliances. She returned several months later to open her own private clinic where she taught other nurses the Dutch methods.[11] Though Stopes refused to join in the accolades to Daniels, incongruously complaining that the nurse had been insubordinate "towards her doctor" and, less forgivable, had failed to consult the Society for Constructive Birth Control, she did agree with those who called for a public inquiry into the Ministry of Health's unsatisfactory ruling.[12]

On 25 July 1923, the birth control question was fleetingly introduced into parliament for the first time when F. A. Broad, the Labour member for Edmonton, sought further clarification from Neville Chamberlain, the Conservative minister of health. Chamberlain merely reaffirmed his predecessor's position.[13] In spite of a dubious New Generation League survey showing that a majority of M.P.s secretly favored permitting birth control instruction in the welfare centers, even though it was politically risky to say so, Broad and his few supporters saw little evidence of it in the Commons and for the time being decided not to press the point.[14] Though most politically conscious birth control advocates in the early 1920s thought that the success of their campaign in parliament would have to await the election of a Labour government, a number of knowledgeable Labourites were less confident. When the Reverend Gordon Lang, standing as a Labour candidate for Monmouth in 1922, raised the issue with party strategists, he was told that birth control was not important to workers. They knew that an equitable redistribution of wealth would make the limitation of families unnecessary. Lang thought this a naive and foolish response that had more to do with prudery, false modesty, and a fear of antagonizing a vocal minority of Catholic constituents than it did with socialist principles. He exhorted voters to emulate the suffragettes and heckle speakers who refused to address the birth control question. The next year he recommended testing public opinion by running a candidate in a by-election pledged to permitting the dissemination of contraceptive information in the infant and maternal welfare centers.[15]

Despite the wary indifference and even animosity that Lang, Broad, and others encountered when they brought the subject up with their colleagues, the formation of the first Labour government in January, 1924, was greeted in birth control circles with a mixture of hopeful enthusiasm and cautious expectation. Both the New Generation League and the CBC, though claiming political neutrality, had sent speakers into working-class districts during the election, and Stopes herself had addressed three thousand members of the Labour Fellowship in Stockport as well as several other worker organizations.[16] Though jubilant that four avowed birth control Labour candidates were returned along with several known sympathizers, the *New Generation* regretted that the base of support was not wider.[17] Little had been expected from the church-oriented Conservatives; there had, however, been considerable anticipation that the divided but more enlightened Liberal party would, at the urging of known sympathizers like John Maynard Keynes and David Lloyd George, seize the initiative and campaign against the Ministry of Health's regressive position.[18] When it failed to do so, the *New Generation* speculated that had the Liberals shown more courage they might have won an outright majority instead of merely holding the balance of power in 1924.[19] Nevertheless, the *New Generation* shared the expectation of many birth control advocates that the new Labour Minister of Health, John Wheatley, would be amenable to a reconsideration of his department's ruling on the welfare centers, which was obviously inimical to the interests of working-class families.

More perceptive analysts, however, pointed out that the fledgling government was heavily dependent upon Catholic votes in industrial areas and that Wheatley himself professed that hostile faith.[20] As early as March

Rose Witcop privately predicted that, in spite of the vigorous efforts being made by some of its members, the Labour party would be unwilling to take a stand and compel its reluctant minister of health to rescind the regressive policy of his Tory predecessors.[21] Her suspicions were confirmed by the Ministry's issuance in June of a circular on maternal mortality (517) in which welfare centers were prohibited from providing birth control information. A discussion the following month in the Commons where Ernest Thurtle, the Labour M.P. for Shoreditch, and Dorothy Jewson, recently returned for Norwich, confronted Wheatley further confirmed Witcop's fears. Jewson, who had campaigned on the birth control issue, reminded the minister that a great many working-class women who were unhealthy and unfit to bear any more children had to revert to dangerous, illegal abortions while their middle-class counterparts were readily provided with contraceptives by their doctors.[22]

In response Wheatley articulated the position that he and his successors, irrespective of party, were to take in subsequent years: because the issue was so controversial and involved public funds, no change could be made in the Ministry's ruling without express directions from parliament.[23] Under prodding Wheatley admitted that his legal authority to withhold grants or to sanction them for birth control in the welfare centers was unclear, but he admitted that even if he had the power to permit money to be used in this way he "would not introduce such a revolutionary change" without parliamentary orders.[24]

Wheatley had given the matter serious thought. A few weeks earlier he had met with a formidable deputation of birth control advocates who presented a petition with six thousand signatures demanding an end to his Ministry's opposition to instruction in the welfare centers. When he refused, the petition, which included the names of twenty of his Labour colleagues in the Commons, was submitted to the National Conference of Labour Women who endorsed it by a vote of 1,000 to 8.[25] The chairman of the Women's Section of the party, Dr. Ethel Bentham, had been able to head off a similar resolution the previous year by establishing a committee to study the sensitive problem. Pressure was obviously building within the ranks; in January 1923 the Women's Section of the Chelsea Labour party became the first of several local branches to urge a change in the Ministry's policy, and the Congress of the Women's Cooperative Guild strongly supported a similar resolution that summer.[26]

The Labour party leadership did all it could to avoid a confrontation, leaving the editor of *Labour Woman*, Dr. Marion Phillips, to remind her militant sisters that their organization had enough difficulty reconciling different socialist points of view without becoming embroiled in something as potentially divisive as birth control. Since many M.D.s and scientists were themselves uncertain, Phillips explained, it was neither reasonable nor politic to expect any government to support the distribution of contraceptives in public facilities. Perhaps in time such a program might be justified, but the central task of the Labour party was to win elections and pass legislation that would redistribute wealth in such a way as to eliminate problems attributed to overpopulation.[27]

This was standard socialist fare, of course, but Phillips, an unmarried economist, personally thought the declining birthrate dangerous and was unconvinced that the control of fertility would have as much effect upon female independence as many of her younger colleagues believed. More importantly, however, as a member of the Labour party executive committee she was sensibly worried about the impact of the birth control issue on the fragile majority that had brought a Labour government to power.[28] She was as determined as the rest of the Labour hierarchy to demonstrate that their party was both responsible and respectable, and championing the dispensing of contraceptives after only a few months in office was obviously not the way.

Neither appeals to political expediency nor doubts about the safety of birth control made any impression on the National Conference of Labour Women when it met in May 1924. Jennie Baker, who introduced the successful resolution, insisted that more than enough was known to proceed and that ignoring the problem would in the end prove politically more disruptive. Most of the delegates thought it was more of a class than a political conflict, and they could see no reason why working-class women should be denied the same advice that middle-class women had been receiving for decades without visible harm. It was, as Dora Russell pointed out, not a question of compulsion but of equal opportunity and accessibility.[29] Only one person spoke against the resolution, which not only had the endorsement of a number of local Women's Sections but was also supported by the CBC and the New Generation League, which acted in a rare display of cooperation.[30] Both organizations were represented in the delegation sent to the minister of health, and when, in the aftermath of the conference, a Workers Birth Control Group was established, it was welcomed as an ally by the older societies.

The Workers Birth Control Group, the third birth control organization founded in Great Britain, was committed to sustaining the momentum built up within the Women's Sections of the Labour party to force the minister of health to soften his stand on the welfare clinics. The composition of its officers, which included Jewson as president and Broad, Thurtle, and several other M.P.s as vice-presidents, reflected the importance placed upon political agitation. Most of the group's activities were actually directed by its chairman, Mrs. L'Estrange Malone, and its secretaries, Dora

Russell and Frida Laski. They concentrated upon the distribution of propaganda, petitioning the Labour leadership and gathering information on the treatment women received when, as the minister of health recommended, they turned to hospitals for for birth control advice.[31] The Workers Birth Control Group recruited most of its members from the Labour party, the cooperatives, and other affiliated bodies. Several of them were also in the CBC or the New Generation League, and the three organizations agreed to assail the government together whenever possible.[32]

Although a number of men lent their support, the group was decidedly female. It benefited in part from the resentment many women felt at being assigned predetermined, subordinate roles in the Labour party. The old guard in the Labour hierarchy frequently held very circumscribed views of female emancipation, which clashed with the expanded feminist demands of the postwar years. Complaints about male insensitivity or indifference to the needs and aspirations of women workers had surfaced in 1923, when the Labour party leadership had failed to support Broad's criticism of the Conservative minister of health in the House of Commons, and feminist resentment was evident in the determination of the National Conference of Labour Women to push ahead with its resolution in 1924.[33]

Class arguments, though often confused with feminist goals, were always more central to the Workers Birth Control Group. Individual equality, its spokesmen argued, was inseparable from class equality. If working-class women were to have the same right as the economically more fortunate to decide how many children they wanted, they had to have equal access to the latest scientific knowledge. Anything less, Russell argued, was to perpetuate the inequities the Labour party was sworn to repudiate.[34] The tragic consequences were partially evident in the disproportionate number of working-class mothers among the three thousand women who died in childbirth each year. It was incongruous to the Workers Birth Control Group that the same Dr. Janet Campbell whose important study, *Maternal Mortality*, described the fatal effects in industrial areas of illegal abortions, multiple pregnancies, and inadequate obstetrical care defended the Ministry of Health's refusal to permit birth control instruction in the grant-aided local clinics.[35]

Those women who refused to be fobbed off with promises of more committees to look into the problem were, Witcop reported, under great pressure from their local sections not to embarrass the government.[36] Nevertheless, Witcop, Russell, Stella Browne, Laski, Cicely Hamilton, and others kept up a steady assault on the leadership. When Wheatley dismissed a deputation from the standing joint committee of the Industrial Women's Organizations with the warning that worker opinion was divided and that Catholics would avoid the welfare clinics if birth control was allowed, he was denounced as a traitor.[37] Stopes thought that the harried minister was under so much pressure in the summer of 1924 that he might have to appoint a birth control commission. If so, she wrote her husband, it was imperative that she be on it, "or it will be tricked—I know how such are worked."[38]

Although the Labour party executives cautioned that the inclusion of the birth control question would divide the party, others, like H. G. Wells, thought it more likely that its exclusion would "split the party into two discordant sections." There was much talk about the revival of suffragette militancy within the ranks of Labour unless the leadership acquiesced to the demands of "younger, more intelligent women" who were neither personally nor politically willing to be diverted any longer by "Roman Catholics, population statistics, army recruiting, racial jealousy, or . . . the unpleasant feelings and imaginations of priests and elderly lady spinsters." Birth control, Wells correctly perceived, had, like the vote before the war, become a symbol for women determined to run their own lives. "Before the next election," he predicted, "every Parliamentary candidate will have to make up his mind whether he stands for knowledge or ignorance on this matter."[39]

Wells's prophecy was put to the test within six months when the Labour government fell and was soundly defeated in the next election. The only issue of interest to the birth control press during the campaign was how candidates stood on the expansion of the functions of the welfare clinics. Politicians as different from one another as Hugh Dalton and Winston Churchill refused to concede that birth control was yet a relevant topic for serious political debate.[40] Dalton's own Labour party had been saved from having to consider eleven birth control resolutions at its annual conference in October 1924 when the political crisis forced cancellation after only two days. It was the first time that the issue had been included on the agenda of a national political assembly, and the Labour chiefs did not look forward to the impending discussions. Whatever the outcome of the elections, they knew that they would have the contentious resolutions brought up again next year, and for many years thereafter, until the women's groups achieved their goal.

Wheatley and his Labour colleagues had proven to be a disappointment to birth control zealots, but some comfort was to be found in the delusion that their Conservative successors would be more receptive since they were not beholden to large numbers of Catholics for their majority. The *New Generation* further rationalized that since Labour ministers, unlike the wealthier Liberals or Conservatives, were totally dependent on the income from their positions, they were inclined to do the safe rather than the heroic thing. Though Neville Chamberlain had not shown himself to be particularly bold during his brief tenure at the Ministry of Health in 1923, he was a Unitarian, not a Catholic, and he would, the *New Generation* believed, be more predisposed to new overtures on the welfare centers in the future.[41]

No one asked him for several months after he returned to that position in 1925; he was not asked until the National Conference of Labour Women had reaffirmed its previous resolution by another overwhelming margin, 876 to 6. In contrast to the preceding year, however, the debate at the conference was at times heated and acrimonious. Beatrice Quinn, a representative of the Leeds garment workers, and, as her opponents noted, an unmarried Catholic, set off a storm of protests when she condemned birth control as "impure and unchaste . . . filth" that was offensive to God and humanity. Once order was restored several Catholic delegates, including a woman with thirteen children, endorsed the resolution, insisting that each individual should at least have the option of regulating her fertility.[42]

Three weeks later in the House of Commons Chamberlain acknowledged to Ernest Thurtle that he had received the resolution but could hold out no hope for altering the decisions of his predecessors.[43] An appeal to the prime minister, Stanley Baldwin, was no more successful.[44] Although the issue continued to be raised periodically and Chamberlain met occasionally with deputations on both sides of the question, he decided after considerable thought that the time for a change in policy was "inopportune."[45] To help him change his mind the New Generation League raised £900 for a summer propaganda campaign, and with the aid of local branches of the Labour party, the Women's Cooperative Guild, and other sympathetic groups, distributed a half million leaflets in fifty-seven industrial cities. The three-month project was launched in Chamberlain's home town of Birmingham, and, although he received a great deal of mail, he remained unpersuaded that the time was right.[46]

As many birth control advocates knew, Chamberlain was not personally opposed to the principle of medical officers' dispensing contraceptives to working-class married women who requested help from the welfare centers. He was simply convinced that public opinion was not ready for such a dramatic change in government policy, and the Commons showed little inclination to debate the question. He had received requests to open the centers from magistrates, teachers, doctors, and other "responsible persons," but the numbers did not, in Chamberlain's opinion, constitute a popular groundswell.[47] The mood in the House of Lords was no more encouraging as Earl Russell and Marie Stopes discovered when they surveyed that chamber for possible support in 1925.[48]

People in the various birth control camps differed about political strategy. Since birth control was legal in Great Britain and legislation was not required, Stopes favored political neutrality and the persuasion of key individuals in each party. Kerr and the *New Generation* wanted to take a page out of the suffragettes' book and stage large rallies, assaulting the front bench of the government where the decision-making power ultimately rested. Others, however, favored constituent education in order to expand the core of M.P.s sympathetic to the cause, and some Liberals, including Keynes, believed that a bold policy linking birth control to such other rights as divorce and equal economic opportunity for women might capture the female vote and revive that party's flagging fortunes.[49] The Women's National Liberal Federation was persuaded by Keynes and Margaret Spring-Rice in 1927 that "scientific birth control provides a means of increasing the efficiency of the nation." The organization endorsed a resolution favoring the local health centers for that end, but the Liberal party as a whole preferred to find its political salvation elsewhere.[50]

The Labour party could not escape so easily. Many of its female members ignored the political appeals of the executive committee. Buttressed by the two decisive votes of the National Conference of Labour Women and similar resolutions from a number of local parties, they forced their demands on the annual party conference held at Liverpool in 1925. To their disgust the executive committee maneuvered consideration of the resolutions to the last item on the agenda and was able to sustain a decree "that the subject of Birth Control is in its nature not one which should be made a political Party issue, but should remain a matter upon which members of the Party should be free to hold and promote individual convictions." Jennie Baker and Dorothy Jewson warned that women felt increasingly deserted by the male-dominated party, and they implied that the struggle for birth control information, already embroiled in class conflict, was fast becoming transformed into a sexual conflict within the ranks of the Labour party. Neither she nor her angry supporters were placated by Mrs. Harrison Bell's assurances that working women could easily obtain birth control information, and it was not for the Labour party to interfere with people's married lives.[51]

The Labour leadership had no illusions about the intensity of feeling surrounding the subject, but it faced a serious dilemma. The party was trying to rebuild after its shattering defeat the previous year. If it took up the question of birth control in the welfare centers, it stood to alienate thousands of Catholic supporters in critical industrial areas and risked offending many other voters who sincerely believed that family limitation was a sensitive matter for the individual conscience. Yet a substantial number of the Labour party's most committed members believed that the alternative policy of noninterference perpetuated class advantages that no sincere socialist could tolerate. Opinion on the executive committee, though divided over the advantages and disadvantages of birth control, was nevertheless unanimous in its negative assessment of the political consequences likely to follow a Labour decision to challenge the minister of health's ruling.

Although other parties were not forced by constituent groups to evaluate their position on birth control, support did cut across political lines. By the end of 1925 it was possible to identify sixty-seven Conservative, Liberal, and Labour M.P.s whose varying degrees of commitment formed the nucleus of what the *New Generation* described as a "birth control committee" in the House of Commons.[52] An opportunity to test the parliamentary waters presented itself on 9 February 1926, when Thurtle introduced a bill permitting local authorities to incur the expenses of providing birth control instruction to married women at the welfare centers. Limited by debate rules to ten minutes, Thurtle hurriedly emphasized the permissive and voluntary nature of the legislation, the need for which was abundantly evident in the persistent differential fertility statistics recorded for rich and poor districts. As a socialist Thurtle knew that smaller families would not cure the workers' basic economic ills, but they would ameliorate much of the suffering, poor health, and feelings of desperation endured by working-class women. Their poverty ought not to bar them from such relief, he pleaded, and, in an era of widening sexual equality, from an equal right to determine what they did with their own bodies.[53]

Thurtle carefully explained that he did not speak for the Labour party, but the only other speaker, the Reverend James Barr, the Labour member for Motherwell, near Glasgow, nevertheless reminded the Commons that his party had declined the previous year to endorse a similar resolution. Though he denied that working-class women were at any disadvantage in obtaining birth control information, his objections were more fundamental. The deliberate thwarting of conception was an immoral affront to God, he told the members, and on this question "religious prejudices are just as sure a guide as science itself."[54]

Barr's personal digressions probably counted for little when the motion was defeated 167 to 82, but they infuriated many of his constituents and triggered a number of angry protests from Scottish labor organizations.[55] These were largely submerged in the general outrage directed against the forty-six Labourites who sided with the majority. To add to the indignity, twice as many Conservatives as Labour members went into the division lobby with Thurtle. The *New Generation* had counted Lloyd George and several of his Liberal followers in its parliamentary "birth control committee," but none of them made an appearance. Only one of four women in the House of Commons, the Labourite Ellen Wilkinson, turned up for the vote but was joined in supporting the measure by three people of cabinet rank in her party, Phillip Snowden, C. P. Trevelyan, and George Lansbury. Not a single left-wing socialist from the Clyde, the *New Generation* noted, came to the aid of working-class women.[56]

The Workers Birth Control Group harassed the Labour M.P.s who voted against the bill by printing their names in a critical pamphlet and distributing it, along with birth control literature, in their districts.[57] When they complained, Stella Browne accused them of betraying their female comrades. Dorothy Thurtle, whose husband introduced the measure, promised to "turn up the heat" even more to remind the party that "some of us do not agree that our function as Labour women is merely to help a few Labour men make careers and sit on the Government front bench."[58] Thurtle himself took the defeat philosophically. He knew there was now much more sympathy for his proposal in the Commons than the vote indicated but that many M.P.s agreed with Chamberlain that for the present no government could afford to outrun public opinion on the issue.[59]

Although birth control enthusiasts made rumblings about Labour women withholding their votes as retribution, they realized that the abbreviated debate was a significant step forward. It not only forced the issue to a vote for the first time in parliament, but it revealed a larger and more varied base of support than had been recognized. Moreover, the willingness of fifty-four Conservatives, several from distinguished families, to disagree with their party, was, as the *New Generation* perceived, the most encouraging sign that birth control was no longer considered "vulgar."[60] Indeed less than three months later the decidedly respectable, educated, middle-class women who led the National Union of Societies for Equal Citizenship approved a resolution embodying Thurtle's motion, thereby becoming the first feminist organization to endorse birth control.[61] It was a cautious, carefully worded statement that made no attempt to link birth control with the broader issue of female emancipation. But in conjunction with other recent developments it was enough to encourage the eminent Liberal barrister, Lord Buckmaster, to adopt its awkward phrasing in proposing to the House of Lords five days later "that His Majesty's Government be requested to withdraw all instructions given to, or conditions imposed on, welfare committees for the purpose of causing such committees to withhold from married women in their district, when sought by such women as to the best means of limiting their families."[62]

Stanley Owen Buckmaster, former lord chancellor in Asquith's wartime government and perhaps the most distinguished of Malthusian League converts, had, with his daughter, the Honorable Mrs. Dighton Pollock, been instrumental in founding the North Kensington birth control clinic the previous year.[63] His motives, as the debate in the House of Lords illustrated, were a mixture of eugenics and Social Darwinism stimulated by fifty years of declining differential fertility. It had led to the number of children conceived by the professional, educated classes falling dangerously below that of the "poorest, the most ignorant, the most destitute, the most shiftless, helpless, hopeless stratum of society." The time had arrived for parliament to have a "rational, restrained and intellectual discussion" of the implications of this trend and the consequences of withholding birth control from the "lowest sedimentary stratum" of the population.[64]

In the ensuing debate the lord privy seal, the Marquess of Salisbury, speaking for the government, raised the practical problem of offending the sensibilities of the many volunteers who supported the two thousand welfare centers. He warned of exacerbating the divisions that already existed in the four hundred county and local committees that governed the facilities. To counter Buckmaster's reference to the National Union of Societies for Equal Citizenship, Salisbury cited a recent contrary resolution from the Church of England's Mother's Union that included a number of lower-class women among its 700,000 members. At the same time the lord privy seal was no less worried about the racial import of recent demographic trends, but, unlike Buckmaster, he was persuaded that the supremacy of the white races, the preservation of western civilization, and the avoidance of French degeneracy could best be achieved if "lazy" and "vicious" modern women would fulfill the obligations they undertook when they married. As for the "unfortunate, the wretched, and the miserable women" who ought to have no more children, they can go to doctors just as rich people do when they need advice "in these matters."[65] Those who recalled the confusion and hostility about birth control within the medical profession itself were reminded that, although disagreements about treatment existed in many branches of medicine, doctors were not prevented from using the best knowledge available.[66]

The Archbishop of Canterbury, Randall Davidson, baffled everyone with his assurances that the motion was unnecessary since several medical officers in the welfare centers had informed him that they were under no restraints from the minister of health if, in their judgment, they wanted to prescribe birth control to patients. He reported that a high official in the Ministry had confirmed this information, but he added that very few women visiting the welfare facilities ever asked for or needed such assistance because their health was rarely endangered from further childbearing. Davidson feared that Buckmaster's resolution, if passed, would morally obligate medical officers to dispense contraceptive advice even if they or their local committees were opposed.[67]

In contrast to the ten-minute discussion in the House of Commons, the Lords debated the issue for three and a half hours before surprising Lord Buckmaster by passing the motion by a vote of 57 to 44. Birth control advocates were as elated as they had been dejected after the division on Thurtle's proposition three months earlier. Many likened it to the bombshell Lord Dawson had dropped on the church congress five years before. F. W. Pethick Lawrence was reminded of August 1914. The country was on the edge of another "vast conflict," he excitedly wrote to Margaret Sanger; "the future is entirely wrapped in mystery." After the unexpected victory in the House of Lords anything was possible.[68]

Though some analysts of the vote assumed that the minority were mostly Catholics and "ultra Churchmen," the *New Generation*, which serialized the lengthy debate, correctly noted that just seven of thirty-six Catholic peers and, aside from Archbishop Davidson, only one Anglican prelate were in attendance. Whether the small turnout was a result of political discretion, indifference, or unawareness of the pending motion, the *New Generation* thought the vote confirmed its belief that support for birth control was more nonpartisan than was commonly believed. It noted that, as in the case of the Commons vote, most of the majority for Buckmaster's resolution were Conservatives who ignored the whip and repudiated their own party's policy. By contrast none of the four Labour peers present voted correctly.[69]

Although she trumpeted the Archbishop of Canterbury's inadvertent "endorsement" of birth control across the front page of her *Birth Control News*, Marie Stopes privately informed him that he had been duped by the minister of health.[70] Suspecting, however, that the Ministry might actually be more equivocal than it seemed, she made careful inquiries of sympathetic medical officers who assured her that though local opinions varied there was no question about the Ministry of Health's directives.[71] Since 1923, when the Stepney Borough Council became the first local authority to propose providing birth control instruction in its public health facilities, four other metropolitan councils had found their way blocked by the Ministry officials. After the passage of Lord Buckmaster's resolution eight other councils, many of them confused by Archbishop Davidson's comments, sought clarification from the government.[72] One of these, the Surrey County Council, was informed that there had been no alteration in the Ministry of Health's previous order, but a rumor persisted for several months that permission had indeed been granted to open the welfare centers. Similarly Dr. Alice Brown at the Pentonville Infant Welfare Clinic thought she had received approval only to be told later that she was mistaken.[73]

Local authorities were clearly receiving mixed signals from the Ministry's standard reply to their inquiries that since "these Centres are maintained out of public funds to which people of all opinions are required to contribute . . . the Minister considers that, without express authority of

Parliament, he would not be justified in assenting to the use of the Centres for a purpose on which public opinion is so acutely divided."[74] As the letter did not explicitly threaten to withhold government grants, however, some authorities, like Surrey, persisted in forcing the issue. Stopes thought that the Ministry was being deliberately vague to avoid local confrontations and would soon cease its interference entirely.[75] By the spring of 1927 Chamberlain made it clear that there was no basis for any such optimism.[76]

Lord Buckmaster's success nevertheless fortified the determination of various labor groups to compel their party to take the lead in forcing the government to relent. Shortly after the vote the Independent Labour party overwhelmingly approved of birth control in the welfare centers and only the disruption caused by the general strike a few weeks later prevented the annual National Conference of Labour Women from reasserting its position. The executive committee of the party took advantage of the absence of another resolution from that troublesome quarter to exclude any discussion of the issue from the agenda of the national meetings scheduled that fall for Margate. When the *Daily Herald* bowed to party pressure and declined to publish an angry letter from Dorothy Jewson on behalf of the "betrayed women" in the Workers Birth Control Group, Robert Kerr printed it in the *New Generation* along with comments about the executive committee's fear of Catholics and appetite for the perquisites of office. He mocked their wanting to send their children to Eton and Oxbridge and recalled the shameful behavior of the Labour peers during the Lords debate earlier that year.[77]

Dora Russell and Dorothy Jewson, supported by hundreds of protest letters and the demands of six local Labour parties, led the fight from the floor of the conference to refer the question back to the national committee for reconsideration and placement on the agenda.[78] They reminded the leadership that before the women's conference was abandoned the previous spring to support the general strike, it had received sixty resolutions from workers' groups advocating birth control in the welfare clinics.[79] Ramsay MacDonald for the first time defended the party's position himself. He acknowledged the great interest Labour women had in the subject, but he reminded them that other members were just as keenly opposed to the use of public funds for birth control even if they did not oppose the practice itself. MacDonald admitted his own reservations about the morality of family limitation, which were intertwined with his longheld dislike of the Malthusian League and its offensive economic philosophy. But in the final analysis he opposed the resolutions for political reasons. Their adoption would divide the membership, discipline would prove impossible in parliament, and it would expose the Labour party to disruptive interests. He therefore pleaded with the dissidents to leave the matter to individuals and to stop "digging ditches" between women and the rest of the party.[80]

Jewson argued that, with two debates and votes in parliament already having taken place, birth control *was* a political issue. Even if the executive committee of the party did not consider it a suitable goal, Dora Russell added, it was as important to female workers as the seven-hour day was to miners. But there was no need for the question to be brought before parliament again, she explained, since the minister of health already possessed the authority to allow birth control to become part of the maternal care and health policies of the welfare centers. If the Labour party Conference demanded it, the next Labourite to hold the post would comply. The alternative, Russell warned, was to force the National Labour Women's Conference to consider forming a separate party.[81]

Visibly angered by the challenge, MacDonald tried to have the topic ruled out of order for three years. Instead, the delegates, by thirty-six thousand votes, forced the executive committee to reconsider its stance and bring the matter forward again the next year.[82] Before then the National Labor Women's Conference reaffirmed its position by a vote of 581 to 74, and a deputation carried the results along with twelve supporting resolutions directly to the party leaders.[83] They remained unmoved, voting ten to one against any alteration in their previous decision. They even rejected a compromise alternative declaring that, although the party took no stand on birth control, it acknowledged the right of women to receive instruction.[84] With the lines so sharply drawn both sides anticipated a bitter confrontation at the annual meeting in 1927. They were not disappointed.

Despite the efforts of the more sympathetic and conciliatory Arthur Henderson to moderate the debate, his pleas for loyalty and unity were ignored. Unlike MacDonald, Henderson had no doubts about the benefits of family limitation, but like other party leaders he thought public opinion was not ready to confront the issue. Its inclusion in the Labour platform would assuredly split constituents along moral and religious lines and further injure the party, already weakened by the collapse of the general strike earlier in the year, in the next election.[85] Several dissenters insisted that the executive committee was foolish to pretend that it was not a political problem worthy of party consideration when the minister of health was a government official responsible to parliament. Helen Pease, a Cambridge magistrate, and H. N. Brailsford, a member of the Independent Labour party, also reminded the assembly that birth control was inevitably linked to female emancipation, a political question if there ever was one, and that the freedom of choice and opportunity it implied should be available to working-class women as it was to middle-class women.[86]

James Sexton, a Labour M.P. and member of the powerful Transport and

General Workers Union, frankly doubted that the National Labour Women's Conference and those who supported its resolutions knew much about working-class women in the real world. He was one of several angry speakers who accused them of living in a "fool's paradise" and bluntly warned that the Catholic men and women who returned a great many Labour members to parliament would never agree to the party sanctioning birth control in any form. One of those M.P.s, Jack Jones, created such an uproar by his insulting remarks that he was unable to continue and was forced to sit down before order could be restored.[87] Birth control, as the acrimonious debate illustrated, had become much too important and fissiparous an issue for the executive committee to risk another defeat from the floor. In contrast to the preceding year it had prepared its ground very carefully. Not even the last-minute appeal from a miner's wife to the miner delegates, reminding them that childbirth was four times more dangerous than work in the pits, could reverse the obvious outcome. Portentous predictions about massive Catholic defections and the collapse of the party's hopes sufficed to smash the birth control forces by more than two million votes. All that could be salvaged was a reluctant agreement to establish a committee to investigate maternal mortality; but the question of birth control and the welfare clinics was ruled out of order for at least three years.[88]

Whatever political momentum had been gained by the Thurtle and Buckmaster motions in parliament and the reversal of the Labour party executive committee in 1926 was largely dissipated by the end of 1927. As the opposition became better organized and the political explosiveness of the issue became apparent, support began to wane. By the following spring Arthur Henderson and Marion Phillips were able to organize an even greater rebuff to the birth control forces when they persuaded the National Labour Women's Conference in 1928 to reverse its previous stand and by a vote of 257 to 254 to support the party leadership. Appeals to priorities and perspective because of an election scheduled for the next year convinced the narrow majority to comply with the conference's decision and another hundred women to abstain. In return Henderson agreed that any investigation into maternal mortality would consider methods of family limitation, and in the future the National Labour Women's Conference would elect its own representatives to the party's executive committee.[89] The latter concession was in part directed against Marion Phillips, who had been appointed to the committee by the Labour leadership with whom she invariably sided on the birth control question. Her criticisms of Stopes and Sanger in *Labour Woman* and her reluctance to publicize the Workers Birth Control Group was a source of continual conflict with many in the conference who, like Dora Russell, viewed her as a "problem" whom "none of us trust."[90]

Although the Labour party retreated from the issue of the welfare centers, parliamentary advocates of differing political allegiance continued to raise the matter during question periods in the Commons, looking in vain for some softening of the minister of health's position. Neither eugenic declamations on the proliferation of the unfit nor appeals to class equity made any difference.[91] It was well understood, as Thurtle recognized, that the state of public sentiment, not the advantages or disadvantages of birth control, were at issue. Most politicians knew their own minds, but few were prepared to fathom those of their constituents. They preferred to await clearer directives.

F. W. Pethick Lawrence and his wife Emmeline had taken up the birth control cause after the war as a logical extension of their earlier support for women's rights. They thought the pending extension of the franchise in 1928 to women between the ages of twenty-one and thirty would prove decisive. Issues of central importance to women would have to be considered by parliament in the near future, they reasoned, and "it will be a very valuable thing if, just as the first suffrage Bill for women coincided with a tremendous reduction in infant mortality, the passage of the full measure of enfranchisement for women synchronises with a reduction in the death-rate of mothers in childbirth."[92] The Pethick Lawrences, like most prominent suffrage leaders, had long been wary of merging birth control with feminism and even after the vote was achieved in 1918 they were uncertain about the effectiveness of that relationship. The firing of Elizabeth Daniels from her Edmonton post in 1923 resolved their doubts; they publicly announced that the right of all women, irrespective of class, to determine the number and frequency of children they would bear was central to true emancipation. They encouraged feminist organizations to adopt the issue.[93]

The *New Generation* was certain that the Pethick Lawrences' conversion signaled the long-awaited widening of the feminist vision. Even such enemies of family limitation as James Marchant recognized that emancipation was moving beyond the limited question of the ballot, and they predicted momentous changes in every sphere of industrial, social, political, educational, and professional life if birth control became integral to the feminist cause. Whether motherhood and the "primal duties of the home" would survive the merger was uncertain.[94] Despite Marchant's pessimism and the *New Generation*'s optimism the feminist societies remained very cautious. Their refusal to provide support or even to send representatives to discuss birth control with women's groups was a continual source of irritation, and it drove radical feminists such as Stella Browne into repeated denuncia-tions of their cowardly sisters.[95] Marie Stopes complained to Maude Kers-lake, president of the conservative, church-oriented National Council of Women of Great Britain and Ireland that far more men than women were willing to address female audiences on the subject of birth control, but little help was forthcoming.[96] The feminist press, like the women's jour-nals, continued to ignore the topic throughout the 1920s, and strategies to divert the militancy once concentrated on achieving the vote to guarantee-ing a woman's rights to sound birth control information met with continued frustration.

The birth control groups found it difficult to persuade the middle- and upper-class membership of the feminist organizations that access to con-traceptive methods was a genuine problem. Women in the vanguard of the feminist movement had been denied the vote but they had not been denied birth control instruction. Suffragists, many of them unmarried or the mothers of small families, had never seen any compelling reason for bringing it into their campaign before the war. In their more leisurely quest for the extension of the franchise to all adult women in the 1920s they remained unconvinced that birth control was either a pertinent or helpful addition to their limited objectives. Moreover, in spite of the greater candor of postwar society, many of the prominent suffrage leaders were of a generation in which well-brought-up ladies did not discuss such subjects—at least not in public.

The birth control movement, unlike the suffrage campaign, had from its origins been primarily concerned with the condition of the working classes. Though working women in some industrial areas of the country were central to the struggle for the vote, they were exceptional, and Sylvia Pankhurst's decision to organize the women of the East End be-fore the war was viewed as a willful aberration by her mother and sister.[97] Even then birth control did not become an objective of most working-class suffragettes. The Neo-Malthusians, not the suffrage organizations, preached family limitation to laboring women as a tactic of emancipation, and they continued to do so when those societies suspended their activities for the duration of the war. When, after the conflict, Marie Stopes and others emphasized birth control not only as an economic and social con-sideration but as a practice affecting the quality of sexual relationships, few thought in terms of the working classes. At the same time, however, the expanded concepts of birth control in the 1920s opened the way for women's organizations to assimilate the regulation of fertility into their differing concepts of women's rights. By discussing contraception as an obvious and beneficial means of permitting natural and mutual sexual enjoyment within marriage, without in any way curtailing a woman's new opportunities for self-fulfillment, Stopes and her disciples articulated dimensions of female emancipation that readily appealed to the postwar generation of activist women.

The vote, though limited, had already been won. The control of fertility, birth control proponents insisted, should now figure prominently among the basic rights still to be achieved. Middle- and upper-class women who dominated the feminist organizations of the 1920s were more sympathetic to the dissemination of contraceptive instruction in the welfare centers when arguments were phrased in terms of an individual woman's rights rather than the advantages of birth control. It was a subtle but important distinction.

Women in the Cooperative Guild, the Workers Birth Control Group, and the Labour party continued to insist that the controversy over the welfare centers was primarily one of class. When, however, the Women's National Liberal Federation, the National Council of Women, and the National Union of Societies for Equal Citizenship embraced the cause in the second half of the decade, they saw it less in terms of class or birth control than as an issue of personal liberty affecting all members of their sex.[98] Consequently, while many of these groups were by the later 1920s prepared to send resolutions to the minister of health calling for a relaxation of restrictions on the welfare centers, they continued to keep their distance from the birth control organizations. In 1926, for example, when the National Union of Societies for Equal Citizenship added its proper name to a petition signed by the Workers Birth Control Group, the Women's Cooperative Guild, the Society for the Provision of Birth Control Clinics, and the CBC, its secretary emphasized that, although individual members were in complete agreement with some of the objectives of Stopes's organization in particular, there was no compelling reason for the National Union to deviate from its policy of nonaffiliation with the birth control cause.[99]

The *New Generation*, its antennae tuned for any alteration in signal, noted in 1926 that general discussions about the rights of women, even in the most staid feminist circles, now included the demand that no wife should be subjected unwittingly to the pain, labor, and risks of unwanted childbirth. Robert Kerr rightly suspected that economic unrest and middle-class concerns about the proliferation of the dysgenic poor were probably more important considerations to many of the conservative and respectable women's societies than were the personal liberties of working-class mothers.[100] It made little difference, however, as long as all of the motives coalesced into an expanding concept of women's rights that included access to reliable birth control information. He was confident the trend would continue as younger, more broad-minded activists moved into positions of authority in the women's movement. Under Kerr's editorship, the *New Generation* overcame its past disappointments and turned more aggressively feminist. It warmly endorsed women M.P.s and campaigned for an even wider franchise on the assumption that most of the women in their twenties who would receive the vote would favor smaller families and greater sexual freedom.[101] While most political analysts tried to calculate what newly enfranchised women would do with their ballots, birth control proponents evaluating age-specific demographic data conjectured about what they would do with their bodies.

Complaints continued throughout the 1920s about the decline of early marriages, low fertility, and the surplus of unmarried women, though the overall frequency of marriage actually increased. Kerr was not distressed, as were many of his contemporaries, by the eugenic consequences of so many unmarried women being in the higher social classes, even though 40 percent of English women over thirty had not yet wed by 1929. A majority of them, he believed, were educated, talented, reform-minded feminists who were not only the backbone of the emancipationist movement, but were sturdy advocates of individual rights and equal opportunities that were especially congenial to the promotion of family limitation.[102] The prospects of changing female values seemed even brighter a few months later, in April 1930, when the young women of the Newnham College Debating Society voted thirty-nine to four "that in the opinion of this House, Birth Control is socially, morally and economically desirable." It would have been unthinkable for a woman's college to even consider such a resolution a few years ago, the *New Generation* observed.[103]

On the surface the Ministry of Health remained obdurate in the face of mounting pressures. It persisted in its claim that poor women in need of birth control guidance could receive it in hospitals, from private practitioners, or in the voluntary clinics. The sporadic expansion of the clinics, after the initial two were opened in 1921, was in large measure a response to the Ministry's continual refusal to allow the local welfare centers to serve that function. Both Stopes and the Malthusian League believed they were merely paving the way for a national system of birth control clinics, which would be attached to local hospitals and maternal and infant care facilities. The league at first agreed with Stopes and the CBC that no further voluntary clinics should be opened, since there could never be a sufficient number to cope with the enormous needs of the British poor. Binnie Dunlop rightly saw that the Ministry of Health would merely point to the clinics as evidence that the need was being met in the private sector. When, however, it became obvious in 1924 that the new Labour government was no more inclined to allow the use of public funds and facilities for birth control than its Conservative predecessor, Dunlop and other Neo-Malthusians bowed to the judgment of the Society for the Provision of Birth Control Clinics that, until the ban was lifted, as many voluntary centers as possible should be established.[104]

Nobody had any illusions that the facilities would aid more than a small number of the populace in the areas in which they were located. They could, however, provide some help, serve as training centers, and, eventually, form the basis of a nationwide network the way the first voluntary schools and religious-oriented educational societies had in the nineteenth century laid the foundations for public education. Clinics were opened in North Kensington, East London, Wolverhampton, Cambridge, Manchester, Salford, Birmingham, Aberdeen, Glasgow, and Oxford during the next two years. Another was established by the Abertillery and District Hospital in Wales, staffed by a nurse trained at Stopes's "Mothers' Clinic." Norman Haire, who quarreled with the Neo-Malthusians and the leaders of the Society for the Provision of Birth Control Clinics, opened his own Welfare and Sunlight Centre in St. Pancras, where patients in the waiting room could view a large painting of the exasperated old woman who lived in a shoe beating one of her innumerable progeny. The domestic drama was accompanied by the obvious admonition:

> There was an old woman who lived in a shoe,
> She had so many children she didn't know what to do.
> Don't be like her. Ask the doctor for birth control advice.

Variations on the rhyme had actually been around for some time. As early as 1906 *The Malthusian* had published an abbreviated version:

> There was a young woman who lived in a shoe,
> She had no children: she knew what to do![105]

Rose Witcop, with the help of the Fulham Labour party and financial infusions from Margaret Sanger, opened her own People's Clinic near the palatial residence of the Bishop of London. Much to her astonishment she even received encouragement from the local Conservative paper.[106] Marie Stopes was less friendly; she denounced the new facility as she did most of the others as being unnecessary and less reliable than her own. Witcop and her husband, Guy Aldred, had hoped to sustain the People's Clinic by publishing some of Sanger's works in England, but they soon discovered that their American friend was now committed to more prestigious firms than the Bakunin Press. The clinic limped along for another two years after which it apparently collapsed.[107]

In addition to the scattered, unaffiliated clinics, the private consultation efforts of Elizabeth Daniels and the nurses she trained provided some birth control instruction for needy women in Mirfield, Ipswich, and Cardiff. The work was obviously frustrating; patients were frequently ignorant and unappreciative. Nurse Daniels complained that when women discovered that they had to buy and insert the Mensinga diaphragms themselves since they were not "charms" that worked magically without any effort on their part, they often left. Results were more encouraging among the wives of the less "primitive" workers, nearly 95 percent of whom gave economic reasons for wanting to curtail their fertility. Many husbands, Nurse Daniels reported, urged their wives to come to her, and men in fact, being less embarrassed, usually initiated the correspondence.[108] All of the clinics reported similar experiences. Norman Himes also found in his study of the North Kensington Clinic in 1927 that anywhere from one-third to one-half of the women who sought assistance were the wives of unskilled workers; nearly 90 percent of the patients were in their late twenties and early thirties and already had on the average slightly more than three children.[109]

As support became available additional clinics were opened in Rother-ham, Newcastle, Exeter, and Nottingham. The endemic fear, timidity, and staggering ignorance encountered in all of these facilities continued to astonish the educated, well-meaning, largely middle-class people who founded and assisted in the running of the clinics.[110] Although, by the early 1930s, they could take considerable pride in having helped more than thirty thousand women, the voluntary supporters were more con-scious than ever of how limited their effect had been.[111] They compared the meager accomplishments of their sixteen or seventeen clinics, most open only a few hours a week, with the enormous potential of the more than 2,200 local infant and maternal welfare clinics closed to them by ministerial decree. It was obvious that millions of people had learned how to limit their families without resorting to the public coffers, but it was equally clear that millions of others were still unable or unwilling to do so. These were people beyond the reach of the estimated fifteen million books, pamphlets, and brochures on contraception that had become avail-able since the war.[112]

The Ministry of Health's position was, however, fast eroding by the end of the decade. It had been predicated on governmental perceptions of public opinion, which, in the judgment of one minister after another, had to demonstrate in some undefined way that it was prepared to accept the dispensing of public funds to assist people in avoiding the consequences of sexual relations. The entire issue was altered by two decisive events: the coming to power in 1929 of a more conciliatory Labour government elected by a clear plurality and the severe economic crisis brought on by the world depression. Neo-Malthusians had predicted for fifty years that in the final analysis economic realities would determine the course of population control. To the disappearing ranks of the more orthodox the depression was the ultimate vindication.

CHAPTER 14
The Walls of the Citadel Fall

As the birth control movement broke free from the narrow constraints of Neo-Malthusianism in the 1920s the orthodox defenders of the old faith continued to preach that the solution to the population question would be determined not by religious, medical, or political considerations but by economic realities. J. M. Robertson was certain that postwar interest in family limitation had much more to do with chronic unemployment, inadequate housing, low productivity, and a scarcity of goods and markets than it did with the conversion of prominent churchmen, physicians, politicians, literary lions, and repentant feminists. In spite of euphoric promises to build a land fit for heroes, demographic truths and financial stringencies had combined to give Malthus a new respectability. Even socialists now understood the relationship, Robertson added, and he predicted that the last outpost of "hidebound hostility," the Catholic church, would soon accommodate itself to the economic imperatives of the new era.[1]

Neo-Malthusian economic determinism was in many ways as consistent as that of its old Marxist adversaries. League spokesmen remained convinced that the altered moral and religious values, changing aspirations, and expectations that had made people receptive to curtailing fertility had been a direct result of a shift in Britain's predominant economic position and a more realistic assessment of current and future economic opportunities. If the brief boom in prosperity that followed the war temporarily disrupted the demographic adjustment and led to a short-lived surge in the birthrate, the subsequent slump starting in 1921 was soon met with an even greater drop in fertility.

It was obvious to Neo-Malthusians and non-Neo-Malthusians alike that the control of conception had become a conscious strategy for the maintenance or improvement of social and economic status. That it had not yet been universally adopted was for the *Malthusian* and its successor, the *New Generation*, strikingly evident in the number of unemployed that reached an unprecedented high of two million in 1922.[2] Each new leap in the number of jobless people provoked another antisocialist diatribe by the Drysdales, who were particularly infuriated by the introduction of a dole based upon family size. But even more restrained analysts took some comfort in the certainty that as the economic situation worsened the acceptance of birth control as a coping mechanism would inevitably increase.

Although Neo-Malthusian opinion was of no great consequence by itself in the 1920s, the problem of surplus labor in a period of economic difficulty was of increasing importance to newspapers, journals, parliamentary commissions, and unofficial commentators who viewed with concern the prospect of providing for a large and expanding population in an era of fierce competition and diminished markets. Some social planners like Sir William Beveridge, noting in 1923 the resurgence of Malthusian pessimism, argued that the country was merely experiencing a temporary economic readjustment rather than suffering the prolonged consequences of overpopulation.[3] When, however, it became apparent that not even a return to relative prosperity in the mid-1920s could reduce unemployment below a million, economists who predicted that the imbalance between population and resources would prove difficult to alleviate appeared to have been correct.[4]

Emigration, halted by the war, was again resurrected as a possible solution. However, not only was the United States more restrictive but Britain's own colonies were no longer receptive to an influx of indiscriminate numbers. Canada and Australia, for example, had recently imposed quotas ranging from twenty to thirty-three thousand people a year. With more than 1,350,000 unemployed in 1925 and the population still increasing by 300,000 a year it seemed obvious that Britain would have to find other alternatives.[5] To Neo-Malthusians the answer was crystal clear. Had the birthrate not already declined so dramatically since the 1870s the crush of excess workers pushing against the diminished opportunities of the postwar years would have been infinitely greater. A. L. Bowley and M. H. Hogg found that nearly 30 percent of the substantial reduction in pauperism since 1913 could be attributed to the falling birthrate. If, as the two economists calculated, most of the advance was a result of wages eclipsing the cost of living, the *New Generation* insisted that the drop in fertility before 1913 was the primary reason that the labor supply had been reduced enough to force the upward trend in wages during and after the war. That the decline was still insufficient in some sectors of the economy was obvious in the persistent unemployment in certain industries.[6]

Nowhere was this more evident than in coal mining. Long the most prolific and least mobile of all occupational groups, miners were particularly vulnerable to postwar economic problems. By the second half of the decade it was evident to the royal commission reporting in 1926 that at least 300,000 miners had become permanently redundant as a consequence of constricted markets, lower productivity, depleted coal seams, and the emergence of alternative sources of energy. The *New Generation* had been reporting the troubles of the coal industry since the war as a vivid example of overpopulation in conflict with diminishing resources and opportunities. It felt vindicated when the commission's chairman, Sir Herbert Samuel, recommended that further recruitment for the mines be carefully restricted, and it quoted with approval the testimony of the secretary of the miners' union, A. J. Cook, who admitted that "if I were still a mine worker I should either commit suicide or should not bring another child into the world."[7]

Birth control activists enthusiastically endorsed the latter alternative. Stella Browne regularly visited the colliery districts to lecture miners and their wives on the advantages and methods of limiting their fabled fertility. In 1928, at the urging of the Women's Section of the Rhondda Borough Labour party, Marie Stopes sent one of two horse-drawn caravans outfitted as birth control clinics into the mining areas of South Wales where the majority of workers were suffering from unemployment and reduced hours.[8] A second caravan was sent into the industrial north where it was set afire by a disgruntled Catholic woman in Bradford. After a predictable cascade of anti-Roman invective from its owner, the mobile clinic was rebuilt and sent on its way.[9] The project had actually been launched the previous year in East London with the help of wealthy supporters, some of whom, like the department-store magnate, H. Gordon Selfridge, preferred to remain anonymous.[10] Women in the Cooperative Guild and in local Labour parties then arranged for the vehicles to visit depressed textile and mining areas.

Stopes's efforts were supplemented by the Workers Birth Control Group, which, led by Frida Laski, carried the gospel of family limitation to Wales and Durham. In spite of their initial misgivings, they found most of their audiences very receptive and interested in the establishment of permanent clinics. The visitors recounted tragic stories of high infant mortality, exhausted mothers, diseased children, and woeful ignorance about the physiology of conception and its prevention. At the end of the meetings the miners' wives overwhelmingly passed resolutions asking that the Ministry of Health's ban on the local welfare centers providing birth control instruction be lifted.[11]

One result of these campaigns was the establishment of clinics in Rotherham and Newcastle, but, like Stopes's inventive rolling caravans, their impact was minimal. Even the most enthusiastic advocates admitted that their voluntary facilities only caused ripples in an ocean of poverty. Both population and unemployment continued to increase, the *New Generation* reported in a new series of statistical "Birth Control Pointers" introduced in 1928. Although the country had to support 2,500,000 more people than in 1914, exports were down 25 percent. Each month the *New Generation*, like other papers throughout the nation, traced the fluctuating curve of unemployment. By the end of February 1929, unemployment exceeded 1,430,000 compared with only 12,988 in France.[12] As the grim statistics from the labor exchanges mounted, birth control coalitions were forming to try to make the population question the most important issue of the upcoming parliamentary elections that spring.

Attempts were made to persuade H. G. Wells, Harold Cox, Edith How-Martyn, and Marie Stopes to stand as birth control candidates in order to force the political parties to confront the relationship between overpopulation and the nation's economic difficulties. Although Stopes toyed with the idea of challenging Neville Chamberlain in his home town of Birmingham, only Edith How-Martyn expressed serious interest in running providing that she could raise £500 and find a constituency near London. Nothing came of it.[13] As the election approached, the *New Generation* published the division list on Ernest Thurtle's 1926 motion to remind voters that birth control was a nonpartisan issue, and it challenged its readers to confront candidates and, if necessary, heckle them into taking a position.[14]

The Workers Birth Control Group and the National Union of Societies for Equal Citizenship proceeded more systematically, submitting questionnaires to 570 candidates to determine if they would support birth control instruction in the welfare centers. In addition, they sent a deputation to the three party leaders, but none of them was willing to make the minister of health's ruling an election issue.[15] The two organizations were trying to attract the attention of the newly enfranchised middle- and working-class women under the age of thirty who would be voting for the first time in the upcoming election. The extension of the vote the previous year meant that the female electorate exceeded that of men by more than two million. New voters were not only more likely to support candidates opposed to the Ministry's restrictions, but they would probably help increase the number of female M.P.s from four. Admittedly only one woman M.P., Ellen Wilkinson, had proved helpful in the past, but when Jenny Lee, a sympathetic, 24-year-old miner's daughter won a by-election in New Lanark in March, it was interpreted as a favorable portent of things to come.[16]

Although no party won a clear majority in 1929 and the second Labour government was, like the first, dependent upon Liberal support, the birth control interests were delighted with the results. Edith How-Martyn reported that 263 of the successful candidates had endorsed the opening of the welfare centers in the preelection questionnaire. Another 85 had chosen to reserve judgment, but How-Martyn was confident that in the final analysis they would be in the birth control corner.[17] If the "flapper vote" failed to turn Britain into a political matriarchy, as some of its opponents had predicted, it did help to increase the number of female M.P.s to fourteen. That some fifty-five other women were defeated, including Dorothy Jewson, was hardly noticed by the excited enumerators in the birth control camp.

There were disappointments: the number of Catholics rose from twenty-one to twenty-five, the *New Generation* groaned, and seventeen of them were Labourites.[18] Nevertheless, Fenner Brockway, Harold Laski, and others assured the Workers Birth Control Group that the victorious Labour party could not long resist their demands.[19] If the new Labour government differed little from the old, and its members showed little sign of sharing Laski's assessment of birth control as the greatest invention since fire, they knew full well that a number of enthusiastic supporters did and would give them little peace.

Throughout the summer and fall of 1929 newspapers and journals were filled with articles discussing the relationship of overpopulation to the parlous state of the economy, and there was more favorable commentary than ever before on the advantages of a diminished, possibly even a stationary population. Some of it was stimulated by an anti-birth control letter from the Italian dictator, Benito Mussolini, whose denunciations of family limitation conjured up recollections of Theodore Roosevelt and the Kaiser. Although the annual conference of the Labour party was still spared from having to discuss the issue, the new minister of health, Arthur Greenwood, was less fortunate. Resolutions and delegations continued to come before him, and he was occasionally badgered in parliament by the persistent Ernest Thurtle.[20]

Though Greenwood professed that no change in the Ministry's position was warranted, the question of birth control in the welfare centers was secretly under review. It was in part prompted by a recent revision of the Local Government Act that expanded the authority of local officials. A number of birth control organizations thought that when the new legislation took effect in April, 1930, it could be used as the wedge needed to allow the governing committees of the individual welfare centers to formulate their own policies in the context of local needs and sentiment. Eva Hubback, chairman of the parliamentary committee of the National Union for Equal Citizenship, saw a number of loopholes in the act, but fearing that the minister might arbitrarily close them if she wrote to him for clarification, she turned instead to the Labour M.P., Ellen Wilkinson.[21] In response to Wilkinson's private inquiries, a Ministry official assured her that in spite of Greenwood's public stance the entire policy was being reassessed. She was, however, reluctant to indicate any wavering to Hubback's group whose members were a "difficult lot."[22]

Far more troublesome for the government were the incipient rebellions brewing in a number of Labour constituencies where local authorities threatened to defy the Ministry's orders. In November 1929 the chairman of the Sheffield Health Committee, supported by some 2,400 people, demanded that the minister of health stop interfering in public facilities.[23] Two months later the Sheffield City Council passed a similar resolution.[24] When, in the first week of 1930, the town council of Bootle, a Liverpool suburb, voted twenty-three to nineteen to join some fifty other local authorities demanding the right to make their own decisions about clinic services, its action was greeted with fiery anathemas from Catholic pulpits. Unless the council rescinded the resolution and publicly apologized, an outraged Monsignor O'Brien threatened to rally thirty thousand Catholic voters against it. "The Battle of Bootle," as the *New Generation* delighted in describing the controversy, was largely fought in the columns of the *Bootle Times*. In the end the council, supported by a number of Catholics, defied the "Mussolini of Bootle," as one of them characterized O'Brien, and added its name to the growing number of communities prepared to challenge the minister of health.[25]

Much of the leadership came from Thurtle's Shoreditch constituency whose council passed a resolution in 1929 to interpret the new Local Government Act in such a way as to permit the prescribing of birth control at local expense in public health facilities. In February 1930, two months before the legislation was to take effect, Greenwood was pressed in the Commons to comment on the legality of the Shoreditch interpretation, but he merely reiterated the Ministry's old position. When asked a week later by what statute he was authorized to prohibit medical officers from providing birth control information, Greenwood bluntly admitted, "I am not aware of any such statute."[26]

In retrospect it is apparent that the minister was stalling while trying to decide what tack to take in the storm churning around him. The deterioration of the economy had become extremely serious as the impact of the depression drove unemployment near the two million mark. Local authorities, especially in older working-class districts, were overwhelmed with problems. The obvious need to help destitute people avoid unwanted children in such a crisis fortified the determination of an expanding minority of local councils, many of them in large industrial and manufacturing centers, to press ahead with their plans with or without the government's blessing. They were supported by the Conference on the Giving of Information on Birth Control by Public Authorities held on 4 April at the Central Hall Westminster. The meeting, organized by a wide coalition of interests, attracted several hundred delegates from the maternity and child welfare centers and other public health agencies. It was carefully scheduled to coincide with the implementation of the new Local Government Act and to remind the minister of health that a substantial number of municipal officials intended to interpret the revised legislation more broadly than he perhaps anticipated. Though Greenwood made no public response to the nearly unanimous resolutions calling on him "to recognize the desirability of making available medical information on methods of Birth Control to married people who need it," he privately prepared to give way.[27] Eight local authorities led by Shoreditch and Poplar had, as Greenwood knew, already ordered their medical officers to provide that information.[28]

Ministry officials discussed the dilemma and in May the assistant secretary, A. B. Maclachan, noted in a memorandum to Greenwood that since "this question has very distinct political risks (as e.g., the Roman Catholic vote, which bulked very large in Mr. Wheatley's time . . .), I am not sure at all that it is not big enough for a special reference to the Cabinet before you act—I should in fact be inclined to recommend such a reference. Birth control is associated in many minds with a definite admission that the nation is starting on the road to decadence." Greenwood concurred and set his staff the task of drawing up a recommendation for cabinet consideration.[29]

After a prolonged discussion about the practical and political difficulties of resolving "so divided a question," it was agreed to stress only medical reasons for birth control. Janet Campbell and Maclachan knew that the more vocal advocates of birth control in the labor ranks would find such a ruling too restrictive and would continue to demand that working-class women should have the same access to information for economic or personal reasons as did those who could afford to purchase it privately.[30] Nevertheless, Ministry officials concluded that a medical restriction would offend the least number of people and could be drawn up to conform to the Notification of Births (Extension) Act of 1915 that permitted local authorities, under existing public health legislation, to assist expectant and nursing mothers at welfare centers or gynecological clinics. If, in the medical officer's judgment, further pregnancies would prove physically detrimental, he would be free to prescribe contraception. By limiting advice to women who were already mothers or pregnant the Ministry hoped to avoid the charge that the welfare centers would become official "rubber shops" where unmarried girls or new brides would be provided with preventive appliances indiscriminately. The recommendations, which were submitted to the cabinet in June and approved a month later, emphasized that birth control assistance was not to be given on demand.[31] Parliament would have to sanction so bold a step and the government obviously wanted to avoid a public debate. By leaving the responsibility for valid medical justification to local officials and their medical advisers, the Ministry of Health hoped to defuse the mounting challenge to its authority while conceding as little as possible.

The Ministry's Memorandum 153/M.C.W., which some enthusiasts in moments of euphoria likened to the Magna Charta, in fact reaffirmed that it was not the function of the maternal and child welfare centers to provide birth control instruction. But, it added, "in cases where there are *medical grounds* for giving advice on contraceptive methods to married women in attendance at the Centres, it may be given, but . . . such advice should be limited to cases where further pregnancy would be detrimental to health, and should be given at a separate session." Having at last decided upon its permissive guidelines, the Ministry cautiously avoided letting anyone know. To minimize reactions it sent copies of the memorandum only to medical authorities who expressly requested guidance. As a result the news of its existence leaked out slowly. When Labour's own paper, the *Daily Herald*, asked for a copy of the guidelines at the end of August, more than a month after its publication, Ministry officials privately expressed astonishment that neither the popular nor the medical press had yet printed the document and were reluctant to release it.[32] Only after considerable debate and delay, involving Greenwood himself, was it decided that since the memorandum was based upon a formal cabinet decision the *Daily Herald*'s request had to be honored.[33]

The Ministry's hand was in part forced by the appearance of its semi-secret directive in the September issue of Marie Stopes's *Birth Control News*.[34] In addition, a newly formed organization, the National Birth Control Council, began printing its own copies of Memorandum 153/M.C.W. and, to the dismay of the Ministry, distributing them to medical officers of health and local authorities along with an explanatory circular broadly interpreting their prerogatives.[35] The NBCC had been established the previous July as a coordinating body for the various birth control societies and committees conducting research into the effectiveness of contraception.[36] Under the chairmanship of Lady Denman and, in 1931, the presidency of Lord Horder, physician-in-ordinary to the Prince of Wales, its list of officers read like a *Who's Who* of the birth control campaign. Old battlers such as Drysdale, Millard, Dunlop, and H. G. Wells joined with John Maynard Keynes, Bertrand Russell, and a host of peers, politicians, physicians, scientists, attorneys, and assorted eugenists. After some hesitation the incorrigible Marie Stopes was also invited to participate, and, although she proposed the formal resolution establishing the association, within three years she had quarreled with the leadership and withdrawn from the council.[37]

In addition to publicizing the Ministry of Health's memorandum the NBCC also made it clear that it intended to monitor the response of welfare centers to women who asked for birth control assistance.[38] It was soon apparent that little help could be expected from the government, and complaints about the Ministry's foot dragging were increasingly heard within the Labour party itself. Since no official publication reaching local authorities had yet published the memorandum, the Independent Labour party in February 1931 threatened to join the NBCC in issuing its own version.[39] Under these pressures the Ministry finally relented and in March, nearly eight months after it had drawn up the directive, it sent official copies to local authorities throughout the country. Furthermore, the memorandum was made available to the public from the Stationery Office at a cost of one pence.[40]

Even if the Ministry of Health was at last willing to permit doctors in public facilities to advise women about how to prevent conception, there was no guarantee, the *New Generation* sensibly cautioned, that the medical officers would be willing to do so.[41] Although a minority of their number had long been sympathetic to the birth control movement and, as Stopes's correspondence reveals, some had quietly tried to assist needy women who came to the welfare centers with contraceptive problems, it was difficult to predict what the majority would do.[42] Many of them were disgusted with the "shiftless" women they treated who were constantly pregnant, and they complained that it was usually the "best type" of working-class mother who wanted information, not the "degenerates" who inundated the welfare centers with their wretched, unhealthy progeny.[43] Whether or not their eugenic concerns would make these physicians more amenable to a more assertive interpretation of Memorandum 153 remained to be seen. Though public health specialists, they were also still members of a profession whose long-held objections to contraception were well known and whose accommodation to the spread of birth control since the war was at best ambivalent.

Before 1930 most medical officers of health obeyed the Ministry either out of fear of losing their grants or out of genuine doubts about contraception. Millard, who had been trying to enlighten his public health colleagues since 1902, recalled in 1924 how deep the feeling had been among medical officers that birth control was a "filthy and unclean" subject. A strong residue of this sentiment persisted, he felt, reinforced by lingering fears of race suicide and the disintegration of the Empire.[44] When other medical officers challenged these arguments, pointing out the eugenic advantages of reducing the proliferation of the unfit while improving the health of mothers and their infants, they met with the usual warnings about sterility, fibroid tumors, and the rest of the familiar glossary of gynecological aberrations associated with preventives.[45]

Nevertheless, as Millard recognized, t'ie views of the profession were changing. For the first half of the 1920s the medical officer's journal, *Public Health*, under the editorship of Robert Lyster, questioned the minister of health's ruling without suggesting defiance. Lyster's successor in 1924, however, was a more cautious barrister and physician who thought it best that medical officers avoid the issue entirely until the legal, medical, and political doubts about birth control were completely resolved.[46] Although most medical authorities were apparently content with this position, a minority continued to challenge it. If *Public Health* declined commentary, other medical publications occasionally noted the arguments within the public health community. The *British Medical Journal*, for example, described the heated debate over birth control that took place at the Conference on Maternity and Child Welfare in 1926. It reported that, although all of the working women in attendance favored instruction in public health clinics, the medical officers were sharply divided.[47] By the end of 1929 fifty-five of them had appealed directly to the minister of health for permission to prescribe contraceptives for their welfare patients.[48]

Like the medical profession in general, however, public health officials were increasingly disturbed by the proliferation of birth control practices without medical supervision and saw in the voluntary clinics a growing challenge to their authority. They were particularly sensitive to the changing interpretation of birth control as a form of preventive medicine, an area of expertise closely associated with the public health movement. The *Lancet*, commenting on this problem in 1927, suggested that the Ministry of Health complicated the solution by its restrictions, and it recommended that the entire matter be left to local authorities and their medical advisers who were more aware of individual and community needs as well as public sentiment.[49]

In effect the *Lancet* supported those medical officers who complained that they were not free to exercise their professional judgment and that the Ministry's refusal to leave the medical aspects of contraception in their hands interfered with their obligation to provide the most appropriate advice for the well-being of their patients. Even the opponents of birth control began to see the implications of centralized control, and they balked at the possibility that, if the birth control forces won, public health officers might be required against their better judgment to prescribe contraceptives to any person who demanded them. Tensions erupted at the annual meeting of the British Medical Association in July 1930 when a number of angry doctors, aware that the government was considering new regulations, asserted that they had no intention of being ordered about by patients, local committees, or the Ministry of Health.

In an attempt to provide some guidance and avoid open conflict between doctors, local health committees, and the government, the association recommended that "where advice on birth control is given at any maternity and child welfare clinic (voluntary or municipal), it should be given on medical grounds only and at the discretion of the medical officer . . . and not merely because it is asked for by the patient." During the ensuing debate doctors on both sides of the birth control issue agreed that every medical practitioner should have the right to advise for or against contraception without being dictated to by patients or employing authorities. A majority of the delegates even found the words "on medical grounds only" too restrictive and forced the resolution to be altered in such a way as to leave any physician free to give contraceptive advice in accordance with his best judgment. The aroused doctors emphasized repeatedly that they alone would decide what was of benefit to their patients.[50]

Memorandum 153/M.C.W. largely reflected the association's position in its insistence on "medical grounds" and in its willingness to permit medical officers full discretion. At the same time the Ministry made no effort to impose medical supervision over the voluntary clinics, as the association recommended. The permissive document in effect turned the controversy over to local authorities, as the *Lancet* and others had suggested years earlier, leaving it up to the medical officers and their governing committees to work out their own policies. Aside from a brief notification of the memorandum without comment in the *BMJ*, the medical press proved very circumspect.[51] Despite the direct bearing the new guidelines had on its readers, *Public Health* did not acknowledge their existence until the following April when the document was at last published and circulated by the Ministry. Even then the journal's response was cool and guarded, stressing the medical limitations of the directive and warning that birth control activities must not interfere in any way with the normal work of the welfare centers. It called attention to another memorandum, which recommended that, whenever possible, birth control clinics be established in a separate facility or hospital.[52] In a front-page commentary the editor recognized that the Ministry's directive raised more questions than it answered. Some authorities viewed it as a license to open birth control clinics; others complained that it was only half a loaf, and they demanded more freedom to dispense contraceptives to anyone who wanted them.[53] Ultimately the responsibility for interpreting the memorandum would rest with the individual medical officer. The birth control groups hoped that most health officials would define "medical grounds" very broadly. If not, the NBCC was prepared to investigate and help reluctant M.D.s broaden their perspectives.[54]

Having at last acknowledged that birth control was medically important, the Royal Institute of Public Health in the fall of 1930 introduced the first formal courses for physicians and senior medical students with Stopes, Millard, and C. P. Blacker among the lecturers.[55] Although the British Medical Association still refused Stopes access to its facilities in Tavistock Square, it opened its meeting rooms to her medical colleagues and to medical officers from the voluntary birth control clinics.[56] Professional resistance weakened noticeably after 1930 as contraception became a subject for serious scientific research and a new generation of physicians allied themselves openly with the birth control movement. In 1933, ten years after it had daringly, but briefly, opened its pages to a birth control symposium, the *Practitioner* took the plunge again. In contrast to the tentativeness, prejudicial moralizing, and anger that had characterized many of the first contributions, the tone was now set by a prominent obstetrical surgeon who summarily asserted that contraception "cannot be said to exert any injurious physiological or psychological effects." The articles then went on dispassionately to describe the various, most reliable methods.[57] Three years later the Dundee branch of the British Medical Association became the first local affiliate of that once-hostile organization to associate itself formally with a birth control clinic.[58]

By then birth control had become a respectable subject for public discussion in the popular press and the women's magazines whose articles would have been inconceivable a decade earlier. Local governments and their health advisers, however, remained frustratingly discreet about availing themselves of their new opportunities. A year after the Ministry of Health issued its memorandum only thirty-five local boards out of more than four hundred had authorized birth control instruction in their welfare facilities.[59] Many officials were keenly sensitive to the religious and moral sensibilities of their constituents who proved to be less advanced in their views than expected. As Lela Florence recalled, the major difficulty in the 1930s was not with the Ministry of Health, but with local authorities who refused to act.[60] For its part the Ministry continued to broaden the categories of women who qualified for birth control assistance, adding in 1934 those "who are suffering from other forms of sickness, physical and mental, which are detrimental to them as mothers."[61]

By 1939 more than 280 local authorities, mainly in large urban areas, approved of some form of birth control assistance in a public health facility. Their activities were supplemented by nearly seventy voluntary clinics, all but five of them affiliated with the new Family Planning Association established shortly before the outbreak of the war. The others remained under the control of Marie Stopes's Society for Constructive Birth Control, which since 1933 had been unwilling to lend its support to the Family Planning Association's predecessor, the National Birth Control Association. As its title suggested, the Family Planning Association reflected a more comprehensive program that emphasized not only voluntary parenthood, but the treatment of sterility, minor gynecological ailments, marriage counseling, education, training, and scientific research. Even with their expanded services, however, the public and voluntary clinics were seeing no more than twenty thousand new patients a year.[62] Like the local welfare centers, the Malthusian League, the CBC, and the numerous other birth control organizations, the clinics essentially assisted, and to a minor extent facilitated, a demographic phenomenon that preceded their existence and would, in all probability, have continued without their encouragement.

Nevertheless, most British birth control advocates believed that their movement had triumphed in the summer of 1930; the major institutional barriers to effective, rational, and scientific population control were at last overcome. Not only did the government relent and, however reluctantly, permit the public welfare centers to chart their own course, but the established church, assembled at Lambeth, also reversed its untenable position. When these dramatic changes were added to the defiant resolutions of doctors at the British Medical Association meetings and the willingness of their profession to study and prevent the physical and psychological ramifications of excessive fertility, they seemed to justify Marie Stopes's proclamation that 1930 "will remain a date to commemorate when the 'Notable Events' in the history of the movement for deliberate parenthood are recorded for posterity."[63] Conveniently forgetting her demographic history as well as the old Malthusian League and the campaign it started before she was born, Stopes dated the commencement of the struggle from her dramatic entrance on the birth control scene twelve years earlier. The result, her old ally Earl Russell excitedly assured her, is that the "walls of the citadel have fallen."[64] Not everyone agreed that Stopes had brought them down alone, as she frequently implied, but at the same time both supporters and opponents of family limitation agreed that a decisive victory for the right of individuals to regulate human reproduction had been won. The problem of birth control in the future was for most people not a matter of principle but of implementation.

Another twenty years would pass before the champions of family planning would again have as much occasion to celebrate. In 1949 a prestigious royal commission, established five years earlier, reported on and thoroughly endorsed their objectives. Though the number of welfare centers and Family Planning Association clinics providing contraceptive advice had multiplied to 500 and the number of annual patients to 150,000, birth control still remained on the fringes of comprehensive family welfare programs.[65] The royal commission recommended that it be fully integrated into the government's postwar plans for domestic assistance.[66] As birth control proponents after World War I turned to the local maternity and infant welfare centers and the Ministry of Health as the best route to reaching the working poor, the next generation of family planners turned to the newly established National Health Service. In contrast to the fragmented interest groups who agitated for reform in the 1920s, leadership after World War II came from a distinguished national body, a fact that in itself was an indication of how much the climate had changed. The appointment of a royal commission had been recommended as early as 1902, when the declining birthrate and the fear of race deterioration was fast becoming a national issue, but no government before World War II thought it politically wise or appropriate and went no further than the 1911 *Fertility of Marriage Census*. In the aftermath of the Beveridge Report (1942) and the planning for a new social service state, however, the issue of population requirements and family size in the postwar world pointed clearly to the need for a more up-to-date comprehensive investigation of demographic trends.

After five years of study and the expenditure of a quarter of a million pounds, the royal commission reported that it could find virtually no evidence that birth control was regarded as improper any longer. Even Catholics, who rejected artificial methods of birth control, accepted the principle of family planning. The commission, however, saw nothing offensive or harmful in medically recommended contraceptives and concluded that it would be sound public policy to endorse their use as an important means of achieving the desirable goal of rational, voluntary parenthood.[67] Neither the voluntary clinics, in spite of their heroic efforts, nor the local maternity and child welfare clinics, still under Ministry of Health restrictions dating from the early 1930s, could, in the judgment of the commission, satisfactorily fulfill the task. Not only should the restrictions be lifted, it argued, but access to free contraceptive advice and appliances should be the right of every patient through the National Health Service. Though initial advice should come from the family doctor, the commission explained, National Health Service birth control clinics should also be established throughout the country.[68]

In its linking of birth control to public health and family welfare, the commission employed in one form or another virtually all of the arguments birth control advocates had been making since the late nineteenth century. These arguments ranged from the economic and physiological consequences of excessive fertility among the poor to the problems of differential overpopulation in a constrained geographical area. Delayed marriage or abstinence were rejected for all of the traditional reasons, and birth control was extolled for the freedom it would permit the modern mother in finding satisfaction outside of the home.

Although the elderly C. V. Drysdale and R. B. Kerr testified before the commission on behalf of the moribund Malthusian League, they were clearly voices from the past—curiosities rather than compelling witnesses. Drysdale interpreted the commission's findings as evidence of a renewed interest in Malthus and the problems of overpopulation, and, along with Kerr and a few other survivors of the old league, he contemplated a revival of the pioneer birth control organization. With the birthrate rising again for the first time in decades and famine threatening portions of the globe, the time seemed opportune. Their pathetic, spasmodic efforts were barely noticed before the infirmities of old age put a final end to their hopes.[69] Marie Stopes did not even appear before the royal commission. Her inability to cooperate with others in the birth control movement and her obvious eccentricities had increasingly relegated her to the sidelines. Moreover, her loathing of the postwar world in general and the Labour government and the welfare state in particular provoked angry eugenic fulminations against the proliferation of degenerate weaklings.[70] On the eve of the triumphs of 1930 she had already concluded that the struggle for birth control had become less important than the genetic improvement of the British race, and she looked for salvation through a national program of sterilization.[71] The passage of the years only intensified that conviction.

The future clearly lay with a new generation whose concepts of birth control were far more expansive. Abortion and contraceptive counseling for unmarried women were now added to the campaign for voluntary parenthood. For Margaret Pyke, chairman of the Family Planning Association, the royal commission's report was everything she and her followers could have desired. As she wrote a few years later, "1949 was the great year."[72] Though another twenty-six years would pass before birth control would be fully integrated into the National Health Service, it had already become a basic cornerstone of family welfare in Great Britain.[73] Neither the Drysdales nor Marie Stopes survived to see the ultimate collectivization of their goals. Moreover, they were scarcely aware of the impending technological and biological developments in family planning that have marked the most recent stage of that social-demographic revolution that began in the closing decades of the nineteenth century.

Notes

Abbreviations in the Notes

BMA   British Medical Association
MH   Ministry of Health
NBCC   National Birth Control Council
NBRC   National Birth-Rate Commission
NCPM   National Council of Public Morals
PRO   Public Record Office
SPBCC Society for the Promotion of Birth Control Clinics

Introduction

1. The term *birth control* was coined by Margaret Sanger and her supporters in 1914 and first used in print in the fourth issue of their new journal, *The Woman Rebel*, in June of that year. See Sanger, *My Fight for Birth Control*, p. 83.

2. See, for example, Glass and Grebenik, *Trend and Pattern of Fertility*; Innes, *Class Fertility Trends*; Lewis-Faning, *Report on an Enquiry into Family Limitation*; Tranter, *Population since the Industrial Revolution*.

3. On birth control in America see Gordon, *Woman's Body, Woman's Right*; Reed, *From Private Vice to Public Virtue*; and Mohr, *Abortion in America*.

4. For the history of contraception see Himes, *Medical History of Contraception*. For more recent developments see Reed, *From Private Vice to Public Virtue*, and Peel and Potts, *Textbook of Contraceptive Practice*.

5. See Ledbetter, *History of the Malthusian League*.

Chapter 1

1. Malthus, *Essay on the Principle of Population*, chap. 1.

2. Mitchell and Deane, *Abstract of British Historical Statistics*, p. 6.

3. Ibid., pp. 29–30.

4. *Daily Mail*, 10 August 1903.

5. Spender, "Population and Agriculture," pp. 102–6.

6. *Lancet*, 10 November 1906, pp. 1290–91.

7. *Malthusian*, May 1906, p. 33.

8. *Lancet*, 11 March 1905, p. 652.

9. Newsholme and Stevenson, "The Decline of Human Fertility," pp. 34–87.

10. Parl. Papers, *Registrar General 82d Report* (1920), Cmd. 1017, p. 5, table 3.

11. *Times*, 15 September 1906; see also Newsholme and Stevenson, "Decline of Human Fertility," pp. 63–64.

12. Webb, *Decline in the Birth-Rate*, p. 4.

13. Elderton, *Report on the English Birth Rate*, pp. 10–11, 19–20.

14. Tranter, *Population since the Industrial Revolution*, p. 98.

15. Pearson, "Reproductive Selection," pp. 78–80.

16. Parl. Papers, *Report of the Inter-Departmental Committee on Physical Deterioration*, Cd. 2175, 2210, 2186; see also Parl. Papers, *Report of the Royal Commission on Physical Training* (Scotland), Cd. 1507, 1508; and *Memorandum by the Director-General, Army Medical Service*, Cd. 1501.

17. See Searle, *The Quest for National Efficiency* and *Eugenics and Politics*; see also Semmel, *Imperialism and Social Reform*, chaps. 1–3.

18. Parl. Papers, *Census of England and Wales 1911: Fertility of Marriage* (hereafter cited as *Fertility of Marriage*).

19. Glass and Grebenik, *Trend and Pattern of Fertility*. For the problems of using the 1911 census see pp. 68–71; see also Innes, *Class Fertility Trends*, pp. 20 ff.

20. Glass and Grebnik, *Trend and Pattern of Fertility*, pp. 87–88.

21. Malthus, *Essay on Population*, chap. 4.

22. Lyttelton, "The Question of Population," pp. 380–83.

23. *Registrar General 82d Report*, p. 5, table 3.

24. Ibid., p. xiv, table 2.

25. Mitchell and Deane, *British Historical Statistics*, pp. 15–16.

26. Wells, *Mankind in the Making*, pp. 83–84.

27. Ellis, *Social Hygiene*, p. 165.

28. *Fertility of Marriage*, pt. 2, p. cix, table 47.

29. Ibid., p. cii, table 46.

30. Ibid.; also Glass and Grebenik, *Trend and Pattern of Fertility*, p. 85, table 13.

31. Elderton, *Report on the English Birth Rate*, p. 5.

32. Yule, "Changes in the Marriage and Birth-Rates," p. 117.

33. *Times*, 31 July 1912.

34. NCPM, *Declining Birth-Rate*, pp. 336–49. The report was edited by the Reverend James Marchant, the Commission's secretary.

35. Ibid., pp. 26–27.

36. Ibid., pp. 149–65.

37. Doubleday, *True Law of Population*.

38. Mill, *Principles of Political Economy*, bk. 1, chap. 10; Spencer, *Principles of Biology*, 2:510–12.

39. Barclay, "Malthusianism and the Declining Birth-Rate," pp. 80–89; Barclay, "The Race Suicide Scare," pp. 895–99.

40. Newsholme, *The Declining Birth-Rate*, pp. 31–32.

41. NCPM, *Declining Birth-Rate*, pp. 350–51.

42. *Principles of Biology*, 2:427.
43. Ibid., pp. 429–31.
44. Ibid., pp. 501–5.
45. Ibid., pp. 528–30.
46. Ibid., pp. 535–37.
47. Greg, *Enigmas of Life*, pp. xxxvii–xxxviii, 84–86.
48. Galton, *Memories*, pp. 287–88; Galton, "Hereditary Talent," pp. 157–66, 318–27.
49. Galton, *English Men of Science*, pp. 28–29.
50. The most comprehensive study of Galton's eclectic career remains Karl Pearson's three-volume *Life of Galton* but a more manageable account is available in Forrest, *Francis Galton*.
51. Spencer, *Social Statics*.
52. Crackanthorpe, "Population and Progress," p. 1004.
53. Saleeby, *Parenthood and Race Culture*, pp. 98–99.
54. Ibid., pp. 90–93, 96.
55. Ibid., p. 103.
56. Ibid., p. 104.
57. Ellis, *Social Hygiene*, p. 185.
58. Saleeby, *Parenthood and Race Culture*, p. 101.
59. Sociological Society, *Sociological Papers*, 1:67 (hereafter cited as *Soc. Papers*).
60. See the following by Galton: *Hereditary Genius*; "Hereditary Improvement," pp. 116–30; *Inquiries into Human Faculty*; *Natural Inheritance*.
61. Galton, "Eugenics," pp. 47–48.
62. Pearson, "Reproductive Selection," p. 77; see also Galton to Pearson, 23 January 1896, Galton Archives, 245/18 B, and Pearson to Galton, 30 October 1901, ibid., 293/E.
63. Pearson, *Groundwork of Eugenics*, p. 32.
64. Crackanthorpe, "Population and Progress," pp. 1004–6.
65. *British Medical Journal*, 3 February 1906, pp. 278–79; see also 20 October 1906, p. 1066; 13 October 1906, p. 980.
66. Newsholme, *Declining Birth-Rate*, pp. 32–33. He was referring to Whetham, *Family and the Nation*.
67. NCPM, *Declining Birth-Rate*, pp. 350–51.
68. Ibid., p. 162.
69. Ellis, *Essays in War-Time*, pp. 215–17.
70. On Ellis's ambivalent role in this controversy see Grosskurth, *Havelock Ellis*, chaps. 11–13.
71. Ellis, *Essays in War-Time*, pp. 225–27.
72. *Times*, 31 May 1911.
73. Hynes, *The Edwardian Turn of Mind*, pp. 279–98; see also *Times*, 31 May 1911.
74. *Times*, 31 October 1913; NCPM, *Declining Birth-Rate*, preface.
75. See, for example, Miles [John Frederick Maurice], "Where to Get Men," pp. 78–86; Maurice, "National Health," pp. 41–56; *Parl. Deb.* (Lords), 4th ser., 6 July 1903, pp. 1326–56; and Jones, *Outcast London*, pp. 128–30.

76. Parl. Papers, *Report of the Inter-Departmental Committee on Physical Deterioration*, 13–14; see also Gilbert, "Health and Politics," pp. 143–53.

77. NCPM, *Declining Birth-Rate*, pp. v–x.

78. Ibid., pp. 20–21.

Chapter 2

1. Pearson, "Reproductive Selection," pp. 78–80.

2. Ibid., p. 83.

3. Ibid., p. 95.

4. Ibid., pp. 101–2.

5. Ibid., pp. 97–99.

6. Ibid., p. 102.

7. Pearson, "On the Inheritance of the Mental and Moral Characters" pp. 179–237; see also *Biometrika*, 3:154.

8. Rowntree, *Poverty*, pp. 119–21, 128, 134–35.

9. Booth, *Life and Labour*, 17:17–30.

10. Ibid., pp. 24–27.

11. Bertillon, "La Natalité Selon le Degré d'Aisance," pp. 163–76.

12. Crackanthorpe, "Population and Progress," p. 1003.

13. Heron, *On the Relation of Fertility*, pp. 11–16.

14. Ibid., pp. 17–20.

15. Yule, "On the Changes in the Marriage and Birth-Rate," pp. 118–21.

16. *Times*, 14 September 1906.

17. Webb, *Industrial Democracy*, pp. 635–37.

18. *Times*, 11 October 1906.

19. Ibid.; also, Webb, *Decline in the Birth-Rate*, pp. 6–7.

20. Ibid.

21. Ibid., pp. 5–6, 9.

22. Ibid., p. 8.

23. Yule, "On the Changes in the Marriage and Birth-Rate," pp. 120–21.

24. Webb, *Decline in the Birth-Rate*, pp. 9–13; *Times*, 16 October 1906.

25. *Times*, 23 October 1906.

26. Pearson had been conducting biometric studies throughout the 1890s in the Department of Applied Mathematics and Mechanics at University College, but the formal designation of a Biometric Laboratory only appeared in the early twentieth century, probably in 1906. *Biometrika* was founded when Pearson, Weldon, and their students found it increasingly difficult to have their work published in the traditional scientific journals, especially those of the Royal Society. Galton's endowment in 1904 was initially for a Eugenics Record Office, but the name was changed by Pearson in 1907 to The Francis Galton Laboratory for the Study of National Eugenics when it was merged with Pearson's Biometric Laboratory and came under his direction. The most complete account of these developments can

be found in Pearson, *Life of Galton*, vol. 3. A useful synthesis is contained in Farrall, "The Origins and Growth of the English Eugenics Movement."

27. Galton, "Hereditary Improvement," pp. 124–25.

28. Galton, *Inquiries*, pp. 24–25.

29. Galton, *Memories*, p. 310.

30. Galton, "The Possible Improvement of the Human Breed," pp. 659–65.

31. *Soc. Papers*, 1:47–50; Pearson, *Life of Galton*, 3:226. For the divisions within the Sociological Society see Sofer, *Ethics and Society*.

32. *Soc. Papers*, 1:50.

33. Galton to Pearson, 2, 16 March 1903, Galton Archives, 245/18F; Pearson, *Life of Galton*, 3:296–97.

34. *Soc. Papers*, 1:53. In his extensive correspondence with Galton, Pearson continually discussed eugenics in terms of the future, once its biometric foundations were secured. See, for example, Pearson to Galton, 22, 25, 29 October 1906 and 2 March 1907, Galton Archives, 293/G.

35. Pearson to Galton, 14 October 1908, Galton Archives, 293/J; Pearson, *Life of Galton*, 3:363. Galton himself was initially wary of the "fanatics" who might be attracted to the new society and delayed joining until assured that "it is in *Safe* management." When Dean Inge joined and Crackanthorpe agreed to become president Galton relented. Galton to Pearson, 25 January, 18 May 1908, Galton Archives, 245/18J; see also Eugenics Education Society Council Minutes, 12 February 1908, Council Minute Books.

36. *Eugenics Review* 1, no. 1 (1909): 29.

37. Pearson, *Groundwork of Eugenics*, pp. 27–30.

38. Whetham and Whetham, *Family and the Nation*, pp. 139–40; "The Extinction of the Upper Classes," pp. 100–103. For a more realistic assessment of the fertility of the peerage see Hollingsworth, "The Demography of the British Peerage," chap. 3.

39. Whetham and Whetham, *Family and the Nation*, p. 140.

40. Ibid., pp. 131–42.

41. Only M.D.s were more numerous, comprising 26 percent of the 100 officers and council members who governed the Eugenics Education Society before the war. Though the total membership only reached 1,654, it was drawn primarily from the professional middle classes, the military, and the clergy, and included about 60 members of the aristocracy. A fifth of the society's officers and council members bore or received titles. Nearly half of the membership was female, 326 of them unmarried, and 24 were also officers or council members. For additional information on the social composition of the society see Farrall, "Origins and Growth of the English Eugenics Movement"; see also MacKenzie, "Eugenics in Britain" and "Karl Pearson and the Professional Middle Class."

42. *Eugenics Review* 3, no. 2 (1911): 109–11.

43. Newsholme and Stevenson, "The Decline of Human Fertility," pp. 69–70.

44. Newsholme, *Declining Birth-Rate*, pp. 43–46.

45. Elderton, *Report on the English Birth Rate*, pp. 211–12, 220–24, 232.

46. Elderton, *On the Correlation of Fertility with Social Value*, pp. 2–5; Elderton,

Report on the English Birth Rate, pp. 219, 225–29.

47. Ibid., p. 223.

48. Ibid., p. 231.

49. Ibid., p. 232.

50. Ibid., preface.

51. *Fertility of Marriage*, pt. 2, lxxvi–lxxxvii. For details of occupational classification see pp. 27–73, 98–143, tables 30, 35.

52. For problems with the 1911 classification see, ibid., p. lxxvi; see also Innes, *Class Fertility*, pp. 38–41, 65; Glass and Grebenik, *Trend and Pattern of Fertility*, pp. 98 ff.

53. NCPM, *Declining Birth-Rate*, pp. 16, 358–65.

54. Stevenson, "The Fertility of Various Social Classes," p. 417.

55. *Fertility of Marriage*, pt. 2, pp. xlvi–xlviii, cxviii.

56. Ibid., pp. cxix–cxxi.

57. Ibid., p. cxviii.

58. Ibid., p. xcviii, table 44; see also Innes, *Class Fertility*, p. 42.

59. Ibid., p. xci.

60. Ibid., pp. xcviii, xciii, table 44.

61. Ibid.

62. Ibid.

63. Ibid., derived from p. 17, table 23.

64. Webb, *Decline in Birth-Rate*, p. 5; Elderton, *Report on the English Birth Rate*, pp. 213–15. Elderton's conclusion was based in part upon personal interviews and questionnaires used in her survey of the northern English counties.

65. *Fertility of Marriage*, pt. 2, pp. lxxviii–lxxx.

66. Ibid., p. cix, table 47, p. cii, table 46, and pp. ci–civ.

67. Ibid.

68. Ibid., pp. xciv, cix.

69. Ibid., p. xcix. For a more recent confirmation of Stevenson's findings and a speculative analysis of contraceptive practices based upon the 1911 *Census* and the *Family Census* of 1946 see Matras, "Social Strategies of Family Formation," pp. 167–81. Matras calculated that although only 20 to 25 percent of married women born between 1831 and 1855 attempted to control their fertility the proportion began to rise rapidly in the closing years of Queen Victoria's reign, reaching 56 percent for the 1870–84 cohort and 67 percent for women born between 1900 and the end of World War I. Though the inadequacy of data made it difficult to correlate fertility with social status for female cohorts born before 1870, the wide class differentials after that date were clearly evident. Matras concluded that whereas nearly 77 percent of wives born between 1870 and 1884 and married to professional or salaried middle- and upper-class husbands attempted to limit their childbearing, only around 42 percent of the wives of general or casual laborers attempted some form of birth control. For the female cohorts born in the 1890s the comparative figures were 77 and 53 percent. Matras, analyzing family size, also speculated that professional and middle-class couples were markedly more successful in their contraceptive efforts.

70. Ibid., p. xciv, table 43, and pp. lxxv–lxxxvii.

71. Ibid., p. xciv.

72. Ibid., p. xci.

Chapter 3

1. NCPM, *Declining Birth-Rate*, pp. 41–42.

2. Banks, *Prosperity and Parenthood*; Banks and Banks, *Feminism and Family Planning*, pp. 82–84.

3. Branca, *Silent Sisterhood*, chap. 7.

4. Courtney, "The Swarming of Men," pp. 331–33.

5. Yule, "Changes in the Marriage and Birth-Rate," pp. 126–30.

6. Newsholme and Stevenson, "The Decline of Human Fertility," pp. 65–69; see also Newsholme, *Declining Birth-Rate*, p. 42.

7. *Times*, 14 February 1912.

8. *Daily Telegraph*, 28 October 1913; see also *Malthusian*, November 1913, pp. 83–84. Between 1890 and 1914 social service expenditures by the local and central governments increased from £27 million to £101. See Read, *Edwardian England*, pp. 81–82.

9. Ellis, *Social Hygiene*, pp. 170–76.

10. Webb, *Decline in the Birth-Rate*, pp. 17–18.

11. NCPM, *Declining Birth-Rate*, pp. 282–84.

12. Pearson, *Problem of Practical Eugenics*, pp. 23–25.

13. Elderton, *Report on the English Birth Rate*, p. viii, 213. Elderton, like others, singled out the Workshop Regulation Act (1867), the Factory and Workshop Act (1878), and the Mines Acts (1887 and 1891), along with the various education acts since 1870, as examples of how social and economic legislation could affect fertility.

14. Elderton, *On the Correlation of Fertility with Social Value*, pp. 8, 10, 19–21.

15. *Malthusian*, December 1894, p. 90; Webb, *Industrial Democracy*, p. 638.

16. Quoted in Drysdale, *Small or Large Families*, p. 15; Shaw, *Three Plays by Brieux*, p. xxxix; see also Newsholme, *Declining Birth-Rate*, pp. 39–40; *Lancet*, 22 April 1911, p. 1060; *Fertility of Marriage*, pt. 2, p. xci; and Stevenson, "Fertility of Various Social Classes," pp. 417–18.

17. Elderton, *Report on the English Birth-Rate*, pp. viii, 234–37.

18. For discussion of Knowlton and the various editions of his work see Himes, *Medical History of Contraception*, pp. 224–31, 460–64. The literature on Knowlton is considerable. Among the more useful summaries are Fryer's *The Birth Controllers*, chap. 10; Reed, *From Private Vice*, chap. 1; Himes, "Charles Knowlton's Revolutionary Influence on the English Birth Rate"; and Riegel, "The American Father of Birth Control." Knowlton described various contraceptive techniques, recommending the sponge or the postcoital douche as reliable, safe, inexpensive, and sexually satisfying.

19. See Himes, *History of Contraception*, pp. 221–31; Fryer, *Birth Controllers*,

chaps. 4–9; Ledbetter, *History of the Malthusian League*, pp. 8–20; McLaren, *Birth Control*, pt. 2; Reed, *From Private Vice*, chap. 1; Field, "The Early Propagandist Movement," pp. 91–129; Himes, "Robert Dale Owen," pp. 529–47.

20. *National Reformer*, 18 May 1861, p. 5; see also Tribe, *President Charles Bradlaugh*, pp. 74–75.

21. Nethercot, *Annie Besant*, pp. 120–22; Fryer, *Birth Controllers*, pp. 107, 161–62.

22. *Queen* v. *Bradlaugh and Besant*, pp. 149, 237; also, Himes, *History of Contraception*, pp. 243–44. Within three months of their arrest Bradlaugh and Besant sold 125,000 copies of the six-penny pamphlet, three times the sales of the previous forty-three years. Another 185,000 copies were sold by the end of the decade along with countless pirated editions.

23. *Queen*. v. *Bradlaugh and Besant*, p. 251.

24. Ledbetter, *Malthusian League*, pp. 36–40.

25. Ibid., pp. 49–52. D'Arcy, "The Malthusian League," pp. 429–30; see also *Malthusian*, February 1879; *National Reformer*, 15 July 1877, pp. 490–91.

26. Micklewright, "The Rise and Decline of English Neo-Malthusianism," pp. 43–44.

27. *Queen* v. *Bradlaugh and Besant*, pp. 220–28. Additional family support was provided by C. R. Drysdale's older brother George (1825–1904), who while still a medical student in the 1850s anonymously published the extremely sucessful treatise on demography and family limitation, *The Elements of Social Science*, which went through some forty-five editions. Though he later modernized some of the medical sections of Knowlton's pamphlet, George always remained aloof from the league's propaganda activities.

28. *National Reformer*, 2 September 1877, p. 599.

29. The league's financial problems were regularly reported in the *Malthusian* and at its annual meetings. See Ledbetter, *Malthusian League*, pp. 74–75; D'Arcy, "The Malthusian League," pp. 430–31; see also *New Generation*, January 1928, p. 2.

30. Ledbetter's study of the Malthusian League was derived from her doctoral dissertation entitled *The Organization That Delayed Birth Control* (1972), a conclusion she modified somewhat in her very useful book.

31. Glass, *Population Policies*, pp. 42–43.

32. *Malthusian*, August 1894, p. 57.

33. Ibid., January 1909, pp. 6–7.

34. Ibid.

35. Ibid., January 1883, p. 381.

36. Ibid., September 1881, pp. 249–50, 254.

37. Ibid., June 1884, pp. 516–18; February 1885, p. 584; July 1887, p. 55; August 1899, p. 60. By the end of the century the league was receiving two thousand requests a month for a variety of "Malthusian Appliances" described or advertised in the *Malthusian*. Although the organization did not sell contraceptives, some of its members did.

38. Himes, *History of Contraception*, pp. 249–50.

39. See Ledbetter, *Malthusian League*, pp. 131–42, for a narrative of the Allbutt

affair; see also Fryer, *Birth Controllers*, pp. 169–72. The case can also be followed in the pages of the *Malthusian*, March 1887, p. 17; April 1887, pp. 28–29; December 1887, pp. 90–95; January–February 1888; August 1889, p. 57.

40. *Malthusian*, August 1899, p. 60.

41. Ibid., December 1891, pp. 89–92; March 1911, pp. 20–22; April 1911, p. 31; May 1911, p. 93; June 1911, pp. 41–42; July 1912, pp. 53–54.

42. Ibid., September 1913, p. 65.

43. NCPM, *Declining Birth-Rate*, pp. 108–9.

44. *Malthusian*, October 1914, p. 66.

45. Ibid., March 1895, p. 18.

46. The *Malthusian* used the term *Neo-Malthusian* in its first issue (February 1879), although it appears to have been coined shortly before by Dr. S. Van Houton, one-time prime minister of Holland and a vice-president of the Malthusian League. See *Malthusian*, September 1910, p. 76; see also Ledbetter, *Malthusian League*, pp. xiv, xxi, n. 6; Glass, *Population Policies*, pp. 35, 424; Himes, "Notes on the Origin of the Terms," pp. 495–96, and his *History of Contraception*, p. 257. Himes mistakenly dated the term from the early 1880s.

47. *Malthusian*, February 1879, p. 8.

48. Cookson, "The Morality of Married Life," pp. 397–412. Upon inheriting an estate in 1888 Cookson assumed the name Crackanthorpe. See also D'Arcy, "The Malthusian League," p. 436, and Besant, *Law of Population*, p. 26.

49. *Malthusian*, October 1880, pp. 166–67; January 1880, p. 95.

50. Ibid., April 1879, p. 24.

51. Ibid., May 1880, p. 122.

52. *Queen* v. *Bradlaugh and Besant*, pp. 107–9; see also Besant, *Law of Population*, pp. 28–29; *Malthusian*, August 1880, p. 147.

53. *Malthusian*, March 1879, p. 12; April 1879, pp. 18–19.

54. Ibid.; see also Besant, *Law of Population*, pp. 29–30.

55. *Malthusian*, May 1879, p. 31; August 1880, pp. 147–48; December 1880, p. 180.

56. Ibid., April 1879, p. 20; January 1880, p. 92; January 1893, p. 5. Actually the French marriage rate at 15/1,000 was not much different from that of the English.

57. *Malthusian*, April 1879, p. 19.

58. Farrar, "Social Problems and Remedies," pp. 351, 359.

59. White, *The Problems of a Great City*, pp. 58–59.

60. Maine, *Popular Government*, p. 37; also *Fortnightly Review*, 1 February 1886, pp. 153–73; Lyttelton, "The Question of Population," 1:151–71; 2:384–87, 393; see also *Malthusian*, May 1886, pp. 34–35.

61. *Malthusian*, March 1909, pp. 17–18.

62. Ibid., July 1903, p. 51; April 1908, pp. 29–30; July 1908, p. 49.

63. Ibid., February 1880, p. 101; April 1880, p. 118; December 1880, p. 181; November 1882, p. 366; see also Parl. Papers, *Registrar General 82d Report* (1920), Cmd. 1017, p. 5, table 3.

64. Snow, "On the Magnitude of the Population," pp. 238–75.

65. NCPM, *Declining Birth-Rate*, pp. 99–100; see also Drysdale, *Small Family System*, pp. 62–63. Drysdale noted similar trends in other European countries

where fertility was declining such as Germany, Holland, and France as well as in low birthrate colonies like Australia and New Zealand.

66. NCPM, *Declining Birth-Rate*, pp. 72–74, 213.

67. Marchant, *Birth-Rate and Empire*, pp. 66–67, 81–83.

68. NCPM, *Declining Birth-Rate*, pp. 74–75.

69. Drysdale, *The Empire and the Birth-Rate*, pp. 3–4, 18; see also *Malthusian*, August 1914, p. 62. For an example of criticism and defense of this viewpoint see Brend, "The Passing of the Child," pp. 584–602; Binnie Dunlop's reply, April 1915, pp. 841–42; and Brend's "Rejoinder," June 1915, pp. 1407–15.

70. NCPM, *Declining Birth-Rate*, pp. 99–100; *Malthusian*, March 1913, p. 23; see also Ellis, *Social Hygiene*, pp. 156–58.

71. Money, "A Little England?," pp. 483–96. Emigration, Money recognized, added greatly to the difference.

72. Ellis, *Social Hygiene*, pp. 136–37, 140–48.

73. Ibid., p. 159.

74. Robertson, *The Economics of Progress*, pp. 248–53.

75. *Malthusian*, April 1912, pp. 27–38.

76. NCPM, *Declining Birth-Rate*, pp. 40–41; *Malthusian*, August 1916, p. 67.

77. *Malthusian*, August 1916, p. 68; October 1916, pp. 90–91.

78. Elderton, *Report on the English Birth Rate*, p. 233.

Chapter 4

1. Cookson, "Morality of Married Life," pp. 406–8, 412.

2. For examples of this argument see *Queen v. Bradlaugh and Besant*, pp. 117–18, 124–38, 147–49, 169.

3. See Billington-Greig, *Commonsense on the Population Question*, pp. 4–10.

4. *Malthusian*, February 1880, p. 101.

5. Besant, *The Social Aspects of Malthusianism*, pp. 1–2.

6. *Malthusian*, June 1879, p. 34; August 1880, pp. 148–49; see also March 1880, pp. 110–11.

7. Ibid., September 1903, pp. 69–70; April 1904, p. 27.

8. Ibid., July 1884, pp. 522–23; June 1888, p. 45.

9. NCPM, *Declining Birth-Rate*, pp. 287–89.

10. Ibid., pp. 40–41.

11. Checkland, *The Rise of Industrial Society*, pp. 33–35, 61–62; see also Thomas, *Migration and Economic Growth*.

12. *Malthusian*, June 1881, pp. 226–28.

13. Ibid., September 1894, p. 68; September 1880, p. 155; December 1897, pp. 90–92; February 1898, pp. 12–13.

14. Thomas, *Migration and Economic Growth*, pp. 153–54; Read, *Edwardian England*, p. 23.

15. NCPM, *Declining Birth-Rate*, p. 127.

16. By 1914 there were an estimated 360,000 aliens in Britain, one-third of

them Jews. See Gainer, *The Alien Invasion*, pp. 2–3, 6–14; see also Gartner, *The Jewish Immigrant in England*, pp. 30, 283.

17. *Malthusian*, May 1879, p. 27; January 1885, p. 570; July 1891, p. 51.

18. Ibid., January 1885, p. 570.

19. Ibid., July 1905, p. 54; February 1903, pp. 11–12.

20. For details of the Aliens Act and its enforcement see Gainer, *Alien Invasion*, pp. 199–211.

21. *Malthusian*, July 1879, p. 42; see also February 1887, p. 12.

22. Ibid., March 1879, p. 14; June 1879, pp. 38–39.

23. Ledbetter, *Malthusian League*, pp. 150–51.

24. *Malthusian*, November 1904; April 1905, p. 28; October 1905, p. 76; June 1907, pp. 41–42.

25. Ibid., October 1905, p. 77. Robertson pointed out that the number of people in parliament who had ever spoken about fertility control could be "counted on one hand." They included Mill, Bradlaugh, John Morley, Leonard Courtney, the Earl of Derby, the Marquis of Dufferin, and, most recently, the labor leader, John Burns.

26. Ibid., June 1907, pp. 41–42.

27. Ibid., May 1879, p. 25; also Drysdale, *Small Family System*, pp. 133–36.

28. *Malthusian*, October 1895, p. 78.

29. Ibid., April 1890, p. 27.

30. For the social composition of the secularist movement see Royle, *Victorian Infidels*, pp. 161, 233–44.

31. *Malthusian*, May 1879, p. 26; Besant, *Social Aspects*, p. 7.

32. See, for example, Alfred Russel Wallace in *Echo*, 24 October 1882; see also *Malthusian*, December 1882, p. 372.

33. Ibid., February 1880, p. 97; July 1886, p. 52; June 1885, p. 618.

34. Ibid., March 1879, p. 11.

35. George, *Progress and Poverty*, bk. 2, chap. 4. George's book and subsequent lecture tour in 1882 sparked excited debate in reformist circles throughout the decade. For the league's response see *Malthusian*, February 1880, pp. 100–101; May 1882, pp. 412–13; November 1882, pp. 36–61. During World War I C. V. Drysdale returned to the league's early conflicts with George, refuting his theories once more in a series of articles entitled "The Fallacies of Henry George." See Ledbetter, *Malthusian League*, p. 92.

36. *Malthusian*, November 1885, p. 649; September 1898, p. 69.

37. Ibid., December 1914, p. 95.

38. Ibid., October 1907, pp. 76–77; October 1906, p. 77. Robertson had been making the same point since the 1880s, but he thought it especially important in the early years of the new century. When elected to parliament in 1905 he knew that his association with the Malthusian League was a liability in his working-class constituency and that it was his Radical-Liberal credentials, not his advocacy of family limitation, that gained him his seat and allowed him to keep it until 1918.

39. Drysdale, *Small Family System*, p. 135.

40. *Malthusian*, January 1916, pp. 9–10.

41. M. G. H., *Poverty*, pp. 11–15. The pamphlet contained a number of quota-

tions from the equally anonymous George Drysdale's writings. See Fryer, *Birth Controllers*, pp. 112–13.

42. See, for example, *Malthusian*, June 1882, p. 321; December 1882, p. 370; February 1884, p. 487; see also Ledbetter, *Malthusian League*, chap. 4.

43. Ibid., May 1883, p. 411; June 1883, p. 420; June 1884, p. 516.

44. Ibid., November 1879, p. 80; May 1883, pp. 409–10; June 1883, pp. 417–19.

45. Ibid., October 1885, pp. 645–46.

46. McLaren, *Birth Control*, pp. 158–62.

47. *Malthusian*, April 1883, p. 406; see also Ledbetter, *Malthusian League*, pp. 93–95.

48. Nethercot, *Annie Besant*, pp. 218–22.

49. Besant, *Autobiography*, pp. 301–2, 306.

50. *Malthusian*, April 1887, p. 31.

51. McLaren, *Birth Control*, pp. 180–81; see also *Malthusian*, May 1888, p. 36; April 1891, p. 28.

52. Pearson, "The Moral Basis of Socialism," pp. 315–19.

53. Pearson, "Socialism and Sex," p. 423. Originally written in 1886 for a small discussion club, "Socialism and Sex" was printed in *To-Day*, February 1887, and as a separate pamphlet.

54. Pearson, "Moral Basis of Socialism," pp. 320–22.

55. Ibid., pp. 322–24.

56. Pearson, "Socialism and Sex," pp. 423–24; see also *Malthusian*, December 1894, p. 90.

57. Webb, *The Difficulties of Individualism*, p. 6; see also McLaren, *Birth Control*, pp. 186–88.

58. *Malthusian*, March 1898, p. 19.

59. Ibid., April 1907, p. 26; February 1909, p. 14.

60. *Clarion*, 24 February, 3, 10, 31 March 1900, 24 July 1903; see also McLaren, *Birth Control*, p. 181.

61. *Justice*, 5 August 1893, p. 5; 14 October 1893, p. 5.

62. McLaren, *Birth Control*, pp. 163–66.

63. In particular see Bax's *The Legal Subjection of Men* and *The Fraud of Feminism* as evidence of his unyielding view.

64. See Aveling and Aveling, *The Woman Question*.

65. *Malthusian*, June 1887, p. 44; Besant, *Autobiography*, p. 240.

66. *Malthusian*, June 1883, p. 427.

67. Ibid., June 1906, pp. 43, 44.

68. Ibid., July 1903, p. 53.

69. Ibid., August 1907, p. 58.

70. Ibid., May 1913, p. 40; December 1913, pp. 91–93.

71. *Malthusian*, May 1912, p. 40.

72. Ibid., March 1912, p. 23; see also Billington-Greig, *Commonsense on the Population Question*, pp. 13–14.

73. Royle, *Victorian Infidels*, pp. 256–58.

74. Nethercot, *Annie Besant*, pp. 242–74; *Malthusian*, November 1889, p. 85.

75. Ibid., March 1890, p. 18; March 1898, p. 19.

76. Ibid., November 1893, pp. 81–82; February 1897, p. 13. The *Malthusian* reported considerable interest on the part of the Amalgamated Society of Carpenters and Joiners.

77. Ibid., October 1905, pp. 76–77; March 1906, pp. 17–18.

78. Ibid., January 1909, p. 8.

79. Ibid., October 1915, pp. 65–66.

80. Ibid., December 1916, pp. 101–4; February 1917, p. 13; June 1917, pp. 46–47.

81. Ibid., November 1918, p. 86.

82. Ibid., January 1918, pp. 7–8; February 1918, pp. 13–14.

83. Ibid., February 1915, p. 9.

84. Ibid., June 1917, pp. 43–44.

85. Ibid., pp. 41–42.

86. Ibid., September 1918, p. 74.

87. George Standring tried to establish a new group in 1919, but his efforts led to nothing more than a short-lived paper with the straightforward title of *Birth Control*.

88. *Malthusian*, June 1884, p. 516; August 1896, p. 58.

Chapter 5

1. *Malthusian*. February 1879, pp. 1–2.

2. *Queen* v. *Bradlaugh and Besant*, p. 119. Later, to expedite the trial, the two clergymen were not called to testify.

3. Headlam was virtually the only clergyman to take much notice of the Neo-Malthusians, and though he disagreed with their economic premises he praised their courage and sincerity. See *Malthusian*, January 1883, p. 383.

4. Ibid., June 1885, pp. 609–10; see also November 1887, pp. 83–84; February 1888, pp. 12–13.

5. Ibid., March 1886, p. 23; March 1887, p. 21.

6. "Report of the 11th Annual Meeting," in ibid., June–July 1888.

7. *Weekly Times and Echo*, 6 November 1886; see also H. R. Haweiss, *"Winged Words"; or, Truth Retold* (London, 1885), quoted in Drysdale, *Small Family System*, pp. 38–39.

8. *Malthusian*, April 1888, pp. 25, 30–31.

9. Whatham, *Neo-Malthusianism*, pp. 5–9.

10. Ibid., p. 8.

11. Drysdale to Whatham, 13 October 1887, in ibid.; see also *Malthusian*, April 1888, p. 25; December 1888, pp. 93–94; January 1889, pp. 3–4.

12. Ibid., December 1891, p. 94; see also Drysdale, *Small Family System*, p. 38.

13. *Malthusian*, May 1885, p. 607.

14. Banks and Banks, *Feminism and Family Planning*, p. 98.

15. Newman and Blackwell, *The Corruption Called Neo-Malthusianism*; see also

Newman, "Malthusianism, True and False," p. 597; Newman, "Two Solutions," pp. 452–53; Banks and Banks, *Feminism and Family Planning*, p. 99.

16. *Malthusian*, August 1891, p. 60.

17. Ibid., April 1897, pp. 29–30.

18. NCPM, *Declining Birth-Rate*, pp. 376–77.

19. *Christian World*, 15 June 1893; see also Glass, *Population Policies*, pp. 429–30, and Banks and Banks, *Feminism and Family Planning*, p. 99.

20. *Economic Review* 8 (1898): 566–67. The work under review was R. Ussher, *Neo-Malthusianism*, a violent, anti-Neo-Malthusian polemic that Lyttelton found to be disorganized and largely without merit.

21. *Daily Express*, 27 April 1904; *Malthusian*, June 1904, p. 46.

22. *Parl. Debates* (Lords), 4th ser., 20 July 1905, 149:1306–7.

23. Ibid., 6 July 1905, 124:1340–46.

24. *Malthusian*, July 1904, p. 51.

25. Winnington-Ingram, *A Charge* (1905), pp. 31–33.

26. Ibid., p. 33.

27. Barry, "Agnosticism and National Decay," pp. 83–93.

28. Taylor, "The Bishop of London," pp. 224–25; see also Newsholme and Stevenson, "The Decline of Human Fertility," p. 69.

29. *Malthusian*, December 1905, p. 89; see also Barclay, "Malthusianism," p. 88.

30. For mid-century religious affiliation see *Census of Great Britain, 1851: Religious Worship in England and Wales*; see also Soloway, *Prelates and People*, chap. 8; Inglis, *Churches and the Working Classes*, pp. 1–20; Chadwick, *The Victorian Church*, pt. 1, pp. 363–69. In the early twentieth century waning religious attendance was reflected in Mudi-Smith, *The Religious Life of London*, based upon a survey made in 1902 for the *Daily News*. See Chadwick, *The Victorian Church*, pt. 2, pp. 233–38, and Gilbert, *Religion and Society in Industrial England*, chaps. 7–8.

31. Taylor, "The Bishop of London," pp. 227–29.

32. Lambeth Conference (1908), *Conference of Bishops*, p. 56.

33. Ibid., pp. 38, 56.

34. Ibid., pp. 144–45.

35. Ibid., pp. 145–46; p. 152, appendix, no. 3.

36. Ibid., p. 146.

37. Ibid., p. 153, appendix, no. 6; see also Sir John MacDonnell, ed., *Civil Judicial Statistics of England and Wales for 1906*, pt. 2, p. 35.

38. Lambeth Conference (1908), *Conference of Bishops*, p. 147.

39. Ibid., pp. 145, 147.

40. *Malthusian*, July 1908, pp. 50–51.

41. Peile, "Eugenics and the Church," p. 172.

42. NCPM, *Declining Birth-Rate*, pp. 377–78, 381.

43. Ibid., pp. 66–67.

44. Drysdale, *Small Family System*, pp. 51–54, 196; see also Ansell, *On the Rate of Mortality*. The average family size of clergymen was not much different from that of aristocrats, merchants, bankers, manufacturers, and members of the legal profession though somewhat larger than the 4.8 recorded for doctors; see also *Fertility of Marriage*, pt. 2, pp. cv–cvii, table 48.

45. See below, chap. 11.

46. Winnington-Ingram, *A Charge* (1911), pp. 25–28; see also *Malthusian*, November 1911, pp. 83–84.

47. *Manchester Guardian*, October 1911; see also Drysdale, *Small Family System*, pp. 40–41.

48. *Times*, 2 October 1912.

49. Ibid., 8 October 1913.

50. *Malthusian*, March 1912, p. 22.

51. *Eugenics Review* 5, no. 3 (1913): 261–62.

52. *Evening Standard*, 4 September 1912.

53. *Daily Telegraph*, 28 October 1913; *Malthusian*, February 1914, p. 9.

54. Drysdale, *Small Family System*, pp. 101–2. The work in question was Horsley, *How Criminals Are Made and Prevented*.

55. *Malthusian*, July 1914, pp. 49–50.

56. Ibid., April 1914, pp. 25–26.

57. NCPM, *Declining Birth-Rate*, pp. 63–64.

58. Ibid., pp. 372–73.

59. Ibid., pp. 374, 378–79.

60. Ibid., pp. 374–77, 380.

61. "The Misuse of Marriage," in ibid., pp. 384–85.

62. Ibid., pp. 365–87.

63. For Bishop Burge's testimony see ibid., pp. 437–47.

64. Ibid., pp. 64–65.

65. Marchant, *Birth-Rate and Empire*, pp. 176–77.

66. *Malthusian*, July 1912, p. 55.

67. Booth, "Religious Belief as Affecting the Growth of Population," pp. 138–42.

68. Ibid., pp. 152–54.

69. NCPM, *Declining Birth-Rate*, pp. 16–17, 425–36.

70. Ibid., pp. 390–400.

71. Ibid., pp. 184–85.

72. Winnington-Ingram, *A Charge* (1905), p. 33; Taylor, "The Bishop of London," p. 224; see also Addinsel, in *Lancet*, 4 November 1905, pp. 1360–61.

73. NCPM, *Declining Birth-Rate*, pp. 65–66.

74. *Malthusian*, October 1914, pp. 75–76.

75. Ibid.

Chapter 6

1. Banks, *Prosperity and Parenthood*, p. 155. For a brief survey of medical opposition to birth control see John Peel, "Contraception and the Medical Profession," pp. 133–46; see also McLaren, *Birth Control*, chaps. 4, 7.

2. *Medical Press and Circular*, October 1878, p. 8. Routh published his address as a separate pamphlet, *The Moral and Physical Evils Likely to Follow If Practices In-*

tended to Act as Checks to Population Be Not Strongly Discouraged and Condemned.

3. Routh, *Moral and Physical Evils*, pp. 9–10.

4. Ibid., pp. 11–13.

5. Ibid., pp. 16–17.

6. Ibid., pp. 13–14; *Malthusian*, October 1879, p. 69.

7. *Malthusian*, November 1880, p. 176.

8. See "Report of Meeting of the Medical Society of London," in ibid., December 1879, p. 84.

9. Ibid., January 1880, p. 94.

10. Ibid., March 1886, p. 17; see also February 1886, p. 12.

11. Ibid., May 1879, p. 30. The *Malthusian* based its figures on Ansell, *On the Rate of Mortality*.

12. Allbutt, *"Wife's Handbook*, pp. 46–50.

13. General Medical Council, *Minutes . . . 1887*, p. 309.

14. *Malthusian*, January 1888, p. 4. Unlike the minutes of the General Medical Council, which contain a brief résumé of the case, the *Malthusian* published the entire transcript.

15. Himes, *Medical History of Contraception*, p. 251.

16. *Malthusian*, September 1893, p. 65.

17. Banks and Banks, *Feminism and Family Planning*, p. 93.

18. Russell, *Autobiography*, 3:116.

19. *British Medical Journal*, 29 June 1901, p. 1630.

20. *Malthusian*, December 1879, p. 84.

21. Drysdale, *Small Family System*, pp. 8–9. Interesting insight into the issue of abortion in the Edwardian period can be found in McLaren, "Abortion in England," pp. 379–400.

22. Drysdale, *Small Family System*, p. 13.

23. Malthusian League, *Fortieth Annual Report*; see also *Malthusian*, November 1916, p. 99; February 1917, pp. 10–11.

24. *British Medical Journal*, 5 October 1901, p. 942.

25. See, for example, ibid., 5 March 1904, p. 578; 13 October 1906, p. 980; 20 October 1906, p. 1066; *Lancet*, 27 January 1906, p. 247; 19 May 1906, p. 1399; see also NCPM, *Declining Birth-Rate*, pp. 149–65, 336–49.

26. *British Medical Journal*, 20 August 1910, pp. 449–57; *Lancet*, 10 September 1910, pp. 815–17; *Times*, 30 July 1910.

27. Taylor, *The Diminishing Birth Rate*, pp. 4–12.

28. Ibid., pp. 13–22.

29. Taylor, "The Bishop of London," pp. 219–22, 226; see also *Lancet*, 27 January 1906, pp. 247–48.

30. *Lancet*, 20 July 1907, pp. 170–71.

31. Drysdale, *Small Family System*, pp. 51–53.

32. *Fertility of Marriage*, pp. cv–cvii, table 48.

33. *British Medical Journal*, 3 September 1910, pp. 637–38; see also Banks, *Prosperity and Parenthood*, pp. 158–59.

34. *British Medical Journal*, 31 May 1913, pp. 1179–80.

35. Drysdale, *Small Family System*, pp. 10, 16, 20–23.

36. *British Medical Journal*, 27 July 1912, pp. 157–63; see also *Malthusian*, September 1912, pp. 63–64.

37. *Malthusian*, September 1908, pp. 65–66; see also August 1912, pp. 57–58.

38. Soloway, "Neo-Malthusians, Eugenists, and the Declining Birth-Rate," pp. 275–78.

39. In addition physicians constituted approximately 10 percent of the 1,400 members of the Eugenics Education Society.

40. Drysdale, *Small Family System*, pp. 27–31; *Malthusian*, August 1913, pp. 60–63; *British Medical Journal*, 2 August 1913, p. 230.

41. Drysdale, *Small Family System*, pp. 31, 35–36; *Malthusian*, September, 1913, p. 70.

42. *British Medical Journal*, 2 August 1913, p. 230.

43. *Malthusian*, July 1913, p. 41.

44. NCPM, *Declining Birth-Rate*, p. 95. In addition to many medical members the Dutch Malthusian League had eight doctors and 50 trained advisers prescribing contraceptive advice and appliances. *Malthusian*, March 1913, p. 24.

45. NCPM, *Declining Birth-Rate*, pp. 247, 256.

46. Ibid., pp. 252, 257–58.

47. Ibid., p. 273.

48. Ibid., pp. 176–77, 181–82.

49. Ibid., pp. 254–55; see also Routh's letter to the *British Medical Journal*, 28 February 1914, p. 510, and other opinions on pp. 566, 625, 686, 793, 891, 943.

50. NCPM, *Declining Birth-Rate*, pp. 116–17.

51. Ibid.

52. *Malthusian*, January 1880, p. 93.

53. Ibid., November 1885, p. 653.

54. NCPM, *Declining Birth-Rate*, p. 127.

55. Drysdale, *Small Family System*, pp. 82–83.

56. Ibid., pp. 61–63; see also *British Medical Journal*, 1914, pp. 510–66, 625, 686, 793, 891, and 943, for examples of medical reaction to Neo-Malthusian correlations of fertility and mortality.

57. *Malthusian*, March 1886, p. 17; September 1893, p. 65.

58. Ibid., June 1890, p. 44; September 1892, p. 70.

59. *John Bull*, 8 October 1910; see also Drysdale, *Small Family System*, p. 19, and *British Medical Journal*, 9 September 1911, pp. 529–33; 17 July 1909, pp. 149–50.

60. Dunlop to Stopes, 15 November 1917, Stopes Papers, Add. MSS. 58564.

61. *Lancet*, 18 November 1905, pp. 1496–97.

62. Lambeth Conference (1908), *Conference of Bishops*, p. 56.

63. Ibid., p. 152.

64. NCPM, *Declining Birth-Rate*, p. 253.

65. *British Medical Journal*, 27 July 1912, pp. 157–58.

66. *Malthusian*, August 1912, pp. 63–64.

67. Quoted in Drysdale, *Small Family System*, pp. 41–42.

68. Ibid., pp. 156–59; see also *Malthusian*, July 1914, pp. 52–53.

69. Rigby, "The Diminishing Birth-Rate," pp. 434–45.

70. Millard, *Population and Birth Control*, pp. 43–44.

Chapter 7

1. Banks and Banks, *Feminism and Family Planning*, pp. 24–25, 41. See Mill, *Principles of Political Economy*, bk. 4, chap. 7, and Mill, *The Subjection of Women*. Angus McLaren contends that the Bankses underestimated the extent of feminist commitment to birth control, and he cites several examples to support his belief that feminist interest in the issue makes it "one of the lost dimensions of Victorian and Edwardian feminism." See McLaren, *Birth Control*, chap. 11. Although there were many individual feminists who were, as McLaren writes, "far from indifferent to the question of fertility control," their numbers and tactics do not, in my judgment, suggest that the Bankses were incorrect in their assessment.

2. Banks and Banks, *Feminism and Family Planning*, pp. 53–54. For a detailed account of the antifeminist movement see Harrison, *Separate Spheres*.

3. Banks and Banks, *Feminism and Family Planning*, pp. 91–93.

4. Ibid., pp. 94–97. For the role of women in the struggle against the Contagious Diseases Acts, see Walkowitz, *Prostitution and Victorian Society*.

5. Banks and Banks, *Feminism and Family Planning*, pp. 110–11, 120–21, 132.

6. *Malthusian*, March 1879, p. 12.

7. See, for example, Drysdale, *The Cause of Poverty*, p. 14.

8. *Malthusian*, March 1880, p. 107; April 1879, p. 18.

9. Ibid., September 1884, p. 546; November 1903; March 1907, pp. 20–21.

10. Banks and Banks, *Feminism and Family Planning*, pp. 100–101.

11. Miller, *The Strike of a Sex*, pp. 27–28. Miller was a former member of the Oneida community.

12. Pearson, *Ethic of Freethought*, pp. 322–23.

13. Pearson, "Socialism and Sex," pp. 414–15.

14. Ibid., pp. 428–29.

15. Ibid., p. 429.

16. Allen, "Plain Words on the Women's Question," pp. 448–52.

17. Ibid., p. 450.

18. Ibid., p. 456.

19. Spencer, *Principles of Biology*, 2:511–13.

20. Galton, *Hereditary Genius*, p. 329.

21. Linton, "The Higher Education of Women," pp. 503–4.

22. Thorburn, *Female Education from a Physiological Point of View*, p. 11; see also Burstyn, "Education and Sex," pp. 79–89.

23. Pearson, "The Woman's Question," pp. 355–56.

24. Ibid., pp. 373–74.

25. Ibid., pp. 360–61.

26. Pearson, "Women and Labour," pp. 241–42.

27. Sidgwick, *Health Statistics of Women Students*, p. 14.

28. Ibid., p. 19.

29. Ibid., p. 90.

30. Ibid., pp. 56–59.

31. Ibid., pp. 62–63, 90.

32. Ibid., pp. 62, 66, 91.

33. Sidgwick, *University Education for Women*, p. 18.

34. Saleeby, *Parenthood and Race Culture*, pp. 101, 106.

35. Whetham, *Family and the Nation*, pp. 143–45; see also "The Extinction of the Upper Classes," p. 106.

36. Whetham, "Decadence and Civilization," pp. 188, 194, 199–200.

37. Whetham, *Heredity and Society*, pp. 100–102.

38. Eugenics Education Society, Council Minute Books, bk. 2, 17 June 1914. D'Arcy, who was elevated to the Archbishopric of Dublin in 1919 and to Armagh in 1920, was president of the Belfast branch of the Eugenics Education Society until it was disbanded in 1915.

39. Saleeby, *Woman and Womanhood*, pp. 22–24.

40. William Bateson to Galton, 2 May 1897, Galton Archives, 198. Bateson, then a Fellow of St. John's, Cambridge, was surprised by Galton's adamant opposition to permitting women to take degrees at Cambridge as well as his rejection of a university exclusively for women. See also Pearson to Galton, 15 December 1908, Galton Archives, 293 J. Galton's opinion can also be found in "The Possible Improvement of the Human Breed (1901)," p. 535.

41. See Saleeby, *Parenthood and Race Culture*, pp. 224–26, see also Wallace, "Evolution and Character," p. 24.

42. Wallace, "Human Selection," pp. 334–37.

43. *Malthusian*, September 1908, pp. 65–66; August 1912, pp. 57–58.

44. Crackanthorpe, *Population and Progress*, p. 117.

45. *Englishwoman*, no. 10 (1909),pp. 163–64.

46. M. E. S., *The Englishwoman's Home*, p. 128.

47. *British Medical Journal*, 5 March 1904, p. 578; 26 March 1904, p. 757.

48. Ibid., 12 March 1904, p. 636.

49. *Lancet*, 10 September 1910, pp. 815–16.

50. Couston, "The Psychological Dangers to Women," pp. 111–12.

51. *Eugenics Review* 2, no. 4 (1911): 284–90.

52. *Sociological Review* 3, no. 1 (1910): 51–54.

53. *Lancet*, 22 April 1911, pp. 1060–62.

54. Ibid., 10 September 1910, p. 816; see also *Times*, 11 July 1910.

55. Ibid., p. 817.

56. See Drysdale, *Small Family System*, pp. 18–19; *Vote*, 25 September 1910; Billington-Greig, *Commonsense on the Population Question*, pp. 4–5.

57. *Englishwoman*, no. 54 (1913), pp. 257–64.

58. Ibid., no. 55 (1913), pp. 105–6; see also no. 10 (1909), pp. 16–22.

59. *Fertility of Marriage*, pp. lxxviii–lxxx, table 34.

60. NCPM, *Declining Birth-Rate*, pp. 18–20. See pp. 322–28 for full evidence.

61. Ibid., pp. 20–21.

62. *Malthusian*, July 1904, pp. 58–59; September 1904, pp. 66–69.

63. *Soc. Papers*, 2:21–22; 1:60.

64. See *Malthusian*, March 1903, p. 19; April 1903, pp. 27–28.

65. Malthusian League, *A Programme of Women's Emancipation*.

66. *Malthusian*, April 1906, p. 27.

67. *Times*, 5 November 1910. The birthrate for England was 26/1,000 com-

pared with 27/1,000 in New Zealand and 26/1,000 in Australia. The Canadian figure was 23/1,000.

68. Billington-Grieg, "The Rebellion of Women," p. 6.

69. Knight, "Woman v. the State," pp. 36–40.

70. *Sociological Review* 3, no. 1 (1910): 53–54.

71. *Votes for Women*, 23 September 1910, p. 829.

72. *Suffragette*, 9 May 1913, p. 503; 29 August 1913, p. 797.

73. Ibid., 9 January 1914, p. 289; see also Pankhurst, *The Great Scourge and How to End It*.

74. Ledbetter, *Malthusian League*, p. 206.

75. NCPM, *Declining Birth-Rate*, p. 93.

Chapter 8

1. Parl. Papers, *Registrar General 82d Report* (1920), Cmd. 1017, p. 5.

2. NBRC, *Problems of Population*, pp. v–vii.

3. Ibid., pp. xxxi–xxxiii.

4. Inge to Ellis, 1 July 1918, Havelock Ellis Papers.

5. NCPM, *Declining Birth-Rate*, pp. 421–23; see also Marchant, *Birth-Rate and Empire*, pp. 42–45, and Snow, "Note on the Future Population," pp. 446–51.

6. NCPM, *Declining Birth-Rate*, pp. 77–80.

7. Marchant, *Cradles or Coffins*, p. 79; see also Marchant, *Birth-Rate and Empire*, p. 12.

8. Marchant, *Birth-Rate and Empire*, pp. 12–31; Marchant, *Cradles or Coffins*, pp. 42–43.

9. Marchant, *Birth-Rate and Empire*, pp. 124, 132–33.

10. Ibid., p. 16.

11. *Malthusian*, August 1918, p. 60.

12. Marchant, *Cradles or Coffins*, p. 96.

13. Ibid., p. 10.

14. Smith, *Race Regeneration*, pp. 10–11.

15. Brend, "The Passing of the Child," pp. 1411–12; see also Brend, "Infant Mortality," pp. 601–2.

16. *Malthusian*, May 1879, p. 29.

17. Ibid., October 1905, p. 76.

18. *Fertility of Marriage*, pt. 2, p. 28.

19. Crackanthorpe, "Population and Progress," pp. 1013–14.

20. Ibid., pp. 128–29.

21. *Malthusian*, November 1908, p. 85; December 1908, p. 94.

22. Ibid., June 1912, p. 47.

23. *National Review*, June 1912, pp. 716–25.

24. Ellis, *Social Hygiene*, pp. 323–33. Ellis quoted from David Starr Jordan, *The Human Harvest* (London, 1907), and Jacques Novikov, *La Guerre et ses Prétendus Bienfaits* (Paris, 1894).

25. Drysdale, *Empire and the Birth-Rate*, pp. 13–15.

26. *Malthusian*, August 1914, pp. 57–58; see also November 1914, pp. 84–85. When Turkey joined the Central Powers she was added to their primitive ranks as further confirmation of the league's thesis. The hesitant decision by the fertile Italians, with their birthrate of 32.7/1,000, to cast their lot with the Allies in 1915 passed without comment.

27. Ibid.

28. Ibid., February 1915, p. 15.

29. Ibid., January, p. 5; see also the *Sunday Chronicle*, 5 December 1917, and Robertson, *The Economics of Progress*, p. 280.

30. Ellis, *Essays in War-Time*, pp. 64–67, 199.

31. *Malthusian*, February 1917, pp. 9–10; see also Drysdale, *Small Family System*, p. 178.

32. Marchant, *Birth-Rate and Empire*, pp. 24–25.

33. Brend, "The Passing of the Child," pp. 584–94; see also "A Rejoinder," pp. 1414–15, and Brend, "Infant Mortality," pp. 606–7.

34. Winter, "Britain's 'Lost Generation,'" p. 454.

35. *Lancet*, 11 December 1915, p. 1306; see also *Times*, 24 November 1915.

36. *Times*, 6 September 1915.

37. Winter, "Britain's 'Lost Generation,'" pp. 456–65.

38. *Eugenics Review* 6, no. 3 (1914): 197.

39. Ibid.

40. Ibid., 7, no. 1 (1915): 2–4.

41. Ibid., no. 2 (1915): 96.

42. Ibid., p. 94.

43. *Times*, 29 June 1916.

44. NBRC, *Problems of Population*, p. 65.

45. *Eugenics Review* 7, no. 3 (1915): 206–7.

46. Ibid., no. 2 (1915): 96.

47. See, for example, Eugenics Education Society, Council Minute Books, 23 March 1915, 16 May 1916.

48. *Eugenics Review* 7, no. 1 (1915): 9.

49. Ibid., no. 2 (1915): 99–101.

50. NCPM, *Declining Birth-Rate*, p. 415.

51. Church of England, *The Chronicle of Convocation*, Upper House, 5, 6 February and 2 May; Lower House, 7, 16 February; see also Parl. Papers, *Report of the Royal Commission on Venereal Disease*, Final Report, 1 (1916), Cd. 8189.

52. *Times*, 13 June 1918.

53. See, for example, *British Medical Journal*, 30 October 1915, pp. 649–50; 15 April 1916, p. 555; *Lancet*, 11 December 1915, p. 1306.

54. *Times*, 5 April 1916.

55. *British Medical Journal*, 30 October 1915, pp. 649–50.

56. Smith, *Race Regeneration*, p. 18.

57. Frazer, *English Public Health*, pp. 247, 323–24, 348; see also Davin, "Imperialism and Motherhood," pp. 9–43.

58. Frazer, *English Public Health*, pp. 327–28. By 1912 medical inspection also

extended to about one-eighth of the secondary schools as well. By 1915 a school medical service was established, but, as it was dependent upon the cooperation of parents, many children were still neglected.

59. See Donnison, *Midwives and Medical Men*.

60. See Davin, "Imperialism and Motherhood," pp. 11–12.

61. Shaw, "The Revolutionist's Handbook and Pocket Companion," in *Man and Superman*; Wells, *Mankind in the Making*, pp. 93–94, 97–99, and *The New Machiavelli*, chap. 4; Saleeby, *Parenthood and Race Culture*, pp. 36 ff.

62. Frazer, *English Public Health*, p. 348. See, for example, *Report of the Proceedings of the National Conference on Infantile Mortality . . . 1908*.

63. Frazer, *English Public Health*, p. 254.

64. *Times*, 16 September 1915; 30 September 1916.

65. See *Votes for Women*, 23 September 1910, p. 829; Selborne, "Imperialism and Motherhood," pp. 985–88.

66. *Times*, 20 August, 21 August 1915, 7 April, 24 June 1916.

67. Ibid., 19 June 1918.

68. Eugenics Education Society, Council Minute Book, 21 October 1914; 15 September 1915; *Eugenics Review* 6, no. 3 (1914): 22–31; 8, no. 4 (1917): 359.

69. *Times*, 2, 3 July 1918. For more details about origins and sponsors of Baby Week see also *Contemporary Review*, July 1917, pp. 97–100.

70. *Malthusian*, October 1941, p. 75.

71. Ibid., December 1914, p. 90; November 1914, pp. 81–82.

72. Drysdale remained at the Admiralty after the war, becoming director of Scientific Research in 1929, a post he held until his retirement in 1934. He was rewarded with an O.B.E. Dunlop, who claimed to suffer from the effects of severe enteric fever since the South African War, was content to live off his private income while devoting his efforts to the population question.

73. *Malthusian*, February 1915, p. 12; April 1915, p. 26; June 1915, p. 42.

74. Ibid., July 1918, p. 49.

75. Ledbetter, *Malthusian League*, p. 64.

76. *Malthusian*, August 1914, p. 64; September 1914, p. 71; December 1914, pp. 89–90.

77. Bessie Drysdale, *War Babies*; see also *The War*; *To Working Men and Women! Get Rid of Poverty*; *Should Working Men and Women Be Urged to Have Large Families*, all in *Malthusian Pamphlets*.

78. Bessie Drysdale, *War Babies*.

79. *Malthusian*, March 1916, p. 31.

80. Millard, *Population and Birth Control*, pp. 24–25; see also NBRC, *Problems of Population*, pp. 106–9.

81. *Malthusian*, September 1917, p. 71.

82. Ibid., pp. 71–73; October 1917, pp. 77–78; see also *New Statesman*, 25 August 1917.

83. *Sunday Times*, 28 October 1917; *Malthusian*, November 1917, pp. 90–91.

84. Ibid., November 1915, p. 88.

85. NCPM, *Declining Birth-Rate*, pp. 418–20; see also *Malthusian*, January

1916, pp. 7–8; February 1917, p. 12; May 1917, p. 39.

86. *New Statesman*, 5 February 1916, p. 419.

87. *Malthusian*, March 1916, p. 31.

88. Marchant, *Birth-Rate and Empire*, pp. 134–35.

89. *Malthusian*, November 1914, pp. 82–83. To support its contention the *Malthusian* compared recruitment in Hastings, where only 277 men out of a population of 62,000 enlisted in a month, with recruitment in the more prosperous town of Eastbourne, where there was an enlistment of 754 men out of 52,000.

90. Ibid., May 1915, pp. 34–35; June 1915, p. 42; November 1914, p. 87.

91. Dunlop to Marie Stopes, 7 July 1917, Stopes Papers, Add. MSS. 58564.

92. For Stella Browne see Rowbotham, *A New World For Women*.

93. Browne, "Women and the Race," pp. 156–57.

94. *Malthusian*, December 1914, pp. 91–92; Browne, "Woman and the Race," pp. 156–57.

95. Pugh, *The Great Unborn*, pp. 28–29.

96. Ibid., p. 28.

97. Ibid., pp. 81, 91–92.

98. Ibid., pp. 114–16, 175–76.

99. Rathbone, *The Disinherited Family*, pp. 256.

100. Havelock Ellis to Margaret Sanger [1915?], Sanger Papers, Carton 4; see also C. V. Drysdale to Sanger, 20 August 1922, ibid., Carton 21.

101. *Times*, 2 July 1918; see also Frazer, *English Public Health*, pp. 412–15.

102. *Times*, 3 July 1918; Marchant, *Birth-Rate and Empire*, pp. 198–99.

103. *Malthusian*, September 1918, pp. 67–89; April 1919, p. 31.

104. Ibid., March 1921, pp. 19–20.

105. Ibid., December 1918, p. 91; October 1918, p. 84.

106. Ibid., December 1918, p. 91; January 1919, pp. 6–7.

107. *New Generation* 1, no. 9 (September 1922): 3.

Chapter 9

1. *Malthusian*, February 1921, p. 16; March 1915, pp. 17–18.

2. *New Generation*, April 1923, p. 49.

3. During the 1930s the birthrate fell to 14.8/1,000. See Mitchell and Deane, *British Historical Statistics*, pp. 29–30, 36–37; Rollett and Parker, "Population and Family," p. 31, table 2.2.

4. *New Generation*, March 1922, p. 3; May 1922, p. 11. The death rate fell to 12.1/1,000 during the 1920s and it remained at that point through the interwar years. Drysdale explained that the death rate was simply equal to the birthrate minus the rate of increase in food. When mortality remained constant while fertility continued to diminish it was obvious that the availability of food was still inadequate. Only a further reduction in fertility, especially among the poor, would reduce pressure on subsistence to the point at which the death rate would start to

drop again. See *Report on the Fifth International Neo-Malthusian and Birth Control Conference*, pp. 61–64 (hereafter cited as *Neo-Malthusian and Birth Control Conference*).

5. Rollett and Parker, "Population and Family," p. 31.

6. Marchant, *Birth-Rate and Empire*, pp. 146–47.

7. Mitchell and Deane, *British Historical Statistics*, pp. 45–46. Though the marriage rate jumped to around 20/1,000 in 1919–20 it soon returned to the prewar norm. At the same time, however, the percentage of people married continued to increase, up from 34.8 in 1901 to 39.7 in 1921 and 42.8 a decade later. This was largely the result of there being fewer children in the population and more people in the marriageable age range. See Halsey, *Trends in British Society*, p. 40, table 2.14; pp. 56–57, tables 2.36, 2.37; see also Glass and Grebenik, *Trend and Pattern of Fertility*, p. 105, table 32; p. 129, table 51; p. 110, table 40.

8. *New Generation*, December 1925, p. 143.

9. Glass and Grebenik, *Trend and Pattern of Fertility*, p. 110, table 40; pp. 112–13, table 42. For categories of social status see p. 21. See also Halsey, *Trends in British Society*, p. 56, table 2.36. In spite of the decline in fertility among all status groups the average number of children born to the most prolific group—unskilled general and casual laborers who married in the years 1920–24—was still twice as large as the number born to the least fertile category—salaried employees in trade, industry, and government service.

10. Marchant, *Birth-Rate and Empire*, p. 47.

11. Stopes, *Wise Parenthood*, p. vii. Bennett wrote the introduction.

12. *New Generation*, October 1923, pp. 118–19.

13. Marchant, ed., *Medical Views on Birth Control*, pp. 136–39. Newsholme estimated that the percentage of people over 65 would nearly double by 1941 and that all population growth would cease sometime in the next 20 years.

14. NCPM, *The Ethics of Birth Control*, pp. 165–76. Beveridge's testimony consisted of a paper delivered to the British Association Meeting in Toronto in 1924.

15. See *Neo-Malthusian and Birth Control Conference*.

16. *Fertility of Marriage*, pt. 2.

17. Pell, *The Law of Births and Deaths*, pp. 7–8, 37–42, 66–67, 96, 104–5.

18. Ibid., pp. 17–24, 30–31. Pell also cited a recent survey of 455 prominent French advocates of large families. On the average, the families had only 1.3 children, and 176 had none. Similarly he recalled that the average fertility of the 188 women who told the NBRC before the war that they never practiced birth control was only 1.6 children, fewer even than the 2.4 claimed by those who admitted employing contraceptive devices.

19. *Neo-Malthusian and Birth Control Conference*, pp. 255–56. Pell was reacting to a gradual increase in childless marriages, which constituted about 15 percent of the total in the 1920s, up about 5 percent when compared with marriages celebrated in the 1890s. Childlessness rose among all groups in society, but it was substantially higher among the middle classes. For nonmanual salaried employees and people in the professions it doubled from 10 to 20 percent when compared with the cohort of the 1890s. Among manual wage earners and laborers sterility rose only half as much, from 8 to slightly more than 13 percent. In spite of lamentations

about the plummeting fecundity of the nobility, the proportion of childless marriages in their elevated ranks was, at 18.6 percent, not much different from other high-status groups. See also Pell, *Births and Deaths*, pp. 27–29, 33–35.

20. Barrett, *Conception Control*, p. 38.

21. *Neo-Malthusian and Birth Control Conference*, pp. 257–78.

22. *Malthusian*, April 1912, p. 27.

23. Ibid., May 1917, p. 38; June 1917, pp. 41–42.

24. Ibid., December 1918, p. 89; February 1919, pp. 14–15; August 1919, p. 60; October 1919, p. 75.

25. Ibid., November 1918, p. 86.

26. Ibid., October 1918, p. 74.

27. Ibid., October 1919, pp. 76–78; December 1919, p. 90; January 1920, pp. 4–5.

28. Ibid., July 1920, pp. 4–5.

29. *New Generation*, June 1922, p. 15.

30. Haire recommended the condom and the Mensinga diaphragm as the safest and most reliable contraceptives. Despite the continued requirement of a signed declaration that the recipient was married or about to wed, more than 91,000 copies were distributed by 1927. See Ledbetter, *Malthusian League*, p. 211.

31. For relations with Dutch Neo-Malthusians see ibid., pp. 172–81.

32. See Bessie Drysdale to Sanger, 9 July 1915, Sanger Papers, Carton 21; Dunlop to Sanger, 11 October 1915, Sanger Papers, Carton 21; see also Sanger, *Diaries, 1914–1915*. The October 1915 issue of the *Malthusian* was dedicated to Sanger. Though the government dropped its case against her, she was convicted in 1917 for running a birth control clinic in Brooklyn and imprisoned for thirty days. See Kennedy, *Birth Control in America*, pp. 86–87.

33. Dunlop to Stopes, 11 November 1917, Stopes Papers, Add. MSS. 58564.

34. Though Sanger insisted that she opposed abortion as a form of birth control she warned that if it was to be done it should take place as early in pregnancy as possible. A Malthusian League memorandum emphasized that the organization was not prepared to consider the subject at all. See *Memorandum Concerning the Prosecution of Mrs. Margaret H. Sanger of New York, U.S.A., for Her Advocacy of Birth Control and Her Issue of a Pamphlet Entitled "Family Limitation" Describing Various Methods of Restricting Families*, by the International Neo-Malthusian Bureau of Correspondence and Defence (London, 1915), p. 2.

35. Sanger to Stopes, 25 May 1920, Stopes Papers, Add. MSS. 58586, and Janet and C. F. Chance to Sanger, 19 July 1920, Sanger Papers, Carton 21.

36. Stopes to Sanger, 26 May 1920, ibid.

37. Dunlop to Stopes, 5 March 1920; Stopes to Dunlop, 12 March 1920, Stopes Papers, Add. MSS. 58564.

38. Dunlop to Stopes, 8 June and 20 October 1920, ibid.

39. For a fuller discussion of Marie Stopes and the birth control clinics see chap. 10.

40. Ledbetter, *Malthusian League*, p. 222.

41. Ibid., pp. 222–23.

42. Dawson of Penn, *Love-Marriage-Birth Control*, pp. 16–24. The *Malthusian*

printed the speech in its entirety in the November 1921 issue, pp. 86–87.

43. B. Drysdale to Sanger, 17 November 1921, Sanger Papers, Carton 21; see also *Malthusian*, December 1921, p. 97, and *Neo-Malthusian and Birth Control Conference*, p. 8. In spite of his doubts C. V. Drysdale gave the new venture £1,000.

44. Dunlop to Stopes, 8 July 1921, Stopes Papers, Add. MSS. 58564.

45. Walworth Women's Welfare Centre, *Annual Report, 1924*.

46. B. Drysdale to Sanger, 17 November 1921, Sanger Papers, Carton 21.

47. *New Generation*, February 1922, p. 16; March 1922, p. 15.

48. J. P. Bland to Sanger, 30 November 1920, Sanger Papers, Carton 21.

49. Russell, *The Tamarisk Tree*, p. 10. See also Grosskurth, *Havelock Ellis*, pp. 376–80.

50. Haire to Stopes, 5 January 1922, Stopes Papers, Add. MSS. 58567.

51. B. Drysdale to Sanger, 26 December 192[2], Sanger Papers, Carton 21.

52. The society opened three more clinics in London and seven in other parts of the country during the 1920s.

53. C. V. Drysdale to Sanger, 25 March 1923, Sanger Papers, Carton 21.

54. B. Drysdale to Sanger, 11 October 192[3], ibid; see also Walworth Women's Welfare Centre, *Annual Report, 1924*, p. 3.

55. *Neo-Malthusian and Birth Control Conference*, p. 211.

56. Barr to Stopes, 5 June 1922, Stopes Papers, Add. MSS. 58566.

57. *New Generation*, January 1922, p. 2; April 1922, pp. 1–2.

58. Ibid., May 1922, p. 3.

59. Ibid., p. 15; April 1922, p. 15.

60. *New Generation*, April 1922, p. 15.

61. *Neo-Malthusian and Birth Control Conference*, p. 38.

62. *New Generation*, February 1923, p. 17.

63. B. Drysdale to Sanger, 6 April and 18 May 1923, Sanger Papers, Carton 21.

64. C. V. Drysdale to Sanger, 20 February 1923, ibid. Bessie Drysdale raised the possibility of discontinuing publication of the *New Generation* and replacing it with Sanger's *Birth Control Review*, with added pages on English developments, but decided it was too complicated. See B. Drysdale to Sanger, 9 January 1923.

65. Ledbetter, *Malthusian League*, p. 226; *Malthusian*, September 1906, p. 65.

66. The *New Generation* assumed its old name, the *Malthusian*, in 1949, but Kerr continued to edit it until his health failed two years later. The elderly C. V. Drysdale tried to continue publication by combining issues, but in 1952 the project was suspended. See Ledbetter, *Malthusian League*, pp. 239–40.

67. Earl Russell to Stopes, 23 January 1923, Stopes Papers, Add. MSS. 58556.

68. C. V. Drysdale to Sanger, 25 March 1923, Sanger Papers, Carton 21.

69. The *Annual Report of the New Generation League* for 1924 listed 1,213 members.

70. *New Generation*, February 1923, p. 77. For the role of the Labour party in the birth control movement see below, chap. 13.

71. Dunlop to Stopes, 7 February 1922 and 21 June 1924, Stopes Papers, Add. MSS. 58564.

72. *New Generation*, January 1924, p. 1.

73. Ibid., March 1925, p. 31.

74. Ibid., April 1925, pp. 39–40; May 1925, pp. 55–56.

75. Ibid., June 1925, p. 66. The cover was changed in the November issue.

76. *Queen* v. *Bradlaugh and Besant*, pp. 96–99. Mrs. Besant quoted from the writings of Darwin, Spencer, and Galton. See also *Malthusian*, March 1879, p. 16; May 1879, pp. 26–27; August 1880, p. 146.

77. *Malthusian*, October 1904, pp. 73–74; *Soc. Papers*, 1:60; 2:21–22.

78. *Malthusian*, September 1908, pp. 65–66; see also *Small Family System*, pp. 131–32.

79. *Malthusian*, December 1909, p. 90.

80. Ellis, *Essays in War-Time*, pp. 205–6; NBRC, *Problems of Population*, pp. 276–77; see also Millard, *Population and Birth Control*, p. 11.

81. Galton, *Inquiries*, pp. 207–10; also *Hereditary Genius*, pp. 356–57; Pearson, *Practical Eugenics*, p. 19; Darwin, *What Is Eugenics?*, pp. 74–75.

82. Drysdale, *Small or Large Families*, pp. 50–51.

83. See note to Havelock Ellis's "Birth Control and Eugenics," in *Eugenics Review* 9, no. 1 (1917): 32.

84. Though the *Eugenics Review* complained about the "cocksure and patronising tone" of the Malthusian League's pronouncements, the Eugenics Education Society's Council began cautious discussions of birth control in 1910. See *Eugenics Review* 1, no. 3 (1909): 146–47, and Eugenics Education Society, Council Minute Books, bk. 1, 7 June 1910.

85. Darwin to Ellis, 17 January 1917, Ellis Papers. Darwin was discussing a forthcoming article Ellis was writing on "Birth Control and Eugenics" for the *Eugenics Review* 9, no. 1 (1917): 32–41. It was the first time the journal had opened its columns to a decidedly pro-birth control argument and Darwin was not pleased. But even eugenists who, like Sir James Barr, favored birth control and disagreed with those of his medical colleagues who believed contraception harmful, declined until after the war to introduce the controversial subject in his numerous eugenic lectures. See, for example, his *The Aim and Scope of Eugenics*, p. 4; see also Searle, *Eugenics and Politics*, pp. 102–3.

86. Darwin to Ellis, 25 September 1920, Ellis Papers.

87. Dunlop to Stopes, 6 February 1920, Stopes Papers, Add. MSS. 58564.

88. Dunlop to Stopes, 23 March 1920, ibid.

89. *New Generation*, January 1922, p. 1; February 1922, pp. 4–5.

90. *Malthusian*, July 1920, p. 56; August 1920, pp. 60–61.

91. *New Generation*, June 1922, p. 15.

92. Ibid., October 1922, pp. 5, 16. Drysdale was particularly impressed by the American Lothrop Stoddard's new book, *The Revolt against Civilization: The Menace of the Under Man* (New York, 1922) for emphasizing the incompatibility of democratic ideas of natural equality with biological and sociological realities.

93. *New Generation*, June 1922, pp. 4–5; February 1924, p. 27.

94. Eugenics Society, "An Outline of a Practical Eugenic Policy." Although undated the document was apparently written about 1922 or early 1923. Shortly thereafter the society began to take a more active, though still discreet, interest in birth control activities.

95. Hodson to Stopes, 11 December 1923, Stopes Papers, Add. MSS. 58644.

96. See Eugenics Society, "Memorandum to Medical Officers and Superintendents: Birth Control Clinics." There is a copy in Stopes Papers, Add. MSS. 58644, and in Breed and How-Martyn, *The Birth Control Movement*, p. 22.

97. Darwin to Twitchin, 30 January 1927, Eugenics Society, "Correspondence with Major Darwin" file.

98. Twitchin to Darwin, 30 October 1928, ibid.

99. Darwin, *What Is Eugenics?*, pp. 74-75. Two years earlier Darwin thought that a minimum of three children would be adequate. See *Case for Eugenic Reform*.

100. *New Generation*, September 1925, pp. 102-3.

101. Ibid., December 1923, p. 147.

102. Ibid., pp. 137-38.

103. Ibid., June 1928, p. 70; September 1928, p. 104.

104. Ibid., July 1929, p. 104.

105. Ibid., February 1924, pp. 22-23.

106. Ibid., July 1928, p. 82.

107. Ibid., June 1925, p. 62; July 1925, p. 76. The Malthusian League became affiliated with Sanger's New York-based International Neo-Malthusian and Birth Control Federation.

108. Ibid., May 1924, p. 50.

109. Ibid., July 1925, pp. 73, 76.

110. Ibid., August 1927, p. 91; see also *Neo-Malthusian and Birth Control Conference*, pp. 61-64.

111. Drysdale to Sanger, 9 February 192[4], Sanger Papers, Carton 21.

112. C. V. Drysdale to Sanger, 10 February 1924, p. 26.

113. *New Generation*, March 1924, p. 26.

114. Ibid., December 1927, p. 133. The vote was 512 to 315.

115. Ibid., July 1925, pp. 73-74, 78; see also Dunlop to Stopes, 21 June 1919; ?November 1919; 6 January 1922, Stopes Papers, Add. MSS. 58564.

116. "Report of the Annual Meeting," *New Generation*, January 1927, p. 3.

117. Ibid., April 1927, p. 45.

118. NCPM, *Medical Aspects of Contraception*, p. 137.

119. *New Generation*, January 1928, p. 6.

120. Ibid., August 1927, pp. 87-88.

121. Ibid., December 1927, pp. 138-39.

122. C. V. Drysdale to Sanger, 14 October 1928 and 1 December 1928, Sanger Papers, Carton 21.

123. *New Generation*, September 1931, p. 107. How-Martyn and a group of other women did organize a "Malthusian ball" in 1933 that attracted a host of aristocratic luminaries, including Princess Alice, Countess of Athlone, who no longer hesitated to associate themselves with the birth control movement. Though its activities were suspended, the Malthusian League stood ready until Drysdale's death in 1961 to take up the populationist cause whenever the world was prepared to receive Malthusian truth. See Ledbetter, *Malthusian League*, chap. 8.

Chapter 10

1. Sanger to Meredith Atkinson, 5 February 1928, Sanger Papers, Carton 21; also Sanger, *My Fight for Birth Control*, pp. 100, 278.

2. Sanger to C. V. Drysdale, 4 March 1925, Sanger Papers, Carton 21.

3. Ibid., B. Drysdale to Sanger, 11 March 1923, ibid.

4. Ibid., 18 May 1923, 9 February 1924, ibid.

5. Breed and How-Martyn, *The Birth Control Movement*, p. 14.

6. Stopes, *Married Love*. Birth control was discussed in chap. 9.

7. The best discussion of Stopes's early life and scientific career can be found in Hall, *Passionate Crusader*, chaps. 1–7. For additional insights see Briant, *Passionate Paradox*, chaps. 1–6.

8. Stopes to Sanger, 6 July 1915, Sanger Papers, Carton 21.

9. Sanger, *An Autobiography*, p. 171; Briant, *Passionate Paradox*, p. 116.

10. Dunlop to Stopes, 15 November 1917, Stopes Papers, Add. MSS. 58564.

11. Ibid.

12. Hall, *Passionate Crusader*, pp. 141–43, 147–48.

13. *Wise Parenthood* sold nearly a half million copies by the mid-1930s. It went through twenty-five editions by the time of its author's death in 1958 and was translated into seven languages.

14. Russell, *Tamarisk Tree*, pp. 168–69.

15. Stopes to Roe, 23 October 1918, Stopes Papers, Add. MSS. 58457.

16. Ibid., 23 September 1918, ibid.

17. Shaw to Stopes, 28 August 1918, ibid., Add. MSS. 58493.

18. The Rev. F. L. Buseton to Stopes, 1 February 1919, ibid., Add. MSS. 58554.

19. Roe (note), 6 May 1919, ibid., Add. MSS. 58457.

20. Briant, *Passionate Paradox*, pp. 97–98; see also Dunlop to Stopes, March 28, 1918, Stopes Papers, Add. MSS. 58564.

21. Dunlop to Stopes, 3 July, 19 July 1919, ibid.

22. Stopes, *A Letter to Working Mothers*. The work passed through sixteen editions by the mid-1950s.

23. Roe to Stopes, 24 August 1918, Stopes Papers, Add. MSS. 58457.

24. Stopes, *Wise Parenthood*, preface; Marchant to Stopes, 18 July 1917, ? February 1918, Stopes Papers, Add. MSS. 58548.

25. Ibid., 21 January 1919.

26. Stopes, *Wise Parenthood*, pp. 9–10.

27. Ibid., pp. 17–25.

28. Stopes, *Letter to Working Mothers*, p. 5.

29. Ibid., pp. 6–13.

30. Ibid., p. 15.

31. See Roe, "Notes," 21 October 1917, Stopes Papers, Add. MSS. 58457.

32. Fryer, *The Birth Controllers*, p. 229.

33. Briant, *Passionate Paradox*, p. 134.

34. See *Queen's Hall Meeting . . . Speeches*.

35. Ibid.; see also Briant, *Passionate Paradox*, pp. 146–48, and Hall, *Passionate Crusader*, pp. 192–95.

36. Maude, *The Authorised Life*, p. 152.

37. Robertson to Stopes, 22 March 1927, Stopes Papers, Add. MSS. 58597.

38. Evan-Thomas to Stopes, 9 May, 20 May 1924, ibid., Add. MSS. 58596.

39. See National Detective Agency Report to Stopes, 14 February 1928, ibid., Add. MSS. 58597.

40. Stopes to Russell, 3 September 1921, ibid., Add. MSS. 58556.

41. Ellis to Stopes, 3 July 1921, ibid., Add. MSS. 58564.

42. Ibid., 15 January 1923, ibid. For Ellis's relations with Stopes see Grosskurth, *Havelock Ellis*, pp. 371–76.

43. Shaw to Stopes, 24 September 1917, Stopes Papers, Add. MSS. 58493.

44. Ibid., 30 June 1921, 5 December, 8 December 1928, ibid.

45. Ibid., 28 October 1928, ibid.

46. Stopes to Millard, 10 May 1921, ibid., Add. MSS. 58564; see also A. Reid to Stopes, 5 November 1919, ibid., Add. MSS. 58565; Stopes to Reid, 1 October 1920; Reid to Stopes, 3 October 1920, ibid.; J. Barr to Stopes, 26 May 1921, 24 January 1922, ibid., Add. MSS. 58566.

47. Barr to Stopes, 24 January 1922, ibid., Add. MSS. 58566; see also 26 May 1921.

48. *New Generation*, May 1923, p. 52.

49. *Birth Control News*, July 1922, p. 3. Circulation reached around 5,000.

50. See Hall, *Passionate Crusader*, pp. 272–79, 299–304.

51. See Stopes Papers, Add. MSS. 58556, for threats against the *Times*, the *Morning Post, John Bull*, and other papers.

52. Russell to Stopes, 30 November 1928, ibid.

53. Stopes, *Our Ostriches*, pp. 69–70.

54. *New Generation*, August 1924, p. 87.

55. Marchant to Stopes, 1 May 1918, Stopes Papers, Add. MSS. 58548.

56. Dunlop to Stopes, 28 March, 7 July 1917, ibid., Add. MSS. 58564; Stopes to the *Malthusian*, 3 January 1919, ibid.

57. Stopes to Dunlop, 11 March 1919, ibid.

58. Ibid., 15 March 1920, ibid.

59. Stopes to Inge, 27 May 1920, and Inge to Stopes, 28 May 1920, ibid., Add. MSS. 58548.

60. T. Winton, NCPM, to Stopes, 29 May 1924, 20 January 1925, ibid., Add. MSS. 58551.

61. NCPM, *Ethics of Birth Control*, pp. 7, 15, 20–25. Stopes was now less charitable toward the NCPM's secretary, Marchant, whom she described as one of the "murderers and muddlers" who vainly opposed birth control. For reasons he never understood she also threatened to sue him. See their correspondence, 14 October 1924 to 8 December 1925, in Stopes Papers, Add. MSS. 58548.

62. Dunlop to Stopes, 19 August 1918, 13 June 1919, ibid., Add. MSS. 58564.

63. Ibid., 14 September 1920, ? May 1921, 16 May 1921; see also Stopes to Dunlop, 14 May 1921.

64. Ibid., 16 May 1921. The Malthusian League viewed the Queen's Hall meeting as a personal rather than an organizational affair and was unwilling to invest its limited resources in a rally not devoted to Neo-Malthusian principles.

65. Briant, *Passionate Paradox*, p. 24.

66. Dunlop to Stopes, 24 May 1921, Stopes Papers, Add. MSS. 58564.

67. Stopes, *Early Days of Birth Control*, pp. 5–11, 19–25.

68. Ibid., pp. 27–28.

69. Ibid., p. 30.

70. Stopes, *Contraception*, pp. 302, 313.

71. Ibid., p. 296. The actual number was closer to 1,200.

72. Marchant to Stopes, 25 November 1921, Stopes Papers, Add. MSS. 58548.

73. *Birth Control News*, July 1922, p. 3.

74. Ibid., p. 2; see also Stopes to Reid, 6 June 1922, Stopes Papers, Add. MSS. 58565.

75. *New Generation* to CBC, 7 March 1922, ibid., Add. MSS. 58596; see also C. V. Drysdale to Roe, ibid., 23 March 1922.

76. Russell to Stopes, 25 January 1922, ibid., Add. MSS. 58556.

77. *New Generation*, March 1922, pp. 4–5. Drysdale also reminded Stopes that Bradlaugh himself had been interested in birth control long before 1877, having raised the question in the *National Reformer* as early as 1861. See pp. 6–7.

78. Stopes, *A New Gospel*. See chap. 11.

79. Dunlop to Stopes, 29 March 1922, November 1922, Stopes Papers, Add. MSS. 58564.

80. See Stopes to Dunlop, 2 December 1922; Dunlop to Stopes, 6 December 1922; 19 July 1923, ibid. Dunlop ceased gossiping about individuals within the league and henceforth provided Stopes little information about its activities.

81. The appeal was signed by H. G. Wells, Arnold Bennett, Gilbert Murray, and Edward Carpenter.

82. Dennett to Stopes, 27 January 1920, ibid., Add. MSS. 58585.

83. Ibid., 5 May, 14 June 1921, ibid. Mrs. Dennett was able to get one hundred copies of *A Letter to Working Mothers* through the Post Office censors and distribute them to congressmen she was lobbying to change the Comstock Law. See her letter of 27 January 1920.

84. For the differences between Mary Ware Dennett and Margaret Sanger see Kennedy, *Birth Control in America*, pp. 218–24.

85. Sanger to Stopes, 29 July 1921, Stopes Papers, Add. MSS. 58586. Sanger charged that Dennett had been repudiated by the medical profession and most other influential people who could help the cause of birth control.

86. Dennett to Stopes, 15 June 1921, ibid., Add. MSS. 58585, and Stopes to Sanger, 6 August 1921, ibid., Add. MSS. 58586.

87. See Stopes to Dennett, 29 October 1921, and Dennett to Stopes, 31 October 1921, ibid., Add. MSS. 58585.

88. Dennett to Sanger (copy), 31 October 1921, and Dennett to Stopes, 31 October 1921, ibid.

89. Stopes to Sanger, 28 October 1921; Sanger to Stopes, 29 October 1921, ibid., Add. MSS. 58586.

90. The Voluntary Parenthood League collapsed in the mid-1920s.

91. Stopes to MacArthur, 23 February 1950, Stopes Papers, Add. MSS. 58586. See also M. F. Bligh, Natl. Council of Women of Great Britain, to Stopes, 8

November 1950, ibid., Add. MSS. 58732/122.

92. Stopes, *Contraception*, pp. 314, 321–23.

93. Ibid., pp. 337–341; see also Breed and How-Martyn, *Birth Control Movement*, p. 24. Stopes noted that the Knowlton pamphlet was condemned because it included obscene pictures that were not in the original tract.

94. *Parl. Debates* (Commons) 5th ser., 31 July 1922, 157:1242–43.

95. *New Generation*, September 1928, p. 107.

96. Mary Abbot to Stopes, 7 December 1921, Stopes Papers, Add. MSS. 58497.

97. Dunlop to Stopes, 23 February 1921; Stopes to Dunlop, 24 February 1921; Dunlop to Stopes, 5 March 1921, ibid., Add. MSS. 58564.

98. *New Generation*, February 1923, p. 18.

99. Ibid., March 1923, p. 30; see also H. Cox to Sanger, 9 February 1923, Sanger Papers, Carton 21. H. G. Wells, Harold Cox, Bertrand Russell, C. V. Drysdale, Sir Arbuthnot Lane, and St. Loe Strachey all offered to testify as well but were not called.

100. Russell, *Tamarisk Tree*, p. 169.

101. B. Russell to Stopes, 13 January 1923, Stopes Papers, Add. MSS. 58556.

102. E. Russell to Stopes, 18 January 1923, ibid.

103. B. Russell to Stopes, 30 January 1923; Stopes to Sonia Bronson, 12 March, ibid., Add. MSS. 58565.

104. Stopes to the editor of *Athenaeum*, 31 January 1923, ibid., Add. MSS. 58596.

105. Dennett to Stopes, 17 April 1923, Stopes Papers, Add. MSS. 58585.

106. Witcop to Sanger, 4 March 1924; Sanger to Witcop, 12 March, 17 March 1924; Witcop to Sanger, 9 May 1924; Sanger to Witcop, 17 May 1924, Sanger Papers, Carton 21.

107. Stopes to Dennett, 7 October 1924, Stopes Papers, Add. MSS. 58585.

108. *New Generation*, November 1923, p. 125.

109. Ibid., August 1924, p. 89, 95; July 1924, pp. 78–79; May 1925, p. 56.

Chapter 11

1. NBRC, *Problems of Population*, pp. 268–70, 275–76.

2. Ibid., p. 270; *Malthusian*, August 1918, p. 62.

3. NBRC, *Problems of Population*, pp. 268–69, 272.

4. Millard to Stopes, 18 October 1919, Stopes Papers, Add. MSS. 58564.

5. Hall, *Passionate Crusader*, pp. 125–26.

6. See Stopes to J. Marchant, 21 November 1917, and to H. R. Wakefield, 8 May 1917; Wakefield to Stopes, 20 June 1917, Stopes Papers, Add. MSS. 58548.

7. Wakefield to Stopes, 17 June 1918, ibid. The bishop's letter was sent the day after Marie and Humphrey Roe were secretly married at a registry office with only Aylmer Maude and Binnie Dunlop as witnesses. Nevertheless, a month later Bishop Wakefield joined the happy couple in matrimony in St. Margaret's Westminster.

8. Stopes to Wakefield, 24 May 1920, ibid. Ten others on the Birth-Rate Commission received similar critical letters.

9. Wakefield to Stopes, 8 December 1924, ibid.

10. Dunlop to Stopes, 6 February 1920, ibid., Add. MSS. 58564.

11. Millard, *Responsible Parenthood*, pp. 3–9. Another copy is in the Stopes Papers (see Millard to Stopes, 2 January 1923, Add. MSS. 58564).

12. *Guardian*, 2 July 1920; see also *Malthusian*, August 1920, p. 62.

13. Inge to Stopes, 26 January 1918, Stopes Papers, Add. MSS. 58548.

14. Ibid., 16 February 1921, ibid.

15. Stopes, *A New Gospel*, pp. 3–8.

16. Ibid., pp. 10–15.

17. Millard to Stopes, 13 July 1920, Stopes Papers, Add. MSS. 58564.

18. Rev. H. Chapman to Stopes, 5, 11, 16, 29 June 1920, ibid., Add. MSS. 58551.

19. See "Canterbury Leaflets: Sex Instruction (The White Cross League)," in ibid.

20. Lambeth Conference (1920), *Conference of Bishops*, pp. 110–12.

21. Ibid., p. 100.

22. *Malthusian*, September 1920, pp. 66–67.

23. *Evening Standard*, 25 August 1920; see also Inge *Diary of a Dean*, p. 60.

24. Fryer, *Birth Controllers*, p. 243.

25. Corner to Stopes, 21 October 1920, Stopes Papers, Add. MSS. 58548.

26. Dudden to Corner, 16 October 1920; sent by Corner to Stopes, 26 October 1920; Corner to Stopes, 29 October 1920, ibid.

27. Stopes to Davidson, 20 October 1922; Davidson to Stopes, 23 October 1922; Stopes to Davidson, 25 October 1922; Davidson to Stopes, 11 December 1922, ibid., Add. MSS. 58551.

28. *Times*, 12 January 1925.

29. See Stopes Papers, [September 1925], Add. MSS. 58551.

30. See, for example, Rev. J. F. Nelson to Stopes, 10 January 1920, Stopes Papers, Add. MSS. 58554; Stopes to Rev. G. K. Allen, 10 January 1919, ibid., Add. MSS. 58551.

31. Rev. A. Champion to Stopes, 1 April 1919, ibid., Add. MSS. 58554.

32. See invitation from unidentified Methodist minister in Stepney, 10 March 1923, ibid.

33. Salvation Army to Stopes, 19 December 1921, ibid.

34. Rev. S. Mellor to Stopes, 27 October 1920, and Stopes to Mellor, 9 November 1920, ibid.; see also Rev. R. W. Cummings (Ashton-under-Tyne), 27 August 1923, ibid., Add. MSS. 58551.

35. See, for example, Rev. J. Taylor to Stopes, 11 February 1923, ibid., Add. MSS. 58554; see also Corner to Stopes, 20 March 1922, ibid., Add. MSS. 58548.

36. Rev. B. H. Streeter to Stopes, 15 November 1919, 24 January, 7 February, 27 September 1920, ibid., Add. MSS. 58554.

37. See Stopes Papers, Add. MSS. 58550, for the questionnaires.

38. Dawson, *Love-Marriage-Birth Control*, p. 18.

39. Ibid., p. 21.

40. Ibid., pp. 22–24.

41. *Sunday Express*, 16 October 1921.

42. Stopes to Roe, 20 October 1921, Stopes Papers, Add. MSS. 58458.

43. Dawson to Stopes, 25 March 1921, ibid., Add. MSS. 58567.

44. Stopes to Dawson, 12 January, 22 February 1922, ibid.

45. Dawson to Stopes, 24 February 1922, ibid.

46. Bessie Drysdale to Sanger, 12 May 1922; Dawson to Sanger, 20 December 1924; Sanger to Dawson, 10 January 1925; Dawson to Sanger, 13 January 1925; Sanger to Dawson, 16 February 1925, Sanger Papers, Carton 21.

47. Curtis Brown, Ltd. to Sanger, 23 March, 18 May, 22 May 1925; Sanger to Curtis Brown, Ltd., 21 May 1925, ibid.; see also Dawson to Sanger, 11 November 1924, 31 October 1927, and Sanger to Dawson, 28 October 1927, ibid.

48. Vaughan, "England's Empty Cradles," pp. 588–601; see also the *Times*, 7 April 1916.

49. *New Generation*, March 1924, pp. 25–26; November 1925, p. 132.

50. Vaughan, "England's Empty Cradles," p. 610.

51. Rev. D. Cameron to Stopes, 2 June, 7 August, 20 October 1923, 30 January 1924, Stopes Papers, Add. MSS. 58554.

52. "Catholic Woman Doctor," *A City Full of Girls and Boys*, p. 19; see also Hall, *Passionate Crusader*, p. 205.

53. *New Generation*, July 1925, p. 84.

54. Ibid., November 1925, p. 132.

55. Ibid., December 1922, p. 6; July 1923, pp. 80–81.

56. Fryer, *Birth Controllers*, p. 230.

57. Stopes to M. Hebbes, 9 April, 11 June 1921, Stopes Papers, Add. MSS. 58596.

58. *Birth Control News*, September 1923, p. 3; January 1924, p. 1.

59. Hall, *Passionate Crusader*, p. 206.

60. Stopes to Dennett, 12 December 1921, Stopes Papers, Add. MSS. 58585. Dennett had described a police raid on one of Sanger's meetings in New York the preceding month. The police had been sent in at the request of Catholic church officials, which created a great row and considerable publicity. See Dennett to Stopes, 25 November 1921 and Stopes to Dennett, 15 February 1922, ibid.

61. Stopes to Dennett, 14 February 1922, ibid.

62. Sutherland, *Birth Control*, pp. 101–2.

63. See Stopes Papers, Add. MSS. 58566, for efforts made to dissuade her from litigation.

64. Hall, *Passionate Crusader*, pp. 207–8.

65. For full account of the proceedings see Box, *The Trial of Marie Stopes*.

66. Briant, *Passionate Paradox*, pp. 159–63.

67. Ibid., pp. 164–68.

68. Sutherland, *Birth Control Exposed*.

69. *Birth Control News*, January 1929, p. 1; August 1929. The entire issue was devoted to Sutherland's unsuccessful libel suit against Stopes for suggesting that he was indirectly responsible for a Catholic woman burning one of the CBC's horse-drawn birth control caravans in 1928.

70. *Morning Post*, 26 January 1928; *Birth Control News*, March 1928, p. 3; July 1928, pp. 3–4; see also Hall, *Passionate Crusader*, pp. 263–64.

71. Hall, *Passionate Crusader*, pp. 266–67.

72. *New Generation*, December 1923, p. 137. The Quakers were the only denomination in the 1920s to formally sanction birth control under "certain circumstances." See Leathard, *The Fight for Family Planning*, p. 24.

73. Norman, *Church and Society*, p. 296.

74. NCPM, *Ethics of Birth Control*, p. 69.

75. *Times*, 1 June 1925; see also *New Generation*, July 1925, p. 81.

76. *Parl. Debates* (Lords), 5th ser., 28 April 1926, 63:1016–26.

77. *Birth Control News*, June 1926, p. 1.

78. Stopes to Davidson, 21, 30 June 1926; Davidson to Stopes, 29 June 1926, Stopes Papers, Add. MSS. 58551; see also *Birth Control News*, January 1927, pp. 1, 3.

79. Inge to Stopes, n.d., 1928, Stopes Papers, Add. MSS. 58548.

80. Stopes to Inge, 15 April 1929; Inge to Stopes, 23 April 1929, ibid.

81. Fryer, *Birth Controllers*, pp. 265–66; see also *New Generation*, August 1929, p. 89.

82. See H. J. Bagge to Stopes, 24 November 1928, Stopes Papers, Add. MSS. 58646.

83. Fryer, *Birth Controllers*, p. 266.

84. *New Generation*, July 1930, p. 77.

85. See copy in Stopes Papers, Add. MSS. 58556.

86. Temple to Stopes, 30 November 1929, ibid., Add. MSS. 58551.

87. Rev. F. W. Jones to Stopes, 30 January 1930, ibid.

88. Stopes, ed., *Mother England*.

89. *Birth Control News*, Nov. 1930, pp. 107–8; see also Leathard, *The Fight for Family Planning*, p. 47.

90. Lambeth Conference (1930), *Encyclical Letter*, pp. 43–44.

91. Ibid.

92. *Birth Control News*, November 1930, pp. 107–8.

93. Lambeth Conference (1930), *Encyclical Letter*, pp. 43–44.

94. Ibid.

95. *Birth Control News*, November 1930, pp. 107–8; December 1930, p. 113; see also *Evening Standard*, 13 November 1930.

96. *Tablet*, 11 October 1930, p. 1.

97. Hall, *Passionate Crusader*, p. 271.

98. *Church Times*, 14 November 1930; see also David and Furse, *Marriage and Birth Control*, a clerical response to the Lambeth Conference demonstrating the cleavage within the clergy's ranks.

99. Fryer, *Birth Controllers*, p. 246.

100. Bishop of Durham's chaplain to Stopes, 21 March 1931, Stopes Papers, Add. MSS. 58551.

101. Inge, *Vale*, p. 81.

102. See Rev. F. Bennett to Roe, 11 October 1930, and to Stopes, 20 October 1930, Stopes Papers, Add. MSS. 58551.

103. Lambeth Conference (1958), *Encyclical Letter*, pt. 2, pp. 143–47.

104. Ibid., pt. 1, p. 122; see also Norman, *Church and Society*, pp. 412–13.

105. Norman, *Church and Society*, p. 413.

106. Briant, *Passionate Paradox*, pp. 125–27.

Chapter 12

1. *Journal of State Medicine*, November 1918, pp. 332–33.

2. Ibid., pp. 333–36.

3. Ibid., p. 336.

4. NBRC, *Problems of Population*, pp. 272–76.

5. *British Medical Journal*, 16 July 1921, pp. 93–94; see also 2 July 1921, pp. 11–12.

6. See *Lancet*, 23 July 1921, pp. 179–81; *Malthusian*, 15 August 1921, pp. 57–58; Stopes, *Contraception*, p. 343.

7. *Lancet*, 23 July 1921, pp. 179–81.

8. Ibid.

9. *British Medical Journal*, 27 August 1921, p. 340; 19 August 1921, pp. 327–28.

10. Ibid., 23 July 1921, p. 131; 30 July 1921, p. 169.

11. Ibid., 23 July 1921, p. 131.

12. Ibid., 27 August 1921, p. 340.

13. Ibid., 21 January 1922, pp. 105–6.

14. *New Generation*, August 1925, p. 88. Mrs. Sprigg's sister-in-law, Margery Spring-Rice, was chairman of the new clinic.

15. Royal Society of Medicine, *Proceedings*, pt. 3, pp. 38–47. The references to birth control were uniformly critical.

16. *Practitioner*, July 1923, p. 2.

17. Ibid., pp. 3–5.

18. Ibid., pp. 23–26, 35.

19. Ibid., pp. 62–73.

20. Ibid., pp. 56–61.

21. Ibid., pp. 74–87.

22. Ibid., p. 90.

23. Ibid., p. 5.

24. *New Generation*, February 1922, pp. 6–7; see also *Neo-Malthusian and Birth Control Conference*, pp. 229–32. Millard sent out 160 questionnaires.

25. *Lancet*, 26 March 1921, p. 677.

26. See Stopes Papers, Add. MSS. 58568, for medical correspondence.

27. Stopes to J. Jeffries, 10 May 1920, ibid.

28. R. Sandilands to Stopes, 15 December 1924, 19, 23 January 1925, ibid., Add. MSS. 58569.

29. R. Moss to Stopes, 4 June 1921, ibid., Add. MSS. 58568.

30. See Stopes Papers, Add. MSS. 58569 for the survey.

31. Blacker to Stopes, 10 August 1924, ibid., Add. MSS. 58655.

32. *Guy's Hospital Gazette*, 11 October 1924, p. 463; see also Fryer, *Birth Controllers*, p. 227.

33. See Blacker's obituary for Stopes in *Eugenics Review* 1, no. 4 (1959): 228–30.

34. See Box, *Trial of Marie Stopes*, pp. 220–21, 252–53; see also *British Medical Journal*, 10 March 1923, pp. 445–48.

35. *Lancet*, 29 November 1924, p. 1137.

36. BMA to Kerslake, 20 February 1924; Kerslake to Stopes, 23 February 1924, Stopes Papers, Add. MSS. 58567.

37. For medical correspondence about *Contraception* see ibid, Add. MSS. 58569.

38. H. Warren to Stopes, 24 November 1925; Dr. M. Fraser to Stopes, ? January 1926 and 17 January 1926, ibid. In late 1926 Stopes was invited to address the South London branch of the BMA which she regarded as a triumph. See *Birth Control News*, December 1926, p. 2.

39. Lancashire/Cheshire Branch, BMA to Stopes, 6 November 1929, Stopes Papers, Add. MSS. 58570.

40. Stopes to Barr, 22 October 1924, ibid., Add. MSS. 58566.

41. *New Generation*, January 1924, p. 13.

42. See Stopes Papers, Add. MSS. 58565 and 58568, for the extensive correspondence and autopsy report on the stillborn child. On the back of a photograph of the dead infant the distraught Stopes wrote, "would have been born alive but for the interference of the doctor."

43. Routh to Stopes, 8, 14, 17 January 1919, ibid., Add. MSS. 58565. Despite Routh sending her a nineteen-page condemnation of all contraceptive devices and techniques, Stopes was determined to have the best medical help available as the birth of her child approached, and Routh's reputation and experience made him an obvious choice. In practice she frequently ignored his advice and over his reservations chose to employ the fashionable new technique of "twilight sleep" to ease the pains of labor. Routh, who was not in attendance at the birth of her child, continued as Stopes's gynecologist though the two remained poles apart over the question of birth control.

44. Stevenson to Roe forwarded to Stopes, 8 June 1921, ibid., Add. MSS. 58458.

45. *British Medical Journal*, 16 July 1921, pp. 93–94.

46. Ibid., 13 August 1921, p. 262.

47. *Birth Control News*, June 1922, p. 3.

48. *British Medical Journal*, 26 November 1921, p. 824; 10 December 1921, p. 1016.

49. *Birth Control News*, June 1926, p. 1; see also Briant, *Passionate Paradox*, pp. 279–80.

50. Stopes to R. Garrett (secretary, Royal Free Hospital), 10 June 1926; Garrett to Stopes, 15 June 1926, Stopes Papers, Add. MSS. 58569.

51. Haire to Stopes, 6 June, 23 September 1921; Stopes to Haire, 27 September 1921, ibid., Add. MSS. 58567.

52. Haire to Stopes, 5 January 1922, ibid.

53. *New Generation*, January 1922, p. 12.

54. Dunlop to Stopes, 24 February, 11 March 1923, Stopes Papers, Add. MSS. 58564.

55. Benevolent Society to New South Wales to Stopes, 17 January 1923, ibid, Add. MSS. 58567.

56. See Box, *Trial of Marie Stopes*, pp. 290–300; see also *British Medical Journal*, 10 March 1923, p. 447.

57. J. Hawthorne to Stopes, 10 January 1925, Stopes Papers, Add. MSS. 58566.

58. G. Armstrong to Stopes, 1 September 1928, ibid.

59. Stopes to Armstrong, 6 September 1928, ibid. Stopes remained convinced that all hypodermic injections were dangerous.

60. Haire to Stopes, 14 March 1934, ibid., Add. MSS. 58567.

61. H. Fawcett to Stopes, 8 March 1927, ibid., Add. MSS. 58570.

62. *Lancet*, 22 January 1927, pp. 165–66; 29 January 1927, p. 259.

63. Ibid., 26 April 1930, p. 925.

64. See *British Medical Journal*, 15 September 1928, pp. 477–79.

65. Barrett, *Conception Control*, pp. 19–23.

66. NCPM, *Ethics of Birth Control*, p. 82.

67. Ibid., pp. 83–86; Barrett, *Conception Control*, pp. 26–34, 41–45.

68. *Public Health*, October 1925, p. 11.

69. Ibid., pp. 9–12.

70. Ibid., p. 13.

71. Barrett, *Conception Control*, p. 31.

72. *Practitioner*, July 1923, p. 34.

73. NCPM, *Ethics of Birth Control*, pp. 90–91.

74. Haire, ed., *Some More Medical Views on Birth Control*, pp. 12–13; see also *New Generation*, February 1927, p. 17.

75. Neo-Malthusian and Birth Control Conference, pp. 268–69, 279–80.

76. Stopes, *"The First Five Thousand."*

77. Stopes to Kerslake, 14 November 1924, Stopes Papers, Add. MSS. 57567.

78. NCPM, *Ethics of Birth Control*, pp. 39–50.

79. Ibid., p. 15; see also *Public Health*, August 1925, p. 327.

80. NCPM, *Ethics of Birth Control*, p. 25.

81. Marchant, ed., *Medical Views*.

82. Ibid., xviii.

83. Ibid., pp. 48–68, 63, 67, 87–88. Stopes's copy is in the Eugenics Society Library.

84. *Lancet*, 28 May 1927, pp. 1165–67.

85. *Public Health*, April 1927, pp. 219–20.

86. Marchant, *Medical Views*, pp. 105–17.

87. See *British Medical Journal*, 6 November 1926, p. 863.

88. Stopes to C. Hodson, 1 March 1926; Hodson to Stopes, 27 March 1926; Stopes to Hodson, 29 March 1926, Stopes Papers, Add. MSS. 58655.

89. Eugenics Society, "Report of the Medical Committee [1926]"; see also Stopes Papers, 16 June 1926, Add. MSS. 58644.

90. Eugenics Society to Stopes, n.d. October 1926, Stopes Papers, Add. MSS. 58644.

91. See NCPM, *Medical Aspects of Contraception*.

92. Crew to Stopes, n.d. February 1927; Stopes to Crew, 22 February 1927; Crew to Stopes, 25 February 1927, Stopes Papers, Add. MSS. 58570. Since Crew was one of the few scientists engaged in the study of sexual physiology and repro-duction, his testimony was considered important. Some of his funding came from C. F. Chance and Margaret Sanger who were interested in new contraceptives. See B. P. Weisner to Sanger, 10 July 1928, Sanger Papers, Carton 21; Crew to Sanger, 13 August 1938, ibid.

93. NCPM, *Medical Aspects of Contraception*, pp. 10–13.

94. *Lancet*, 17 December 1927, p. 1325; *Public Health*, January 1928, pp. 100–101; *British Medical Journal*, 19 November 1927, pp. 952–53.

95. *British Medical Journal*, 29 October 1927, p. 806; *Lancet*, 19 November 1927, p. 1110. Members of the committee included Blacker, A. M. Carr-Saunders, and Julian Huxley, among others.

96. *British Medical Journal*, 15 September 1928, pp. 499–500; see also 5 April 1930, p. 658.

97. Ibid., 6 October 1928, p. 634; *Public Health*, October 1928, pp. 11–12.

98. *Birth Control News*, April 1930, p. 189.

99. Florence, *Birth Control on Trial*. For example see Dr. Louise Hunter and Dr. Helena Wright's report on the North Kensington Clinic in *British Medical Journal*, 6 October 1928, p. 634, and *Public Health*, October 1929, pp. 11–12.

100. Florence, *Birth Control on Trial*, pp. 30, 56; see also Stopes, *First Five Thousand*, pp. 49–51.

101. Florence, *Birth Control on Trial*, pp. 30, 35–36.

102. *Birth Control News*, April 1930, p. 189; June 1930, p. 22.

103. For a tentative confirmation of these observations based upon oral inter-views see Gittins, "Married Life and Birth Control," pp. 53–64. In addition, after World War II the Royal Commission on Population estimated that only 5 percent of working-class couples used any artificial appliances to control their fertility. The vast majority still practiced coitus interruptus. See Lewis-Faning, *Report . . . into Family Limitation*, p. 58.

104. Florence, *Birth Control on Trial*, p. 119.

105. Haire to Stopes, 24 October 1929, Stopes Papers, Add. MSS. 58567.

Chapter 13

1. Stopes to M. Hebbes, 12 April 1922, Stopes Papers, Add. MSS. 58596.

2. Stopes, *Contraception*, pp. 382–83.

3. *Malthusian*, May 1917, p. 2.

4. Dunlop to Stopes, 6 January 1922, Stopes Papers, Add. MSS. 58564.

5. *Times*, 29 March 1922; see also *New Generation*, May 1922, p. 10; August 1922, p. 4. Young, *County Palatine of Chester: Report of the Medical Officer of Health*, p. 6; *Birth Control News*, August 1922, pp. 1, 3.

6. *British Medical Journal*, 22 July 1922, p. 133.

7. *New Generation*, July 1922, p. 12; August 1922, p. 3; October 1922, p. 7.

8. *British Medical Journal*, 11 March 1922, p. 419.

9. *New Generation*, January 1923, pp. 3, 8.

10. Fryer, *Birth Controllers*, p. 257.

11. *New Generation*, May 1923, p. 59; October 1924, p. 11.

12. *Birth Control News*, January 1923, p. 3; February 1923, p. 1.

13. *Parl. Debates* (Commons), 25 July 1923, 167:480; see also C. V. Drysdale to Sanger, 25 March 1923, Sanger Papers, Carton 21.

14. *New Generation*, April 1923, p. 45.

15. Ibid., April 1922, pp. 8–9; September 1923, p. 108.

16. *Birth Control News*, December 1923, p. 2. The Stockport meeting was under the chairmanship of Meredith Young, the medical officer of health for Chester.

17. *New Generation*, January 1924, p. 1.

18. Dunlop to Stopes, 6 December 1922, Stopes Papers, Add. MSS. 58564.

19. *New Generation*, April 1924, p. 38.

20. Ibid., February 1924, pp. 13–14, 21.

21. R. Witcop to Sanger, 4 March 1924, Sanger Papers, Carton 21.

22. *Parl. Debates* (Commons), 5th ser., 30 July 1924, 176:2050; see also Peel and Dowse, "The Politics of Birth Control," p. 184.

23. *Parl. Debates* (Commons), 5th ser., 30 July 1924, 176:2050.

24. Ibid., 6 August 1924, pp. 2908–9.

25. *New Generation*, May 1924, p. 53; June 1924, pp. 63–64; July 1924, p. 73.

26. Ibid., September 1925, pp. 87–88; see also B. Drysdale to Sanger, 18 May 1923, Sanger Papers, Carton 21; *Public Health*, September 1923, p. 322.

27. *Labour Woman*, 1 March 1924, pp. 34, 46. The other signatories were Marjorie Allen, Ruth Dalton, Joan Malleson, and Mrs. L'Estrange Malone.

28. Ibid., 1 June 1924, p. 85.

29. Ibid., pp. 96–97.

30. D. Russell to Stopes, 31 March, 4, 8 April 1924, Stopes Papers, Add. MSS. 58556.

31. *New Generation*, July 1924, p. 89.

32. *Birth Control News*, July 1924, pp. 2, 4.

33. *New Generation*, August 1923, p. 91; May 1924, p. 50.

34. Russell, *Tamarisk Tree*, p. 170; see also *Socialist Review*, September 1924, p. 62.

35. Ibid., p. 59; see also Campbell, *Maternal Mortality*.

36. Witcop to Sanger, June or July 1924, Sanger Papers, Carton 21.

37. *New Generation*, August 1924, p. 86; September 1924, pp. 97–98; see also *Public Health*, September 1924, p. 303.

38. Stopes to Roe, 15 August 1924, Stopes Papers, Add. MSS. 58458.

39. *Westminster Gazette*, 7 June 1924; see also *Public Health*, July 1924, pp. 264–65.

40. Birth control advocates were sent to various political meetings with the express purpose of questioning candidates about their position. See *New Generation*, December 1924, pp. 143–44.

41. Ibid., June 1924, p. 65; September 1924, p. 104; November 1924, pp.

109–10; December 1924, p. 144.

42. "Report of the National Conference of Labour Women," *Labour Woman*, 1 July 1925, p. 123; see also *New Generation*, August 1925, p. 87.

43. *Parl. Debates* (Commons), 5th ser., 11 June 1924, 184:2213–14.

44. Ibid., 18 June 1925, 185:783.

45. Ibid., 6 August 1925, 187:1556.

46. See J. Chance to Sanger, 13 May 1925, Sanger Papers, Carton 21, for plans; see also *New Generation*, July 1925, p. 75; November 1925, p. 123.

47. *Parl. Debates* (Commons), 5th ser., 23 June 1925, 185:1292; 19 November 1925, 188:611.

48. E. Russell to Stopes, ? May 1925, Stopes Papers, Add. MSS. 58556.

49. *New Generation*, October 1925, p. 116; see also *Nation and the Athenaeum*, 15 August 1925, pp. 587–88.

50. *Birth Control News*, May 1927, p. 4; *New Generation*, July 1927, p. 62.

51. *Report of the . . . Conference of the Labour Party* (1925), p. 44.

52. *New Generation*, December 1925, pp. 133, 136.

53. *Parl. Debates* (Commons), 5th ser., 9 February 1926, 191:849–53.

54. Ibid., pp. 854–56.

55. See *Socialist Review*, April 1926; *New Generation*, April 1926, pp. 40–42, for a list of protests.

56. Ibid., March 1926, p. 26.

57. Russell, *Tamarisk Tree*, p. 183.

58. *New Generation*, April 1926, pp. 40–42. Even Marion Phillips was offended by Barr's views and the brief amount of time allowed for debate. See *Labour Woman*, March 1926, p. 38.

59. *New Generation*, February 1926, p. 17.

60. Ibid., March 1926, p. 26.

61. Ibid., May 1926, p. 52.

62. *Parl. Debates* (Lords), 5th ser., 28 April 1926, 63:995.

63. *New Generation*, August 1925, p. 88.

64. *Parl. Debates* (Lords), 5th ser., 28 April 1926, 63:996–1007.

65. Ibid., pp. 1007–11.

66. Ibid., pp. 1042–46.

67. Ibid., pp. 1016–26.

68. Pethick Lawrence to Sanger, 3 May 1926, Sanger Papers, Carton 21.

69. *New Generation*, May 1926, p. 52; see also E. Russell to Stopes, 10 May 1926, Stopes Papers, Add. MSS. 58556.

70. *Birth Control News*, June 1926, p. 1.

71. See Stopes to R. Garrett, 10 June 1926, Stopes Papers, Add. MSS. 58569.

72. *New Generation*, June 1923, pp. 65, 69; August 1925, p. 86; September 1925, p. 98; see also *Birth Control News*, December 1926, p. 2.

73. A. Brown to Stopes, 19 January 1927, Stopes Papers, Add. MSS. 58570.

74. Ministry of Health to Surrey County, 25 June 1926, ibid., Add. MSS. 58597.

75. Stopes to A. Brown, 11 February 1927, ibid., Add. MSS. 58570.

76. *Parl. Debates* (Commons), 5th ser., 12 May 1927, 206:568.

77. *New Generation*, September 1926, pp. 85, 88.

78. "Resolutions for the Twenty-Sixth Annual Conference," in *Report of the . . . Conference of the Labour Party* (1926), p. 39.

79. Ibid., pp. 204–5.

80. Ibid., pp. 32–33, 205–6.

81. Ibid., pp. 201–5.

82. Ibid., p. 207. The vote was 1,656,000 to 1,620,000.

83. *Labour Woman,* June 1927, p. 82; see also *Report of the . . . Conference of the Labour Party* (1927), p. 54.

84. Ibid., p. 16.

85. Ibid., pp. 233–34.

86. Ibid., pp. 230–31.

87. Ibid., pp. 232–33.

88. Ibid., p. 234.

89. *New Generation,* June 1928, p. 63.

90. D. Russell to Stopes, 2 October 1929, Stopes Papers, Add. MSS. 58556; see also *Labour Woman,* October 1924, p. 165; October 1926, p. 151; November 1926, p. 168. In 1929 Stopes, disguised as a "working woman," attended a meeting in Dorchester in which Dr. Phillips was the principal speaker. After challenging Phillips's position on birth control and angering the speaker, Stopes dramatically revealed her true identity to the astonished assembly.

91. *Parl. Debates* (Commons), 5th ser., 15 May 1928, 217:962–89.

92. Ibid., p. 969.

93. *New Generation,* April 1923, p. 42.

94. Marchant, *Birth-Rate and Empire,* pp. 179–83.

95. *Neo-Malthusian and Birth Control Conference,* pp. 40–43; *New Generation,* November 1922, p. 3.

96. Stopes to Kerslake, 14 November 1923, Stopes Papers, Add. MSS. 58567.

97. See Liddington and Norris, *One Hand Tied Behind Us,* for an example of working-class activity in Manchester; see also E. S. Pankhurst, *The Suffragette Movement.*

98. Breed and How-Martyn, *Birth Control Movement,* pp. 27–28; see also *New Generation,* November 1929, p. 122.

99. Secretary of National Union to Roe, 18 February 1930; Secretary of National Union to Stopes 3, 10 July 1930, Stopes Papers, Add. MSS. 58597.

100. *New Generation,* January 1926, p. 1.

101. Ibid., March 1928, p. 26.

102. Ibid., October 1929, p. 114.

103. Ibid., April 1930, pp. 38, 46.

104. Ibid., August 1925, p. 88.

105. Fryer, *Birth Controllers,* pp. 255–56.

106. Witcop to Sanger, 12 May, 1 July 1925, Sanger Papers, Carton 21.

107. Ibid., 27 April 1926, ibid., Sanger to Witcop, 22 May 1926; Witcop to Sanger, 14 November 1928, ibid.

108. *New Generation,* October 1924, p. 111.

109. See *Eugenics Review* 20, no. 3 (1928): 157–65. For more complete results

see Himes and Himes, "Birth Control for the British Working Classes," pp. 578–617.

110. See Florence, *Birth Control on Trial*.

111. SPBCC, *Birth Control and Public Health*.

112. Himes and Himes, "Birth Control for the British Working Classes," p. 580.

Chapter 14

1. *New Generation*, June 1923, pp. 70–71.

2. Ibid., October 1922, p. 3.

3. *Birth Control News*, October 1923, pp. 1–2, 4.

4. *Times*, 15 February 1923; *New Generation*, January 1923, p. 8; March 1923, p. 36; July 1923, p. 79.

5. *New Generation*, November 1925, p. 124; see also *Times*, 13 October 1925.

6. Bowley and Hogg, *Has Poverty Diminished?*; *New Generation*, February 1926, p. 14.

7. *New Generation*, April 1926, p. 38; June–July, p. 64; see Parl. Papers, *Report of the Royal Commission on the Coal Industry* (1926), Cmd. 2600.

8. G. Evans to Stopes, 26 July 1927, Stopes Papers, Add. MSS. 58621.

9. The arsonist served two months in prison. See *Birth Control News*, January 1929, pp. 1, 4; see also Stopes to *Daily Telegraph*, 21 November 1928, Stopes Papers, Add. MSS. 58597.

10. H. G. Selfridge to Stopes, 24 February 1927, Stopes Papers, Add. MSS. 58621.

11. See *New Generation*, May 1928, p. 50; May 1929, p. 53; July 1929, p. 73. The mission was financed by Mrs. G. A. Gaskell, an early Malthusian League member.

12. *New Generation*, August 1928, p. 86; September 1928, p. 98; October 1928, p. 110; April 1929, p. 38.

13. Ibid., February 1929, pp. 13–14; March 1929, pp. 34.

14. Ibid., April 1929, p. 42; May 1929, pp. 54–55.

15. Ibid., December 1928, p. 140; July 1929, pp. 77–78.

16. Ibid., April 1929, p. 40.

17. Ibid., November 1929, p. 125. Breed and How-Martyn, *Birth Control Movement*, p. 31.

18. *New Generation*, August 1929, p. 88.

19. Ibid., November 1929, p. 125.

20. *Parl. Debates* (Commons), 5th ser., 31 October 1929, 231:342.

21. Hubback to Wilkinson, 4 December 1929, Ministry of Health Papers, PRO/MH 55/289.

22. A. S. Laurance to Wilkinson, 19 December 1929, ibid.

23. Stopes to Arthur Greenwood, 9 November 1929, Stopes Papers, Add. MSS. 58597. Greenwood replied that no changes in the Ministry's position were con-

templated. See Greenwood to Stopes, 14 November 1929, ibid.

24. Medical Officer of Health Sheffield to Stopes, 24 January 1930, ibid., Add. MSS. 58570.

25. See *Bootle Times*, January–February 1920; see also *New Generation*, March 1930, pp. 29–30.

26. *Parl. Debates* (Commons), 5th ser., 13 February 1930, 235:605–6 and 20 February 1930, 235:1590.

27. *Report of Conference on the Giving of Information on Birth Control*, p. 32.

28. J. Halford, Secretary of the National Association for the Prevention of Infant Mortality, to Minister of Health, n.d., 1930, PRO/MH 55/289.

29. W.A.R. to A. Greenwood, 8 May 1930; Greenwood to W.A.R., 13 May 1930, ibid.

30. J. Campbell to A. B. MacLachan, ibid.

31. The Memorandum CP 201 was sent to the cabinet on 6 June and approved 2 July, PRO/MH 55/289.

32. See comments on letter from the Labour party to A. Greenwood, 29 August 1930, ibid.

33. M H Memorandum, 8, 12 September 1930, ibid.

34. *Birth Control News*, September 1930, p. 72.

35. Fryer, *Birth Controllers*, p. 263.

36. Leathard, *The Fight for Family Planning*, pp. 44–46; see also Stopes Papers, 26 June 1930, Add. MSS. 58643.

37. Hall, *Passionate Crusader*, p. 268.

38. See NBCC, "Summary of Meeting," 20 November 1930, Stopes Papers, Add. MSS. 58643.

39. Independent Labour party to MH, 9 February 1931, PRO/MH 55/289; see also MH Memorandum, 17 February 1931.

40. Ibid., MH Minutes, 18 February 1931. The memorandum was sent the following month.

41. *New Generation*, November 1930, p. 121.

42. See, for example, J. Patterson, M.D., to Stopes, 26 July 1926, Stopes Papers, Add. MSS. 58597.

43. See Superintendent of South Clerkenwell Maternity and Child Welfare Centre to Stopes, 15 October 1925, ibid., Add. MSS. 58596.

44. *Public Health*, March 1924, p. 129.

45. Ibid., November 1922, p. 37; April 1923, pp. 185–88; July 1923, pp. 291–92.

46. Ibid., September 1923, p. 322; July 1923, p. 295.

47. *British Medical Journal*, 10 July 1926, p. 73.

48. *Parl. Debates* (Commons), 5th ser., 29 January 1929, 224:781; 30 January 1930, 234:1174.

49. *Lancet*, 28 May 1927, p. 1141.

50. Ibid., 2 August 1930.

51. The Ministry was surprised by the lack of comment in medical publications. See MH Memorandum, 8 September 1930, 17 February 1931, PRO/MH 55/289.

52. *Public Health*, April 1931, pp. 193–94.

53. Ibid.

54. *New Generation*, November 1930, p. 121.

55. Ibid., p. 124. British medical schools, in general, yielded slowly. The first to provide a regular course was the British Post-Graduate Medical School in 1936. See Leathard, *The Fight for Family Planning*, p. 58.

56. *Lancet*, 22 November 1930, p. 1165.

57. *Practitioner*, September 1933, p. 255. The journal was now edited by a strong advocate of birth control, Sir Humphrey Rolleston.

58. Fryer, *Birth Controllers*, p. 326, n. 73.

59. *British Medical Journal*, 12 September 1931, p. 516.

60. Florence, *Progress Report on Birth Control*, pp. 26–29.

61. Ibid.; see MH Circular 1408 (1934).

62. See Family Planning Association, *Report . . . 1939*; Leathard, *The Fight for Family Planning*, p. 66.

63. *Birth Control News*, September 1930, p. 73.

64. E. Russell to Stopes, 15 October 1930, Stopes Papers, Add. MSS. 58556.

65. Glass, "Western Europe," p. 189, n. 16.

66. Parl. Papers, *Report of the Royal Commission on Population*, Cmd. 7695, p. 194.

67. Ibid., pp. 158–59.

68. Ibid., pp. 193–94.

69. Ledbetter, *Malthusian League*, pp. 238–40.

70. Hall, *Passionate Crusader*, p. 296.

71. See Stopes to F. D. Saner, M.D., 3 June 1930, Stopes Papers, Add. MSS. 58570. Starting in 1929 the *Birth Control News* began to publish much more about mental defectives and sterilization, frequently citing the experience of various American states. In these issues Stopes reflected the enhanced interest of the Eugenics Society in negative eugenics and often devoted several pages of an issue to advantages of sterilization for the racially undesirable. See, for example, *Birth Control News*, July 1929, pp. 42–45; see also Searle, "Eugenics and Politics in Britain in the 1930s."

72. Glass, "Western Europe," p. 190, n. 18.

73. For a survey of developments since World War II see Leathard, *The Fight for Family Planning*, chaps. 10–23.

Bibliography

Primary Sources

MANUSCRIPT COLLECTIONS

Cambridge
Kings College Library
  John Maynard Keynes Papers

Champaign-Urbana, Illinois
University of Illinois Library
  H. G. Wells Archives

London
British Library
  William Boyd Carpenter Papers
  George Bernard Shaw Papers
  Marie Stopes Papers
British Library of Political and
  Economic Science
  C. V. Drysdale Papers
Eugenics Society Library
  Reports, Council Minute Books,
  Correspondence. The society's corre-
  spondence since 1920 has recently
  been deposited in the Wellcome In-
  stitute of the History of Medicine in
  London. The Eugenics Education

Society became the Eugenics Society
  in 1926.
National Maritime Museum (Green-
  wich)
  Arnold White Papers
Public Record Office
  Ministry of Health Papers
University College
  Francis Galton Archives
  Karl Pearson Papers

New Haven, Connecticut
Stirling Library, Yale University
  Havelock Ellis Papers

Philadelphia, Pennsylvania
Library of the American Philosophical
  Society
  Charles B. Davenport Papers

Washington, D.C.
Library of Congress
  Margaret Sanger Papers

GOVERNMENT DOCUMENTS AND OFFICIAL PUBLICATIONS

Parliamentary Debates
Great Britain (Hansard).
  Parliamentary Debates
  3d series, 1856–91

4th series, 1892–1908.
5th series, 1909–30.

Parliamentary Papers

Annual Reports of the Registrar General (England and Wales).

Census of England and Wales, 1911: Fertility of Marriage. Part 1. Cd. 8678 (1917). Part 2. *Report*. Cd. 8491 (1923).

Census of Great Britain, 1851. Religious Worship in England and Wales. London, 1854.

Glass, D. V., and Grebenik, E. *The Trend and Pattern of Fertility in Great Britain: A Report on the Family Census of 1946*. Part 1. Papers of the Royal Commission on Population, vol. 6. London, 1954.

Legge, James. *49th Report of the Inspector of Reformatory and Industrial Schools*. London, 1900.

Lewis-Fanning, E. *Report on an Enquiry into Family Limitation and Its Influence on Human Fertility during the Past Fifty Years*. Papers of the Royal Commission on Population, vol. 1. London, 1949.

Memorandum by the Director-General, Army Medical Service, on the Physical Unfitness of Men Offering Themselves for Enlistment in the Army. Cd. 1501 (1903).

Ministry of National Service, 1917–19. *Report upon the Physical Examination of Men of Military Age by National Service Medical Boards from November 1, 1917– October 31, 1918*. Cmd. 504 (1920).

Report of the Inspector General of Recruiting. Cd. 1501 (1903).

Report of the Inter-Departmental Committee on Physical Deterioration. Cd. 2175, 2210, 2186 (1904).

Report of the Royal Commission on Alien Immigration with Minutes of Evidence and Appendix. Cd. 1741–43 (1903).

Report of the Royal Commission on the Care and Control of the Feeble Minded. Cd. 4202 (1908).

Report of the Royal Commission on the Coal Industry. Cmd. 2600 (1926).

Report of the Royal Commission on Divorce and Matrimonial Causes. Cd. 6478–82 (1912–13).

Report of the Royal Commission on Physical Training (Scotland). Cd. 1507, 1508 (1903).

Report of the Royal Commission on Population. Cmd. 7695 (1949). *Papers*. 6 vols. 1950–54.

Report of the Royal Commission on Venereal Diseases. Cd. 8189, 8190 (1916).

NONGOVERNMENT OFFICIAL PUBLICATIONS

Church of England. *The Chronicle of Convocation: Being a Record of the Proceedings for the Convocation of Canterbury for the Session 1916*. London, 1917.

General Medical Council. *Minutes of the General Medical Council, of Its Executive and Dental Committees, and of Its Three Branch Councils, for the Year 1887*. Vol. 24. London, 1888.

In the High Court of Justice, Queen's Bench Division. June 18, 1877. The Queen v. Charles Bradlaugh and Annie Besant. 2d ed. London, 1888.

———. *February 1, 1878. The Queen. v. Edward Truelove, for Publishing the Hon.*

Robert Dale Owen's Moral Physiology and a Pamphlet, Entitled 'Individual, Family and National Poverty.' London, 1878.

National Birth-Rate Commission. *Problems of Population and Parenthood, Being the Second Report of and the Chief Evidence Taken by the National Birth-Rate Commission, 1918–1920.* New York, 1920.

National Council of Public Morals. *The Declining Birth-Rate, Its Causes and Effects, Being the Report of and the Chief Evidence Taken by the National Birth-Rate Commission, Instituted, with Official Recognition, by the National Council of Public Morals–for the Promotion of Race Regeneration–Spiritual, Moral, and Physical.* Edited by James Marchant. London, 1916.

_____. *The Ethics of Birth Control, Being the Report of the Special Committee Appointed by the National Council of Public Morals in Connection with the Investigations of the National Birth-Rate Commission.* London, 1925.

_____. *Medical Aspects of Contraception, Being the Report of the Medical Committee Appointed by the National Council of Public Morals in Connection with the Investigations of the National Birth-Rate Commission.* London, 1927.

REPORTS OF CONFERENCES

Lambeth Conference, 1908. *Conference of Bishops of the Anglican Communion: Holden at Lambeth Palace, July 27 to August 5, 1908. Encyclical Letter from the Bishops, with the Resolutions and Reports.* London, 1908.

Lambeth Conference, 1920. *Conference of Bishops of the Anglican Communion: Holden at Lambeth Palace, July 5 to August 7, 1920. Encyclical Letter from the Bishops, with the Resolutions and Reports.* London, 1920.

Lambeth Conference, 1930. *Encyclical Letter from the Bishops with Resolutions and Reports.* London, 1930.

Lambeth Conference, 1958. *The Encyclical Letter from the Bishops Together with the Resolutions and Reports.* London, 1930.

Report of the Conference on the Giving of Information on Birth Control by Public Health Authorities, Friday, April 4th, 1930. London, 1930.

Report of the Fifth International Neo-Malthusian and Birth Control Conference, London, 11–14 July 1922. London, 1922.

Report of the Proceedings of the National Conference on Infantile Mortality, Held at the Caxton Hall, Westminster, on the 23rd, 24th, and 25th March, 1908. Westminster, 1908.

Report of the Proceedings of the Sixth International Neo-Malthusian and Birth Control Conference. New York, 1926.

Report of the Twenty-Fifth Annual Conference of the Labour Party, Liverpool, 1925. London, 1925.

Report of the Twenty-Sixth Annual Conference of the Labour Party, Margate, 1926. London, 1926.

Report of the Twenty-Seventh Annual Conference of the Labour Party Held in Blackpool, 1927. London, 1927.

JOURNALS, PERIODICALS, NEWSPAPERS

Anti-Suffrage Review.
The Army Quarterly.
Army Review.
Athenaeum.
The Beehive.
Biometrika.
Birth Control News.
Birth Control Review.
Blackwood's Edinburgh Magazine.
The Bootle Times.
Britannia.
British Friend.
British Medical Journal.
British Quarterly Review.
British Weekly.
Brotherhood.
Bulletin de l'Institute International de Statistique.
Cambridge Magazine.
Cassell's Saturday Journal.
The Catholic Crusader—A Challenge to Capitalism.
Catholic News.
Catholic Times.
Chamber's Journal.
Charity Organization Society Review.
The Child.
Child-Study: The Journal of the Child Study Association.
Christian Commonwealth.
Christian Socialist.
Church Family Newspaper.
Church Quarterly Review.
Church Reformer.
Church Socialist.
Church Socialist Quarterly.
Church Times.
The Clarion.
Common Cause.
The Commonwealth: A Socialist Review.
Congregational Review.
Conservative and Unionist Women's Franchise Review.
The Contemporary Review.

The Cornhill Magazine.
Daily Chronicle.
The Daily Herald.
The Daily Mail.
The Daily Mirror.
Dublin Review.
Ecclesiastical Gazette.
The Economic Review.
The Edinburgh Review.
The English Churchman.
The Englishwoman.
Eugenics Review.
The Evening Standard.
Fabian Journal.
The Fortnightly Review.
Fraser's Magazine.
Freewoman.
Friend.
Friend's Quarterly Examiner.
Good Words.
The Guardian.
Guy's Hospital Gazette.
Hibbert Journal.
Hospital.
Hospital Social Service.
The Humanitarian.
Independent Labour Party [I.L.P.] *News.*
The Independent.
John Bull.
Journal of the Anthropological Institute of Great Britain and Ireland.
Journal of the Ethnological Society.
Journal of Hygiene.
Journal of the Royal Statistical Society.
Journal of the Royal United Services Institute.
Journal of Science.
Journal of State Medicine.
Jus Suffragii.
Justice.
Labour Leader.
Labour Record.
The Labour Woman: A Monthly Journal for Working Women.

Lancet.
Lansbury's Labour Weekly.
The London Magazine.
London Quarterly Review.
Macmillan's Magazine.
The Malthusian.
Medical Officer.
The Medical Press and Circular.
The Medical Times and Gazette.
Methodist Recorder.
The Methodist Times.
Methodist Weekly.
The Miner.
Modern Churchman.
The Month.
The Morning Post.
National and English Review.
The National Church.
National Health.
The National Reformer.
The National Review.
Nature.
New Church Magazine.
The New Generation: For Rational Birth Control.
The New Leader.
The New Statesman.
The Nineteenth Century (changed to *The Nineteenth Century and After* in 1901).
Noncomformist.
Obstetric Journal.
Our Corner.

Pall Mall Gazette.
Pearson's Magazine.
The Practitioner.
Prevention: An Illustrated Quarterly Journal Devoted to Public Morals.
Primitive Methodist Magazine.
Proceedings of the British Association for the Advancement of Science.
Public Health.
Review of Reviews.
Royal Army Service Corps Quarterly.
The Saturday Review.
The Scout.
Socialist Review.
The Sociological Review.
The Spectator.
Suffragette.
The Tablet.
Time and Tide.
The Times.
Transactions of the Medico-Legal Society.
Truth.
United Services Magazine.
The Universe.
The Vote.
Votes For Women.
War Cry.
The Weekly Times and Echo.
The Westminster Gazette.
The Westminster Review.
Woman's Leader and Common Cause.
The Woman Rebel.

BOOKS AND PAMPHLETS

"A Doctor of Medicine." *The State Remedy for Poverty*. London, 1904.
Aldred, Guy. *No Traitor's Gate: The Life and Times of Guy Aldred*. Glasgow, 1955.
Allbutt, Henry Arthur. *The Wife's Handbook: How a Woman Should Order Herself during Pregnancy, in the Lying-In Room, and After Delivery, With Hints on the Management of the Baby, and on Other Matters of Importance Necessary to Be Known by Married Women*. 2d ed. London, 1886.
Ansell, Charles. *On the Rate of Mortality at Early Periods of Life . . . and Other Statistics of Families in the Upper and Professional Classes*. London, 1874.
Aveling, Edward B. *Darwinism and Small Families*. London, 1882.

————, and Aveling, Eleanor Marx. *The Woman Question*. London, 1886.

Balfour, Arthur James. "Decadence." In *A Collection of the More Important and Interesting Passages in His Non-Political Writings, Speeches, and Addresses, 1879–1912*. London, 1912.

Barr, Sir James. *The Aim and Scope of Eugenics*. Edinburgh, 1911.

Barrett, Lady Florence E. *Conception Control and Its Effects on the Individual and the Nation*. London, 1922.

Barry, William. *Literature: The Word of Life or of Death*. London, 1912.

Bateson, William. *Biological Fact and the Structure of Society: The Herbert Spencer Lecture, Wed. Feb. 28, 1912*. Oxford, 1912.

Beale, Dr. G. Courtenay. *Wise Wedlock: The Complete Treatise on Birth Control and Marriage*. London, 1924.

Beale, Octavius Charles. *Racial Decay: A Compilation of Evidence from World Sources*. London, 1911.

Bertillon, Jacques. *Essai de statistique comparée du surpeuplement des habitations à Paris et dans les grandes capitales européenes*. 2d ed. Paris, 1895.

Bertillon, Louis Adolphe. *Le Démographie figureé de la France mortalité selon l'âge, le sexe, l'etat-civil, en chaque département et pour la France entière comparée aux pays ètrangers*. Paris, 1874.

Besant, Annie. *An Autobiography*. London, 1893.

————. *Essays, Political and Social*. London, 1881.

————. *The Law of Population: Its Consequences and Its Bearing upon Human Conduct and Morals*. London, 1881.

————. *The Social Aspects of Malthusianism*. Malthusian Tracts no. 10. London, 1881.

Beveridge, William H. *Unemployment: A Problem of Industry*. Rev. ed. London, 1931.

Billington-Greig, Teresa. *Commonsense on the Population Question: The Substance of a Lecture Delivered to the Glasgow Clarion Scouts on December 13, 1914*. Westminster, 1914.

————. *The Militant Suffrage Movement*. London, 1911.

Birth Control and Public Health: A Report on Ten Years Work of the Society for the Provision of Birth Control Clinics. London, 1932.

Blacker, C. P. *Birth Control and the State: A Plea and a Forecast*. London, 1926.

Blackwell, Elizabeth. *Medical Sociology*. London, 1902.

Blatchford, Robert. *Merrie England*. London, 1894.

Blunt, Wilfred Scawen. *My Diaries, Being a Personal Narrative of Events, 1888–1914*. 2 vols. New York, 1921.

Bond, C. J. *Natural Capacity in Relation to Vocation*. London, 1921.

————. *Racial Decay*. London, 1930.

Booth, Charles. *Life and Labour of the People in London*. 17 vols. London, 1902–4.

Bowley, Arthur L., and Hogg, Margaret H. *Has Poverty Diminished? A Sequel to "Livelihood and Poverty."* London, 1925.

Box, Muriel, ed. *The Trial of Marie Stopes*. London, 1967.

Breed, Ruth, and How-Martyn, Edith. *The Birth Control Movement in England*. London, 1930.

Brittain, Vera. *Testament of Youth: An Autobiographical Study of the Years 1900–1925.* New York, 1933.

Campbell, Janet. *Memorandum on Maternal Mortality.* London, 1924.

———. *The Protection of Motherhood.* London, 1927.

Cantlie, James. *Degeneration amongst Londoners.* Parkes Museum of Hygiene Lecture. London, 1885.

———. *Physical Efficiency: A Review of the Deleterious Effects of Town Life upon the Population of Britain, with Suggestions for Their Arrest.* London, 1906.

Carr-Saunders, A. M. *Eugenics.* New York, 1926.

———. *Population.* Oxford, 1925.

"Catholic Woman Doctor, A." *A City Full of Girls and Boys.* London, 1923.

Chesser, Elizabeth S. *Woman, Marriage, and Motherhood.* London, 1913.

Clapperton, Jane Hume. *Scientific Meliorism and the Evolution of Happiness.* London, 1885.

———. *A Vision of the Future Based on the Application of Ethical Principles.* London, 1904.

Clark, George W. *Race Suicide: England's Peril.* London, 1917.

Clayton, I. M. *The Shadow on the Universe or the Physical Results of War.* London, 1915.

Cox, Harold. *The Problem of Population.* London, 1922.

Crackanthorpe, Montague. *Population and Progress.* London, 1907.

Crambe, John A. *Reflections on the Origin and Destiny of Imperial Britain.* London, 1900.

D'Arcy, Charles. *A Short Study of Ethics.* 2d ed. London, 1901.

Darwin, Charles. *The Descent of Man and Selection in Relation to Sex.* London, 1871.

———. *The Origins of Species by Means of Natural Selection or the Preservation of Favored Races in the Struggle for Life.* London, 1859.

———. *The Variation of Animals and Plants under Domestication.* 2 vols. New York, 1896.

Darwin, Leonard. *The Case for Eugenic Reform.* London, 1926.

———. *Evolution and Eugenics: The Stevenson Lecture, Bedford College for Women, University of London, Oct. 25, 1927.* London, 1928.

———. *First Steps towards Eugenic Reform.* London, 1912.

———. *Organic Evolution: Outstanding Difficulties and Possible Explanations.* Cambridge, 1921.

———. *What Is Eugenics?* London, 1928.

David, the Rt. Revd. A. A., and Furse, the Rt. Revd. M. B. *Marriage and Birth Control.* London, 1930.

Dawson of Penn. *Love-Marriage-Birth Control.* London, 1922.

Dennett, Mary Ware. *Birth Control Laws.* New York, 1926.

Doubleday, Thomas. *True Law of Population, Shewn to be Connected with the Food of the People.* London, 1842.

Drysdale, Bessie. *Labour Troubles and Birth Control.* London, 1920.

———. *War Babies.* [London, 1915].

Drysdale, Charles Robert. *The Cause of Poverty.* London, 1891.

———. *Large Families and Over-Population.* London, 1879.

————. *The Population Question According to Malthus and Mill.* London, 1892.

————, ed. *Clerical Opinions on the Population Question.* London, 1904.

————, ed. *Medical Opinions on the Population Question.* London, 1901.

Drysdale, Charles Vickery. *The Empire and the Birth Rate: A Paper Read before the Royal Colonial Institute, March 24, 1914.* London, 1914.

————. *Neo-Malthusianism and Eugenics.* London, 1922.

————. *The Small Family System: Is It Injurious or Immoral?* Rev. and enl. ed. New York, 1917.

————. *Small or Large Families: Birth Control from the Moral, Racial, and Eugenic Standpoint.* New York, 1917.

Drysdale, George. *The Elements of Social Science; Or, Physical, Sexual, and Natural Religion: An Exposition of the True Cause and Only Cure of the Three Primary Social Evils: Poverty, Prostitution, and Celibacy.* 2d ed. London, 1859.

Dunlap, K. *Personal Beauty and Racial Betterment.* London, 1920.

Elderton, Ethel M. *The Relative Strength of Nurture and Nature.* Eugenics Laboratory Lecture Series 3. 2d ed. Cambridge, 1915.

————. *Report on the English Birth Rate.* Part 1. *England North of the Humber.* Eugenics Laboratory Memoirs 19 and 20. Cambridge, 1914.

————, and Pearson, Karl. *A First Study of the Influence of Parental Alcoholism on the Physique and Ability of the Offspring.* Eugenics Laboratory Memoir 10. London, 1910.

————; Barrington, Amy; Jones, H. Gertrude; Laski, Harold; and Pearson, Karl. *On the Correlation of Fertility with Social Value: A Cooperative Study.* Eugenics Laboratory Memoir 18. London, 1913.

Ellis, Havelock. *Essays in War-Time: Further Studies in the Task of Social Hygiene.* Boston and New York, 1917.

————. *The Problem of Race Regeneration.* London, 1911.

————. *Studies in the Psychology of Sex.* 2 vols. New York, 1940.

————. *The Task of Social Hygiene.* Boston and New York, 1912.

Eugenics Education Society. *Problems in Eugenics: Papers Communicated to the First International Eugenics Congress and Report of Proceedings. Held at the University of London, July 24th to 30th, 1912.* 2 vols. London, 1912–13.

Everitt, H. *The Falling Birth Rate and Its Significance.* London, 1909.

Fallon, V. *Eugenics.* London, 1923.

Family Planning Association. *Report of the Family Planning Association, 1939.* London, 1939.

Fawcett, Millicent G. *What I Remember.* London, 1924.

————. *Women's Suffrage.* London and Edinburgh, 1911.

————. *The Women's Victory and After.* London, 1920.

Finch, A. Elley. *Malthusiana: Illustrations of the Influence of Nature's Law of the Increase of Human Life Discovered and Verified by Malthus.* London, 1904.

Florence, Lella Secor. *Birth Control on Trial.* London, 1930.

Galton, Francis. *English Men of Science: Their Nature and Nurture.* London, 1874.

————. *Hereditary Genius: An Inquiry into Its Laws and Consequences.* New York, 1871.

————. *Inquiries into Human Faculty and Its Development.* 2d ed. London, 1907.

_____. *Memories of My Life.* 3d ed. London, 1909.

_____. *Natural Inheritance.* London, 1889.

Gates, R. Ruggles. *Heredity and Eugenics.* London, 1923.

George, Henry. *Progress and Poverty: An Inquiry into the Cause of Industrial Depressions and of the Increase of Want with Increase of Wealth: The remedy.* London, 1884.

Gerrard. Thomas J. *The Church and Eugenics.* London, 1912.

Gorst, John Eldon. *Education and Race Regeneration.* London, 1913.

Greg, William Rathbone. *Enigmas of Life.* London, 1872.

Greville, Frances E., Countess of Warwick. *A Nation's Youth: Physical Deterioration, Its Causes and Some Remedies.* London, 1906.

Haire, Norman. *Hygienic Methods of Family Limitation.* London, 1922.

_____, ed. *Some More Medical Views on Birth Control.* London, 1928.

Harben, Henry D. *The Endowment of Motherhood.* Fabian Society Tract 149. London, 1910.

Hart, Heber. *Woman Suffrage: A National Danger.* London, 1912.

Haycraft, John Berry. *Darwinism and Race Progress.* London, 1895.

Heitland, W. E. *Behind and Before: Two Essays on the Relation of History, Politics, and Eugenist Warnings.* Cambridge, 1924.

Heron, David. *A First Study of the Inheritance of the Insane Diathesis.* Eugenics Laboratory Memoirs 2. London, 1907.

_____. *The Influence of Defective Physique and Unfavourable Home Environment on the Intelligence of School Children, Being a Statistical Examination of the London County Council Pioneer School Survey.* Eugenics Laboratory Memoirs 8. London, 1910.

_____. *On the Relations of Fertility in Man to Social Status, and on the Changes in This Relation That Have Taken Place during the Last Fifty Years.* Drapers Company Research Memoirs 1. London, 1906.

Hobson, John A. *Free Thought in the Social Sciences.* London, 1926.

Holmes, S. J. *Studies in Evolution and Eugenics.* London, 1923.

_____. *The Trend of the Race: A Study of Present Tendencies in the Biological Development of Civilized Mankind.* London, 1921.

Holyoake, Austin. *Large or Small Families? On Which Side Lies the Balance of Comfort?* London, 1870.

Horsley, J. W. *How Criminals Are Made and Prevented.* London, 1912.

Houghton, Robert F. *National Ideals and Race Regeneration.* London, 1912.

Howe, Mark DeWolfe, ed. *Holmes-Laski Letters: The Correspondence of Mr. Justice Holmes and Harold J. Laski, 1916–1935.* 2 vols. Cambridge, 1953.

Hubbard, A. J. *The Fate of Empires, Being an Inquiry into the Stability of Civilization.* London, 1913.

Huxley, Leonard. *Progress and the Unfit.* Conway Memorial Lecture, May 27, 1926. London, 1926.

Huxley, Thomas. *Evolution and Ethics and Other Essays.* New York, 1896.

Hyndman, Henry M. *The Records of an Adventurous Life.* New York, 1911.

Inge, William Ralph. *Diary of a Dean: St. Paul's, 1911–1934.* London, 1949.

_____. *Outspoken Essays.* London, 1919. 2d series. London, 1922.

————. *Vale*. London, 1934.

Jackson, Holbrook. *The Eighteen-Nineties*. London, 1913.

Jordan, David Starr. *The Human Harvest*. London, 1907.

Kelynack, T. N., ed. *Human Derelicts: Medico-Sociological Studies for Teachers of Religion and Social Workers*. London, 1914.

Kenney, Annie. *Memoirs of a Militant*. London, 1924.

Kerr, Robert Bird. *Is Britain Overpopulated?* London, 1927.

Kidd, Benjamin. *Social Evolution*. 2d ed. London, 1894.

Knowlton, Charles. *Fruits of Philosophy: An Essay on the Population Question*. London, 1877.

Lankester, Ray. *Degeneration: A Chapter in Darwinism*. London, 1880.

League of National Life. *The Disastrous Influence of a Declining Birth Rate on the Life of the Nation*. London, 1929.

Lofthouse, K. L., and W. F. *Purity and Racial Health*. Epworth, 1920.

Lyttelton, Edward. *The Christian and Birth Control*. London, 1929.

McDougall, William. *National Welfare and National Decay*. London, 1921.

Malthus, Thomas Robert. *An Essay on the Principle of Population as It Affects the Future Improvement of Society*. London, 1798.

Malthusian League. *Fortieth Annual Report of the Malthusian League*. London, 1917.

————. *Hygienic Methods of Family Limitation*. London, 1913.

———— [George Standring]. The *Malthusian Handbook, Designed to Induce Married People to Limit Their Families within Their Means*. 4th ed. London, 1898.

————. *A Programme of Women's Emancipation*. London, 1905.

————. *Unemployment, Its Causes and Remedy: A Manifesto Issued by the Malthusian League*. London, 1908.

Malthusian Pamphlets. London, variously dated. Available at the British Library of Political and Economic Science, London.

March, N. H. *Towards Racial Health*. London, 1918.

Marchant, James. *Birth-Rate and Empire*. London, 1917.

————. *Cradles or Coffins?: Our Greatest National Need*. London, 1916.

————. *Social Hygienics: A New Crusade*. London, 1909.

————, ed. *The Claims of the Coming Generation*. London, 1923.

————, ed. *The Control of Parenthood*. London, 1920.

————, ed. *Medical Views on Birth Control*. London, 1926.

Masterman, C. F. G. *The Condition of England*. London, 1909.

————; Pigou, A. C.; et al. *The Heart of the Empire: Discussions of Problems of Modern City Life in England, with an Essay on Imperialism*. London, 1902.

Maurice, G. T. K. *Birth Control and Population. An Essay*. London, 1922.

[M. E. S.]. *An Englishwoman's Home*. London, 1909.

————. *Mixed Herbs: A Working Woman's Remonstrance against the Suffrage Agitation*. London, 1908.

Meyer, F. B. *Religion and Race Regeneration*. London, 1912.

Mill, John Stuart. *Principles of Political Economy*. 2 vols. London, 1848.

————. *The Subjection of Women*. London, 1869.

Millard, Charles Killick. *Population and Birth Control, Being the Presidential Address Delivered before the Leicester Literary and Philosophical Society, October 8, 1917*.

Leicester, 1917.

———. *Responsible Parenthood and Birth Control: Memorandum Respectfully Submitted for Consideration by the Archbishops and Bishops of the Anglican Communion.* London, 1920.

Miller, George Noyes. *The Strike of a Sex.* London, 1891.

Mills, Elliott. *The Decline and Fall of the British Empire.* Oxford, 1905.

Money, L. G. Chiozza, *The Peril of the White Race.* London, 1925.

More, Adelyne. *Fecundity versus Civilization: A Contribution to the Study of Over-Population as the Cause of War and the Chief Obstacle to the Emancipation of Women, with Special Reference to Germany.* London, 1916.

Morgan, Charles L. *Eugenics and Environment.* London, 1919.

Mother's Union. *Some Facts and Opinions in Reply to Dr. Killick Millard's Memorandum on Responsible Parentage and Birth Control, compiled in Support of the Mother's Union Appeal to the Members of the Lambeth Conference, 1920.* London, 1920.

Mudi-Smith, R. *The Religious Life of London.* London, 1904.

Nasmyth, George. *Social Progress and the Darwinian Theory.* London, 1916.

Newman, Francis W., and Blackwell, Elizabeth. *The Corruption Called Neo-Malthusianism.* London, 1889.

Newsholme, Arthur. *The Declining Birth-Rate: Its National and International Significance.* London, 1911.

———. *Fifty Years in Public Health: A Personal Narrative with Comments.* London, 1935.

Nisbet, John F. *Insanity of Genius and the General Inequality of Human Faculty.* London, 1891.

Nordau, Max. *Degeneration.* London, 1892.

Owen, Robert Dale. *Moral Physiology; Or, a Brief and Plain Treatise on the Population Question.* New ed. London, 1870.

"Oxoniensis." *Early Marriage and Late Parentage: The Only Solution of the Social Problem.* 1883. Reprint. London, 1906.

Pankhurst, Christabel. *The Great Scourge and How to End It.* London, 1913.

Pankhurst, E. Sylvia. *The Suffragette.* London, 1911.

Pankhurst, Emmeline. *My Own Story.* London, 1914.

Paul, Eden. *Socialism and Eugenics.* London, 1911.

———, and Paul, Cedar, eds. *Population and Birth Control: A Symposium.* New York, 1917.

Pearson, Charles H. *National Life and Character: A Forecast.* London, 1893.

Pearson, Karl. *The Academic Aspect of the Science of National Eugenics: A Lecture Delivered to Undergraduates.* Eugenics Laboratory Lecture Series 7. Cambridge, 1911.

———. *The Chances of Death and Other Studies in Evolution.* 2 vols. London, 1897.

———. *Darwinism, Medical Progress, and Eugenics: The Cavendish Lecture, 1912. An Address to the Medical Profession.* Eugenics Laboratory Lecture Series 9. Cambridge, 1912.

———. *The Ethic of Freethought and Other Addresses and Essays.* 2d ed. London, 1901.

———. *The Grammar of Science.* London, 1937.

————. *The Groundwork of Eugenics.* Eugenics Laboratory Lecture Series 2. 2d ed. Cambridge, 1912.

————. *National Life from the Standpoint of Science.* London, 1901.

————. *"Nature and Nurture—the Problem of the Future": A Presidential Address—at the Annual Meeting of the Social and Political Education League April 28, 1910.* London, 1910.

————. *On the Handicapping of the First Born.* Eugenics Laboratory Lecture Series 10. Cambridge, 1914.

————. *The Problem of Practical Eugenics.* Eugenics Laboratory Lecture Series 5. 2d ed. Cambridge, 1912.

————. *Some Recent Misinterpretations of the Problem of Nurture and Nature.* Eugenics Laboratory Lecture Series 3. Cambridge, 1915.

————, and Elderton, Ethel. *A Second Study of the Influence of Parental Alcoholism on the Physique and Ability of the Offspring, Being a Reply to Certain Medical Critics of the First Memoir and an Examination of the Rebutting Evidence Cited by Them.* Eugenics Laboratory Memoirs 13. London, 1910.

Pethick Lawrence, Emmeline. *My Part in a Changing World.* London, 1938.

Pethick Lawrence, F. W. *Fate Has Been Kind.* London, 1943.

Pell, Charles Edward. *The Law of Births and Deaths, Being a Study of the Variation in the Degree of Animal Fertility under the Influence of the Environment.* London, 1921.

Petrie, William Flinders. *Janus in Modern Life.* New York, 1907.

Ponsonby, Arthur. *The Decline of Aristocracy.* London, 1912.

The Position of Women: Actual and Ideal. London, 1911.

Pugh, Edwin. *The Great Unborn: A Dream of Tomorrow.* London, 1918.

Queen's Hall Meeting on Constructive Birth Control: Speeches and Impressions. London, 1921.

Rathbone, Eleanor F. *The Disinherited Family: A Plea for the Endowment of the Family.* London, 1924.

Rentoul, Robert Reid. *Race Culture; Or, Race Suicide? (A Plea for the Unborn).* London, 1906.

Robertson, John Mackinnon. *The Economics of Progress.* London, 1918.

————. *Overpopulation: A Lecture Delivered for the Sunday Lecture Society, London, October 27, 1889, under the title: The Law of Population: Its Meaning and Menace.* London, 1890.

————. *The Saxon and the Celt: A Study in Sociology.* London, 1897.

————. *Socialism and Malthusianism.* London, 1885.

Robinson, W. J. *Small or Large Families: Birth Control from the Moral, Racial, and Eugenic Standpoint.* New York, 1917.

Rout, Ettie. *The Morality of Birth Control.* London, 1925.

Routh, Charles Henry Felix. *The Moral and Physical Evils Likely to Follow If Practices Intended to Act as Checks to Population Be Not Strongly Discouraged and Condemned.* London, 1879.

Rowntree, B. Seebohm. *Poverty: A Study of Town Life.* London, 1901.

Royal Society of Medicine. *Proceedings of the Royal Society of Medicine.* Part 3, *Session 1921–22.*

Russell, Bertrand. *The Autobiography of Bertrand Russell, 1872–1914.* 3 vols.

Boston, 1967.

_____. *Marriage and Morals*. London, 1929.

_____, and Russell, Patricia, eds. *The Amberley Papers: The Letters and Diaries of Lord and Lady Amberley*. 2 vols. London, 1937.

Russell, Dora. *Hypatia: Or Women and Knowledge*. London, 1925.

_____. *The Tamarisk Tree: My Quest for Liberty and Love*. New York, 1975.

Saleeby, Caleb. *The Creed of Eugenics: History and Biology*. London, 1908.

_____. *The Eugenic Prospect: National and Racial*. New York, 1921.

_____. *Evolution: The Master-Key*. London, 1906.

_____. *The Methods of Race Regeneration*. New York, 1911.

_____. *Parenthood and Race Culture: An Outline of Eugenics*. New York, 1910.

_____. *The Progress of Eugenics*. London, 1914.

_____. *The Whole Armour of Man*. London, 1919.

_____. *Woman and Womanhood: A Search for Principles*. London, 1911.

Sanger, Margaret. *An Autobiography*. New York, 1938.

_____. *Family Limitation*. 2d ed. London, 1920.

_____. *My Fight for Birth Control*. New York, 1931.

Scharlieb, Mary. *Womanhood and Race Regeneration*. London, 1912.

Schiller, F. C. S. *Eugenics and Politics*. London, 1926.

Schreiner, Olive. *Woman and Labour*. London, 1911.

Schuster, Edgar. *Eugenics: A Science and an Ideal*. London, 1913.

_____. *The Promise of Youth and the Performance of Manhood, Being a Statistical Inquiry into the Question Whether Success in the Examination for the B.A. Degree Oxford Is Followed by Success in Professional Life*. Eugenics Laboratory Memoir 3. London, 1907.

_____, and Elderton, Ethel. *The Inheritance of Ability, Being a Statistical Study of the Oxford Class Lists and of the School Lists of Harrow and Charterhouse*. Eugenics Laboratory Memoir 1. London, 1907.

Shaw, George Bernard. *Man and Superman: A Comedy and a Philosophy*. New York, 1947.

Sidgwick, Mrs. Henry. *Health Statistics of Women Students of Cambridge and Oxford and of Their Sisters*. Cambridge, 1890.

_____. *University Education for Women: Presidential Address Delivered to the Education Society, Manchester University, on 21 November 1912*. Manchester, 1913.

Simpson, George. *Infantile Mortality and the Birth Rate*. Salford, c. 1911.

Smith, E. J. *Race Regeneration*. London, 1918.

Smyth, A. Watt. *Physical Deterioration: Its Causes and the Remedy*. New York, 1904.

Snowden, Ethel. *The Feminist Movement*. London, 1913.

Society for the Promotion of Birth Control Clinics. *Birth Control and Public Health*. London, 1932.

Sociological Society. *Sociological Papers*. 3 vols. London, 1905–17.

Spencer, Herbert. *The Principles of Biology*. 2 vols. London, 1864, 1867.

_____. *Social Statics: Or the Conditions Essential to Human Happiness Specified, and the First of Ten Developed*. London, 1851.

Stocks, [Lady] Mary. *My Commonplace Book*. London, 1970.

Stopes, Marie C. *Contraception (Birth Control): Its Theory, History, and Practice. A*

Manual for the Medical and Legal Professions. London, 1923.

―――. *Early Days of Birth Control*. 3d ed. London, 1923.

―――. "*The First Five Thousand*," *Being the First Report of the First Birth Control Clinic in the British Empire*, "*The Mothers' Clinic*" *for Constructive Birth Control*. London, 1925.

―――. *A Letter to Working Mothers on How to Have Healthy Children and Avoid Weakening Pregnancies*. Leatherhead, 1919.

―――. *Married Love: A New Contribution to the Solution of Sex Difficulties*. London, 1918.

―――. *A New Gospel: A Revelation of God Uniting Physiology and the Religion of Man, Delivered to the Bishops in Session at Lambeth*. London, 1920.

―――. "*Our Ostriches*": *A Play of Modern Life*. London, 1923.

―――. *Radiant Motherhood: A Book for Those Who Are Creating the Future*. London, 1920.

―――. *Roman Catholic Methods of Birth Control*. London, 1933.

―――. *Wise Parenthood: A Sequel to Married Love*. London, 1918.

―――, ed. *Mother England: A Contemporary History, Self-Written by Those Who Have Had no Historians*. London, 1929.

Strachey, Ray. *The Cause*. London, 1928.

Strahan, Samuel A. K. *Marriage and Disease: A Study of Heredity and More Important Family Degenerations*. London, 1892.

Sutherland, Halliday G. *Birth Control: A Statement of Christian Doctrine against the Neo-Malthusians*. London, 1922.

―――. *Birth Control Exposed*. London, 1925.

Swanwick, H. M. *Autobiography*. London, 1935.

Swinburne, James. *Population and the Social System*. London, 1924.

Talbot, Eugene S. *Degeneracy: Its Causes, Signs, and Results*. London, 1898.

Taylor, John W. *On the Diminishing Birth Rate: The Presidential Address Delivered before the British Gynaecological Society, February 11, 1904*. London, 1904.

Thomson, J. Arthur. *Darwinism and Human Life*. London, 1911.

Thorburn, John. *Female Education from a Physiological Point of View: A Lecture, Introductory to the Summer Course on Obstetric Medicine, 1884*. Manchester, 1884.

Ussher, R. *Neo-Malthusianism: An Enquiry*. London, 1897.

Vaughan, Bernard. *The Menace of the Empty Cradle*. London, 1917.

―――. *The Problem of Motherhood*. London, 1911.

Vickery, Alice D. *A Woman's Malthusian League*. London, c. 1905.

Wallace, Alfred Russel. *The Revolt of Democracy*. London, 1913.

Walston, Charles. *Eugenics, Civics, and Ethics*. Cambridge, 1920.

Walworth Women's Welfare Centre, *Annual Report of the Walworth Women's Welfare Centre, 1924*. London, 1924.

Watts, Charles. *A Refutation of Mr. Bradlaugh's Inaccuracies and Misrepresentations, as Contained in the National Reformer of February 11th under the Title of a So-called* "*Plain Statement of Facts*." London, 1877.

Webb, Beatrice. *My Apprenticeship*. London, 1926.

―――. *Our Partnership*. London, 1948.

Webb, Sidney. *The Decline in the Birth-Rate*. London, 1907.

Webb, Sidney, and Webb, Beatrice. *Industrial Democracy*. London, 1902.
_____. *The Letters of Sidney and Beatrice Webb, 1873–1947*. Edited by Norman MacKenzie. 3 vols. Cambridge, 1978.
Wells, H. G. *Mankind in the Making*. London, 1903.
_____. *A Modern Utopia*. London, 1905.
_____. *The New Machiavelli*. London, 1911.
_____. *Socialism and the Family*. London, 1906.
Whatham, A. E. *Neo-Malthusianism: A Defence, Being a Reply to a Paper Read before the London Junior Clergy Society, On the Population Questions and Its Modern Aspects by the Hon. and Rev. A. T. Lyttleton, M.A.*. Walthamstow, 1907.
Whetham, William Cecil Dampier. *Eugenics and Unemployment: A Lecture Delivered in Trinity College, Cambridge, January 24, 1910*. Cambridge, 1910.
_____. *Heredity and Society*. London, 1912.
_____. *The War and the Nation: A Study in Constructive Politics*. London, 1917.
Whetham, William Cecil Dampier, and Whetham, Catherine Durning. *The Family and the Nation: A Study in Natural Inheritance and Social Responsibility*. London, 1909.
_____. *An Introduction to Eugenics*. London, 1912.
White, Arnold. *The Destitute Alien in Great Britain*. London, 1892.
_____. *Efficiency and Empire*. London, 1901.
_____. *English Democracy: Its Promises and Perils*. London, 1894.
_____. *The Problems of a Great City*. London, 1887.
White, F. *Birth Control and Its Opponents*. London, 1935.
Whitehead, George. *Birth Control and Race Culture*. London, 1925.
_____. *Birth Control: Why and How*. London, 1929.
_____. *Socialism and Eugenics*. London, 1907.
Winnington-Ingram, A. F. *A Charge Delivered to the Clergy and Churchwardens in the Diocese of London, October 1911*. London, 1911.
_____. *A Charge Delivered to the Clergy and Churchwardens of London in St. Paul's Cathedral, October 19, 1905, at his Primary Visitation of the Diocese of London*. London, 1905.
Women's Cooperative Guild. *Maternity: Letters from Working Women*. London, 1915.
Wright, Almroth E. *The Unexpurgated Case against Woman Suffrage*. London, 1913.
Wright. Harold. *Population*. London, 1923.
Young, Meredith. *County Palatine of Chester: Report of the Medical Officer of Health for the Year 1921*. Chester, 1922.
Yule, G. Udny. *The Fall in the Birth Rate*. Cambridge, 1920.

ARTICLES

Allen, Grant. "Plain Words on the Women's Question." *Fortnightly Review*, n.s. 46 (October 1889): 448–52.
Barclay, James W. "Malthusianism and the Declining Birth Rate." *Nineteenth Century* 59 (January 1906): 80–89.

————. "The Race Suicide Scare." *Nineteenth Century* 60 (December 1906): 895–99.

Barry, Rev. William. "Agnosticism and National Decay." *National Review* 45 (March 1905): 83–97.

Bertillon, Jacques. "La Natalité Selon le Degré d'Aisance: Etude à ce Point de Vue de Paris, Londres, Berlin et Vienne." *Bulletin de l'Institute International de Statistique* 11, pt. 2 (1899): 163–76.

Billington-Greig, Teresa. "The Rebellion of Women." *Contemporary Review* 94 (July 1908): 1–10.

Bisset-Smith, George T. "The Census: Population and Progress." *Westminster Review* 173 (1910): 605–18.

Booth, Meyrick. "Religious Belief as Affecting the Growth of Population." *Hibbert Journal* 13 (October 1914): 138–42.

Brend, William A. "Infant Mortality: A Problem of the Land." *Nineteenth Century* 79 (March 1916): 606–26.

————. "The Passing of the Child." *Nineteenth Century* 73 (March 1915): 584–602.

————. "The Passing of the Child: A Rejoinder." *Nineteenth Century* 73 (June 1915): 1407–15.

Brunton, Sir Lauder. "The National League for Physical Education and Improvement." *National Review* 44 (November 1904–5): 489–98.

Cannan, Edwin. "The Malthusian Anti-Socialist Argument." *Economic Review* 2 (February 1892): 71–87.

————. "The Probability of a Cessation of the Growth of Population in England and Wales during the Next Century." *Economic Review* 5 (December 1895): 505–15.

Carr-Saunders, A. M. "Some Recent Eugenic Work." *Economic Review* 21 (January 1911): 19–27.

Chatterton-Hill, George. "Race Progress and Race Degeneracy." *Sociological Review* 2 (April 1909): 140–51; (July 1909): 250–59.

Cookson, Montague. "The Morality of Married Life." *Fortnightly Review*, n.s. 12 (October 1872): 392–412.

Courtney, Leonard. "The Swarming of Men." *Nineteenth Century* 23 (March 1888): 331–53.

Crackanthorpe, Montague. "Eugenics as a Social Force." *Nineteenth Century* 63 (June 1908): 962–72.

————. "Population and Progress." *Fortnightly Review*, n.s. 80 (December 1906): 1001–16.

Drysdale, Charles Robert. "The Malthusian Theory of Population: A Reply to 'Statistics versus Malthus.'" *Westminster Review* 131 (1889): 561–73.

Drysdale, Charles Vickery. "The Empire and the Birth-Rate." *United Empire: The Royal Colonial Institute Journal* 5 (May 1914): 398–416.

Dunlop, Binnie. "The Truth about Birth and Death Rates: A Reply to Dr. Brend." *Nineteenth Century* 77 (April 1915): 841–47.

Dunn, Henry Percy. "Is Our Race Degenerating?" *Nineteenth Century* 36 (August 1894): 301–14.

Edmond, James. "The Birth Rate—and Afterwards." *National Review* 59 (June

1912): 713–25.

Ellis, Havelock. "Birth Control and Eugenics." *Eugenics Review* 9 (April 1917): 32–41.

———. "Eugenics and Genius." *Contemporary Review* 104 (October 1913): 519–27.

———. "Eugenics and St. Valentine." *Nineteenth Century* 59 (May 1906): 779–87.

Elsdale, H. "Why Are Our Brains Deteriorating?" *Nineteenth Century* 46 (August 1899): 262–72.

Ewart, J. Cossar. "The Saving of Child Life." *Nineteenth Century* 82 (July 1917): 117–35.

Farrar, F. W. "Social Problems and Remedies." *Fortnightly Review*, n.s. 49 (February 1888): 350–63.

Fite, Warne. "Birth Control and Biological Ethics." *International Journal of Ethics* 27 (1916): 50–63.

Foard, Isabel. "The Power of Heredity." *Westminster Review* 151 (1899): 538–53.

Gale, Annabel Clark. "Heredity: A Plea for Women's Suffrage." *Westminster Review* 172 (1909): 186–90.

Galton, Francis. "Eugenics: Its Definition, Scope, and Aims." *Sociological Papers* 1 (1905): 45–50.

———. "Hereditary Improvement." *Fraser's Magazine* 7 (January 1873): 116–30.

———. "Hereditary Talent and Character." *Macmillan's Magazine* 12 (June 1865): 157–66; (August 1865): 318–27.

———. "Our National Physique-Prospects of the British Race—Are We Degenerating?" *Daily Chronicle*, 29 July 1903.

———. "The Possible Improvement of the Human Breed under the Existing Conditions of Law and Sentiment." *Nature* 64 (November 1901): 659–65.

———. "The Relative Supplies from Town and Country Families to the Population of Future Generations." *Journal of the Royal Statistical Society* 36 (March 1873): 19–26.

———. "Restrictions in Marriage." *Sociological Papers* 2 (1905).

———. "Studies in National Eugenics." *Sociological Papers* 2 (1905).

Hannan, Thomas. "One of War's Warnings—'Take Care of the Child.'" *Nineteenth Century* 78 (July 1915): 137–50.

Harris, John. "The Degenerates." *Westminster Review* 177 (1912): 624–26.

———. "The Eugenics Congress." *Westminster Review* 178 (1912): 390–92.

———. "Our Defectives." *Westminster Review* 178 (1912): 25–27.

———. "Unfit for Parenthood." *Westminster Review* 177 (1912): 579–81.

Hartog, Marcus. "The Transmission of Acquired Characters." *Contemporary Review* 94 (September 1908): 307–17.

———. "The Transmission of Acquired Characters: A Rejoinder." *Contemporary Review* 94 (November 1908): 635–40.

Herbert, S. "The Discovery of the Fittest: A Eugenic Problem." *Westminster Review* 175 (1911): 39–45.

———. "Eugenics in Relation to Social Reform." *Westminster Review* 180 (1913): 377–86.

Hill-Climo, William. "A Healthy Race: A Woman's Vocation." *Westminster Review* 173 (1910): 11–19.

Himes, Norman, and Himes, Vera. "Birth Control for the British Working Classes: A Study of the First Thousand Cases to Visit an English Birth Control Clinic." *Hospital Social Service* 19 (1929): 578–617.

Humphries, Moyra. "Racial Responsibility." *Englishwoman* 18 (April 1913): 97–104.

Hutchins, B. L. "Higher Education and Marriage." *Englishwoman* 18 (June 1913): 257–64.

Inge, W. R. "The Birth-Rate." *Edinburgh Review* 225 (January 1917): 62–83.

————. "The Question of Population." *Economic Review* 3 (February 1893): 103–11.

Kidd, Benjamin. "Social Evolution." *Nineteenth Century* 38 (February 1895): 226–40.

Kirkup, T. "Darwinism and Socialism." *Economic Review* 1 (October 1891): 531–36.

Knight, Mary. "Woman v. the State." *Westminster Review* 172 (July 1909): 36–41.

Laski, H. J. "The Scope of Eugenics." *Westminster Review* 174 (1910): 25–34.

Lindsay, J. A. "The Case for and against Eugenics." *Nineteenth Century* 72 (September 1912): 546–57.

Linton, E. Lynn. "The Higher Education of Women." *Fortnightly Review*, n.s. 40 (September 1886): 498–510.

Lissenden, George B. "Racial Suicide: The Reply of the Masses." *Westminster Review* 172 (1909): 267–74.

Lyttelton, Arthur T. "The Question of Population." *Economic Review* 1 (March 1891): 151–71.

————. "The Question of Population II." *Economic Review* 2 (June 1892): 378–94.

————. "The Question of Population." *Economic Review* 3 (February 1893): 107–10.

Lyttelton, Edward. "Eugenics, Ethics, and Religion." *Nineteenth Century* 74 (July 1913): 155–63.

————. Review of *Neo-Malthusianism*, by R. Ussher. *Economic Review* 8 (December 1898): 562–68.

McDougall, William. "A Practicable Eugenic Suggestion." *Sociological Papers* 3 (1907).

MacGregor, Malcolm Evan. "A Plea for the Reduction of the Birth-Rate." *Westminster Review* 177 (1912): 348–52.

McIlroy, Anne Louise. "Some Factors in the Control of Birth Rate." *Transactions of the Medico-Legal Society*, 1921–22. (1922): 137–51.

Macrosty, Edith. "Men and Marriage." *Englishwoman* 14 (April 1912): 20–27.

Maurice, Sir John Frederick. "National Health: A Soldier's Study." *Contemporary Review* 83 (January 1903): 41–56.

Meath, Earl of. "Have We the 'Grit' of Our Forefathers." *Nineteenth Century* 64 (September 1908): 421–29.

Miles [Sir John Frederick Maurice]. "Where to Get Men." *Contemporary Review* 81 (January 1902): 78–86.

Millard, Charles Killick. "The Problem of Birth Control with Special Reference to the Public Health Aspect." *Journal of State Medicine* 26 (November 1918): 321–37.

Money, Leo G. Chiozza. "A 'Little' England?" *Nineteenth Century* 71 (March 1912): 483–97.

Newman, Francis W. "Malthusianism, True and False." *Fraser's Magazine*, n.s. 3 (May 1881): 597–602.

———. "Two Solutions: By the Author of Ginx's Baby." *Fraser's Magazine*, n.s. 3 (April 1881): 452–53.

Newmarch, Eugenia. "Woman and the Race." *Englishwoman* 10 (April 1911): 33–39.

Newsholme, Arthur. "Alleged Physical Degeneration in Towns." *Public Health* 17 (February 1905): 293–300.

———. "The Enemies of Child Life." *Nineteenth Century* 83 (January 1918): 76–98.

———, and Stevenson, T. H. C. "The Decline of Human Fertility in the U.K. and Other Countries as Shown by Corrected Birth Rates." *Journal of the Royal Statistical Society* 69 (January 1906): 34–87.

Ogilvy, A. J. "The Malthusian Doctrine." *Westminster Review* 136 (1891): 289–97.

Ogle, William. "On Marriage-Rates and Marriage Ages with Special Reference to the Growth of Population." *Journal of the Royal Statistical Society* 53 (June 1890): 253–89.

Paget, Stephen. "Heredity and Life." *Cornhill Magazine* 32 (May 1912): 638–45.

Pearson, Karl. "The Moral Basis of Socialism." *Ethic of Freethought* (1901).

———. "On the Inheritance of the Mental and Moral Characters in Man, and Its Comparison with the Inheritance of the Physical Characters: The Huxley Lecture for 1903." *Journal of the Anthropological Institute of Great Britain and Ireland* 33 (1903): 179–237.

———. "Politics and Science." *Chances of Death* 1 (1897).

———. "Socialism and Natural Selection." *Chances of Death* 1 (1897).

———. "Socialism and Sex." *Ethic of Freethought* (1901).

———. "Socialism in Theory and Practice." *Ethic of Freethought* (1901).

———. "Woman and Labour." *Chances of Death* 1 (1897).

———. "The Woman's Question." *Ethic of Freethought* (1901).

Peile, J. H. F. "Eugenics and the Church." *Eugenics Review* 1 (October 1909): 163–73.

Phelps, L. R. "Population." *Edinburgh Review* 176 (October 1892): 431–52.

Richardson, A. M. "The Professional Classes, the War, and the Birth-Rate." *Nineteenth Century* 77 (March 1915): 603–8.

Rigby, James A. "The Diminishing Birth-Rate: Is It a National Danger?" *Nineteenth Century* 75 (February 1914): 434–45.

Rogers, Ethel. "The Professor, the Woman, and the Superman." *Englishwoman* 4 (November 1909): 16–24.

Saleeby, Caleb W. "The Dysgenics of War." *Contemporary Review* 107 (March 1915): 331–38.

Scharlieb, Mary. "The Hope of the Future: An Inquiry into the Causes of Infantile Mortality—and Some Suggestions." *Nineteenth Century* 79 (May 1916): 1035–57.

———. "The Nation's Children and Our Duty towards Them." *Nineteenth Century*

81 (June 1917): 1277–89.

Selborne, Maude. "Imperialism and Motherhood." *National Review* 43 (August 1914): 985–88.

Snow, E. C. "Note on the Future Population of the Self-Governing Portion of the British Empire." *Journal of the Royal Statistical Society* 78 (May 1915): 446–51.

———. "On the Magnitude of the Population of England and Wales Available for Emigration." *Journal of the Royal Statistical Society* 78 (March 1915): 238–75.

Spender, J. A. "Population and Agriculture." *Fortnightly Review*, n.s. 81 (January 1907): 102–6.

Sprigge, S. Squire. "Mating and Medicine." *Contemporary Review* 96 (November 1909): 578–87.

Stevenson, T. H. C. "The Fertility of Various Social Classes in England and Wales from the Middle of the Nineteenth Century to 1911." *Journal of the Royal Statistical Society* 80 (May 1920): 401–44.

Stopes, Marie C. "Positive and Negative Control of Conception in Its Various Technical Aspects." *Journal of State Medicine* 39 (1931): 354–60.

Taylor, J. Lionel. "The Social Application of Eugenics." *Westminster Review* 170 (1908): 416–24.

Taylor, John W. "The Bishop of London on the Declining Birth Rate." *Nineteenth Century* 59 (February 1906): 219–29.

Vaughan, Bernard. "England's Empty Cradles." *Nineteenth Century* 80 (September 1916): 586–611.

Wallace, Alfred R. "Evolution and Character." *Fortnightly Review*, n.s. 83 (January 1908): 1–24.

———. "Human Selection." *Fortnightly Review*, n.s. 48 (September 1890): 325–37.

Warwick, Countess of. "Race Suicide." *Hibbert Journal* 14 (July 1916): 751–59.

Whetham, William Cecil Dampier. "Inheritance and Sociology." *Nineteenth Century* 65 (January 1909): 74–90.

———. "The War and the Race." *Quarterly Review* 227 (January 1917): 17–38.

———, and Catherine D. "Decadence and Civilization." *Hibbert Journal* 10 (October 1911): 179–200.

———. "Eminence and Heredity." *Nineteenth Century* 69 (May 1911): 818–32.

———. "The Extinction of the Upper Classes." *Nineteenth Century* 66 (July 1909): 97–108.

White, Arnold. "The Cult of Infirmity." *National Review* 34 (October 1899–1900): 236–45.

Yule, G. Udny. "On the Changes in the Marriage and Birth-Rates in England and Wales during the Past Half Century, with an Inquiry as to Their Probable Causes." *Journal of Royal Statistical Society* 69 (March 1906): 88–132.

Secondary Sources

B O O K S

Abrams, Philip. *The Origins of British Sociology*. Chicago, 1968.

Anderson, Michael. *Family Structure in Nineteenth-Century Lancashire*. Cambridge, 1972.

Arnstein, Walter L. *The Bradlaugh Case: A Study in Late Victorian Opinion and Politics*. Oxford, 1965.

Bailey, Peter. *Leisure and Class in Victorian England: Rational Recreation and the Contest for Control, 1830–1885*. London and Toronto, 1978.

Banks, Joseph A. *Prosperity and Parenthood: A Study of Family Planning among the Victorian Middle Classes*. London, 1954.

_____, and Banks, Olive. *Feminism and Family Planning in Victorian England*. Liverpool, 1964.

Barnes, John. *Ahead of His Age: Bishop Barnes of Birmingham*. London, 1980.

Bealey, Frank. *Social and Political Thought of the British Labour Party*. London, 1970.

Bell, Enid. *Storming the Citadel: The Rise of the Woman Doctor*. London, 1953.

Bentley, Michael. *The Liberal Mind, 1914–1929*. Cambridge, 1976.

Blacker, C. P. *Eugenics: Galton and After*. London, 1952.

Boner, Harold A. *Hungry Generations: The Nineteenth-Century Case against Malthusianism*. New York, 1954.

Bonner, H. B., and Robertson, J. M. *Charles Bradlaugh: A Record of His Life and Work by His Daughter with an Account of His Parliamentary Struggle, Politics, and Teaching*. 2 vols. London, 1894.

Branca, Patricia. *Silent Sisterhood: Middle-Class Women in the Victorian Home*. Pittsburgh, 1975.

Brand, Jeanne L. *Doctors and the State: The British Medical Profession and the Public Health, 1870–1912*. Baltimore, 1966.

Branson, Noreen, and Heinemann, Margot. *Britain in the Nineteen Thirties*. London, 1971.

Braybon, Gail. *Women Workers in the First World War*. London, 1980.

Briant, Keith. *Passionate Paradox: The Life of Marie Stopes*. New York, 1962.

Brittain, Vera. *Pethick Lawrence: A Portrait*. London, 1963.

Burrow, J. W. *Evolution and Society: A Study in Victorian Social Theory*. Cambridge, 1966.

Carpenter, S. C. *Winnington-Ingram*. London, 1949.

Chadwick, Owen. *The Victorian Church*. Part 1. London, 1966.

_____. *The Victorian Church*. Part 2. London, 1970.

Chappelow, Allen. *Shaw–"The Chucker-Out": A Biographical Exposition*. London, 1969.

Chase, Allan. *The Legacy of Malthus: The Social Costs of the New Scientific Racism*. New York, 1977.

Checkland, S. G. *The Rise of Industrial Society in England, 1815–1885*. London, 1964.

Comfort, Alex. *The Anxiety Makers*. London, 1967.

Crossick, Geoffrey, ed. *The Lower Middle Class in Britain, 1870–1914*. London, 1977.

Crow, Duncan. *The Edwardian Woman*. London, 1978.

———. *The Victorian Woman*. London, 1971.

Cullen, Michael. *The Statistical Movement in Early Victorian Britain: The Foundations of Empirical Social Research*. Brighton, 1973.

Dangerfield, George. *The Strange Death of Liberal England*. London, 1936.

Davidoff, Leonore. *The Best Circles: Women and Society in Victorian England*. London, 1973.

Davies, Horton. *Worship and Theology in England: The Ecumenical Century, 1900–1965*. Princeton, 1965.

Delamont, Sara, and Duffin, Lorna, eds. *The Nineteenth Century Woman: Her Cultural and Physical World*. London, 1978.

Donnison, Jean. *Midwives and Medical Men: A History of Inter-Professional Rivalries and Women's Rights*. London, 1977.

Drake, Michael, ed. *Population in Industrialization*. London, 1969.

Eiseley, Loren. *Darwin's Century*. New York, 1958.

Emy, H. V. *Liberals, Radicals, and Social Politics, 1892–1914*. Cambridge, 1973.

Eversley, D. E. C. *Social Theories of Fertility and the Malthusian Debate*. London, 1959.

Field, James A. *Essays on Population and Other Papers*. Chicago, 1931.

Fletcher, Sheila. *Feminists and Bureaucrats: A Study in the Development of Girl's Education in the Nineteenth Century*. Cambridge, 1980.

Florence, Lella S. *Progress Report on Birth Control*. London, 1956.

Forrest, D. W. *Francis Galton: The Life and Work of a Victorian Genius*. London, 1974.

Frankfort, Roberta. *Collegiate Women: Domesticity and Career in Turn-of-the-Century America*. New York, 1977.

Frazer, W. M. *A History of English Public Health, 1834–1939*. London, 1950.

Freeden, Michael. *The New Liberalism: An Ideology of Social Reform*. Oxford, 1977.

Fryer, Peter. *The Birth Controllers*. London, 1965.

———. *British Birth Control Ephemera, 1870–1947: The Collis Collection*. Leicester, 1969.

Gainer, Bernard. *The Alien Invasion: The Origins of the Aliens Act of 1905*. Ithaca, 1972.

Garrard, John A. *The English and Immigration: A Comparative Study of the Jewish Influx, 1880–1910*. Oxford, 1971.

Gartner, Lloyd P. *The Jewish Immigrant in England, 1870–1914*. London, 1960.

Gauldie, Enid. *Cruel Habitations: A History of Working-Class Housing in Britain, 1780–1918*. New York, 1974.

Gilbert, A. D. *Religion and Society in Industrial England: Church, Chapel, and Social Change, 1740–1914*. London, 1976.

Gilbert, Bentley B. *British Social Policy, 1914–1939*. Ithaca, 1970.

_____. *The Evolution of National Insurance in Great Britain: The Origins of the Welfare State*. London, 1966.

Glass, David V., ed. *Introduction to Malthus*. London, 1953.

_____. *Population Policies and Movements in Europe*. Oxford, 1940.

_____, and Eversley, D. E. C., eds. *Population in History: Essays in Historical Demography*. Chicago, 1965.

Gloversmith, Frank, ed. *Class, Culture, and Social Change: A New View of the 1930s*. Brighton, 1980.

Gordon, Linda. *Woman's Body, Woman's Right: A Social History of Birth Control in America*. New York, 1976.

Gray, Madeline. *Margaret Sanger: A Biography of the Champion of Birth Control*. New York, 1979.

Griffith, G. T. *Population Problems in the Age of Malthus*. Cambridge, 1976.

Grosskurth, Phyllis. *Havelock Ellis: A Biography*. London, 1980.

Habakkuk, H. J. *Population Growth and Economic Development since 1750*. Leicester, 1971.

Hall, Ruth, ed. *Dear Dr. Stopes: Sex in the 1920s*. London, 1978.

_____. *Passionate Crusader: The Life of Marie Stopes*. New York, 1977.

Haller, Mark H. *Eugenics: Hereditarian Attitudes in American Thought*. New Brunswick, 1963.

Halsey, A. H., ed. *Trends in British Society since 1900: A Guide to the Changing Social Structure of Britain*. London, 1972.

Harris, José. *Unemployment and Politics: A Study in English Social Policy, 1886–1914*. Oxford, 1972.

_____. *William Beveridge: A Biography*. Oxford, 1977.

Harrison, Brian. *Drink and the Victorians: The Temperance Question in England, 1815–1872*. London, 1971.

_____. *Separate Spheres: The Opposition to Women's Suffrage in Britain, 1867–1928*. London, 1978.

Harrison, Fraser. *The Dark Angel: Aspects of Victorian Sexuality*. London, 1967.

Harrod, R. F. *The Life of John Maynard Keynes*. London, 1951.

Hartman, Mary, and Banner, Lois, eds. *Clio's Consciousness Raised: New Perspectives on the History of Women*. New York, 1974.

Himes, Norman E. *Medical History of Contraception*. Baltimore, 1936.

Himmelfarb, Gertrude. *Victorian Minds*. New York, 1968.

Hogben, Lancelot, ed. *Political Arithmetic: A Symposium of Popular Studies*. London, 1938.

Holcombe, Lee. *Victorian Ladies at Work: Middle-Class Working Women in England and Wales, 1850–1914*. Newton Abbot, 1973.

Hopkinson, D. *Family Inheritance: A Life of Eva Hubback*. London, 1954.

Hull, David. *Darwin and His Critics*. Oxford, 1973.

Hutchinson, Edward P. *The Population Debate: Development of Conflicting Theories Up to 1900*. Boston, 1967.

Huxley, G. *Lady Denman, G. B. E., 1884–1954*. London, 1961.

Hynes, Samuel. *The Edwardian Turn of Mind*. Princeton, 1968.

Inglis, K. S. *Churches and the Working Classes in Victorian England*. London, 1963.

Innes, John W. *Class Fertility Trends in England and Wales, 1876–1934*. Princeton, 1938.

James, Patricia. *Population Malthus: His Life and Times*. London, 1979.

Johnson, Paul Barton. *Land Fit for Heroes: The Planning of British Reconstruction, 1916–1919*. Chicago, 1969.

Jones, Gareth Stedman. *Outcast London: A Study in the Relationship between Classes in Victorian Society*. Oxford, 1971.

Jones, Greta. *Social Darwinism and English Thought: The Interaction between Biological and Social Theory*. Brighton, 1980.

Jones, Peter d'A. *The Christian Socialist Revival, 1877–1914*. Princeton, 1968.

Kapp, Yvonne. *Eleanor Marx*. 2 vols. London, 1972, 1976.

Kendall, Walter. *The Revolutionary Movement in Britain, 1900–1921*. London, 1969.

Kennedy, David. *Birth Control in America: The Career of Margaret Sanger*. New Haven, 1970.

Knodel, John E. *The Decline of Fertility in Germany, 1871–1939*. Princeton, 1974.

Koss, Stephen. *Nonconformity in Modern British Politics*. London, 1975.

Kynaston, David. *King Labour: The British Working Class, 1850–1914*. London, 1976.

Laslett, Peter. *The World We Have Lost*. New York, 1965.

Lawton, Richard, ed. *The Census and Social Structure: An Interpretative Guide to Nineteenth-Century Censuses for England and Wales*. London, 1978.

Leathard, Audrey. *The Fight for Family Planning: The Development of Family Services in Britain, 1921–1974*. London, 1980.

Ledbetter, Rosanna. *A History of the Malthusian League, 1877–1927*. Columbus, Ohio, 1976.

Lesthaeghe, Ron J. *The Decline of Belgian Fertility, 1890–1970*. Princeton, 1978.

Levine, David. *Family Formation in an Age of Nascent Capitalism*. New York, 1977.

Liddington, Jill, and Norris, Jill. *One Hand Tied Behind Us: The Rise of the Women's Suffrage Movement*. London, 1978.

Lloyd, Roger. *The Church of England, 1900–65*. London, 1967.

McBriar, A. M. *Fabian Socialism and English Politics, 1844–1918*. Cambridge, 1962.

McHugh, Paul. *Prostitution and Victorian Social Reform*. London, 1980.

MacKenzie, Norman, and MacKenzie, Jean. *The First Fabians*. London, 1977.
———. *The Time Traveller: The Life of H. G. Wells*. London, 1973.

McKeown, Thomas. *The Modern Rise of Population*. New York, 1977.

McLaren, Angus. *Birth Control in Nineteenth-Century England*. London, 1977.

McLeod, Hugh. *Class and Religion in the Late Victorian City*. London, 1974.

Macquarrie, John. *Twentieth-Century Religious Thought*. London, 1963.

Malchow, Howard. *Population Pressures: Emigration and Government in Late Nineteenth-Century Britain*. Palo Alto, California, 1979.

Marcus, Steven. *The Other Victorians: A Study of Sexuality and Pornography in Mid-Nineteenth-Century England*. New York, 1966.

Marquand, David. *Ramsay MacDonald*. London, 1977.

Marrin, Albert. *The Last Crusade: The Church of England in the First World War*.

Durham, 1974.

Marsh, David C. *The Changing Social Structure of England and Wales, 1871–1951.* London, 1958.

Martin, Kingsley. *Harold Laski (1893–1950): A Biographical Memoir.* New York, 1953.

Marwick, Arthur. *The Deluge: British Society and the First World War.* Harmondsworth, 1967.

————. *Women at War, 1914–1918.* London, 1977.

Matthew, H. C. G. *The Liberal Imperialists: The Ideas and Politics of a Post-Gladstonian Elite.* Oxford, 1973.

Maude, Aylmer. *The Authorised Life of Marie C. Stopes.* London, 1924.

Mayor, Stephen. *The Churches and the Labour Movement.* London, 1967.

Meacham, Standish. *A Life Apart: The English Working Class, 1890–1914.* London, 1977.

Meek, Ronald, ed. *Marx and Engels on Malthus.* London, 1953.

Mitchell, Brian R. *European Historical Statistics, 1750–1970.* London, 1975.

————, and Deane, Phillis. *Abstract of British Historical Statistics.* Cambridge, 1962.

Mitchell, David. *Queen Christabel: A Biography of Christabel Pankhurst.* London, 1977.

Mitchison, Rosalinde. *The British Population Change since 1860.* London, 1977.

Mohr, James. *Abortion in America: The Origins and Evolution of National Policy, 1800–1900.* Oxford, 1978.

Morgan, Kenneth. *Keir Hardie: Radical and Socialist.* London, 1975.

————, and Morgan, Jane. *Portrait of a Progressive: The Political Career of Christopher, Viscount Addison.* Oxford, 1980.

Noonan, John J. *Contraception: A History of Its Treatment by Catholic Theologians and Canonists.* Cambridge, 1965.

Norman, E. R. *Church and Society in England, 1770–1970.* Oxford, 1976.

Oliver, John. *The Church and Social Order: Social Thought in the Church of England, 1919–1939.* London, 1968.

Packe, Michael St. John. *The Life of John Stuart Mill.* London, 1954.

Parry, Noel, and Parry, José. *The Rise of the Medical Profession: A Study of Collective Social Mobility.* London, 1976.

Past and Present Society. *The Roots of Sociobiology: Past and Present Society Conference in Conjunction with the British Society for the History of Science.* Oxford, 1978.

Pearsall, Ronald. *The Worm in the Bud: The World of Victorian Sexuality.* London, 1969.

Pearson, E. S. *Karl Pearson: An Appreciation of Some Aspects of His Life and Work.* Cambridge, 1938.

Pearson, Karl. *The Life of Francis Galton.* 3 vols. London, 1914–30.

Peel, J. D. Y. *Herbert Spencer: The Evolution of a Sociologist.* London, 1971.

Peel, John, and Potts, Malcolm. *Textbook of Contraceptive Practice.* Cambridge, 1969.

Peterson, M. Jeanne. *The Medical Profession in Mid-Victorian London.* Los Angeles and Berkeley, 1978.

Pickens, Donald R. *Eugenics and the Progressives.* Nashville, 1968.

Pierson, Stanley. *Marxism and the Origins of British Socialism: The Struggle for a New Consciousness*. Ithaca, 1973.

Pinchbeck, Ivy, and Hewitt, Margaret. *Children in English Society: From the Eighteenth Century to the Children Act 1948*. London, 1973.

Provine, William B. *The Origins of Theoretical Population Genetics*. Chicago, 1971.

Rabb, Theodore, and Rotberg, Robert, eds. *Marriage and Fertility*. Princeton, 1981.

Ramsey, A. M. *From Gore to Temple: The Development of Anglican Theology between LUX MUNDI and the Second World War, 1889–1939*. London, 1960.

Read, Donald. *Edwardian England, 1901–1915: Society and Politics*. London, 1975.

Reader, W. J. *Professional Men: The Rise of the Professional Classes in Nineteenth-Century England*. New York, 1966.

Reed, James. *From Private Vice to Public Virtue: The Birth Control Movement in American Society since 1830*. New York, 1978.

Robinson, Victor. *Pioneers of Birth Control in England and America*. New York, 1919.

Rosen, Andrew. *Rise Up, Women!: The Militant Campaign of the Women's Social and Political Union, 1903–1914*. London, 1974.

Rover, Constance. *Love, Morals, and the Feminists*. London, 1970.

―――. *Women's Suffrage and Party Politics in Britain, 1866–1914*. London, 1967.

Rowbotham, Sheila. *A New World for Women*. London, 1976.

―――, and Weeks, J. *Socialism and the New Life: The Personal and Sexual Policies of Edward Carpenter and Havelock Ellis*. London, 1976.

Royle, Edward. *Radicals, Secularists, and Republicans: Popular Free-thought in Britain, 1866–1915*. Manchester, 1980.

―――. *Victorian Infidels: The Origins of the British Secularist Movement, 1791–1866*. Manchester, 1974.

Ryder, Judith, and Silver, Harold. *Modern English Society: History and Structure, 1850–1970*. London, 1977.

Saville, John. *Rural Depopulation in England and Wales, 1851–1951*. London, 1957.

Searle, G. R. *Eugenics and Politics in Britain, 1900–1914*. Leyden, 1976.

―――. *The Quest for National Efficiency: A Study in British Politics and British Political Thought, 1899–1914*. Berkeley and Los Angeles, 1971.

Sellers, Ian. *Nineteenth-Century Nonconformity*. London, 1977.

Semmel, Bernard. *Imperialism and Social Reform: English Social Imperial Thought, 1895–1914*. New York, 1968.

Shorter, Edward. *The Making of the Modern Family*. London, 1975.

Skelley, Alan R. *The Victorian Army at Home: The Recruitment and Terms of the British Regular, 1859–1899*. London, 1977.

Smith, F. B. *The People's Health, 1830–1914*. London, 1979.

Smith, Kenneth. *The Malthusian Controversy*. London, 1951.

Smith, Warren Sylvester. *The London Heretics, 1870–1914*. London, 1967.

Sofer, Reba. *Ethics and Society in England: The Revolution in the Social Sciences, 1870–1914*. Berkeley, 1978.

Solden, Norbert. *Women in British Trade Unions, 1874–1976*. London, 1978.

Soloway, Richard A. *Prelates and People: Ecclesiastical Social Thought in England,*

1783–1852. London, 1969.

Stevenson, John. *Social Conditions in Britain between the Wars*. London, 1977.

———, and Cook, Chris. *The Slump: Society and Politics during the Depression*. London, 1977.

Stone, Lawrence. *The Family, Sex, and Marriage in England, 1500–1800*. New York, 1977.

Stott, Mary. *Organization Women: The Story of the National Union of Townswomen's Guilds*. London, 1978.

Thatcher, David S. *Nietzsche in England, 1890–1914*. Toronto, 1972.

Thomas, Brinley. *Migration and Economic Growth: A Study of Great Britain and the Atlantic Economy*. Cambridge, 1954.

Thompson, D. M. *Nonconformity in the Nineteenth Century*. London, 1972.

Thompson, F. M. L. *English Landed Society in the Nineteenth Century*. London, 1963.

Thompson, Laurence. *The Enthusiasts: A Biography of John and Katherine Bruce Glasier*, London, 1971.

Thompson, Paul. *The Edwardians: The Remaking of British Society*. London, 1975.

Tilley, Louise A., and Scott, Joan W. *Women, Work, and Family*. New York, 1978.

Titmuss, R. and K. *Parents Revolt: A Study of the Declining Birth Rate in Acquisitive Societies*. London, 1942.

Tranter, N. L. *Population since the Industrial Revolution: The Case of England and Wales*. New York, 1973.

Tribe, David. *President Charles Bradlaugh, M.P.*. London, 1971.

Trudgill, Eric. *Madonnas and Magdalens: The Origins and Development of Victorian Sexual Ideas*. London, 1976.

Tsuzuki, Chushichi. *Edward Carpenter, 1844–1929: Prophet of Human Fellowship*. Cambridge, 1980.

———. *H. M. Hyndman and British Socialism*. Oxford, 1961.

———. *The Life of Eleanor Marx*. Oxford, 1967.

Turner, F. M. *Between Science and Religion: The Reaction to Scientific Naturalism in Late Victorian England*. New Haven, 1974.

Vicinus, Martha, ed. *Suffer and Be Still: Women in the Victorian Age*. Bloomington, 1972.

Walkowitz, Judith R. *Prostitution and Victorian Society: Women, Class, and the State*. Cambridge, 1980.

Watson, Francis. *Dawson of Penn: A Biography*. London, 1951.

Weeks, Jeffrey. *Sex, Politics, and Society, 1875–1975*. London, 1981.

Wiltshire, David. *The Social and Political Thought of Herbert Spencer*. Oxford, 1978.

Winter, J. M. *Socialism and the Challenge of War: Ideas and Politics in Britain, 1912–1918*. London, 1974.

Wohl, Anthony S., ed. *The Victorian Family: Structure and Stresses*. New York, 1978.

Wolfe, Willard. *From Radicalism to Socialism: Men and Ideas in the Formation of Fabian Socialist Doctrines, 1881–89*. New Haven, 1975.

Wood, Clive, and Suitters, Beryl. *The Fight for Acceptance: A History of Contraception*. Aylesbury, 1970.

Woodward, John, and Richards, David, eds. *Health Care and Popular Medicine in*

Nineteenth-Century England: Essays in the Social History of Medicine. New York, 1977.

Wrigley, E. A., ed. *An Introduction to English Historical Demography*. London, 1966.
_____. *Nineteenth-Century Society: Essays in the Use of Quantitative Methods for the Study of Social Data*. Cambridge, 1972.
_____, and Schofield, R. S. *The Population History of England, 1541–1871*. Cambridge, 1981.

ARTICLES

Armytage, W. H. G. "The Stock Question." *British Journal of Education Studies* 26 (June 1978): 119–36.

Banks, J. A. "Historical Sociology and the Study of Population." *Daedalus* 97 (Spring 1968): 397–413.

Banks, Joseph A., and Banks, Olive. "The Brandlaugh-Besant Trial and the English Newspapers." *Population Studies* 8 (July 1954): 22–34.

Beaver, M. W. "Population, Infant Mortality, and Milk." *Population Studies*. 27 (July 1973): 243–54.

Burstyn, Joan N. "Education and Sex: The Medical Case against Higher Education for Women in England, 1870–1900." *Proceedings of the American Philosophical Society* 117 (April 1973): 78–89.

Campbell, Flann. "Birth Control and the Christian Churches." *Population Studies* 14 (November 1960): 131–47.

Carrier, N. H. "An Examination of Generation Fertility in England and Wales." *Population Studies* 9 (July 1955): 3–23.

Clements, R. V. "Trade Unions and Emigration, 1840–80." *Population Studies* 9 (November 1955): 167–80.

Coale, Ansley J. "The Decline of Fertility in Europe from the French Revolution to World War II." In *Fertility and Family Planning*, edited by S .J. Behrman, Leslie Corsa, and Ronald Freedman, pp. 3–24. Ann Arbor, 1967.

Cominos, Peter. "Late-Victorian Sexual Respectability and the Social System." *International Review of Social History* 8 (1963): 18–48; 216–50.

Corning, C. H. "Francis Galton and Eugenics." *History Today* 23 (October 1973): 724–32.

Cunningham, A. R. "The New Woman Fiction of the 1890s." *Victorian Studies* 17 (December 1973): 177–86.

D'Arcy, F. "The Malthusian League and the Resistance to Birth Control Propaganda in Late Victorian Britain." *Population Studies* 31 (November 1977): 429–48.

Davidoff, Leonore. "Mastered for Life: Servant and Wife in Victorian and Edwardian England." *Journal of Social History* (Summer 1974): 406–28.

Davin, Anna. "Imperialism and Motherhood." *History Workshop: A Journal of Socialist Historians* 5 (Spring 1978): 9–65.

Dyhouse, Carol. " 'Good Wives and Little Mothers': Social Anxieties and the Schoolgirl's Curriculum, 1890–1920." *Oxford Review of Education* 3 (1977): 21–35.

———. "Working-Class Mothers and Infant Mortality in England, 1895–1914." *Journal of Social History* 12 (Winter 1978): 248–67.

Erickson, Charlotte. "The Encouragement of Emigration by British Trade Unions, 1850–1900." *Population Studies* 3 (December 1949): 248–73.

Farid, S. M. "On the Tempo of Childbearing in England and Wales." *Population Studies* 28 (March 1974): 69–83.

Farrall, Lyndsay. "The History of Eugenics: A Bibliographical Review." *Annals of Science* 36 (March 1979): 111–23.

Fee, Elizabeth. "The Sexual Politics of Victorian Social Anthropology." *Feminist Studies* 1 (Winter-Spring 1973): 23–39.

Freeden, Michael. "Eugenics and Progressive Thought: A Study in Ideological Affinity." *Historical Journal* 22 (September 1979): 645–71.

Friedlander, Dov. "Demographic Characteristics of the Coal Mining Population in England and Wales in the Nineteenth Century." *Economic Development and Cultural Change* 22 (October 1973): 39–51.

Gibson, Colin. "The Association between Divorce and Social Class in England and Wales." *British Journal of Sociology* 25 (March 1974): 79–93.

Gilbert, B. B. "Health and Politics: The British Physical Deterioration Report of 1904." *Bulletin of the History of Medicine* 39 (1965): 145–53.

Gittins, Diana. "Married Life and Birth Control between the Wars." *Oral History* 3, no. 2 (1975): 53–64.

———. "Women's Work and Family Size between the Wars." *Oral History* 5, no. 2 (1977): 84–100.

Glass, David V. "Western Europe." In *Family Planning and Population Programs: A Review of World Developments*, edited by Bernard Berelson, pp. 183–206. Chicago, 1966.

Haldane, J. B. S. "Karl Pearson." *New Biology* 25 (1958): 7–26.

Halliday, R. J. "Social Darwinism: A Definition." *Victorian Studies* 14 (June 1971): 389–405.

Harrison, Brian. "Women's Health and the Women's Movement in Britain: 1840–1940." In *Roots of Sociobiology*, by Past and Present Society, pp. 1–40. Oxford, 1978.

Heer, David M. "Economic Development and the Fertility Transition." *Daedalus* 97 (Spring 1968): 447–62.

Himes, Norman. "Charles Knowlton's Revolutionary Influence on the English Birth Rate." *New England Journal of Medicine* 149 (September 1928): 461–65.

Hollingsworth, T. H. "A Demographic Study of the British Ducal Families." *Population Studies* 11 (July 1957): 4–23.

———. Demography of the British Peerage." *Population Studies* 18 (November 1964): 3–108.

Hyde, William J. "The Socialism of H. G. Wells in the Early Twentieth Century." *Journal of the History of Ideas* 17 (April 1956): 217–34.

Jeger, Lena M. "The Politics of Family Planning." *Political Quarterly* 33 (January–March 1962): 48–58.

Krause, J. T. "Changes in English Fertility and Mortality, 1781–1850." *Economic History Review* 2d ser. 11, no. 1 (1958–59): 52–70.

Langer, William. "The Origins of the Birth Control Movement in England in the Early Nineteenth Century." *Journal of Interdisciplinary History* 5 (Spring 1975): 669–86.

Laslett, Peter. "Size and Structure of the Household in England Over Three Centuries." *Population Studies* 23 (July 1969): 199–223.

Logan, W. P. D. "Mortality in England and Wales from 1848 to 1947." *Population Studies* 4 (September 1950): 132–78.

Love, Rosaleen. "Alice in Eugenics-Land." *Annals of Science.* 36 (March 1979): 145–158.

McGregor, O. R. "The Social Position of Women in England, 1850–1914: A Bibliography." *British Journal of Sociology* 6 (March 1955): 48–60.

MacKenzie, Donald. "Eugenics in Britain." *Social Studies of Science* 6 (September 1976): 499–532.

———. "Karl Pearson and the Professional Middle Class." *Annals of Science* 36 (March 1979): 125–43.

McKeown, Thomas; Brown, R. G.; and Record, R. G. "An Interpretation of the Modern Rise of Population in Europe." *Population Studies* 26 (November 1972): 345–82.

———. "Reasons for the Decline of Mortality in England and Wales during the Nineteenth Century." *Population Studies* 16 (November 1962): 94–122.

McKibbin, R. I. "Social Class and Social Observation in Edwardian England." *Transactions of the Royal Historical Society* 28 (1978): 175–99.

McLaren, Angus. "Abortion in England." *Victorian Studies* 20 (Summer 1977): 379–400.

———. "Contraception and the Working Classes: The Social Ideology of the English Birth Control Movement in Its Early Years." *Comparative Studies in Society and History* 18 (1976): 236–51.

MacRae, Donald G. "Darwinism and the Concept of Social Evolution." *British Journal of Sociology* 10 (June 1959): 105–13.

Matras, Judah. "Social Strategies of Family Formation: Data for British Cohorts Born 1831–1906." *Population Studies* 19 (November 1965): 167–82.

Micklewright, F. H. Amphlett. "The Rise and Decline of English Neo-Malthusianism." *Population Studies* 15 (July 1961): 32–51.

Noonan, John T. "Intellectual and Demographic History." *Daedalus* 97 (Spring 1968): 463–85.

Oren, Laura. "The Welfare of Women in Laboring Families: England, 1860–1950." *Feminist Studies* 1 (Winter–Spring 1973): 107–25.

Peel, John. "Birth Control and the British Working Class Movement." *Society for the Study of Labour History* 7 (Autumn 1963): 16–22.

———. "Contraception and the Medical Profession." *Population Studies* 18 (November 1964): 133–46.

———. "The Manufacture and Retailing of Contraceptives in England." *Population Studies* 17 (November 1963): 113–25.

———, and Dowse, R. E. "The Politics of Birth Control." *Political Studies* 13 (June 1965): 179–97.

Pugh, Martin. "Politicians and the Woman's Vote, 1914–1918." *History* 59 (October 1974): 358–74.

Rollett, Constance, and Parker, Julia. "Population and Family." In *Trends in British Society*, edited by A. H. Halsey, pp. 20–63.

Rowntree, Griselda, and Carrier, Norman H. "The Resort to Divorce in England and Wales, 1853–1957." *Population Studies* 11 (March 1958): 188–233.

Rowntree, Griselda, and Pierce, Rachel M. "Birth Control in Britain." *Population Studies* 15 (July 1961): 3–31; (November 1961): 121–60.

Rubinstein, W. D. "Wealth, Elites, and Class Structure of Modern Britain." *Past and Present* 76 (August 1977): 99–126.

Sauer, R. "Infanticide and Abortion in Nineteenth-Century Britain." *Population Studies* 32 (March 1978): 81–93.

Searle, Geoffrey R. "Eugenics and Class." In *Roots of Sociobiology*, by Past and Present Society, pp. 1–26. Oxford, 1978.

————. "Eugenics and Politics in Britain in the 1930s." *Annals of Science* 36 (March 1979): 159–69.

Semmel, Bernard. "Karl Pearson: Socialist and Darwinist." *British Journal of Sociology* 9 (June 1958): 111–25.

Shorter, Edward. "Female Emancipation, Birth Control, and Fertility in European History." *American Historical Review* 78 (June 1973): 604–40.

Smith-Rosenberg, Carroll, and Rosenberg, Charles. "The Female Animal: Medical and Biological Views of Woman and Her Role in Nineteenth-Century America." *Journal of American History* 60 (September 1973): 332–56.

Sofer, Reba N. "The Revolution in English Social Thought." *American Historical Review* 75 (December 1970): 1938–64.

Soloway, Richard A. "Neo-Malthusians, Eugenists, and the Declining Birth Rate in England, 1900–1918." *Albion* 10 (Spring 1979): 264–86.

Spengler, J. J. "[Alfred] Marshall on the Population Question." *Population Studies* 8 (March 1955): 264–87; 9 (July 1955): 56–66.

Thomas, David. "The Social Origins of Marriage Partners of the British Peerage in the Eighteenth and Nineteenth Centuries." *Population Studies* 26 (March 1972): 99–111.

Turner, Frank M. "Rainfall, Plagues, and the Prince of Wales: A Chapter in the Conflict of Religion and Science." *Journal of British Studies* 13 (May 1974): 46–65.

Winter, J. M. "Britain's 'Lost Generation' of the First World War." *Population Studies* 31 (November 1977): 449–66.

————. "The Impact of the First World War on Civilian Health in Britain." *Economic History Review* 30 (August 1977): 487–507.

Wrigley, E. A. "Family Limitation in Pre-Industrial England." *Economic Historical Review* 2d ser. 19 (April 1966): 89–109.

Young, Robert M. "Malthus and the Evolutionists: The Common Context of Biological and Social Theory." *Past and Present* 43 (May 1969): 109–45.

DISSERTATIONS

Cowan, Ruth. *Sir Francis Galton and the Study of Heredity in the Nineteenth Century*. Ph.D. dissertation, Johns Hopkins University, 1969.

Farrall, Lyndsey A. *The Origins and Growth of the English Eugenics Movement, 1865–1925*. Ph.D. dissertation, Indiana University, 1970.

Index